Lecture Notes in Computer Science 8547

Commenced Publication in 1973
Founding and Former Series Editors:
Gerhard Goos, Juris Hartmanis, and Jan van Leeuwen

Editorial Board

Klaus Miesenberger   Deborah Fels
Dominique Archambault   Petr Peňáz
Wolfgang Zagler (Eds.)

Computers Helping People with Special Needs

14th International Conference, ICCHP 2014
Paris, France, July 9-11, 2014
Proceedings, Part I

 Springer

Volume Editors

Klaus Miesenberger
Johannes Kepler University, Linz, Austria
E-mail: klaus.miesenberger@jku.at

Deborah Fels
Ryerson University, Toronto, ON, Canada
E-mail: dfels@ryerson.ca

Dominique Archambault
Université Paris 8 Vincennes-Saint-Denis, France
E-mail: dominique.archambault@univ-paris8.fr

Petr Peňáz
Masaryk University, Brno, Czech Republic
E-mail: penaz@fi.muni.cz

Wolfgang Zagler
Vienna University of Technology, Austria
E-mail: zw@fortec.tuwien.ac.at

ISSN 0302-9743   e-ISSN 1611-3349
ISBN 978-3-319-08595-1   e-ISBN 978-3-319-08596-8
DOI 10.1007/978-3-319-08596-8
Springer Cham Heidelberg New York Dordrecht London

Library of Congress Control Number: 2014941710

LNCS Sublibrary: SL 3 – Information Systems and Application, incl. Internet/Web
and HCI

Typesetting: Camera-ready by author, data conversion by Scientific Publishing Services, Chennai, India

Printed on acid-free paper

Springer is part of Springer Science+Business Media (www.springer.com)

Preface

Welcome to the ICCHP 2014 Proceedings!

Twenty-five years ago, after an intense state-of-the-art analysis, a group of computer science experts from the Austrian Computer Society, led by Prof. Roland Wagner and Prof. A Min Tjoa, started this conference. ICCHP is proud of this history and to this day it provides one of the few comprehensive and complete collections of scientific work in the field of assistive technologies (AT) and eAccessibility. All 19 volumes of past proceedings, covering more than 2,200 reviewed articles,[1] are a unique source for learning and understanding the theoretical, methodological, and pragmatic specializations of our field. This collection of work, with its unique user focus, offers a significant body of evidence for the enormous but often neglected impact on usability for all users regardless of their abilities.

In 2014, the proceedings of the 14th conference are delivered to you as a compendium of new and exciting scholarly and practical work going on in our field. The Call for Papers received 362 submissions. Each submission was carefully reviewed by at least three members of the international Program Committee, comprising 136 experts from all over the world listed in these proceedings. The panel of 18 conference chairs analyzed the review results and prepared the final decisions. Based on this intense and careful analysis, ICCHP 2014 accepted 132 submissions as full papers (36%) and 55 (15%) as short papers. As evidenced by these data, the proceedings and the conference are based on a highly competitive process guaranteeing the scientific quality.

As in the past, we welcomed over 500 participants from more than 50 countries in Paris at Université Paris 8 – Vincennes-St. Denis. The modern campus and, in particular, the team of researchers and teachers running a master's program in assistive technologies and the experienced team of service provision for students with disabilities at the university guaranteed an accessible, inclusive, and enjoyable event.

The program covered a broad spectrum of users of AT as well as domains where eAccessibility must be implemented. The concept of organizing "Special Thematic Sessions" again helped to structure the proceedings and the program in order to support a deep focus on highly desirable selected topics in the field as well as to bring new and interesting topics to the attention of the research community. One particular emphasis of this year's conference was on inclusive

---

[1] Due to the increasing interest in ICCHP, the five conferences published their proceedings in two volumes.

education and was based on the co-operation with Masaryk University Brno in organizing one track under the umbrella of "Universal Learning Design." The second focus was given to media accessibility (television, video, and animated content) using the unique occasion of co-locating the Media4D conference. The ICCHP Roland Wagner Award, the European finals of the SS12 Coding Competition, the Young Researchers Consortium, the ICCHP Summer University on Math and Science, and a series of parallel workshops and meetings again made ICCHP a unique meeting place for promoting assistive technologies and eAccessibility.

ICCHP 2014 was proud to once again be held – after 2010 and 2012 – under the patronage of the United Nations Educational, Scientific and Cultural Organization (UNESCO).

We thank all those who helped in putting together ICCHP and thereby supporting the AT field and a better quality of life for people with disabilities. Special thanks go to all our supporters and sponsors, displayed at: http://www.icchp.org/sponsors.

July 2014   Klaus Miesenberger
                                                      Deborah Fels
                                          Dominique Archambault
                                                       Petr Peňáz
                                                 Wolfgang Zagler

Organization

ICCHP 2014 General Chair

Fels, Deborah   Ryerson University, Canada

Program Chairs

Fitzpatrick, D.   Dublin City University, Ireland
Manduchi, R.   University of California at Santa Cruz, USA
Ramesh S.K.   CSUN, USA
Watanabe, T.   University of Niigata, Japan
Weber, G.   Technische Universität Dresden, Germany

Program and Publishing Chairs

Archambault, D.   Université Paris 8, France
Miesenberger, K.   University of Linz, Austria
Peňáz, P.   Masaryk University Brno, Czech Republic
Zagler, W.   Vienna University of Technology, Austria

Young Researchers Consortium Chairs

Fels, D.   Ryerson-University, Canada
Fitzpatrick, D.   Dublin City University, Ireland
Gelderblom, G.-J.   Zuyd University, The Netherlands
Kobayashi, M.   Tsukuba University of Technology, Japan
Lam, S.   Project:Possibility, USA
Mihailidis, A.   University of Toronto, Canada
Morandell, M.   Austrian Institute of Technology, Austria
Pontelli, E.   New Mexico State University, USA
Prazak-Aram, B.   Austrian Institute of Technology, Austria
Weber, G.   Technische Universität Dresden, Germany
Zimmermann, G.   Stuttgart Media University, Germany

Workshop Program Chairs

Petz, A.   University of Linz, Austria
Pühretmair, F.   KI-I, Austria

International Program Committee

Abascal, J	Euskal Herriko Unibertsitatea, Spain
Abbott, C.	King's College London, UK
Abou-Zahra, S.	W3C Web Accessibility Initiative (WAI), Austria
Abu Doush, I.	Yarmouk University, Jordan
Abu-Ali, A.	Philadelphia University, Jordan
Andrich, R.	Polo Tecnologico Fondazione, Italy
Arató, A.	KFKI-RMKI, Hungary
Azevedo, L.	Instituto Superior Tecnico, Portugal
Banes	Qatar Assistive Technology Center, Qatar
Batusic, M.	Fabasoft, Austria
Bernareggi, C.	Università degli Studi di Milano, Italy
Bosse, I.	Technische Universität Dortmund, Germany
Bu, J.	Zhejiang University, China
Bühler, C.	TU Dortmund University, FTB, Germany
Chorbev, I.	Ss. Cyrill and Methodius University in Skopje, Macedonia
Christensen, L.B.	Sensus, Denmark
Chutimaskul, W.	University of Technology Thonburi, Thailand
Conway, V.	Edith Cowan University, Australia
Coughlan. J.	Smith-Kettlewell Eye Research Institute, USA
Craddock, G.	Centre for Excellence in Universal Design, Ireland
Crombie, D.	Utrecht School of the Arts, The Netherlands
Cudd, P.	University of Sheffield, UK
Cummins Prager, M.	California State University Northridge, USA
Darvishy, A.	Zürcher Hochschule für Angewandte Wissenschaften, Switzerland
Darzentas, J.	University of the Aegean, Greece
Debeljak, M.	University of Ljubljana, Slovenia
DeRuyter, F.	Duke University Medical Centre, USA
Diaz del Campo, R.	Antarq Tecnosoluciones, Mexico
Dupire, J.	CNAM, France
Emiliani, P.L.	Institute of Applied Physics "Nello Carrara", Italy
Engelen, J.	Katholieke Universiteit Leuven, Belgium
Galinski, C.	InfoTerm, Austria
Gardner, J.	Oregon State University, USA
Hanson, V.	University of Dundee, UK
Holzinger, A.	Medical University of Graz, Austria
Hoogerwerf, E.-J.	AIAS Bologna, Italy
Inoue, T.	National Rehabilitation Center for Persons with Disabilities, Japan

Iversen, C.M.	U.S. Department of State, USA
Jaworek, G.	Karlsruhe Institute of Technology, Germany
Jemni, M.	University of Tunis, Tunisia
Kalinnikova, L.	Pomor State University, Russia
Koronios, A.	University of South Australia, Australia
Kouropetroglou, C.	ALTEC, Greece
Kouroupetroglou, G.	University of Athens Greece
Kremser, W.	OCG, HSM Austria
Lauruska, V.	Siauliai University, Lithuania
Leahy, D.	Trinity College Dublin, Ireland
Leblois, A.	G3ict, USA
Lopez-Krahé, J.	Université Paris 8, France
Magnussen, M.	Stockholm University, Sweden
Matausch, K.	KI-I, Austria
Mathiassen, N.-E.	Statped, Norway
Mayer, C.	Austrian Institute of Technology, Austria
McDonagh, D.	University of Illinois at Urbana-Champaign, USA
McMullin, B.	Dublin City University, Ireland
Mohamad, Y.	Fraunhofer Institute, Germany
Muratet, M.	INS HEA, France
Normie, L.	GeronTech, Israel
Nussbaum, G.	KI-I, Austria
O Connor	NCBI Centre For Inclusive Technology, Ireland
Ohnabe, H.	Niigata University of Health and Welfare, Japan
Oku, H.	Kobe Gakuin University, Japan
Ono, T.	Tsukuba University of Technology, Japan
Paciello, M.	The Paciello Group, USA
Panek, P.	Vienna University of Technology, Austria
Petrie, H.	University of York, UK
Petz, A.	University of Linz, Austria
Rassmus-Groehn, K.	Lund University, Sweden
Rice, D.	National Disability Authority, Ireland
Sanchez, J.	University of Chile, Chile
Sax, C.	San Diego State University, USA
Sik Lányi, C.	University of Pannonia, Hungary
Simsik, D.	University of Kosice, Slovakia
Sloan, D.	The Paciello Group, UK
Snaprud, M.	University of Agder, Norway
Stephanidis, C.	University of Crete, FORTH-ICS, Greece
Stiefelhagen, R.	Karlsruhe Institute of Technology, Germany
Stoeger, B.	University of Linz, Austria
Suweda, O.	The Hyogo Institute of Assistive Technology, Japan

Svensson, H.	National Agency for Special Needs Education and Schools, Sweden
Takagi, H.	IBM, Japan
Takahashi, Y.	Toyo University, Japan
Tauber, M.	University of Paderborn, Germany
Teshima, Y.	Chiba Institute of Technology, Japan
Traunmüller, R.	University of Linz, Austria
Trehin, P.	World Autism Organization, France
Truck, I.	Université Paris 8, France
Uzan, G.	Université Paris 8, France
Velasco, C.A.	Fraunhofer Institute, Germany
Velleman, E.	Bartimeus, The Netherlands
Vigo, M.	University of Manchester, UK
Vigouroux, N.	IRIT Toulouse, France
Vlachogiannis, E.	Fraunhofer Institute, Germany
Votis, K.	CERTH/ITI, Greece
Wagner, G.	Upper Austria University of Applied Sciences, Austria
Weber, H.	ITA, University of Kaiserslautern, Germany
Weisman, J.	Rehab Technology Service, USA
Wöß, W.	University of Linz, Austria
Yamaguchi, K.	Nihon University, Japan
Yeliz Yesilada	Middle East Technical University, Cyprus
Zangla, K.	University of New Orleans, USA
Zetterstrom, E.	Qatar Assistive Technology Center, Qatar

Organizing Committee

Austrian Computer Society, Vienna, Austria
Göbl, R. (President)
Bieber, R. (CEO)
Kremser, W. (Working Group ICT with/for People with Disabilities)

Institute Integriert Studieren, Johannes Kepler University of Linz, Linz, Austria:
Feichtenschlager, P.
Heumader, P.
Koutny, R.
Miesenberger, K.
Murillo Morales, T.
Petz, A.
Pölzer, S.
Radu, N.
Schult, Ch.
Wagner R.

Masaryk University Brno, Brno, Czech Republic (ULD):
Peňáz, P.
Damm, Ch.

Université Paris 8 – Vincennes - St. Denis, Paris, France:
Archambault, D.
Dupire, J.
Muratet, M.
Parvanova, E.
Truck, I.
Uzan, G.

ICCHP Roland Wagner Award

We thank the Austrian Computer Society for announcing and sponsoring the Roland Wagner Award on Computers Helping People with Special Needs.

The Austrian Computer Society decided in September 2001 to endow this award in honor of Prof. Dr. Roland Wagner, the founder of ICCHP.

The Roland Wagner Award is a biannual award in the range of € 3,000. It is handed over at the occasion of ICCHP conferences.

Award Winners

- Award 0: Prof. Dr. Roland Wagner on the occasion of his 50th birthday, 2001
- Award 1: WAI-W3C, ICCHP 2002 in Linz
- Award 2: Paul Blenkhorn, University of Manchester, ICCHP 2004 in Paris
- Award 3: Larry Scadden, National Science Foundation, ICCHP 2006 in Linz
- Award 4: George Kersher, Daisy Consortium, ICCHP 2008 in Linz
- Award 5: ICCHP 2010 in Vienna
  - Harry Murphy, Founder, Former Director and Member Advisory Board of the Centre on Disabilities USA and
  - Joachim Klaus, Founder, Former Director of the Study Centre for Blind and Partially Sighted Students at the Karlsruhe Institute of Technology, Germany
- Award 6: The TRACE Centre of the University Wisconsin-Madison, ICCHP 2012 in Linz

Table of Contents – Part I

Accessible Media

Digital Content and Media Accessibility

25 Years of the Web: Weaving Accessibility

Towards e-inclusion for People with Intellectual Disabilities

The Impact of PDF/UA on Accessible PDF

Accessibility of Non-verbal Communication

Emotions for Accessibility (E4A)

Games and Entertainment Software: Accessibility and Therapy

Implementation and Take-up of eAccessibility

Accessibility and Usability of Mobile Platforms for People with Disabilities and Elderly Persons

Portable and Mobile Platforms for People with Disabilities and Elderly Persons

People with Cognitive Disabilities: AT, ICT and AAC

Autism: ICT and AT

Access to Mathematics, Science and Music

Blind and Visually Impaired People: AT, HCI and Accessibility

Table of Contents – Part II

Smart and Assistive Environments: Ambient Assisted Living (AAL)

Text Entry for Accessible Computing

People with Motor and Mobility Disabilities: AT and Accessibility

Assistive Technology: Service and Practice

ICT-Based Learning Technologies for Disabled and Non-disabled People

Universal Learning Design: Methodology

Universal Learning Design: Hearing Impaired and Deaf People

Universal Learning Design: Sign Language in Education

Sign Language Transcription, Recognition and Generation

Universal Learning Design: Accessibility and AT

Differentiation, Individualisation and Influencing Factors in ICT Assisted Learning for People with Special Needs

Developing Accessible Teaching and Learning Materials within a User Centred Design Framework

Using Mobile Technologies to Support Individuals with Special Needs in Educational Environments

Accessible Media

Introduction to the Special Thematic Session

Deborah I. Fels

Ryerson University, Toronto, Ontario, Canada
dfels@ryerson.ca

Abstract. The Special Thematic Session of ICCHP 2014 entitled Accessible Media promises to yield exciting research and development from around the world in the areas of access to television and audio-video content, eBooks, and social media. The scholarly works in this session report on and discuss a wide range of activities under the umbrella of this important theme, which are all working towards the United Nations specified goal of providing more equal access to the cultural environment for person with disabilities.

1 Introduction

Inclusive design refers to design methodology and practices as well as business models that account for a wide range of users, abilities and functionalities at the outset of the design process [1]. It is not something that is an afterthought to the process but rather infused into design thinking, user analysis, business strategy and resulting products or service provisions. When new features or upgrades are considered, inclusive design should also be part of the process.

Inclusive media is a term that describes techniques, methods and theories for making media, in its many forms, more accessible to persons with disabilities. However, it also implies that as many people as possible are included in the efforts to produce more inclusive media. In general, inclusive media objects refers to closed captioning/subtitles for the hard of hearing (CC), audio description (AD) for blind/low vision audiences, alternative access to print-based media, and low literacy tracks for various media. Specifically, CC refers to the verbatim translation of spoken dialogue from television, film and video content and AD is "a second audio track produced in conjunction with the original audio track, to provide descriptions of important visual elements" [2, pg 1] of that content.

The United Nations Convention on the Rights of Persons with Disabilities [3] "recognizes the importance of accessibility to the physical, social, economic and cultural environment..." (para 1). The cultural environment includes media and other cultural artefacts and providing access in alternative formats makes them more inclusive of a wide range of audiences. Many different signatory countries in the world have introduced regulations and legislation that attempt to operationalize these recommendations. For example, the Canadian Radio-television and Telecommunications

K. Miesenberger et al. (Eds.): ICCHP 2014, Part I, LNCS 8547, pp. 1–3, 2014.

Commission has regulations that govern the quantity of closed captioning/subtitling and audio description required by Canadian Broadcasters. By 2016, all Finnish broadcasters will be required to have 100% of their Finnish and Swedish language programming captioned. Alternative access to print-based media is considered an allowable exception to copyright legislation in many countries. What is important to recognize is that most of the regulations and standards do not mention the notions of quality, engagement, entertainment or understanding when specifying the need for access to media. However, whenever there is a translation/interpretation from one medium to a second one, meaning can be lost because contextual cues are missing. This is compounded by the fact that most inclusive media is produced by a third party after the original is finished rather than by the people responsible for creating that original so much of the context or purpose for specific elements is unavailable. As a result, there is usually no supervision or approval of the inclusive form even though it is for the consumption of that media by audiences.

As the world goes through change and upgrading driven by technology, particularly in the media industries, there are incredible opportunities to bring in inclusive design thinking to address missing or new elements that are enabled by the new technologies. For instance, CC has always been static text with limited font properties and styles due to the limitations of the television technology that could display it. Television and production technologies have changed dramatically as have consumption and viewing models. CC, however, has not changed much even though the limitations imposed by the television technologies of the 1970s no longer exist. Innovation for CC is needed because it is incomplete in its current form and thus it could convey more of the content (e.g., techniques for conveying non-dialogue sound could be developed and provided with new digital technologies). The inclusive media domain is ripe with opportunity for research, development and new ways of thinking about access to media.

In this special thematic session, there are three short papers and four long papers that focus on the broad theme of inclusive media from a diverse group of international researchers from the United States to Europe to Japan. Authors will be presenting research related to subtitles for the hard of hearing/captioning, audio description, access to social media and ebooks. Specifically, papers will describe: a three-dimensional framework describing eInclusion opportunities and elements for social media; a novel technique for expressing non-speech audio using tactile captions; a method for generating real-time remote captions for mathematical formulae; attitudes of and desires for subtitling for the hard of hearing or captioning in Japan; an analysis technique to determine non-dialogue spaces for more efficient production of audio description; LIA, a project that involves providing ebook publishers with a simple method for integrating accessibility features into mainstream production flows; and Synote allows teachers and students to annotate video using a second mobile technology and then make it available to others.

References

1. Clarkson, J., Coleman, R., Keates, S., Lebbon, C.: Inclusive Design. Springer, London (2003)
2. Udo, J., Fels, D.: The rogue poster children of universal design: closed captioning and audio description. Journal of Engineering Design 21, 207–221 (2009)
3. United Nations ad hoc committee on disabilities. Convention on the rights of persons with disabilities, United Nations (2014),
   `http://www.un.org/disabilities/`
   `convention/conventionfull.shtml` (cited: April 2, 2014)

The Case of LIA – Libri Italiani Accessibili

Cristina Mussinelli

Associazione Italiana Editori, Milan, Italy
cristina.mussinelli@aie.it

Abstract. The paper present the case study of the LIA services aimed at providing accessible e-books for blind and visual impaired readers in the mainstream publishing distribution channels. The service had been launched in June 2013 and the catalogue offers at the time of the publication of the paper more than 6.000 accessible e-books of fiction and non fiction, mainly new titles and best sellers. More than 400 titles are added every month thanks to the collaboration of more than 65 Italian publishers.

Keywords: e-Book, Accessible, Accessibility, e-Pub, Mainstream, Visually Impaired, Interoperability.

1 Introduction

LIA is a service carried out by the Italian Publishers Association (AIE) – through its subsidiary Ediser – in collaboration with the Italian Union of the Blind and Visually Impaired. The project was started in January 2011 by a partnership among Ediser (the service company owned by AIE – Associazione Italiana Editori), AIE and mEDRA srl (a joint venture between AIE and the University Consortium CINECA). Such partners had obtained the contribution to be allocated under the fund created by the Ministry for Culture. The development stage has been preceded by the analysis of the reading habits of blind readers as well as of the publishing production workflows (along with the ICT company Cefriel) and international standards (activity developed with IDPF - International Digital Publishing Forum and EDItEUR, the two main international standard setting organizations of the publishing sector)[1].

2 The Service

After two years of preliminary studies and activities, whose steps are available for consultation in the project website www.progettolia.it/en, the project eventually resulted in a service available from June 2013 at the address www.libriitalianiaccessibili.it, with more than 6,000 Italian e-books in EPUB format accessible to blind and partially sighted readers, offering a wide variety of titles: from classics to best sellers, literary

---

[1] A detailed description of the preliminary stages of the project was published in ICCHP 2012, LNCS 7382, part I, pp 550 – 553, Springer Berlin Heidelberg (2012).

K. Miesenberger et al. (Eds.): ICCHP 2014, Part I, LNCS 8547, pp. 4–7, 2014.

prizes and books for kids. The website, developed for traditional and mobile devices, can be navigated in full autonomy also by visually impaired users and offers different sections: the catalogue section displays accessible e-book titles, each going with a rich description of content and the accessibility features of the single e-book file; the guide to digital reading section includes a large data base of tested reading devices and software, classified on the basis of visual impairment; a support section includes FAQs and a dedicated telephone and e-mail help desk to provide users with real time assistance; an on demand section allows users to require e-book titles not included in the catalogue.

Users with visual impairments can access mainstream on line bookstores or digital libraries directly from the LIA website to purchase or lend chosen e-books and get them on their reading devices, in the same channels and ways as any other reader.

Thanks to the efforts of some 65 Italian publishers and publishing groups that joined LIA, the accessibility features of e-books, whose provision LIA included in mainstream e-book metadata flows, have been progressively integrated into mainstream production flows, and presently allow the on line catalogue to expand of a couple hundred titles per month.

3   From Design to Implementation of the Service

Two keywords characterize the approach adopted by LIA: digital and interoperability. The first, without the second, does not allow reaching real equal opportunities, since it may bind visually impaired readers in a narrow fence of dedicated services.

Interoperability means standards: for both formats and description. Standard also means international. Therefore, accessible e-books are in EPUB format, as they already are in most cases both in Italy and abroad. The EPUB 3 version incorporates the accessibility features of the DAISY format, the main standard for blind and visually impaired. LIA has been working in tight cooperation with IDPF, the international body that rules the standard, with the LIA scientific director in its Board. The theme of accessibility enters in publishing production processes as an integrating element, no longer as a feature to add ex post.

When an e-book is put in commerce, it goes with a series of descriptive metadata on the accessibility features provided. The standard used worldwide to spread them is ONIX, managed by Editeur, in particular the 196 code list. This grants the interoperability among the information systems of all the actors of book e-commerce. The work flows between publishers and LIA have been shaped into a dedicated technological platform, called VCC (Verification, Conversion and Certification) designed and implemented by LIA in collaboration with the project partners mEDRA and Cefriel. The files are collected, converted and/or certified by the LIA staff and, once checked, returned to publishers with additional metadata on their compliance with the LIA accessibility requirements for distribution in mainstream distribution platforms.

The LIA website works first of all as a display with all the LIA certified titles available for sale or digital lending in mainstream digital book stores and libraries. To now, there are no Italian bookstores that offer such opportunity to blind and VIPs, thus the need to create an environment fitting to their needs. The LIA display site allows users to purchase chosen titles, each presented with a rich info sheet including accessibility features in detail, in the bookstores that joined the project and changed their purchase section into an accessible one.

Other on line stores display the LIA accessible e-books, thanks to an electronic label that goes with each certified title, a clickable tag including details on its accessibility features. This is possible because info on accessibility has been included in the national books in print catalogue.

4   User Involvement

Since the very beginning, a distinctive characteristic of LIA has been the steady involvement of visually impaired users, directly or through their advocacy organizations, to define and test the different steps and developments of the project.

Starting from the preliminary analyses carried out in 2011 to properly shape the project design activities, blind and visually impaired users advocacy organizations, namely UICI (the Italian Blind and Visually Impaired Union) and CNUDD (National Conference of University Representatives of Disabilities) were involved to sketch a survey on blind and visually impaired reading habits and use of technologies. The results of the survey provided relevant indications on the key needs to meet for a service valuable in terms of users' satisfaction as well as from a scientific perspective.

The introductory definition of digital contents requirements was also shared with a group of final users, thanks to the collaboration of the Institute for the blind "F. Cavazza" of Bologna and its long expertise in technology and visual disabilities. The Institute engineers also played a relevant role in the design and implementation of the front end of the technological infrastructure developed to display the project information website and the website with the catalogue of the LIA accessible titles, in compliance with domestic ruling legislation (Legge 9 gennaio 2004, n. 4, or "Stanca Act") as well as international accessibility and usability protocols (W3C).

Users have been also constantly involved in two main testing activities: first, the screening of the accessibility features of reading devices, software and applications, resulting in a series of evaluation charts available for consultation in the dedicated section of the catalogue website, second, the analysis of the interaction of the best performing technologies resulting from the screening with the accessible EPUBs produced by publishers under the guidance of LIA. As regards reading applications, a group of selected testers has worked specifically on their usability and accessible shaping in order to grant a satisfactory reading experience with mobile devices, considering their growing diffusion among users.

Furthermore two cycles of training modules have been carried out, involving trainers of local sections of the Italian Union of the Blind and Visually Impaired and of the Cavazza Institute, with further sessions to come in 2014.

A dedicated help desk service is active, offering support via e-mail and a toll free phone number to LIA service users. The catalogue website features a section dedicated to digital reading, with FAQs and interactive pages for requests, suggestions and comments. The involvement of final users provides a valuable evaluation and support instrument to optimize the LIA service in terms of actual usability.

5   Planned Activities

The project life span of LIA under the funding of the Ministry expired on February 28th, 2014; to grant sustainability for the development of the activities included in the service, the involvement of new partners and funding channels will play a key role in the short and medium term. The highly innovative value of the LIA approach and solutions has been acknowledged at domestic and international level – organizations like Daisy Consortium, BISG Book Industry Study Group, Editeur and FEP Federation of European Publishers have expressed their support in this sense – while some European countries show interest in the possible replication of the LIA model.

6   Results and Perspectives

Significant results in terms of opportunities and difficulties for the actual accessibility of the whole e-reading eco-system, sometimes in broader perspective for e-commerce at large (as in the case of accessible electronic payment forms) emerged from the test activities with final users, and are at the core of the ongoing work for the next future.

On the one hand lots of opportunities are rising from the ongoing technological development and the diffusion of digital devices, and significant progress has already been made by forward-looking companies which pay attention to the issue of accessibility in the design of their products and services.

On the other hand there are still several issues with the end-to-end accessibility of the chain that need to take further actions which will have a positive impact in improving the experience of partially sighted end users. Activities such as the joint letter written in 2013 by Daisy Consortium, IDPF, EDItEUR and AIE to the Big Player Apple aim to encourage the deployment of accessibility features to serve the needs of the widest possible consumer market, through all the links in the digital publishing value chain. Further international joint actions at all levels would be highly beneficial to raise awareness to the theme of accessible reading and to go on from the starting point outlined by the LIA experience.

Reference

1. Mussinelli, C.: The LIA Project-Libri Italiani Accessibili. In: Miesenberger, K., Karshmer, A., Penaz, P., Zagler, W. (eds.) ICCHP 2012, Part I. LNCS, vol. 7382, pp. 550–553. Springer, Heidelberg (2012)

Semi-automatic DVS Authoring Method

Inseon Jang[1], ChungHyun Ahn[1], and Younseon Jang[2]

[1] Realistic Broadcasting Media Research Department
Electronics and Telecommunications Research Institute
218 Gajeong-ro, Yuseong-gu, Daejeon, Korea
{jinsn,hyun}@etri.re.kr
[2] Deptment of Electronic Engineering
Chungnam National University
99 Daehak-ro, Yuseong-gu, Daejeon, Korea
jangys@cnu.ac.kr

Abstract. Descriptive video service (DVS) is the main method of making programs accessible to those with seeing disabilities, but only a few of conventional broadcasting programs have been reproduced in the form of DVS contents because of practical limitations. It takes much of the time and professional manpower to produce the DVS contents so it is quite costly. In this paper, we propose semi-automatic DVS authoring method. Non-dialog sections detected through audio/subtitles analysis are recommended and then the author is able to insert appropriate audio description (AD) scripts and to produce their synthesized AD using TTS easily. Currently we have completed a basic study and developed the trial version of the proposed.

Keywords: the Blind, Descriptive Video Service, Non-dialog Section Detection, Text-to-Speech.

1 Introduction

Since the broadcasting environments are developed, the digital divide is increased more. Especially, the disabled have trouble in access to the media normally so that this imbalance has been shifted from social and welfare issues to human rights. In order to reduce a gap between the handicapped and healthy people, various kinds of media service have been provided for the disabled. A typical example is DVS (Descriptive Video Service) which makes visual media more accessible to those with seeing disabilities [1]. It provides audio descriptions which explain what is happening visually in the picture with video. Though social requirement, only a few of conventional broadcasting programs have been reproduced in the form of DVS contents so that the actual organization ratio of the DVS program has been insignificant. Because it takes much of the time (for example, generally over 24 hours/program for a soap opera) and professional manpower to produce the DVS contents so it is quite costly. In this paper, we propose a semi-automatic DVS authoring method as a solution. It features the non-dialog section detection based on audio and subtitles analysis, which

K. Miesenberger et al. (Eds.): ICCHP 2014, Part I, LNCS 8547, pp. 8–12, 2014.

are contained in the broadcasting stream. Also it supports to mix the master audio with synthesized AD (Audio Description) using TTS (Text-To-Speech) so that the proposed enables the DVS contents to be produced semi-automatically by one author.

2   Background

The conceptual diagram shown in Fig. 1 illustrates the typical procedure for the DVS contents. For the traditional production, AD (or DVS) scripts are first written in appropriate form which can be inserted into the master audio track by the subjective judgment of the DVS writers. Then voice actor's narrations according to the scripts are mixed with original master audio by the producer.

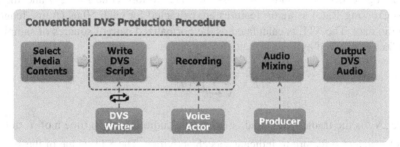

Fig. 1. Block diagram of the conventional DVS authoring method

As mentioned in the previous section, producing the DVS contents is quite costly because it takes much of the time and professional manpower. In order to improve these practical limitations, TTS based AD have been proposed [2,3]. Especially in [2], the results of the survey demonstrated that the majority of the blind and partially sighted respondents accepted TTS AD as an interim solution, while many others also favored TTS AD becoming a permanent option for voice actor's AD. However, they have described synthesized AD using TTS but have not resolved all of inconveniences to overall DVS production.

3   Proposed Method

Fig. 2 shows the block diagram of the proposed method. First, the audio and subtitles data are extracted from imported media contents, then the non-dialog sections are detected from them automatically. Detected non-dialog sections are recommended as candidates where the AD can be entered and then the author inputs the DVS scripts with appropriate length into them selectively. Inserted DVS scripts are synthesized using TTS with the author's intention (e.g. voice selection, speech speed/volume control and pitch control). A TTS converts normal language text into speech with a smooth and natural sounding voice. Its automatic intonation reflects the meaning of the text, with respect to pauses, breath groups, punctuation and context. Finally, the DVS audio is generated to mixed original mater audio with synthesized AD.

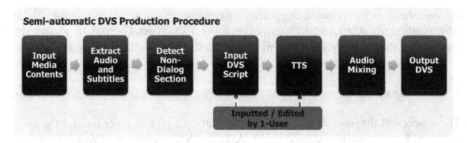

Fig. 2. Block diagram of the proposed semi-automatic DVS authoring method

In proposed method, the audio and subtitles analysis are performed to detect the non-dialog section. For audio analysis, the STE (Short-Time Energy) and the ZCR (Zero Crossing Rate) as audio features are extracted for each 50ms (frame length) of an audio data. The STE is calculated as the normalized sum of squares of samples for each frame, as given by

$$STE = \frac{1}{N} \sum_{n=1}^{N} |x_i(n)|^2 \tag{1}$$

where N is the frame length and $x_i(n)$ is the audio sample at time n of i-th frame. It is classic audio feature to indicate speech activities. The STE value of the speech is generally more than that of silence in the case of small background noise.

The ZCR measures the number of times that the time domain signal changes its sign and is given by

$$ZCR = \frac{1}{N} \sum_{n=2}^{N} sign(n) \tag{2}$$

where $sign(n) = \begin{cases} 1, & \text{for } x(n)x(n-1) < 0 \\ 0, & \text{otherwise} \end{cases}$. It is used to discern unvoiced speech which usually has low STE. Through the comparison between these values and their thresholds, the segmentation is performed and then the non-dialog section is detected.

For the subtitles analysis, the information related to subtitles such as text and its presentation time are extracted from broadcasting stream. For example, the terrestrial digital broadcasting services with MPEG-2 TS (Transport Stream) in Korea and its subtitles text data is contained inside the Picture User Data area of ES (Elementary Stream) of Video TS (Transport Stream) Packet [4, 5]. For subtitles analysis, the subtitles text is first extracted. It performed with a sentence as a unit. In order to recognize one sentence, it detects the punctuation marks which indicate the end of the sentence such as a period '.', an exclamation mark '!' and a question mark '?'. If one of them exists in the text buffer, two PTS (Presentation Time Stamp) values are outputted. One is the PTS of TS packets including first character and the other is the PTS of the TS packet including the punctuation mark which indicates the end of the sentence, respectively. They are utilized as inverse time information of non-dialog section.

4   Implementation

Fig. 3 shows the GUI (Graphic User Interface) of the proposed semi-automatic DVS authoring tool. The media contents captured from the real broadcasting with subtitles, whose format is MPEG-2 TS was imported and its video and audio waveform displayed on the 'Preview' and the 'Audio Track' window, respectively.

If the author clicks the 'analysis' icon on the top of the authoring tool, both audio and subtitles analysis are performed and the non-dialog sections are detected. Their results are displayed on the 'DVS Audio' located in the bottom of the authoring tool. Non-dialog sections through audio and subtitles analysis are indicated by red and blue respectively. Also overlapped sections of two results are indicated by violet. Watching the media, the author is able to find an appropriate timing to entering the AD with these recommended non-dialog sections. AD scripts are able to be written in the 'DVS Card' located in the center of the authoring tool. After entering the AD script, the author can listen and make the TTS audio by clicking the 'Play' and 'Make' button on the each 'DVS Card', respectively. In this implementation, the Power TTS of Diotek was used [6]. Waveforms of generated TTS audio are displayed on the 'DVS audio' and edges of the box where the audio waveform of focused 'DVS Card' is displayed are highlighted by yellow bold lines.

Fig. 3. An example of the proposed semi-automatic DVS authoring tool's GUI

After inserting and editing the AD, the DVS audio to mix an original mater audio with related synthesized ADs is generated by 'export' function, whose format is 'wav'. It also supports to re-generate the video with DVS audio in the form of the 'wmv' (window media video) file.

5   Summary and Future Work

This paper described a semi-automatic DVS authoring method. In this method, non-dialog sections based on the audio/subtitles analysis are recommended as candidate sections where ADs can be entered. Referring to the suggestions, the author can make appropriate AD scripts and its synthesized AD using TTS more easily so that the DVS contents can be semi-automatically produced by one-author.

Currently we have developed the trial version of the proposed and we proceed with adding more advanced functions and making its UI more convenient. Through fruitful tries such as the proposed method to improve the practical problem, it is expected that more services and contents for the blind will be distributed so that the blind will be able to access the media service like sighted people.

Acknowledgments. This research was funded by the MSIP (Ministry of Science, ICT & Future Planning), Korea in the ICT R&D Program 2014.

References

1. ITU-T BT.2207-2, Accessibility to broadcasting services for persons with disabilities (November 2012), http://www.itu.int/pub/R-REP-BT.2207-2-2012
2. Szarkowska, A.: Text-to-speech audio description: towards wider availability of AD. Journal of Specialised Translation (15), 142–163 (2011)
3. Lim, W., Ahn, C.: Descriptive Video Service using Text to Speech. In: Proc. Conference of the Korean Society of Broadcast Engineers (June 2013) (in Korean)
4. CEA-708-D, Digital Television (DTV) Closed Captioning (August 2008)
5. KCS.KO-07.0050, The Standard for DTV Closed Caption System (January 2009)
6. http://www.diotek.com/eng/?page_id=28

Gaps between the Expectations of People with Hearing Impairment toward Subtitles and the Current Conditions for Subtitle Creation in Japan

Sawako Nakajima[1], Naoyuki Okochi[2], Kazutaka Mitobe[1], and Tetsujiro Yamagami[3]

[1] Akita University, 1-1 Tegatagakuenmachi, Akita-shi, Akita, Japan
{nakajima,mitobe}@gipc.akita-u.ac.jp
[2] The University of Tokyo, 4-6-1 Komaba, Meguro-ku, Tokyo, Japan
okochi@bfp.rcast.u-tokyo.ac.jp
[3] Media Access Support Center, 2-9-1-401 Chuo, Nakano-ku, Tokyo, Japan
yamagami@cine.co.jp

Abstract. In this study, questionnaire surveys were conducted with film producers/directors and deaf and hard-of-hearing people to consider the issues surrounding subtitling of films for people with hearing impairment in Japan. The results show that only a small number of film producers taking part in this study have engaged in subtitling, and a majority pointed out the low profitability of producing subtitles under circumstances where the actual movie-viewing demand of hearing-impaired people is unclear. On the other hand, the survey of deaf and hard-of-hearing people revealed the actual movie-viewing tendencies of people with hearing impairment equal to that of hearing people and their high expectations regarding subtitles, despite limited opportunities to watch Japanese films in movie theaters. These results suggest possibilities of creating new economic models for increasing production and access to subtitles for hearing-impaired people sustainably.

Keywords: Subtitle, Deaf People, Hard-of-hearing People, Film Producer, Film Director, Film, Cinema, Audio-Visual Media.

1 Introduction

Audio and visual media play a crucial role in our daily lives—not only in securing information, but also in our cultural lives. However, subtitling and the equipment for presenting subtitles for hearing-impaired people are insufficient. The percentage of audio-visual media that are subtitled in Japan is rather low: the rate for films was 11% in 2012, for DVD & Bluray 4% in 2011, and for television broadcast hours 48.4% in 2012 (according to a survey by the Media Access Support Center, MASC). In the field of television broadcasting, the Japanese government has established a policy aiming to ensure that 100% of programs are subtitled by 2017. Furthermore, with the 2013 decision of Japan's National Diet to ratify the UN Convention on the Rights of Persons with Disabilities and the establishment last year of the Parliamentary League

K. Miesenberger et al. (Eds.): ICCHP 2014, Part I, LNCS 8547, pp. 13–16, 2014.

of Art and Culture for Persons with Disabilities, it can be forecast that Japan's various government agencies will be forced to follow suit in undertaking efforts to ensure not only TV programs but also movies are more accessible, and thus that the need for subtitles will increase in the future. In parallel with these political developments, professional training of subtitle producers has commenced in the private sector, and a robust movement has started to ensure television, films, and commercials are fully accessible. Meanwhile, with regard to subtitle display technology, we have witnessed the spread of second screens (mobile-phone, tablet PC, etc.) and the development of compact head-mounted displays (HMD), as well as the introduction of advanced subtitle presentation apps using audio watermarking in movie theaters; thus the mechanisms are beginning to be put into place that will enable hearing-impaired people to watch the films they want to watch at any time (developed by MASC). In addition, a variety of research regarding subtitles for hearing-impaired people has been conducted, including studies on the effects of caption rates and text reduction on comprehension [1] and methods for expressing emotions using animated text captions [2].

Despite this social context, in which awareness and understanding of subtitles for the hearing-impaired people have spread while technical development has advanced, neither demand nor supply has kept pace. One reason for this is that film/television producers tend not to consider subtitling for people with hearing impairment as work—in fact, there is a lingering association with volunteer activities or welfare. In this study, surveys of film directors/producers and of people with hearing impairment were conducted to clarify current issues surrounding subtitling and the potential movie-going population of people with hearing impairment.

2   Survey on the Current Issues of Subtitling for the Film Directors/Producers

First, a survey of 52 film producers and 6 film directors was conducted in 2012, with the cooperation of the Motion Picture Producers Association of Japan. The survey showed that only 19.2% of these film producers had engaged in the production of subtitles for people with hearing impairment, either at the time of the movie's theatrical release or its release on DVD. These producers covered the costs of the subtitles from their production or distribution budgets, but they noted the difficulty of doing so at a time when these budgets are decreasing, and nearly all of them indicated the problem of cost-effectiveness, given the small number of screenings and low levels of utilization of the subtitled films after their release. Noting that government support is provided for the subtitling of foreign-language editions of Japanese films, the producers (regardless of whether they had engaged in producing subtitles) requested government funding support for subtitling. In this way, the present lack of cost-effectiveness serves as a barrier for film producers to actively embrace subtitle production for deaf and hard-of-hearing people. However, a number of comments reflected a positive orientation; for example, "I would like the opportunity to actually observe the effective process of production," and "I would like to know the extent of the movie-going population of hearing-impaired people and the level of demand for the subtitles." Further, the survey of film directors generated the following comments: "People with hearing impairments should be involved in reviewing the subtitles before they are completed," and "I want to know techniques for subtitling that express the style of each film." These comments suggested a positive orientation toward subtitling for people with hearing impairments, and a desire to make the process more creative and expressive.

3 Survey on the Expectations Regarding Film Subtitles of People with Hearing Impairment

Next, a questionnaire survey of 100 hearing-impaired people was conducted in 2012. The subjects were 48 deaf people (mean [±SD] age, 54.1±13.3 years; 19 males, 29 females) and 52 hard-of-hearing (HOH) people (mean [±SD] age, 61.2±15.2 years; 17 males, 35 females) which were classified on self-identification.

Figure 1 shows the responses of deaf and HOH people to the question "How many films have you watched in movie theaters in the past year?" The results show that 46.8% of deaf and 59.6% of HOH people had watched a film at a movie theater at least once in the past year. According to research carried out by a private-sector re-search institute on about 2600 people living within 30 kilometers of Tokyo, 55.9% had attended a theatrical movie screening in 2012 [3]. This rate of movie attendance is about the same as that of the hearing-impaired people of relatively advanced age that comprised our study. However, when it came to Japanese films (based on the numbers of films viewed at movie theaters in the past year), it was found that the average percentage having watched Japanese films was 22.0% across both deaf and HOH people (23.9% for deaf and 20.8% for HOH people), which was 43.7% lower than the national average for the Japanese movie-going population of 65.7%, estimated from nationwide box office takings in 2012 [4]. Further, when asked whether they had decided against viewing movies at the cinema that were not supported by subtitles, 40.4% of deaf and 51.0% of HOH respondents answered "many times," 48.9% of deaf and 31.4% of HOH respondents answered "several times," while 10.6% of deaf and 17.7% of HOH respondents answered that they had never decided against viewing such a movie. On the other hand, in regard to the possibility of increased opportunities to view movies with subtitles, when asked "If more Japanese films were subtitled, would the frequency of watching Japanese movies in the theater increase?", the responses "Would increase a lot," "Would increase somewhat," "Would not change," and "Other" accounted for 36.2%, 29.8%, 29.8% and 4.3% of responses of deaf people, and 54.2%, 33.3%, 10.4% and 2.1% of responses of HOH people, respectively.

These results suggest that, in the same manner as hearing people, people with hearing impairments do visit movie theaters and enjoy watching movies at theaters. If an environment can be established in which subtitling is promoted and people with hearing impairments can thus appreciate Japanese movies with subtitles, there would be a shift toward viewing Japanese movies (which they had previously decided against viewing). Even if this was not extremely lucrative, it would be expected to produce enough profit to partially cover the costs of subtitling.

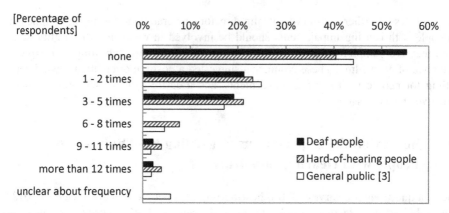

Fig. 1. Results of film attendance including both Japanese and foreign films per year of people with hearing impairments obtained from this study in 2012 and of general public living within 30 km of Tokyo obtained from the previous research in 2012 [3]

4   Conclusion

One of the main findings of this research is that despite missing opportunities to enjoy Japanese films in the movie theaters, the movie-going tendencies of people with hearing impairments is equal   to that of hearing people. On the other hand, while the production of subtitles for hearing-impaired people cannot at present be expected to bring much profit from a business perspective, it is clear that some producers and directors of films, in addition to understanding the significance and the enjoyment of subtitles, are also eager to know their societal effects. As national policy favoring the production of subtitles and technical support for this effort increase, the potential for hearing-impaired people to watch movies in theaters perceived in this study enables us to draw the details of a path toward a sustainable system for subtitling that goes beyond the issue of cost-effectiveness to facilitate new media experiences.

Acknowledgements. This work was supported by grants-in-aid for Strategic Information and Communications R&D Promotion Programme (SCOPE) (no. 112103024).

References

1. Burnham, D., Leigh, G., Noble, W., Jones, C., Tyler, M., Varley, A.: Parameters in Television Captioning for Deaf and Hard-of-Hearing Adults: Effects of Caption Rate Versus Text Reduction on Comprehension. J. Deaf Stud. and Deaf Educ. 13(3), 391–404 (2008)
2. Rashid, R., Vy, Q., Hunt, R., Fels, D.I.: Dancing with Words: Using Animated Text for Captioning. Int. J. Hum-Comput. Int. 24(5), 505–519 (2008)
3. A research for Information and Media Society: In: Dentsu Innovation Institute, Tokyo, p. 92. DIAMOND, Inc. (2013)
4. Motion Picture Producers Association of Japan, Inc.,
   http://www.eiren.org/statistics_e/

Empowerment by Digital Media of People with Disabilities

Three Dimensions of Support

Christian Bühler[1] and Bastian Pelka[2]

[1] TU Dortmund University -Rehabilitation Technology-, Dortmund, Germany
c.buehler@reha-technologie.de
[2] Social Research Centre - Central Scientific Institute, Technische Universität Dortmund,
Dortmund, Germany
pelka@sfs-dortmund.de

Abstract. The paper differentiates three dimensions of access for eInclusion instruments: Firstly, digital media are understood as environments that offer multiple channels for interaction between persons with disabilities and their environment. This dimension is challenged by barriers that hinder people to use digital media. Peer support could be understood as a second dimension: Social media can empower people to act as social innovators and help people with disabilities. Barriers are identified in the effort that has to be done or in unsuitable ICT-applications. On a third dimension, the advantages of "space" are explored: Public internet access points can be understood as a "space" that offers ICT access, support for individual needs and competences, facilitated by specialized staff. The high costs, missing political backing and need for competences could be understood as main barriers here. The paper suggests to capitalize on social innovation approaches to design new support instruments for eInclusion.

Keywords: Digital Media, Social Media, Public Access Point, People with Disability, Empowerment, eInclusion, Telecentre.

1 The Digital Society – Potentials and Barriers for People with Disabilities

Computers are widely accepted as instruments for people with disabilities supporting their ADL (activities of daily living) tasks at home and at work. This is very much supported by the institutional support setting and accepted by people with disabilities. Digital media are entering the everyday life tasks of people with disabilities at two sides: Firstly, digital media are offering support for traditional offline tasks. Examples are digital devices that support communication or orientation. Secondly, with the ubiquity of digital media in every single social sub system (education, politics, economics, health etc), digital media establish a new access mode to societal offers and discourses [1]. The education system strongly builds on ICT mediated learning environments [2], political decision making is increasingly affected by online discourses

K. Miesenberger et al. (Eds.): ICCHP 2014, Part I, LNCS 8547, pp. 17–24, 2014.
© Springer International Publishing Switzerland 2014

and economic procedures are widely transferred into online booking, shopping and selling. This transfer of social routines into digital net-works is supporting the participation of people with disabilities, as certain restrictions are decreased. At the same time, new barriers (accessibility, demand for new competences etc) arise and are about to dig new cleavages between mainstream and disadvantaged persons. It is an information society challenge to shape these environments in a way that persons with disabilities can exercise their rights in the same way than other people [3]. Against this backdrop, this article discusses three access dimensions for instruments aiming at empowering disabled people to use digital media and participate in the digital society.

2   Three Dimensions of Support

2.1   Networking Dimension: Social Media

Besides pure information retrieval from the web and communication by means of telephones combined platforms create new options for information, communication, shared interests, expression of opinions, gaming, entertainment, business etc. Although there exist profound skepticism and criticism with regard to security and privacy of such platforms, they are well accepted and part of the daily lives of very many people. The published numbers of users of the most common networks underpin the widespread acceptance (e.g. Facebook is accessed by 1.19 billion active users every month as of September 30, 2013 [4]). In Germany for example 46% of the people who go online maintain a profile in social networks, 89% of those on Facebook [5]. So, obviously for many people advantages of social networks outbalance the reservations. It is interesting to note that technical accessibility of social networks is still an issue which is not fully solved. An approach following the concept of universal design and computers [6] seems to be necessary. A particular problem occurs in Web 2.0 applications, where users create content which does often not address accessibility at all. In user generated content, frequently used media like pictures and videos remain inaccessible. In this respect ATAG 2.0[1] Part B (candidate recommendation) introduces guidelines how to support authors to produce accessible content.

Generally incomplete accessibility in user generated content seems to be more accepted compared to accessibility problems of the platforms and content of the providers. Therefore, the accessibility of the platforms and its content need to follow WCAG 2.0[2].

Unfortunately, further non-technical barriers can be observed for people with restrictions in cognition [7]. Among those barriers range financing combined with the living situation (e.g. in nursing homes), but also related to the content e.g. complexity, difficult language, orientation and navigation options, mass of information, etc. [7]. Part of the problems are obviously related to the online content: the used language is too difficult and not easy to read; controls are ambiguous and inconsistent; websites provide too much content and too many operation options at a time; advertisements

---

[1] http://www.w3.org/TR/ATAG20/#part_b

[2] http://www.w3.org/TR/WCAG20/

attract the users' focus; captchas, pop-ups, unexpected content change on the page, timed response requirements irritate and distract the users. Many of those problems can be avoided following WCAG 2.0. However, additional measures seem to be necessary. The use of easy to read, plain language are very relevant in this context, but also new ways of presenting the various options of platforms combine with online tutorials and online-help systems are required.

Another part of the problems is connected to the users' settings. As long as the problems with the content and operation are recognized a general hesitation to go online can be observed. Users miss appropriate support ("it is anyway too complicated") or are kept on special private platforms for smaller "safe" communities ("we need to protect against improper and offensive content and economic online traps"). Hence people with learning difficulties and people with cognition problems seem to some extend being excluded from the online development and the inherent potential. Thinking in inclusive terms, it is necessary to investigate, how this kind of exclusion can be overcome. Remaining technical barriers (WCAG 2.0, ATAG 2.0) need to be removed but also content related issues solved. Appropriate assistance, access through simplified/ individualized interfaces, increase of media competence through training and courses, online resources are some of the measures to further investigate. A combination of training in secure environments, online help and assistance in groups is one promising approach. On the other hand, the idea of simplification the interface to access mainstream platforms as in principle proposed in GPII[3] is very much needed.

2.2   Peer Dimension: Peer Support Platforms

Peer support is a principle employed as self-help mechanism in many areas especially in the disability field. It follows the motto of the European Disability Forum (EDF) "Nothing about us without us") and constitutes a powerful instrument unlocking the valuable experience of the peers with high credibility. Of course a direct contact face to face is often desired and also supporting the peer support process. However, nowadays peer support is no longer limited to face to face situations but has already entered the Web with several resulting advantages: First of all it is not restricted to a local community and hence possible to reach many more peers with a request, in principle world-wide. So one can address many peers or in case of orphan diseases/ disabilities at least some of the few existing. Secondly, it makes particular sense in Web and technology related issues, such as software problems, accessibility requirements, use of assistive technology or services. Blogs, FAQ, Fora, groups, Wikis, example videos, special websites provide a lot of options and huge potential for online peer support. A very special form of peer support is based on crowd sourcing where voluntary contributions either very small or maybe bigger are combined with a very profound result. Very good examples in the area of disability are "Universal Subtitles"[4] for provision of subtitles, "Meldestelle Digitale Barrieren"[5] handling access problems to digital

---

[3] www.gpii.net
[4] Subtitling with Universalsubtitles: http://universalsubtitlesorg.html
[5] Meldestelle für digitale Barrieren: http://www.meldestelle.di-ji.de

media, "Wheelmap"[6] for documenting low barrier locations for wheelchair users, "Selfpedia"[7] responding to individual requests, "Knoffit"[8] [8] providing an online glossary. Many of those are mainly based on voluntary contributions, but also financed peer support. More informal peer information can be found within the social networks by direct contacts or search e.g. in groups or channels. A difficult issue for the many good ideas is the wide dissemination and the sustainability on the one hand and the quality of the service e.g. correctness, thematic coverage, response time on the other. It further needs to be combined in a synergetic way with existing more traditional services by the self-help communities and professional providers. It needs to be understood as a complement of service structures rather than a replacement. Of course restricted capacity leads to the question of the most effective and efficient way of spending the available resources or raise further ones.

2.3   Organizational Dimension: Public Internet Access Points and the "Space" Concept

Next to help found on networks or from peers, we can distinguish a third dimension of support for digital competences in actual existing "brick and mortar" welfare institutions (like senior residences, nurseries or community welfare centers). Among these, the possibilities and demands of the information society have been scrutinized during the recent years and several forms of actual offline support institutions for the online world have been developed. More and more public institutions (like libraries, cultural centres and youth clubs for example) and welfare organizations offer free IT infrastructure, internet access, courses and individual support for disadvantaged persons on their way to the digital society as part of their empowerment services. South American and Mediterranean countries have shown a strong movement towards founding special dedicated spaces for eInclusion: the "Telecentre", which is defining itself primarily as an eInclusion actor. In other countries, public internet access points are part of existing welfare institutions and foster eInclusion empowerment as one branch among other welfare services. Libraries for example have recently strongly adopted their role as mediators of digital skills throughout Europe. Both types – dedicated "telecentres" or public internet access points as parts of existing welfare institutions with a broad variety of offers – could be understood as a third dimension of support for eInclusion which is using "space" and "proximity" as means of a low threshold target group approach. "Proximity" in this context does not only refer to geographical proximity, but also includes Boschma's understanding of cognitive, organizational, social and institutional proximity as supporting ingredients of learning [9]. In this sense, telecentres combine different facets of proximity in order to style eInclusion offers that suit best for their specific target groups, acknowledging the high demand of a target group specific approach of eInclusion. The physical space of a

---

[6] Wheelmap: http://wheelmap.org/en/
[7] Selfpedia: http://selfpedia.de
[8] Das Mitmach Wörterbuch: http://www.knoffit.de

telecentre is therefore used as a means to establish proximity to persons that are not profiting from ICT mediated forms of proximity (cf chapter 2.2).

Rissola/Garrido estimate that there are "almost 250,000 eInclusion organizations in the EU27, or an average of one eInclusion organization for every 2,000 inhabitants" [10]. More than a quarter of these institutions (25.8 % of the public and 28.4 % of the third sector funded institutions) are targeting individuals with physical disabilities 18.8 % of the public and 24.1 % of the third sector funded organizations are targeting individuals with mental disabilities ([10]: 59). These institutions, predominantly publicly funded, operate with mostly less than 10 employees and a budget of less than 100,000 EUR per year [10] – shaping the "physical" eInclusion support structure in Europe as widely spread, but consisting of small institutions. The individual public internet access point (may it be a dedicated telecentre or a branch of a library, cultural club or senior residence) can be distinguished by the support it offers and the proximity to its target group. A four level pattern can be developed [2] that is reflecting Boschma's five layers of proximity by referencing to geographical, social, organizational, cognitive and institutional proximity between telecentre and users:

Level 1: On demand assistance	Passive role; the telecentre only reacts to user's demand of help.
Level 2: Level 1 + Training	Provider of digital literacy training, the telecentre can also look for/attract the users and give a social orientation to his/her intervention.
Level 3: Level 2+ User empowerment	Provider of social inclusion services, the telecentre promotes the digital autonomy of the users and their achievement of personal goals taking advantage of the many resources available at the Information Society
Level 4: Level 3 + Active participation in community	Provider of community service-learning, the telecentre promotes the critical use of ICT and the engagement of the users with their local communities/social belonging groups through their active participation of community/social projects.

Fig. 1. Telecentre - Four levels of telecentres

Ongoing research [11,12,13] indicates that albeit public internet access centers are well spread in Europe, there is a need to raise the competences of their staff in addressing disadvantaged persons' digital needs adequately. It is difficult to estimate the number of persons working with end users in the field of eInclusion, but taking 250,000 organisations as a basis, it seems safe to argue that around 250,000-375,000 persons in the EU are working on digital competences of disadvantaged persons. Only tentative research has been done on the socio demographic characteristics of this field of employment [9], but it seems to prevail a young, female and highly educated workforce with a high diversity of educational profiles. This staff can be regarded as

---

[9] Cf.: http://www.efacilitator.eu/wordpress/wp-zontent/uploads/
2010/12/VET4e-i_Multi-Country_Context_AnalysisDEF.pdf

persons with high interest in social innovation and strong links between this person group and social innovators could be traced through different social entrepreneurship organizations. This staff is in need of constant training and issues such as means to initiate and sustain fundraising, certification of competences and a high crew change rate have to be tackled. Recent re-search and development activities are aiming at these issues by developing customized and certifiable curricula for telecentres' staff (see http://www.trans-efacilitator.eu). The aim of this ongoing research and development activities is to support and secure professionalization within this new arising working field in order to make it more efficient for end users and more attractive for staff working on eInclusion issues.

3   Conclusion

Support structures for digital empowerment and eInclusion show a broad variety of approaches – digital, social or institutional; but mostly have just recently started. The short overview provided in this paper illustrates the pioneer status of many approaches and challenges their impact and sustainability. Web 2.0 and interactive social networks seem to provide very good potential to increase participation. But they also create new threats. Inaccessible user generated content and complexity issues create problems. People with intellectual problems are not sufficiently supported in this context. More effort as well online as in offline settings is required. To some extent online peer support and crowd-sourcing can be of help. Research has to show which concepts work and how existing concepts of care for people with disabilities might be connected to the eInclusion question. Many activities in this field are driven by individuals or small organizations, while traditional welfare is organized within large institutions with long established practices and strong connections to policy. The eInclusion scene at the moment is catalyzed by "social innovations" – new social practices and/or social configurations that are aiming at providing better solutions for societal challenges [14], whose origins, rules, behavior patterns, economic underpinnings and sustainability are widely unknown. Actual research has to explain how social innovation works for empowerment of digitally disadvantaged persons, which mechanism work and how policy could use social innovation as a pillar of its eInclusion activities (e.g. the "Digital Agenda Flagship initiative" under the "Europe 2020" strategy). Again, research is only on tentative level by now. But some suggestions from the field of social innovation research include (cf. [15]): The micro layer of innovation – the individual innovator and the individual process of up taking something new – seems to be of important for the "success" of a social innovation. Social innovations seem to rather occur in a stream of small innovations that being introduced as one big new idea. The preparedness of society and its willingness to co-construct an innovation is for social innovations much more important than for technological innovations. Imitating social practices seems to be the heart chamber of social innovation. Seeing these preliminary findings of recent research on social innovation as a binding element of the three support dimensions of empowerment by digital media of people with disabilities, the role of innovative individuals and their networks for providing digital inclusion should be valued highly. To this extend, eInclusion instruments could profit from social innovation research results and scrutinize the process of bringing social ideas to practice. But in contrast to national innovation systems for technological innovations, there is no innovation supporting frame for social innovations. Crowd funding and social media based cooperation seem to fill a gap at the moment, but policy will have to design their role within the context of social innovation for digital inclusion. One way could be to include social entrepreneurs and a combination of "new" and "small" eInclusion approaches with the practice of "old" and "powerful" welfare organizations that are step by step discovering the field of digital inclusion.

Acknowledgement. This paper is partly based on findings produced in a EU LLP funded project ("Trans eFacilitator"): http://www.adam-europe.eu/adam/project/view.htm?prj=9831#.Uuo8_vuj93s and the project Di-Ji (Digital informiert - im Job integriert) funded by BMAS (German Federal Ministry of Labor and Social Affairs): http://di-ji.de

References

1. Paraguay, A.I.B.B.: eInclusion: Policies and Concepts Regarding Persons with Disabilities – Considerations about Brazil and Portugal. In: Stephanidis, C. (ed.) Universal Access in HCI, Part I, HCII 2011. LNCS, vol. 6765, pp. 507–516. Springer, Heidelberg (2011)
2. Kaletka, C., Pelka, B., Diaz, A., Rastrelli, M.: eScouts: Intergen-erational Learning in Blended Environments and Spaces (ILBES) for social inclusion. In: European Distance and eLearning network (EDEN) (Hrsg.), Conference, June 6-9. Book of abstracts, Porto (2012),
http://www.eden-online.org/system/files/
Annual_2012_Porto_BOA.pdf
3. United Nations: The Convention on the Rights of Persons with Disabilities, CRPD (2008),
http://www.un.org/disabilities/default.asp?navid=13&pid=150
4. Facebook 2013 (2013)
5. Busemann, K.: Wer nutzt das Social Web? Ergebnisse der ARD/ZDF-Onlinestudie 2013 in Media Perspektive 7-8/2013 Frankfurt am Main (2013),
http://www.ard-zdf-onlinestudie.de/fileadmin/
Onlinestudie/PDF/Busemann.pdf
6. Bühler, C.: Universal Design - Computer. In: Stone, J., Blouin, M. (eds.) Center for International Rehabilitation Research Information and Exchange (CIRRIE): International Encyclopedia of Rehabilitation (2010),
http://cirrie.buffalo.edu/encyclopedia/en/article/146/
(Abruf: January 29, 2014)
7. Berger, A., et al.: Web 2.0 barrierefrei. Eine Studie zur Nutzung von Web 2.0 Anwendungen durch Menschen mit Behinderung. Aktion Mensch e.V. Online verfügbar unter, Bonn (2010),
http://publikationen.aktion-mensch.de/
barrierefrei/Studie_Web_2.0.pdf

8. Schaten, M., Lexis, M., Roentgen, U., Bühler, C., de Witte, L.: User Centered Design in Practice – Developing Software with/ for People with Cognitive and Intellectual Disabilities. In: Assistive Technology: From Research to Practice, AAATE 2013, pp. 815–822. IOS Press (2013)
9. Boschma, R.A.: Proximity and Innovation: A Critical Assessment. Regional Studies 39, 61–74 (2005)
10. Rissola, G., Garrido, M.: Survey on eInclusion Actors in the EU27 (2013), http://ftp.jrc.es/EURdoc/JRC84429.pdf
11. Lohrmann, L.: Trans eFacilitator comparative report (2013), http://www.adam-europe.eu/prj/9831/prd/1/1/3.6%20Comparative%20Report.pdf
12. Pelka, B., Kaletka, C.: eFacilitators: Functional Hybrids between ICT Teaching and Community Management. In: Deitmer, L., Gessler, M., Manning, S. (eds.) Proceedings of the ECER VETNET Conference 2012: Papers Presented for the VETNET Programme of ECER 2012 at Cádiz, September 18-21. EERA Network: 02. Vocational Education and Training (VETNET), Wissenschaftsforum Bildung und Gesellschaft e.V, Berlin (2012a), http://www.ecer-vetnet.wifo-gate.org, http://www.b.shuttle.de/wifo/vetnet/ecer12.htm, http://vetnet.mixxt.org/networks/files/file.111156
13. Pelka, B., Kaletka, C.: Blended Learning Spaces as a Social Innovation for Local Inclusion, Integration and Employability. In: EIRP Proceedings, vol. 7 (2012b), http://www.proceedings.univ-danubius.ro/index.php/eirp/article/view/1362/1308
14. Howaldt, J., Schwarz, M.: Social Innovation: Concepts, Research Fields and International Trends. In: Henning, K., Hees, F. (eds.) Studies for Innovation in a Modern Working Environment - International Monitoring, vol. 5, p. 2011. Eigenverlag, Aachen (2010), http://www.sfs-dort-mund.de/odb/Repository/Publication/Doc%5C1289%5CIMO_Trendstudie_Howaldt_Schwarz_englische_Version.pdf (June 9, 2011)
15. Howaldt, J., Kopp, R., Schwarz, M.: Social innovations as drivers of social change – Tarde's disregarded contribution to social innovation theory building. Social Frontiers. The next edge of social innovation research (2014)

Tactile Captions: Augmenting Visual Captions

Raja Kushalnagar, Vignesh Ramachandran, and Tae Oh

Rochester Institute of Technology, Rochester, New York, USA
http://www.rit.edu/avd

Abstract. We explore the efficacy of tactile captions as a supplement to online captioned video. Closed captions are not fully accessible, because many auditory signals are not easily represented by words, e.g., the sound of the ball being hit by a bat, or to describe a ring tone. The goal is to explore whether audiovisual information can be effectively represented through an equivalent tactile-visual interface. We compare viewers preferences between viewing video with captions alone, and captions plus tactile captions. Our study showed that viewers significantly preferred tactile captions to captions.

Keywords: Accessible Technology, Educational Technology, Deaf and Hard of Hearing Users, Dual Tasks.

1 Introduction

Modern user interfaces increasingly mirror physical and social interaction, as this leverages existing human interactive knowledge. However, the range and experience of this interaction, such as gesture and speech is incredibly diverse and can be a barrier for users with different abilities and cultures. It is difficult to represent all auditory information through captions. First, many environmental sounds are not easily expressed in text, as they are perceptually meaningful, but semantically vague. Even if these sounds are expressed as onamatoepic wprds, different cultures use different words to represent these sounds [8]. Second, it is hard to read captions at normal to fast speech, especially deaf viewers who are likely to be less fluent readers [7]. Third, viewers have to split their attention between the video and the captions and this reduces the amount of time they can spend on each [4],[6]. We explore viewers preferences of tactile captions that enhance auditory information, such as a phone ring. We use the Pebble Smartwatch to provide the tactile feedback via vibrations. The pattern of vibration is programmed into the watch and synchronized with the video and captions so as to ensure that the vibration occurs at the same time as the video events.

By varying the various frequencies and intensities of vibrations, it becomes possible to interpolate and simulate environmental sounds in everyday activities through vibrations; for example a phone ring, wake-up-alarm, and so on.

2 Related Work

Tactile feedback, also called haptics, conveys information through the sense of touch through vibrations or motions. There is scant prior research on combining

K. Miesenberger et al. (Eds.): ICCHP 2014, Part I, LNCS 8547, pp. 25–32, 2014.

Fig. 1. A viewer watching a video with the pebble watch strapped on

video captions with tactile feedback for videos. One line of research has focused on simulating the hearing experience by providing a rich, whole body tactile experience. Prior research has explored sensory substituion via a tactile chair. The tactile chair provided a tactile sensory system to provide sensory substitution for music. It provided a high-resolution audio-tactile version of music to the body [2,3]. The system uses eight separate audio-tactile channels to deliver sound to the body, and provides an opportunity to experience a broad range of musical elements as physical vibrations. The other line of research has focused on augmentation of audio or visual information with tactile information. For example, Apostolopoulos et al. [1] and Khoo et al. [5] used the vibration function of smart phones to provide tactile information in parallel with auditory information for navigation for blind and low vision users.

We used a Pebble smart-watch as shown in Figure 1 to convey vibrations synchronized with the captions. The watch can receive notifications from a personal phone and transmit tactile feedback.

3   Design Criteria

Based on feedback from deaf and hard of hearing consumers, we tried to satisfy the following criteria:

Fig. 2. An example of an environmental sound: a warning sign falling over

1. The tactile information should correlate with the auditory information.
2. The choice of words in the captions that describe the auditory event to be translated to tactile information should occur slightly after the tactile information for best clarity.
3. The hardware and software requirements must not minimize cost and intrusiveness.

4   Tactile Captions Evaluation

For deaf or hard of hearing people the captions provide a way to understand the scene in place. Video-tactile vibration can provide perception and understanding of a scene that is more in depth when just reading a caption along with the video.

4.1   System

We recorded a video that included several routine activities that have associated environmental sounds. For example, we developed a specific vibration pattern to mimic the feel of the thud when an object falls, as shown in Figure 2.

Next, we programmed corresponding vibrations for each environmental sound in the video. Finally, we created two versions of the video: one with tactile captions and the other without tactile feedback.

The experimental system had three components: a computer, watch and a tablet. There are two connections between the computer and the watch. The first connection is between the computer and the Pebble Application over the

Fig. 3. An example of an environmental sound: crumpling up a paper sheet

network. So it is essential that the application and the computer be on the same network for it to function smoothly. The second connection is between the application and the smart watch over a Bluetooth connection. The smart watch needs to have its Bluetooth interface enabled and paired with the device that is hosting the application.

4.2   Programming

The vibration of the watch can be programmed and thus controlled by appropriate programming. The video with captions is analyzed and the synchronization of the video and the vibration is done. The video and the vibrations are loosely coupled i.e. manually synchronized and the vibrations occur at the occurrence of a particular event in the video, for example when the actor crumples up his homework and throws it away, as shown in Figure 3.

This time synchronization is achieved by manually programming it to vibrate at a particular time or at regular time intervals. Although we do not have direct control over the intensity of the vibration, we can simulate varying levels of intensity and patterns by setting the gap between individual vibrations and the total duration of each vibration.

5   Study

We evaluated whether adding tactile feedback would increase deaf and hard of hearing consumer satisfaction in following audiovisuals with captions.

Fig. 4. An example of an environmental sound: large printer running a print job

We recorded a 4-minute long captioned video that followed a student's activities on campus. There were ten aural events that were supplemented with tactile captions. In Figure 4, the viewer will feel vibrations that suggest "whirring."

The usual way to caption this environmental sound: "(printer whirring)" is not onamatopic, nor does it carry any information about the noise itself. In the absence of sound, when the video is viewed with captions alone, a viewer who merely reads "whirring", does not have a clear idea of what is being shown on TV. On the other hand, when the viewer experiences the tactile vibration of whirring, while watching this particular event, the viewer will be able to relate to the feeling a hearing person gets when they hear the whirring.

5.1   Participants

We recruited 20 subjects (12 male, 8 female, ages 18-29). All participants typically watched videos with captions. We recruited through flyers and word of mouth on the campus. We asked students to contact and schedule through email appointment. All of them were reimbursed for their participation. Each person was directed to an online web page that explained the purpose of the study. Next, the students were asked to complete a short demographic questionnaire in order to determine eligibility for the test and asked for informed consent. Before the start of the study, the participants viewed a 30-second introduction video that enabled them to familiarize themselves and get comfortable with the experience of tactile captions. We picked the sound of water running as shown in Figure 5. It has mostly high frequency components, yet is something that is often felt.

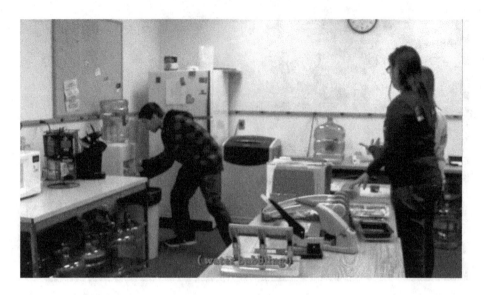

Fig. 5. An example of an environmental sound: water running

It is hard for most deaf and hard of hearing people to hear it as it is common to be more deaf at higher frequencies rather than lower frequencies.

The participants then answered a user preference questionnaire after watching each video. The questionnaire measured user preferences using Likert scale and open-ended questions.

Half of the viewers watched the captioned video and then the tactile-captioned video; the other half watched the tactile captioned video first and then the captioned video. The total time for the study was about 20 minutes. We measured user preferences using Likert scale and open-ended questions.

After the participant completed watching the sequence of segments, they were asked to complete a questionnaire. Then they were asked to answer in their own words in response to the questions that asked for their thoughts.

The Likert rating questionnaire asked the following questions on a scale of 1-5:

1. "The [tactile captions/captions] was easy to use."
2. "I like the [tactile captions/captions]."
3. "How helpful were the [tactile-captions/captions] in understanding the environmental sounds in the video?"
4. "I would recommend [tactile captions/captions] for use by other deaf/hard-of-hearing students."
5. "I am confident in using [tactile captions/captions] in class."

6 Results

The [tactile captions/captions] was easy to use I like the [tactile captions/captions]. I would recommend [tactile captions/captions] for use by other deaf/hard-of-hearing students. I am confident in using [tactile captions/captions] in class. How helpful were the [tactile-captions/captions] in understanding the environmental sounds in the video?

The participants rated captions and tactile captions equally in terms of ease of use: The average rating of captions was 4.3 (SD=0.3), while the average rating of tactile captions was 4.2 (SD=0.4). Next, the participants liked the tactile captions more than the captions: the average rating for tactile captions was 4.5 (SD=0.4) whereas the rating for plain captions was only 3.9 (SD=0.3). Similarly, the participants rated the tactile captions as more helpful at 4.7 (SD=0.5), while their average rating for captions was 4.0 (SD=0.5). The participants also were more willing to recommend the tactile captions for others to use: the average rating for captions was 4.2 (SD=0.5), while the average rating for tactile captions for 4.3 (SD=0.5). Finally, participants rated tactile captions very highly in terms of understanding the caption sounds as compared to the captions: the average rating for understanding events based on tactile captions was 4.8 (SD=0.2), while the average rating for captions was 4.2 (SD=0.3).

These findings are supported by participant comments. For example, one participant noted: "Tactile captions let me feel the doorbell rather than just looking at the description: "doorbell ringing"". Another participant commented: "videos and labs would be good, and field trips. lectures are possible but if its entirely verbal, I am not sure how it would be useful." On the other hand, some students felt it was too distracting: "I like the vibration to get my attention, but at the same time, it was distracting when trying to watch the video."

7 Future Work

There is great potential for further work with the tactile caption paradigm. We will do evaluation studies in which viewers will be asked to describe what they saw and felt. We will rate these descriptions for accuracy in relation to the actual auditory events, such as different phone ringtones, or a car turn signal versus a seat-belt signal. The current research work has laid a foundation for taking the idea behind the research to the next level. In terms of accuracy, a more accurate vibration motor than the pebble watch could be used. The aim is to explore more and more patterns and intensities of vibrations in order to build a continuous vibration system rather than the current discrete vibration system. Further exploration leads us towards custom-built vibration products rather than using the pebble smart-watch. Use of custom-built product will provide us the freedom to explore the various intensities and patterns of vibrations as well as control them more efficiently.

The future prospect is to build a system that not only conveys broad range of everyday activities but also a deeper range of vibrations that are able to communicate the emotions in the video to the user. The current product that we have used, i.e. pebble smart watch is tied on to the wrist of the user. The extent of impact it creates on the users senses is a point of consideration. Hence, one other important feature that needs to be kept in mind is the type of product that is built. It is important that the sensitive points of the user are stimulated to the maximum extent so that the desired results are achieved and the user is satisfied completely.

Acknowledgements. We thank our participants for their time and comments in evaluating the captions. This work is supported by a grant from the National Science Foundation IIS-1218056.

References

1. Apostolopoulos, I., Fallah, N., Folmer, E., Bekris, K.E.: Integrated online localization and navigation for people with visual impairments using smart phones. ACM Transactions on Interactive Intelligent Systems 3(4), 1–28 (2014), http://dl.acm.org/citation.cfm?doid=2567808.2499669
2. Baijal, A., Kim, J., Branje, C., Russo, F., Fels, D.I.: Composing vibrotactile music: A multi-sensory experience with the emoti-chair. In: 2012 IEEE Haptics Symposium (HAPTICS), pp. 509–515. IEEE (March 2012), http://ieeexplore.ieee.org/lpdocs/epic03/wrapper.htm?arnumber=6183839
3. Branje, C., Karam, M., Fels, D., Russo, F.: Enhancing entertainment through a multimodal chair interface. In: 2009 IEEE Toronto International Conference Science and Technology for Humanity (TIC-STH), pp. 636–641. IEEE (September 2009), http://ieeexplore.ieee.org/lpdocs/epic03/wrapper.htm?arnumber=5444421
4. Jensema, C.: Viewer reaction to different television captioning speeds. American Annals of the Deaf 143(4), 318–324 (1998), http://www.ncbi.nlm.nih.gov/pubmed/9842059
5. Khoo, W.L., Seidel, E.L., Zhu, Z.: Designing a virtual environment to evaluate multimodal sensors for assisting the visually impaired. In: Miesenberger, K., Karshmer, A., Penaz, P., Zagler, W. (eds.) ICCHP 2012, Part II. LNCS, vol. 7383, pp. 573–580. Springer, Heidelberg (2012), http://link.springer.com/10.1007/978-3-642-31534-3
6. Kushalnagar, R.S., Lasecki, W.S., Bigham, J.P.: Captions Versus Transcripts for Online Video Content. In: 10th International Cross-Disclipinary Conference on Web Accessibility (W4A), pp. 32:1–32:4. ACM Press, Rio De Janerio (2013), http://dl.acm.org/citation.cfm?id=2461142
7. Kushalnagar, R.S., Lasecki, W.S., Bigham, J.P.: Accessibility Evaluation of Classroom Captions. ACM Transactions on Accessible Computing 5(3), 1–24 (2014), http://dl.acm.org/citation.cfm?doid=2568367.2543578
8. Sundaram, S., Narayanan, S.: Classification of sound clips by two schemes: Using onomatopoeia and semantic labels. In: 2008 IEEE International Conference on Multimedia and Expo, pp. 1341–1344. IEEE (June 2008), http://ieeexplore.ieee.org/lpdocs/epic03/wrapper.htm?arnumber=4607691

Captioning System with Function of Inserting Mathematical Formula Images

Yoshinori Takeuchi[1], Yuji Sato[1], Kazuki Horiike[2], Daisuke Wakatsuki[3], Hiroki Minagawa[3], and Noboru Ohnishi[2]

[1] Department of Information Systems, School of Informatics, Daido University, 10-3 Takiharu-cho, Minami-ku, Nagoya 457-8530 Japan
ytake@daido-it.ac.jp, db10044@stumail.daido-it.ac.jp
[2] Graduate School of Information Science, Nagoya University, Furo-cho, Chikusa-ku, Nagoya 464-8603 Japan
horiike@ohnishi.m.is.nagoya-u.ac.jp, ohnishi@is.nagoya-u.ac.jp
[3] Faculty of Industrial Technology, Tsukuba University of Technology, Amakubo 4-3-15, Tsukuba, Ibaraki 305-8520 Japan
{waka,minagawa}@a.tsukuba-tech.ac.jp

Abstract. We propose a captioning system with a function of inserting mathematical formula images. [We match/The system matches?] mathematical formulas presented orally during a lecture with those simultaneously projected on a screen in the lecture room. We then manually extract the mathematical formula images from the screen for displaying on the monitor of the system. A captionist can input mathematical formulas by pressing a corresponding function key. This is much easier than inputting mathematical formulas by typing. We conducted an experiment in which participants evaluated the usefulness of the proposed captioning system. Experimental results showed that 14 of the 22 participants could input more sentences when using the function of inserting mathematical formula images than when not using it. Furthermore, from the results of a questionnaire, we could confirm that the proposed system is effective.

1 Introduction

Hearing-impaired students go to university and attend lectures with hearing-able students. They cannot listen to lecturers, so they need complementary technologies, such as sign-language interpretation and PC captioning, which is already used at several universities, and a system is being developed that will remotely transcribe a lecturer's speech.

Kato *et al.* investigated information required by a remote transcriber and methods of displaying that information on a transcriber's monitor [1]. With this approach, content keywords are displayed on the monitor, and the transcriber can use these keywords to input the summarized text of the lecture. Miyoshi *et al.* developed a remote real-time captioning system [2] that sends audiovisual signals from a classroom to a remote location where captionists type captions in

K. Miesenberger et al. (Eds.): ICCHP 2014, Part I, LNCS 8547, pp. 33–40, 2014.

real time. Miyoshi *et al.* also developed a support system for real-time captioning by using automatic speech recognition software [3]. This system uses the "re-speak" method, in which a captionist listens to the instructor and then repeats what the instructor said into the system. The acoustic model of the automatic speech recognition system is trained on the captionist's speech, so the recognition rate is high. The output text of the system is then checked and modified with modifiers, and the system creates a complete caption. Another technology that has captured much interest is real-time speech recognition. Wald and Bain proposed an automatic speech recognition system for universal access to communication and learning [7]. Takeuchi *et al.* proposed a system to extract an object such as a mathematical formula in a screen of a classroom[4]. The system uses automatic speech recognition to extract the demonstrative speech phrase[5] and pointing gesture recognition to extract the pointing object on the slide. The system then matches the pointing object with the demonstrative speech phrase and extracts the object pointed to by the lecturer along with the corresponding demonstrative phrase. The extracted object is displayed on the transcriber's screen to help the transcription. Takeuchi et al. reported on the effectiveness of this system[6].

An even more difficult task is the transcription of mathematical formulas. Complex mathematical formulas are often presented in a lecture. It is quite difficult to transcribe complex mathematical formulas by using a PC keyboard; therefore, transcribers need an easy mathematical-formula input method.

Takeuchi *et al.* are developing a system for matching mathematical formulas presented orally during a lecture with those simultaneously projected on the lecture room screen [8]. The system recognizes the utterance of mathematical formulas by automatic speech recognition and the pointing gesture of the lecturer by analyzing the locus of the pointing stick. It then integrates the utterance and pointing gesture and extracts the pointed mathematical formulas on the slide with a corresponding utterance. The extracted and matched formulas are then shown to the transcriber to help him or her transcribe the formulas correctly.

We propose a captioning system that enables the easy input of mathematical formulas. Mathematical formulas are extracted from the screen in the lecture room and presented on the computer screen for the captionist. The captionist can input the mathematical formulas by pressing the corresponding function key assigned to the extracted mathematical formula.

2   Captioning System with a Function of Inserting Mathematical Formula

Figure 1 shows the screen of the captioning system. The bottom part of the screen is for text input and top is for displaying mathematical formulas. Mathematical formulas are displayed with the corresponding function key such as 'F1' and 'F2.' We match mathematical formulas presented orally during a lecture with those simultaneously projected on the screen in the lecture room. We then manually extract the mathematical formula images from the screen for display on the

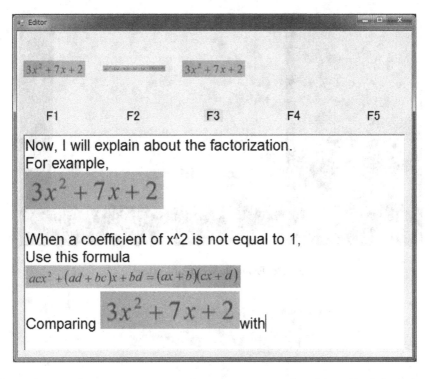

Fig. 1. Screen of captioning system: Sentences are translated into English. Original sentences were in Japanese.

mathematical formula display part of the captioning system. When the first mathematical formula image is extracted, it is displayed in the area labeled 'F1'. Then, the next image is displayed in the area labeled 'F2', and so on until 'F5'. After the image is displayed on 'F5', it goes back to 'F1'. The color of the newly displayed label turns yellow. Therefore, the captionist can be aware which mathematical formula is the most newly extracted. The captionist can input the mathematical formula by pressing the corresponding function key. This is much easier than inputting mathematical formulas by typing. We call this function "easy insertion" for short.

Figure 2 shows an example scene of a lecture. This image is just after the lecturer pointed to the mathematical formula $3x^2 + 7x + 2$ with a corresponding utterance. We are currently developing a system that extracts the mathematical formula images with the corresponding utterance automatically. However, in the system proposed for this research, the image is extracted manually. After the lecturer points to the mathematical formula shown in Fig. 2, we extract the mathematical formula image, as shown in Fig. 3. The extracted mathematical formula image is copied to a particular shared folder that the system

Fig. 2. Example scene of lecture

$$3x^2 + 7x + 2$$

Fig. 3. Example of extracted mathematical formula

monitors. Once the new mathematical formula image is copied to this folder, the system shows this image on the mathematical formula display part. The input summary text with the mathematical formula image can be saved as a rich-text format text document.

3 Experimental Results

We conducted an experiment in which participants evaluated the usefulness of our captioning system. We created short scenes of a mathematics lecture, as shown in Fig. 2. The lecturer always points to mathematical formulas on the screen, each with a corresponding demonstrative word.

We showed the participants these lecture scenes. When the lecturer pointed a mathematical formula on the screen, we extracted and displayed it on the screen for the participants. We showed them two scenes. The details of the scenes are summarized in Table 1. The scenes were almost the same length and same difficulty level in captioning. We recruited 22 graduate and undergraduate students who could type very quickly and who would understand the content of the lecture.

Table 1. Two scenes used for captioning evaluation

	scene A	scene B
duration	3m 30s	3m 8s
no. of sentences to be written	15	15

Table 2. Grouping for captioning evaluation

group	1st experiment	2nd experiment
A	scene A without easy insertion	scene B with easy insertion
B	scene A with easy insertion	scene B without easy insertion
C	scene B without easy insertion	scene A with easy insertion
D	scene B with easy insertion	scene A without easy insertion

We grouped the participants into four groups. Each group viewed the scenes in a different order and with or without the easy insertion. Table 2 lists the details of each group. We gave the participants a practice lecture scene and allowed them about two minutes to study it before each captioning experiment. Figure 4 shows the arrangement of the experiment. The left monitor displayed the screen of the proposed system and right monitor displayed the lecture clip. This situation simulated remote captioning. The participants watched the lecture through the monitor from a distant location and typed a summary text.

We selected the important sentences in the lecture that should be written as captions in advance. The number of sentences to be written is shown in Table 1. We counted the number of important sentences that appeared in the sentences the participants input. The number of input sentences by each participant is given in Table 3.

After a participant finished captioning, we asked about the usefulness of the system. We asked two questions. One was about the easiness of captioning, and the other was about the usefulness of the easy insertion. Figures 5 and 6 show the histograms of each answer, respectively.

Table 3. Number of input sentences

group	A					B					
participant	1	2	3	4	5	6	7	8	9	10	11
with easy insertion	8	10	9	9	10	8	14	8	10	10	12
without easy insertion	4	5	7	9	12	8	8	0	4	3	3

group	C					D					
participant	12	13	14	15	16	17	18	19	20	21	22
with easy insertion	7	2	3	5	4	4	3	4	4	9	6
without easy insertion	2	5	4	5	4	3	5	3	2	6	2

Fig. 4. Arrangement of captioning experiment

4   Discussion

In Table 3, 14 of the 22 participants could input more sentences when using the easy insertion than when not using it. Four participants input the same sentences, and 4 participants could not input more sentences when using the easy insertion. A Wilcoxon signed-rank test showed that both results were significant at the 1%

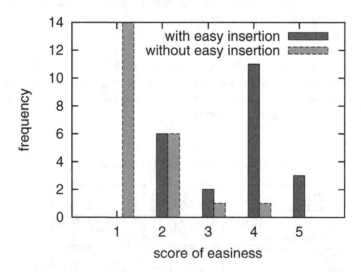

Fig. 5. Histogram of easiness: 1-hard, 2-somewhat hard, 3-moderate, 4-somewhat easy and 5-easy

level. These results show that the proposed system can help captionists easily input captions with mathematical formulas.

In Fig. 5, the average score of easiness increased to 3.5 when using the easy insertion from 1.5 when not using it. Captioning of mathematical formulas is difficult; however, it becomes easy when the captionist uses the proposed system. Six participants answered that captioning was somewhat difficult even when they used the easy insertion. Each participants typing skills were different; therefore, the task of inputting summary text was somewhat difficult for those who did not have good typing skills even when they used this function. All participants answered that the proposed system is useful or somewhat useful, as shown in Fig. 6.

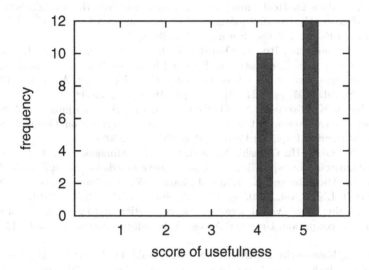

Fig. 6. Histogram of usefulness: 1-not useful, 2-somewhat not useful, 3-moderate, 4-somewhat useful and 5-useful

5 Conclusion

We proposed a captioning system with the function of inserting mathematical formula images. With this system, a captionist can easily input mathematical formulas into the text by pressing the corresponding function key.

Experimental results show that a captionist can input more sentences when using the easy insertion than when not using it. The results from the questionnaire show that the system makes it easy to input caption mathematical formulas.

Further work should be done to automatically extract mathematical formula images, and experiments during an actual lecture should be conducted. We should also consider a display method of inputting summary text with mathematical formula images for hearing impaired students.

This work was supported by JSPS KAKENHI Grant Number 24500642.

References

1. Kato, N., Kawano, S., Miyoshi, S., Nishioka, T., Murakami, H., Minagawa, H., Wakatsuki, D., Shirasawa, M., Ishihara, Y., Naito, I.: Subjective Evaluation of Displaying Keywords for Speech to Text Service Operators. The Transactions of Human Interface Society 9(2), 195–203 (2007) (in Japanese)
2. Miyoshi, S., Kawano, S., Nishioka, T., Kato, N., Shirasawa, M., Murakami, H., Minagawa, H., Ishihara, Y., Naito, I., Wakatsuki, D., Kuroki, H., Kobayashi, M.: A Basic Study on Supplementary Visual Information for Real-Time Captionists in the Lecture of Information Science. IEICE Transactions on Information and Systems (Japanese edition) J91-D(9) 2236–2246 (2008)
3. Miyoshi, S., Kuroki, H., Kawano, S., Shirasawa, M., Ishihara, Y., Kobayashi, M.: Support Technique for Real-Time Captionist to Use Speech Recognition Software. In: Miesenberger, K., Klaus, J., Zagler, W.L., Karshmer, A.I. (eds.) ICCHP 2008. LNCS, vol. 5105, pp. 647–650. Springer, Heidelberg (2008)
4. Takeuchi, Y., Saito, K., Ito, A., Ohnishi, N., Iizuka, S., Nakajima, S.: Extracting Pointing Object with Demonstrative Speech Phrase for Remote Transcription in Lecture. In: Miesenberger, K., Klaus, J., Zagler, W.L., Karshmer, A.I. (eds.) ICCHP 2008. LNCS, vol. 5105, pp. 624–631. Springer, Heidelberg (2008)
5. Ito, A., Saito, K., Takeuchi, Y., Ohnishi, N., Iizuka, S., Nakajima, S.: A Study on Demonstrative Words Extraction in Instructor Utterance on Communication Support for Hearing Impaired Persons, ibid, 632–639 (2008)
6. Takeuchi, Y., Ohta, H., Ohnishi, N., Wakatsuki, D., Minagawa, H.: Extraction of Displayed Objects Corresponding to Demonstrative Words for use in Remote Transcription. In: Miesenberger, K., Klaus, J., Zagler, W., Karshmer, A. (eds.) ICCHP 2010, Part II. LNCS, vol. 6180, pp. 152–159. Springer, Heidelberg (2010)
7. Wald, M., Bain, K.: Universal access to communication and learning: role of automatic speech recognition. Universal Access in the Information Society 6(4), 435–447 (2007)
8. Takeuchi, Y., Kawaguchi, H., Ohnishi, N., Wakatsuki, D., Minagawa, H.: A System for Matching Mathematical Formulas Spoken during a Lecture with Those Displayed on the Screen for Use in Remote Transcription. In: Miesenberger, K., Karshmer, A., Penaz, P., Zagler, W. (eds.) ICCHP 2012, Part I. LNCS, vol. 7382, pp. 142–149. Springer, Heidelberg (2012)

Synote Second Screening: Using Mobile Devices for Video Annotation and Control

Mike Wald, Yunjia Li, George Cockshull, David Hulme, Douglas Moore,
Aidan Purdy-Say, and James Robinson

ECS, University of Southampton, Southampton, United Kingdom
m.wald@soton.ac.uk

Abstract. This paper describes a new important enhancement to Synote, the freely available, award winning, open source, web based application that makes web hosted recordings easier to access, search, manage, and exploit for learners, teachers and other users. The feature supports 'flipped' classrooms and allows students to ask questions through annotations on their personal mobile devices while also being able to remotely control and play relevant video fragments.

Keywords: Second Screen, Recorded Lectures, Learning, Flipping Classroom.

1 Introduction

In their study of eLearning tools Rohani and Yazdani [1] identified several issues including a lack of social networking, a failure to use tags to categorise resources and an inability to raise questions or share comments. The award winning web application Synote helps address these issues as captioned video can be tagged and users can add comments as accessible synchronised annotations [2]. Text, audio, images, annotation and video can enhance the effectiveness of conveying information through eLearning [3] and a recorded lecture allows a student to decide when and where they wish to study. At home students can work at their own pace taking regular breaks to reduce fatigue and can play a video with their preferred screen size, audio volume, lighting and assistive technologies, pausing or rewinding when necessary to make it easier for them to take notes. 'Flipping the Classroom' (3) means teachers can ask students to watch videos at home and then discuss them in class afterwards. Students finding some of the content difficult to understand may not actually ask the questions in class that they had prepared at home due to communication difficulties, lack of confidence, or time pressures. Synote Second Screening helps address these issues by allowing students to ask questions through annotations on their personal devices while also being able to remotely control and play the relevant video fragments. The lecturer or the other students in the room can use media fragment annotations to respond to these questions or post additional information about the video. Kam et al. [4] showed that 66% of users preferred collaborative to independent note taking and Synote Second Screening could help facilitate this.

K. Miesenberger et al. (Eds.): ICCHP 2014, Part I, LNCS 8547, pp. 41–44, 2014.

2   Example Use Case

Synote Second Screening enables annotations to be made in real time on mobile second screen devices when a video is replayed on a main screen. Students using controls on their mobile device can navigate through the presenter's video while being able to add annotations to the video for a chosen duration with an optional fragment added to highlight a particular region of the video. The ability to control a video from a second screen can be disabled by the presenter. All text and image thumbnail annotations are available on each participant's second screen. Thumbnails alt attributes are automatically made relevant and correct for the image, so a screen reader will announce "The thumbnail for [video name] at [timecode]". Synote Second Screening promotes interactive, collaborative working in real-time and allows reviewing of annotations from previous sessions.

Participants are undergraduate geologists who are beginning to learn about Hydraulic Fracking. They were asked by their lecturer, Laura to watch half of an introductory BBC Documentary video at home and are now discussing it in class. Figure 1 shows John's tablet in front of the main screen as he joins the new discussion session with Description 'Review of BBC Hydraulic Fracking Documentary' and Location '46/3001'. Figure 1 also shows that before John joins the session Laura is the only participant and she has selected the three options: 'show annotations from other sessions' which makes annotations added in any previous sessions also visible in this session; 'allow participants to control video player' so they can show Laura which media fragments they wish to discuss; 'pin annotations to player timeline' to give a quick overview on the timeline of which parts of the video have been annotated and whether they are important and questions or comments.

Fig. 1. (a) Laura creates session from tablet fragment on main screen; (b) John selects timecode to play video

Fig. 2. (a) Laura marks media fragment and timeline flags as important. (b) Fragment on main screen video and timeline pips.

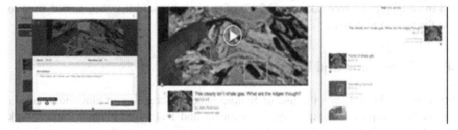

Fig. 3. (a) John selects area, writes annotation thumbnail and flags as question. (b) John's annotation and fragment appears on all screens.

All participants now join the session by selecting from the session list. Laura gives an overview of the video, and then asks the participants if they have any questions. John explains he had an issue understanding a part of the explanation of the fracking process. John had created an annotation from 5:03-5:26 at home stating that he found it confusing. He selects the time code on this annotation to play this video fragment on the main screen (Figure 2). The video starts at 5.03 and stops automatically at 5.26. Laura is then able to explain the fracking process in more detail and to John's satisfaction before asking if there are any more questions. Sarah asks Laura to explain the image of rock more thoroughly and uses the timeline on her device to jump to the appropriate point in the video which is 17:46 to 17:49. Laura draws a rectangular fragment on a dark pore region and explains that this is where the gas collects and flags it as important (Figure 3). Laura continues the explanation and replays the video which now shows the marked fragment as a yellow rectangle with the importance of the annotation shown on the timeline by pip colour (Figure 4). John then creates the annotation 'this clearly isn't Shale Gas, what are the ridges though?' with a fragment on a light region of the thumbnail image and flags it as a question (Figure 5) and it appears on all screens as a yellow rectangle (Figure 6). When the class ends and

Laura signs out on the main screen an alert box on John's second screen shows that the session has ended.

3   Testing and Evaluation

The final version of Synote Second Screening was developed following evaluation and comment on an initial prototype by a focus group of seven students. PowerMapper and Webaim's Wave toolbar for Firefox and The Paciello Group Coour Contrast Analyser were used to help confirm accessibility. Testing and user evaluations took place through 10 participants simulating real classroom tasks using keyboard and mouse input on laptops and touchscreen input on tablets and smartphones. The tasks were: Joining a session; Adding an annotation; Adding a media fragment; Marking a new annotation as a question; Deleting a personal annotation; Controlling the video playback; Playing a media fragment; Viewing session comments only and Creating a session. Analysis of results showed that Synote Second Screening was accessible, effective and intuitive to use and 80% of participants agreed the system would help aid in collaborative note taking and 90% of participants said that they would want to use the system in classes.

4   Conclusion and Future Work

Students would welcome the use of Synote Second Screening in classrooms and it would help improve accessibility, engagement and learning. Planned future work includes: the addition of a `one-click' button to notify a lecturer that something in the video was confusing; a more advanced, permission-based authorisation system to enable the teacher to allow only certain participants to control playback from their second screen device; providing a text box to search for a timecode rather than only moving the timeline slider to a specific location in a video; and classrooms trials.

References

1. Rohani, M.B., Yazdani, K.: Web 2.0 Embedded E-Learning: A Case Study. In: International Conference on Innovation Management and Technology Research (ICIMTR 2012), pp. 603–608. IEEE (2012)
2. Wald, M.: Important new enhancements to inclusive learning using recorded lectures. In: Miesenberger, K., Karshmer, A., Penaz, P., Zagler, W. (eds.) ICCHP 2012, Part I. LNCS, vol. 7382, pp. 108–115. Springer, Heidelberg (2012)
3. Wallace, A.: Social learning platforms and the flipped classroom. In: Second International Conference on e-Learning and e-Technologies in Education (ICEEE), pp. 198–200. IEEE (2013)
4. Kam, M., Wang, J., Iles, A., Tse, E., Chiu, J., Glaser, D., Tarshish, O., Canny, J.: Livenotes: a system for cooperative and augmented note-taking in lecture. In: Proceedings of the SIGCHI Conference on Human Factors in Computing Systems, CHI 2005, pp. 531–540. ACM (2005)

Digital Content and Media Accessibility

Introduction to the Special Thematic Session

David Crombie and Pierre Mersch

HKU University of the Arts Utrecht, Utrecht, The Netherlands
{david.crombie,pierre.mersch}@hku.nl

Abstract. This Special Thematic Session (STS) on Digital Content and Media Accessibility is intended to provide a focus on activities related to making digital content and audio-visual media accessible for people with sensory impairements. The eACCESS+ Thematic Network (eACCESS+) was established to bring together different stakeholders in the eAccessibility chain and foster the take-up of accessibility by mainstream players. It has largely concentrated on these issues and produced a large pool of resources dealing with eAccessibility-related information. The Technology and Innovation for Smart Publishing Thematic Network (TISP) aims to bring together publishing companies and ICT enterprises, in order to stimulate new partnerships and business models. This short paper introduces the STS on Digital Content and Media Accessibility and the related papers.

Keywords: eAccessibility, Audio-Visual Media, Digital Content, Publishing, Accessible Services.

1 Introduction

Digital content accessibility refers to the inclusive practice of making digital contents usable by people of all abilities and disabilities. This is closely linked to the wider issue of web accessibility, where significant progress has been made to improve the accessibility of digital content.

Reading technologies offer such an opportunity to create a more inclusive society and the Publishers Association, the Society of Authors, the Association of Authors' Agents and the Right to Read Alliance have recommended that publishers routinely enable text to speech on all eBooks.

Nowadays, if a large portion of top-selling titles is available as braille, audio and large print, this proportion falls dramatically when talking about less popular titles. Readers who have to rely on specialist provision have therefore a very restricted choice. [1]

From the user perspective, the more a document is adaptable for diverse needs (e.g. legibility, readability, use paradigms, a possibility to annotate, enrich, convert and translate) the more it is accessible. Despite some encouraging moves in the International legislation regarding the cross-border circulation of books in an accessible

K. Miesenberger et al. (Eds.): ICCHP 2014, Part I, LNCS 8547, pp. 45–48, 2014.
© Springer International Publishing Switzerland 2014

formats (as with the recently adopted WIPO Marrakesh Treaty to Facilitate Access to Published Works for Persons Who Are Blind, Visually Impaired, or Otherwise Print Disabled and the European ETIN initiative) obstacles however still exist when it comes to the mere possibility to edit the published content.

In the publishing sector the evolution of electronic formats has created new opportunities to produce and deliver digital contents accessible from scratch, needing less additional processing or adaptation.

Yet digital reading is a complex process that involves not only formats, but also instruments (reading software, apps and devices) and containers (websites, e-commerce channels). As new technologies emerge, innovative approaches and solutions offer impaired people new ways of delivering and interacting with content. All the stakeholders across the value chain should be involved in this dialogue, as promoted by the TISP Network that brings together publishers and ICT providers. [2]

(Audio-visual) Media provide an efficient way of gaining access to information and entertainment and over recent years new technologies have emerged with a great potential for increased accessibility raising high expectations from people with sensory disabilities. At the dawn of the 21st century television is an almost universally used technology. For this reason and for many years, solutions, standards and legislation have been developed in order to enhance the accessibility of audio-visual media. The convergence of digital media offer both opportunities and challenges to media accessibility in a field that is evolving at an ever-increasing pace.

As the digital switch-over is being completed in Europe, the hopes for an increased accessibility of AV media have been poorly met while the up-and-coming technologies in the media arena bring along new accessibility challenges and fears that the progress done so far may be forgotten. Limitations and barriers preventing AV media accessibility from becoming a mainstream reality now lie in various broader issues and are no-longer limited to technological problems. These are related to usability, interoperability and standards issues as well as lack of business-case for take-up by mainstream actors, legal barriers (for example for the transnational reuse of accessible content), difficulties in the reuse of accessible content over time and across different platforms as AV content is longer viewed on television only and the life-time of content is often longer than that of the delivery platform etc [1], [3,4].

2   Areas Covered by This STS

In their paper Fume et al. present an innovative system and propose a new transliteration method of Text-to-speech DAISY content creation. DaisyRings features versatility of input document (by making use of plain text and not making use of preventive document formats), limited edit functions at reduced costs and presents the advantage of being compatible with current working processes. It can convert plain text to DAISY content including formatted HTML and audio data via automatic Text-to-Speech Technology. The approach to DAISY Content creation proposed by Fume et al. will facilitate the work of transliteration workers who will be able to make and edit content more easily and dramatically more quickly than is currently possible with the conventional method.

This paper presented by Sorin et al. deals with an ongoing experiment aiming at improving structural information accessibility by blind people, using text-to-speech along with audio cues. Their approach consists of looking closely at textual objects in a text. Textual objects have different properties and the relationships among them and are of crucial importance to the readers but hardly accessible and comprehensible for blind readers using screen readers or a braille document. Despite this importance and despite the fact that most of the digital documents have a very rich layout and many visual properties, only a few initiatives try to restore part of this structural information to blind users. The approach suggested in this research is to annotate the different textual objects along with their properties in XML and to restore them during document presentation with a Text-to-Speech software using prosody variation, audio cues and discursive descriptions of the properties. In the longer term, Sorin and al. intend to explore further restitution modalities such as specialized audio or haptic feedback.

In their research, Argyroploulos et al. present the results of a series of experiments in the field of haptic representation of typographic meta-information embedded in rich texts documents. The study aimed at studying patterns and characteristics of hand movements of blind readers when they receive typographic metadata (bold and italic) by touch through a braille display. The results from the experiments depict the types of participants' phonological errors and the performance of usage of six-dot and eight-dot braille codes. The paper discuss the educational implication of their results and the importance of the development of a suitable design of tactile rendition of typographic signals metadata through six or eight-dot braille code in favor of a better perception and comprehension.

In their paper, Lee et al. present the results of a series of comparative studies of listen-ing speed of Korean Text-to-Speech technologies for blind users based on their screen reader experience.

The paper presented by Ošlejšek et al. discusses the concept of "communicative images" and aims to provide graphical information by means of dialogue interaction, which is suitable for people with various disabilities. This paper deals with the utilization of formal ontologies for the process of image annotation and dialogue-based investigation of images in the context of assistive technologies.

Petrie et al. present the results of a series of experiments of crowd sourcing descriptions of images available on museum websites for visually impaired visitors. These experiments were conducted with the support of Museum Victoria and were based on the observation that despite the fact that guidelines advocate describing images on the Web for visually impaired Web users, there are very few guidelines available on how to write images description. Based on their study, Petrie et al. propose a refined version of the guidelines and examples of good practice.

The paper presented by Lim et al. deal with the closed captions for hearing impaired viewers and proposes an approach making use of dynamic subtitles to convey non-verbal emotional information to the viewers. The approach suggested by Lim et al. analyses pitch and speech energy as a kind of emotional information and suggest to use of dynamic captioning scheme to render these emotional information to the viewers in the form of variation in colors (color) and font size and thickness (voice level).

References

1. eACCESS+ Network: Roadmap to eAccessibility (2013),
   http://www.eaccessplus.eu
2. TISP Thematic Network, http://www.smartbook-tisp.eu
3. Looms, P.O.: Making Television Accessible, G3ict-ITU, ITU, Geneva, Switzerland (2011)
4. Looms, P.O.: Standardization of Audiovisual Media Accessibility: from vision to reality. In: Biswas, P., et al. (eds.) A Multimodal End-2-End Approach to Accessible Computing. Human-Computer Interaction Series. Springer, London (2013)

A Comparison of the Listening Speed of the Korean TTS for the Blind: Based on Their Screen Reader Experiences

Heeyeon Lee[1], Yujin Jang[2], and Ki-Hyung Hong[2]

[1] Center for QoLT, Seoul National University, Seoul, Korea
heeyeonlee@hotmail.com
[2] Department of Computer Science, Sungshin University, Seoul, Korea
jangy100@nate.com
kihyung.hong@gmail.com

Abstract. The purpose of this study was to examine the listening speed of the Korean TTS for the blind based on their screen reader experiences. Among ten participants, five people have used a screen reader and the other five had few experiences of using a screen reader. Participants were asked to recall what they heard after they listened to the same sentences for ten repeated sentence sets, and they were asked to recall what they heard after they heard different sentences for the five random sentence sets. For all sentence sets, sentences were provided with fifteen differentiated speeds ranged from 0.8 to 3.6. The results showed that there were positive correlations between participants' screen reader experiences and their listening speed of the Korean TTS, and between the familiarity of sentences and the differences in the listening speed.

Keywords: The Blind, Screen Reader, TTS, Listening Speed.

1   Introduction

With the help of rapid development of technology, nowadays, many people who are blind can access a lot of information by using a screen reader. A screen reader is a useful tool for the blind to gain access to various educational opportunities, employments, and social interactions. Many people think that the blind will process auditory stimuli much faster than ordinary people. However, there are few research studies regarding the listening speed of the blind.

The purpose of this study is to examine the maximum and the best listening speed of the Korean TTS (Text-to-Speech) for the blind in order to provide screen reader developers meaningful information by comparing the Korean TTS listening speeds among the individuals with screen reader experiences and those without the experiences.

2   Related Works

Not many studies have been conducted regarding the listening speed of the screen reader for the blind. Asakawa and Ino [1] examined the fastest and the most suitable

K. Miesenberger et al. (Eds.): ICCHP 2014, Part I, LNCS 8547, pp. 49–52, 2014.
© Springer International Publishing Switzerland 2014

listening speed of the Japanese TTS for the blind using the objective and subjective test procedures. The results presented that (1) advanced participants recognized the spoken test sentences 1.6 times faster than the fastest speed of TTS engine used for the test, so they suggested that Japanese TTS should support faster speeds, and (2) participants' listening speed was affected by the familiarity of the test sentences.

In the previous study [3], we found that (1) participants' recall accuracy tended to increase as the TTS speed decreases, (2) participants' subjective recall accuracy was higher than objective recall accuracy in the repeated tests and vice versa in the random tests.

3   Methodology

In order to apply Asakawa and Ino [1]'s study to the Korean TTS, we developed Korean sentence sets [2]. Most sentence sets consist of 7 chunks (words) considering participants' recall capabilities. In order to examine the effect of the sentence familiarity on the listening speed, sentence sets were classified as familiar sentences and unfamiliar sentences [2,3]. Familiar sentences were chosen from the websites where the blind has been frequently visiting and from the final report of the 21st century Sejong project [4] which contains familiar Korean idiomatic expressions. Unfamiliar sentences were selected from the websites with academic jargons and unfamiliar Korean idiomatic expressions.

A total of 10 people who were blind (three females/seven males, aged from 23 to 63) participated in this study. Five of them have used a screen reader in their daily lives (an advanced group), and the other five people have few experiences of using a screen reader (a novice group).

In a repeated test, participants were asked to recall what they heard after they heard the same sentences from the fastest to the slowest speed (15 differentiated speeds, Range=0.8-3.6, SD=0.2) for the ten sentence sets. The standard speed 1.0 means 285.96 syllables per minute which is similar to the Korean's ordinary communication speed of 300.00 syllables per minute. In a random test, participants were asked to recall what they heard after they heard the different sentences for the five sentence sets. Participants' objective listening accuracy was calculated by the number of correctly recalled syllables out of the total number of syllables in a sentence. Each participant's maximum listening speed was defined as at least 50% correctly recalled speed and the best listening speed was defined as at least 90% correctly recalled speed. Each participant's maximum and best listening speed were calculated by objective recall accuracy.

4   Results

Figure 1 present the maximum and the best listening speeds in the repeated test. As shown in Figure 1, the advanced group's listening speeds were faster than the novice group's listening speeds for all of the repeated sentence sets. Differences in the maximum speeds between two groups ranged from 0.48 to 0.86, and those in the best listening speeds ranged from 0.36 to 0.88 (See the dotted lines in Figure 1). The average difference of the maximum listening speeds was 0.59 and that of the best listening speeds was 0.61.

In the repeated test, the biggest difference of the maximum and the best listening speeds between two groups was found at the sentence set number 7 and the smallest difference was found at the sentence set number 10. The sentence set number 7 was an unfamiliar sentence containing English words. The sentence set number 10 was a familiar Korean proverb. In the sentence set number 9, even participants in the advanced group showed slow listening speeds compared to their listening speeds in the other sentence sets, and those in the novice group did not reach the best listening speed even at the slowest listening speed (see Figure 1). The sentence set number 9 was too difficult for participants to recall, so it was excluded from the analysis.

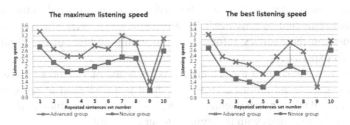

Fig. 1. The listening speed in the repeated test

Figure 2 presents the maximum and the best listening speeds in the random test. As shown in Figure 2, the advanced group's listening speeds were faster than the novice group's listening speeds for all of the random sentences sets. Differences in the maximum listening speeds between two groups ranged from 0.32 to 0.68, and those in the best listening speeds ranged from 0.24 to 0.96 (See the dotted lines in Figure 2). The average difference of the maximum listening speeds was 0.54 and that of the best listening speeds was 0.50.

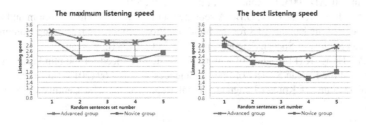

Fig. 2. The listening speed in the random test

In the random test, the biggest difference of the maximum listening speeds between two groups was found at the sentence set number 2 and 4, and the smallest difference was found at the sentence set number 1. The biggest difference of the best listening speeds between two groups was found at the sentence set number 5, and the smallest difference was found at the sentence set number 1. The sentence set number

2 consisted of unfamiliar Korean proverbs, and the sentence set number 4 and 5 contained academic jargons, abbreviation of English words or numbers. The sentence set number 1 consisted of familiar Korean proverbs.

These results presented that the differences in the listening speeds between two groups for the familiar sentences were larger than those for the unfamiliar sentences in both the random and repeated test.

5   Conclusion and Future Work

In this study, we found out that there were positive correlations between participants' screen reader experiences and their listening speeds of the Korean TTS. The result also showed that, in both the random and repeated test, the difference in the listening speeds between the advanced group and the novice group was related to the familiarity of sentences. This finding provides TTS developers and special educators meaningful information on the auditory information processing abilities of the blind with a variety of TTS experiences.

In this study, we have used the sentence sets consisted of 7 chunks (words) considering participants' recall abilities. However, there is a limitation of not controlling the number of syllables in each sentence. Therefore, in further studies, it is recommended to use the sentences with the same number of syllables.

Acknowledgements. This research was supported by the R&D grant of rehabilitation services by Korean National Rehabilitation Center Research Institute, Ministry of Health & Welfare.

References

1. Asakawa, C., Takagi, H., Ino, S., Ifukube, T.: Maximum listening speeds for the blind. In: Proceedings ICAD 2003, Boston, USA, pp. 276–279 (2003)
2. Lee, H.Y., Hong, K.-H., Park, D.B.: A sentence set for evaluation in maximum and best listening speed of the Korean TTS for the blind. In: Proceedings of 2013 Spring Conference of the Korean Society of Speech Sciences, pp. 242–244 (2013) (in Korean)
3. Lee, H.Y., Hong, K.H.: A study of Korean TTS listening speed for the blind using a Screen Reader. J. of the Korean Society of Speech Sciences 5(3), 63–69 (2013) (in Korean)
4. National Institute of Korean Language: Final Report of the 21st Century Sejong Project (2011)

Dynamic Subtitle Authoring Method Based on Audio Analysis for the Hearing Impaired

Wootaek Lim, Inseon Jang, and Chunghyun Ahn

Electronics and Telecommunications Research Institute, Realistic Broadcasting Media
Research Department, 218 Gajeong-ro, Yuseong-gu, Daejeon, Korea
{wtlim,jinsn,hyun}@etri.re.kr

Abstract. The broadcasting and the Internet are important parts of modern society that a life without media is now unimaginable. However, hearing impaired people have difficulty in understanding media content due to the loss of audio information. If subtitles are available, subtitling with video can be helpful. In this paper, we propose a dynamic subtitle authoring method based on audio analysis for the hearing impaired. We analyze the audio signal and explore a set of audio features that include STE, ZCR, Pitch and MFCC. Using these features, we align the subtitle with the speech and match extracted speech features to subtitle as different text colors, sizes and thicknesses. Furthermore, it highlights the text via aligning them with the voice and tagging the speaker ID using the speaker recognition.

Keywords: The Hearing Impaired, Media Accessibility, Dynamic Subtitle, Speaker Recognition.

1   Introduction

Media technologies for the broadcasting and the Internet have been widely increasing and now enable viewers what they want to select among a variety of video contents according to their personal taste. However such an environment evolves, digital divide of the people with disabilities is increasing.

Today, there are 650 million people with disabilities in the world and their number and proportion is growing as humanity lives longer. Especially, there are more than 66 million people suffering from hearing impairment and it brings them difficulty in video content understanding due to the loss of audio information [1]. The main method to make media programs accessible to them is providing subtitles with the video. A typical example is broadcasting with subtitles, which is now a common media service. However, the general media service with subtitle provides only a basic function to display the actor's dialogue in the form of text, so hearing impaired people are limited to understand not only the context but also the atmosphere.

In this paper, new dynamic subtitle authoring method based on the audio analysis is proposed. It supports to analyze the audio signals contained in the media contents and to display the subtitles dynamically according to the analysis results so that hearing impairment users are able to understand the media content more readily.

K. Miesenberger et al. (Eds.): ICCHP 2014, Part I, LNCS 8547, pp. 53–60, 2014.

2   Background

In this section, we introduce subtitles in the media for the hearing impaired and review the related works for this field.

2.1   Subtitles in Media

Subtitles are typically used to transcribe the speech and additional information for the hearing impaired, which are provided primarily for them. Viewers with normal hearing can easily experience this if they ever attempt to watch TV without sound. Fig. 1 shows examples of the many type of subtitles used with video content.

Fig. 1. Examples of the many type of subtitles used with video content

For the television, the line 21 in the vertical blanking interval has been allocated to carry subtitle information. At a television station, a subtitle encoder is used to put the data onto line 21. At home, either a recent model television or set-top box may be used to decode the subtitles and display the text on the screen [2]. Online video streaming and media content also offer subtitle formats for video. The video can be played with a SAMI (*.smi), SubViewer (*.sub), SubRip (*.srt) or Advanced Substation Alpha (*.ass) file.

2.2   Related Works

Many researchers have developed methods for subtitling in various ways. Adjusting the subtitle to a suitable speech level and speed can improve the understanding of content for hearing impaired was proved in [3]. A dynamic subtitling scheme to enhance the accessibility of content for the hearing impaired was proposed in [4]. This method suggests synchronous highlighting of the script by aligning it with the speech signal to help the hearing impaired audience keep better track and to perceive the scripts. It also locates the subtitle in a suitable region by applying face detection and tracking algorithms. This method, however, requires the heavy algorithm and the database because of the face recognition and the dictionary based script-speech alignment. Another study has proposed an ambient font technique for visualizing the non-verbal information for the hearing impaired through adjustments of font size, color, and so on [5]. This method has a drawback of using only sound level and pitch features. Therefore, a simple method to reduce complexity while maintaining the quality of the dynamic subtitle is required.

3   The Proposed Dynamic Subtitle Authoring Method

Our major goal is to enhance the video accessibility for the hearing impaired. Fig. 2 demonstrates the schematic of our proposed dynamic subtitle authoring method.

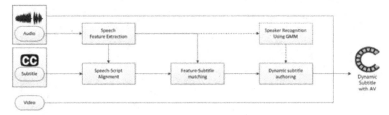

Fig. 2. The schematic illustration of the dynamic subtitle authoring method

3.1   Speech Feature Extraction

Short Time Energy. The short time energy (STE) indicates the magnitude of each signal frame. Let $x_i(n)$ (where n=1, ... ,N) represents the audio samples of the i-th frame whose length is N. Then, for each frame energy is calculated according to the following equation:

$$E(i) = \frac{1}{N}\sum_{n=1}^{N}|x_i(n)|^2 \tag{1}$$

In addition, some studies reveal that variations in voice volume impart important information about human emotions [6].   Therefore, in the proposed, we symbolize the speech energy as a form of emotional information to obtain more cues about the dialogue.

Zero-Crossing Rate. Zero-Crossing Rate (ZCR) refers to the number of zero crossings in a given frame. Sequential samples in a speech signal have different algebraic signs. ZCR is a measurement of frequency composition in signals. In general, voiced segments have lower ZCR compared to unvoiced segments [7].

$$Z(i) = \frac{1}{2N}\sum_{n=1}^{N}|sgn[x_i(n)] - sgn[x_i(n-1)]| \tag{2}$$

Pitch. Pitch is the fundamental frequency in a speech, musical note or tone. Detection of the pitch from monophonic music or speech signals has been studied [8]. Current study indicates that the voice pitch frequency is related to human emotional states [6]. Therefore, in our study, we used a pitch characteristic to represent the speaker's feelings.

MFCC. Mel-frequency cepstral coefficients (MFCCs) are commonly used as a valid feature in speech signal processing such as speech/speaker recognition. This feature is based on the known characteristic of the human ear's critical bandwidth with frequency. The MFCC makes use of two types of filter based on human ear characteristics: linearly spaced filters and logarithmically spaced filters. The phonetically important characteristics of speech are captured by expressing the signal in the Mel frequency scale. As shown in Fig. 3, this scale has linear frequency spacing below 1000 Hz and a logarithmic spacing above 1000 Hz [9].

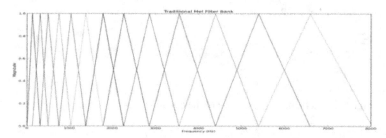

Fig. 3. Mel-scale filter bank

After conducting Mel-frequency filter wrapping, the log mel-spectrum has to be converted back to time domain. This result is called the MFCC which provides a good representation of the spectral properties of the signal for the given frame. The MFCCs can be converted to a time domain using the Discrete Cosine Transform (DCT). A block diagram of the MFCC extraction process is given in Fig. 4 [9], [10].

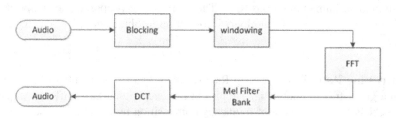

Fig. 4. A block diagram of MFCC extraction process

3.2   Speech-Subtitle Alignment

The speech and the subtitle in a broadcasting system tend to be unsynchronized due to the program production process. When subtitling is done during a live broadcast, synchronization is not possible due to manufacturing and transmission delays. For multimedia applications, we extract the subtitle data from MPEG-2 Transport Stream of the ATSC-based digital TV signal and generate a subtitle file using the extracted subtitle data and time information [11]. The extracted subtitle data time is compensated using the default value and Voice Activity Detection (VAD) algorithm. The ITU Making TV Accessible Group recommends a subtitle delay between on-screen speech and the subtitles being displayed from 5 to 14 seconds in the case of live subtitling

[12]. In South Korea, the delay time in DTV broadcasting is recommended as 2-4 seconds, so the time delay must be compensated uniformly [11]. After that, we conduct the VAD algorithm for more elaborate time synchronization. Use of the VAD method categorizes the signal frames into Voiced/Unvoiced frames. In this paper, we simply implement the VAD using STE and ZCR.

In other cases, a pre-authored subtitle with video content that has a start/end point that is created manually can be also used for dynamic subtitling.

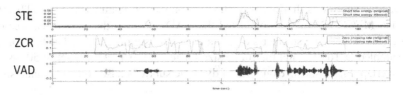

Fig. 5. Example of VAD using STE and ZCR

3.3   Speech Feature-Subtitle Matching

The fundamental frequency of speech can vary from 40 Hz for male voices to 600 Hz for children or female voices. Based on it, human voice tone-color matching method was proposed in [13]. In our research, we match the high-pitched voice to red color and low-pitched voice to violet color, as shown in Fig. 6. This method was devised by proportionally connecting the relationship between the wavelength of light and the frequency of sound.

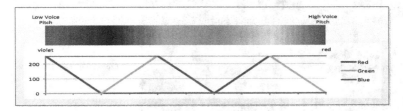

Fig. 6. Color-tone matching method based on color wavelength and voice pitch

The signal energy is one of the important features that represent the speaker's emotions, as previously mentioned. Therefore, in this study we match the speech energy level and energy variation to the text size and thickness of the letters.

3.4   Speaker Recognition

For speaker recognition, the Gaussian Mixture Model (GMM) was trained using the extracted MFCCs. GMM is a parametric probability density function represented as a weighted sum of Gaussian component densities. It is commonly used as a parametric model of the probability distribution of continuous measurements or features in a biometric system, such as vocal-tract related spectral features in a speaker recognition system [14]. Speaker recognition process is conducted in only script sections and tagging the speakers ID to a subtitle.

4   Experiment Result

For dynamic subtitle authoring, we extracted the speech features such as STE, ZCR, Pitch and MFCCs. Next, we conducted the VAD and map the speech features onto subtitles for express the speaker's emotion as previously mentioned. The test contents were sampled at 16 kHz and the frame size for feature extraction is set to 50 ms with 50 % overlap. Fig. 7 shows examples of dynamic subtitles based on audio analysis.

Fig. 7. Examples of dynamic subtitles based on audio analysis

Furthermore, the speaker recognition using GMM was applied. The test contents are composed of diverse genres, including drama, news, sports and documentary. Each test contents are 5~10 minutes-long and the number of test set is 10. We trained the 20 speakers for modeling database and the identification accuracy is about 85 %. Fig. 8 shows examples of speaker recognition in dynamic subtitles.

Fig. 8. Examples of speaker recognition in dynamic subtitles

5   Conclusion

This paper describes a new dynamic subtitle authoring method by analyzing the speech signal. In the proposed, we extracted the speech features such as STE, ZCR, Pitch and MFCCs. Using these features, we created the dynamic subtitle for the hearing impaired to understand the scene contexts. The proposed method was achieved with simple algorithm and it can be readily applied to conventional subtitle production system. It confirmed that the proposed subtitles authoring system provides the acceptable quality through the experiments using the various media contents.

Acknowledgment. This research was funded by the MSIP (Ministry of Science, ICT & Future Planning), Korea in the ICT R&D Program 2014.

References

1. BSeries, B.T.: Accessibility to broadcasting services for persons with disabilities (2011)
2. Abrahamian, S.: N. T. S. C. In: EIA-608 and EIA-708 closed captioning (2006)
3. Boyd, J., Vader, E.A.: Captioned television for the deaf. Am. Ann. Hearing Impaired 117(1), 32–37 (1972)
4. Hong, R., et al.: Dynamic captioning: video accessibility enhancement for hearing impairment. In: Proceedings of the International Conference on Multimedia. ACM (2010)

5. Seto, S., et al.: Subtitle system visualizing non-verbal expressions in voice for hearing impaired-Ambient Font. In: Proceeding of the 10th Asia-Pacific Industrial Engineering and Management Systems (2010)
6. Ververidis, D., Kotropoulos, C.: Emotional speech recognition: Resources, features, and methods. Speech Communication 48(9), 1162–1181 (2006)
7. Jalil, M., Butt, F.A., Malik, A.: Short-time energy, magnitude, zero crossing rate and autocorrelation measurement for discriminating voiced and unvoiced segments of speech signals. In: International Conference on Technological Advances in Electrical, Electronics and Computer Engineering (2013)
8. Hess, W.: Pitch Determination of Speech Signals. Springer (1983)
9. Hasan, M.R., Jamil, M., Rabbani, M.G., Rahman, M.S.: Speaker identification using mel frequency cepstral coefficients (2004)
10. https://instruct1.cit.cornell.edu/courses/ece576/FinalProjects/f2008/pae26_jsc59/pae26_jsc59/
11. Kim, N.: A Study on Multimedia Application Service using DTV Closed Caption Data. Journal of Broadcast Engineering (2009)
12. Peter, O.L.: Making Television Accessible. Report published by the International Telecommunications Union, in collaboration with The Global Initiative for Inclusive Information and Communication Technologies. ITU. Media accessibility 101 (2011)
13. Maryon, E.: The Science of Tone-Color. CC Birchard & Co., Boston (1924)
14. Reynolds, D.A., Quatieri, T.F., Dunn, R.B.: Speaker verification using adapted Gaussian mixture models. Digital Signal Processing 10(1) (2000)

Communicating Text Structure to Blind People with Text-to-Speech

Laurent Sorin[1], Julie Lemarié[2], Nathalie Aussenac-Gilles[1], Mustapha Mojahid[1], and Bernard Oriola[1]

[1] Université de Toulouse; UPS & CNRS; IRIT; ELIPSE et MELODI, Toulouse, France
{sorin,aussenac,mojahid,oriola}@irit.fr
[2] Université de Toulouse; Laboratoire CLLE, 5 Allées Antonio Machado, Toulouse, France
lemarie@univ-tlse2.fr

Abstract. This paper presents the results of an experiment conducted with nine blind subjects for the evaluation of two audio restitution methods for headings, using Text-To-Speech. We used specialized audio and two voices to demarcate headings. This work is part of a research project which focuses on structural information accessibility for the blind in digital documents.

Keywords: Accessibility of Digital Documents, Blind People, Document Structure, Text-to-Speech, Specialized Audio.

1   Introduction

Accessibility of information contained in digital documents is a crucial challenge for visually impaired people, especially for blind users. Indeed, blind users should be in the center of design issues since Internet and new technologies are an unprecedented opportunity for them to perform tasks that they can hardly do without [1]. Even though there has been much effort on designing assistive technologies and accessible information, the situation often remains frustrating for blind users [2], [3]. Indeed, digital documents in general (web pages, text-documents, spreadsheets, etc.) are primarily designed to be visually displayed, so that the expressive means offered by a spatial layout are often intensively used to create complex objects like tables, graphs, outlines, menus, etc. In this context, our project aims at allowing blind users to access a document's visual properties and logical structure and at designing new reading tools.

In the frame of our project, we focus on documents "textual objects", i.e. every block or portion of the text visually distinct from the rest via its disposition and typography, which we could call the "contrast" principle. The Textual Architecture Model [4], a linguistics model, states that every salient block (or textual object) in a document was created by the author in order to structure his message. The different types of textual objects in a document each have different properties and relationships between them. This structural information coming from the visual properties of a

K. Miesenberger et al. (Eds.): ICCHP 2014, Part I, LNCS 8547, pp. 61–68, 2014.

document is crucial for the understanding of its content from a sighted reader point of view (see [5] for a review).

Most of the digital documents have a very rich layout and many visual properties. Yet, only few existing projects try to restore part of this structural information to blind users: for instance [6] focuses on HTML tables and frames, whereas [7] focuses on enumerations (lists of items in a document) and [8] focuses on hierarchical structures in general. Our global approach in this research project is to annotate the different textual objects along with their properties (as described by the Textual Architecture Model and SARA), and to restore them during document presentation with a Text-To-Speech software. The aim is to restore the multi-level logical structure of the documents, for instance local emphasis and global structure.

In this paper we present our results about the restitution of headings properties to blind people using Text-To-Speech, in order to validate our global approach. We made the hypothesis that providing blind users with headings properties will help them build a better mental representation of the document.

In the first part we describe what structural information is and why we want to make it accessible. The second part describes the methodology used to test our hypothesis. Finally, we present and discuss the obtained results.

2   Structural Information Restitution to Blind People

As mentioned before, logical information about documents structure conveyed by the text formatting and layout is crucial in order to comprehend the text content. We chose to focus on the restitution of headings because of their important role in text comprehension. Indeed, according to [9], headings help (sighted) readers to build a global representation of the text topic structure, which improves memorization in general and also activates the reader's relevant prior knowledge.

However, blind people almost never have access to this information while using a Text-To-Speech (TTS) software (for instance via a screen-reader) on a computer. In fact, TTS still struggle to render text objects like headings [10]. Indeed, with a screen-reader a heading is signaled with the sentence "Heading Level N", either on a braille terminal or orally with a TTS. This restitution method doesn't emphasize the heading over the rest of the content, so that the headings are not as distinct from the rest of the text in the audio modality as compared to the printed text. It may consequently hamper the identification of the different text headings by the blind people, what could impair text processing. Indeed, [10] showed that it is easier for sighted readers to catch the text structure when a text containing headings is printed than in an auditory presentation via a TTS. In their second experiment, they also showed that it is possible to improve text structure processing in an auditory presentation by systematically restoring the headings information functions. Our goal in the present study is to assess the efficiency of different restitution methods with blind people. We conducted an experiment with blind volunteers who were instructed to listen to a text oralized by a TTS and then, to answer questions about the text structure.

In order to make the headings more salient, we compare three different restitution methods. The first is the basic restitution provided by a TTS. The second is to use two different voices, one to enunciate the headings and the other one for the rest of the text. The third chosen method is to use spatialized audio to simulate one enunciation location on the left of the participant and another on his right, at head level. We used the left location to enunciate the headings and the right location to enunciate the rest of the text. The principle was to enrich the text presentation by restoring structural information through voice modifications without adding any discursive content to avoid cognitive overload for the listeners. .

The main hypothesis was that enriching the auditory presentation with voice modification to signal headings results in a better comprehension of the text structure than the basic restitution.

3   Methodology

The global principle of the experimentation was to present several documents to participants using different restitution methods, and to measure the general comprehension of the documents contents along with the outline retention.

3.1   Experimental Design

Nine legally blind volunteers participated in our study, without particular hearing problems, all using synthetic voices on everyday basis. We used a synthetic voice reading text at about 175 words per minute, which is far slower than maximum listening speed for blind people using Text-To-Speech [11]. Three different conditions were defined for documents reading.

The first was the control condition which was equivalent to what a screen-reader would read of a web page containing headings and raw text, that is to say a discursive segment indicating "Heading level N" before the heading oralization. The text in this condition was read using a male voice. The second condition used a female voice to enunciate the headings and a male voice for the documents contents. Note that we used free voices from the MRBOLA Project.[1] Finally, the third condition used spatialized audio and defined two "reading" locations: one on the left in front of the listener and one on the right, both at head level. We chose those particular locations since it appears that the left/right arc in front of the listener is where the locations discrimination works best [12], [13]. In every condition headings were announced by saying "Heading level N" (and "Main title" for the first title of each document). Subjects had the possibility to pause the reading using the space-bar, but couldn't play it back so that each subject listened one time to every part of every text.

We used five documents in total. Three of them contained about 875 words (5 minutes of listening) and were used to test each of the three conditions. They were expository texts which topics were chose so the subjects would have enough basic

---

[1] Mbrola page : http://tcts.fpms.ac.be/synthesis/mbrola.html1

knowledge to understand them, but were unlikely experts of the concerned fields; the topics of those three documents were energy problems, firefighting and energy solutions. Each of those three texts had 3 levels of headings: main title, headings level 1 and headings level 2. Two other short documents containing about 450 words (3minutes of listening) were used as distractors during the experiment, and dealt with random topics, namely Brazil and French Louisiana.

In order to avoid a possible rank bias, each condition and each text were played in total three times at each rank (i.e. three times in first position, three times in second and three times in third position during the different tests).

The procedure was the following one: after signing a consent form, we asked subjects few questions about themselves. Then, the three long texts were read, each in a different condition, either in control, dual-voices or spatialized audio condition. After each text we asked the subject to recall the outline of the text, ideally the headings with their level in the hierarchy, along with a self-evaluation of the difficulty they had to comprehend and memorize it, on a scale ranging from 1 to 7, 7 being very difficult and 1 very easy. After that, comprehension questions about the text were asked, each question being related to one or several text sections.

The two "distracting" texts were read after text 1 and text 2. Once the subject heard them, we asked them three questions about details of each text. The aim of the distractors was to prevent subjects from over-focusing on the text headings and to try to understand the whole texts.

Finally, after all the text readings, subjects would give us feedback about the experiment.

3.2   Measures

We measured mainly two variables: outline recall and comprehension (through the questions asked after each reading).

Three scores were extracted from the outline recall. First we evaluated the number of topics recalled over the total number of topics, each topic corresponding to a heading, which gave us a score between 0 (no topic recalled) and 1 (all the topics recalled). A second score concerned the recalled hierarchy: we computed the distance between the recalled outline and the original outline, using the absolute difference between the level of recalled headings and the level of the corresponding headings in the documents. Score ranged between 0 (recalled hierarchy identical to the original) and 1 (recalled hierarchy completely different). Finally, we computed a third score corresponding to the correlation between the recalled order of the headings and the original order (normalized between 0 and 1).

Lastly, we rated each of the answers to comprehension questions. The constructed questions dealt with the text macrostructure and the correct answers were the headings contents (e.g. what are the consequences of dwindling fuel resources? correct answer: hazardous productions methods, increasing costs of fuel resources). For each expected topic, we calculated a correctness score to the total of the question, each score ranging between 0 and 4 (0: topic not recalled, 1-3: more or less semantic equivalent, 4: exact literal topic). For instance, if a question dealt with three different headings, the answer rate ranged between 0 and 12.

4   Results

The first graph shows the results regarding outline recall for each tested condition with the three measures we performed on this data (topic recall, hierarchy recall and order recall).

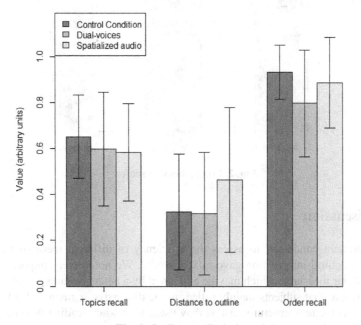

Fig. 1. Outline recall scores

The second graph shows the results regarding comprehension scores for each tested condition.

There were no statistically significant differences between the conditions, either in terms of outline recall, comprehension score and mental effort. As our sample is small, this absence of difference might be due to a lack of statistical power. Looking at the data with a descriptive approach shows that the differences observed for the outlining task and reported mental effort are not compatible with our hypothesis. However, the differences observed for the comprehension task, albeit small, are in line with our predictions: both restitution methods entail better comprehension scores than the control condition.

Concerning the user preferences, 5 subjects preferred the dual-voices condition re-gardless of the text content, 2 preferred the spatialized audio condition, 1 liked them both, while the last subject had no particular preference.

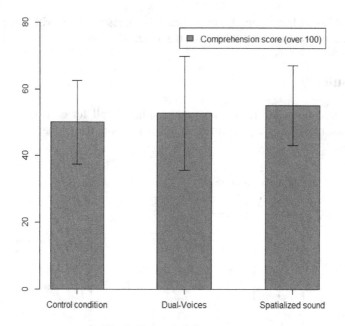

Fig. 2. Comprehension scores

5   Discussion

This experiment conducted to assess the efficiency of different methods to restore headings structural information gave mixed results. We note a very important variability in all our measures, which may be explained by a heterogeneous sample.

It is possible that subjects mainly relied on the discursive segment "Heading level N" to process the text structure, just as they usually do when reading web pages with their screen readers, all of them being everyday users of screen readers with a Text-To-Speech software. Consequently, our manipulation had no effect on the topic structure identification. However, text comprehension was slightly improved by our restitution methods. Moreover, the post-test results showed some individual preferences. A deeper analysis of data showed that subjects who preferred the spatialized audio condition performed better in this condition than in the control condition, and at the same time had worse performance in the dual-voices condition than in the control condition. The same trend occurred for 3 of the 5 subjects who preferred the dual-voices condition (they performed better in this condition than in the control condition, and worse in the spatialized audio condition than in the control condition). This analysis is also consistent with the post-test questions which showed that subjects who preferred spatialized audio disliked the dual-voices condition. At the same time, subjects who preferred the dual-voices condition disliked the spatialized audio condition. This could mean that blind users have preferences on how to contrast synthesized speech. This fact might also explain why we haven't any global trend on the overall data, since some of the subjects preferred one tested method over the other and performed better in the preferred method.

We also had positive qualitative feedback from all the subjects who reported that "I felt the demarcation" (subject 5), "it draws attention" (subject 6), "I had an idea of what the next section will deal with" (subject 7), "I can see the structure well" (subject 8), "it is an interesting idea" (subject 9), etc.

One last interesting fact is that even though the two tested restitution methods don't induce more mental effort than the control condition, there is a trend in the spatialized audio condition showing an increase of mental effort. This increase of mental effort could be due to the lack of familiarity with spatialized audio.

6   Conclusion

Even though the results don't show statistical evidences that either the dual-voices method or the spatialized audio method has better performance than current TTS oralization, we found that blind users may have preferences on which methods to use. Here, those preferences may have impacted performance.

The feedback from the users encourages us to pursue our research. Future work will focus on creating a new reading system which combines the tested restitution methods (spatialized audio and voice change) with intra-document navigation techniques. This system should be able to take into account individuals preferences. We will also study other textual objects than headings, and possible ways for blind people to access their properties.

Acknowledgements. We would like to thank all the volunteers from the IJA (Institute for Blind youths) of Toulouse who took part in our study and especially Claude Griet; their contribution was greatly appreciated. We are also grateful to the "PRES Toulouse" and the "Région Midi-Pyrénées" for funding this work.

References

1. Giraud, S., Uzan, G., Thérouanne, P.: L'accessibilité des interfaces informatiques pour les déficients visuels. In: Dinet, J., Bastien, C. (eds.) L'ergonomie des objets et environnements physiques et numériques. Hermes - Sciences Lavoisier, Paris (2011)
2. Lazar, J., Allen, A., Kleinman, J., Malarkey, C.: What Frustrates Screen Reader Users on the Web: A Study of 100 Blind Users. Int. J. Hum. Comput. Interact. 22(3), 247–269 (2007)
3. Petit, G., Dufresne, A., Robert, J.: Introducing TactoWeb: A Tool to Spatially Explore Web Pages for Users with Visual Impairment. In: Stephanidis, C. (ed.) Universal Access in HCI, Part I, HCII 2011. LNCS, vol. 6765, pp. 276–284. Springer, Heidelberg (2011)
4. Pascual, E., Virbel, J.: Semantic and Layout Properties of Text Punctuation. In: Proceedings of the Association for Computational Linguistics Workshop on Punctuation, pp. 41–48 (1996)

5. Lemarié, J., Lorch, R.F., Eyrolle, H., Virbel, J.: SARA: A Text-Based and Reader-Based Theory of Signaling. Educ. Psychol. 43(1), 27–48 (2008)
6. Pontelli, E., Gillan, D., Xiong, W., Saad, E., Gupta, G., Karshmer, A.I.: Navigation of HTML tables, frames, and XML fragments. In: Proceedings of the Fifth International ACM Conference on Assistive Technologies, ASSETS 2002, pp. 25–32 (2002)
7. Maurel, F., Lemarié, J., Vigouroux, N., Virbel, J., Mojahid, M., Nespoulous, J.-L.: De l'adaptation de la présentation oralisée des textes aux difficultés perceptives et mnésiques du langage. Rev. Parol. 2004–29–30, 153–187 (2005)
8. Smith, A.C., Cook, J.S., Francioni, J.M., Hossain, A., Anwar, M., Rahman, M.F.: Nonvisual tool for navigating hierarchical structures. In: Proceedings of the ACM SIGACCESS Conference on Computers and Accessibility, ASSETS 2004, pp. 133–139 (2004)
9. Lemarié, J., Lorch, R.F., Péry-Woodley, M.-P.: Understanding How Headings Influence Text Processing. Discours. Rev. Linguist. Psycholinguistique Informatique 10 (2012)
10. Lorch, R.F., Chen, H.-T., Lemarié, J.: Communicating headings and preview sentences in text and speech. J. Exp. Psychol. Appl. 18(3), 265–276 (2012)
11. Asakawa, C., Takagi, H.: Maximum Listening Speed For The Blind. In: Proceedings of the 2003 International Conference on Auditory Display, pp. 276–279 (2003)
12. Rumsey, F.: Spatial audio, pp. 1–233. Taylor & Francis (2001)
13. Goose, S., Möller, C.: A 3D Audio Only Interactive Web Browser: Using Spatialization to Convey Hypermedia Document Structure. In: Proceedings of the Seventh ACM International Conference on Multimedia (Part 1), pp. 363–371 (1999)

TTS-Based DAISY Content Creation System: Implementation and Evaluation of DaisyRings™

Kosei Fume, Yuka Kuroda, Taira Ashikawa,
Yoshiaki Mizuoka, and Masahiro Morita

Corporate Research & Development Center, Toshiba corporation 1,
Komukai-Toshiba-cho, Saiwai-ku, Kawasaki, 212-8582, Japan
{kosei.fume,yuka.kuroda,taira.ashikawa,
yoshiaki.mizuoka,masahiro.morita}@toshiba.co.jp

Abstract. Digital Accessible Information System (DAISY) content is expected to gain popularity gradually among the visually impaired according to the prevalence of e-book reading devices and the development of text-to-speech (TTS) technology. However, the development of DAISY-formatted e-books, which is undertaken by volunteers, is a time-consuming process, making it difficult to meet end user requirements. In this report, we propose a content transliteration system that can convert plain text to DAISY content including formatted HTML and audio data via automatic TTS technology. Furthermore, using the graphic user interface of the proposed system, users can correct text and accent information by inputting ruby-type data. Through this functionality, we aim to target support for transliteration workers such as volunteers, teachers, and parents to make and edit contents easily and quickly for the visually impaired. Finally, we present the results of a preliminary evaluation using the proposed method in order to compare it with the conventional method.

Keywords: Transliteration, Text-to-speech, DAISY, Accessibility, Visual disability, Dyslexia.

1 Introduction

The popularity of e-books has increased recently, leading to the development and availability of some unique applications and functions related to e-books. Obviously, users have benefited from the Internet and cloud services for content distribution and management. They can enjoy listening to audio versions of e-books using TTS or customize the font size or font type as per their choice. However, audiobook CDs and tapes are created by volunteers at the Braille Library or at public libraries. Recently, these audiobooks provided not only audio data but also DAISY formatted data that includes text and index data for synchronous play [10].

K. Miesenberger et al. (Eds.): ICCHP 2014, Part I, LNCS 8547, pp. 69–76, 2014.

2   Related Work

2.1   Immediacy Prioritized Approach

Considering the need for quick reporting, exploiting TTS in reading applications and devices is a practical mothod for visually impaired and for people with reading disabilties [2],[8],[13]. To make the content more accesible, an interactive approach that targets graphics information is poposed by [3]. [14],[21] focuses on the document logical structure approaches are done, and [17] proposes a real-time document-handling approach and skimming approach for information acquisition [1]. Another proposal to improve accessibility for dyslexics is made by [15], who presents layout guidlines for online text.

2.2   Accuracy Prioritized Approach

At the same time, other approaches that involve adding metadata or annotation to contents in advance serve as helpful reading guidelines. A few useful meta-data editing or annotation applications [6],[9],[12],[16],[18] are already in the market. Many tools and plugins for DAISY content creation have recently been made available, such as those described in [4,5],[7],[19]. Using "Daisy pipeline" [4], users are able to convert various documents to a DAISY related format. The "Daisy Producer"[7] supports time-consuming and corporative workflow of creating DAISY contents.

3   Background and Problem

While recently introduced mobile devices are much more useful than their predecessors for persons with disabilities, and while some visually impaired people enjoy reading, or writing blogs or tweets on these, current methods are insufficient on the whole to cater to disabled end-users.

Considering in terms of information utilization, the transliteration contents are categorized into three types:

- Flow information: As in email messages, blog articles and tweets, immediate perusal is prioritized, and a few grammatical errors or incorrect pronounciation are considered negligible.
- Stock information: Reuseable documents, like important lists, schedules and memos, and some public documents that the authors are expected to verify only cursorily.
- Archive information: Library books and textbooks that many people frequentry refer to. The contents of these are meticulously verified by publishers.

Our target contents are those of stock and archive information. These are expected to contain a higher quality of audible content than the flow information, depending upon the cost of reading and accent correction.

However we will focus on limiting information types. Content creation processes in general take anywhere from two to three months to a year from receiving a request to deliver DAISY contents (Fig.1).

4   Concept

Considering the above issues, we propose a system that emphasizes the following:

- To meet the various demands of readers regardless of document genre or categories (**Versatility of input document**).
- To enable users to create content as quickly as they want through a simple operation (**Limitation of edit function**).
- To reduce the requisite computer literacy to accommodate volunteers (**Minimize initial cost and maximize ease of use**).
- To design the system to be used seamlessly in currently common scenarios, such as face-to-face readings and transliterations (**Compatibility with current working processes**).

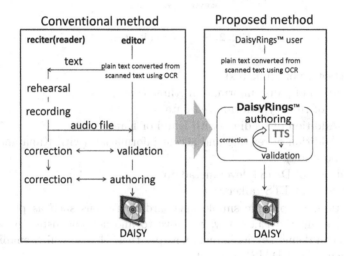

Fig. 1. Content creation process

4.1   Approach

Considering the above-mentioned limitations with the conventional method of DAISY content creation, our proposed system has following features:

- **Versatility of input document:** Regardless of document genre or type, to meet the users reading requirements, we support not preemptive document format but plain text that can easily be converted from scanned text using optical character recognition, email messages, or other documents. In addition, we employ our TTS system. The advantages of TTS are that it negates the need for recording equipment, and it allows for easy correction of reading and pronounciation.
- **Limitation of edit function:** The system realizes quick and simple user-demanded contents creation. We adopt a ruby-based format input graphic user interface (GUI) and limit the edit operations as follows:

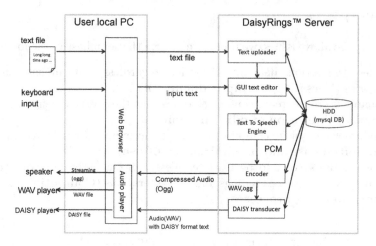

Fig. 2. System architecture

- Correction of input text
- Insertion of pause information (three types)
- Input of ruby-type formatted data
  * Addition of reading (with Kanji or Kana)
  * Addition of reading and accent information (with Kana and special notation)
- Addition of DAISY-level metadata
- Selection of TTS talker

In addition, we provide simple keyboard operations such as play or stop reading, using the Enter key, or move to another line using cursor keys. Editors can define key assignments as per their choice, which enables them to efficiently edit DAISY content.

- **Minimize initial cost and maximize ease of use:** For volunteers, to maintain PC skill requirements and initial costs to a minimum and comply with needs, we implemented the system as a Web application as shown in Fig.2.
- **Compatibility with current working processes:** For volunteers, the proposed system should not detract from their usual working processes but should support or replace sub process. Our proposed transliteration processes would have some characteristic steps as stated below:

1. Extract plain text from books or digital contents.
2. Generate audio data from text by TTS.
3. Generate synchronized data between audio and text.
4. Combine mid-output data, add extra metadata, and build targeting e-book format.

Our proposed system mainly supports step 2 and 3, and a part of step 4 as DAISY output.

5   Overview of DaisyRings™

Our proposed system, DaisyRings™, provides a content creation environment. The basic edit GUI is shown in Fig.3.

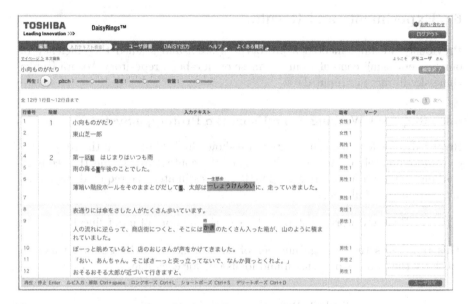

Fig. 3. Edit view in DaisyRings™

5.1   Details

The following are the details of our system. A main feature is the edit function and GUI incorporating with TTS. In paticular, using the ruby-based input GUI shown in Fig.4, editors can change input modes between the ruby-format and plain text using a toggle key such as Ctrl<space>. In general, ruby is used for reading or description with Hiragana or Katakana. We expand this notation,

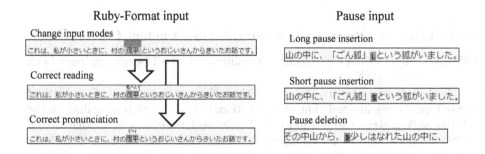

Fig. 4. Ruby-format and pause input method

and therefore, our system can accept Kanji or accent symbols from the ruby-formatted input. Further, our system supports the insertion of three types of pauses with simple key combinations shown in Fig.4. Owing to our previous survey, one of the most frequently corrected data types is pause-related data.

6   Experiments and Results

Previously, we implemented a prototype system and studied the efficiency of our concept using content from Japanese open e-book repository Aozora Bunko (blue-sky library) as input data.

6.1   Required Working Time Using the Prototype System

Required steps for each content item are shown in Table.1. From the results, we can approximately estimate the lengths of the content items, and the required working steps can be coorrelated. Further, we estimated the required steps that are described as follows (1):

$$\text{Required working steps} = 1.89 \times \text{(the number of input lines)} \quad (1)$$

This represents the average number of keystorokes used by editors, which is precisely the number of focus-in and focus-out for each line.

Table 1. Preliminary experimantal results

Book Title	Author	The number of lines	Working steps
Gon-Gitsune	Niimi Nankichi	213	508
Wagahaiwa Nekodearu	Natsume Soseki	290	699
Ho-ro-ki	Hayashi Fumiko	398	940
Show White	Grim brothers	379	84
Oiteke-bori	Tanaka Kotaro	93	137
The Wolf and the Kids	Grim brothers	156	149
Amenimo Makezu	Miyazawa Kenji	62	119
Enpitsu-no Shin	Yumeno Kyusaku	26	26

6.2   Estimated Required Time for a DAISY Content Creation

We also conducted an experimental transliteration of a 15-page children's book using DaisyRings^{TM}.

Table.2 shows a comparison between the estimated woking cost of our method based on the results and that of conventional transliteration according to the Japanese Ministry of Education [11]. These results are then extrapolated to a 150-page book, that is, a book having ten times the number of pages of the book used in our evaluation. In advance, we conduct the optional character recognition (OCR) preprocess, and the plain text is ready for input.

Our results show that whereas conventional book transliteration takes 44 days, we are successfully able to reduce the time taken to seven days using our proposed method. There are various factors to be considered in actual scenario; however, because editors can use our system in parallel, the actual required time can be further reduced.

Table 2. Estimated required working time using DaisyRings™

Working contents	Preparation	DAISY level	Recording	Page metadata	Correction	Building book	Total
Conventional method	8 days	8 days	600min (≈3weeks) = 21 days	1 day	5 days	1 day	44 days
Proposed method	1 day	6 days					7 days

6.3 Future Work

This system has been available free of charge at a demonstration site in Japan [20], particularly to the public library or Braille library staff and volunteers. In consultation with such users, we intend to develop additional functions such as utilizing edit history and indicating correction to candidates and preparing a framework for sharing the editors' knowledge such as a glossary or domain-constrained dictionary.

7 Conclusions

We developed the TTS-based transliteration system, DaisyRings™. This system provides:

- An environment for content creation using TTS and web-based applications.
- The capability to correct misreading or mispronunciation through a direct ruby-format input.
- Support for DAISY output, so that users can directly exploit it by using other tools with the imported data.

Our system is currently being used by a growing number of library staff or volunteers, and we continue to collect and analyze correction data.

References

1. Ahmed, F., Borodin, Y., Puzis, Y., Ramakrishnan, I.V.: Why read if you can skim: Towards enabling faster screen reading. In: Proceedings of the International Cross-Disciplinary Conference on Web Accessibility, W4A 2012, pp. 39:1–39:10. ACM, New York (2012)
2. Apple: VoiceOver, http://www.apple.com/accessibility/

3. Carberry, S., Elzer Schwartz, S., Mccoy, K., Demir, S., Wu, P., Greenbacker, C., Chester, D., Schwartz, E., Oliver, D., Moraes, P.: Access to multimodal articles for individuals with sight impairments. ACM Trans. Interact. Intell. Syst. 2(4), 21:1–21:49 (2013)
4. DAISY Consortium: DAISY Pipeline, http://www.daisy.org/project/pipeline
5. Daniel, W.: DAISY Tobi: an extensible software tool to author next-generation accessible publications. In: The DAISY International Technical Conference (2009)
6. Dolphin Computer Access: Dolphin Publisher, http://www.yourdolphin.com/products.asp
7. Egli, C.: Daisy producer: An integrated production management system for accessible media. In: The DAISY International Technical Conference (2009)
8. Freedom Scientific: Jaws, http://www.freedomscientific.com/jaws-hq.asp
9. Innovative Rehabilitation Technology: eclipsewriter, http://www.irti.net/eclipse/eClipseWriter
10. Japanese Braille Library: SAPIE, https://sapie.or.jp
11. Japanese Society for Rehabilitation of Persons with Disabilities (JSRPD): Utilizing assistive technology and private organizations, special education research project (final report) (2011), http://www.mext.go.jp/component/a_menu/education/micro_detail/__icsFiles/afieldfile/2011/09/09/1310526_3_1.pdf
12. Yamaguchi, K., Suzuki, M.: Accessible Authoring Tool for DAISY Ranging from Mathematics to Others. In: Miesenberger, K., Karshmer, A., Penaz, P., Zagler, W. (eds.) ICCHP 2012, Part I. LNCS, vol. 7382, pp. 130–137. Springer, Heidelberg (2012)
13. Kochi System Development: PC-Talker, http://www.pctalker.net/
14. Miyashita, H., Sato, D., Takagi, H., Asakawa, C.: Aibrowser for multimedia: Introducing multimedia content accessibility for visually impaired users. In: Proceedings of the 9th International ACM SIGACCESS Conference on Computers and Accessibility, Assets 2007, pp. 91–98. ACM, New York (2007)
15. Rello, L., Kanvinde, G., Baeza-Yates, R.: Layout guidelines for web text and a web service to improve accessibility for dyslexics. In: Proceedings of the International Cross-Disciplinary Conference on Web Accessibility, W4A 2012, pp. 36:1–36:9. ACM, New York (2012)
16. Science Accesibility Net, http://www.sciaccess.net/jp/ChattyInfty/index.html
17. Shaik, A.S., Hossain, G., Yeasin, M.: Design, development and performance evaluation of reconfigured mobile android phone for people who are blind or visually impaired. In: Proceedings of the 28th ACM International Conference on Design of Communication, SIGDOC 2010, pp. 159–166. ACM, New York (2010)
18. Kenshi, S.: Plextalk recording software pro, http://www.plextalk.com/americas/top/products/prs
19. The Urakawa Project, http://urakawa.sourceforge.net
20. Toshiba: Demonstration site DaisyRings™, https://daisyrings.jp
21. Yu, C.H., Miller, R.C.: Enhancing mobile browsing and reading. In: CHI 2011 Extended Abstracts on Human Factors in Computing Systems, CHI EA 2011, pp. 1783–1788. ACM, New York (2011)

Patterns of Blind Users' Hand Movements

The Case of Typographic Signals of Documents Rendered by Eight-Dot and Six-Dot Braille Code

Vassilios Argyropoulos[1], Georgios Kouroupetroglou[2], Aineias Martos[1,2],
Magda Nikolaraizi[1], and Sofia Chamonikolaou[1]

[1] University of Thessaly, Department of Special Education, Volos, Greece
{vassargi,mnikolar,chamonik}@uth.gr, eniasmartos@yahoo.gr
[2] National and Kapodistrian University of Athens,
Department of Informatics and Telecommunications, Athens, Greece
koupe@di.uoa.gr, eniasmartos@yahoo.gr

Abstract. The main focus of the present study lies on patterns and characteristics of hand movements when participants with blindness receive typographic meta-data (bold and italic) by touch through a braille display. Patterns and characteristics were investigated by the use of six-dot braille and eight-dot braille code in conjunction with types of reading errors. The results depicted that the participants' reading errors (phonological type) were similar in both braille codes. In addition, the participants performed more fluid hand movements when they used the six-dot braille code, whereas they spent less time when they were reading through eight-dot braille. The focus of the discussion was placed on the importance of the development of a suitable design of tactile rendition of typographic signals through six or eight-dot braille code in favor of better perception and comprehension.

Keywords: Typographic Signals, 6-dot Braille, 8-dot Braille, Braille Display, Blindness, Patterns of Hand Movements, Reading Errors.

1 Introduction

This paper reports on the results from a series of experiments in the field of haptic representation of typographic meta-information embedded in rich texts documents. Typographic signals [1] is the information that sighted readers get from the documents at the typographic layer (such as, type, size, color, background color, etc.) or/and font style such as bold, italics, underline [2,3]. These attributes play a crucial role in text reading comprehension.

The way blind people's hands are moved while reading has been considered a critical parameter in Braille reading and comprehension [4]. The Braille reading process is considered to be a complex one because the readers need to: a. decode with the tips of their fingers each symbol-letter of each word of the text, b. extract the meaning of the text, and c. combine the movements of the fingers with the cognitive reading

K. Miesenberger et al. (Eds.): ICCHP 2014, Part I, LNCS 8547, pp. 77–84, 2014.
© Springer International Publishing Switzerland 2014

process [5]. In addition to this, the evolution of assistive technology in braille technology has opened up new possibilities to interact with computers and specialized hardware such as braille displays (i.e. electro-mechanical devices for displaying braille characters in real time [6]. Hence, investigating patterns and characteristics of hand movements of tactile reading position on a Braille display in real-time, when people with blindness attempt to figure out typographic meta-information, constitutes a challenge and promising approach for educational implications.

Thus, the main focus of the present study lies on patterns and characteristics of hand movements when participants with blindness receive typographic meta-data (bold and italic) by touch through a braille display. Patterns and characteristics will be investigated by the use of six-dot braille and eight-dot braille code. It is characteristic that the six-dot braille code has limited number of characters-symbols (64 combinations), resulting in an overlap in the use of symbols and meanings. The advantage of eight-dot braille code is the increase in number of combinations of dots from 64 to 256 extremely facilitating the use of symbols in scientific fields such as the Nemeth Code for Mathematics and Science Notation [7]. In essence, the research objectives of the present study are the following:

1. to compare the type of reading errors when braille readers use six-dot braille and eight-dot braille respectively through a braille display, and
2. to investigate the hand movements that braille readers conduct when use six-dot braille and eight-dot braille respectively through braille display.

Both research objectives refer to typographic meta-data and specifically to bold and italic. The reason of choosing these specific typographic signals is their frequency of use: a total of 2,927 entities, of which 1,866 were occurrences of "bold" and 1,061 of "italics" were manually identified and labeled in a corpus of 2,000 articles of a Greek newspaper [8].

2   Method

2.1   Participants

Twelve individuals with blindness participated in haptic tests. All participants had a visual acuity of no better than light perception, they were all braillists and they lack additional diagnosed disabilities. Their age range was from 20 to 40 years (mean= 31.58, SD= 4.79).

2.2   The Research Design

The research design of the study had a strict structure similar to that of experiments [9]. All participants were asked to read from a braille display different scripts within which meta-information was included such as bold and italic. The scripts were divided into two categories. The first one comprised sentences in which bold and italic were rendered by the eight-dot braille code, by the use of the seventh and eighth dot of the expanded braille cell and the second one consisted of an equivalent number of sentences in which bold and italic were rendered by the six-dot code, by the use of tags [10]. The participants were invited to read aloud every single script and mention all the meta-information (bold and italic) they met.

All experiments were conducted with the same braille display and a training period preceded the experimental procedure to assure that all participants had the same baseline regarding renderings for bold and italic by a braille display. Additionally, the participants were informed that the whole process would be video-recorded and that the camera shot would focus only on their hands. The camera was positioned on a tripod behind the participants' right shoulder after some recording trials. In this way it was feasible to describe all participants' hand movements on the braille display when they were reading in six-dot and the eight-dot braille code respectively.

2.3   Data Analysis

The data analysis for the first research objective was the following: The authors were interested only at errors of phonological type. For this they based their analysis on a classification system which met the peculiarities of the Greek language. The error pattern used in this research was a synthesis of other similar patterns [11,12] and consists of two broad categories. The first refers to errors of phonological type and the second to errors of non-phonological type.

Errors of phonological type are considered those which change the acoustic image of the word (e.g., fin for fine). This type of error can be organized into many subtypes such as: omission of needed letters, addition of unneeded letters, reversal of whole words, addition of syllables, omission of syllables and so on (Table 1).

Table 1. Errors of Phonological Type

Category of Errors of Phonological Type	Abbreviations
Addition of Letters	AL
Omission of Letters	OL
Letter Transpositions	LT
Letter Substitutions	LS
Addition of Syllables	AS
Omission of Syllables	OS
Syllable Transpositions (e. g. reversals)	ST
Syllable Substitutions	SS

On the contrary, errors of non-phonological type do not alter the auditory representation of the word (e.g., night for knight); instead, this type refers to errors which are opposed: a. to the correct spelling of the word in terms of the historical evolution of the language (historical type), and b. to common spelling rules (morphological type) [13].

Regarding the analysis of the second research objective, the authors used the findings of Wormsley's study [14] where she distinguishes six main characteristics of blind persons' hand movements when they read braille:

1. Scrubbing (Sc), involves the motion that the finger makes when it moves up and down over a braille character,
2. Regression (R), involves motions such when the finger(s) is/are moving back across the page to reread or check something,
3. Searching (Se), when the hands are looking for information but without reading,
4. Pausing (P), when the hand rests on the page,
5. Erratic movements (EM), when the movements include all type of motions except reading, and
6. Normal Braille Reading (NBR), when fluid movements take place on the paper by the user's hands.

3   Results

3.1   First Research Objective: Type of Reading Errors

Figure 1 provides a description of the phonological errors that the participants made while reading the General informative text (G) by the 8-dot (8d) and the 6-dot (6d) Braille code. Based on the data it was noticed that the participants' Phonological Errors (PE) were similar in both Braille codes. The only noticeable divergence that was found between the two Braille codes was in the category Syllable Substitution (SS) (min.PE6dGSS=19 & max.PE8dGSS=28).

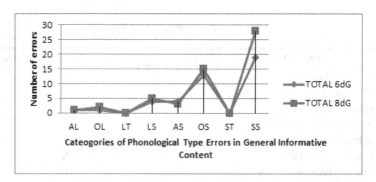

Fig. 1. Phonological Errors in General informative text (G) by 8-dot & 6-dot Braille code

The same analysis took place regarding the texts with the scientific content. In particular, all participants seemed to perform the same quality of phonological type of errors and at the same analogy when they read the Scientific text (S) by the 8-dot (8d) and the 6-dot (6d) respectively (Figure 2). In general, the number of the PEs with the 8-dot Braille code is bigger than that of the 6-dot Braille code (total PE6dSLS=4 & total PE8dSLS=7, total PE6dSAS=5 & total PE8dSAS=8, total PE6dSOS=2 & total PE8dSOS=6, and total PE6dSSS=15 & total PE8dSSS=17).

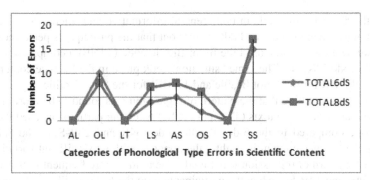

Fig. 2. Phonological Errors in Science content (S) by 8-dot & 6-dot Braille code

3.2   Second Research Objective: Patterns of Hand Movements

The second research question was confronted by a detailed description of the partici-pants' hand movements when receiving typographic meta-data (bold and italic) by touch through a braille display. As mentioned in the "data analysis section" the au-thors adopted the categorization of Wormsley's study [14] where she distinguishes six main characteristics of blind persons' hand movements when they read braille.

Table 2 shows all types of the participants' hand movements when they read texts with General informative content (G) and Science content (S) respectively. The read-ing procedure was conducted through 6-dot braille (6dG & 6dS) and 8-dot braille code (8dG & 8dS). The findings indicated that the participants spent less time to read

Table 2. Types of the participants' hand movements in General informative content (G) and Science content (S) by 6-dot and 8-dot Braille Code

	Braille Code and Content			
	6dG	8dG	6dS	8dS
Partici-pants				
A	6R	6R	1R, 5R-Sc	5R, 1NBR
B	4R, 2NBR	5R, 1NBR	5R, 1NBR	3R, 3R-Sc
C	4R, 1NBR, 1R-Sc	5R, 1R-Sc	3R, 3Sc	4R, 2R-Sc
D	2R, 1Sc, 3R-Sc	1R, 5R-Sc	1R, 1Sc, 2R-Sc, 2NBR	3R, 1R-Sc, 1Sc, 1NBR
E	6R	1R, 1Sc, 2NBR, 2R-Sc	5R, 1R-Sc	4R, 2R-Sc
F	4R, 1R-Sc, 1NBR	4R-Sc, 1Sc, 1NBR	3R, 2R-Sc, 1Sc	3R, 1Sc, 2NBR
G	5R, 1NBR	6R-Sc	6R, 4NBR	4R, 2NBR
H	2R, 4NBR	5R, 1NBR	2R, 5NBR	1R, 5NBR
I	4R	4R, 2NBR	1R, 4R-Sc	4R, 1NBR
J	4R, 1NBR	3R, 1NBR	3R, 2NBR	1R, 3R-Sc
K	4R, 1NBR	5R-Sc	4R, 2NBR	3R, 1NBR
L	2R, 3NBR	4R, 1NBR	2R, 4NBR	1R, 4NBR
TOTALS	47R, 5R-Sc, 1Sc, 14NBR	34R, 23R-Sc, 2Sc, 9NBR	36R, 14R-Sc, 5Sc, 20NBR	37R, 8R-Sc, 2Sc, 17NBR

through the 8-dot Braille code in both general informative and science texts. Thus, a comparison between the 6dG and 8dG leaves out that the participants performed more fluid movements when they used the 6-dot Braille code (14NBR) compared to the 8-dot Braille code (9NBR). The same "situation" took place in the Science content (6dS and 8dS); 20NBR for the 6-dot Braille and 17NBR for the 8-dot Braille.

Also it is worth noting that the pattern of regression was found to be more frequent in the General informative texts (47R and 5R-Sc) when the participants used the 8-dot Braille code compared to the 6-dot Braille code (34R and 23R-Sc). The "picture" regarding the Science content is slightly the opposite without significant variations. In specific, the pattern of regression was found to be a little more frequent in the Science content (36R and 14R-Sc) when the participants used the 6-dot Braille code compared to the 8-dot Braille code (37R and 8R-Sc).

4   Discussion and Conclusions

This paper addresses issues of Braille reading accuracy and patterns of hand movements, when blind users receive typographic meta-data (bold and italic) by touch through a braille display in 6-dot Braille and 8-dot Braille code in matched texts (general content and scientific content).

Based on the results, it was found that the participants' Phonological Errors (PE) did not differ significantly in both Braille codes and for both type of content (G & S). Hence, it may be argued that the different renderings of the specific typographic meta-data (bold & italic) by 6-dot and 8-dot Braille code respectively did not have an impact on the participants' Braille reading accuracy. Instead, it seems that the prevalent PE type was captured by the category Syllable Substitution (SS). Vakali and Evans [15] also indicated the prevalence of this PE type in their own research. In sum, it seems that the type of reading errors may be attributed to the specific location of the dots as well as their density in the braille cell (6-dot or 8-dot Braille cell) and the different renderings of the meta-data occupy a neutral role in the reading process.

Regarding the results which referred to the second research objective, participants' hand movements were more fluid with the 6-dot Braille, but less time was spent reading by the 8-dot Braille. These two results seem somewhat contradictory. In specific, the participants performed in total more "regression" movements with the 8-dot Braille code (84R) and less "Normal Braille Reading" movements (26NBR) compared to the 6-dot Braille code (70R and 34NBR). This situation was unsatisfactory to the participants and may led them to a. ineffective reading scanning, and b. the trend to predict the word instead of decoding it [16]. In this way they could manage to finish the task earlier, whereas the Normal Braille Reading movement might offer satisfaction and a normal rate of reading which helped the braille readers to: a. decode with the tips of their fingers each symbol-letter of each word of the text, b. to extract the meaning of the text, and c. to combine the movements of the fingers with the cognitive reading process [5].

   To conclude, typographic signals [17-19] is the information that readers get from the documents at the typographic layer which includes font (type, size, color, background color, etc.), and font style such as bold, italics, underline [18-21]. These attributes play a crucial role in comprehension. Young readers may not be able to distinguish what is associated with a particular task, since they have not fully developed the metacognitive process. Therefore, typographic signals act as a kind of signal to structure the argument of text and eventually facilitate comprehension [19]. Hence, it is suggested that the focus of research should be placed on the educational implications of the results developing a suitable design of tactile rendition of typographic signals meta-data through six or eight-dot braille code in favor of better perception and comprehension.

Acknowledgements. This research has been co-financed by the European Union (European Social Fund – ESF) and Greek national funds through the Operational Program "Education and Lifelong Learning" of the National Strategic Reference Framework (NSRF) under the Research Funding Project: "THALIS-University of Macedonia- KAIKOS: Audio and Tactile Access to Knowledge for Individuals with Visual Impairments", MIS 380442.

References

1. Lorch, R.F.: Text-Signaling Devices and Their Effects on Reading and Memory Processes. Educational Psychology Review 1, 209–234 (1989)
2. Kouroupetroglou, G., Tsonos, D.: Multimodal Accessibility of Documents. In: Pinder, S. (ed.) Advances in Human-Computer Interaction, pp. 451–470. I-Tech Education and Publishing, Vienna (2008)
3. Tsonos, D., Kouroupetroglou, G.: Modeling Reader's Emotional State Response on Document's Typographic Elements. Adv. in Human-Computer Interaction (January 2011)
4. Millar, S.: Reading by touch. Routledge, New York (1997)
5. Hughes, B.: Movement Kinematics of the Braille-reading Finger. Journal of Visual Impairment & Blindness 105, 370–381 (2011)
6. Cook, Miller Polgar, J.: Essentials of Assistive Technologies, Mosby (2012)
7. Dure, I.K., Durre, I.: Instant Print-Braille Compatibility with COMBRA. Journal of Visual Impairment & Blindness 93, 140–152 (1999)
8. Fourli-Kartsouni, F., Slavakis, K., Kouroupetroglou, G., Theodoridis, S.: A Bayesian Network Approach to Semantic Labelling of Text Formatting in XML Corpora of Documents. In: Stephanidis, C. (ed.) HCI 2007. LNCS, vol. 4556, pp. 299–308. Springer, Heidelberg (2007)
9. Robson, C.: Real world research: a resource for social scientists and practitioner-researchers. Blackwell, Oxford (2002)
10. Argyropoulos, V., Martos, A., Kouroupetroglou, G., Chamonikolaou, S., Nikolaraizi, M.: An Experimental Approach in Conceptualizing Typographic Signals of Documents by Eight-dot and Six-dot Braille Code (to be published)
11. Tindal, G.A., Marston, D.B.: Classroom-based Assessment. Evaluating Instructional Outcomes. Maxwell Macmillan, New York (1990)

12. Kotoulas, V., Padeliadu, S.: The Nature of Spelling Errors in the Greek Language: The Case of Students with Reading Disabilities. In: Nikolaidis, K., Mattheoudakis, M. (eds.) 13th International Symposium on Theoretical and Applied Linguistics – Proceedings, pp. 330–339. School of English AUTH, Thessaloniki (1999)
13. Beers, K.: When kids can't read: What teachers can do. A guide for Teachers 6-12. Portsmouth, pp. 6–12. Heinemann, NH (2003)
14. Wright, T., Wormsley, D.P., Kamei-Hannan, C.: Hand movements and braille reading efficiency: data from the alphabetic braille and contracted braille study. Journal of Visual Impairment & Blindness 103, 649–661 (2009)
15. Vakali, A., Evans, R.: Reading strategies employed by Greek braille readers: miscue analysis. Early Child Development and Care 177, 321–335 (2007)
16. Millar, S.: Reading by Touch. Routledge, London (1997)
17. Lorch, R.F.: Text-Signaling Devices and Their Effects on Reading and Memory Processes. Educational Psychology Review 1, 209–234 (1989)
18. Morrison, G.R., Ross, S.M., Kemp, J.E., Kalman, H.: Designing effective instruction. John Willey & Sons, Inc., United States (2011)
19. Waller, R.: Typography and reading strategy. In: Britton, B.K., Glynn, S.M. (eds.) Executive Control Process in Reading, pp. 81–106. Lawrence Erlbaum, Hillsdale (1987)
20. Kouroupetroglou, G., Tsonos, D.: Multimodal Accessibility of Documents. In: Pinder, S. (ed.) Advances in Human-Computer Interaction, pp. 451–470. I-Tech Education and Publishing, Vienna (2008)
21. Tsonos, D., Kouroupetroglou, G.: Modeling Reader's Emotional State Response on Document's Typographic Elements. Advances in Human-Computer Interaction, 1–18 (2011)

Dialogue-Based Information Retrieval
from Images

Pavel Hamřík, Ivan Kopeček, Radek Ošlejšek, and Jaromír Plhák

Faculty of Informatics, Masaryk University Botanicka 68a,
602 00 Brno, Czech Republic
{xhamr,kopecek,oslejsek,xplhak}@fi.muni.cz

Abstract. Our concept of communicative images aims to provide graphical information by means of dialogue interaction, which is suitable for people with various disabilities. Communicative images are graphical objects integrated with a dialogue interface and linked to an associated knowledge database which stores the semantics of the objects depicted. This paper deals with the utilization of formal ontologies for the process of image annotation and dialogue-based investigation in the context of assistive technologies.

Keywords: Ontologies, Picture Semantics, Dialogue Systems.

1 Introduction and Related Work

This paper deals with the utilization of formal ontologies for the process of image annotation and dialogue-based investigation. The role of ontology in relation to information systems is described in [5]. The paper [11] thoroughly describes the process of building user and expert models, as well as the Web Ontology Language and its use. A system for ontology based annotation and indexing biomedical data is studied in [15] and [4]. The paper [14] introduces medical ontology. Paper [17] describes how CHIP and iCITY systems communicate and exchange user data to obtain a more exact view of the users' interests.

A "communicative image", originally introduced and discussed in [9], is a graphical object integrated with a dialogue interface and linked to an associated knowledge database which stores the semantics of the objects depicted.

The interface between natural language and a formalized ontology framework provides an engine that transforms natural language into corresponding formal schemes. Typically, we can restrict ourselves to a small fragment of natural language, so that the engine can be based on relatively simple grammars in combination with the frames technology and standard techniques for misunderstanding solving. For instance, the question *"How far is it from this hotel to the nearest beach?"* is resolved using the template *"How far is it from SLOT1 to SLOT2?"*. The system expects both the SLOT1 and the SLOT2 to be filled by the specific entries from the ontology. Main principles and details of the dialogue management have been discussed in [7].

K. Miesenberger et al. (Eds.): ICCHP 2014, Part I, LNCS 8547, pp. 85–92, 2014.

A single communicative image consists of three data structures: (a) graphical data, (b) identification of objects in the image and (c) their semantic data, i.e. picture annotations and their associated knowledge base. In our approach we exploit the SVG format [3] to encode all these data structures in a single file. The semantics are encoded as OWL ontologies [10]. Formal ontologies present the key feature of communicative images because they define and structure the vocabulary that is shared across different pictures with similar content. Moreover, they provide a suitable formalism for information retrieval and machine-generated dialogues.

Because users can communicate with standard images, either on the Internet or locally, it is necessary to provide an automatic conversion of common images into a communicative form. The necessary infrastructure is cloud-based, with thin clients and a shared server. The role of the clients is to handle a user's interactions with the image, whether mouse clicking, keyboard typing or voice recognition, and to redirect these interactions to a remote server which contains the core application logic. It is responsible for semantic analysis, reasoning, knowledge storing, management and sharing, and dialogue management.

At the beginning of the communication the client sends the original image to the server. The server acquires as much information about the image as possible using image archives, auto-detection and image recognition algorithms, EXIF data extraction, inspection of shared knowledge database, etc. Then it drives the communication, generates dialogues, searches and filters semantic data stored in the knowledge database, learns from the dialogue and updates the knowledge database.

The cloud-based server approach allows the development of variable thin clients. These clients can be either specialized such as those adapted to the specific needs of people with disabilities, or at the other extreme, generic, such as plug-ins to web browsers which permit interaction with common images on the web via a dialogue interface.

2   Experimental Implementation

The whole concept of communication images is implemented within the GATE project – Graphics Accessible To Everyone [8]. The server is designed as a modular component-based Java enterprise application which provides session-oriented remote services available through *SOAP* and *RESTfull* APIs. It consists of the following three modules, as shown on the UML component diagram in Fig. 1.

The **SVG Module** enables the user to upload an image and to inspect its graphical data by going through the SVG DOM tree. Either SVG or raster images can be uploaded. Raster images are automatically wrapped with initial SVG content. The suggested *Image Recognition* interface is used to extend the abilities of the module with automatic image recognition, which is very useful especially in the case of ordinary images, e.g. photos, that have no semantic data embedded so far. Image recognition algorithms must be provided by external component and connected to the *SVG Module*. Although the image recognition

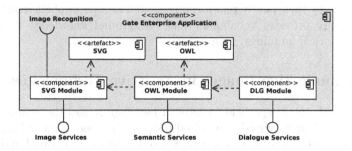

Fig. 1. Component architecture of GATE server

and auto detection techniques are still far from being able to fully describe an analyzed picture in general, specific domains, e.g. face recognition [2,13] or similarity search algorithms in large image collections [6,1] are applicable for the initial image content retrieval and can be integrated to our system.

The **OWL Module** provides semantic-related services. This module cooperates with the SVG module to get annotation data stored directly in the image and to associate them with the available knowledge database. Both the annotation data and the knowledge database are described by OWL. The implemented services cover the ontology management, low-level traversal of the OWL DOM tree, ontology reasoning and information filtering.

The **DLG Module** is responsible for the dialogue subsystem, i.e. parsing and understanding questions in natural language and then composing answers. This module cooperates closely with the OWL Module to analyze the meaning of words. At present, a simplified version of this module is implemented. This version supports questions in *What-Where Language*, WWL [8], having the format "where is what", "what is where" or "what some object is". Moreover, the engine can be configured for domain-specific utterances enabling the user to ask picture-specific questions, e.g. questions on family relationships.

Several ontologies have been proposed and integrated to the GATE project so far. *Graphical ontology* [12], for instance, prescribes important global visual characteristics of the objects such as their unusual size, dominant color or significant shape, enabling the dialogue module to express significant or unusual visual features of the objects depicted. The graphical ontology also supports the description of location and mutual position of objects (e.g. "at the upper left corner", "on the right side of another object", etc.).

Graphical ontology represents upper ontology (also known as a top-level ontology or foundation ontology [16]) describing general concepts that are the same across different knowledge domains. However, it does not handle the non-visual information required to understand the meaning of the individual depicted objects. This kind of information is supported by the domain ontologies defining vocabulary and knowledge base for concrete knowledge domain. We have developed several domain ontologies. For example, *Family* ontology can be used to classify people by their family relationships as well as infer implicit relationships. *Sights* ontology provides vocabulary and background knowledge to describe interests, historical buildings, monuments.

3   Communicative Images in Assistive Technologies

A dialogue with the image held in natural language makes the graphical data accessible especially to visually impaired people. The users are not limited to a simple summary of the image's content. Since the data is structured and related to different parts, objects and aspects of the image, a complex dialogue can be undertaken, ultimately leading to a more natural and fulfilling experience of the users.

The nature of spoken dialogue is also suitable for improving the accessibility for other groups of users with special needs. Elderly people and people with lower technological literacy would benefit from the ease of access to the information in and about the image provided by the dialogue system. The desired information does not have to be obtained manually, which might prove to be difficult for them, but on the basis of a simple request in natural language. This is also useful to motor-impaired people, people with dyslexia and some other cognitive disorders.

Moreover, a cloud-based solution enables the integration of communicative images into social media sites. These technologies support easy information sharing and on-line user collaboration, which helps to manage the knowledge in a decentralized way. The activity of one user publishing some historical facts about a monument, for example, can be utilized by other users to improve their exploration of a photo downloaded from the web. For communicative images, this kind of crowdsourcing presents an efficient way of building up knowledge bases with a long term perspective and making graphical data more accessible to everyone.

Another aspect of a collaborative structure is the social element – communication over images of mutual interest offers sharing knowledge, avocations, contacts, relations and leads to increase in a general social cohesiveness rather than the typical social inadequacy and exclusion.

These functions utilizing the ontology based information not only fulfill the user's need for information, but they also help them to exercise their memory, perception and other cognitive functions. The users with neurological or cognitive dysfunction can browse family pictures while being reminded of the age and names of the people in the photos, their birthdays, names of family pets, the time and occasion the picture was taken. Therefore, apart from the advantages concerning the access to information, communicative images can play inconsiderable role in the development of the psycho-social domain.

4   Evaluation

To evaluate the usability of the concept of communicative images, we prepared a simple experiment, where the users was aimed at exploring a given photo

Fig. 2. Annotated painting: Last Supper by Leonardo da Vinci

by means of What-Where Language. We chose the Last Supper by Leonardo da Vinci as the reference picture, as shown in Fig. 2. This picture was precisely annotated by hand and then inspected by users via the GATE system. Da Vinci's Last Supper is one of the world's most famous paintings capturing the final meal that Jesus shared with his Apostles in Jerusalem before his crucifixion. The picture consists of several dominant objects: Jesus, 12 Apostles and a table. These objects was linked with thorough semantic data. The annotation data include historical facts about Jesus and his Apostles, their position in the picture, mutual position of the figures and the table, dominant colors of clothes, activities of figures (e.g. sitting, talking, etc.) as well as expression on their faces (e.g. curious, angry, etc.). The annotation of important figures, namely Jesus, Judas and Peter, went into more details. Their annotation was supplemented with the position of hands, for instance. Besides the annotation of picture content, the facts about the painting itself is included, e.g. when the painting was completed, its size, etc. The experiment was attended by several students of the Masaryk University with different IT skills. All the participants was sighted, therefore we hide the picture from them. Before the testing, they have been informed about the principles of communicative images. To help us understand the nature of the interaction, they have been requested to speak aloud as they communicate with the image, which enables us to record their intents, expectations or things that surprise them. After the testing, the participants filled in a questionnaire which provided us with quantitative as well as subjective evaluation.

During the experiments we used two modes, with and without guidance. Without guidance, the participants had no idea what is depicted. They communicated with the picture in any way they liked without any support. On the contrary, users with guidance was instructed what pieces of information are present and how they are structured.

Following fragment of dialogue was recorded during the free communication without guidance. This example represents a typical questions, answers and limitations in the communication (our comments are surrounded by square brackets):

User: What is in the picture?
System: In the picture, there are Andrew, Table, Philip, Peter, ... [A long list of all objects depicted follows. The user would prefer a brief description instead.]

User: What is in the top left corner?
System: In the top left corner there is no object.

User: What is in the middle?
System: In the middle there are James Major, Jesus, Thomas, Peter, Philip, John and Judas. [User asked for various locations one by one. Then he was wondering about the exact order of figures. Some questions failed at this moment.]

User: What is on the left side of Jesus?
System: On the left side of the Jesus are Andrew, Peter, Bartholomew, Judas, Right Hand of Judas, James Minor and John.

User: Is Peter on the left side of Andrew?
System: The position "left side of andrew" is not valid for searching for object Peter. Please, re-type your query.

User: Is Peter in the left of Andrew?
System: The position "left of andrew" is not valid for searching for object Peter. Please, re-type your query. [Several attempts continued.]

User: Describe Table.
System: The table around which are Jesus and all the Apostles sitting. [This is misunderstanding. In fact, the user was interested in objects on the table, not description of the table.]

User: Describe Jesus.
System: Jesus (72 BC to 3033 AD), also referred to as Jesus of Nazareth, is the central figure of Christianity, whom the teachings of most Christian denominations hold to be the Son of God. Christianity regards Jesus as the awaited Messiah of the Old Testament and refers to him as Jesus Christ, a name that is also used in non-Christian contexts. He is also a major figure in Islam. In the painting, Jesus appears to be calm, tranquil. [Another misunderstanding. The user would prefer to put emphasis to the last sentence, i.e. it would be better to distinguish between "Describe Jesus" and "Who is Jesus".]

In what follows, there is a transcription of guided dialogue, i.e. the user knew what kind of information is available:

User: Describe the picture.
System: Object cannot be recognized. Please, re-type your query.

User: Detailed information about picture.
System: This photo presents the painting called "The Last Supper", which portrays the reaction given by each apostle when Jesus said one of them would betray him.

User: Who painted the picture?
System: This painting was created by Leonardo da Vinci.

User: What people are in the picture?

System: Sorry, I don't understand your query. Please, enter another query.
User: Who is in the picture?
System: In the picture, there are Andrew, Philip, Peter, Bartholomew, James Major, Judas, Thomas, Thaddeus, Simon, Matthew, James Minor, John and Jesus.
User: Where is Judas?
System: Judas is in the middle.

Subjective impression of all the participants was very positive. All the people were able to recognize the painting, reconstruct the layout in their mind and imagine the scene. However, we have to point out that the sighted people participating in the experiment were probably familiar with this popular painting. For blind users this task could be more difficult.

Users usually assessed the interaction with the image as funny, quite easy and natural. On the contrary, effectiveness of the dialogue based interaction varied from "very effective" to "not very effective". Users frequently criticized weak misunderstanding solving, the lack of hints and missing support of general questions that do not belong to the scope of WWL.

5   Conclusions and Future Work

In this paper, we have outlined basic principles of communicative images as well as the general architecture of the system. The aim of the performed experiment was to make sure that the concept is viable, implementable and useful. The implementation is still very simplified and the concept of communicative images has many open problems. For instance, there is the gap between semantic models and dialogue strategies. At the moment, we have to carefully prepare and finetune the dialogue subsystem for each concrete domain ontology by hand instead of generating dialogue strategies automatically from the internal structure of provided ontology. Also continual enhancement and enlargement of knowledge base as well as automatic learning from dialogues pose a big challenge.

The preliminary results show that this approach promises valuable utilization in many application domains like e-learning, smart management of large photo collections or assistive technologies. However, more experiments especially with visually impaired people have to be performed to verify feasibility of communication images.

References

1. Abbasi, R., Chernov, S., Nejdl, W., Paiu, R., Staab, S.: Exploiting flickr tags and groups for finding landmark photos. In: Boughanem, M., Berrut, C., Mothe, J., Soule-Dupuy, C. (eds.) ECIR 2009. LNCS, vol. 5478, pp. 654–661. Springer, Heidelberg (2009)
2. Bartlett, M., Movellan, J.R., Sejnowski, T.: Face recognition by independent component analysis. IEEE Trans. on Neural Networks 13(6), 1450–1464 (2002)

3. Dahlström, E., et al.: Scalable vector graphics (svg) 1.1, 2nd edn. (2011), http://www.w3.org/TR/SVG/
4. Faro, A., Giordano, D., Spampinato, C.: Combining literature text mining with microarray data: advances for system biology modeling. Briefings in Bioinformatics 13(1), 61–82 (2012), http://bib.oxfordjournals.org/content/13/1/61.abstract
5. Guarino, N.: Formal ontology and information systems, pp. 3–15. IOS Press (1998)
6. Jaffe, A., Naaman, M., Tassa, T., Davis, M.: Generating summaries and visualization for large collections of geo-referenced photographs. In: Proc. of ACM Int. Workshop on Multimedia Information Retrieval, New York, USA, pp. 89–98 (2006)
7. Kopecek, I., Ošlejšek, R., Plhák, J.: Dialogue management in communicative images. In: Text, Speech and Dialogue - Students' section, Proceedings Addendum, pp. 9–13. University of West Bohemia in Pilsen in Pilsen, Publ. House, Pilsen (2011)
8. Kopeček, I., Ošlejšek, R.: GATE to accessibility of computer graphics. In: Miesenberger, K., Klaus, J., Zagler, W.L., Karshmer, A.I. (eds.) ICCHP 2008. LNCS, vol. 5105, pp. 295–302. Springer, Heidelberg (2008)
9. Kopecek, I., Oslejsek, R.: Communicative images. In: Dickmann, L., Volkmann, G., Malaka, R., Boll, S., Krüger, A., Olivier, P. (eds.) SG 2011. LNCS, vol. 6815, pp. 163–173. Springer, Heidelberg (2011)
10. Lacy, L.W.: OWL: representing information using the Web Ontology Language. Trafford Publishing, Victoria BC, Canada (2005), http://www.worldcat.org/search?qt&=1412034485
11. Linton, F., Joy, D., Peter Schaefer, H.: Building user and expert models by long-term observation of application usage. In: Proceedings of the Seventh International Conference on User Modeling, pp. 129–138. Springer (1999)
12. Ošlejšek, R.: Annotation of pictures by means of graphical ontologies. In: Proc. Int. Conf. on Internet Computing, ICOMP, pp. 296–300 (2009)
13. Rowley, H., Baluja, S., Kanade, T.: Neural network-based face detection. In: Proceedings of the 1996 IEEE Computer Society Conference on Computer Vision and Pattern Recognition, CVPR 1996, pp. 203–208 (June 1996)
14. Satria, H., Priya, R.S., Ismail, L.H., Supriyanto, E.: Building and reusing medical ontology for tropical diseases management. International Journal of Education and Information Technologies 6, 52–61 (2012)
15. Shah, N., Jonquet, C., Chiang, A., Butte, A., Chen, R., Musen, M.: Ontology-driven indexing of public datasets for translational bioinformatics. BMC Bioinformatics 10(suppl. 2), 1–10 (2009), http://dx.doi.org/10.1186/1471-2105-10-S2-S1
16. Staab, S., Studer, R.: Handbook on Ontologies, 2nd edn. Springer Publishing Company, Incorporated (2009)
17. Wang, Y., Cena, F., Carmagnola, F., Cortassa, O., Gena, C., Stash, N., Aroyo, L.M.: RSS-based interoperability for user adaptive systems. In: Nejdl, W., Kay, J., Pu, P., Herder, E. (eds.) AH 2008. LNCS, vol. 5149, pp. 353–356. Springer, Heidelberg (2008), http://dblp.uni-trier.de/db/conf/ah/ah2008.html#WangCCCGSA08

Annotation Tool for the Smart Web Accessibility Platform

Sébastien Aupetit and Vincent Rouillé

Université François Rabelais Tours, Laboratoire Informatique (EA6300) 64,
Avenue Jean Portalis, 37200 Tours, France
`aupetit@univ-tours.fr`

Abstract. Active and passive accessibility are two manner to improve
web accessibility. While active accessibility mostly relies on norms and
recommendations, it is practically proved that it is not sufficient. Passive accessibility is achieved by *a posteriori* content transformations. The
Smart Web Accessibility Platform (SWAP) is a set of open source tools
designed to tackle the passive accessibility problem of web contents. This
article presents the goals and aims of SWAP through its main components: the proxy, the server and the annotation tool. The annotation tool
is built using the proxy of SWAP. We explain how such design allows the
annotation tool to be maintainable, independent of the browser and very
flexible compared to other design.

Keywords: Web Accessibility, Annotation Tool, Proxy, Smart Web
Accessibility Platform, Web Page Transformation.

1 Introduction

Web accessibility means that people can access contents of web pages whichever
disabilities they suffer (aging, impairment. . .). Active and passive web accessibility are two ways to achieve such universal access. Active accessibility relies
on norms, recommendations[1] and laws [1] to enforce a proper structuring and
tagging of documents during their creation by webmasters. Tools[2] and methodologies [2] complete the set to easy achievement. Besides lobbies strongly encourage on active web accessibility, it is not sufficient. A great part of the web
remains not accessible for many reasons: "it costs too much", "constraints are
too high", lots of web sites are not maintained anymore, lots of web sites are
not professional works, web sites evolve, enforcing laws are country specific and
have various requirements. . . A fully accessible web is not for tomorrow. Passive accessibility is a complementary approach which can handle those flaws. It
mainly consists in using assistive technologies (zoom, speech synthesis. . .) or in
transforming web pages contents *a posteriori* when pages are already available

---

[1] `http://www.w3.org/TR/WCAG10/`, `http://www.w3.org/TR/WCAG20/`
[2] `http://achecker.ca/checker`, `http://www.binaryblue.com.au/access_wizard...`

K. Miesenberger et al. (Eds.): ICCHP 2014, Part I, LNCS 8547, pp. 93–100, 2014.

on the Internet . Web pages transformation is what we are concerned here. Many tools[3] and authors tried to handle the problem [3,4,5,6,7,8,9,10,11]. Those tools can be categorized by the location where the transformation occurs: on the web site, on a dedicated web site or on the user computer. Each location has pros and cons. On the web site or on a dedicated server, specific data can be used (database, templates...) but the server must be stronger to handle more tasks, webmasters must provide all what is necessary for the transformation and accessibility features can not be personalized for a user's disabilities. On the user computer, the tool can do specific transformations for the user and webmaster help is not required (if he cooperates, it is better). The main concern is that the tool does neither have access to the data used, nor to the templates to built the page. On user computer, the tool can be a specific process or an extension of a browser (plugins). Plugins have access to all the features of the browser but are highly dependent of the browser, of its evolution, of its support and of how web technologies advances through time. Dedicated processes are usually proxy software. The main advantage is that a proxy does neither enforce the user to a specific browser, nor to change his current assistive technologies. Moreover, the proxy evolution is independent of the browser and its evolution. The only requirement is that access to the web is made through the proxy. The main disadvantage is that some processing are done by both the proxy and the browser (e.g. document parsing and analysis).

The Smart Web Accessibility Platform (SWAP)[4] developed by the computer science laboratory of Université François Rabelais Tours aims to provide tools for passive accessibility using a client side proxy transformation approach. SWAP is an open source modular and extensible set of tools. Previous works on web accessibility demonstrated how SWAP can be used for textual color improvement [10,11,12,13]. To develop smarter transformations of the contents, we are faced with the problem of annotating contents for pattern recognition and automatic assessments of the results. A flexible annotation tool is required. In the following, we discuss the SWAP platform and demonstrate why and how the annotation tool can be defined as a specific component of the platform.

2   Smart Web Accessibility Platform for Passive Accessibility

SWAP is both a research tool, an experimentation tool and a final user tool. SWAP is built to be portable, easily extensible and modular allowing the assembling of any custom applications. It is written in Java using components, a design patterns approach and the Spring framework[5] for the Inversion of Control (IoC) part. Maven[6] is used to manage dependencies and to create specific

---

[3] http://www.bbc.co.uk/education/betsie,
  http://apache.webthing.com/mod_accessibility/,   http://muffin.doit.org/,
  http://rabbit-proxy.sourceforge.net/...
[4] https://projectsforge.org/projects/swap
[5] http://www.springsource.org/
[6] http://maven.apache.org/

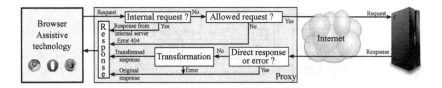

Fig. 1. Request processing by the proxy

custom assembly of components. The SWAP platform is currently composed of three high level applications: the proxy, the server and the annotation tool. Each application relies on a set of common components (the core) and specific components. A Java Virtual Machine (JVM) can be bundled with the applications removing the need of administrator privileges on a computer to use the applications. Consequently, the tools can be used even on very software standardized or constrained computers (bank...). The one and only constraint is that accessing the web is made through the proxy by both the browser and the assistive technologies.

2.1 The Core Components

The core components provide a simplified self expressive management of the components, of the dependencies (IoC) and of the database. This is mostly achieved using Java annotations with Spring, Hibernate[7] and Java Persistence API (JPA)[8] using Spring JPA. Core components provide HTTP protocol support, request and response caching, HTML Document Object Model (DOM) facilities and Cascading Style Sheets (CSS) facilities.

2.2 The Proxy Tool

The proxy tool is composed of the core components and of specific ones. The main specific component is the one handling the communication with the browser. It is realized using the Jetty web server[9]. Depending on which domain is accessed, the component does either the proxying of the request or forwards the request to the internal HTTP server (see Fig. 1). The internal HTTP server allows either the communication between a page in the browser and the proxy using Javascript (see section 3), or the configuration of the tool. This internal server is managed by the Web MVC (Model View Controller) component of Spring. To proxy a request, the component forwards the request to the web site. The obtained response can then be transformed if needed. The original or transformed response is finally sent to the browser. Since the proxy tool is executed on the user computer, HTTPS requests (secured contents) can also be transformed.

---

[7] http://hibernate.org/

[8] https://www.jcp.org/en/jsr/detail?id=317

[9] http://www.eclipse.org/jetty/

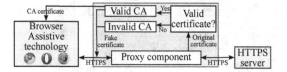

Fig. 2. *Man-in-the-middle* approach used for secured exchanges

To not compromise security, a *man-in-the-middle* approach (see Fig 2) is used. Two internal Certification Authorities (CA) are used (self signed CA). The valid CA is used to create fake certificates for servers having valid certificates. The invalid CA is used in the other cases. The CA certificate of the valid CA is exported by SWAP and imported by the browser. Consequently, any certificate emitted by the valid CA is recognized as a valid certificate by the browser. Security is maintained while secured contents can be transformed if needed.

Multiple transformations can be applied on a web page. The proxy handles the proper parallel execution of all the transforming components using read/write locks and components synchronization. Transformations can be done at low level (bytes) or at high level (DOM). [10,11,12,13] shows the use of specific transformation components with the proxy tool. The annotation tool is another example of the use of the proxy tool with specific components (see section 3).

2.3   The Server Tool

The server tool includes the core components. One specific component allow a simple communication protocol between the proxy tool and the server tool (Remote Procedure Call). Another component handle database storage. For now, the server tool is only used for global knowledge storage. It is planned to use the server to do some learning calculus when pattern recognition will be used.

3   The Annotation Tool

The annotation tool is the proxy tool for which specific components are added (see below). The tool aims to collect data on web pages and to store them on the server as global knowledge.

3.1   The Problem

To create smart transformations, it becomes necessary to have a database of knowledge on web pages samples to tackle web variability. Such knowledge can be gathered using experts (paid service, volunteers...) and a dedicated annotation tool. The knowledge database allows the use of machine learning, the use of pattern recognition methods or automated validations of transformations.

3.2   Which Form for the Annotation Tool?

The annotation tool can take many forms such as a dedicated software, a plugins for a browser or a set of components for SWAP. By integrating a web browser into a dedicated software, it is possible to have access to all features of the browser almost without limits (internal representation, interaction...). However, browsers and technologies evolve rapidly increasing the risk on durability and maintainability of the tool. Browser plugins have similar pros and cons as the dedicated software. They are highly dependent on the API (Application Programming Interface) of the browser. The plugins API are browser specific and evolve rarely with an ascending compatibility. In both cases, the integration of the annotation tool with the page requires the interactive parts (selection, marking...) to be linked to the DOM of the page. A simpler way to integrate the interactive part can be done using injection of scripts in the page like a transformation using SWAP. In this case, the annotation tool is independent of the browser, of the browser API and of the evolution of the browser. Moreover, as being integrated in the page, the scripts have access to all features of the pages without limits. The main drawback is that the injection can lead eventually to a breakage of the page structure, of the aspect or of the behavior. A proper handling of the isolation of the DOM, of the styles and of the scripts of the annotation tool and of the page is necessary.

3.3   Isolation

The Document Object Model (DOM) is a hierarchical representation of the elements of a web page. Any element must be in the DOM to be visible. Javascript allow to manipulate and interact with the DOM to do things. There is not permissions for accessing the DOM: any script can modify the DOM. Consequently, the scripts of the page and the injected scripts both have access to the same content. Moreover, when an unexpected element is inserted in the DOM, it can lead to lots of consequences such as script errors or styles breakage. To reduce the consequence of the annotation tool on the page, scripts isolation, DOM isolation and styles isolation must be done. We identified three ways to isolate the DOM (see Fig. 3).

One way to isolate the DOM consists in creating a specific page containing all what is necessary for the annotations (scripts, CSS) and in embedding an `iframe` containing the web page to annotate. The contained DOM is isolated from the containing DOM by the `iframe` but the scripts of the containing page can access the content of the annotated web page. This approach seems simple but to interact with the annotated page, a complex Javascript API must be used and some features of the browsers can conflict with the annotation process. For example, popup or windows opening create new tab/window which does not contain the annotation tool. As a solution, we can consider that an injected script checks for the presence of the annotation tool and, if not, reload the annotation tool with the page as a parameter. This is not usable since the reloading of a page does not guarantee to obtain an identical page. It is even less the case

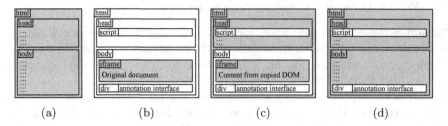

Fig. 3. The three ways to isolate the DOM. Parts of the original document are represented in grey. (a) Original DOM, (b) Specific `iframe` isolation, (c) The DOM is moved as a child of an `iframe`, (d) A root node is added at the end.

when POST request are used. Then this approach is not appropriated for the annotation tool.

The second way to isolate is similar to the previous but without a dedicated web page for the annotation. A script is injected in every page passing by the proxy. On page loading, the script copies the DOM of the document, replaces the current DOM by a simpler one containing an `iframe` and puts the copied DOM in the `iframe`. In this case, the DOM of the annotated page is isolated from the annotation tool and browser features does not interfere with the tool. This approach seems miraculous but it suffers major drawbacks. An important latency is introduced for the annotation tool since the complete DOM needs to be loaded before being copied and replaced. Since the complete DOM of the page is loaded, the embedded scripts of the page can not be unloaded or blocked leading in frequent cases to infinite loops or errors. Moreover, ours tests with recent browsers showed important stability and performance issues. This approach is appropriated only for simple static contents.

The third and also the simplest way to isolate consists in adding an element to the DOM. This element is used as a root node for any element added to the page for the annotation tool. It is simple and browser performances are preserved. The main drawbacks is that the DOM is modified. By regrouping the changes under an unique root node at the end of the document, we experimentally devised that it provokes no breakage on lots of page. Theoretically, it can lead to breakage of scripts or of styles but it is very infrequent. This approach is the most suited for the injection of the annotation tool in the page. To limit the influence of the page on the tool, styles isolation and scripts isolation must be performed.

Styles isolation is performed by marking the root element of the annotation tool with an unique class identifier and by resetting the style properties for any child element. The properties are marked as important to take precedence over any defined style in the annotated web page. Element properties evolve with standards and can sometimes be specific to the used browser. To increase maintainability and durability of the tool, we defined a script which compare the styles of the element with a neutral element outside the DOM (then not affected by styles of the page). If properties differ then they are reset to the neutral values. Performance degradation introduced by this script is insignificant.

Fig. 4. A screenshot of the annotation tool on a web page with the `Zone` component

Scripts isolation is achieved through methodology. The scripts are injected at the highest location in the DOM (first child of `head`). It implies that ours scripts are the first to be executed in the page, whichever the page's scripts, when the Javascript execution environment is clean. To eliminate any conflict between the annotation tool scripts and the page's scripts, ours scripts never create or modify global variables. Scripts are made anonymous and not callable by others scripts using anonymous function. Those functions and theirs local variables are not visible to the other scripts. We use: `(function() {/* isolated code */})();`.

3.4 Annotation Tool Components

SWAP is designed to be modular. The scripts of the annotation tool follows the same principles. The annotation tool is mainly composed of Javascript scripts designed like components having dependencies. The main component is the `Loader`. It provides an API for the components allowing to describe their names, their dependencies and theirs implementations. The loader is the first executed script on the page. It loads the required components using the isolation principle described above and the described dependencies. Many components are actually implemented. The *Communication* component defines an API simplifying the exchange between the page and the internal web server of the proxy. It relies on jQuery[10] to be browser neutral. The *EventEmitter* component implements the Observer pattern (subscription and emission of signals) to simplify the communication between the isolated components and to handle events. In the current implementation, those components are completed with the *Zone* component whose aim is to allow the marking, the identification and the annotation of zones in the page. It handles the transmissions of information on the zones to the proxy (type, anonymized DOM, Xpath...). The proxy forwards the information to the server for storage in the knowledge database. Figure 4 presents a screenshot of the annotation tool with the `Zone` component.

4   Conclusion

In this work, we extend the modular platform SWAP with components dedicated to the creation of an annotation tool. We discussed how it can be implemented using the proxy tool of the project and how the isolation problem can be resolved

---

[10] `http://jquery.com/`

efficiently. The modular feature of SWAP is applied even for the Javascript code providing a flexible annotation tool. An example of specific components for zones annotation is presented but the tool can easily be extended with others kind of annotations by creating new components. The isolation principle and infrastructure are used for the annotation tool. They can also be reused for the injection of scripts in web page, for example, for nagivation assistance or for any interactive assistive task.

References

1. République Française: Loi no 2005-102 du 11 février 2005 pour l'égalité des droits et des chances, la participation et la citoyenneté des personnes handicapées. JO no 36 du 12 février 2005, p. 2353 (2005)
2. Colas, S., Monmarché, N., Burger, D., Mohamed, S.: A web site migration support tool to reach european accessibility standards. In: 9th European Conference for the Advancement of Assistive Technology in Europe (AAATE 2007), San Sebastian, Spain, vol. 20, pp. 907–911 (2007)
3. Brown, S.S., Robinson, P.: A world wide web mediator for users with low vision. In: Proceedings of Conference on Human Factors in Computing Systems (CHI 2001 Workshop No. 14), Seattle, WA (2001)
4. Colajanni, M., Grieco, R., Malandrino, D., Mazzoni, F., Scarano, V.: A scalable framework for the support of advanced edge services. In: Yang, L.T., Rana, O.F., Di Martino, B., Dongarra, J. (eds.) HPCC 2005. LNCS, vol. 3726, pp. 1033–1042. Springer, Heidelberg (2005)
5. Parmanto, B., Ferrydiansyah, R., Zeng, X., Saptono, A., Sugiantara, I.: Accessibility transformation gateway. In: Proceedings of the 38th Annual Hawaii International Conference on System Sciences, HICSS 2005, p. 183a. IEEE (2005)
6. Han, R., Bhagwat, P., LaMaire, R., Mummert, T., Perret, V., Rubas, J.: Dynamic adaptation in an image transcoding proxy for mobile web browsing. IEEE Personal Communications 5(6), 8–17 (1998)
7. Gupta, S., Kaiser, G.: Extracting content from accessible web pages. In: International Cross-Disciplinary Workshop on WebAccessibility, p. 26. ACM Press (2005)
8. Gupta, S., Kaiser, G.E., Grimm, P., Chiang, M.F., Starren, J.: Automating content extraction of HTML documents. World Wide Web 8(2), 179–224 (2005)
9. Hermsdorf, D., Gappa, H., Pieper, M.: WebAdapter: A prototype of a WWW-browser with new special needs adaptations. In: Proceedings of the International Conference on Computers Helping People with Special Needs, pp. 151–160 (1998)
10. Mereuță, A., Aupetit, S., Slimane, M.: Improving web accessibility for dichromat users through contrast preservation. In: Miesenberger, K., Karshmer, A., Penaz, P., Zagler, W. (eds.) ICCHP 2012, Part I. LNCS, vol. 7382, pp. 363–370. Springer, Heidelberg (2012)
11. Aupetit, S., Mereuță, A., Slimane, M.: Automatic color improvement of web pages with time limited operators. In: Miesenberger, K., Karshmer, A., Penaz, P., Zagler, W. (eds.) ICCHP 2012, Part I. LNCS, vol. 7382, pp. 355–362. Springer, Heidelberg (2012)
12. Mereuta, A., Aupetit, S., Monmarché, N., Slimane, M.: Web page textual color contrast compensation for CVD users using optimization methods. Journal of Mathematical Modelling and Algorithms in Operations Research (October 2013)
13. Mereuta, A., Aupetit, S., Monmarché, N., Slimane, M.: An evolutionary approach to contrast compensation for dichromat users. In: Proceedings of Evolution Artificielle 2013. LNCS. Springer (2013) (to appear)

Iberoamerican Observatory of Web Accessibility

A Benchmarking and Educative Tool

Carlos Benavidez[1], Claudia Cardoso[2], Jorge Fernandes[2],
Emmanuelle Gutiérrez y Restrepo[1], Henry Gutiérrez[1], and Loïc Martínez-Normand[3]

[1] Fundación Sidar – Acceso Universal, Madrid, Spain
{carlos,emmanuelle,henry}@sidar.org
[2] Fundação para a Ciência e a Tecnologia, Lisboa, Portugal
{Jorge.Fernandes,Claudia.Cardoso}@fct.pt
[3] Universidad Politécnica de Madrid, Spain
loic@fi.upm.es

Abstract. The web content accessibility guidelines (WCAG) were first published 15 years ago. Since then, there has been a lot of progress in web accessibility, but much work is still needed to reach good levels of accessibility. It is therefore important to measure the degree of accessibility of current websites and the rate of improvement. There have been several studies on the implementation of web accessibility in Europe and the world, but such studies are unstable, with a methodology and sample that changes from year to year. The Iberoamerican Observatory presented in this paper aims to correct this situation, coordinating the work of the observatories of the different participating countries, so that all use the same methodology and a consistent sampling and data structure. Thus, results can be compared within the same country and with the other countries of the region.

Keywords: Web Accessibility, Review, Benchmarking, Monitoring.

1 Introduction

In 2014 we celebrate 25 years of the web, and 15 of the publication of WCAG 1.0 (Web Content Accessibility Guidelines) [1] that indicate how web content has to be to provide equal access to all users, including persons with disabilities.

The WCAG have become an internationally accepted standard as the basis of accessibility legislation in most countries [2] and version 2 (WCAG 2.0) [3], published in 2008, has also been published as the ISO / IEC 40500:2012 standard [4]. However, evidence indicates that neither the regulations nor the existing standards are being properly implemented in most websites, which still present significant barriers for users with and without disabilities.

Studies on the implementation of web accessibility criteria in Europe and the world are published regularly (i.e. [5,6]), but such studies are partial and unstable, with methodologies and sampling changing from year to year. The Iberoamerican Observatory aims to correct this situation, coordinating the work of observatories of the

K. Miesenberger et al. (Eds.): ICCHP 2014, Part I, LNCS 8547, pp. 101–108, 2014.

participating countries, so that all use the same methodology and consistent sampling and data structures. Thus, results can be compared within the same country and with the other countries of the region. In addition, the evolution over time can also be measured.

The Observatory will serve a dual purpose. On the one hand, it will provide clear and precise information about the evolution over time of the conformance to the sub-set of success criteria and sufficient techniques that can be automatically checked (not only showing accessibility errors but also highlighting good practices). On the other hand, it will fulfil a pedagogical function, as it will provide those in charge of each country's websites with specific guidelines on how to check for and repair the errors found, based on the combination of an internal communication system and outreach public activities.

2   Related Work

In America's Spanish-speaking and Portuguese-speaking countries, large scale accessibility monitoring projects are hard to find. In Spain, there are various observatories for IT [7], disability [8] and Public Administration [9]. One example is the e-Government Website Accessibility Observatory, set up in 2010 by the General Directorate for the Promotion of e-Government. The activity of this Observatory ended in 2011 and its reinstatement for 2014 is currently being considered. Unfortunately, most of the observatories do not publish information enough about their investigations, or they publish sector-specific studies that do not have continuity over time.

In Portugal, Unidade Acesso of Fundação para a Ciência e a Tecnologia [10] has been monitoring Public Administration websites since 2006, but without releasing the benchmarking directories. This activity has resulted in the publication of four reports about the Portuguese Central Public Administration in 2002, 2003, 2008 and 2010.

Out of the Iberoamerican area, the most immediate antecedent is the European Internet Accessibility Observatory (EIAO), founded in September 2004 and active until 2008. In that year they published a report with their results [11]. EIAO was part of a cluster of European projects on web accessibility, WAB CLUSTER [12]. After EIAO, the eGovMon [13] project was carried out in the Nordic countries, and it is intended to be continued in the European Internet Inclusion Initiative project (EIII) [14].

Some other projects have been carried out, such as SMART 2008-0066 "Monitoring eAccessibility in Europe" [15]. This activity was commissioned by the European Commission as a follow-up to the study "Measuring Progress of eAccessiblity in Europe" (MeAC) [16], developed during the period 2006 - 2008. One of the goals of the SMART 2008-0066 activity is to draw up an annual report, taking as a starting point the data provided by the MEAC study. The results have been two reports published in 2010 and 2011.

Recently, a Study on Assessing and Promoting E-Accessibility [6] was published. It is a study prepared for the European Commission DG Communications Networks, Content & Technology, whose main aims were to describe the extent of e-accessibility across the EU27 countries and some third countries, as well as the policy efforts that have emerged in this area.

At present, the main problem is that there are no means of obtaining accurate data on the evolution of web accessibility, neither in Europe nor the rest of the world. This is due to various reasons: documentation and databases disappear; reports do not compile all the desired and necessary information to make a follow-up; samples are not constant; methodologies and criteria change from one report to the next, etc.

The conclusion of the analysis of related work is that the existing projects of large-scale web accessibility benchmarking have so far failed to reach the goal of showing the evolution of web accessibility in a region, given the difficulties of comparing different reports that do not share sampling nor evaluation methodologies. We believe that part of the problem is the need of a large amount of resources for launching and maintaining the activity of transnational web accessibility observatories. That is the reason why our proposal distributes the workload into national observatories that are coordinated in Spain by the Sidar Foundation.

3   Observatory Needs and Objectives

The publication of WCAG 1.0 in 1999 [1] leaded to many changes. Proof of those changes are the large number of legislation's modifications adopted across the Latin American countries [2] that intend to enforce compliance to WCAG 1.0 regulations. Even so, the advances over the region in WCAG conformance are partial and uneven. And, as described above, there is no reliable data collected in Latin America, Europe or globally, that allows an objective vision.

The sporadic publication of lack-of-compliance reports is not enough; to really en-courage improvements in WCAG compliance, it is necessary the publication of regulated and standardized reports on a regular basis. Such publications should be on publicly accessible media, not only on specialized magazines.

In addition, if such an observatory is to become an advocacy tool and an educational instrument for more and better accessibility, it is necessary to complement the information on the degree of accessibility compliance with qualitative identification of problems found to enable point solutions. It is important to know the current degree of accessibility, but it is even more important to know how to correct the situation and exit the non-compliance status.

Over the 15 years of the WCAG 1.0 history, many attempts were made to explain the difficulties of a wide adoption of the regulations. Given the uneven format and periodicity of the reports, it is not possible to obtain a conclusion based on them. A regularity on publication as well as a standard methodology of the tests performed would mean the feasibility of benchmarks among different sectors, countries or in-country organizations.

Therefore, the main aims of this Observatory are: (1) to preserve regularity in the methodology, sampling and periodicity of the evaluations; (2) to enable the creation of reports with manual revisions by experts to achieve more detailed results; (3) to enable the creation of reports with usability tests with people with disabilities of some pieces of content and technologies of Web content contributing to arise of new techniques of accessibility design; (4) to create culture about good practices in the evaluation and repair of accessibility problems; and (5) to make public campaigns about the most common errors and their resolution.

4   OIA's Methodology

The Iberoamerican Observatory of Accessibility (Observatorio Iberoamericano de la Accessibilidad - OIA) has established a network of autonomous observatories that apply a common methodology, using an even set of data collection and producing an even set of measurements and reports.

Each national observatory is responsible on the selection of statistical marks over its own country, and the resulting data is collected and grouped on predetermined categories named following the European Network for Administrative Nomenclature (ADNOM) [17].

National observatories have to follow a common approach: they have to report the result of the test performed; the test has to include all the sub-categories of the 10 categories previously defined; the test is performed on at least 10 pages on every site; the test has to include the HTML source to enable comparing automatic results and making complementary studies. This way, the results obtained can be compared, measurements are consistent and reports are meaningful.

To guaranty the uniformity of calculations, the observatories are spread among different web servers while every one of them makes use of a specifically designed application that produces a metric (or accessibility score). Reports are updated on a monthly basis and every single observatory produces its own statistical results to be collected on the OIA so as to produce global statistics.

4.1   Metric

The calculations are performed using an automatic evaluation tool specifically created for OIA, based on a previous tool called eXaminator [18]. The tool uses a quantitative metric that indicates a ratio of successful tests. This metric is an indication of the degree of accessibility that users will experience on a site. The metric obtained, quantified on a 1 to 10 scale, is used to compare the results and variations of tests, and to record the variations upon time.

The evaluation algorithm of eXaminator is based on 96 individual tests related to techniques or failures of WCAG 2.0. The results of each test are then averaged to obtain a general score for each page. Out of those 96 tests, 60 are known to offer a large accuracy upon automatic evaluation test, and are used to identify errors that, along with the page's evaluation score, constitute the main source of statistical data.

4.2   Categorization

The OIA presents the challenge to obtain comparable reports from public administration websites of different Latin American countries. There is a lot of diversity in the structure of national governments, the terminology of public functions and even the political way of governments. Even the concept of public administration differs from one country to another. For instance, in Argentina, neither the legislative power nor the justice power are included as part of public administration. In addition, we have found significant differences in the organization of public administration websites, complicating the search for equivalent sites for comparison.

Such remarkable differences, lead us to define a common glossary and a common classification system that enables a proper classification of the web pages that are part of the sample in each country.

For these purposes, OIA has adapted the nomenclature system specified at the CWA 15526 European Network for Administrative Nomenclature (ADNOM) [17], which is based on the COFOG (Classification of the Functions of Government) [19] that was developed in 1999 the United Nations.

OIA can describe websites based on function, organism and jurisdiction. The values for function and organism are based on the ADNOM terms and the terminology for jurisdiction has been specifically developed for OIA. A document has been produced to explain the terminology and its application to 3 different Iberoamerican countries with different government forms.

In addition to a common nomenclature, OIA also includes a definition of a common set of websites to be monitored, so that results can be compared. Also, each country can freely select additional sites to be tested and monitored for their own needs.

5   From eXaminator to OIA: Lessons Learned

Since 2006, the eXaminator tool has been widely used on large-scale monitoring projects and its inner algorithm has been modified according to such direct experiences. The first version of eXaminator was based on WCAG 1.0 and was used in Portugal. And updated version, AccessMonitor, was based on WCAG 2.0.

AccessMonitor can evaluate single pages, but its main capacity is to perform large-scale benchmarking of Portugal's public administration sites. The test results are published only among the responsible individuals (site owners) of the evaluated sites; the reports are then incorporated to fill the reports published by Unidade Acesso.

The authors of AccessMonitor published in 2010 the Web Accessibility Frame-Work [20], a demonstration tool that intends to demonstrate how large-scale benchmarking could be applied to improve the accessibility on the web.

In 2012, based on the idea of the Web Accessibility FrameWork, the first two national observatories were created in Argentina [21] and Mexico [22]. Both of those projects were the launching platform for recommendations and improvements to the system later used by the OIA.

Even though there were operational issues on those two attempts that forced the discontinuation of the projects, the experience was valuable and helped to confirm the real usefulness of continuous evaluation that appears after continued work.

A hard lesson learned was that an observatory is an ongoing project that takes its time to shows its benefits. In addition, it requires a large amount of economic and technical resources to be run. The authors expect to take advantage of these previous experiences to avoid the difficulties in reaching the full potential of OIA.

6   Expected Impact and Contributions to the Accessibility Field

There have been several attempts to define metrics that represent the degree of conformance to WCAG ([11], [23,24,25,26,27,28,29]). In addition the latest Working Draft of the Website Accessibility Conformance Evaluation Methodology (WCAG-EM) [30] prompts for the use of a score card on manual revisions.

OIA uses a new metrics similar to the one used by the AccessMonitor [31], but improved to facilitate large scale comparisons and without the intention to provide relationships between the obtained score and the accessibility level compliance.

OIA can contribute to the creation of better instruments to observe and compare accessibility, which is one of the main issues on proposed new European Directive on the accessibility of public sector bodies' websites [32] that could be enforced during 2014.

The Observatory has recently appeared and it is soon to talk about its impact. However, the experiences of the Sidar Foundation and the Portuguese government on accessibility awareness campaigns point to expecting a strong positive impact of OIA.

As an example of the results of the performed tests we have observed that some pages frequently disappear because of URL changes. This is an issue for the user and for the Observatory. Hence, the observatory will contribute to eliminate such a bad practice by informing its members about content negotiation as a way to ensure the localization of resources both to the general public and to the Observatory itself, so that stable analysis can be generated and data comparison can be achieved over the years. The Observatory will also allow addressing other studies, performing analysis of global data, developing joint projects in all countries involved and measuring the impact of these projects.

An especially attractive feature of OIA is that the results are shown in a graphical way, making easy to understand the statistical data. Even more, information is offered about which type of user results positively or negatively affected for any particular result and to what extent. This will end up on a better comprehension of the impact that a particular -easy to solve- failure can have. Our hope then is that this helps to increase awareness and help developers to increase the accessibility of their websites.

7   Conclusions and Future Work

After 15 years of the WCAG 1.0 publication, no global wide data can be obtained regarding accessibility conformance. There only have been some isolated and non-constant reports. The lack of consistent and stable data makes it difficult to assess the validity of the reports about web content compliance, thus reducing their reliability and impact.

An observatory such as OIA is not able to perform a complete measurement of conformance (as manual evaluation is required for that), but it can provide a reasonably good knowledge of the current and future state.

It is still uncertain what the actual contribution of OIA will be in the general improvement of accessibility, mainly because never before this information was available in a standardized and constant form. However it is expected to become a platform that will enable new projects and research that propose specific actions in favor of accessibility.

As per future work on the Observatory, we are currently working on the generation of machine-readable reports, using the EARL format [33], as was already available on the sister tool HERA [34]. We are also working on a system for offering information related to the implementation of good practices when creating mobile applications that overlap general accessibility guidelines.

References

1. W3C. WCAG 1.0 (1999), http://www.w3.org/TR/WCAG10/
2. Legislación sobre Accesibilidad para la Sociedad de la Información. Sidar website (in Spanish), http://www.sidar.org/recur/direc/legis/index.php
3. W3C. WCAG 2.0 (2008), http://www.w3.org/TR/WCAG20/
4. ISO/IEC 40500:2012 Information technology – W3C WCAG 2.0 (2012)
5. Nomensa: United Nations global audit of Web accessibility (2006), http://www.un.org/esa/socdev/enable/documents/fnomensarep.pdf
6. EU Study on Assessing and Promoting E-Accessibility, http://ec.europa.eu/digital-agenda/en/news/study-assessing-and-promoting-e-accessibility
7. Inteco (in Spanish), http://www.inteco.es
8. Observatorio de Accesibilidad (in Spanish), http://administracionelectronica.gob.es/pae_Home/pae_Estrategias/pae_Accesibilidad/pae_observatorio_accesibilidad_eng.html#.UurBwPuwVr0
9. Observatorio de Accesibilidad TIC (in Spanish), http://www.discapnet.es/Castellano/areastematicas/Accesibilidad/Observatorio_infoaccesibilidad/informesInfoaccesibilidad/Paginas/default.aspx
10. Unidade Acesso de la Fundação para a Ciência e a Tecnologia (in Portuguese), http://www.acessibilidade.gov.pt/
11. Bühler, C., Heck, H., Nietzio, A., Olsen, M.G., Snaprud, M.H.: Monitoring Accessibility of Governmental Web Sites in Europe. In: Miesenberger, K., Klaus, J., Zagler, W.L., Karshmer, A.I. (eds.) ICCHP 2008. LNCS, vol. 5105, pp. 410–417. Springer, Heidelberg (2008)
12. The EU Web Accessibility Benchmarking Cluster: http://www.wabcluster.org/
13. eGOVMON project, http://tingtun.no/research-archive
14. European Internet Inclusion Initiative project, http://eiii.eu/
15. SMART 2008-0066 Monitoring eAccessibility in Europe, http://www.eaccessibility-monitoring.eu/
16. MeAC, http://ec.europa.eu/digital-agenda/en/news/assessment-status-eaccessibility-europe
17. CWA 15526 European Network for Administrative Nomenclature (ADNOM). European Committee for Standardization (CEN) (2006)
18. eXaminator, http://examinator.ws/

19. COFOG, http://unstats.un.org/unsd/cr/registry/regcst.asp?Cl=4
20. Web Accessibility Framework, http://walidator.net
21. Observatorio argentino (in Spanish), http://wcag.com.ar
22. Observatorio mexicano (in Spanish), http://ati.org.mx/observatorio
23. Hackett, S., Parmanto, B., Zeng, X.: Accessibility of Internet websites through time. In: Proceedings of 6th International ACM SIGACCESS Conference on Computers and Accessibility, pp. 32–39. ACM, New York (2004)
24. Parmanto, B., Zeng, X.: Metric for Web Accessibility Evaluation. Journal of the American Society for Information Science and Technology 56(13), 1394–1404 (2005)
25. Snaprud, M.H., Ulltveit-Moe, N., Pillai, A.B., Olsen, M.G.: A Proposed Architecture for Large Scale Web Accessibility Assessment. In: Miesenberger, K., Klaus, J., Zagler, W.L., Karshmer, A.I. (eds.) ICCHP 2006. LNCS, vol. 4061, pp. 234–241. Springer, Heidelberg (2006)
26. Sullivan, T., Matson, R.: Barriers to use: usability and content accessibility on the Web's most popular sites. In: Proceedings of ACM Conference on Universal Usability 2000, pp. 139–144. ACM, New York (2000)
27. Vigo, M., Arrue, M., Brajnik, G., Lomuscio, R., Abascal, J.: Quantitative Metrics for Measuring Web Accessibility. In: Proceedings of W4A 2007, pp. 99–107. ACM Press (2007)
28. Mirri, S., Muratori, L., Roccetti, M., Salomoni, P.: Metrics for Accessibility: Experiences with the Vamolà Project. In: Proceedings of W4A 2009, pp. 142–145. ACM Press (2009)
29. Vigo, M., Brajnik, G.: Automatic web accessibility metrics: where we are and where we can go. Interacting with Computers 23(2), 137–155 (2011)
30. W3C: WCAG-EM, http://www.w3.org/TR/WCAG-EM/
31. Fernandes, J., Benavidez, C.: A zero in eChecker equals a 10 in eXaminator: a comparison between two metrics by their scores. In: Proceedings of the Online Symposium Website Accessibility Metrics (2011),
    http://www.w3.org/WAI/RD/2011/metrics/paper8/
32. Proposal for a directive of the European parliament and of the Council on "The Accessibility of Public Sector Bodies' Websites",
    http://ec.europa.eu/information_society/newsroom/
    cf/dae/document.cfm?doc_id=1242
33. W3C: EARL, http://www.w3.org/TR/EARL10-Schema/
34. Benavídez, C., Fuertes, J.L., Gutiérrez, E., Martínez, L.: Semi-automatic evaluation of web accessibility with HERA 2.0. In: Miesenberger, K., Klaus, J., Zagler, W.L., Karshmer, A.I. (eds.) ICCHP 2006. LNCS, vol. 4061, pp. 199–206. Springer, Heidelberg (2006)

Checking Web Accessibility with the Content Accessibility Checker (CAC)

Eduard Klein[1], Anton Bolfing[2], and Markus Riesch[2]

[1] E-Government-Institute, BUAS – Bern University of Applied Sciences, Bern, Switzerland
eduard.klein@bfh.ch
[2] «Access-for-All» Foundation, Zurich, Switzerland
{anton.bolfing,riesch}@access-for-all.ch

Abstract. The internet has become an indispensable tool for the access of information. However, most websites are not sufficiently accessible for people with disabilities. Accessibility problems originate from either the underlying CMS systems or from content authors disregarding fundamental accessibility requirements. With the Content Accessibility Checker CAC we give a tool at hand to specifically red-flag possible accessibility issues to authors. The checking criteria form a subset of the WCAG 2.0 standard and are published as a checklist for authors and publishers. CAC is available as a browser plugin and is published as open source on github. It is based on JavaScript and can be extended with specific checking rules. In checking mode it detects accessibility issues on a website, highlights it with an overlay in the web browser and gives hints and recommendations on improving web accessibility.

Keywords: Web Accessibility, E-Inclusion, Design for All.

1 Introduction

The World Wide Web is an essential tool for people when accessing information, using web applications, shopping on the internet, and participating in communication and social networks. For users with disabilities the user experience is very poor on most websites [1]. Even assistive technologies such as screen readers do not improve the situation because of poor semantic website structure or multimedia content without alternative representation. Conservative estimates suggest that 15-20% of internet users have sensory, motor or cognitive limitations. Taking into account demographic shifts with the first internet user generations entering more advanced ages, the proportion of people with various limitations surfing the internet must be expected to quickly rise in the near future.

As part of the EU funded TAO project (thirdageonline.eu), the German Wikipedia web site was assessed according to the WCAG accessibility guidelines (w3.org). The assessment was performed according to the three levels mentioned in the WAI (Web Accessibility Initiative) recommendations: expert based evaluation, conformity analysis, and user studies with people with disabilities. The resulting study [2] contains recommendations for improvement, which is published as part of a MediaWiki

K. Miesenberger et al. (Eds.): ICCHP 2014, Part I, LNCS 8547, pp. 109–112, 2014.

Accessibility Tracking Group[1] for the developer community, indicating the state of implementation.

The paper is structured as follows: after the problem description, a motivation for tool development is given, presenting requirements and evaluation of existing checking tools. Afterwards we explain the usage of CAC, its architecture and results achieved so far. The conclusion also suggests areas of possible further improvement.

2   Checking Web Accessibility

The Access for all foundation is campaigning for accessible ICT in Switzerland. It has established the most respected national website accessibility certification scheme and conducts expert reviews, WCAG 2.0 conformity tests and user tests with blind and multiply disabled people. From its studies[2], we could deduce that only about one percent of the most important websites to be WCAG2.0 accessible.

Typical accessibility issues are missing keyboard support and clean semantic site structure, where assistive technologies are further reliant on. Moreover, inappropriate contrasting color schemes and unclear heading structures in articles are a problem. Paragraphs and lists ought to be tagged as such; tables must be set up semantically correctly; table dimensions must be stated in the table headers. Alternative text for images must be provided. An extensive list and explanations are given in [3].

3   Comparison with Other Tools

We selected five popular tools (WAVE, Web Accessibility Inspector, Web Thing, Cynthia Says, Accessibility Toolbar) from an extensive set[3] of tools for evaluation against the following functionalities:

- Checking during development: e.g. during editing or in preview mode
- Environment independence: analysis is HTML based (not CMS dependent)
- Category of messages: the tool shows messages on specific page elements, and gives recommendations which are valid for the whole website
- User experience: messages are shown as an overlay for better error localization
- Extendibility: user defined rules can be integrated

It turned out that none of these tools fulfilled all the requirements mentioned above; in particular none of them met the extendibility requirement. This led to the decision to implement the CAC tool.

---

[1] https://www.mediawiki.org/wiki/Groups/Proposals/
Accessibility_Tracking
[2] http://access-for-all.ch/ch/publikationen.html
[3] http://www.w3.org/WAI/ER/tools

4   The CAC Content Accessibility Checker

CAC indicates accessibility issues which are caused by authors, and not by the CMS. The tool is based on the Accessibility Checklist for authors and publishers[4], comprising a subset of WCAG 2.0 criteria, which can be split in three categories:

- automatic test: based on the structure of the web page it can be decided if a criterion fails. Example: check hierarchical properness of heading levels.
- heuristic test: based on experience, the system makes a guess about failing of a criterion. E.g. for a download link (indicated through file suffix analysis), CAC recommends adding file size and format information.
- not testable (by a tool): it cannot be determined, if the description of an image sufficiently explains its contents. In this case, CAC gives a warning.

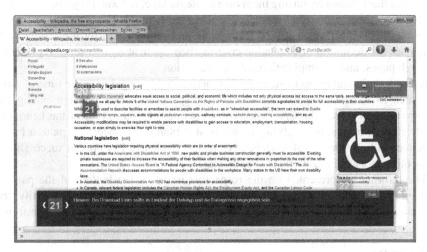

Fig. 1. CAC in action

CAC can be turned on/off as a browser plugin (see blue button in navigation bar in figure 1). If activated, the accessibility issues are presented as clickable overlay icons, at the bottom of the window the respective issues are explained in more detail. From the platform analysis in [3], it turned out that the realization in JavaScript promised the most benefits such as easy integration in web browsers and independence from a CMS. The checking process is solely based on HTML code.

The JavaScript code analyzes the structure of the web page based on its DOM by help of the popular jQuery library. It implements the checking rules, each of which consists of a pattern and an action. When a pattern is matched in a web page, i.e. the respective accessibility issue has occurred, an information item containing the location on the page and the error category is added to an intermediate storage in a

---

[4] http://access-for-all.ch/barrierefreiheit/
barrierefreies-webdesign/checklist-2.html

de-fined format. This storage is realized as a set of DOM nodes which are rendered by the popular pageguide library.

CAC is open source (github.com/Access4all/ContentAccessibilityChecker) for further development. It comes in several distribution versions: as a Firefox plugin or as pure JavaScript code which can be integrated e.g. in a web page or a CMS.

5   Conclusion and Further Activities

CAC is to date the only tool providing accessibility error warnings to authors using accessible CMS. The approach to clearly differentiate between CMS and content regarding accessibility is novel. CAC helps authors identify possible and actual accessibility errors and helps raise awareness of accessibility issues. Moreover, it is helpful to prevent these issues by raising them on a strategic level for web projects.

Ongoing research and development on CAC are twofold. First, the evaluation of the tool with respect to quality of test results and implications on users/authors. It comprises the definition of evaluation criteria, their application to a set of representative web pages, and the implications of the evaluation.

Second, optimization and extension of functionality is ongoing at the time of writing, such as localization, the de-/selection of specific criteria, and optimizing the keyword list by which the CAC analysis is operated. Optimization of the heuristics for detecting possible accessibility issues is also planned. Concerning pattern based issue recognition, the use of a declarative pattern language has proven successful in many other tools and thus will also be integrated.

The information presented on the respective issues at the bottom of the page is planned to contain links with detailed information on the specific issues. Finally, the upcoming version of CAC will be available on the Mozilla Firefox Add-ons platform.

References

1. Kerkmann, F.: Web Accessibility. Informatik-Spektrum 36(5), 455–460 (2013)
2. Ritter, P., Riesch, M., Bolfing, A.: German Language Wikipedia Accessibility Test According to WCAG 2.0. Test Report. (2011),
   http://www.thirdageonline.eu/wp-content/uploads/2012/02/
   Accessibility_Test_Report_Wikipedia.pdf (accessed April 11, 2014)
3. Lehmann, R.: Entwicklung eines Accessibility-Assistenztools für Autoren von Online-Inhalten; Bachelor Thesis; BUAS-Bern University of Applied Sciences (May 2013)

AdaptNow – A Revamped Look for the Web:
An Online Web Enhancement Tool for the Elderly

Roberto Dias and Sergi Bermúdez i Badia

Universidade da Madeira, Madeira-ITI, Funchal, Portugal
roberto.dias@loopbug.com, sergi.bermudez@uma.pt

Abstract. Elderly population will become the largest age group of our society in the next twenty years. Consequently, we need to be able to accommodate technologies to the needs of this population. AdaptNow is a web-based application that allows users to adapt existing webpages and turn them more accessible and user friendly. Users can do so directly from any web browser thanks to AdaptNow's user personalization and automatic adaptation artificial intelligence algorithms. In this paper we present the design and implementation of Adapt-Now, a solution that improves navigation on the web for elderly users.

Keywords: Web Enhancements, Elderly Users, Accessibility, Human Computer Interaction.

1 Introduction

A recent study predicts that elderly population will become the largest age group of our society in the next twenty years [1]. Consequently, we need to be able to accommodate technologies to the needs of this population. Policy makers are already working in accessibility and inclusive design methods in an attempt to provide a barrier free society with initiatives like [2,3]. Universal design aggregates a wide group of ideas that have the objective of producing buildings, products and environments that are built to be usable to the greatest extent possible by everyone, regardless of their age, ability, or status in life [4]. The difficulty in using computer systems by people with impairments is a well know problem. Despite the current efforts in accessibility, computer interfaces are still an accessibility barrier for elderly users. Interfaces are typically designed with the assumptions that 1) they are going to be used by able-bodied individuals; 2) using an typical set of input/output devices and; 3) that users will be in a static environment [5]. Further, elderly users are generally associated with impairment due to the loss of motor and visual capabilities due to the ageing process [6]. Hence, complex and multi-functional systems may present substantial cognitive challenges for elderly. In an attempt to make the usage of technology more comfortable some applications have been developed to aid in the interaction with technology [7]. These are divided in two groups, hardware and software. For the first there are devices such as special computer mice that increase the user's control, and larger screen monitors that ease the reading. As for software, there exist client-side

K. Miesenberger et al. (Eds.): ICCHP 2014, Part I, LNCS 8547, pp. 113–120, 2014.

applications that enhance the font size, colour and font family of the operation system [8]. Unfortunately, many of these approaches have been discontinued either by lack of funds, their complexity, expensive maintenance, or because the target audience is a minority with low resources [9].

One particular case in point is that of web pages. Web 2.0 technologies are quickly gaining popularity due to their power in terms of design, flexibility but also because of their tremendous reach. Unfortunately, there is still a poor adherence to accessibility standards. Consequently, people with disabilities meet barriers of all types while navigating the web that make it hard for them to understand what they should do [10]. These barriers come in form of confused webpages, abundance of misleading ads, unnecessary videos, moving information, etc. Moreover, the abilities of elderly users can fluctuate throughout the day due to several factors (fatigue or medication), or evolve across days or months following longer-terms age related changes [5]. This makes it hard to create general purpose interfaces that can be a best fit to everyone. Hence, the ideal solution needs to be adapted according to the environment and the specific needs of the user.

With all this in mind, the goal of AdaptNow is to provide a web enhancement navigation tool that simplifies and eases web experience. AdaptNow is a web platform that dynamically enhances the original webpages through an artificial intelligence (AI) system trained with elderly user data. By using AdaptNow to enhance navigation and remove all undesired noise around the desired action we want to provide a simple and adaptable solution for web navigation. AdaptNow provides users with a simple way to configure enhancement settings. Further, AdapNow improves its AI by tracking user behaviour and extrapolating settings from similarly designed websites.

2   Methods

AdaptNow is a web based enhancement system for elderly and impaired users. AdaptNow was designed after several field studies and development iterations in an attempt to understand how to improve web experience and minimize the effect of age related conditions and/or the lack of web experience.

2.1   Web Enhancements and Artificial Intelligence (AI) Modelling

To understand what elderly would do to enhance usability of webpages we performed a first experiment with a system that was able to modify several features of web pages, such as 1) highlighting (box/underline) clickable objects with user defined colours; change the mouse pointer 2) size and 3) visual aspect; modify 4) zoom as well as 5) font sizes; and 6) page scrolling mode (Fig. 1). We interviewed and evaluated the prototype with 12 users with ages between 51 and 63 years old to understand how elderly users would adapt the above mentioned features in web pages to improve navigation. For that purpose we tested 10 different web page examples in several domains such as social, news, travel, mail and search engines.

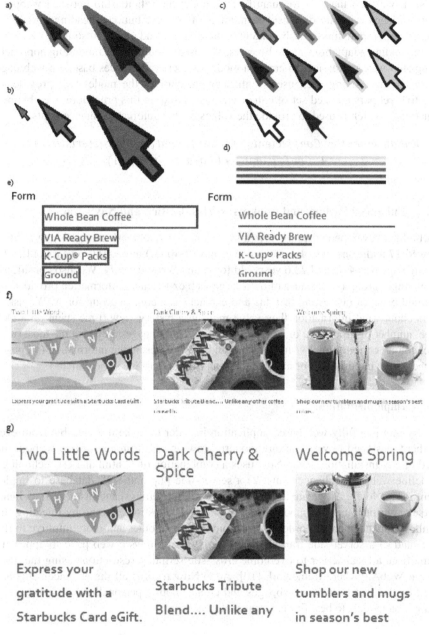

Fig. 1. Some of the features present during the first user experiment. a) Mouse cursor sizes; b) Mouse cursor over links; c) Available cursor colours; d) Link enhancement colours; e) Link enhanced with box/underline; f) Webpage with high zoom and low font size; g) Page with low zoom and high font size.

Next, we used the data to quantify and model the relationship between webpage characteristics (website dimensions; number of images, buttons, heading tags, divisions, scripts, and links; flash content; image sizes; and screen resolution) and the corresponding adaptations made by users. We used a multi linear modelling approach, using step-wise regression, to create a model of users preferences based on web page characteristics. Using each user's enhancement choices the model will provide an adaptive yet personalized set of enhancements. Based on this procedure, we obtained equation 1, which is used to provide the values for the automatic enhancements.

$$Enhancement = Coefficient_0 + Coefficient_1 * Characteristic_1 + ... + Coefficient_n * Characteristic_n \quad (1)$$

2.2   Enhanced History and Bookmark Visualization and Navigation

To build a revamped history view and a dynamic bookmark navigation we interviewed 17 additional people of two age groups (>40 (A) and <40 (B) years old). The average age was 47.8 and 22.6 years old for A and B respectively. We also considered the younger group (B) because of their large web experience. Information provided by B could bring in interesting insights and can acts as a control group for A. We asked users about what information they value more in a history view (time spent on a web page, number of visits, type of content), how to highlight pages they visit the most (icon size, colour, contrast, total visits counter), and how to present the information (all pages at once, showing the order of navigation, grouping pages of the same domain).

2.3   Implementation

The system is a fully web based application in order to make it accessible from everywhere, designed to work on any modern browser and from any device without the need of any installation. AdaptNow uses a combination of 1) html and css technology to define webpage enhancements; 2) a server-side php and SQL database to implement AdaptNow's AI, create user profiles, store user settings, and history; 3) a client-side Javascript/JQuery to modify the original webpages in real-time by injecting the html/css enhancements in order to make navigation smother and more intuitive to the user; and 4) a server-side transformation proxy that allows a web page to appear to come from a local server to overcome cross-site scripting restrictions using the open source WebAnywhere framework [10]. AdaptNow records all the enhancements applied by the user to visited webpages and creates both a personal and global website adaptation models to best fit the learnt preferences.

3   Results

The first experiment allowed us to define the core AI that models each web enhancement (zoom factor, font size, mouse cursor, etc) as a multivariate linear regression of the variables that define the web page characteristics (resolution, page height, number of words, etc). Interestingly, our modelling approach allows us to identify and quantify to what extent web site features do determine the enhancement choices made by elderly (Table 1). From these results we were able to fully model zoom and text enhancements with an average error of 6-7% (Table 2). The border and button enhancements could also be satisfactorily modelled using the multivariate approach. Some of the enhancements could not be satisfactorily modelled with a linear approach due to their underlying bimodal nature.

All statistically significant enhancement models were implemented in AdaptNow to enable the system to learn from the data collected from the user and automatically build adaptation model for each user, making the automatic adaptations system a best fit for each one (Fig. 2).

Table 1. Web page characteristics and their corresponding web enhancement AI model. The used web page characteristics are a) Screen Width, b) Page Height, c) Number of words, d) Biggest image Width, e) Average image width, f) Number of scripts, g) Number of H1 tags, h) Number of H2 tags, i) number of divisions.

Propriety		a)	b)	c)	d)	e)	f)	g)	h)	i)
Zoom (0-100)		0,0001	-	-	-	0,0088	-	0,0005	0,0237	-
Text Size (0-100)		-	0,0001	0,0008	-	-	-	0,0001	-	0,0001
Link Enhance-ment	Box (0-1)	-	-	-	-	-	-	-	-	-
	Underline (0-1)	-	-	-	-	-	-	-	-	-
	Colour	-	-	-	-	-	-	0,0108	-	-
	Border Size (0-100)	-	0,0001	-	-	-	-	-	-	0,0001
Button	Enhanced (0-1)	-	-	-	-	-	-	-	-	-
	Colour	-	-	-	-	-	0,0003	-	-	-
	Border Size	-	-	-	0,0003	-	-	-	-	-

From the second inquiry, the feature that was chosen as the most important for automatically adding a bookmark to a webpage was the number of visits. Group B, the more experienced group, classified the amount of time spent on a page also as very important. Therefore, both time spent on the webpage and number of visits is used for dynamically adding a page to the "most visited" section. To avoid a history of visited pages that current web browsers use containing long lists of redundant information that are very difficult to search we asked users about how they would prefer information to be presented. Interestingly, users preferred grouping all pages of the same domain, what is the opposite of what current browsers do. Users also reported the importance of showing the navigation order of the visited pages. Finally, we presented users with three models of possible history views and asked them about what they would do in order to identify the most visited ones. The most consensual answer was showing the number of visits to each website, following the icon size and the contrast of the displayed icon (Fig. 3).

Table 2. Web page characteristics and their corresponding model significance and error. * p<0.05, ** p<0.01, and *** p<0.001.

Propriety		P-VAL	Model significance.	Mean Error
Zoom (0-100)		2,61E-10	***	5,5739%
Text Size (0-100)		3,06E-18	***	6,6132%
Link Enhancement	Box (0-1)	0,4264	-	42,07%
	Underline (0-1)	0,4264	-	42,07%
	Colour	0,1851	-	70,08%
	Border Size (0-100)	0,0034	**	7,8799%
Button	Enhanced (0-1)	3,60E-173	***	0,23%
	Colour	0,0356	*	58,33%
	Border Size (0-100)	1,38E-09	***	5,5729%

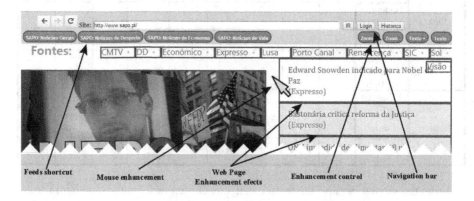

Fig. 2. AdaptNow interface visualization of an enhanced webpage

After 2 field studies, we implemented the beta version of AdaptNow. AdaptNow is currently composed of 3 main visual components: navigation, adaptation, and webpage. The first component presents the user with: 1) an address bar to choose where to navigate, and a back, forward and refresh buttons; 2) A login button/functionality is also available where the user can access and modify his/her settings and default information; and 3) a button to the history view. The second component shows the complete list of feeds (RSS) that a specific website is broadcasting to visualize the feeds in AdaptNow's own web enhanced RSS reader. In addition, direct buttons to web page enhancement options such as zoom and text alterations can be used at any time. The third and most important component is a large frame containing the enhanced web pages and where all the adaptations take place (both web page and mouse cursor and scrolling enhancements) (Fig. 2). With this design we want to achieve a layout similar to a regular web browser window in an attempt to reduce the amount of changes from what is expected by users.

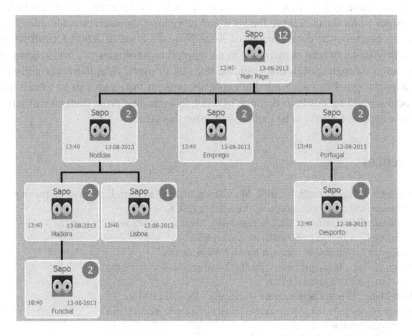

Fig. 3. AdaptNow visualization of the history visits of a webpage

4   Conclusion

We believe that AdaptNow provides useful insights as how simple alterations on regular web pages can make the web more accessible to elderly. Further, the AdaptNow tool is web based, making it worldwide accessible though all computer platforms that support a modern web browser. AdaptNow is developed after 2 field studies that informed us on how enhancements are used depending on the characteristics of each web page, and how we can improve history visualization and bookmark navigation with contextual information. An interesting feature of the system is that the more we use the system the more data we collect, consequently making our AI more accurate and personalized to each user to deliver more accurate enhancement.

A similar web enhancement was done by [11] where they proposed an adaptation of the a particular web page by decomposing it in its different divisions and reordering them to create a new navigation experience. Our approach differs from previews because AdaptNow is completely web-based and does not require any installation and the user profile and data is available everywhere. Another aspect that differs is our automatic enhancement system that changes the web page based on the learnt preferences and web page characteristic. Something similar can be achieved in more generic terms for a larger group of webpages if the new tag system from HTML5 is used. With this in mind we think that a deeper study of HTML5 and CSS3 functionalities is necessary to determine what can be achieved once most web pages start using these standards. These types of enhancements work well in responsive webpages because these pages adapt the content to the view and reorganize themselves automatically.

As we continue the development of AdaptNow we hope to achieve a full integration with WebAnywhere allowing us to use speech technologies to provide additional information through speech that could be relevant to users. AdaptNow currently does not support pages like Facebook that explicitly prevent their pages to be rebuilt locally. Local rebuilding needs to be done in order to overcome cross domain restrictions, so a new approach needs to be explored to solve this issue.

References

1. Emiliani, P.L., Burzagli, L., Billi, M., Gabbanini, F., Palchetti, E.: Report on the impact of technological developments on eAccessibility (2008)
2. European Commission, "Web Accessibility," http://ec.europa.eu/digital-agenda/en/web-accessibility
3. European Commission, "Design for all for eInclusion," http://ec.europa.eu/digital-agenda/en/content/design-all-einclusion
4. Ron Mace, "North CarolinaState University - Ronald L. Mace," http://www.ncsu.edu/ncsu/design/cud/about_us/usronmacespeech.htm
5. Gajos, K.Z., Weld, D.S., Wobbrock, J.O.: Automatically generating personalized user interfaces with Supple. Artif. Intell. 174(12-13), 910–950 (2010)
6. Gregor, P., Newell, A.F., Zajicek, M.: Designing for dynamic diversity: interfaces for older people. In: Proc. of the Fifth International ACM Conference on Assistive Technologies, pp. 151–156 (2002)
7. Impairments, M.: Working Together: People with Disabilities and Computer Technology Providing access to technology, DO-IT (2012)
8. Hanson, V.L.: Web access for elderly citizens. In: Proc. 2001 EC/NSF Work. Univers. Access. Ubiquitous Comput. Provid. Elder, WUAUC 2001, p. 14 (2001)
9. Gajos, K.Z., Weld, D.S., Wobbrock, J.O.: Decision-Theoretic User Interface Generation, interactions (2008)
10. Arch, A.: (W3C): Web Accessibility for Older Users: A Literature Review (2008), http://www.w3.org/TR/wai-age-literature
11. Chen, J., Zhou, B., Shi, J., Zhang, H., Fengwu, Q.: Function-based object model towards website adaptation. World Wide Web (49), 587–596 (2001)

Accessibility of E-Commerce Websites
for Vision-Impaired Persons

Roopa Bose and Helmut Jürgensen

Department of Computer Science,
The University of Western Ontario, London, Ontario, Canada

Abstract. We report the results of a detailed analysis of the problems encountered by blind or vision-impaired persons when accessing web sites which use technologies like, for example, flash animation, JavaScript, HTML 5. We also examine typical accessibility problems found in e-commerce websites, especially in on-line shopping. We check our findings against the WCAG 2.0 accessibility guidelines and provide detailed recommendations for changes or additions to these guidelines.

Keywords: Web Accessibility, WCAG, Screen Readers, E-Commerce Website Accessibility.

1 The Issue

For persons with vision disabilities, computers and the internet can offer easy access to information and to activities like communication, learning, banking, shopping and so on; on the other hand, many features offered in computer interfaces and on web pages turn into hardly surmountable obstacles. In this paper we analyse, in detail, the sources of access problems. We focus on websites, mainly those for e-commerce. We compare our findings with the *Web Content Accessibility Guidelines* (WCAG 2.0) [18] and recommend concrete changes or additions to these. The modifications, if implemented and adhered to, would make such pages significantly easier to use. While our work concerns web access for vision-impaired persons in general, our main focus is on problems encountered by blind persons. In the sequel, when we mention only the latter group, we imply that many of the findings would also apply to the larger group when properly adjusted.

Our present paper is based on the thesis [2] by the first author. In that thesis additional details of the analysis and many examples of unusable or hard to use websites are provided.

A detailed survey of methods and devices used for presenting information to vision-impaired persons as of 2010 is given in [11]. For dynamic access to information like browsing the web, the list of suitable techniques reduces to: refreshable tactile media like Braille displays, screen readers or special web browsers – and, for input, keyboard or voice.

Screen readers are the popular choice among the three output media [19]. Among these, some of the options are: JAWS, NVDA (Non Visual Desktop Access), Window Eyes, VoiceOver, SpeakUp and Thunder – to be installed locally

K. Miesenberger et al. (Eds.): ICCHP 2014, Part I, LNCS 8547, pp. 121–128, 2014.

– or web-based WebAnywhere [1]. When web pages are accessed, screen readers have severe limitations as illustrated by the WebAIM screen reader simulation[1]. Navigation, reading out the content exactly according to the page layout, conveying image and graphic contents, accessing dynamic content or special text like formulæ, reading tables, providing a page overview – these are some of the challenges. Some screen readers can handle dynamic content to some extent; some cannot. A major reason for such limitations is that syntactic and semantic information is lost when content is linearised for a screen reader [15],[23].

Many blind people use Braille displays along with screen readers. There are also planar tactile displays like the BrailleDis 9000 and its predecessor, the DMD 120060, which can display text, tables, graphics and diagrams by raising, lowering or vibrating the pins in a 60×120 matrix; finger position feedback is available on these devices (see [14],[17]). Tactile web browsing is discussed in [13], for instance. A rendering technique for tables on such a device is proposed in [3]. Many further related studies have been or are being conducted.

Special web browsers and browser extensions exist, which provide access to web pages for vision-impaired persons. Some of them convert the web content into a format which is better suitable for a screen reader, while other ones have special built-in screen readers with an improved interpretation of the HTML objects. Some such web browsers offer improved navigation or support formulæ. Examples include WebbIE [5], MozBraille [10] and ChromeVox [12].

WebbIE distinguishes the main content and the navigation links. The user interface present the web pages as plain text using Internet Explorer control objects. Each component in the HTML Document Object Model structure is presented with an appropriate title.

ChromeVox conveys the page overview as a hierarchy of groups, objects, sentences, words and characters [12]. The user can navigate within this hierarchy.

A web browser, based on Mozilla Firefox, for a planar tactile display is described in [13]. It can handle small tables, certain static graphical contents and mathematical formulæ written in MathML.

WAB (World-wide-web Access for Blind and visually impaired computer users) [4] deals with page overview and navigation problems. WAB implements a proxy server which acts between the web browser and the web server. It modifies the web document by adding a list of titles and links to facilitate navigation. There is no mechanism to deal with dynamic or graphic web content.

A web browser described in [9] is reported to provide features which make multimedia contents accessible to screen readers.

Modern web pages use many new techniques to present the information in a more flashy way than before, presumably with the intent to gain the readers' attention, for instance graphics, images, videos, animations. Often accessibility is not or only superficially considered when such pages are designed. A study of popular websites showed that around 82% of those considered were partly or

---

[1] The simulation, to be found at http://webaim.org/simulations/, shows typical cognitive issues; admittedly, it is old and, hence, not representative of the current state of screen reader technology.

completely inaccessible [16]. According to a survey of 2012, almost 65% of the participants stated that websites have become less accessible or that not much improvement has been noticed [21]. Another survey had Flash-based websites and shopping websites at the top of the list of websites to be avoided [20]. Many studies point out that non-standard page layout, embedded graphical elements and dynamic HTML, especially JavaScript and Flash animation, make web content inaccessible [5],[11],[13]. Our paper presents the results of a detailed study of web accessibility problems and leads to recommendations for improved web design.

Accessibility guidelines exist. The WCAG are developed as a part of the Web Accessibility Initiative (WAI) by the World Wide Web Consortium (W3C). WCAG 1.0 was finalized in 1999. These earlier guidelines have been superseded by WCAG 2.0. There are four basic principles: perceivability, operability, understandability and robustness. An overview is given in [22], and the details are found in [18]. Below we recommend modifications and additions to these guidelines to address issues found in our study.

To arrive at this report, we proceeded as follows: After consultation with a highly experienced blind person, the former head of the accessibility centre of Western University, popular websites were analysed from the perspective of a screen reader user to identify the accessibility problems. Experiments were conducted using the screen readers NVDA and WebAnywhere (and, occasionally, also JAWS). With a combination of screen readers and computer monitors the various accessibility problems were identified and grouped according to the four categories listed above. This allowed us to identify even the logical problems behind the accessibility issues.

2   Problem Identifications and Recommendations

We list accessibility problems on websites in general according to the four categories and our respective recommendations regarding WCAG 2.0. Following that, we list accessibility problems specific to e-commerce websites and recommendations for these cases.

2.1   Inaccessible Dynamic Content

Problems. 1. Graphic links and buttons do not have alternate text. 2. Some graphic buttons cannot be invoked using the enter key. 3. The actions of some buttons are different on mouse hover and enter key. 4. Information about the landing page, not even its title, is conveyed before the animation starts. 5. Screen reader audio is masked by the audio on the page. 6. Lack of control over animation including when it starts. 7. The screen reader user is not aware of the presence of animation. 8. No indication about flashing content and periodic updates. 9. It is difficult to manoeuvre dynamic contents like slide shows.

Recommendations. Problems 1,2,3 and 5 can be solved to a great extent by following the relevant guidelines. However, conformance to the highest level (AAA) may not suffice for a basic level of accessibility in case of dynamic contents. Guideline 1.1.1 on non-text content: A recommendation should be added that page descriptions provide an overview of dynamic content for pages having animations. A recommendation to implement slide shows by grouping images and hyperlinks together and providing descriptions of both in the alternate text should be added. Guideline 2.4.4 on link purpose should include: A recommendation on implementing graphic links by providing details of hyperlinks and their associated images in the alternate text and by conveying the purpose and context of interactive buttons through alternate text.

Guideline 2.1.1 on accessing functionalities through the keyboard can be improved: a list of keys and their purposes along with audio descriptions should be given when mouse events are replaced by keystrokes. Implementing auto-updating content using lists and providing an indication that the content will be auto-updated will offer better accessibility of such contents. A suggestion to add appropriate audio descriptions to informative animations played in the background has to be attached to guideline 1.2.1. Guideline 3.2.1 should be modified to include audio alert to inform about page content change. Problems 5 and 6 can be solved by ensuring that audio and animation both can be controlled using the buttons provided for interaction and by following guideline 2.1.1.

2.2   Confusing Page Layout

Problems. 1. Tables are used for storing layout information. 2. Main content is not recognizable. 3. Tabular data structure presented without using HTML tables. 4. Frames used to store values of hyperlinks for JavaScript functions and using frames dynamically by JavaScript. 5. Use of HTML elements like hyperlinks as column values in tables. 6. Title and labels missing for HTML elements like tables, forms, frames. 7. No alternative text for graphs and charts.

Recommendations. Problems 2 and 6 can be solved by adhering to the relevant guidelines. Guideline 1.1.1 on non-text content should provide a clear definition of non-text content. Frames used to store JavaScript functions can be tagged to be ignored by assistive technology if such frames are identified as decorative content as per this guideline. This guideline should also include a precise specification that charts and graphs must be presented as one entity without any text or numbers floating outside. The content required in the alternative text should be specified. Guideline 1.3.1 on information and relationship should include: The restriction to using HTML tables only for tabular data; that table should not be used to store layout information; that HTML elements like hyperlinks should not be used as column values in a table; that there not be unnecessary blank lines inside a table. A recommendation enforcing a summary attribute giving an overview of tables with more than 2 dimensions should be added to Guideline 1.3.1. The conformance level of Guideline 2.4.6 for descriptive title and label should be raised to A. Section headings specified by Guideline

2.4.10 and skip functionality by Guideline 2.4.1 should be made mandatory for pages having vertical scroll and a listing of h1, h2 headings should be enforced to ensure easy access to the main contents.

2.3 Complicated Navigation

Problems. 1. Navigation menus require mouse specific events. 2. Main menu and corresponding submenu conveyed as two separate lists. 3. Submenu space contains text and even images rather than essential hyperlinks. 4. Unable to identify a particular table during navigation. 5. Only limited navigation possible in a table. 6. Unable to identify particular frames or overview of their contents during navigation. 7. Numerous headings in web page. 8. Hyperlinks do not convey their purpose. 9. User is not aware of which web page he has landed on during navigation.

Recommendations. Problems 1 and 4 can be solved by making menus keyboard accessible by adhering to Guideline 2.1.1 and by providing descriptive title labels based on Guideline 2.4.6. A new section solely for navigation menus should be added to WCAG. Recommendations to implement navigation menus using ordered and unordered lists, providing short secondary menus of navigation menus containing numerous items, restricting the content of navigation menus only to hyperlinks, preserving the relationship between a main menu and its submenus in all pages in a website and indicating start and end of navigation menus to differentiate hyperlinks associated with navigation menus should be included in this new section. Guideline 1.1.1 (non-text content) should include a recommendation to provide titles for frames and iframes when necessary and to ignore iframes which are used for alignment purposes. Guideline 2.4.6 regarding headings and labels should be modified to accommodate the restriction that headings can be shown as hyperlinks as well only under necessary conditions and also only h1, h2, h3 tags should be used to show the main headings and section headers in a web page. Guideline 2.4.10 dealing with section headings should include the suggestion to present section headers with h2 or h3 headings and that all the headings under the section should take a heading level below h3. The conformance level of Guideline 2.4.9 on link purpose should bee raised to A from AAA. The recommendations for Guideline 1.3.1 in Section 2.2 above are also necessary to reduce navigation difficulties.

2.4 Difficulty to Get Page Overview

Problems. 1. To recognize the category of a web page one needs to read numerous headings or hyperlinks. 2. The presence of different types of content becomes known only after encountering them. 3. To get at least some kind of information about the overview of a page, one has to go through numerous headings or hyperlinks. 4. It is difficult to assess the amount of information in a page. 5. It is difficult to identify the presence of structures like a navigation menu.

Recommendations. Web pages should be designed according to W3C standards to gain at least a basic level of page overview information. Problem 3 can be solved by adhering to the modifications proposed for Guidelines 2.4.6 and 2.4.10 as discussed in Section 2.3 above. A recommendation to add tags to indicate a navigation menu as discussed in Section 2.3 above is also relevant to solve the problems in this category. Guideline 2.4.2 regarding page titles should be modified to provide overview information as a textual or audio description concerning the page organisation, type of contents etc.

2.5 E-Commerce Websites

As discussed earlier, E-commerce websites, especially on-line shopping websites, are far less accessible than others. It is interesting to know that in the study of 50 popular websites only one on-line shopping website was found to be highly accessible [16].

Problems with the Navigation Menu. 1. Complex navigation menu with numerous items in the main menu and submenu. 2. Navigation menu inaccessible using keyboard.

Recommendations. By following Guideline 2.4.1 regarding bypassing blocks and implementing menus using HTML lists as mentioned in Section 2.3 above, Problem 2 can be solved. To avoid the complication with numerous items in the navigation menu, a recommendation to add textual or audio descriptions to the main menu items explaining the list of items and products under its submenu should be included in the new guideline section for navigation.

Problems with Information Searches. 1. To check complete list of items in the search result one has to traverse through different pages. 2. No shortcuts available to access detailed information on the product. 3. The search result set is large. 4. Many hyperlinks and contents are read out before reading out the search result.

Recommendations. No proper guidelines were found in WCAG 2.0 which will provide an efficient solution for search complexity. We recommend adding a new section to WCAG 2.0 to deal with search complexities addressing the following points:

The search option should appear right after the page title with the 'skip to' functionality implemented following Guideline 2.4.1 which deals with bypass blocks to access search results readily. Advanced sort and filter options should be provided and easily accessible. To avoid traversing through different pages, our suggestion is to display the entire result set in one page and remove images if necessary.

Problems with Images and Graphics. 1. Images and graphics do not have alternate text. 2. Graphic links cannot be accessed using the keyboard. 3. Slide shows are difficult to manoeuvre. 4. Buttons or links in slide shows do not have informative alternate text. 5. The whole text displayed on the image is not conveyed through its alternate text.

Recommendations. Not much discussion is required on the solutions for the above mentioned problems since they are already discussed in the Sections 2.1 and 2.2. By following Guidelines 1.1.1, 2.1.1 and our recommendations to these guidelines, Problems 1–4 can be solved. Adding a new recommendation which enforces the textual content on the image to be present in the alternate text as well to Guideline 1.1.1 deals with Problem 5.

3 Solutions?

One cannot expect that guidelines like WCAG 2.0 with our recommendations included will change web page design unless there is some pressure, commercial or political, according to which the guidelines could not be circumvented. Nevertheless the guidelines can serve a purpose in the presence of formal validation methods. Clearly, lazy or careless designers can easily evade such evaluations. But, optimistically, a badly designed web page will have few customers.

On another note, design of web pages for visually impaired persons may profit from the necessity to put large amounts of information onto the very small screens of mobile devices. The problems are not quite the same, but sufficiently related.

Guidelines cannot change anything unless they are adhered to, not just in words, but in the spirit. Much education will be required to make web designers aware of the issues – not just to follow the guidelines, but also to anticipate potential accessibility problems even before guidelines for them have been drawn up.

Currently we are looking at more sophisticated solutions to the kind of problems presented here. We are still uncertain what a good approach would be.

Acknowledgements. This work was supported by a grant of the Natural Sciences and Engineering Research Council of Canada.

References

1. Bigham, J.P., Prince, C.M.: Webanywhere: A Screen Reader On-the-go. In: Pontelli, E., Trewin, S. (eds.) ASSETS 2007, pp. 225–226. ACM Press, New York (2007)
2. Bose, R.: Accessibility of e-commerce websites for vision-impaired persons. MSc Thesis, Western University, London, Ontario, Canada (2014)
3. Chiousemoglou, M., Jürgensen, H.: Setting the table for the blind. In: PETRA 2011, 8 p. ACM Press, New York (2011), Published on CD
4. Kennel, A., Perrochon, L., Darvishi, A.: WAB: World Wide Web access for blind and visually impaired computer users. SIGCAPH Newsletter 55, 10–15 (1996)

128   R. Bose and H. Jürgensen

5. King, A., Evans, G., Blenkhorn, P.: Webbie: A browser for visually impaired people. In: Proc. 2nd Cambridge Workshop on Universal Access and Assistive Technology, pp. 35–44 (2004)
6. Lazar, J., Allen, A., Kleinman, J., Malarkey, C.: What frustrates screen reader users on the web: A study of 100 blind users. Int. J. Human-Computer Interaction 22(3), 247–269 (2007)
7. Leporini, B., Paternò, F.: Increasing usability when interacting through screen readers. Univ. Access Inf. Soc. 3(1), 57–70 (2004)
8. Leuthold, S., Bargas-Avila, J.A., Opwis, K.: Beyond web content accessibility guidelines: Design of enhanced text user interfaces for blind internet users. Int. J. Human-Computer Studies 66(4), 257–270 (2008)
9. Miyashita, H., Sato, D., Takagi, H., Asakawa, C.: Making Multimedia Content Accessible for Screen Reader Users. In: Harper, S., Yesilada, Y. (eds.) Internat. Cross-Disciplinary Conference on Web Accessibility, W4A 2007, pp. 126–127. ACM Press, New York (2007)
10. MozBraille (July 2013), http://mozbraille.mozdev.org/index.html
11. Power, C., Jürgensen, H.: Accessible presentation of information for people with visual disabilities. Univ. Access Inf. Soc. 9(2), 97–119 (2010)
12. Raman, T.V., Chen, C.L., Mazzoni, D., Shearer, R., Gharpure, C., DeBoer, J., Tseng, D.: ChromeVox: A Screen Reader Built Using Web Technology. Google Inc. (2012)
13. Rotard, M., Taras, C., Ertl, T.: Tactile web browsing for blind people. Multimed. Tools Appl. 37(1), 53–69 (2008)
14. Schiewe, M., Köhlmann, W., Nadig, O., Weber, G.: What you feel is what you get: Mapping GUIs on planar tactile displays. In: Stephanidis, C. (ed.) UAHCI 2009, Part II. LNCS, vol. 5615, pp. 564–573. Springer, Heidelberg (2009)
15. Spiliotopoulos, D., Xydas, G., Kouroupetroglou, G., Argyropoulos, V.: Experimentation on Spoken Format of Tables in Auditory User Interfaces. In: Smith, M.J., et al. (eds.) 11th HCI International, pp. 22–27. Lawrence Erlbaum Associates, Mahwah (2005)
16. Sullivan, T., Matson, R.: Barriers to Use: Usability and Content Accessibility on the Web's Most Popular Sites. In: Thomas, J. (ed.) ACM Conference on Universal Usability, pp. 139–144. ACM Press, New York (2000)
17. Völkel, T., Weber, G., Baumann, U.: Tactile graphics revised: The novel BrailleDis 9000 pin-matrix device with multitouch input. In: Miesenberger, K., Klaus, J., Zagler, W.L., Karshmer, A.I. (eds.) ICCHP 2008. LNCS, vol. 5105, pp. 835–842. Springer, Heidelberg (2008)
18. W3C: Web Content Accessibility Guidelines (WCAG) Overview (October 2012), http://www.w3.org/WAI/intro/wcag.php
19. WebAIM: Visual Disabilities, Blindness. Web Accessibilit. In: Mind (August 2013), http://webaim.org/articles/visual/blind
20. WebAIM: Survey of Preferences of Screen Readers Users. Web Accessibility in Mind (January 2009), http://webaim.org/projects/screenreadersurvey/
21. WebAIM: Screen Reader User Survey 4 Results. WebAIM: Web Accessibility in Mind (May 2012), http://webaim.org/projects/screenreadersurvey4
22. WebAIM: Web Content Accessibility Guidelines. Web Accessibility in Mind (August 2013), http://webaim.org/standards/wcag
23. Yesilada, Y., Stevens, R., Goble, C., Hussein, S.: Rendering Tables in Audio: The Interaction of Structure and Reading Styles. In: Jacko, J.A., Sears, A. (eds.) Proc. ASSETS 2004, pp. 16–23. ACM Press, New York (2004)

jCAPTCHA: Accessible Human Validation

Matthew Davidson[1], Karen Renaud[2], and Shujun Li[3]

[1] BT, London, UK
matthew.davidson@bt.com
[2] School of Computing Science, University of Glasgow, UK
karen.renaud@glasgow.ac.uk
[3] Department of Computing, University of Surrey, UK
shujun.li@surrey.ac.uk

Abstract. CAPTCHAs are a widely deployed mechanism for ensuring that a web site user is a human, and not a software agent. They ought to be relatively easy for a human to solve, but hard for software to interpret. Most CAPTCHAs are visual, and this marginalises users with visual impairments. A variety of audible CAPTCHAs have been trialled but these have not been very successful, largely because they are easily interpreted by automated tools and, at the same time, tend to be too challenging for the very humans they are supposed to verify. In this paper an alternative audio CAPTCHA, jCAPTCHA (Jumbled Words CAPT-CHA), is presented. We report on the evaluation of jCAPTCHA by 272 human users, of whom 169 used screen readers, both in terms of usability and resistance to software interpretation.

1 Introduction

One of the blights on the web is the pervasiveness of automated software agents that masquerade as humans to attack websites [8]. To counteract this, the **C**ompletely **A**utomated **P**ublic **T**uring tests are used to tell **C**omputers and **H**umans **A**part (CAPTCHA) [16]. These are interactive tests that human users can pass but which are difficult for software attackers to solve. We will refer to this metric as the **E**asy **4 H**umans, **H**ard **4 S**oftware (E4H-H4S) test.

Generally CAPTCHAs are visual and consist of distorted text that users are required to decipher. Sometimes the shape and positioning of letters are changed (Figure 1) or background noise is added [12]. Such CAPTCHAs are often difficult to read or easy to break using specially designed crackers, failing the E4H-H4S test [4],[11].

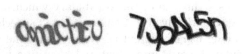

Fig. 1. Example of letter shape distortion CAPTCHAS (Google & Yahoo)

K. Miesenberger et al. (Eds.): ICCHP 2014, Part I, LNCS 8547, pp. 129–136, 2014.

Offering only visual CAPTCHAs ignores a sizeable portion of the online community. Hence audio CAPTCHAs have been introduced: users transcribe the characters that they hear, instead of those they see. Many have, thus far, failed the E4H-H4S test [13,10].

The World Wide Web Consortium lists CAPTCHAs as one of the greatest security-related problems for users who "have low vision, or have a learning disability such as dyslexia" [2] and accommodating these users is a legal requirement in the UK [1]. Accordingly, we have developed a novel audio CAPTCHA that our user study shows is usable and accessible.

The rest of the paper is structured as follows. Section 2 reviews the current state of play with respect to audio CAPTCHAs. Section 3 then presents the jCAPTCHA solution, and explains how it was evaluated. Section 4 reflects on the results and Section 5 concludes.

2   Background

Suggested success rates for human users of CAPTCHAs should be around 90% and 0.01% for automated systems [5]. Achieving this is non-trivial. Bigham *et al.* [3] found that an audio CAPTCHA used to secure a high school course website was impenetrable by any of his 15 blind students. A 2008 study into the usability of the 8 digit audio CAPTCHA reported only a 46% pass rate. Based on a review of the literature, three particular design aspects are pertinent: *content, timing* and *accessibility.*

2.1   Content

Most audio CAPTCHAs require a user to hear, recognise and transcribe what they hear. As a first step, CAPTCHAs have to make sure that the articulated words are relatively common and easy to spell, then that the accent is easily understandable. In reality, most audio CAPTCHAs exclusively use digits to avoid spelling errors.

Similarly to visual CAPTCHAs, audio CAPTCHAs have to resist automated attacks. Often the digits are distorted, or background noise added, to resist automated recognition efforts. A popular resistance method is to add formatted human speech, perhaps played backwards or at a different volume to the characters of the actual CAPTCHA. This is supposed to make it harder for automated attacks to segment the digits. Unfortunately attackers have quickly found a way to strip this from the CAPTCHAs [6]. Moreover, composing audio CAPTCHA clips of digits, a very limited vocabulary, weakens the CAPTCHA unacceptably [15].

Using words increases the size of the vocabulary which makes CAPTCHAs harder to decipher automatically [15]. Language-based speech recognition tools have adapted by making use of contextual clues to ease the attacking process. They examine articulated words in context and identify a word by using both the audio characteristics of the word itself and the probability of such a word occurring, given the surrounding words. Contextual clues within phrases ease recognition for humans too [14].

Using words unfortunately re-introduces the spelling issue. One way of addressing this is to relax the exactness requirement. Non-exact matching will assist humans but not necessarily improve the success rates of automated attacking systems [15] so this is a technique that would be worth considering to improve E4H.

2.2 Timing

The duration of audio CAPTCHA clips usually ranges from 3 to 25.1 seconds. Solving may well require multiple replays of the clip. The previously reported solve time is 65.64s [10]. Using radio clips to form the audio CAPTCHA could reduce the solve time to only 35.75s . Using words instead of nonsense characters also decreases the solve time since the context assists recognition [10],[14].

2.3 Accessibility

CAPTCHAs require the user to enter an answer in a text box. Screen reader users are disadvantaged as they do not have access to their problem source whilst entering their answer, ergo, the answer must be entered from memory. Screen reader users have likened this to having visual CAPTCHAs with the problem image and answer text box on different webpages. Playing the audio clip also usually requires leaving the text entry field. The screen reader will normally narrate the page contents as the user navigates to the playback controls, and can then can talk over the audio CAPTCHA, inadvertently confusing the user.

3   jCAPTCHA Evaluation

In proposing a new kind of CAPTCHA we have attempted to address content and timing by using words derived from public media (to improve usability), and to design specifically to accommodate screen readers.

jCAPTCHA is an audio CAPTCHA that uses words as content *out of context*. As such, they rely on grammatical noise to fool language model-based speech recognition tools. The presence of grammatical noise avoids the need for further noise to be added to the audio clip. Therefore the answer can be 'hidden in plain sight' allowing humans to have a pleasant and straightforward experience in solving the jCAPTCHA but rendering current automated speech recognition tools unreliable.

The jCAPTCHAs were generated by manually concatenating audio clips from publicly available media to construct unusual phrases. The text used for the jCAPTCHAs can be viewed in Table 1.

Table 1. jCAPTCHA ID with the expected answer text

ID	jCAPTCHA text	ID	jCAPTCHA text
1	very impressive helping hand	2	in britain vanilla look like
3	move on completely silent	4	into the water slightly forward
5	silent industry lift days	6	lift dinner push beauty
7	prize electric car ages	8	push food list guests
9	prize days screw push	10	bone fitness age glorious

An evaluation webpage that allowed users to solve the ten jCAPTCHAs was implemented. High contrast colours were used and extraneous html elements removed to improve screen reader navigation and control. Bespoke user controls were offered to visually impaired users allowing them to transcribe jCAPTCHAs without needing to switch back and forth between media controls and the text entry field. Screen reader users use the 'full stop' key to play the audio file while the text field is active, and use the standard alphanumeric keys to enter their answer during or while the audio is playing.

The evaluation follows a design very similar to other studies assessing the usability of CAPTCHAs [7],[10],[13]. To accommodate human error or spelling mistakes, a Levenshtein distance [7] of two was allowed when judging the correctness of an answer. For the purpose of this experiment a distance of one was allowed for each word, with a possibility of one word being completely incorrect, whilst the answer as a whole still being judged as correct. Therefore in the answer to a 5-word jCAPTCHA 4 of the words must have at most a Levenshtein edit distance of one. The edit distance was chosen to allow for differences in pluralisation of words and typos, without accepting majorly different phrases. By evaluating, we wanted to answer the following questions:

- What is the success rate of jCAPTCHAs (i.e. can users comprehend them?)
- Is the experience more enjoyable for users compared to other audio CAPT-CHAs?
- How long does it take to solve?
- Do the embedded controls ease the process?

The evaluation involved the following steps:

1. Demographic Questionnaire, to collect name, email address, age range, visual impairments, use of screen reader, IT expertise, hearing problems, other disabilities and spoken languages.
2. An initial training was given to allow participants to familiarise themselves with use of the site and solving jCAPTCHA.
3. Ten jCAPTCHAs were presented, one at a time. The users listened to an audio clip and attempted to type the words that they heard. Participants were then given the expected answer along with their own answer, as well as an indication of whether their answer was deemed close enough to the expected answer to have been accepted.
4. An exit questionnaire to gather satisfaction ratings and to collect additional comments.

After obtaining ethical approval, participants were recruited using social media and advertisements within the visually impaired community (talking newspapers and blind institutions). Respondents used the website with their traditional web-browsing set up, with or without screen readers.

3.1   Evaluating E4H (Easy 4 Humans)

272 individuals (173 Male, 96 Female, 3 Undisclosed) participated (138 aged between 18 and 30, 72 between 31 and 50 and 55 were 51 or over; 7 participants chose to not disclose their age range). 169 participants used a screen reader whereas 103 did not.

A number of user behaviours were monitored on the answer pages of the experiment. Time taken to submit an answer to each jCAPTCHA [1], key presses on input box and number of plays of jCAPTCHA audio were recorded. These measurements can be used to determine the process the user went through when typing their answer (multiple changes to words, misspellings, multiple plays, etc.).

Figure 2 shows the time taken to submit an answer for each jCAPTCHA with and without a screen reader. The mean time was 27.12 seconds. This measurement includes the time taken to load the page, listen to the audio at least once and to submit an answer. The graph also shows the success rate for users with and without a screen reader.

89 of the 103 non-screen reader users found jCAPTCHA easy to use. One non-screen reader user reported that they *were frustrating to use, would rather use normal way of doing it*. Luckily this was the only participant to express a purely negative opinion on the jCAPTCHA system.

139 of 169 screen reader users felt that jCAPTCHA was easy to use. Most users went on to say that the idea was much easier than alternatives. 22 of 169 users commented negatively about the clarity of the words in the audio clips. Common problems were the rate of the words in the audio or the pitch. A small number wanted the word segmentation improved, or wanted the speech rate slowed down. The general consensus from participants was mostly positive except for these issues.

3.2   Evaluating H4C (Hard 4 Computers)

Traditionally a paper that introduces a new security mechanism would include a summary of its resiliency against attacks. The robustness of the technique could be demonstrated by showing an expression of the entropy of possible solutions or by attacking the CAPTCHA. The results of a brief evaluation of freely available ASR tools is offered but these do not simulate a motivated CAPTCHA breaking attempt.

---

[1] The time used in the calculation is measured server side. It is a measure of the time (in seconds) from the page being sent until the answer is received.

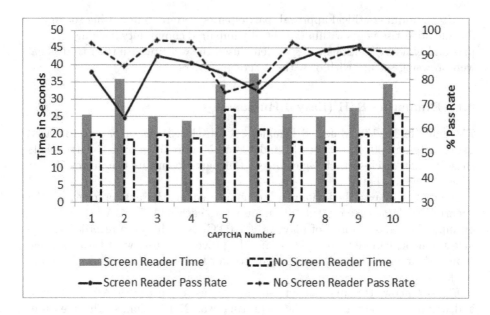

Fig. 2. Timings and Pass Rates

Two popular dictation programs (Dragon: Naturally Speaking[2] and iSpeech[3]) were used to test the resilience of jCAPTCHAs to automated software interpretation. The dictation software was first calibrated using clips of the same speaker for 31 words or phrases. The dictation software then attempted to interpret each jCAPTCHA. The responding transcription was manually recorded and evaluated for correctness using the same metric as used for participants.

Two of the 10 jCAPTCHAs were correctly interpreted: jCAPTCHA 4 was a perfect match. jCAPTCHA 5 was partially solved, with two words correctly identified and the Levenshtein edit distance [9] permitted the word 'gift' instead of the expected 'lift'.

jCAPTCHA 4 is, in hindsight, a suboptimal phrase since the word order could feasibly be used in normal conversation. It thus fails to meet the intended design goals. In the case of jCAPTCHA 5, the software submitted five words for the four word jCAPTCHA. Future heuristics for judging the correctness of the jCAPT-CHAs should limit the number of possible words submitted in given answers, else multiple homonyms could be entered and used to break the jCAPTCHA.

4   Discussion

jCAPTCHAs approach the desired 90% pass rate [5]. However, it should be acknowledged that these jCAPTCHAs only use one speaker, and the results

---

[2] http://www.nuance.co.uk/dragon/index.htm

[3] www.ispeech.org

may well differ if multiple speakers, accents and languages are employed in the audio clip formation stage.

The pass rate for all visually impaired users is 83.78% which is a remarkable improvement on the 46% pass rate given in [13]. It should be noted that Sauer's experiment [13] used a much smaller sample size (6) and ages were between 28 and 54, so the results may well be a worst-case scenario. The pass rate for reCAP-TCHA is 70% [15] but for this study no demographic information was reported. The mean answer submission time for screen reader users (31.46 seconds) is slightly faster than the reported time of 35.75 seconds in [10]. Only 10 screen reader users participated in the Lazar study whereas 169 participated in this study, making it difficult to conclude definitively which is the faster. Moreover, Lazar does not describe the method for recording answer times, it may only have measured time spent between the page having loaded and the answer message being sent to the server which would shorten the given time compared to the timings collected in our study. The mean answer submission time for non-screen reader users is 20.35 seconds, similar to the reported time of 22.8 seconds in [10]. It is likely that jCAPTCHAs do not offer significant improvements in answer submission time compared to radio clip based CAPTCHAs [10].

Before jCAPTCHA can be advanced as a viable alternative CAPTCHA a system needs to be created that can generate jCAPTCHAs automatically. To do this a corpus of audio clips and a reverse language model need to be created. The system should be tested with specially configured audio recognition toolkits to ensure that the words and ordering are resilient to more rigorous attacks.

5   Conclusion

The concept of a CAPTCHA was introduced and the accessibility issues explored. We then proposed a new, more accessible CAPTCHA called jCAPTCHA. We presented the results of our evaluation, which included participants using screen readers as well as those without visual impairments.

The results show that jCAPTCHAs are moderately resistant to recognition by off-the-shelf audio recognition programs. The jCAPTCHAs should be tested more rigorously with use of a toolkit that has been customised to recognise the types of clips used in the CAPTCHA. These jCAPTCHAs utilised only one speaker. Future jCAPTCHAs should use multiple speakers, accents and languages in order to diversify the vocabulary and thwart automated attacks.

The CAPTCHAs were created by hand, and, as such, it is not possible to give the entropy of all possible generated jCAPTCHAs. Given an automated system we would need to carefully consider how likely a training based attack can be developed. At this point we could then express the limits of the generation algorithm. If jCAPTCHA were ever deployed in the wild, it is predictable that attackers and defenders would enter a cat and mouse game of creating, updating and breaking the language models employed.

References

1. Equality act,
   http://www.legislation.gov.uk/ukpga/2010/15/contents
   (accessed: November 18, 2013)
2. World Wide Web Consortium (W3C). Inaccessibility of CAPTCHA (2007),
   http://www.w3.org/TR/turingtest/ (accessed: November 13, 2013)
3. Bigham, J., Cavender, A.: Evaluating existing audio captchas and an interface optimized for non-visual use. In: Proceedings of the 27th International Conference on Human Factors in Computing Systems, pp. 1829–1838. ACM (2009)
4. Bursztein, E., Bethard, S., Fabry, C., Mitchell, J.C., Jurafsky, D.: How Good Are Humans at Solving CAPTCHAs? A Large Scale Evaluation. In: Proceedings of the 2010 IEEE Symposium on Security and Privacy, pp. 399–413 (2010)
5. Chellapilla, K., Larson, K., Simard, P., Czerwinski, M.: Designing human friendly human interaction proofs (HIPs). In: Proceedings of the SIGCHI Conference on Human Factors in Computing Systems, pp. 711–720. ACM (2005)
6. Gao, H., Liu, H., Yao, D., Liu, X., Aickelin, U.: An audio captcha to distinguish humans from computers. In: 2010 Third International Symposium on Electronic Commerce and Security (ISECS), pp. 265–269. IEEE (2010)
7. Gilleland, M.: Levenshtein distance, in three flavors. Merriam Park Software (2009),
   http://www.merriampark.com/ld.htm
8. Gossweiler, R., Kamvar, M., Baluja, S.: What's up CAPTCHA? A CAPTCHA based on image orientation. In: Proceedings of the 18th International Conference on World Wide Web, WWW 2009, pp. 841–850. ACM, New York (2009),
   http://doi.acm.org/10.1145/1526709.1526822
9. Heeringa, W.J.: Measuring dialect pronunciation differences using Levenshtein distance. Ph.D. thesis, University Library Groningen (2004)
10. Lazar, J., Feng, J., Adelegan, O., Giller, A., Hardsock, A., Horney, R., Jacob, R., Kosiba, E., Martin, G., Misterka, M., et al.: Assessing the usability of the new radio clip-based human interaction proofs. In: Proceedings of ACM SOUPS Symposium On Usable Privacy and Security, pp. 1–2 (2010)
11. Li, S., Shah, S.A.H., Khan, M.A.U., Khayam, S.A., Sadeghi, A.R., Schmitz, R.: Breaking e-Banking CAPTCHAs. In: Proceedings of 26th Annual Computer Security Applications Conference (ACSAC 2010), pp. 171–180 (2010)
12. Mori, G., Malik, J.: Recognizing objects in adversarial clutter: Breaking a visual CAPTCHA. In: Proceedings of the 2003 IEEE Computer Society Conference on Computer Vision and Pattern Recognition, vol. 1, p. I-134. IEEE (2003)
13. Sauer, G., Hochheiser, H., Feng, J., Lazar, J.: Towards a universally usable CAPTCHA. In: Proc. of the 4th Symp. on Usable Privacy and Security (SOUPS 2008), Pittsburgh, PA, USA (2008)
14. Schlaikjer, A.: A dual-use speech CAPTCHA: Aiding visually impaired web users while providing transcriptions of audio streams. LTI-CMU Technical Report, pp. 07–014 (2007)
15. Tam, J., Simsa, J., Hyde, S., Ahn, L.V.: Breaking audio CAPTCHAs. In: Advances in Neural Information Processing Systems, pp. 1625–1632 (2008)
16. Von Ahn, L., Blum, M., Hopper, N., Langford, J.: CAPTCHA: Using hard AI problems for security. In: Biham, E. (ed.) EUROCRYPT 2003. LNCS, vol. 2656, pp. 294–311. Springer, Heidelberg (2003)

Benefits and Challenges of Combining Automated and User Testing to Enhance e-Accessibility – The European Internet Inclusion Initiative

Mikael Snaprud[1], Kamyar Rasta[1], Kim Andreasson[2], and Annika Nietzio[3]

[1] Tingtun AS, Norway
mikael.snaprud@tingtun.no, kamyar.rasta@tingtun.no
http://www.tingtun.no
[2] DAKA advisory AB, Sweden
kim@dakaadvisory.com
http://www.DAKAadvisory.com
[3] Forschungsinstitut Technologie und Behinderung (FTB)
der Evangelischen Stiftung Volmarstein, Germany
eiii@ftb-esv.de
http://www.ftb-esv.de

Abstract. The European Internet Inclusion Initiative (EIII) presents a new approach by combining the benefits of automated and user testing in order to improve both the quality and the coverage of evaluation results. This paper provides an overview of the challenges posed by online accessibility assessment and outlines the initial steps towards the combination of automated and user testing in the form of crowd sourcing.

1 Introduction

The Internet has been a great success over the last 25 years. In the beginning, it seemed hard to believe that people with disabilities would use the Web but Accessibility soon emerged as a mainstream topic.

The formation of the W3C Web Accessibility Initiative (WAI) led to the creation of the Web Content Accessibility Guidelines (WCAG) 1.0 in 1999. Soon afterwards the first automated tools (such as *Bobby approved* or *Cynthia says*) emerged. Although the tools could identify only a fraction of all potential accessibility issues in a web site, they became quite popular as they met the need to develop a big picture of web accessibility with less effort than expert evaluation.

As the Web grew, policies like legal obligation to create accessible (public) web sites and regular monitoring were introduced. With more content, new devices and technologies, the guidelines and approaches for evaluation and monitoring have also evolved. Algorithms are more sophisticated so that automated tools can check more aspects. WCAG 2.0 offers a clearer understanding of good practices and common failures. Computing power and bandwidth allow large scale monitoring. Manual evaluation schemes have also evolved, such as the Unified

K. Miesenberger et al. (Eds.): ICCHP 2014, Part I, LNCS 8547, pp. 137–140, 2014.

Web Evaluation Methodology (UWEM)[6] and the W3C Website Accessibility Conformance Evaluation Methodology (WCAG-EM) 1.0 [7]. There also exist several national evaluation methodologies, such as the Dutch *Webrichtlijnen*, the Norwegian *Kvalitet på nett*, or the German *BITV-Test*.

Both the automated and manual approach have their advantages and limitations. While automated testing can process many pages in a short time and yield repeatable results, manual evaluation can produce detailed and accurate reports for a small number of pages and instances. Building on the advantages of both approaches, the EIII project is developing a methodology and an implementation that will allow user input to complement automated accessibility evaluations. Thus reaching a broader coverage of web sites as well as a deeper insight.

2   Related Work

The idea of combining automated and user testing has been suggested before. A first simple approach was the presentation of "warnings": The tools highlight areas that might contain an accessibility problem and leave the decision to the user. Later on, tools (such as *Walidator*[5]) prompted users to enter their findings and presented them together with the automated WCAG 1.0 evaluation results for the web page. Naftali and Clúa [2] discuss the general challenges arising when combining evaluation results from different sources including false positives in tools results, variability among results produced by (different) humans, and noise introduced by less experienced evaluators. But to our knowledge there are currently no tools that combine automated and user testing results based on WCAG 2.0.

For automated accessibility testing EIII builds on the experience from the European Internet Accessibility Observatory (EIAO) project [1], which delivered the first open source application for large scale web site evaluation and the eGovMon project [3] which implemented large scale WCAG 2.0 evaluation. These applications provide a system architecture to handle a large number of web sites, including the sampling and downloading of the individual web pages and the storage and retrieval of the collected accessibility data.

Methodologies for expert evaluation describe procedures to produce reliable and repeatable results. EIII draws on the lessons learned from UWEM, a first harmonised methodology for web accessibility evaluations according to WCAG 1.0 and experiences from national evaluation methodologies. The currently developed WCAG-EM also provides helpful input on sampling and reporting, although individual tests are not covered.

3   The EIII Approach

EIII is developing a methodology to combine results from different sources to overcome the shortcomings of the individual evaluation approaches.

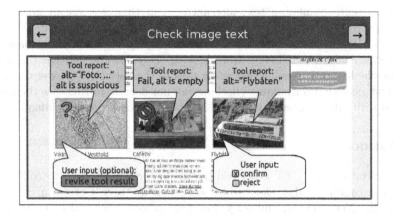

Fig. 1. Tool supported user testing of images

3.1   Challenges and Potential Solutions

Automated checks can run quickly and produce a large volume of evaluation results. The combination with human input poses theoretical challenges: How can different types of results be combined so that the human input is well represented in the overall results? And practical challenges: How can people be empowered and motivated to carry out manual checks of web accessibility?

The EIII User Testing Tool (UTT) is designed with a low threshold for participation. Users don't need to be accessibility experts as they are guided through the testing procedure. The UTT directs their attention to objects to be examined and provides clear and easy to understand questions. The UTT also takes care of the sampling of web pages and the selection of elements that require human judgement.

The mission of EIII is to work not only **for** persons with disabilities but **with** them. The UTT interface is designed to be accessible so that many people can contribute. This will help assure a reasonable coverage of devices, assistive technologies, and client software. In this way crowd-sourcing techniques can be used to collect input from users. EIII will draw on previous experiences from crowd-sourcing, for instance the Norwegian *Rett fram* project, which focuses on making public services accessible for families with disabled children, and the project *Lavterskel IKT for eldre* which offers ICT training for the elderly.

3.2   Towards an Implementation of the EIII User Testing Tool

When the automated accessibility checker is applied to a web page, the tests can produce three different results, namely: *pass*, *fail* or *to be verified*. The *to be verified* results are the input to the UTT.

Figure 1 illustrates how images and their corresponding texts can be assessed. First the tool determines the applicability and extracts the relevant information from the page. In this case, it identifies the images and extracts any existing alternative text. A missing text alternative – in this case on an image that is the only content of a link – will lead to a fail report without further user interaction. The tool can also apply heuristics [4]. In the example a suspicious text alternative is detected (text starting with "Foto:"). The user has the option to revise the heuristic results. The main task of the user is to answer questions about instances that automated checking can not decide. In this case the user is asked to verify if the alternative text describes the corresponding image.

4   Outlook

The EIII system and UTT described in this paper will be used to collect and compare accessibility data for public web sites in three European countries: Norway, the Netherlands, and Italy. Coverage of countries will be extended as the approach is refined. The first results will be published in fall 2014.

Plans for future development include adding different perspectives to the UTT interface: the expert evaluator, the visitor, the evaluation commissioner, or the web developer. The EIII system will not only support user testing but will also provide an API to import test results from other tools or even integrate other accessibility evaluation tools directly.

Acknowledgements. The EIII project (`http://eiii.eu`) is co-funded by the European Commission under FP7 Project no.: 609667.

References

1. Bühler, C., Heck, H., Nietzio, A., Olsen, M.G., Snaprud, M.: Monitoring Accessibility of Governmental Web Sites in Europe. In: Miesenberger, K., Klaus, J., Zagler, W.L., Karshmer, A.I. (eds.) ICCHP 2008. LNCS, vol. 5105, pp. 410–417. Springer, Heidelberg (2008)
2. Naftali, M., Clúa, O.: Integration of Web Accessibility Metrics into a Semi-automatic Evaluation Process. In: W3C Online Symposium on Web Accessibility Metrics (2011)
3. Nietzio, A., Eibegger, M., Goodwin, M., Snaprud, M.: Following the WCAG 2.0 Techniques: Experiences from Designing a WCAG 2.0 Checking Tool. In: Miesenberger, K., Karshmer, A., Penaz, P., Zagler, W. (eds.) ICCHP 2012, Part I. LNCS, vol. 7382, pp. 417–424. Springer, Heidelberg (2012)
4. Olsen, M.G., Snaprud, M., Nietzio, A.: Automatic Checking of Alternative Texts on Web Pages. In: Miesenberger, K., Klaus, J., Zagler, W., Karshmer, A. (eds.) ICCHP 2010, Part 1. LNCS, vol. 6179, pp. 425–432. Springer, Heidelberg (2010)
5. Walidator: Web Accessibility Frame Work (2010), `http://walidator.net/en/` (retrieved March 26, 2014)
6. Web Accessibility Benchmarking Cluster: Unified Web Evaluation Methodology (UWEM) 1.2., `http://www.wabcluster.org/uwem1_2/` (retrieved March 26, 2014)
7. World Wide Web Consortium: Website Accessibility Conformance Evaluation Methodology. W3C Working Draft (January 30, 2014), `http://www.w3.org/TR/WCAG-EM/` (retrieved March 26, 2014)

Accessibility of MOOCs

Marco Bohnsack[1] and Steffen Puhl[2]

[1] Data-quest Suchi & Berg GmbH, Göttingen, Germany
bohnsack@data-quest.de
[2] Justus Liebig University, Gießen, Germany
steffen.puhl@hrz.uni-giessen.de

Abstract. The paper gives a short overview on the topic of Massive Open On-line Courses and providers of MOOC infrastructure. Selected MOOC-platforms are reviewed for accessibility with different set-ups of common screen-reading software and browsers. No platform was fully accessible, most lacked correct language markers and an accessible design. The results show that accessibility was not in focus when the platforms where built, thus excluding impaired people and not fulfilling the claim that MOOCs are open to everyone.

Keywords: Accessibility, MOOCs.

1 Introduction

The term "MOOC" is an acronym for Massive Open Online Courses. Extensive publications, often with an enthusiastic undertone, described MOOCs as "a revolution" and "the future of learning" [1]. The New York Times declared 2012 to "The year of the MOOCs"[2]. The idea which fascinated the authors was the availability and easy access to lectures. Knowledge, open and accessible to everyone, is an alluring idea? If MOOCs are really meant to be open for everyone, they have to fulfill many different requirements, even in terms of accessibility. The subject of the scientific research on MOOCs was mainly the didactic methods (or their absence thereof) [3]. Sanchez-Gordon and Luján-Mora investigated the accessibility of MOOC for elderly students [4], but until the time this paper was written, no publication on the accessibility of MOOCs for disabled persons has been released.

2 Definition and History of MOOCS

The term MOOC was introduced by Dave Cormier in 2008 as a response to an online course, in which the massive number 2,200 participants from the general public enrolled [5,6]. A typical MOOC has no on-site attendance and is solely held online. It consists of a mix of video lecturing and online tests. In 2011 Stanford Professor Sebastian Thrun held an open online course on artificial intelligence. 160,000 people enrolled, triggering extensive media coverage. Within a few weeks, two more MOOCs were launched by Daphne Koller and Andrew Ng. Due to the high number of

K. Miesenberger et al. (Eds.): ICCHP 2014, Part I, LNCS 8547, pp. 141–144, 2014.
© Springer International Publishing Switzerland 2014

participants, Thrun, Ng and Koller suspected a broader demand for knowledge. They founded the companies "Udacity" and "Coursera", which act as providers for infrastructure and aspire to partnerships with universities, which are to deliver the content. Media started an extensive coverage on MOOCs in 2012. In Germany and other European countries media coverage started with a delay in early 2013, when other companies started to provide platforms for MOOCs and searched for partnership with universities. Examples are "P2PU" (UK), "Iversity" (GER), "Open MOOC" (Spain) or "Futurelearn" (UK). Potential revenue sources are fees for participation or certification, applicant screening, employee recruitment or sponsorships.

3   Methodology

In our research, we attempted to examine whether a MOOC-platform is accessible in real life, or if there are "show stoppers". We intentionally did not check the platforms against the W3C-catalogue with recommendations for accessibility. We opted for protocol observation as our research design. A blind test person familiar with our test-setup was given the URLs of the MOOC. The assignment was to register to the platform, then select and enroll to a random course. The experiment was stopped the moment the person ran into a situation in which proceeding without help by a non-impaired person would have been impossible. The tests took place on November 5th, 2013. Our intent was to examine the most successful platforms both in the US and in Germany. Since the numbers of active users were and still are hard to obtain, we opted for the number of courses offered as criteria. This led to the choice of Udacity, Coursera, edX (USA) and OpenCourseWorld and Iversity (Germany).

For our research we chose two setups of hard- and software. The configurations represent the most widespread aids for blind people, which means Microsoft Windows, the screen reading software JAWS and Internet Explorer as browser [7]. Alternative browsers, such as Mozilla Firefox, suffer from incompatibilities with JAWS. Our test setup consisted of two computers with common, every day configurations derived from the survey:

- Configuration 1: Notebook running Windows XP, Internet Explorer 8, Java 7 and JAWS 11.0
- Configuration 2: Notebook running Windows Vista, Internet Explorer 8, Java 7 and JAWS 9.0

4   Results

4.1   Coursera[1]

The start page identified Internet Explorer 8 as outdated. It displayed a message with the recommendation to update to an actual browser. Even though this is a good

---

[1] https://www.coursera.org

advice, it was not possible for technical reasons. We were unable to access the platform and had to stop the experiment at this point.

4.2   Udacity[2]

The start page lacks the tags which sets the screen reader software to the appropriate language. Since our test setup was running in another language, the JAWS started to read English texts using German pronunciation. The result was incomprehensible, thus making the platform inaccessible for the visual impaired.

4.3   edX[3]

The start page contained the correct mark-up for English speech. All graphics were provided with correct descriptions. The registration page contained an invisible but, with a screen reader, accessible message indicating that the installation of a special plug-in for rendering formulas could be useful – a thoughtful hint. The learning content in our sample course consisted of inaccessible PDFs. With Configuration 2, it was impossible to log out.

4.4   OpenCourseWorld[4]

The landing page included three landmark roles for the banner, the main and the content area. Unnecessary was a constantly changing element which did nothing more than rotate banners, but delivered a massive distraction to the screen reader in configuration 1. The course directory was hard to understand because all metadata were condensed into one, long link. After completing the user profile, the platform led to a page with half a dozen frames and many unnamed buttons. Further navigation was not possible.

4.5   Iversity[5]

The home page of iversity lacked correct language markers, which made test configuration 1 read the German text with English pronunciation, rendering the page almost unusable. Test configuration 2, with the older version of JAWS, read and spoke German text correctly, but English words in a German text were not marked as such and thus pronounced as German. Pictures did not have a meaningful description. The registration via mail and password did not work for the duration of our test.

---

[2] https://www.udacity.com
[3] https://www.edx.org
[4] http://opencourseworld.de
[5] http://iversity.org

5   Conclusion

From the five examined MOOC-platforms only one was accessible with our real-life test-configurations for visually disabled persons. Nearly every platform tested suffered from technological shortcomings. The only platform which proofed accessible was edX, which was also the only open source software in our test sample. During an extended post-test in February 2014, the outcome was the same, despite the fact that iversity and Open Course World had been relaunched in the meantime. Even with Windows 7, JAWS 13.0 and Internet Explorer 11 the problems remained. This leads to the conclusion that MOOCs, despite their promise to be open to everyone [8], currently exclude visually impaired people. This finding is backed in December 2013 by Professor Wenju Wu of Beijing University, who claimed "Regarding accessibility, we think most MOOC framework hasn´t given consideration to that" [9].

References

1. Meister, J.: How Moocs Will Revolutionize Corporate Learning and Development, Forbes Online (2013),
   http://www.forbes.com/sites/jeannemeister/2013/08/13/
   how-moocs-will-revolutionize-corporate-learning-development/
2. Pappano, L.: The Year of the MOOC, The New York Times (2013),
   http://www.nytimes.com/2012/11/04/education/edlife/
   massive-open-online-courses-are-multiplying-at-a-
   rapid-pace.html?pagewanted=all
3. Schulmeister, R. (ed.): MOOCs – Massive Open Online Courses. Waxmann, Münster (2013)
4. Sanchez-Gordon, S., Luján-Mora, S.: Web accessibility of MOOCs for elderly students. In: 12th International Conference on Information Technology Based Higher Education and Training (ITHET 2013), Antalya (Turkey), October 10-12, pp. 1–6 (2013)
5. Stokes, P.: The Particle Accelerator of Learning, p. 31. Inside Higher Ed. (May 2013)
6. Parr, C.: Mooc creators criticise courses' lack of creativity. Times Higher Education (2013),
   http://www.timeshighereducation.co.uk/
   news/mooc-creators-criticise-courses-lack-of-
   creativity/2008180.fullarticle
7. WebAIM, http://webaim.org/projects/screenreadersurvey5/
8. Bildungsprojekt Udacity, Hochschulbildung, kostenlos und für alle,
   http://www.zeit.de/studium/uni-leben/2012-01/udacity-thrun
9. Wu, W.: During the Online Symposium for Accessible E-Learning (December 16, 2013), Transcript at http://www.w3.org/WAI/RD/2013/e-learning/

A First Look into MOOCs Accessibility

The Case of Coursera

Najd A. Al-Mouh[1], Atheer S. Al-Khalifa[1], and Hend S. Al-Khalifa[2]

[1] King Abdulaziz City for Science and Technology, Riyadh, Saudi Arabia
{nalmouh,aalkhalifa}@kacst.edu.sa
[2] King Saud University, Riyadh, Saudi Arabia
hendk@ksu.edu.sa

Abstract. Since the inception of Massive Open Online Courses (MOOCs), millions of people have benefitted from their provided content. Yet, the question we need to ask is: how accessible are MOOCs especially to the Visually Impaired People (VIP)? In this paper we look thoroughly into the accessibility problems VIP face while using one of the well-know MOOCs environments (Coursera.org) and provide some recommendations to improve its accessibility.

Keywords: Accessibility, WCAG, MOOCs, e-Learning, Screen readers, Blinds.

1 Background and Related Work

According to World Health Organization (WHO), there are about 39 million people who are totally blind among 285 million people with visual impairment. Visual impairment people (VIP) use different assistive technologies (ATs) especially screen readers and screen magnifiers that help them access the web. However, there are still a number of difficulties a VIP faces when using such ATs to browse the web; these problems might come from the ATs or from the website itself. The studies in [2,3] compared the time visually impaired and non-visually impaired need to complete a task. The results showed that VIP using screen readers needed triple amount of time in comparison to non-impaired people. In both cases the VIP have faced difficulty accessing an application and its content.

In educational environments, such as Learning Content Management Systems (LCMS), VIP often encounter difficulties when accessing courses' websites. Both ATs and resources need to be accessible, thus VIP can overcome the accessibility problems they face to reach the required learning content [4].

For VIP, distance learning, e-learning and MOOCs are considered good choices to improve one's education. They have opened the doors for learning to many people around the world, even VIP; they offer courses which can elevate one's knowledge in many ways. MOOCs are like any other online courses; they have syllabi, resource materials, activities, assessment quizzes, and discussion forums. All of these components need to be accessible for VIP, which raise the importance of implementing accessibility in such systems by web developers.

K. Miesenberger et al. (Eds.): ICCHP 2014, Part I, LNCS 8547, pp. 145–152, 2014.

Accessibility of Learning Management Systems (LMS) for people with disabilities was discussed in few research. For instance, [7] evaluated accessibility of four LMSs: Blackboard 4, Blackboard 5, Prometheus 4, and WebCT 3.0 using W3C/WAI guidelines. Its findings indicate that LMSs are continually improving, but they still need more work to comply with Priority 1 of the W3C/WAI guidelines. Moreover, [8] evaluated the accessibility of LMSs' tools. The results showed that there is no one correct application that complies with WCAG guidelines and specifications; thus it is important to adopt a design for all methodology which can make tools adaptable to each user separately.

From this brief overview, we can see that MOOCs accessibility have not been studied before for VIP. Therefore, in our paper we aim at contributing to this domain by conducting accessibility evaluation of MOOCs. The MOOC environment we choose for this case study is Coursera.org. Coursera[1], with about 4.4 million students and 420 courses presented by about 84 universities around the world, is considered one of the leading MOOCs environments nowadays [5].

2   Evaluation Design

This section describes the two evaluation approaches we used with Coursera.org, namely: user testing and heuristic evaluation. At first we explain the evaluation objectives for each approach, followed by the evaluation environment, the selected courses, and the evaluation method for each.

2.1   Evaluation Objective

This study aims to evaluate Coursera accessibility, using two methods: (a) VIP evaluation with the assistance of screen readers. This approach focuses on accessibility in general and tries to analyze problems VIP face when performing and completing mundane tasks e.g. course enrollment. (b) Heuristic evaluation, which is a test performed by experts to evaluate the interface of a website according to a recognizable set of principles [9]. Therefore this study aims at assessing the compliance of Coursera's different courses with W3C and WCAG 2.0 through manual examination which helps to assure that web content is more accessible to people with disabilities.

2.2   Evaluation Environment

This study was conducted on Courseras' English interface and carried out on devices running Microsoft Windows 7, Mac OS X 10.8.5, and iOS7. As for the web browsers: IE9, Mozilla Firefox, and Safari were used with two screen readers: Window's NonVisual Desktop Access (NVDA)[2] and Mac's OS preinstalled VoiceOver.

---

[1] https://www.coursera.org/about
[2] http://www.nvaccess.org/

In this experiment, NVDA was used with IE on a desktop that runs Microsoft Windows 7. VoiceOver was used with Safari on an iPhone, which runs iOS7 operating system. The expert evaluation was carried out on Firefox with the help of several accessibility add-ons to facilitate the process of conforming to specific guidelines. The add-ons include: WAVE Toolbar 1.1.6[3], WCAG Contrast checker 1.4.3[4] and Accessibility Evaluator Toolbar 1.5.7.1[5].

2.3 Evaluation Methods

For a sufficient user evaluation, an expert as well as user experience must be taken into consideration. So, our method of evaluation tried to combine these two angles together. Based on W3C evaluation methodology, and using other evaluation studies [10,11], we first chose a set of essential tasks to be evaluated. These tasks are important in joining a course in MOOCs. The tasks evaluated are presented in Fig 1.

As for the heuristic evaluation, two accessibility experts used WCAG guidelines checklist and semi-automated tools to perform the evaluation.

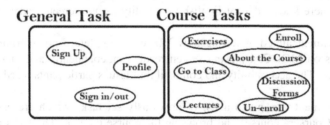

Fig. 1. Tasks Evaluated

2.4 Heuristic Evaluation Method

In this evaluation we selected 10 different Coursera courses from different universities that were open for enrollment at the time of the study. All the courses were in English and cover variety of subjects including: information, technology & design, business & management, engineering, arts, humanities, medicine, biology & life sciences, education and physics. In the evaluation process, each course in the dataset was manually checked in order to confirm its compliance with WCAG 2.0 guidelines. The used checklist inspects 105 accessibility problematic issues within 12 guidelines, which are classified under four main principles: perceivable, operable, understandable, and robust. Each guideline has a set of Success Criteria (SC) or requirements to be fulfilled with different priority levels: lowest A to the highest AAA[6].

---

[3] http://wave.webaim.org/
[4] https://addons.mozilla.org/en-us/firefox/addon/
  wcag-contrast-checker/
[5] https://code.google.com/p/accessext/
[6] http://www.w3.org/WAI/intro/wcag.php

However, some SC needs the assistance of a semi-automated tool to determine the contrast level between foreground and background of different elements in the web page like the SC 1.4.3 Contrast (Minimum): "The visual presentation of text and images of text has a contrast ratio of at least 4.5:1 (Level AA)". Moreover, accessibility toolbars were used to help facilitate confirming other SC by: (1) listing different components and their properties or (2) disabling the stylesheet to determine the text sequence within the page.

2.5   User Evaluation Method

In this experiment, two blind females and one male took part in the evaluation. All of them are good at English and use computers efficiently. The first female and male have been totally blind since they were born. The second female is an accessibility and IT expert who is not blind but was blind-folded and turned the computer screen off to simulate blindness.   The two blind participants have been chosen as representative of any blind individual who needs a screen reader to use Internet applications. The main criteria we focused on when choosing the participants to test MOOCs accessibility, where knowledge of English and ability to use screen readers to browse the web.

The experiment aimed at testing how VIP can complete a predetermined set of specific tasks on MOOCs by using screen readers independently and identify problems they face. The accessibility and compatibility issues participants faced have been recorded.

Each participant was given a list of previously set tasks which are essential for enrolling in Coursera courses and browsing the course content. The tasks are shown in Figure 1. To conduct the experiment in the best way, participants fulfilled the tasks independently without any help of technicians or accessibility experts. Then, each of the participants commented on the success of the tasks completion and on any difficulty faced while performing the tasks.

3   Evaluation Results

3.1   Heuristic Evaluation

The results of the heuristic evaluation of ten Coursera courses with respect to WCAG 2.0 showed that all the courses failed to confirm with all priority levels (A-AA-AAA). Table 1 shows the number of open issues in each course along with the level of conformity for each priority level. The open issues rates varies between 23 and 34 out of 105 testable SC. Whereas the level of conformity of level A was the highest among other levels (70%-84%), showing that the minimum level of conformance is highly achieved compared to other levels. Whereas level AAA is the lowest in conformance with a rate between (56%-69%), since it depends on the conformance of level A and AA.

Table 1. Number of Open Issues in Coursera Courses

Course / University	A	AA	AAA	Open issues
Online Games: Literature, New Media, and Narrative / Vanderbilt University	78%	78%	56%	30
Plagues, Witches, and War: The Worlds of Historical Fiction / University of Virginia	76%	69.6%	59%	32
Design: Creation of Artifacts in Society / University of Pennsylvania	82%	74%	68.75%	25
Bioelectricity: A Quantitative Approach / Duke University	78%	74%	62.5%	29
Synapses, Neurons and Brains / Hebrew University of Jerusalem	82%	74%	68.75%	25
Drug Discovery, Development & Commercialization / University of California, San Diego	78%	82.6%	68.75%	25
Experimental Genome Science / University of Pennsylvania	78%	74%	59%	30
Neural Networks for Machine Learning / University of Torronto	84%	78%	69%	23
Blended Learning: Personalizing Education for Students / New Teacher Center	70%	74%	59%	34
Writing in the Sciences / Stanford University	80%	74%	62.5%	28
Average	79%	75%	63%	28.1

In the following, we present the most common failed SC found in the evaluation among courses based on their priority level.

Level A. One of Coursera's fundamental features is its video lectures. However, even with all the courses providing text transcripts of their videos, they have failed to follow guideline 1.2.3, which assures that time-based media must have written text or audio description to allow VIP to understand audio-visual material. This failure is extended to guidelines 1.2.5(AA), 1.2.7(AAA) and 1.2.8(AAA) that deal with extended audio description.

Another commonly failed guideline is 1.3.1 that focuses on presenting information, structure and relationships of a content programmatically. It was noticed that some of the authors would neglect marking up appropriate headings and use instead other properties such as underline or bold HTML tags, while others would not use appropriate HTML tags when creating lists, instead they would add a dash or a number to a list item. On the other hand, special texts e.g. citations or long quotations are not marked up with their appropriate HTML elements which make reading long lists of syllables a hard task for a VIP. Moreover, most of data tables have missing titles and summaries.

The evaluation showed that Coursera's video lectures page violate 2.1.2 guideline that assures a user cannot be trapped when using the keyboard only. However, our tester has found that the video lecture captures the keyboard focus without advising the user in advance about a way to exit such a situation.

Skip links for repetitive blocks of information were absent in the evaluated courses, which did not fulfill the guideline 2.4.1 that aims at facilitating user navigation within a web page. It was also noted that some courses' authors fail to provide titles of web pages that describe the topic presented (SC 2.4.2).

Furthermore, in concern with web pages readability, none of the courses had a correct language declaration in every page which fails to fulfill guideline 3.1.1.

Level AA. According to guideline 1.4.3, the contrast ratio between the front and the background colors should be at least 4.5:1 that applies to all text, borders around input fields and texts in information graphics. However, having a button in the courses would violate this guideline along with its enhanced version in guideline 1.4.6 (AAA).

With respect to guideline 1.4.4 about defining font sizes in the CSS in terms of % or em, results showed that all the courses failed to use such measurements which are important to implement, in order to assist VIP's readability that depends on the enlargement functions of the browser.

Some courses did not fulfill guideline 2.4.5, regards providing multiple ways to access an element of content either by a search function or a sitemap. The search function was present in most of the courses, but none provided a sitemap.

Level AAA. Concerning guideline 1.4.8 related to the visual presentation of blocks of texts, Coursera platform fails to provide a mechanism for the user to select foreground and background colors in this case. Moreover, it was noticed that the width of text blocks are more than 80 characters and line spacing within paragraphs are larger than 1.5. It also failed this SC by the inability to scale-up these texts to read them without the need of horizontal scrolling.

Another noticeable issue found from some course providers is that links' texts alone do not identify the purpose of these links. For example, some uses the URL as a text of the label, or use a single word that is insufficient to convey the content of the link, which defies guideline 2.4.9.

Moreover, in readability of the text content, observations showed that courses lacked an explanation of unusual words presented in the content. Unusual words such as technical terms were not linked to a glossary or other mechanism to describe their meanings which defies guideline 3.1.3. Additionally, abbreviations were not explained in a glossary or were marked-up with appropriate tags such as <abbr>.

3.2   User Evaluation

The users, as mentioned previously, were two blinds and a sighted person who was blind-folded. The blindfolded test subject was added to confirm whether the barriers faced by the other subjects exist due to accessibility problems rather than language barrier. The accessibility problems participants faced when using MOOCs were analyzed and the results from the three participants were compared. All the users have reflected on their general satisfaction with MOOCs; however, the accessibility difficulties they all faced are similar. Although tasks were fulfilled, the participants identified specific accessibility problems when completing the tasks.

The problems are as follows:

1. No assistance was available for the VIP in the text input control;
2. Pages refresh and new pages open with no notification;
3. Instructions for registering in a new course were difficult to understand by the participants;
4. Text alternatives did not include well described text or were read incorrectly by the screen reader;
5. When there is an error, no messages are given for correction or termination;
6. There was no alt text in the images linked to other websites;
7. Using keyboard was difficult to reach some functions;
8. Using heading inappropriately conflicted with screen readers;
9. It was not compatible with mobile browsers.

In one hand, we have to highlight the fact that most of the required tasks were fulfilled. Nevertheless, there were yet some accessibility problems that faced the users and impeded the use of Coursera.

4   Recommendation and Conclusion

In this study, we evaluated the accessibility of one of the well-know MOOCs environments from two different perspectives: users as well as experts. We have resolved that Coursera still have limitations regarding accessibility to screen readers' users. Also, it failed to conform to WCAG 2.0 guidelines.

Based on the outcomes of our evaluation, we suggest a set of recommendations to enhance Coursera accessibility and reduce the difficulty faced by visually impaired when using its courses. The recommendations target courses' authors as well as Coursera platform. The following suggestions are aimed at the course author:

1. Information presented needs to be divided into small and easily understandable pieces using appropriate layout elements, such as headings.
2. Text alternatives must be available for any non-text content, whether an audio or text description.
3. Form input labels in quizzes and assignments should have descriptive labels for easier understanding by VIP.
4. In quizzes, authors should indicate fill-in blanks in a question instead of using multiple underscores (__), otherwise the screen-reader will not notify the user about them.
5. Links, tables and images are among content elements that need to have descriptive alternatives.

On the other hand, the following are recommendations for Coursera platform to take into consideration for more accessible content:

1. The platform should provide an authoring tool to ensure that the content is compatible with A, AA, or AAA levels of WCAG 2.0 guidelines.
2. The student should be able to change some interface features regarding auto-saving, colors, font size, etc.
3. There should be Input Assistance tools to help VIP correct mistakes and avoid them.
4. There should be substitutions for time-based media.
5. Search options in headings, lists, and tables should be allowed.
6. Keyboard focus indicator should be visible.
7. There should be a mobile version that fits the mobile screen size.
8. The platform should provide a mechanism or help to allow the user to perform the quiz within a video lecture, as a sighted person would do.
9. The platform should provide help to users when starting a video lecture, since the help option when clicked will take the user to a new window while the video is still playing in the previous page.

References

1. World Health Organisation (WHO): World report on disability. WHO (2011)
2. Disability Rights Commission (DRC): The Web: Access and Inclusion for Disabled People. TSO, London, UK (2004)
3. Craven, J.: Access to electronic resources by visually impaired people. Information Research 8(4), 156 (2003)
4. Fisseler, B., Bühler, C.: Accessible e-learning and educational technology - extending learning opportunities for people with disabilities. In: Proceedings of ICL, 2007, hal-00257138, pp. 26–28. Archives Ouvertes (2007)
5. Liyanagunawardena, T.R., Adams, A.A., Williams, S.A.: MOOCs: A Systematic Study of the Published Literature 2008-2012. The International Review of Research in Open and Distance Learning 14(3), 202–227 (2013)
6. Sanchez-Gordon, S., Lujan-Mora, S.: Web accessibility of MOOCs for elderly students. In: Proceedings of ITHET 2013, pp. 1–6. IEEE, Washington (2013)
7. Johnson, A., Ruppert, S.: An evaluation of accessibility in online learning management systems. Library Hi Tech 20(4), 441–451 (2002)
8. Guenaga, M.L., Burger, D., Oliver, J.: Accessibility for e-learning environments. In: Miesenberger, K., Klaus, J., Zagler, W.L., Burger, D. (eds.) ICCHP 2004. LNCS, vol. 3118, pp. 157–163. Springer, Heidelberg (2004)
9. Nielsen, J.: Finding usability problems through heuristic evaluation. In: Proceedings of CHI 1992, pp. 373–380. ACM, New York (1992)
10. Abou-Zahra, S.: Web accessibility evaluation. In: Harper, S., Yesilada, Y. (eds.) Web Accessibility, pp. 79–106. Springer, London (2008)
11. Harper, S., Yesilada, Y.: Web accessibility: a foundation for research. Springer, London (2008)

How to Increase Contrast Using Color Inversion

Josef Köble

SAP AG, Accessibility Competence Center, Walldorf, Germany
josef.koeble@sap.com

Abstract. This paper discusses why the inverted foreground and background colors should also be considered when calculating contrast with regard to accessibility. It is even possible to achieve an enhanced contrast for a pair of inverted colors while the pair of non-inverted colors meets the minimum contrast according to the WCAG 2.0. Implementing this benefit would support users with low vision, especially those who need high contrast.

Keywords: Luminance contrast, High contrast, Color inversion, Inverted Color.

1 Introduction

It can definitely be assumed that users with low vision in combination with severe light sensitivity prefer bright text on a dark background, for example, white text on a black background, to reduce brightness and increase readability. When working with a personal computer or an electronic device, these users might choose a theme called "High Contrast Black", which includes a black background color and a white foreground color [4]. The operating system Windows 7, for example, enables users to switch to High Contrast [10], and it offers different themes with a black background.

Unfortunately, there are web pages which are not accessible to this kind of user setting. Hard-coded black text or UI elements will not be visible on the black background of the High Contrast Black theme. In the worst case the user sees just a black page without any text or UI elements, because all texts and UI elements are also black. This can especially cause trouble when filling in forms. A workaround in this case would be to use the default theme (or another theme with white background color) and to invert the screen colors with a screen magnifier tool. Most screen magnifier tools offer color inversion [3].

Some operating systems do not offer any High Contrast Black themes by default, rather a function to invert the colors on the screen. Apple Mac OS X and Apple iOS, for example, include color inversion [1,2]. Pictures and videos are obviously not viewable with color inversion. But apart from that, text and UI elements can be perceived well with color inversion as long as the contrast is also sufficient for the inverted colors. Contrast is usually measured in the non-inverted mode, and not in the inverted mode. Thus, how can sufficient contrast be ensured for the inverted mode? Furthermore, is it possible to increase the contrast in the inverted mode? It seems that neither of these questions have been discussed yet.

K. Miesenberger et al. (Eds.): ICCHP 2014, Part I, LNCS 8547, pp. 153–156, 2014.

2   Basics

A color in the standard RGB color space is usually indicated by three integer values (r, g, b) where "r" is the standard red value, "g" the standard green value, and "b" the standard blue value. For example, (0, 255, 0) produces the standard green value. An integer value in the range from 0 to 255 requires one byte of memory. As one byte has eight bits, the binary values for the standard green color are (0000 0000, 1111 1111, 0000 0000). Another way to indicate an RGB color is to use a preceding "#" and three two-digit hexadecimal color values for red, green, and blue. For example, #00FF00 stands for Red = 00, Green = FF, and Blue = 00. [5,6], [8]

In this paper, the term "inverted color" is used to mean a bit inversion of the RGB color values, for example: The standard blue color has the binary RGB values (0000 0000, 0000 0000, 1111 1111). A bit inversion of these values produces the RGB values (1111 1111, 1111 1111, 0000 0000), which is known as yellow [5].

From an accessibility perspective, the visual presentation of a webpage should support the minimum contrast based on the requirement 1.4.3 of the Web Content Accessibility Guidelines (WCAG) 2.0.[9] But even if the minimum contrast requirement is given for a pair of colors, what about the contrast ratio of the pair of inverted colors? As a matter of fact, the contrast ratio of the foreground color to the background color is not necessarily equal to the contrast ratio of the inverted foreground color to the inverted background color. For example, a blue foreground (#0000FF) on a white background (#FFFFFF) has a contrast ratio of 8.6:1.[1] With inverted colors the blue foreground becomes yellow, and the white background becomes black. A yellow foreground (#FFFF00) on a black background (#000000) has a contrast ratio of 19.6:1.

3   Solution

Inverted colors will only support users with low vision if the combination of the inverted foreground color and the inverted background color has sufficient contrast. Users with low vision may desire an enhanced contrast based on the requirement 1.4.6 of WCAG 2.0. Minimum contrast requires a contrast ratio of at least 4.5:1 (3:1 for a large text), while enhanced contrast requires a contrast ratio of at least 7:1 (4.5:1 for a large text).

One approach is to provide users who are visually impaired with enhanced contrast on an inverted screen presentation, while providing all users with minimum contrast on the normal (non-inverted) screen presentation. This is possible because there are pairs of foreground colors and background colors, which provide a contrast ratio of

1. at least 4.5:1 in normal presentation and
2. at least 7:1 in inverted presentation.

Table 1 lists some pairs of colors (Color 1, Color 2) which support these two conditions.

---

[1] All contrast ratios in this article are calculated by the Color Contrast Analyzer tool from The Paciello Group, which is based on the algorithm in WCAG 2.0.[7][9].

Table 1. Pairs of colors which support at least 4.5:1 in normal mode and 7:1 in inverted mode

Color 1	Color 2	Contrast ratio color 1 / color 2	Color 2 inverted	Color 1 inverted	Contrast ratio of inverted colors
White #FFFFFF	Black #000000	21:1	White #FFFFFF	Black #000000	21:1
White #FFFFFF	Blue #0000FF	8.6:1	Yellow #FFFF00	Black #000000	19.6:1
White #FFFFFF	(darker) gray #666666	5.7:1	(brighter) gray #999999	Black #000000	7.4:1

Of course, not all pairs support these conditions. For users with low vision those pairs which fulfill the minimum contrast in normal presentation, but not in inverted presentation, are the worst. Table 2 shows four of these color combinations. (Although these pairs can be considered as rare combinations, they were chosen since their inverted colors are easy to calculate.) The combination of red text color on a black background color, for example, fulfills the minimum contrast of 4.5:1. But this combination will have a bad impact on the inverted presentation, because the contrast ratio of the inverted colors (cyan text on a white background) is 1.3:1 only.

Table 2. Pairs of colors which support at least 4.5:1 in normal mode, but not in inverted mode

Color 1	Color 2	Contrast ratio color 1 / color 2	Color 2 inverted	Color 1 inverted	Contrast ratio of inverted colors
Red #FF0000	Black #000000	5.3:1	White #FFFFFF	Cyan #00FFFF	1.3:1
Green #00FF00	Black #000000	15.3:1	White #FFFFFF	Magenta #FF00FF	3.1:1
Cyan #00FFFF	Black #000000	16.7:1	White #FFFFFF	Red #FF0000	4.0:1
Yellow #FFFF00	(darker) gray #666666	5.3:1	(brighter) gray #999999	Blue #0000FF	3.0:1

Provided that the minimum contrast ratio of at least 4.5:1 is fulfilled for given pairs of colors in default presentation, there are three categories for the inverted presentation of these given pairs:

- A pair of inverted colors supports the enhanced contrast of at least 7:1.
- A pair of inverted colors does not support the enhanced contrast of at least 7:1, but does support the minimum contrast of at least 4.5:1.
- A pair of inverted colors does not support the minimum contrast of at least 4.5:1.

It is obvious that the third category in the list will not support users with low vision, but it can be assumed that the first category in the list will optimally support users with low vision. Thus, color pairs of the third category should be avoided while color pairs of the first category should be preferred.

4   Conclusion

If software designers want to support users with low vision who use color inversion, they should consider the described aspects and use color pairs which fulfill a contrast ratio of at least 4.5:1 in normal presentation and optimally of at least 7:1 in inverted presentation. They will also support users with light sensitivity if they use white background for the normal presentation, because the inverted presentation results in a black background and can be compared to a "High Contrast Black" theme.

References

1. Apple: Accessibility – iOS. A wide range of features for a wide range of needs, http://www.apple.com/accessibility/ios/
2. Apple: Mac OS X displays inverted image colors (white on black, reverse type), http://support.apple.com/kb/ht3488
3. Evans, G., Blenkhorn, P.: Screen Readers and Screen Magnifiers. In: Hersh, M.A., Johnson, M.A. (eds.) Assistive Technology for Visually Impaired and Blind People, pp. 449–495. Springer, London (2008)
4. Köble, J.: New High Contrast Black Theme in SAP GUI for Windows 7.20. In SAP Design Guild: Edition 12: Accessibility Edition (March 2012), http://www.sapdesignguild.org/editions/edition12/high_contrast.asp
5. Microsoft: Color Table, http://msdn.microsoft.com/en-us/library/ie/ms531197(v=vs.85).aspx
6. Microsoft: RGB Color Model, http://msdn.microsoft.com/en-us/library/dd355244.aspx
7. The Paciello Group: Colour Contrast Analyser (Win/Mac), http://www.paciellogroup.com/resources/contrastAnalyser
8. Stokes, M., Anderson, M., Chandrasekar, S., Motta, R.: A Standard Default Color Space for the Internet - sRGB. Version 1.10, http://www.w3.org/Graphics/Color/sRGB.html
9. W3C: Web Content Accessibility Guidelines (WCAG) 2.0; W3C Recommendation (December 11, 2008), http://www.w3.org/TR/WCAG20/
10. Windows: Turn on High Contrast, http://windows.microsoft.com/en-us/windows7/turn-on-high-contrast

Easy to Surf - What Makes Websites Accessible to People with Intellectual and Learning Disabilities

A Study Resulting in Prototypical Guidelines

Gabriela Antener[1], Anton Bolfing[2], and Stefania Calabrese[1]

[1] University of Applied Sciences and Arts Northwestern Switzerland FHNW,
School of Social Work, Institute Integration and Participation, Olten, Switzerland
{gabriela.antener,stefania.calabrese}@fhnw.ch
[2] Stiftung «Zugang für alle», Schweizerische Stiftung zur behindertengerechten
Technologienutzung, Zurich, Switzerland
anton.bolfing@access-for-all.ch

Abstract. Special needs of intellectually and mentally challenged people are generally not considered in ICT, not even in exemplary accessible websites. In this paper we reveal our scientific approach on how to develop guidelines closing this gap. We describe the process of extracting relevant and easy-to-understand directives from scientific literature addressing different aspects of user interfaces and different cognitive abilities. Considerations on how to further develop and improve these beta guidelines and on how to implement the gained insights in the World Wide Web are discussed.

Keywords: Intellectual Disability, Learning Disability, Guidelines, Projects, Development, E-Inclusion, Evaluation, Accessible Websites, Need for Development and Research.

1 Introduction

Compared to normal population, persons with intellectual and learning disabilities are detained from getting web access in many ways. We suppose that they have restricted access to devices with internet access (i.e. no wifi in residential accommodation, restricted personal budget with no or little means for electronic devices); little media competence (i.e. lack of media education and experience, lack of peer support) problems to handle the devices; problems to use the information available in the internet because of illiteracy, problems with navigation and problems with display of information.

The internet demands a lot of prerequisites to participate. People with intellectual and learning disabilities are disadvantaged due to reduced financial means, reduced intellectual abilities, insufficient education and a lack of websites optimized and adapted for this target group. (Matausch et al. 2012, Einfach für alle 2011, Berger et al. 2010; Bohman 2007).

K. Miesenberger et al. (Eds.): ICCHP 2014, Part I, LNCS 8547, pp. 157–160, 2014.
© Springer International Publishing Switzerland 2014

2   The Project

Easy-to-Surf lays a foundation for continuing initiatives and projects in Switzerland. Need for research, action and development are subjects of the project. Therefore the project is split in two parts.

A systematic capture of the issue allows the definition of relevant aspects and future work to be done. The review of scientific findings und publications leads to an overview about planned, ongoing and finished research, projects and initiatives in Switzerland and abroad. These findings are used to develop guidelines for accessible websites and to define the need for further research and development.

2.1   Literature Research

At the moment, there are almost no guidelines nor instructions available for organizations intending to provide accessible websites for people with intellectual and learning disabilities. The WCAG 2.0 guidelines do not, or only marginally, take into account the special demands and needs of these people and are therefore not sufficient for this target group. There is a necessity to develop relatively simple and clear guidelines for website suppliers and webmasters in order to make their websites accessible and thereby enhance the participation of people with intellectual disabilities in the inter-net. (Einfach für alle 2011; Karreman et al. 2007; Bohman 2007).

These guidelines must consider not only the users functional characteristics (i.e. problems or differences in perception and processing of information, literacy, language comprehension, visual comprehension, memory, problem solving, action planning, attention, communication and interaction with others). But they must also take into account different kinds of using the internet and different types of barriers (i.e. technical, editorial, content, design, organizational). (Einfach für alle 2011, Ellies and Kent 2011, Inclusion Europe n.d.; Karreman et al. 2007).

2.2   The Guidelines

As a scientific fundament for the first prototype of our guidelines we come back to the literature studies presented in the previous section. The findings regarding functional characteristics of the users have mainly been used for identifying the most relevant cognitive aspects for ICT-consumption and interaction: thinking, memory, attention, perception, language and communication. Here, it turned out that all aspects of perceiving and interacting with websites can be subsumed by nine user interface categories: language/text, font design, content area design, navigation/orientation, interaction/forms, layout design, images/multimedia, help/assistance and privacy protection.

Each relevant text passage from the literature studies was now assigned to one or more of the six and nine categories identified. Following this approach we managed to represent the whole complex of problems as a matrix of the two dimensions 'cognitive abilities' and 'user interface aspects'. This representation as a matrix allows narrowing down the search regarding special needs, being a web developer, a content author or a caretaker who wants to know what solution fits best the needs of the target group.

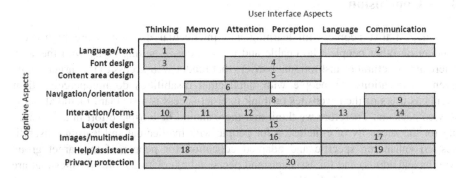

Fig. 1. Schematic presentation of the 20 guideline recommendations assigned to the two dimensions Cognitive Aspects and user Interface Aspects

The Guidelines exist in a preliminary beta version which is in evaluation now. The evaluation encompasses the implementation of at least three test websites and the feedback from the responsible webmasters according to the comprehensibility and applicability of the guidelines. It also includes user tests with people belonging to the target group. The testing will be conducted by means of the thinking-aloud-method and TalkingMats – an AAC communication framework that enables people with communication or intellectual disabilities to express their views (Murphy/Cameron 2005).The evaluation results in a revised version of the easy-to-surf guidelines which are planned to be published and spread in late 2014.

3   Exploitation

Accessibility requirements after WCAG 2.0 generally affect html source code and, with the exception of minimum contrast ratios, have no implications on web design flexibility. As it can be seen in our guidelines, this does not apply to accessibility requirements regarding cognitive impairments.

Any strategy to spread our findings in the World Wide Web must distinguish between essential requirements for general low-threshold, easy-to-use interaction and specific requirements for different specific and usually more severely cognitive impaired people. The first requirements apply to all websites including online shops, e-banking etc. and are addressing people with foreign language, poor literacy skills or learning disabilities as well as elderly people. The last more specific requirements apply to specific target groups such as community platforms of services and facilities for people with more severe impairments. For these groups our guidelines will cover the most important aspects, but it is indispensable to adapt and optimize them for specific groups together with the future users and their caretakers. However, both aspects can be included in ICT accessibility consulting.

4   Conclusion

We suggest that people with learning and intellectual disabilities are highly dependent on other people who enable and assist them in getting along with the web. There are structural or institutional barriers that hinder web-access to the target group. Even organizations for people with intellectual disabilities do not perceive their clients as users of their websites or think internet-access is a standard included in the service package. Therefore we think that there should be a triple effort in a) sensitizing for the necessity of e-inclusion for people with intellectual and learning disabilities, b) enhancing specific and adapted education for people of the target group (youths and adults) and for assistants and peers and c) creating more websites that are interesting and accessible for the target-group.

References

1. Berger, A., et al.: Web 2.0/barrierefrei. Eine Studie zur Nutzung von Web 2.0 Anwendungen durch Menschen mit Behinderung, http://publikationen.aktion-mensch.de/barrierefrei/Studie_Web_2.0.pdf
2. Bohman, P.R.: Web Accessibility for Cognitive and Learning Disabilities: A Review of Research-Based Evidence in the Literature (2007),
   http://www.digitalaccessibility.org/accessibility/cognitive/litreview2007
3. Einfach für alle, Das Angebot der Aktion Mensch für ein barrierefreies Internet – Web Content Accessibility Guidelines (2011),
   http://www.einfach-fuer-alle.de/wcag2.0
4. Ellies, K., Kent, M.: Disability and New Media. Routledge, New York (2011)
5. Karreman, J., Van der Geest, T., Buursink, E.: Accessible Website Content Guidelines for Users with Intellectual Disabilities. Journal of Applied Research in Intellectual Disabilities 20, 510–518 (2007)
6. Kelly, B., et al.: Accessibility 2.0: Next Steps for Web Accessibility. Journal of Access Services 6(1-2), 265–294 (2009)
7. Matausch, K., Peböck, B., Pühretmair, F.: Accessible Content Generation an Integral Part of Accessible Web Design. Procedia Computer Science 14, 274–282 (2012)
8. Murphy, J., Cameron, L.: The effectiveness of Talking Mats with people with intellectual disabilities. British Journal of Learning Disabilities 36(4), 232–241 (2008)

"Easy-to-Read on the Web": State of the Art and Needed Research

Klaus Miesenberger and Andrea Petz

Institute Integriert Studieren, University of Linz, Linz, Austria
{klaus.miesenberger,andrea.petz}@jku.at

Abstract. In this paper, we present results from work done within the project WAI-Act and an online-symposium [1] initiated and put in place by the W3C/WAI RDWG (Research and Development Working Group) aiming at raising awareness and collecting / de-riving concise and up-to-date recommendations, guidelines, standards and tools for enhancing the web experience for users with cognitive disabilities and other groups facing problems with "standard" information on the Web and its applications.

Keywords: Easy to Read, Web, Cognitive Disability, SPLD, Inclusion.

1   Introduction

Research on "Easy to Read on the Web" addresses the needs of user groups whose needs are beyond requirements more related to the accessibility of the technical infrastructure and "legibility" in terms of being able to reach and get hold of information. Over the last decades (as W3C/WAI will celebrate 25 years of web accessibility in 2014), the needs of users with physical or sensory disabilities formed the foundation of most research and development activities in web accessibility leading to a profound body of knowledge in web accessibility including recommendations, guidelines, standards, legislation and tools.

The last years, aspects like content design, structure, wording in use and "Easy-to-Read on the Web" became more important. Aspects supporting readability, legibility, understandability and "memorability" for people with cognitive disabilities, people with learning disabilities and other user groups facing problems with standard wording and information design became more important.

As our daily lives get more and more globalized with a growing number of citizens on the move and/or with migration background, these aspects became important also for a more mainstream audience – as well as considerations concerning the usability of information outside someone´s expertise. "Easy to Read on the Web" is understood as a key factor to make oneself informed, understood and getting/staying in touch with people, clients and customers.

2   State of the Art

Even without this opening to the mainstream audience, the definition of 'the' target group benefitting from "Easy to Read on the Web" is a complex, if not impossible

K. Miesenberger et al. (Eds.): ICCHP 2014, Part I, LNCS 8547, pp. 161–168, 2014.
© Springer International Publishing Switzerland 2014

task due to the broad variety of reasons which might lead to reduced reading and understanding skills and the diverse needs resulting from them:

- People with cognitive disabilities related to functionality such as [2]
  - Memory / Problem solving (conceptualizing, planning, sequencing, reasoning and judging thoughts and actions)
  - Attention (Attention-Deficit / Hyperactivity Disorder - ADHD) and awareness
  - Reading, linguistic, and verbal comprehension (Dyslexia)
  - Visual Perception and Comprehension
  - Mental health disorders
- People with low language skills incl. people who are not fluent in a language [3]
- People with auditory disabilities impacting reading / perception of written content [3]

There is common understanding that besides for these primary groups, Easy to Read significantly contributes to the more general concept of usability in terms of ISO 9241-11 [4] "the extent to which a product can be used by specified users to achieve specified goals with effectiveness, efficiency, and satisfaction in a specified context of use.", dealing with learnability, memorability, error prevention and handling, guessability, trust, safety, security, privacy and satisfaction.

Common denominator of all these concepts is the importance of language use and thereby recommendations and guidelines contributing to an increased general usability, whereas Plain Language is a concept and area addressing these aspects in a more mainstream oriented Web usability context.

The more ICT becomes part of our everyday lives, the more the impact of usability has to be taken into account. There is evidence that Plain Language and Easy to Read significantly contribute to usability in general and impact on users much beyond the primary groups outlined above.

Concerning persons depending on Easy to Read or Plain Language, international studies outline that in most (also highly industrialized) countries every fourth adult does not reach the reading skills expected after nine years of formal education. In several countries, this figure is as high as 40-50 percent [5].

Combined with the globalization aspects from before, this demands for information that is usable and readable cross borders and cultures as well as understood by the biggest possible user group. Political initiatives and according legislation aiming at fostering the equal participation of people with disabilities and the aging population and beyond are other drivers for increased accessibility and usability and in particular for better readability for all user groups. "Easy-to-Read on the Web" matches with this demand and expands it towards the requirements for people with cognitive disabilities and other user groups experiencing problems with the language in use and information presentation on the Web in a globalised context – underlined by the UN-Convention on the Rights of People with Disabilities [6] and a growing number of international and national legislation.

3   Methodology and Results

Web Accessibility provides a profound body of knowledge emphasizing a more technical focus allowing people to adapt the display and interaction on standard and assistive devices. Quality aspects in terms of a content´s readability, understandability, memorability and usability seemed to be postponed, even if general statements underline the key role of "Easy to Read on the Web", but this is not accordingly reflected in the recommendations, guidelines, standards and tools. [7]

Furthermore, the development follows a possible natural trend which is not specific to web accessibility for people with disabilities following Looms [8] presenting a hierarchical structure of domains in his "inclusion pyramid of digital media" amongst

1. Availability
2. Accessibility
3. Usability
4. Digital literacy

Although all aspects have to be addressed to reach accessibility and usability in a holistic and not only technical sense, availability and accessibility, what matches with the mentioned aspect of access in a more technical sense of getting hold of the information, is prior, as the later can only be based on prior ones. Following this the mainstream term and concept of usability, includes and puts emphasis on aspects like [27]:

- Effectiveness,
- Efficiency,
- Learnability / guessability (intuitive use),
- Memorability,
- Error rates,
- Safety, security, privacy, trust,
- Reliability,
- Satisfaction,

going beyond a pure technical level of access to content and questions if users are enabled to reach their goals in an easy and appropriate manner. It is evident that the focus on usability followed the basic attempts to provide access in a more technical sense. In particular today when ICT and the Web are a global phenomenon and are of importance for almost anybody and in almost any context of our lives.

Taking up this broader sense of accessibility in terms of also implementing usability, W3C/WAI went beyond a primarily technical access to content and interface elements with the concept of "usable accessibility" [9]. Furthermore. WCAG2.0 demand for making content and Web pages understandable as the third of four principles - further detailed in guidelines and techniques for making content readable and understandable.

4   Conclusions and Next Steps

Activities follow the line of distinguishing and separating between the two concepts of Plain Language and Easy to Read in terms of what can be asked from any author or content provider and what has to be done by specialized services. The analysis provided is seen as a first step to come to more targeted recommendations, guidelines, standards and tools for both domains of practice concerning: [27]

4.1   Awareness

Experience and research on the state of the art reveal the necessity of increased awareness for the importance and need for both: Plain Language for a more general understandability and usability and Easy to Read as a specialized and individualized adaptation service for specific user groups. Benefits for users, service providers, business and society have to be quantified and need specific attention to come up with more compelling arguments for the implementation of Easy to Read on the Web.

4.2   User Needs

Both Plain Language and Easy to Read are sets of recommendations and guidelines supporting authors or translators based on a sound understanding of "the user" in terms of "the reader". For both domains it becomes evident that there is a strong need for tools supporting practice (end users as well as service providers publishing information and authors, designers, developers, owners and also providers of specialized services - translators). [9]

4.3   Guidelines

First sets of elaborated rules, guidelines and recommendations on Plain Language and Easy to Read exist. Some first approaches, tools, and heuristics are available. [10,11,12,13].

Multimedia elements get more important – also because of the availability of flexible and affordable end user devices – enriching the quality and understandability of content and interaction for Easy to Read as well as Plain language. First sets of recommendations and guidelines to support the integration of multimedia elements into text to enrich usability and user experience are available. [14]

Mainstream research areas share similar goals or include complementary development efforts. For example, research in Web usability contributed considerably to the concept of Plain Language and the development of different methods and tools to measure (technical) readability, e.g. Flesch Reading Ease, Wiener Sachtextformel, SMOG or FOG. [15] These domains also provide a wide spectrum of guidelines and methods comprising design guidelines for homepage usability [16] and international user interfaces [17]. Considerable potential in supporting Easy-to-Read on the Web [18] can be found in research activities dealing with "text normalization".

With all these activities, investigations regarding overlap (and contradiction) of general Web usability with the needs of the target groups need further research before profound integration of Plain Language and Easy to Read into WCAG 2.0 and other WAI activities (e.g. ATAG and UAAG) can take place.

4.4 Implementation Tools

Large scale implementation of Easy to Read on the Web or Plain Language asks for efficient tools supporting developers, designers and content providers. These tools in best case allow a seamless integration into every day working or development environments making Plain Language feasible for the mainstream and Easy to Read more efficient and widespread.

Work originating from other domains such as linguistics and language technologies, including Natural Language Processing (NLP) are potential facilitators making significant progress in grammar and style-checking (or "Controlled Language" [19]), translation [20], annotation and enhancement [21], and summarizing. [22, 23]

Research and tools have been developed to support content authors and users, and there is mutual benefit of further investigating the deployment of these tools in the domain of Plain Language and Easy to Read: [27]

- Enriching content with acronyms, alternative expressions, images and multi-media: Plain language and Easy to Read on the Web addressed first the design and use of text but also goes beyond making use of alternative ways of information representation. Research and development in Augmentative and Alternative Communication (AAC as well as CAA) provides a related set of resources on user requirements, guidelines, methods, techniques and tools for accessing information and the use of language in written or audio format, including symbol systems and symbolic languages [24]. As described above, concepts like Natural Language Processing [25] deriving from research and development for people with speech disabilities showed high potential to impact the needs of "our" target groups.
- Text-audio integration: Following research, written information is causing most accessibility / usability problems for our target groups. For them, switching from written format to audio might considerably increase accessibility.
- Access to written information: Access for blind and partially sighted people as well as people with other disabilities like dyslexia significantly progressed over the last years. The possibility to switch to audio or to use both formats in parallel and adaptation features also considerably contribute to Easy to Read on the Web. Assistive Technologies meant for visually impaired persons (e.g. TTS, screen reader, enlargement, audio description) and systems/ services making information accessible contribute to Easy-to-Read on the Web.
- Captioning: Captioning was designed to translate an audio or video source in different languages, but also for persons with sensory disabilities. These services have a profound potential for our target groups when descriptions, dynamic information and texts are displayed following principles of Easy-to-Read. This includes recommendations and guidelines e.g. regarding length, display, structuring,... [15]

- Designing layout to meet user requirements: Research in text customization showed high potential for enhancing readability and understandability.

Tools that provide broad selections of functionalities supporting the user to implement the above options range from automated or supported: [27]

- Analysis and checking tools ("readability evaluation") over
- Integration and adaptation of assistive functionalities such as text and layout adjustment ("Text Customization") and easy to understand audio playback towards
- Translation of information into Easy to Read text and
- Annotation with alternative cues like synonyms, explanations, definitions, symbols, pictures and other multi-media resources from e.g. cloud-based services to
- Translation into standardized or individually developed symbol/picture systems or languages based on infrastructures like the Concept Coding Framework [26]

Working on a shared and re-usable open source framework for creating a set of tools is seen as a viable way towards an efficient implementation and support of Easy to Read and Plain Language in practice. Bringing these concepts to prototype level would demonstrate their feasibility; allow user evaluations and product development.

Needed activities include adaptations and refinements of functionalities of Assistive Technologies (AT) towards the needs of people with cognitive disabilities. Text to Speech (TTS), Screen Readers, screen adaptation functionalities or Augmented and Alternative Communication solutions (AAC) then could be part of Plain Language and Easy to Read tools. Existing functionalities of the OS or browsers might also support users with cognitive disabilities – research and awareness raising is needed.

Furthermore, tools supporting to keep a necessary workflow provide guidance on how to implement Plain Language and even more Easy to Read to reach the goal of an accessible and usable Web experience. Due to the diversity of issues addressed, there is clear evidence that the set of already available recommendations, guidelines, techniques and tools, but also future developments should integrate into a one stop user experience providing efficient guidance and support to users, evaluators, designers, developers, content providers, Easy to Read service / support providers and any other stakeholders. This should be accompanied by a collection of examples and templates raising understanding and making concepts clearer and easier to follow.

4.5   Education and Getting Used to the Web

The Web provides a broad range of interaction, communication paradigms and means to access content and services. To increase the level of accessibility, research is needed on how educational and support programs (also in AT) allow our target groups to access the web more efficiently and independently. The implementation of any Easy to Read standards and tools needs education, "show case examples", best practice and "up and running" offers, e.g. in social media, online shops, and blogs.

4.6   Design and Easy to Read

Easy to Read should be part of a holistic Web experience. Aspects and components of "usable web accessibility" such as language use, design, layout, navigation and their relation to Easy to Read have to be discussed. Therefore Easy to Read has to be analyzed following to what extent it is linked with the basic layout and the used / implemented navigation elements / navigation possibilities of a website. The final question must be if - and if yes, to what extent elaborated accessibility rules and guidelines (e.g. no fixed fonts and font sizes) support or interfere with the requirements of groups using Easy to Read has to be taken into account.

4.7   Transferability

The Web is a global phenomenon and tool and therefore readability and Easy to Read have to be addressed accordingly. The diverse range of different requirements and needs of people with cognitive disabilities as well as national languages/linguistics and social / cultural conditions ask for research activities on if and how far common recommendations, guidelines, standards and tools like those provided by W3C/WAI can meet with real life and whether an international approach to Plain Language and Easy to Read is possible or not.

References

1. Research Report on Easy to Read on the Web,
   http://www.w3.org/WAI/RD/2012/easy-to-read/
2. WebAIM, http://webaim.org/articles/cognitive/
3. W3C/WAI, Diversity of the Web, http://www.w3.org/WAI/intro/
   people-use-web/diversity#learning
4. International standards for HCI and usability,
   http://www.usabilitynet.org/tools/
   r_international.htm#9241-1x
5. International Adult Literacy Surveys (IALS),
   http://www.oecd.org/education/innovation-
   education/39437980.pdf
6. UN Convention on the Rights of Persons with Disabilities,
   http://www.un.org/disabilities/convention/
   conventionfull.shtml
7. WebAIM: Evaluating Cognitive Web Accessibility,
   http://webaim.org/articles/evaluatingcognitive
8. Looms, P.O.: Design Models for Media Accessibility. Chinese Journal of Design (2012)
9. Usable Web Accessibility, http://www.icchp.org/node/234
10. Sbattella, L., Tedesco, R.: The authoring of highly accessible texts. In: Proceedings of Adaptive Content Processing Conference (ACP 2008), Amsterdam, Netherlands, Paper 4 (2008)
11. W3C/WAI: G153,
    http://www.w3.org/TR/2012/NOTE-WCAG20-TECHS-20120103/G153

12. European Standards for making information Easy-to-Read and understand, http://cop.health-rights.org/files/c/1/c1fbaaeb17db47800782d8721bd8b0db.pdf
13. Guidelines for easy to read materials, http://www.ifla.org/files/assets/hq/publications/professional-report/120.pdf
14. The Principles of readability, http://almacenplantillasweb.es/wp-content/uploads/2009/11/The-Principles-of-Readability.pdf
15. Mikk, J.: Textbook Research and Writing. Lang, Frankfurt (2000)
16. Nielsen, J., Tahir, M.: Homepage Usability: 50 Websites Deconstructed. New Riders, Indianapolis (2002)
17. Nielsen, J.: International User Interfaces. Wiley, Chichester (1996)
18. Han, B., Baldwin, B.: Lexical normalisation of short text messages: Makn sens a #twitter. In: Proceedings of the 49th Annual Meeting of the ACL HLT, pp. 368–378. Stroudsburg, Pennsylvania (2011)
19. Fuchs, N.E. (ed.): CNL 2009. LNCS, vol. 5972. Springer, Heidelberg (2010)
20. Chiang, D.: Grammars for Language and Genes. Springer series in Theory and Applications of Natural Language Processing. Springer, Heidelberg (2012)
21. Nikolova, S., Boyd-Graber, J., Fellbaum, C.: Collecting Semantic Similarity Ratings to Connect Concepts in Assistive Communication Tools. In: Mehler, A., Kühnberger, K.-U., Lobin, H., Lüngen, H., Storrer, A., Witt, A., et al. (eds.) Modeling, Learning, and Proc. of Text-Tech. Data Struct. SCI, vol. 370, pp. 81–93. Springer, Heidelberg (2011)
22. Hovy, E.: Automated Text Summarization. In: Mitkov, R. (ed.) The Oxford Handbook of Computational Linguistics, pp. 583–598. Oxford University Press, Oxford (2005)
23. Nenkova, A., McKeown, K.: A Survey of Text Summarization Techniques. In: Aggarwal, C.C., Zhai, C.X. (eds.) Mining Text Data, pp. 43–76. Springer, Heidelberg (2012), doi:10.1007/978-1-4614-3223-4_1
24. Fager, S., et al.: Access to augmentative and alternative communication: New technologies and clinical decision-making. Journal of Pediatric Rehabilitation Medicine 5(1) (2012)
25. Higginbotham, D.J., Lesher, G.W., Moulton, B.J., Roark, B.: The Application of Natural Language Processing to AAC. Assistive Technology: The Official Journal of RESNA 24(1), 14–24 (2012)
26. Lundälv, M., Derbring, S.: Towards General Cross-Platform CCF Based Multi-Modal Language Support. In: Miesenberger, K., Karshmer, A., Penaz, P., Zagler, W. (eds.) ICCHP 2012, Part II. LNCS, vol. 7383, pp. 261–268. Springer, Heidelberg (2012)
27. Miesenberger, K., Petz, A.: Easy to Read on the Web – State of the Art and Research Directions. In: DSAI 2013. Procedia Computer Science, vol. 27, pp. 318–326. Elsevier (2014)

Testing the Perceived Ease of Use in Social Media

Acceptance Testing for People with Intellectual and Cognitive Disabilities

Julia George, Nils Dietzsch, Michael Bier, Hannes Zirpel, Alexander Perl,
and Susanne Robra-Bissantz

Departement for Information Systems,
University of Braunschweig Institute of Technology, Braunschweig, Germany
{j.george,n.dietzsch,m.bier,h.zirpel,a.perl,
s.robra-bissantz}@tu-braunschweig.de

Abstract. In the last few years, social media spread around the globe. Being a substantial and integral part in today's everyday life of many people, especially online social networks (OSNs) changed communication behavior fundamentally. Unfortunately, not everybody is integrated in this "new everyday life" yet. In our research, we focus on this important issue of e-inclusion and participation of people with intellectual disabilities in social media. In the context of this paper, we will present a methodology on how to evaluate the perceived ease of use of social media applications by people with intellectual disability. Moreover, we will pre-validate this methodology by applying it in a test setting with a customized barrier-free OSN, developed in our research group. This is the first step for developing a target group specific acceptance model, based on the technology acceptance model.

Keywords: Acceptance Testing, Online Social Networks, Experiment, Triangulation.

1 Introduction

The International Classification for Functioning, Disability and Health (ICF) provides a method to describe and classify aspects of health status and health-related terms. According to ICF, the existence of a disability is based on personal and environmental factors. Participation is a fundamental environmental factor of health and is defined as "involvement in a life situation". Limitations in participation describe problems a person encounters in daily life situations. Environmental factors can either reduce the influences of a disability (facilitators) or increase them (barriers). [1]

Environmental factors are, as specified by the ICF, for instance also "products and technologies for communication" (e125), [2] which also includes OSNs such as Facebook or Google+. And these have fundamentally changed today's communication behavior and social life. [3]

K. Miesenberger et al. (Eds.): ICCHP 2014, Part I, LNCS 8547, pp. 169–176, 2014.

But according our own experience, participation of people with special needs in OSNs is still often limited. Whereas there exists a bandwidth of resources supporting physically disabled people in using the internet and social media (e.g. screen readers, virtual keyboards or eye-tracking systems), intellectual disabilities affect such a wide area that standard methods supporting their special needs while using social media applications cannot be found yet. [4] Thus our research group started to develop a specialised OSN. The questions we want to answer with this paper: How can we know, whether people with intellectual disabilities will use it? Especially how can we investigate whether the target group finds the system to be easy to use?

2   Reference Implementation

During the pre-testing phase of our research work we developed several test web pages to analyse the effect of different web-designs and concepts relating to the use of icons and buttons, different graphical designs and structural concepts for a barrier-free OSN. According to our pre-testing results and in line with the Web Content Accessibility Guidelines (WCAG 2.0) [5] we built a reference implementation of an OSN for people with an intellectual and/or cognitive disability such as text blindness, learning disability, or dysgraphia. Hereby, we chose a certain design of buttons, a standard webpage structure as well as a layout logic, which proved to be the most accepted approach during the pre-testing phase.

3   Acceptance Testing

To date and the authors' knowledge there exists no established methodology to verify the usefulness and quality of information systems, much less of OSNs, for people with intellectual and cognitive disabilities. But such a tool would help researchers and developers alike to predict and explain system use. [6] Having detailed knowledge of both factors would foster e-inclusive applications and their spread amongst users. In order to develop such a methodology we rely on the, in information systems research well established, Technology Acceptance Model (TAM) by DAVIS [7]. The general methodology for applying TAM is to acquire test persons who have direct or indirect experiences with the new technology and investigate different constructs including the Perceived Ease of Use (PEoU) and Perceived Usefulness (PU). Each construct is supposed to be tested by four to six questions that have been tested for validity, rigour and significance of impact on the users' technology acceptance. [7]

3.1   Constraints in Acceptance Testing for People with Intellectual Disabilities

The TAM in general is applicable to the case at hand. But its items cannot be implemented in the way they were originally designed. As the constraints are numerous and there exists no research so far, we will focus on the construct of PEoU in this paper. Following general issues with respect to intellectual disabilities are addressed:

- Performing a PEoU analysis requires experienced participants concerning the assessed technology, who complete a questionnaire after using the system in focus. As our target group has a lack of experience concerning OSNs it is necessary to give them the possibility to get in touch with the tested application. Furthermore, the target group often has limited access to information technology, which makes web based studies difficult. Thus, an onsite experimental setup is necessary.
- Although TAM is based on the test persons' perception of the investigated system and draws its conclusions towards acceptance and future system use from it, we realize that our target group is very heterogeneous in computer and internet experience which likely results in very heterogeneous interpretations of the concept of ease of use. To be able to analyze, and if necessary account for, these effects more objectively, technical measurements should be collected.
- To deal with participant specific and individual characteristics qualitative information sources, such as additional remarks and observations from the researchers, should be included in the experimental design. Especially we propose the Observed Ease of Use (OEoU), which represents the researchers' observation of the participants' ease of use during the experiment.

Fig. 1. Scale selection tool for finger pointing during an interview (original width about 15 cm) [authors' development]

Additionally, experience shows that it is difficult for our target group to differentiate between fine-grained scale values. For this reason we used a scale selection tool (see Fig. 1), which had been developed within our research group: The study participant was invited to point a finger at the scale section where he or she considered most appropriate. For the researcher the scale represented 5 distinct values.[1]

3.2   TAM-Based Perceived Ease of Use Assessment Methodology

Our first part of a TAM-based methodology is designed to perform a structured evaluation of the PEoU of social media applications by people with an intellectual and cognitive disability. The PU is collected too, but will not be further analyzed within this paper. Based on the assumptions above the experiment is structured in four phases:

1. Introduction: The study starts with an introduction phase creating a pleasant atmosphere for the following dialogue and experimental phase.
2. Testing the PU: For assessing the PU, the participant is asked how much he likes / would like using OSNs, such as facebook, to keep contact to friends and family.

---

[1] (Sad smiley) extremely unlikely | unlikely | (neutral smiley) neither | likely | extremely likely (happy smiley), or scale labels corresponding to the construct at hand.

3. Testing for the PEoU: This part of the analysis focuses on investigating the PEoU of our reference implementation by presenting four specific scenarios. During the experiment the time and clicks as well as the help needed to complete the scenarios are recorded. After each scenario the participant reveals his own PEoU by using the scale selection tool and the researcher team records its OEoU.
4. Re-Assessment PU: A final re-assessment of the PU will determine potential changes in the participants' perception after using the specialized OSN.

In general we propose using triangular study techniques by observing the participants while working on scenarios, analyzing their answers on our questions and simultaneously collecting quantitative data. Our general triangulation design can be ascribed to the so-called "within-method", which stipulates using a method-mix in order to test and validate the same construct [8]. This approach can help to further qualify the assessed PEoU and thus rigidify the assessment overall.

4   Designing the Pre-validation of the Perceived Ease of Use Assessment

4.1   Setup of the Pre-validation Experiment

With a first experiment we pre-validate our approach of assessing the PEoU of people with intellectual disabilities. We used Tablets to accommodate a quick learning curve for the usage of a computational device and therefore eliminate possible constraints due to e.g., the lack of competence in the usage of a mouse.

After getting a brief introduction into the research project and a simple explanation of OSNs in general, one by one participant sat together with two researchers. Whereas on of the latter embodied the experimental guide, who led through the experiment and offered help where needed, the second researcher observed the participant and protocolled all data. The technical measures were recorded automatically.

4.2   Hypotheses and Mixed Method Design for the Pre-validation

To be able to validate the PEoU we used a special setup of test scenarios. In step 3 during the experiment we alternately presented scenarios with optimised (A) and non-optimised (B) representations of our OSN. For the non-optimised version we intentionally ignored the basics of web accessibility. We assume that following web accessibility guidelines leads to more accessible applications and thus to a higher PEoU of the users. Therefore there should emerge significant differences with the comparison of these expected outcomes (less acceptance for non-optimised OSN). In order to have data on both OSN types we separated the participants into two groups in which we started the alternation differently (A-B-A-B | B-A-B-A). Thus the first hypothesis accounts for the validation of the outcome of the PEoU measurement:

- H1: Our method shows a significant difference in the PEoU of the participants between the optimised and the complex version of our OSN.

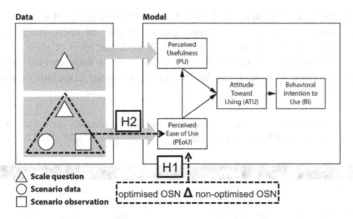

Fig. 2. Overview of the TAM (right) [based on [7]] and the in the proposed methodology acquired data (left), overlaid with the research hypotheses from this paper

Furthermore, the original PEoU's items demand a rather high level of abstraction.[2] In order to avoid overstimulation of the participants' motivation and cognitive load we reduced the PEoU's items to one. But as the original items are intended to cross-validate each other, we needed to add validation measurements for the PEoU construct. We thus on the one hand, measured the time, clicks and help needed by each participant to complete each scenario. On the other hand we had the observer and researcher record their observation of the participants' ease of use, the OEoU and further remarks. Thus the second hypothesis constitutes:

- H2: The OEoU, the additional recorded remarks, the measurements of the click efficiency and the amount of time taken as well as the amount of help given to complete a task help to qualify the answers given on the PEoU by the participants.

5   Evaluation and Hypothesis Testing

5.1   Pre-conditions and Variable Analysis

Overall we had 42 participants (and corresponding demographic data), who helped to generate 168 datasets on the 4 scenarios that each of them worked on (see Table 1).

We cannot finally validate the approach undertaken with the scale selection tool due to an often occurring three polar distribution[3] of the values.

According the on-going discussion about the data type of scales overall, we chose to treat the values on PEoU, OEoU, reading, computer and internet skill to be ordinal. [9] The Kolmogorov-Smirnov-Test on all concerning parameters[4] showed significant at a 99% confidence level, which means they are not normally distributed.

---

[2] The original items by DAVIS include "My interaction with the system would be clear and understandable", "I would find the system to be flexible to interact with" [6].

[3] Only the extreme values and the middle of the scale were chosen.

[4] (Time, clicks and age).

Thus overall the Mann-Withney-U-Test will be used for testing on significant differences and Spearman's Rank Correlation Test for testing on interconnections within the dataset. We chose to rely only on the high confidence level of 99%, as the mentioned tests on ordinal scales cannot be as reliable as tests with interval data. For the same reason we were looking for at least moderately strong correlations (correlation coefficient higher than 0,4).

Table 1. Variables used in this paper: Variables within 168 datasets on overall 4 scenarios (left), variables on each of 42 participants (right)

variable	datatype		variable	datatype
PEoU	Ordinal		Age	Ratio
OEoU	Ordinal		Computer skill	Ordinal
Time taken for task completion	Ratio		Reading skill	Ordinal
Clicks taken for task completion	Interval		Internet Skill	Ordinal
Group (A-B-A-B|B-A-B-A)	Grouping variable (1,2)		Supplementary remarks	Qualitative
OSN type (complex|optimised)	Grouping variable (1,2)			
Amount of help needed	Interval			

Testing for H1. In order to accept H1 we presuppose a significant difference in the PEoU between the non-optimised and optimised OSN. As we recorded the supporting variables time, clicks, help needed and OEoU we also considered these for analysis. But the Mann-Whitney-U-Test does only show significant differences in the OEoU.[5] H1 therefore cannot be accepted. We could not finally prove, that our PEoU items and supporting data really reflect the participants' perceived ease of use.

Although we were confident, that the design modifications would be reflected in the PEoU we cannot prove this with the data. As we did not want to risk the participants' frustration during the experiment we did not intentionally make the non-optimised OSN difficult by implementing stumbling blocks, for example supplementary pop-up windows or similar. Only the observers obviously made a significant difference between ease of use of both OSNs.[6] But as time and click values are not significantly different this phenomenon could be traced to the fact, that the observers simply expected that there would be a difference in the ease of use.

In consequence we analysed all 168 datasets together for the approval of H2, as both OSNs are being evaluated as being equally easy to handle by the participants.

Testing for H2. For testing H2 we considered the variables time, clicks, help count, OEoU and PEoU in a Spearman correlation analysis. There are overall seven significant correlations: three weak (lower or equal to 0,4) two moderately strong and two strong correlations (correlation coefficient higher than 0,7). One expected correlation is the moderately strong connection between time and clicks.

The correlation between the OEoU and the PEoU is rather low (correlation coefficient of 0,351). This effect will be further detailed in following paragraphs.

---

[5] The Mann-Withney-U-Test showed low significance, confidence level 95%, in help needed.
[6] The help count only shows different at a 95% confidence level.

Additionally, weak ties are found between the help count and PEoU (correlation coefficient 0,252) as well as time and PEoU (0,400). There is no connection between PEoU and clicks. Which leads to the assumption that participants don't consider the factors time, clicks and help as being very relevant for the ease of use.[7]

The strong correlations between the factors time and amount of help and the OEoU are explicable because the observer expects these factors to influence the ease of use and can easily observe them. The correlation between the OEoU and clicks is not as strong.[8] Due to the ordinal nature of the OEoU we cannot compute a regression. But as the time and clicks are not influenced by the observer and the OEoU is assessed after each scenario and therefore after giving support to a participant the causality can assumed to be: When time, clicks or help increase the OEoU drops.

In general our research group aims at developing an OSN that is easy to use without additional help. Therefore the amount of support that a user needs to complete a task is relevant for the ease of use score. We also think, that the click efficiency is an important determinant for the ease of use, as each click in a wrong menu caters the chances of clicking the wrong actionable item and therefore, e.g., publish content in the OSN that was not intend for publishing and thus possibly frustration.[9] The OEoU seems to account for these measures.

A supplementary core question that arose during the analysis of the qualitative data, and comparing it with the results of the PEoU, is the one after the authenticity of the answers given by the participants. A central indicator for a partial lack of authenticity could be the participants' self-assessment of their reading and writing skills. Especially for the latter we could observe a rather large difference between the participants' answers and reality. For example many answered being able to write very well. But during a task that involved writing they needed a lot of help[10] with writing words or could not write at all. Of course the question after the reading and writing skills is a very private one and it might be difficult to answer authentically. But couldn't it also be difficult to tell us, that our system is not easy to use? These and other similar cases lead to the assumption that the PEoU scores cannot be used without further assessment. In many cases though we can observe that the answer on the ease of use seems to be authentic. Looking at it in general, there is a mean difference of 0,75 scale grades between the PEoU and the OEoU. This can on the one hand be explained through the lower influence of above-mentioned determinants, but also in referencing qualitative observations. The goal in H2 of qualifying the PEoU with supplementary data can partially be accepted.

We propose to record the OEoU alongside the PEoU, which will give the researcher the opportunity to probably explain differences in the PEoU that have the potential to be caused by misunderstandings or other biases. Depending on the results the researcher should consider weighing the OEoU versus the PEoU in an overall formula.

---

[7] The participants' self-assessed skills in reading, computer and internet usage show no correlation with the PEoU. Thus there must be other determinants not recorded in this study.

[8] Time <> OEoU correlation coefficient: -0,728; help <> OEoU correlation coefficient: -0,785; clicks <> OEoU correlation coefficient: -0,495.

[9] The analysis of our qualitative data did reveal such misguided steps.

[10] This help was not counted as 'help needed' to complete the scenarios.

6   Conclusion

With this paper we took the first step to adapt the assessment methodology of the known acceptance model TAM. We introduced a method for investigating the users' Perceived Ease of Use, which is an integral part of the TAM. Although there are limits to this study, such as the amount of participants and the newly introduced and so far not validated scale selection tool, we can constitute, that it is important to record and analyse supplementary data besides the items that have originally been designed for the PEoU construct. The Observed Ease of Use, and other variables help to qualify the possibly non-authentic PEoU, which is an abstract construct for our target group.

For future research on the PEoU assessment with people with cognitive disabilities, we recommend expanding the participants' base, taking steps to validate the scale selection tool and overall aiming at developing a weighing methodology between the PEoU and OEoU for final PEoU scores.

In general the other constructs of the TAM need to be adapted for a target group specific assessment and evaluated.

References

1. The International Classification of Functioning, Disability and Health, vol. 18(4), p. 267. WHO Library Cataloguing-in-Publication Data, Geneva (2001)
2. ICF Browser, http://apps.who.int/classifications/icfbrowser
3. Lin, K.-Y., Lu, H.-P.: Why people use social networking sites: An empirical study integrating network externalities and motivation theory. Computers in Human Behavior 27, 1152–1161 (2011)
4. Weber, H., Edler, C.: Supporting the Web Experience of Young People with Learning Disabilities. In: Miesenberger, K., Klaus, J., Zagler, W., Karshmer, A. (eds.) ICCHP 2010, Part I. LNCS, vol. 6179, pp. 649–656. Springer, Heidelberg (2010)
5. Web Content Accessibility Guidelines 2.0, http://www.w3.org/TR/WCAG20
6. Davis, F.D.: Perceived Usefulness, Perceived Ease of Use, and User Acceptance of Information Technology. MIS Quarterly 13, 319–340 (1989)
7. Davis, F.D., Bagozzi, R.P., Warshaw, P.R.: User Acceptance of Computer Technology: A Comparison of Two Theoretical Models. Manage. Sci. 35, 982–1003 (1989)
8. Jick, T.: Mixing qualitative and quantitative methods: Triangulation in action. Administrative Science Quarterly 24, 602–611 (1979)
9. de Winter, J.C.F., Dodou, D.: Five-Point Likert Items: T Test versus Mann-Whitney-Wilcoxon. Practical Assessment, Research & Evaluation 15, 1–16 (2010)

People with Learning Disabilities Using the iPad as a Communication Tool - Conditions and Impact with Regard to e-inclusion

Cordula Edler[1] and Matthias Rath[2]

[1] Inbut, Integrative Consulting and Support, Zell u.A., Germany
cordula.edler@t-online.de
[2] Ludwigsburg University of Education, Germany
rath@ph-ludwigsburg.de

Abstract. This paper presents results of an interdisciplinary pre-study that involved people with and without learning disabilities using iPads as a communication tool in their everyday life for self-confidence and empowerment. Main results highlight the accessibility challenges still prevalent: not usability leading to a lack of acceptance; but poor level of awareness of the relevance of media-literate action for the target group; insufficient coaching / personal support; insufficient technical accessibility and assistance.

Keywords: Cognitive Disabilities, Empowerment, Usability, Accessibility.

1   Introduction

In the past the predominant view on accessibility for people with disabilities referred solely to technological issues, see e. g. the W3C/WAI guidelines and techniques.

It is however apparent that for people with various learning difficulties (intellectual and cognitive disabilities) the key challenges in using digital media are not primarily of technical nature, but often a result of lack of suitable approaches to build up media literacy. In this context accessibility means for this target group much more than the ability to read and understand written text. People with cognitive disabilities face different challenges. For instance, conventional information design, navigation or exclusively text-based content often introduce insurmountable obstacles to them.

It is also important to see how this people are involved in development and introduced to new technologies like digital devices. What are they "allowed" to do, and what is expected of them in making own choices and options for action? These are not only technical or educational questions but also ethical ones. We have to assure the critical and responsible use of the technology and contents, whether content is self-produced or originates through web-based access. We have to find a balance between trust in and protection of users with regard which level of media literacy can be achieved and must not stop them in using digital devices or accessing online content!

Until now, in the first place information and communication technologies (ICT) were made accessible, to facilitate autonomous participation and to reduce user's

K. Miesenberger et al. (Eds.): ICCHP 2014, Part I, LNCS 8547, pp. 177–180, 2014.

personal dependence on professional support through "special" applications. Today, younger people with cognitive disabilities are using digital access devices everyday with no special adaptations. They grew up with multi-media technology, they have learned many ways of using the media world and they would like to use it independently for their own goals and purposes. It was assumed that special solutions would be best for the target group, without questioning it. Experience and teaching media literacy including Internet and "social media" has taught us to take a new view of the Web for and with people with cognitive disabilities. "Social media" and the Web have become an important part in their lives. Furthermore, these media have the potential to enable people with disabilities to act as independent and equal participants, to stay in touch with friends and family wherever they are. The new generation of Table PCs and mobile apps could be a quantum leap for the accessibility of digital devices and for participation and communication possibilities for people with cognitive disabilities and to assist them.

2   Proceeding

The study presented interdisciplinary pre-study to understand how people with learning disabilities use or deal with the challenges presented by the new type of tablets including touch screen, voice output, voice input and camera. In the research detailed below, we first observed the intuitive approach using the iPad in three different residential groups where people with and without disabilities live together and support each other. During the entire observation period we tried to motivate and increasingly involve the participants, also to observe themselves, their environment and their activities. We wanted to find out to what extent the existing applications are sufficient for daily information and communication between family, assistants, friends, etc., and what improvements are required. Through the existing access to the target group, it was possible to start directly with the observations and to get relatively quick initial results. The following individual steps are described development of accessible new applications.

3   Design and Method

Aims for a qualitative research in general are to gather an in-depth understanding of human behavior and the reasons that govern such behavior. Respective qualitative methods investigate the why and how of decision making, not only what, where and when. Hence, smaller but focused samples are more often used in qualitative research than large samples.

We approached the topic using Action Research [1] as a participative method. As far as methodology was concerned, we mainly used different instruments such as observations, interviews, questionnaires, photos, videos, case studies etc., and collected these as qualitative data. We have tried to realize a participatory / inclusive approach [2]. The target group takes the role of user experts. Ahead of their participation, they received information on the project and on the purpose of their potential participation, phrased in understandable language. The following issues refer to methodological challenges and to the central research question:

1. Is a user-centered design for digital devices necessary and if yes, when, where and what is the best way to involve people with intellectual and cognitive disabilities in the process of development to achieve and hence meet the requirements in the best possible way?
2. Which applications for iPad are available or which applications for that device can be adapted to strengthen e-inclusion for people with intellectual and cognitive disabilities?

The study was carried out between September 2013 and January 2014 in three residential groups, with 28 participants: 16 were people with disabilities (5 male, 4 female) aged between 19 and 39 years, and 12 different assistants (6 male, 6 female) aged between 18-47 years. Five case studies were developed in that process. The participants had 6 iPads available. In the beginning all participants were interviewed, as to their person and their use of digital devices such as PC, mobile phone and tablet. Then there was a short introduction of how to use iPads, and finally the iPads were handed over to the members of the groups and to their assistants. The next step was an observation via protocol and video, and an analysis of the use of the iPad within the group and by different individuals. The five case studies, people with cognitive disabilities, who were observed along different criteria, showed also a variety of ways in accessing the iPad. An interview with a focus group and a survey of supporters (professional assistants) completed the study.

4   Results

4.1   Acceptance of the iPads by the Participants with Disabilities

First, it should be noted that all participants with and without disabilities were excited at the prospect of using the iPad together. When the iPads were installed, however, working together proved extremely difficult, because of the lack of time and cooperation by the part of the assistants (see 'Coaching and Personal support for the target group' below). Various different types of reservation were observed. It was difficult to communicate that their participation and support was required.

Participants with disabilities showed the most patience and the least reservation. They easily became familiar with the iPad. They tried it out by themselves and always discovered something new. They independently asked for and planned their meetings to learn more. The recognition of apps and also the use of known and formerly learned applications was not a problem after a few repetitions (2 to 3). Even a female participant with severe multiple disabilities who does not speak was one of the first to use the new generation of iPad. For example, she drew attention to herself by pointing at the Skype app to indicate that she wants to communicate with somebody. As long as the app worked reliably, she was almost completely independent, because she was also able to select the person she wants to reach. She communicates so with the family via videochat with her special behavior. Unfortunately, she has not yet accepted a special app, a flexible picture communication system like "go talk now"[3].

Remarkable in the project is the quick comprehension of the learner that was not significantly different from that of people without learning difficulties, like the mutual support within the peer group.

4.2   Coaching and Personal Support for the Target Group

Some times coaching for the participants from the researcher was available. But additional input from assistants, which would have be helpful and necessary, failed. Mostly because the assistants, although initially showing interest, quickly drew back when they realized that the use of these devices did not make their work easier.

4.3   Accessibility and Technical Assistance

Support the target group is not only a question of the provision of technical aids. It also encompasses everyday circumstances that must not be barriers in themselves. Accessibility like for example a user-friendly environment, understandable language and structure, and a set-up with a working Wi-Fi must be granted.

4.4   Media Literacy and Other Competences

In addition to general media knowledge all the participants have, we noticed their skills and strategies, to familiarize with the new technology available for them. These skills are different for each individual person. Remarkable is the independent using of digital devises without much support and coaching. Social competences were observed, like peer counseling.

5   Discussion and Conclusion

First of all, the study participants are in no way representative for the target group. The presented results, however, serve as impressions to give stimulus for further studies on e-inclusion, orientation in authenticity, and identity of people with cognitive disability. Developments on further increasing the accessibility of mobile digital media for this target group should take more realistic, i.e. everyday conditions for mobile use of digital devices, into consideration.

References

1. Moser, H.: Grundlagen der Praxisforschung. Lambertus, Freiburg Breisgau (1995)
2. Walmsley, J., Johnson, K.: Inclusive Research with People with Learning Disabilities: Past, Present and Future. Jessica Kingsley, London (2003)
3. GoTalk: http://www.attainmentcompany.com/gotalk-now

Implementing PDF/UA in Microsoft Word - How Can PDF/UA Become an Everyday Part of Document Authoring?

Roberto Bianchetti[1], Samuel Hofer[1], and Markus Erle[2]

[1] xyMedia GmbH, Volketswil, Switzerland
{bianchetti,hofer}@xymedia.ch
[2] Wertewerk, Tuebingen, Germany
erle@wertewerk.de

Abstract. The ISO-standard PDF/UA-1 with its clearly-defined requirements promises a new era of accessible document creation. But users of word processing software are often overwhelmed when they try to understand how to fulfill the requirements. This leads to our focus in this paper: how can every document author using Microsoft Word be able to create a PDF/UA compliant PDF document without deep knowledge of PDF accessibility or time-consuming quality assurance and remediation? We present a workflow model which enables in combination with a special Word-Add-In the easy creation of accessible PDF documents without special training.

Keywords: PDF, Accessibility, PDF/UA, Document, Template, Workflow, Microsoft Word.

1 Introduction: Is PDF/UA Only for Insiders, Geeks and Experts?

The ISO-standard PDF/UA-1 (ISO 14289-1) with its clearly-defined and WCAG 2 orientated requirements [3] - elaborated in the so called Matterhorn Protocol [4] - is a big progress in the field of document accessibility. But a standard can only be successful if there are easy to handle tools for the creation and evaluation of compliant documents. A vast amount of PDF documents are created with Microsoft Word which is a wide-spread word processing software especially in the fields of e-government, education and business. In the majority of cases to meet the requirements of accessible documents is the responsibility of one small part of an organization with deep PDF accessibility knowledge [5]. But with this strategy it is not possible to make accessibility as an everyday part of document authoring.

The support in mainstream authoring tools like Microsoft Word is not sufficient in order to generate PDF/UA conforming documents. Even if the author fulfills all accessibility requirements in the source document, it is not possible to create a fully complying PDF document by using the PDF export function in Word itself [2] or the common Add-In Adobe PDF-Maker for Word. The technical side of this issue is

K. Miesenberger et al. (Eds.): ICCHP 2014, Part I, LNCS 8547, pp. 181–184, 2014.

ad-dressed by a special conversion tool. The concept of that tool as a Word-Add-In was presented by the authors of this paper at ICCHP 2012 [1]. The remaining problem however is the workflow itself.

Till today the common strategy is to train all document authors to become a PDF accessibility expert. We want to choose another approach: what role based model or workflow model is necessary in order to empower Microsoft Word authors without deep PDF accessibility knowledge to create PDF/UA documents?

2   The Concept: A New Role Based Model - Only the Template Creator Has to Be the PDF Accessibility Expert

In a first step we tried to make clear what we mean with "to empower". Based on our experiences in teaching document accessibility to office workers and power users for many years we worked out the goals of a new workflow model:

- to easily create accessible PDF documents without any special training
- to relieve the authors of dealing with PDF accessibility problems or special knowledge about PDF tagging
- to enable the authors to focus on content issues
- to facilitate semantic authoring without calling it semantic
- to support the creation of "born accessible" documents
- to minimize the effort of PDF/UA checking

In a second step we tried to define roles and their special tasks according to accessibility issues. We identified 3 different roles:

1. The template developer: responsible for the basic layout and the styles – he determines the look of the document and the possibilities to structure the content by using different styles.
2. The document author: responsible for the content and the document structure – he writes the content and marks it by using the available styles.
3. The document evaluator: responsible for the quality assurance – he checks the PDF for accessibility (in this case for conformance with PDF/UA).

Every role needs a special knowledge in order to execute the according tasks.

2.1   The First Role: The Template Developer

The template developer needs deep knowledge about the creation of tem-plates, PDF accessibility and axesPDF for Word features and settings. He provides the authors with templates that are prepared for accessible authoring. His tasks are in detail:

- prepare all styles and complex elements already with accessibility features in the template
- determine the PDF-tags processing in the template

- name styles according to their usage
- determine settings and metadata according to accessibility in the template
- add protection to a template to help prevent authors from changing the styles

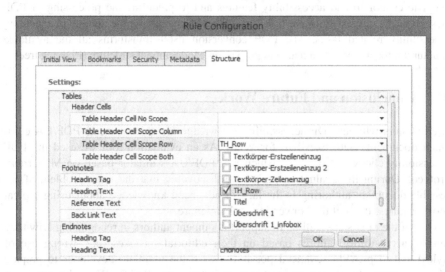

Fig. 1. Window for predefining the processing of PDF tags: in this example you see the mapping of the style TH_Row to the processing as Table Header Cell Scope Row

2.2   The Second Role: The Document Author

The document author only needs advanced knowledge about using predefined styles and typical Word features (e.g. how to create a table of content or how to anchor images). According to document accessibility the author needs only basic knowledge (on editorial level) in order to execute the following tasks:

- decide which picture or graphic is decorative and which is relevant for the content
- determine alternate text for the relevant graphics
- complete metadata (e.g. document title)
- check the language setting

The last two tasks can be executed right before the conversion to PDF in the conversion window.

2.3   The Third Role: The Document Evaluator

In our concept we canceled the third role of a document evaluator because the document author should be able check his document for PDF/UA compliance on his own and this should not take more than - in worst case - five minutes. And if there are failures he should be able to correct them in the source document.

3   Implementation of the Role Based Model

In the first basic implementation in the add-in axesPDF for Word it is possible for the template creator to add accessibility features and to predefine the processing of PDF tags. By using context sensitive task panes the add-in supports the authors in executing accessibility related tasks. The PDF conversion itself transforms all the available structural information into a lean and proper logical document structure (PDF tag tree).

4   Conclusion and Future Work

Even authors without PDF accessibility knowledge are able to create PDF/UA compliant documents with axesPDF for Word. As an evaluation tool we used the PDF accessibility checker PAC 2 [6] which is a PDF/UA validator based on Matterhorn Protocol. During the evaluation period we discovered that the main problem of accessible document authoring is the lack of advanced knowledge about using typical Word features. It is not the conversion tool any more.

One of the next steps will be to support document authors in recognizing how they can fix accessibility failures based on their editorial mistakes (e.g. wrong use of styles) and to provide advanced possibilities for the template developer to prepare Word templates. In addition we will implement into axesPDF for Word the support of further document elements (e.g. content controls and building blocks).

References

1. Bianchetti, R., Erle, M., Hofer, S.: Mainstreaming the Creation of Accessible PDF Documents by a Rule-Based Transformation from Word to PDF. In: Miesenberger, K., Karshmer, A., Penaz, P., Zagler, W. (eds.) ICCHP 2012, Part I. LNCS, vol. 7382, pp. 595–601. Springer, Heidelberg (2012)
2. Creating accessible Word documents with Microsoft Word 2010 or higher,
   http://office.microsoft.com/en-us/word-help/
   creating-accessible-word-documents-HA101999993.aspx
3. Drümmer, O.: PDF/UA (ISO 14289-1) – Applying WCAG 2.0 Principles to the World of PDF Documents. In: Miesenberger, K., Karshmer, A., Penaz, P., Zagler, W. (eds.) ICCHP 2012, Part I. LNCS, vol. 7382, pp. 587–594. Springer, Heidelberg (2012)
4. MatterhornProtocol_1-0 PDF/UA Conformance Testing Model developed by the PDF/UA Competence Center,
   http://www.pdfa.org/wp-content/uploads/2013/12/
   MatterhornProtocol_1-0.pdf
5. McNaught, A., Featherstone, L.: Alternative Approaches to Alternative Formats – Changing Expectations by Challenging Myths. In: Miesenberger, K., Karshmer, A., Penaz, P., Zagler, W. (eds.) ICCHP 2012, Part I. LNCS, vol. 7382, pp. 43–50. Springer, Heidelberg (2012)
6. PDF Accessibility Checker (PAC) 2 from the Access for All Foundation (Switzerland), is a free PDF/UA checker, http://www.access-for-all.ch/en/pdf-lab/
   pdf-accessibility-checker-pac.html

PAVE: A Web Application to Identify and Correct Accessibility Problems in PDF Documents

Luchin Doblies, David Stolz, Alireza Darvishy, and Hans-Peter Hutter

ZHAW Zurich University of Applied Sciences InIT Institute of Applied Information Technology Winterthur, Switzerland
alireza.darvishy@zhaw.ch

Abstract. This paper describes the implementation of the PDF Accessibility Validation Engine (PAVE). PAVE is a web based application for identifying and correcting accessibility issues in PDF documents. The accessibility analysis is based on the PDF/UA standard.

We previously introduced the idea of such a system in [1]. The entire application runs on a web server, allowing users to both analyze a PDF document in regard to accessibility issues and then to directly fix these issues within the browser, thus relieving them from installing software. A simple and intuitive user interface allows both experts as well as users with only little previous knowledge of PDF accessibility to work with PAVE.

Keywords: Accessibility, Document Accessibility, Visual Impairment, Tagged PDF, PDF/UA, Web Content Accessibility Guidelines, Screen Readers.

1 Introduction

The Portable Document Format (PDF) standard [2] is concerned with the creation, processing and display of documents which shall be represented true to original on all devices and platforms. PDF documents are widely disseminated in today's information society. For example, PDF is the format of choice for scientific publications and documents of public institutions.

Early specifications of PDF, for the most part, put no special emphasis on compatibility with assistive technology (especially for people with visual impairments) but aimed primarily for consistent visual presentation. Since the first version of the standard in 1993, accessible PDF documents were made possible and standardized by Tagged PDF [3] and then especially by PDF/UA [4]. Documents that conform to PDF/UA adhere to the requirements of the Web Content Accessibility Guidelines (WCAG) 2.0 [5].

Yet, the largest part of PDF documents which are available on the web today does not conform to the very recent PDF/UA standard. Furthermore, many of the PDF documents that are written nowadays still do not comply with PDF/UA

K. Miesenberger et al. (Eds.): ICCHP 2014, Part I, LNCS 8547, pp. 185–192, 2014.

upon publishing. This is in spite of the fact that popular, modern authoring tools like the newest versions of Adobe Acrobat Pro [6] or Microsoft Word [7] offer extensive accessibility guidance tools to authors.

To conclude, nowadays most of the available PDF documents are not (or only partially) accessible, imposing restrictions on people using assistive technology. If one wants an accessible version of a document, one way would be to contact the author and let him republish his work. This would, however, in most cases be very tedious or even impossible.

In order to solve the mentioned problems, we identified two major tasks: First, we need an accessibility checker that allows users to assess an existing PDF document in a simple and comprehensive fashion. And second, we need a tool that allows to correct an existing PDF document in regard to accessibility. Since these two functionalities are often used in conjunction (e.g., checking, correcting, checking the result), we decided to address both tasks within a single application. We already introduced the architecture for such an application in [1]. The proposed web application requires very little knowledge about accessibility and can thus be used by a broad audience. In this paper, we discuss this system in more detail and present an implementation.

2   Related Work

The idea of a software architecture for a web application that evaluates the accessibility of PDF documents and provides means to make them accessible has been introduced in [1]. Users get an accessibility evaluation report and are able to use the tool to fix the encountered issues directly within a web browser. The proposed system includes a user interface component as well as a PDF analysis and tagging engine.

Adobe Acrobat Pro [6] provides a commercial desktop solution to recognize accessibility issues in existing PDF documents and to correct them. Common-Look PDF [8] is a third-party commercial add-on to Adobe Acrobat Pro. It claims to bring more efficiency and comprehensiveness to the accessibility evaluation and correction process within Adobe Acrobat Pro. These two are the only solutions that we know of that include correcting capabilities, apart from our system.

There are also some pure PDF accessibility evaluators which do not offer a correction framework. The PDF Accessibility Checker (PAC) 2 [9] evaluates documents for compliance with PDF/UA. PAC 2 implements all machine checkable conditions of the Matterhorn Protocol [10], which provides a list of tests to evaluate PDF/UA conformance of documents. As for online checkers, among others, there's the Tingtun PDF Checker [11], which evaluates PDF documents for compliance with WCAG 2.0 guidelines.

All existing solutions have at least one of the following three shortcomings: They are non-free (thus hindering wide usage), require extensive accessibility knowledge, or do not offer a correction facility.

3 Approach

Since one of our goals was to relieve users of the application from installing additional software, PAVE can directly be accessed within a web browser. Initially, a user uploads an existing PDF document to PAVE, where it then gets analyzed for any accessibility issues. The result of this analysis is presented to the user, showing potential problems. This information enables her to make an informed decision about whether or not she wants to correct the PDF document. If she decides not to perform any corrections, she is at least assured about the degree of accessibility conformance of the PDF document. However, if she decides to correct the issues presented in the accessibility analysis, she can do so directly within PAVE.

After correcting the issues, she can proceed to download a PDF document that reflects these corrections, while visually being identical to the original document. Figure 1 shows an overview of this process. The accessibility issues that PAVE reports are based on the Matterhorn Protocol [10]. Note that some of the issues that are defined in the Matterhorn Protocol can be corrected automatically. Hence, PAVE corrects those issues without any user interaction.

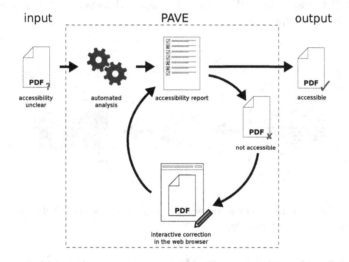

Fig. 1. System overview

The PDF/UA standard defines the criteria for accessibility conformance of PDF documents on a very technical level. When designing an application that shall enable people to correct documents with regard to this standard, it would be straightforward to design a user interface that reflects the criteria of the standard directly. However, this would result in a rather unintuitive user interface, which would only be usable by people who are very familiar with the internals of the PDF standards. Therefore, we decided to design the user interface in such a way, that we expose as little of the PDF internals as possible, without limiting the user in her correcting capabilities.

In the following, we provide an example of how we hide PDF internals from the user. Assume that a user uploaded a PDF document that is not tagged at all, i.e., the text inside the PDF document has no logical information attached to it. The user gets informed about this issue. Within our tool, she can then draw a rectangular box with her mouse around the first block of text, providing the information that this text represents a paragraph. This is a very intuitive user interface design, but it does not correspond to the PDF internals. Inside of an (untagged) PDF document, there is no such thing as a paragraph, instead, there is a multitude of drawing commands within a content stream. When the user selects a certain block of text in the user interface in order to mark it as one group of text, the application must analyze the drawing commands within the content stream to match them with the selection. Figure 2 illustrates how the system matches the selection of the user with the according drawing commands. From a technical point of view, it would be easier to present the different drawing commands to the user, and require the user to tag all these commands one by one. Yet, such a work would be quite tedious and unintuitive for the user, and thus we decided to design the user interface in such a way, that we put the focus on accessibility and hide PDF technical details wherever it does not add any benefit to the user experience.

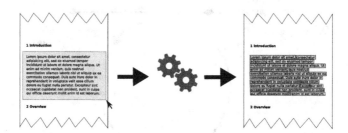

Fig. 2. Left: User selects an entire paragraph. Right: The system automatically finds the according drawing commands.

In addition to the intuitive user interface, the correction process is further enhanced by correcting certain issues automatically. Examples include the reconciliation of inconsistencies in metadata, or the removal of invalid tags. Fortunately, a large fraction of commonly encountered accessibility issues in PDF documents can be fixed in this fully automated way. We hope that the combination of the intuitive user interface and the fully automated corrections lowers the entry barrier and reduces the amount of time used for the correction process substantially, in comparison to existing solutions.

4   Current State of Development

As PAVE is currently still being developed, we only address a small section to the current state of the application. Figure 3 shows a screenshot of the accessibility report generated by PAVE. The hierarchically structured report can be expanded and collapsed by the user, enabling her to either get a high-level overview of the problems in the document, or to dig deeper into the details. With the help of the hierarchical structure, it is straightforward to assess the accessibility conformance.

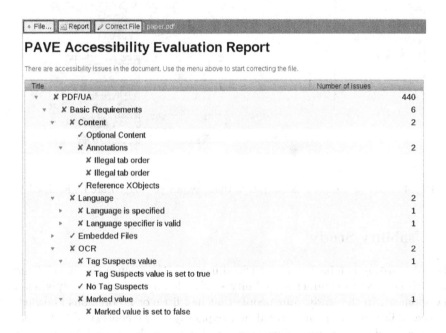

Fig. 3. Accessibility report

The screenshot in Figure 4 shows the page view, i.e., the view in which the user can add and modify the tags and the reading order. On the left, the current reading order is presented to the user, allowing her to reorder it using drag & drop. On the right, a page of the PDF document is displayed. The currently untagged elements on the page are highlighted, allowing the user to quickly identify the next action she wants to perform. Note that there are different highlighting options; for example, the user can also highlight existing tags, or both existing and missing ones with different colors. Additionally to these rather static overlays, we also added dynamic content highlighting; e.g., when the user hovers an existing tag, its position in the reading order and all elements contained in this tag are highlighted. Note that the creation and editing of tags within the page view is according to the intuitive user interface approach that we introduced in Section 3. In particular, we implemented the selection mechanism depicted in Figure 2.

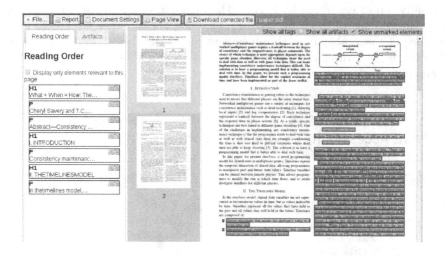

Fig. 4. The tagging process. Elements that are not yet tagged are highlighted.

5   Usability Study

We put a strong emphasis on user friendliness of PAVE since the start. Therefore, we decided to conduct a usability study already in a very early stage of development. In the study, four people that had little or no previous knowledge of accessibility problems in general, nor explicitly in the context of PDF documents, worked with the tool. They were asked to assess the accessibility problems in a given test document and then to correct the document using PAVE. The test document consisted of two pages, which contained different types of elements, such as text and images, as well as headers and footers.

The main result of the study was that all people were able to correct the PDF document properly, i.e., so that the document was fully accessible, within less than twenty minutes.

In the following we point out two additional results learned from the usability study. The first result is that without PAVE, users were unable to assess the degree of accessibility conformance of the PDF document at all. However, once they uploaded the PDF document to PAVE, they were assured that there exist issues within the document. The second result concerns the process of tagging the document: Users quickly understand the concept of tagging a document, and even when using PAVE for the first time, it only took them less than eight minutes on average to tag the two pages completely.

Summarizing the results of the usability study, users mentioned a handful of small changes in regard to the user interface, but overall, all users were easily able to assess and correct the given PDF document. All users also stated that if they were given the task to either assess or correct a PDF document (in regard to accessibility) in the future, they would want to use PAVE.

In a later stage of the development, we will assert the usability of PAVE by a more extensive user study. This study will target a larger number of users with strongly varying previous knowledge of document publishing and accessibility.

6   Future Work

Since PAVE is currently work in progress, there are multiple features that we have planned to implement. The next step is to complete the tagging functionality, by extending it so that complex elements such as lists and tables can be tagged. Afterwards, we plan to implement semantic checks. An example for such a check is verifying that headings are properly nested.

Furthermore, we plan to change and extend the user interface, in order to make it easier and even more intuitive to use, and thus to reduce the amount of time required to correct a PDF document. We hope that by achieving these goals, the effort of making PDF documents accessible is reduced by such a significant amount, that checking for accessibility and correcting issues accordingly will become a well-established step in the publishing process of PDF documents.

7   Conclusion

PDF documents are a prevalent means to publish content to people. The problem that many of those documents are insufficiently accessible originates mainly from the fact that it is often too tedious to create and validate accessible PDF documents. All the existing tools suffer from shortcomings: They are commercial, require expert knowledge, or provide insufficient functionality. These shortcomings prevent many people, companies and administrations from using such tools, which leads to a substantial amount of inaccessible PDF documents being published. We address these shortcomings with PAVE, a web application that allows people to evaluate and correct existing PDF documents in an intuitive and straightforward manner. PAVE provides an accessibility report based on PDF/UA and offers means to correct the identified problems.

References

1. Darvishy, A., Hutter, H.-P., Mannhart, O.: Web application for analysis, manipulation and generation of accessible PDF documents. In: Stephanidis, C. (ed.) Universal Access in HCI, Part IV, HCII 2011. LNCS, vol. 6768, pp. 121–128. Springer, Heidelberg (2011)
2. Adobe Systems Incorporated. Portable Document Format (PDF 1.7). ISO 32000 (2008)

3. Adobe Systems Incorporated. PDF Reference, 3rd edn., PDF 1.4 (2001)
4. Use of ISO 32000-1 (PDF/UA-1). ISO 14289-1 (2012)
5. World Wide Web Consortium. Web Content Accessibility Guidelines (WCAG) 2.0, http://www.w3.org/TR/WCAG20/ (Online; accessed January 29, 2014)
6. Adobe Systems Incorporated. Adobe Acrobat XI Pro, http://www.adobe.com/products/acrobatpro.html (Online; accessed January 29, 2014)
7. Microsoft Corporation. Microsoft Word, http://office.microsoft.com/word/ (Online; accessed January 29, 2014)
8. NetCentric Technologies. CommonLook PDF, http://www.commonlook.com/CommonLook-PDF (Online; accessed January 29, 2014)
9. Access for all Foundation. PDF Accessibility Checker (PAC2), http://www.access-for-all.ch/en/ pdf-lab/pdf-accessibility-checker-pac.html (Online; accessed January 29, 2014)
10. PDF Association. Matterhorn Protocol 1.0, http://www.pdfa.org/wp-content/uploads/ 2013/08/MatterhornProtocol_1-0.pdf (Online; accessed January 29, 2014)
11. eGovMon project. Tingtun PDF Checker, http://accessibility.tingtun.no/en/pdfcheck/ (Online; accessed January 29, 2014)

Correcting "Last Mile" Errors - Quality Assurance of PDF/UA Documents without Being a Developer

Roberto Bianchetti[1], Samuel Hofer[1], and Markus Erle[2]

[1] xyMedia GmbH, Volketswil, Switzerland
{bianchetti,hofer}@xymedia.ch
[2] Wertewerk, Tuebingen, Germany
erle@wertewerk.de

Abstract. With the ISO-standard PDF/UA-1 and the free PDF accessibility checker (PAC) 2 it is possible to validate PDF documents for accessibility very easily based on clearly defined requirements. But users who evaluate their documents are often faced with hard to correct errors because the mainstream authoring programs do not fully support PDF/UA yet. Remediation is tedious and time-consuming and sometimes even impossible with available tools. Therefore we worked out the main "last mile" errors and developed a special tool for "quickfixing" these errors – even for document authors without PDF accessibility knowledge on expert level. In this paper we present this approach and the tool.

Keywords: Accessibility, Evaluation, PDF, PDF/UA, Remediation.

1 Introduction: No Authoring Software Yet with Full Support for PDF/UA

Although the ISO-standard PDF/UA-1 (ISO 14289-1) with its clearly-defined requirements [3] – elaborated in the so called Matterhorn Protocol [4] – is two years old in summer 2014, there are no mainstream programs around which support the creation of fully PDF/UA compliant documents. Document authors evaluating their accessible PDF documents are often faced with hard to correct errors because the authoring tools or the conversion tools are not good enough. We call such evaluation failures "last mile" errors. You have to go the last mile - that is often very stressful – because you have to fix the errors manually at PDF content level – a kind of PDF source code for most of the users.

2 The Concept: Defining "Last Mile" Errors and Developing a Combined Checking and Fixing Tool

2.1 Typical "Last Mile" Errors

In a first step we defined typical last mile errors. Last mile errors are evaluation failures which cannot be fixed by optimizing the source document for accessibility.

K. Miesenberger et al. (Eds.): ICCHP 2014, Part I, LNCS 8547, pp. 193–196, 2014.
© Springer International Publishing Switzerland 2014

We looked at the different workflows (from word processing programs like Microsoft Word, layout processing programs like Adobe InDesign and PDF editors like Adobe Acrobat Pro) and tried to find out the most common errors.

In cooperation with leading international document accessibility companies from Canada, Denmark, Germany and Switzerland we analyzed the workflows according to common programs with the best PDF/UA support. Typical errors are for example missing PDF/UA identifier, wrong language settings on marked content level, limited range of available PDF tags, missing descriptions for link annotations, path objects that are not marked as artifacts, wrong zoom settings of bookmarks, figures and forms with wrong placement attributes. Up to now these errors have to be fixed manually element by element.

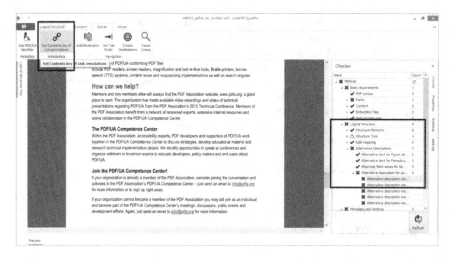

Fig. 1. The user interface of the "quickfixing" tool: on the right hand the PDF/UA checker with precise failure report and on the left hand above the corresponding buttons to fix it

2.2   Levels of "Last Mile" Errors

We divided the last mile errors into 3 levels:

- Level 1: ISO 32000 (PDF 1.7) and ISO 14289 (PDF/UA) - example: fix role map-ping, insert missing spaces between words, missing note ID's.
- Level 2: Web Content Accessibility Guidelines (WCAG) 2.0 - example: accessible bookmarks as a combination of navigation bar and sitemap.
- Level 3: usability for people with disabilities - examples: reset zooms (in order to keep user settings), create destinations (screen reader usable internal links), fix placement attributes (so that assistive technologies can render images, forms, formulas and notes correctly), apply PDF standard tags.

2.3   Combined Checking and Remediation Tool

We implemented a PDF/UA checker [5] based on Matterhorn Protocol [4] and our paper "Validity and Semantics – Two Essential Parts of a Backbone for an Automated PDF/UA Compliance Check for PDF Documents" [2] which we presented at ICCHP 2012 as a starting point. For remediation the user has only to click the corresponding button or to change a few settings e.g. the role mapping. The tool enables the user to fix typical errors at one blow through the whole document. By refreshing the checker the user will get immediate evaluation feedback.

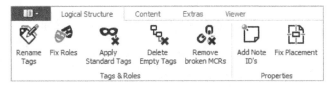

Fig. 2. Tab "Logical Structure" with the buttons to solve typical "last mile" errors

3   Evaluation

We evaluated the beta version of our solution – called axesPDF QuickFix [1] – with the experts of the international document accessibility companies mentioned above. During that period we received feedback about additional features we should implement. We added some document views for professional users. These views enables to locate reported errors easily and precisely in the document.

Furthermore the tool is used by the PDF/UA competence center to evaluate PDF documents for accessibility and identify best practice files in order to publish these documents and to promote that ISO standard.

4   Results, Impact and Future Work

The "quickfixing" tool enables even users without expert knowledge to correct "last mile" errors according PDF/UA very fast and easily. The user can check and remediate in one step - often by clicking a button. The tool enables – in combination with the best authoring tools – lean workflows for the creation of PDF/UA compliant documents. Next step will be to implement additional features especially on the level "usability for people with disabilities" because this aspect is often ignored.

References

1. axesPDF QuickFix: http://www.axespdf.com
2. Erle, M., Hofer, S.: Validity and Semantics – Two Essential Parts of a Backbone for an Automated PDF/UA Compliance Check for PDF Documents. In: Miesenberger, K., Karshmer, A., Penaz, P., Zagler, W. (eds.) ICCHP 2012, Part I. LNCS, vol. 7382, pp. 617–620. Springer, Heidelberg (2012)

3. Drümmer, O.: PDF/UA (ISO 14289-1) – applying WCAG 2.0 principles to the world of PDF documents. In: Miesenberger, K., Karshmer, A., Penaz, P., Zagler, W. (eds.) ICCHP 2012, Part I. LNCS, vol. 7382, pp. 587–594. Springer, Heidelberg (2012)
4. MatterhornProtocol_1-0 PDF/UA Conformance Testing Model developed by the PDF/UA Competence Center, http://www.pdfa.org/wp-content/uploads/2014/03/MatterhornProtocol_1-011.pdf
5. PDF Accessibility Checker (PAC) 2 from the Access for All Foundation (Switzerland), is a free PDF/UA checker, http://www.access-for-all.ch/en/pdf-lab/pdf-accessibility-checker-pac.html

PDF Accessibility Checker (PAC 2): The First Tool to Test PDF Documents for PDF/UA Compliance

Andreas Uebelbacher[1], Roberto Bianchetti[2], and Markus Riesch[1]

[1] «Access for all», Zurich, Switzerland
{andreas.uebelbacher,riesch}@access-for-all.ch
[2] xyMedia GmbH, Volketswil, Switzerland
bianchetti@xymedia.ch

Abstract. In 2012, the new standard PDF/UA (ISO 14289-1) was published, specifying the requirements for accessible PDF documents. The Matterhorn Protocol by the PDF Association details the list of 136 test conditions that need to be fulfilled, but so far, there was no test tool to check a given PDF document against these requirements. This paper presents the PDF Accessibility Checker 2.0 (PAC 2), which is the first tool that allows for an automatic test of those 108 test conditions which can be tested fully automatically. The tool provides a detailed report of a document analysis, and various features such as visual inspection of standard violations, supporting further improvement of the PDF document. As the PAC 2 is free of charge and can be used without technical knowledge, the tool promotes PDF accessibility among a wider user group and has the potential to increase compliance of PDF documents with the respective accessibility standard.

Keywords: Accessible PDF, PDF/UA, ISO 14289-1, PDF Analysis.

1 General Introduction

An enormous body of information on the internet is made available in the Portable Document Format (PDF), from general terms and conditions when doing online shopping to scientific publications, or the form you need to complete when applying for a new passport. As Google trends reveal, there is also a steady growth of interest in PDF-related content over the last 5 years [1]. However, most PDF documents today are not accessible for people with disabilities, as they do not comply with PDF accessibility standards [e.g. 2]. Consequently, people with disabilities using assistive technology (e.g. a screenreader) cannot effectively use the respective information resources.

The relevant standard is PDF/UA ('universal accessibility'; ISO 14289-1:2012-07), which was published in summer 2012 [3]. It specifies the technical requirements for a PDF document to be accessible for a wide variety of processing systems, including assistive technology, thereby aiming to achieve for PDF documents what WCAG 2.0 achieves for websites [4]. The Matterhorn Protocol [5], developed by the PDF

K. Miesenberger et al. (Eds.): ICCHP 2014, Part I, LNCS 8547, pp. 197–201, 2014.

Association, supports the implementation of the standard in practice, as it details 136 specific test conditions accessible PDF documents have to fulfill.

In many countries, providing accessible PDFs is required by law for government agencies. However, the actual implementation of the law proceeds disappointingly slow. While the ISO standard finally provided clear specifications for accessible PDFs, a tool to evaluate their application within PDFs was still missing. This gap is filled by PAC 2.

2   PDF Accessibility Checker 2.0 (PAC 2)

Back in 2010, the foundation 'Access for all' released the first version of the PDF Accessibility Checker, performing 14 tests on PDF documents. Since then, PAC has been downloaded more than 20'000 times worldwide, and it is recommended as one of the primary tools for PDF accessibility checking by the World Wide Web Consortium [6]. In August 2013, PAC 2 was released for Windows, and is now adapted to the new ISO Standard 14289-1 (PDF/UA). To our knowledge, it is the first tool to check PDF/UA compliance and provides an easy to use automated testing functionality.

2.1   Features of PAC 2

The main features of PAC 2 are as follows.

1. At the push of a single button, it provides a check of those 108 failure conditions in the Matterhorn Protocol, which can be tested fully automatically.
2. A detailed report is presented which allows the user to analyze the specific errors in the document. There is a display available for an easy visual identification of the elements in the PDF, which cause the test failures.
3. The preview offers a simplified view of the document structure, to allow for a manual check of the semantic information in the document (the tag structure), and the reading sequence.
4. Document statistics are provided, which give an overview of the used structural elements in the document.
5. The complete tag structure can be viewed, with a visual mapping of the elements in the PDF document to the tag structure.

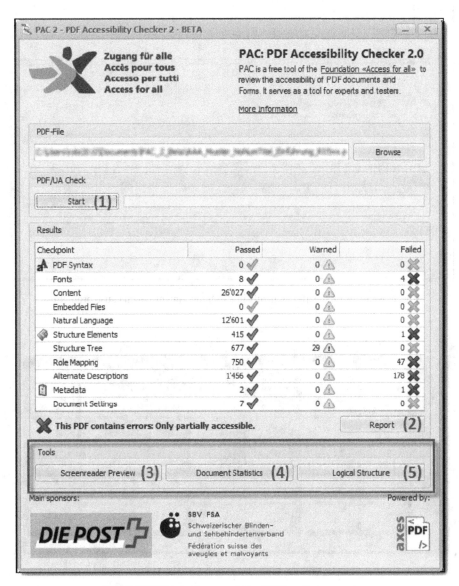

Fig. 1. PAC 2 interface providing PDF analysis report

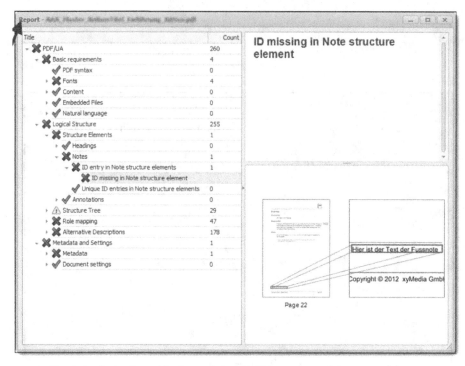

Fig. 2. Analysis of specific elements in a PDF document which cause problems

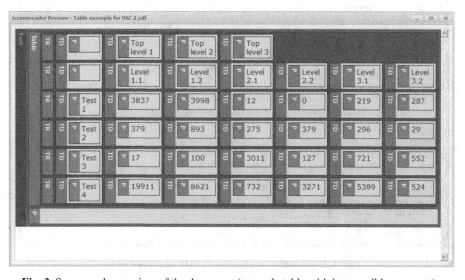

Fig. 3. Screenreader preview of the document (example table with inaccessible structure)

2.2   Strengths and Limitations

PAC 2 provides an easy to use tool to check PDF accessibility. This is especially useful for government agencies and private sector companies contracting third parties to create accessible PDFs. Finally, they are able to check standard compliance of the delivered products. Communication and digital design agencies receive a tool which supports their creation of accessible PDFs. The analysis provides them with specific information about the causes of the respective standard violations, a prerequisite of corrections to reach full document compliance.

In contrast to other available tools, one of the major advantages of PAC 2 is that it can be downloaded and used for free. This allows the software to effectively promote the topic of PDF accessibility among a wider user group and to increase compliance of PDF documents with the respective accessibility standard.

However, the remaining failure conditions, which cannot be tested automatically, still require human accessibility experts analyzing the PDF document. The tool cannot be a substitute for an expert assessment of document accessibility.

3   Outlook

PAC 2 is currently only available for the Microsoft Windows operating system. As soon as the financing is secured for this purpose, there will also be a version for alternative operating systems.

References

1. Google: Google Trends for 'PDF' (2014),
   https://www.google.com/trends/explore#q=pdf
2. Zugang für alle: Schweizer Accessibility-Studie 2011. Bestandesaufnahme der Zugänglichkeit bedeutender Schweizer Websites für Menschen mit Behinderungen. Stiftung 'Zugang für alle' (2011),
   http://access-for-all.ch/images/Accessibilty_Studie/
   Accessibility_Studie_2011_de_komplett.pdf
3. ISO: ISO 14289-1:2012. Document Management Applications - Electronic Document File Format Enhancement for Accessibility - Part 1: Use of ISO 32000-1, PDF/UA-1 (2012)
4. Drümmer, O., Erle, M.: PDF/UA – A New Era for Document Accessibility: Understanding, Managing and Implementing the ISO Standard PDF/UA (Universal Accessibility): Introduction to the Special Thematic Session. In: Miesenberger, K., Karshmer, A., Penaz, P., Zagler, W. (eds.) ICCHP 2012, Part I. LNCS, vol. 7382, pp. 585–586. Springer, Heidelberg (2012)
5. PDF Association. Matterhorn Protocol (2014),
   http://www.pdfa.org/wp-content/uploads/
   2014/03/MatterhornProtocol_1-011.pdf
6. World Wide Web Consortium (W3C). PDF Techniques for WCAG 2.0 (2014),
   http://www.w3.org/WAI/GL/WCAG20-TECHS/pdf.html

A Strategic Approach to Document Accessibility: Integrating PDF/UA into Your Electronic Content

Adam Spencer[1] and Karen McCall[2]

[1] Accessibil-IT, Oakville, Ontario Canada
[2] Karlen Communications, Paris, Ontario Canada

Abstract. Many countries, provinces and states have legislation mandating the accessibility of documents and formatted content. There are now existing and emerging standards for specific content formats such as PDF. The question remains as to why there are so many recently produced inaccessible documents if we have tools, legislation and standards clearly mandating accessible documents.

Keywords: PDF/UA, AODA, Accessibility for Ontarians with Disabilities Act, Information Communication Technology, ICT, Procurement, Training, Standard, Organizational Policy.

1   Organisational Policy

It is critical that any organization have a policy on the accessibility of Information Communication Technology (ICT)[1]. The best way to develop policies on accessible content or any aspect of inclusive design is to incorporate inclusion and accessibility into the overall organisational policy and not to have a separate policy that ad-dresses any legislative or standards based inclusion. For the PDF/UA [2] or accessible PDF standards, there must be an under-standing of what this standard represents to the work flow. For example, will the tools currently used for creating PDF documents support the standard, how much remediation will be required for documents and most importantly, who will be doing the remediation (staff or external contractor).?

An organisation must have a senior level department or entity charged with the oversight and implementation of the inclusive standards and legislation within the entire organization [3]. Everyone and every department within the organisation must be accountable to this entity for compliance and enforcement. As we've seen in the province of Ontario Canada, without enforcement, legislation and standards are meaningless and propagate barriers [4].

2   Procurement Policy

Once an inclusive policy is established, the elements of that policy must be non-negotiable in the procurement process. All requests for tenders and quotes must clearly identify that PDF/UA (in this example) is the supported benchmark of the deliverable.

K. Miesenberger et al. (Eds.): ICCHP 2014, Part I, LNCS 8547, pp. 202–204, 2014.

This policy must be clearly stated and defined on the organization's website even before it is stated in a procurement document. The fact that the accessibility of content must be accessible upon delivery should be an integral part of what defines the organisation.

A procurement process [5] should reiterate the policy and standards and not be the mechanism of introducing them.

3   Training Staff versus Outsourcing PDF/UA

The role of staff in strategic planning and policy development is important in determining the expectations of duties [6]. For example, if an organisation has thousands or millions of PDF documents, is the expectation that staff will spend time remediating them to PDF/UA compliance or is it more cost effective and resource effective to outsource the remediation for the high volume of documents and train some staff on remediating time sensitive documents such as memos or inter-office correspondence.

4   Document Development Cycle

The development cycle of a document should resemble the development cycle of any technological entity and be included in the accessibility standards of an organisation. The designations of the steps are different, but the development cycle remains evolutionary:

Fig. 1. The development cycle of documents

Organisations should implement a standard of file management and naming conventions to allow for easy archival and retrieval of documents by any staff member. These standards should be included in any policy or procurement documents for easy integration.

5   Summary

Organisations must find a way to work as an organisation rather than islands of departments working independently of each other with no overarching policy or implementation for the creation of accessible PDF documents or content in general.

Ad hoc implementation of accessibility is not fiscally viable. By developing an organisational, team-based strategy and sharing it with every employee what appear to be mountains of unachievable accessibility for PDF documents become "molehills" that can be achieved, and in a short period of time, become milestones of "what we do" as an organisation for everything produced.

References

1. Access Ontario, Developing Accessibility Policies for your Organization, ISBN: 978-1-4435-9778-4 (PDF)
2. PDF Association, Matterhorn Protocol, PDF/UA Conformance Testing Model, 1.0
3. Charting A Path Forward: Report of the Independent Review of the, Accessibility for Ontarians with Disabilities Act, p. 25 (2005),
   http://www.mcss.gov.on.ca/documents/en/mcss/accessibility/
   Charles%20Beer/Charles%20Beer.pdf
4. Implementing Accessibility in the Enterprise, Web Accessibility: Web Standards and Regulatory Compliance, ch. 3, http://jimthatcher.com/book2/chapter03.html
5. World Bank, STRATEGIC PLANNING: A TEN-STEP GUIDE:
   http://siteresources.worldbank.org/INTAFRREGTOPTEIA/
   Resources/mosaica_10_steps.pdf
6. Ontario College AODA Procurement Toolkit, Olga Dosis (January 2014)

Accessibility of Non-verbal Communication

Introduction to the Special Thematic Session

Andreas Kunz[1] and Klaus Miesenberger[2]

[1] Swiss Federal Institute of Technology, Zurich, Switzerland
kunz@iwf.mavt.ethz.ch
[2] Johannes Kepler University, Linz, Austria
Klaus.Miesenberger@jku.at

Abstract. This Special Thematic Session describes the elements of an IT system that allows for a better integration of blind people in a MindMap brainstorming session together with sighted users. Software components will be introduced that convert the parallel information visualization to a serialized information representation, which will then be output on a special blind user interface using screen reader and Braille display. Moreover, non-verbal communication elements are another important carrier of information, which also need to be captured and displayed to the blind user. Thus, this session also describes the necessary hardware components and the overall setup, which will allow for a more efficient teamwork in such a mixed team.

1   Introduction

Today, many devices exist that allow for an easier accessibility for blind people to digital content on screens. Braille displays or text-to-speech-software are typical tools for the blind user to interact with the content on the screen. However, these technologies are only of limited benefit for a collocated teamwork in the ideation process together with sighted persons.

Such teamwork in the ideation process typically goes along with a lively discussion between all participants, and the artifacts on the common workspace guide the way to a common solution for a given task. However, the discussion during such a teamwork is accompanied by non-verbal communication elements such as pointing, posture, gaze or facial expression. Together with the artifacts and the verbal communication, these non-verbal communication elements also carry a significant amount of information, which is partly unconsciously perceived and interpreted by the sighted participants. With exception of the audio channel, such information is not accessible anymore for blind people.

Consequently, such mixed groups attempt to consciously place more information on the verbal communication channel, which slows down the whole teamwork since is causes an additional cognitive workload. If the participants are not used to such a communication style, the working behavior typically falls back to a communication style that is less accessible for blind users.

K. Miesenberger et al. (Eds.): ICCHP 2014, Part I, LNCS 8547, pp. 205–208, 2014.
© Springer International Publishing Switzerland 2014

This situation becomes even worse, since blind users sometimes could also not use their text-to-speech output, since this might disturb other users or prevents the blind user from having full access to the ongoing verbal communication.

2   Session Goal

This session will present a new approach how blind people could be better integrated in such a brainstorming session within a mixed team of blind and sighted users. Using the scenario of a MindMap application on a common workspace to capture the volatile generated ideas and to guide the discussion within the group, new technologies and algorithms will be introduced in this session that allow a better integration of blind users. The application of a MindMap was consciously chosen, since it typically provokes a significant amount of non-verbal communication elements such as pointing gestures (and in particular deictic gestures). Moreover, this application also contains other situations, a blind user is typically confronted with, e.g. dynamic content of a common workspace, non-explicit artifact information such as clusters of objects or spatial distances, or on-screen interaction.

The session will discuss in detail, how current information technology can help to improve the overall information flow without the need for the blind user to learn new devices or technology.

3   Challenges to Be Addressed

Integrating blind users into such a MindMap-based brainstorming session imposes the following challenges that have to be met:

3.1   Parallel-to-Serial Conversion of Screen's Content

Visible content on a screen such as a MindMap can be parallel accessed by sighted users. They see the content written on the cards, their orientation to each other, but also clusters and other annotations. Such parallel information must be serialized in order to become accessible for blind users using their normal Braille display. Moreover, a MindMap is altered and extended during such a session, and thus continuously changes its layout and visual appearance. This implies that also these changes will be translated in order to be displayed to the blind users together with a corresponding change notification.

3.2   Capturing of Non-verbal Communication Elements

Non-verbal communication in the chosen scenario mainly consists of pointing gestures onto artifacts on the common workspace. A direct interaction with the MindMap elements on the so-called "Artifact Level" (e.g. for moving the elements) could be directly captured, if an interactive table such as PixelSense would be used. However, deictic gestures typically do not touch the surface and thus cannot be captured by the table's sensors anymore. Here, new sensors have to be integrated into the overall system, which offer a sufficiently high resolution for the detecting fingers together with their orientation and inclination. This is in particular important for deictic gestures, since they have to be precisely assigned to an artifact on the screen in order to avoid a wrong interpretation and translation for the blind user.

3.3   Sensor Fusion

Having various sensors in the technical setup would provide partially redundant information of different resolution. Such information – even though some signals might be noisy – can still be used to increase the overall system's accuracy by fusing the sensor signals. Since mainly deictic gestures are relevant for the chosen scenario, also multimodal sensor signals such as audio, artifact position, artifact content, and pointing orientation could be used to further improve accuracy. Saying "I mean this" for example will only give relevant information if it goes along with a pointing gesture. Carefully filtering and refining such information could help to avoid false alerts to the blind user, since not every pointing gesture would carry information and thus could be ignored.

However, such a sensor fusion also requires a complex data model, which supports various sensors, user applications, as well as models that contain the logical context of the complete system to guarantee the persistence.

3.4   Applications

As mentioned before, the chosen application consists of a brainstorming session, which uses a MindMap tool for capturing and visualizing volatile ideas. These common ideas should than be displayed on an interactive table as common workspace. This requires a MindMap software that can be simultaneously edited by the sighted users around the table, who can also rotate the artifacts, or cluster them in groups. The blind user can access this MindMao tool via the blind user interface, which shows a serial representation of the MindMap on the screen. Within this application, the blind user is also able to modify the tree, and all changes will then also be mapped to the MindMap tool on the screen.

3.5   New Input Procedure for Large Interactive Surfaces

So far, the blind user reads messages via the Braille display, and enters them over the regular keyboard, which is the most common interface. However, also applications for smart phones became very accepted within the last years. But using smart phones for entering text is still limited, mainly due their size and due to their missing haptic cues as feedback. On a first glance, it thus seems to be impossible to realize text input even on larger surfaces like tablet PCs or even interactive tables, as they exist in the chosen scenario. Here, new approaches are required that will use the system's intelligence to automatically adapt the keyboard to the blind user while he is entering text.

4   Summary

Within this session, a system was introduced in detail, which will allow for a blind user integration in MindMap-based brainstorming sessions. This system addresses several challenges that have to be overcome in order to capture and translate non-verbal communication elements, while also the blind user should have full access to the artifacts being generated on the screen during the discussion. The technical solutions in hard- and software were discussed in detail, which could build the basis for many other applications in this field.

Multimodal Fusion and Fission within W3C Standards for Nonverbal Communication with Blind Persons

Dirk Schnelle-Walka, Stefan Radomski, and Max Mühlhäuser

Technische Universität Darmstadt, Darmstadt, Germany

Abstract. Multimodal fusion and multimodal fission are well known concepts for multimodal systems but have not been well integrated in current architectures to support collaboration of blind and sighted people. In this paper we describe our initial thoughts of multimodal dialog modeling in multiuser dialog settings employing multiple modalities based on W3C standards like the Multimodal Architecture and Interfaces.

1 Introduction

Research in the domain of communication with disabled, especially blind persons usually implies the use of multiple modalities to enable or ease access to information. These range from audio feedback [14] over tactile feedback [2] to tangible objects [6]. While most of the research focuses on how a certain piece of information can be delivered to the blind, there is hardly any research on architectures that ease the development of such multimodal interfaces. With the advent of the *W3C Multimodal Architecture and Interfaces* recommendation[1] a first promising candidate to standardize multimodal systems is available. A first analysis of the *nuts and bolts* is provided by [12]. However, the actual approach on how input coming from multiple sources is fused into a coherent meaning (multimodal fusion [5]) as well as state-of-the-art concepts on how to deliver information using more than a single available modality (multimodal fission [5]) is vaguely specified in the respective standards.

In this paper, we introduce our first thoughts on how to translate communication elements, inaccessible to blind persons onto accessible modalities. We aim at a scenario in a current project to improve the participation of blind people in a brain-storming process with sighted people. Here, a mind map[2] is used on a touch table. Usually, these scenarios feature high dynamics in the communication, including speaker changes, nonverbal communication elements like deictic gestures as well as frequent changes of the artifacts. In [9] we focused on the artifact level while in this publication we describe on how the architecture can be extended to include communication of nonverbal communication elements with multimodal fusion and multimodal fission.

The architecture proposed by the W3C decomposes a multimodal application into a nested structure of *interaction managers* (IM) for dialog control and

---

[1] http://www.w3.org/TR/mmi-arch/
[2] http://come.sourceforge.net

K. Miesenberger et al. (Eds.): ICCHP 2014, Part I, LNCS 8547, pp. 209–213, 2014.

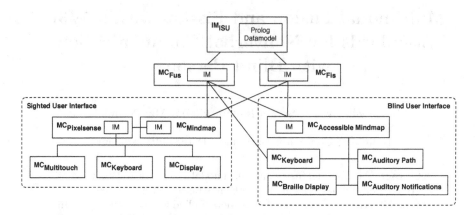

Fig. 1. Constituting components of the prototype

modality components (MC) for in- and output. An application is conceived as a set of control documents expressed e.g. in SCXML [3] for the interaction managers and a set of presentation documents with modality-specific markup for the modality components.

2   Related Work

MICOLE [8] introduces an architecture based on agents to "support the computer use and communication of disabled people" [8]. Input and output devices implement an agent that communicates with the application via a bus. Sender agents function as a driver to the application to hide the message exchange. Hence, the main advantage of MICOLE is the ability to provide abstractions to input and output modalities. It does, however, not offer any support for fusing input or fission of output.

Doulens et al. present in [4] an agent based system to enable understanding of "what is happening in the environment in a situational context" [4]. The architecture is applied to an assistant robot that helps blind or disabled people to cross a road in a virtual reality environment. Inputs are provided via SOAP services and forwarded to fusion agents. Meaning is inferred with the help of ontologies in semantic agents (which can be nested). On the output side fission agents are used to control the actual hardware actuators. While this provides a flexible architecture it does not make use of standards (SOAP being the only exception). The emphasis of this approach is also on multimodal fusion while multimodal fission is not explored in detail.

3   Dialog Management for Multiple Users and Modalities

In this section the components for building a multimodal and multiuser dialog management are presented.

---

[3] http://www.w3.org/TR/2012/WD-scxml-20120216/

The W3C suggests the use of SCXML as the dialog manager which has been proven to be suitable to decouple the control flow and presentation layer in dialog management [15]. It has been used in several applications to express dialog states [3] or to easily incorporate external information [13]. However, multimodal fusion to combine the input from multiple input modalities and multimodal fission to use multiple modalities to deliver information has not been discussed in -depth so far.

3.1 Multimodal Fusion

In multimodal systems users are able to express their dialog move by more than a single modality. Multimodal fusion combines the input coming from the various modalities into a single semantic interpretation that expresses the user's interaction intent [1]. The MCs send their input as EMMA [4] events to the upper IM for further refinement. The fusion engine needs an application independent representation of the current context to infer meaning [4]. Here, we suggest that the MC_{fus} can query IM_{ISU} for information that is present in the datamodel but also for the state of the different MCs. The latter can be achieved by a registry of available services that is maintained by the IM_{ISU}. Such a service allows for a direct connection to an MC e.g. to query for information. Hence, it works as an overlay to the actual structure of IMs and MCs. The use of Prolog as a scripting language also allows for reasoning capabilities in the multimodal fusion. Finally, the MC_{fus} sends the results of the multimodal fusion to the topmost IM_{ISU}.

For our demo scenario, deictic gestures are captured with the Leap Motion which may be augmented by some spoken comment. For instance, users may point at a certain location stating e.g. *"Maybe, we should move that to here."*. Here, the meaning of *that* and *here* is fused with the semantic interpretation of the spoken utterance *move* into a coherent meaning which we send as an EMMA event to the IM_{ISU} dialog manager.

3.2 The Root Interaction Manager

The individual EMMA events received from the MC_{fus} already represent the user's application specific interaction intent and will update the information state. Depending on the change, this topmost interaction manager will reason about the next steps to take and will communicate the new (derived) information to MC_{fis}. Thereby, it must consider the personal attributes of the participants containing information about output settings like *blind user*, *available* and *preferred* modalities.

3.3 Multimodal Fission

Multimodal systems allow for the combined or alternative use of different input modalities and to select output modalities most appropriate for a given context. Besides the advantages named by Oviatt and Cohen[7], namely that the system

---

[4] http://www.w3.org/TR/2009/REC-emma-20090210/

gains robustness and is less prone to errors, an appropriate selection and combination of output modalities has the potential to ease or enable communication, e.g. when communicating with disabled people. One approach for fusion was introduced as WWHT by Rousseau et al. [10]. (i) **What** is the information to process, (ii) **Which** modalities should we use to present this information, (iii) **How** to present the information using these modalities and (iv) and **T**hen, how to handle the evolution of the resulting presentation [11]. These questions also shape the processing stages during fission.

In the *What* stage, a message is decomposed into elementary information units, e.g. (i) the fact that a new node was added, (ii) the name of the new node and (iii) the parent node. There may be other information units as well like *location of the new node*, but we restrict it to these three for traceability. This data is sent from the topmost interaction manager IM_{ISU} to the MC_{fis}.

The *Which* stage allows for the selection of appropriate modalities based on rules and the affordances of the individual modalities. Employing Prolog as part of the interaction managers also allows us to include reasoning capabilities and global knowledge in this step. E.g. to deduce that a change in context justifies to reestablish an explicit reference by playing an auditory path to a node on the mind map.

In the *how* stage, we actually rendering the output. This is done by the specific MCs.

As it comes to multiuser support, we are using multiple instances of the fission engine: One per user.

4   Conclusion

This paper describes our approach to model multiuser, multimodal applications using recently finalized W3C recommendations to communicate nonverbal communication elements. We exemplify the approach by employing it to a brainstorming session with blind and sighted participants. This scenario shows the potential of using fusion and fission in a multimodal environment.

Another aspect is that the integration of fusion and fission engines in the W3C MMI architecture needs some further refinement. An integration as in comparable state-of-the-art architectures violate the tree structure as suggested in the specification for arranging modality components [12]. A main reason is the enforced split of modality components into modality components that are either responsible to contribute to the multimodal fusion or those that will be triggered by the multimodal fission. In the W3C MMI architecture modality components can play both roles at the same time.

The extension of SCXML via Prolog enables SCXML documents to include reasoning capabilities in the dialog manager as well as in the fusion and fission. In a next step, we will continue the implementation and evaluate the approach with a larger group of sighted and blind people.

Acknowledgments. This work has been partially supported by the DfG (German Research Foundation) and it has been produced out of the D-A-CH project.

The D-A-CH project is a joined project between TUD, the ETH and JKU with the respective founding organizations DFG (German Research Foundation), SNF (Swiss National Science Foundation) and FWF (Austrian Science Found).

References

1. Atrey, P.K., Hossain, M.A., Saddik, A.E., Kankanhalli, M.S.: Multimodal fusion for multimedia analysis: a survey. Multimedia systems 16(6), 345–379 (2010)
2. Brock, A., Truillet, P., Oriola, B., Jouffrais, C.: Usage of multimodal maps for blind people: why and how. In: ACM International Conference on Interactive Tabletops and Surfaces, pp. 247–248. ACM (2010)
3. Brusk, J., Lager, T., Hjalmarsson, A., Wik, P.: Deal: dialogue management in scxml for believable game characters. In: Proceedings of the 2007 Conference on Future Play, pp. 137–144. ACM (2007)
4. Dourlens, S., Ramdane-Cherif, A., Monacelli, E.: Multi levels semantic architecture for multimodal interaction. Applied Intelligence, 1–14 (2013)
5. Landragin, F.: Physical, semantic and pragmatic levels for multimodal fusion and fission. In: Proceedings of the Seventh International Workshop on Computational Semantics (IWCS-7), pp. 346–350 (2007)
6. Manshad, M.S., Pontelli, E., Manshad, S.J.: Micoo (multimodal interactive cubes for object orientation): a tangible user interface for the blind and visually impaired. In: The Proceedings of the 13th International ACM SIGACCESS Conference on Computers and Accessibility, pp. 261–262. ACM (2011)
7. Oviatt, S.L., Cohen, P.R.: Multimodal interfaces that process what comes naturally. Communications of the ACM 43(3), 45–53 (2000)
8. Pietrzak, T., Martin, B., Pecci, I., Saarinen, R., Raisamo, R., Järvi, J.: The micole architecture: multimodal support for inclusion of visually impaired children. In: Proceedings of the 9th International Conference on Multimodal Interfaces, pp. 193–200. ACM (2007)
9. Pölzer, S., Schnelle-Walka, D., Pöll, D., Heumader, P., Miesenberger, K.: Making brainstorming meetings accessible for blind users. In: Proceedings of the 12th European AAATE Conference (Pre-print 2013)
10. Rousseau, C., Bellik, Y., Vernier, F.: WWHT: Un modèle conceptuel pour la présentation multimodale d'information. In: Proceedings of the 17th International Conference on Francophone sur l'Interaction Homme-Machine, pp. 59–66. ACM (2005)
11. Rousseau, C., Bellik, Y., Vernier, F., Bazalgette, D.: A Framework for the Intelligent Multimodal Presentation of Information. Signal Processing 86(12), 3696–3713 (2006)
12. Schnelle-Walka, D., Radomski, S., Mühlhäuser, M.: JVoiceXML as a Modality Component in the W3C Multimodal Architecture. Journal on Multimodal User Interfaces (April 2013)
13. Sigüenza Izquierdo, Á., Blanco Murillo, J.L., Bernat Vercher, J., Hernández Gómez, L.A.: Using scxml to integrate semantic sensor information into context-aware user interfaces. In: International Workshop on Semantic Sensor Web, in Conjunction with IC3K 2010, Telecomunicacion (2011)
14. Ward, J., Meijer, P.: Visual experiences in the blind induced by an auditory sensory substitution device. Consciousness and cognition 19(1), 492–500 (2010)
15. Wilcock, G.: SCXML and voice interfaces. In: 3rd Baltic Conference on Human Language Technologies. Citeseer, Kaunas (2007)

A Mind Map for Brainstorming Sessions with Blind and Sighted Persons

Dirk Schnelle-Walka[1], Ali Alavi[2], Patrick Ostie[1],
Max Mühlhäuser[1], and Andreas Kunz[2]

[1] Technische Universität Darmstadt, Darmstadt, Germany
[2] Eidgenössisch Technische Hochschule Zürich, Zürich, Switzerland

Abstract. Accessible mind maps tools are, due to their visual nature hardly available and, if available, they focus on rendering the structure, not considering nonverbal communication elements in ongoing discussions. In this paper, we describe the need for this type of communication as well as a mind map tool that is capable of processing the respective information, coming from a Leap tracking system attached to the interactive surface.

Keywords: Accessibility, Non-verbal Communication Clements, Computer Supported Collaborative Work, MindMap.

1 Introduction

Mind maps usually are tree-based diagrams that are used to outline ideas related to a central topic. "Major topics or categories associated with the central topic are captured by branches flowing from the central image. Each branch is labeled with a keyword or image. Lesser items within each category stem from the relevant branches" [1]. They can be used to generate, visualize, structure and classify ideas in a multitude of scenarios, e.g problem solving or decision making [8]. As they are predominantly visual, they are inaccessible to blind persons. Moreover, explanatory gestures are used above the mind map on non-verbal communication levels [2]. Consequently, an inclusive mind mapping tool must be designed to support both (i) access for the blind participants to the artifacts displayed on the mind map and (ii) access to the artifacts for translation tools of non-verbal communication elements. However, these nonverbal communication elements cannot be captured anymore by sensors of the interactive surface. Thus, additional sensors are required to precisely detect deictic gestures such as pointing. In the following, we describe our approach to such a mind map tool based on focus groups, where we identified relevant requirements to consider in the design of such a tool.

2 Related Work

A project started by Roy Grubb aims at helping a blind student who was forced to use mind maps during his course[1]. He, along with 30 contributors, analyzed

---

[1] http://www.informationtamers.com/WikIT/
   index.php?title=Mind_mapping_for_people_who_are_blind

K. Miesenberger et al. (Eds.): ICCHP 2014, Part I, LNCS 8547, pp. 214–219, 2014.

available tools with regard to accessibility. Here, XMind[2] was considered to be the most accessible tool. Its main advantage lies in the integration with available text reading software like NVDA[3] or JAWS[4] on Windows or VoiceOver[5] on MacOSX and iOS. Another tool is FreeMind[6] that can be controlled by spoken commands using Simon with some adaptations[7]. They consider "touch or sound [...] to be the only options", e.g. to synthesize the labels. While this would work if the blind user is working on her own, the applicability in collaborative settings with sighted users is problematic.

One of the most interesting tools is described by Sanchez et al. in the domain of concept mapping for blind children [7]. Here, children can navigate the tree-like structure of concept maps with the help of audio cues. They found that blind users tend to create the maps in a sequential order rather than more elaborate structures. However, they developed an interface that was mainly meant to be used by blind persons only. Thereby, they did not consider e.g. nonverbal communication or problems that might occur because the interface should be able to support both, blind and sighted participants simultaneously.

Capturing hand gestures as a main carrier of nonverbal information and translating them to a blind user is a new approach to better integrate them in such kind of vivid discussions. Tang et al. [9] introduced VideoArms to relate hand gestures to artifacts displayed on the screen. VideoArms captured the users' arms with the help of a color camera, and separated them from the screens content employing color segmentation. This approach proved to be problematic in presence of a dynamic background, or colors shared both by the screen content and the users' arms. Kunz et al. [5] overcame these issues with the CollaBoard system, which benefits from the fact that an LC screen emits linearly polarized light. Placing an additional linear polarization filter that is rotated by 90° in front of the camera will blind it for the content on the screen, while the user is still visible. This allows separating a person in front of a highly dynamic background on the LC screen. A more recent approach by Kunz et al. [4] use Microsoft Kinect to capture hand gestures above an interactive table. However, in all cases the remote station receives the content of the digital surface together with the video overlay, which is an unsuitable representation in a mixed group of blind and sighted users.

3   Focus Group about Brainstorming Tools

We conducted a focus group since we were interested which nonverbal communication elements would be most interesting to be communicated to the blind besides the artifacts.

---

[2] http://www.xmind.net/
[3] http://www.nvaccess.org/
[4] http://www.freedomscientific.com/products/fs/jaws-product-page.asp
[5] http://www.apple.com/accessibility/voiceover/
[6] http://freemind.sourceforge.net/wiki/index.php/Main_Page
[7] http://kde-files.org/content/show.php/
%5BEN%2BVF%5D%2BFreeMind%2B0.9.0RC7?content=137915

Four persons participated (3 female, 1 male). Two persons were blind from birth, one became blind at the age of one year and one could partially see shapes. They distinguished three kinds of nonverbal communication elements (i) deictic gestures, (ii) pose and (iii) facial expressions. They were generally not actively using these and saw the danger that they are likely to be misinterpreted. On the one hand, they feel that something is missing. On the other hand they stated that it is hard to miss something which is unknown. However, they think that this may change once they learn more about it. First approaches are stated by one person. She participated in a training about nonverbal communication.

Generally, they considered deictic gestures to be the most important ones. This category is well known known and also sometimes used, e.g. to raise the hand to stop a bus. However, they mostly rely on someone to verbalize this kind of communication. They feel that, since deictic gestures may happen frequently during a conversation, an interpretation of all gestures may result in information overload.

Postures are hardly known and considered to be of less importance. It may be used to express the user's affective state but is hard to interpret correctly.

Facial expressions are considered to be the least important. Also it is again no reliable source of information.

With regard to possible translations they raised doubts that it can happen via auditory icons alone. They prefer verbal descriptions since this is a known world. Also, they fear an information overload. Consequently, it will be hard to follow both, an ongoing discussion as well as the descriptions. A better solution would be to use pauses as a human translator would do.

4   Collaborative Mind Map

The focus group described in the previous section suggests that a mind map tool should primarily support deictic gestures, e.g. when pointing at a certain node of the mind map. Additionally, we regard collaborative settings were multiple persons can modify the mind map. General requirements to such a tool are described in [6]. They identified requirements for such a tool as to (i) be accessible by blind people not interfere other users, (ii) always synchronize visual and non-visual representations, (iii) offer the same functionalities as all users, (iv) guarantee that the blind user has to be made aware of any changes done and (v) allow tracking changes. As concluded above, such a tool must also cope with nonverbal communication. Therefore, we developed CoME, a **Co**llaborative **M**ind Map **E**ditor, which runs on the Microsoft PixelSense and which is available as open source[8].

CoME features communication capabilities that allows to propagate addition or modification of nodes as well as receiving them externally and integrate them into the current view. Here, we follow the observation from Kamel et al. [3]. They suggest using different representations to cope with individual presentation needs resulting in higher synchronization needs. We are using messages that are

---

[8] http://come.sourceforge.net

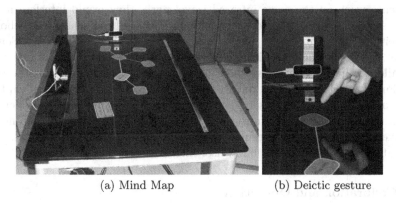

(a) Mind Map   (b) Deictic gesture

Fig. 1. Collaborative Mind Map Editor running on the Microsoft PixelSense

sent over uMundo[9] as ProtoBuf messages. Messages can indicate (i) a new map, (ii) addition and (iii) deletion of a node as well as (iv) updates. A node has the following attributes (i) the node id, (ii) the text displayed, (iii) the node's parent id, (iv) the issuer, (v) a time-stamp, (vi) the screen coordinates and (vii) the color of the node. Thanks to uMundo's publish-subscribe capabilities, a client can receive or publish these messages as long as it knows the name of the communication channel. A client for blind users has already been presented in [6]. Changes of the screen coordinates are sent over another channel since they are not relevant for each client.

These messages are also the basis to include e.g. pointing gestures as shown in Figure 1 (b). Visually overlaying deictic gestures on digital content gives information to sighted users only, but is not useful for blind users. The visual computation of such an overlay is complicated and also the depth information of the pointing gestures is completely lost in a two-dimensional representation. Thus, a new system for reliable tracking is required. In this case, a Leap Motion is used to capture the pointing and fused with knowledge about the screen coordinates of the nodes.

5   Capturing Pointing Gestures

For capturing pointing gestures above the table, we mounted three Leap motion sensors on the sides of the table, while the fourth side (the blind user's position) does not require to sense pointing information (see section 3). Since tracking of pointing gestures is computationally expensive, the Leap motion sensors have to run on separate machines. Here, uMundo's publish/subscribe capabilities help to ease the communication across machines. The motion sensor machines publish their information to CoME as the subscriber. All the mentioned software is developed for Windows 7 using C#. Since the Leap motion sensors and the

---

[9] https://github.com/tklab-tud/umundo

PixelSense work on the same infrared wavelength, they would interfere if the devices see each other. However, the inclination of the Leap sensors was chosen that neither the Leap sensors see each other, nor do they see the PixelSenses surface. The Leaps field of view is oriented in such a way that its one edge is parallel to the PixelSenses surface, since this orientation allows for the best detection of pointing gestures on artifacts on the screen. The sensors capture the pointing fingers of the users, calculating their target on the PixelSense's screen, and send the final results to the PixelSense. The software running on the PixelSense displays the results as a highlighter to the sighted users. The information is also sent to the blind user interface

5.1   Calibration and Operation

Prior to a brainstorming session, the tracking system needs to be calibrated. Although the geometric position of the sensors with regard to the table only needs to be calibrated once, it is important to take also into account the user's position and height, in order to achieve reliable results. For the calibration process, every user has to touch the PixelSense's screen several times. The touch point is detected by the PixelSense, but also by the Leap sensor. Next, the measured data needs to be unified, since the table and the sensor work in different coordinate systems. After performing these transformations, the system compares the calculated touch point with the measured data from the PixelSense in order to find constant shifts and slopes (see Figure 2).

Fig. 2. Calibration of the system

During normal operation, gestures are detected and the target point is highlighted on the screen. This will help the sighted user to perform more precise pointing and consequently avoid wrong notifications of the blind user.

6   Conclusion and Outlook

In this paper, we described CoME, a collaborative mind map editor that can be used in collocated brainstorming sessions with blind and sighted persons. It features communication capabilities that allow for the presentation of the mind map in user interfaces that consider special information presentation needs. Further, we described the results of a focus group that provided us with those nonverbal communication elements that should be considered in the first place. We showed, how these pointing gestures and deictic gestures are captured using Leap sensors.

As a next step, we will work on a noise filtering of the tracking data, which will make the detection of deictic gestures more stable. We foresee an exponential or double-exponential smoothing of the signals. Although this will come to cost of a slightly increased latency, we do not expect any negative impact on the users performance, since pointing gestures are not time critical. On the other hand, a filtering will eventually improve the stability of the highlighter and thus will allow a smoother interaction with the system. Further, we will also work on a data refinement using this filtered data and the knowledge about the artifacts positions on the PixelSense. Together with other information such as audio, this will allow an unequivocal and stable input for the blind user interface. Finally, we also envision to also integrate other gestures then pointing to make our system also applicable to other collaboration scenarios such as net-based collaboration.

Acknowledgments. This work has been partially funded by the D-A-CH project #CR21I2L_138601.

References

1. Budd, J.W.: Mind maps as classroom exercises. The Journal of Economic Education 35(1), 35–46 (2004)
2. Ellis, C.A., Gibbs, S.J., Rein, G.: Groupware: some issues and experiences. Communications of the ACM 34(1), 39–58 (1991)
3. Kamel, H.M., Landay, J.A.: A study of blind drawing practice: creating graphical information without the visual channel. In: Proceedings of the Fourth International ACM Conference on Assistive Technologies, pp. 34–41. ACM (2000)
4. Kunz, A., Alavi, A., Sinn, P.: Integrating pointing gesture detection for enhancing brainstorming meetings using kinect and pixelsense. Proceedings of the 8th International Conference on Digital Enterprise Technology pp. 1–8 (2014)
5. Kunz, A., Nescher, T., Küchler, M.: Collaboard: A novel interactive electronic whiteboard for remote collaboration with people on content. International Conference on Cyberworlds - CW 2010 pp. 430–437 (2010)
6. Pölzer, S., Schnelle-Walka, D., Pöll, D., Heumader, P., Miesenberger, K.: Making brainstorming meetings accessible for blind users. In: AAATE Conference (2013)
7. Sanchez, J., Flores, H.: Concept mapping for virtual rehabilitation and training of the blind. IEEE Transactions on Neural Systems and Rehabilitation Engineering 18(2), 210–219 (2010)
8. Shui, W., Le, W.: Mindmap-ng: A novel framework for modeling effective thinking. In: 2010 3rd IEEE International Conference on Computer Science and Information Technology (ICCSIT), vol. 2, pp. 480–483 (2010)
9. Tang, A., Neustaedter, C., Greenberg, S.: Videoarms: Embodiments for mixed presence groupware. In: Proceedings of HCI, pp. 85–102 (2006)

Presenting Non-verbal Communication to Blind Users in Brainstorming Sessions

Stephan Pölzer and Klaus Miesenberger

Johannes Kepler Universität Linz, Institute Integriert Studieren, Linz, Austria
{stephan.poelzer,klaus.miesenberger}@jku.at

Abstract. In co-located meetings, which are part of our professional and educational lives, information exchange relies not only on information exchange using artifacts like bubbles in mind-maps or equations presented on electronic whiteboards in classrooms, but also to a large extent on non-verbal communication. In the past much effort was done to make the artifact level accessible but also non-verbal communication heavily relies on the visual channel to which blind people do not have access. Thereby co-located meetings are seen as first domain to research accessibility of non-verbal communication, which are well defined and should lead to more general research on access to non-verbal communication. We present a first prototypical system which allows experimenting with access to non-verbal communication elements by blind people using both the input from a "human" transcriber or automatic tracking and recognition of non-verbal communication cues.

Keywords: Co-located meetings, Non-verbal Communication, Blind User.

1 Introduction

Non-verbal communication plays an important role in social interaction [1,2]. Such communication heavily relies on the visual channel. Examples are nodding of the head to agree or disagree with the current speaker, pointing at artifacts (as for instance bubbles of a mind-map in brainstorming meetings), smiling or gazing to other persons. Further speaker regulation is influenced by non-verbal communication. Non-verbal behavior can include hints of a listener's interest on an ongoing discussion or talk. Blind people do not have access to such information and therefore not only miss information exchange done by an inaccessible artifact layer, but also miss information exchange, which is done by visual non-verbal communication.

This paper presents a tool, which can be used to present non-verbal communication elements to blind people. At the moment, the tool is especially designed for brainstorming sessions based on mind-maps as described in [3]. Such a tool allows investigating the importance of different non-verbal communication elements to blind people, and if the presentation of non-verbal communication elements to blind users could ease the participation of blind persons in co-located meetings.

This work on the presentation layer of non-verbal communication for blind people is embedded in a larger research project which focuses on the access to non-verbal communication in a more general sense.

K. Miesenberger et al. (Eds.): ICCHP 2014, Part I, LNCS 8547, pp. 220–225, 2014.
© Springer International Publishing Switzerland 2014

2   State of the Art in Tracking and Reasoning for Non-verbal Communication and Research Questions

Much effort has been done during the last years to make the artifact level of communication accessible for blind persons, as for instance mathematical equations, graphs and pictures (examples are [4,5,6]). But also non-verbal communication heavily relies on the visual channel to which blind people don't have access. So far topics as

1. the importance of occurring visual non-verbal communication for blind participants in co-located and also distance meetings,
2. the feasibility of transcribing or tracking and automatic translation of non-verbal communication and
3. the usefulness or added value, restrictions and requirements of such transcript

are not well studied. Especially point 2 and 3, the importance and usefulness, of non-verbal communication will depend also on the way how the non-verbal information is presented to the blind user. Which leads to further research questions how much information can be reasonably presented to the blind user and how to present the information to the blind user? Is it better and feasible to present the gathered information via haptic devices, vibrations, audio cues, non-speech sounds or any other thinkable modalities?

Hardware for tracking movements (e.g. video cameras or sensors which give also 3D data as the Leap Motion (https://www.leapmotion.com) and the Microsoft Kinect (http://www.xbox.com/kinect) becomes more affordable. Further, sensors attached to the body (e.g. acceleration sensors, MyoTM sensor (https://www.thalmic.com/en/myo/)) can be used to track motions. All such devices can be integrated in the described scenario, of course still restricted to settings as being in front of a background for good contrast. They all show potential for a better access to non-verbal communication for blind people and a more detailed description of tracking in co-located meeting can be found in [7], which was prepared in the same project.

However, despite the fact that tracking devices become more accurate and many well-defined scenarios can be found, in which tracking works fine, tracking of the whole occurring non-verbal communication of all persons who are participating in a co-located meeting is not yet possible today. But not only limitation of hardware accuracy is responsible for the limitation of non-verbal communication tracking but also the reasoning algorithms to interpret humans' movements are limited. The interpretation of non-verbal communication by human being is not only done by analyzing the data of one single channel (visual), but much more by the combination of different channels (acoustic, visual and tactile). A human being interprets the occurrence of a stretched finger in the combination with a spoken sentence "Look at this" as a pointing gesture. In most situations human being can interpret gestures with similar appearance but with different meanings easily and sensibly. So tracking and reasoning of non-verbal communication today done by a machine is far away from the interpretation capabilities of non-verbal communication by human beings.

3   Tool for Simulating Non-verbal Communication Elements

3.1   General Description of the Simulating Tool

Considering the fact that an automatic tracking of non-verbal communication today is still very limited, transcribing by a human being is the only reasonable way to do research and considering a service for better access to important aspects of non-verbal communication. The tool provides an UI (see figure 1) for fast entering information on gestures and other non-verbal elements a transcriber identifies during a brainstorming session. A second possibility is to use time protocols and video recordings. In the second case, a co-located meeting has to be recorded, the video has to be analyzed and a time protocol has to be designed. Afterwards the video and the defined gestures can be presented to the blind user. Both possibilities are included in the system architecture of the mind-map tool presented in [3]. In the current version, the blind user is informed via a message box about the transcribed gesture. In a later stage, automatic import of recognized gestures and other non-verbal cues can be supported.

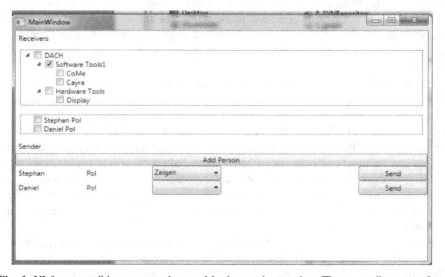

Fig. 1. UI for transcribing gestures in a real brainstorming session: The transcriber can select the gesture from a predefined list (here "zeigen (pointing)"), and the originator as well as a receiver by selecting it with a tick. At the moment possible receivers are bubbles of the mind-map and persons taking part in the meeting, who have to be added at the beginning of the session via the "add Persons" button.

For the presentation of the non-verbal communication elements to the blind user with standard AT, a machine readable format has to be defined. The structure used at the moment is described by the following attributes:

- Sender: Is the originator of a message
- Message Type: can be for instance pointing, gaze or smiling

- Receiver: The "object" the originator is interacting with, can be another person or a mind-map bubble
- Timestamp: Time when the non-verbal communication element occurred

These attributes are highly related to an information exchange in a typical conversation, in which a sender generates a message and interacts with a receiver. The timestamp is not immediately presented to the blind user but can be used afterwards to allow chronologically looking up gestures in a history view. For the beginning, it seems that the fields selected are satisfying. However if important fields are missing as for instance repetition, duration or starting- and end time they can be added easily.

3.2   First Experimental Setup

Two different experiment setups were tested. One experiment setup was based on a real time meeting and the graphical user interface for gesture transcription and the second one was based on recording of a brainstorming session which was presented to a blind person afterwards. The blind person, who was taking part in the real time meeting, was also the person, who took part in the video based experiment. In both experiment setups only pointing gestures were considered as a representative of non-verbal communication.

During the first experiment setup in a short meeting, between a sighted and a blind participant, a small mind-map with only a few bubbles was created. The CoME tool (http://sourceforge.net/projects/come/) which is also developed in the same project was used for the presentation of the mind-map to the sighted person and the BlindUserView, which is described in [3] was used for the presentation of the mind-map to the blind user. During the generation of the mind-map the sighted person tried to make a high number of pointing gestures, which were presented to the blind user using the UI for transcribing. The transcribed gestures were presented to the blind user by message boxes. During the generation of pointing gestures, the sighted user consciously avoided spoken hints of the focused targets. Sentences like "can you add a node with the content meeting as a child to this bubble" were used instead of telling the bubble names.

For the second experiment setup a video of a brainstorming session between two sighted persons was prepared. Afterwards a time-protocol including the pointing gestures and the generation of the bubbles was generated. The video was presented to the blind user and in parallel the BlindUserView was used for the representation of the mind-map. Based on the time-protocol the bubbles and the gestures were presented to the blind user at the corresponding times to the video. Again message boxes were used to present the occurrence of pointing gestures. The record was presented twice to the blind user. In the second case the message boxes, which informed the user that a bubble was added, were deactivated. Instead only a beep, which indicated a creation of a bubble, was given as a hint to the blind user that a change of the mind map occurred. The blind user had to figure out where the bubble was added.

From a short discussion with the blind user about the importance of the pointing gestures, it turned out that they might have the possibility to support the blind in brainstorming meetings but it has to be taken care that only important gestures are presented to the blind user and not to overload him/her. Blind users also urged that the output interface has to be designed in a clever way. At the moment the alert messages, which present changes of the mind-map and occurring gestures are judged by the blind user as too time consuming to follow the ongoing discussion. The blind user has also the impression that only generating a beep, when a bubble is added, and to allow him to use the time to search for the changes in the tree instead of reading the message boxes and jumping to the change, gives him a better understanding of the structure of the mind-map (generating only a beep was done during the second time the blind user watched the video).To reduce time effort for the blind user to read message boxes presentation of the gestures via audio might be a good idea. But audio often conflicts with the ongoing discourse. Braille allows more "catching up in parallel". Another way to reduce reading effort is to shorten question by using clever structures and not to ask whole questions. To give an example: In case of a pointing gesture instead of presenting a message box with the content "Person is pointing to bubble. Jump to node?" it might be enough to use a specific beep for an occurring pointing gesture and just present the bubble, where the user is pointing to, on the Braille display. If the blind user likes to put the focus to the bubble he/she just hits the space button on the keyboard.

4   Outlook and Goals

Today, tracking and reasoning of non-verbal communication is only possible for special scenarios and setups as for instance sign recognition. Automatic tracking and reasoning of non-verbal communication cues will only be possible at an experimental level the next years. The presented tool gives a possibility already today to investigate the importance of different non-verbal communication cues for blind persons taking part in co-located meetings and supports research in automatic tracking.

The subjective importance of gestures to a blind user will not only depend on the information benefit which the blind user gets but also on the presentation method. As pointed out above special care has to be given not to overload the blind user by less important gestures in a conversation so he/she is not distracted from the ongoing verbal communication. One important step not to overload but still present as much as possible of information of non-verbal communication to the blind user is to find the right presentation technique.

The next goals are to figure out important gestures in brainstorming session to propose non-verbal communication elements an automatic detection and presentation should focus on. In addition it allows experimenting to the mentioned important step in what way non-verbal communication is presented best to blind users (e.g. audio or message boxes). Finally, it proposes considering new services for important meetings, be it by human or automatic support. Moreover, other co-located or distant meetings in which e.g. a teacher points at artifacts on a white-/blackboard will be analyzed.

Acknowledgements. This work has been partially supported by the FWF (Austrian Science Found) with the regional project number I867-N25 and it has been produced out of the D-A-CH project. The D-A-CH project is a joint project between TUD, the ETH and JKU with the respective funding organizations DFG (German Research Foundation), SNF (Swiss National Science Foundation) and FWF (Austrian Science Found).

References

1. Goldin-Meadow, S.: The role of gesture in communication and thinking. Trends in Cognitive Sciences (1999)
2. M. Argyle: Non-Verbal Communication in human social interaction. In: Non-Verbal Communication. Cambridge University Press, USA (1972)
3. Pölzer, S., Schnelle-Wlka, D., Pöll, D., Heumader, P., Miesenberger, K.: Making Brainstorming Meetings Accessible for Blind Users. In: Encarnação, P., Azevedo, L., Gelderblom, G.J., Newell, A., Mathiassen, N.E. (eds.) Assistive Technology: From Research to Practice, Assistive Technologies Research Series, vol. 33, pp. 653–658. IOS Press, Amsterdam (2013)
4. Archambault, D., Fitzpatrick, D., Gupta, G., Karshmer, A.I., Miesenberger, K., Pontelli, E.: Towards a universal maths conversion library. In: Miesenberger, K., Klaus, J., Zagler, W.L., Burger, D. (eds.) ICCHP 2004. LNCS, vol. 3118, pp. 664–669. Springer, Heidelberg (2004)
5. Ramloll, R.S., Yu, W., Brewster, S., Riedel, B., Burton, M., Dimigen, G.: Constructing Sonified Haptic Line Graphs for the Blind Student: First Steps. In: Proceedings of the Fourth International ACM Conference on Assistive Technologies, Assets 2000 (2000)
6. Stöger, B., Batušić, M., Miesenberger, K., Haindl, P.: Supporting Blind Students in Navigation and Manipulation of Mathematical Expressions: Basic Requirements and Strategies. In: Miesenberger, K., Klaus, J., Zagler, W.L., Karshmer, A.I. (eds.) ICCHP 2006. LNCS, vol. 4061, pp. 1235–1242. Springer, Heidelberg (2006)
7. Schnelle-Walka, D., Alavi, A., Ostie, P., Mühlhäuser, M., Kunz, A.: A Mind Map for Brainstorming Sessions with Blind and Sighted Persons. In: Miesenberger, K., Fels, D., Archambault, D., Penaz, P., Zagler, W. (eds.) ICCHP 2014, Part I. LNCS, vol. 8547, pp. 214–219. Springer, Heidelberg (2014)

Towards an Information State Update Model Approach for Nonverbal Communication

Dirk Schnelle-Walka, Stefan Radomski, Stephan Radeck-Arneth,
and Max Mühlhäuser

Technische Universität Darmstadt, Darmstadt, Germany

Abstract. The Information State Update (ISU) Model describes an approach to dialog management that was predominantly applied to single user scenarios using voice as the only modality. Extensions to multimodal interaction with multiple users are rarely considered and, if presented, hard to operationalize. In this paper we describe our approach of dialog modeling based on ISU in multiuser dialog settings employing multiple modalities, including nonverbal communication.

1 Introduction

Although the Information State Update Model (ISU) as introduced by Larsson and Traum [9] describes a general concept to implement dialog managers, most implementations like TrindiKIT [1] or Dipper [2] primarily focus on spoken dialog systems. The approach originated in Dynamic Information Theory (DIT) as introduced by Bunt [3]. While Bunt based his *dialog acts* as the "functional units used by the speaker to change the context" [3] on linguistic aspects, the concept is not restricted to spoken language. Extensions to multimodality have already been successfully employed, e.g. [6]. These systems, however, primarily target single user settings while ISU based systems dealing with more than a single user are still focused on spoken interfaces. Furthermore, they are more interested in understanding *who is speaking to whom* [5] [12] which is relevant to include the computer as a homologous conversational counterpart. This research question may also include nonverbal aspects like gaze and gestures in order to detect turn-taking cues in multiparty conversations [1].

In contrast to that we aim at interfaces where both input and output are multimodal and the computer takes a solely supportive role. The information is presented to the users by a combination of modalities that best suits the kind of information to deliver while taking into account the special needs of the users, in our case blind users in a brainstorming session together with sighted persons. They require a special sort of interface that allows them to follow the discussion and the visual artifacts that are employed. The interface should enable them to actively contribute to the discussion but the selection of available modalities is limited. In this paper we introduce a novel way to model information states

---

[1] http://www.ling.gu.se/projekt/trindi/trindikit/

K. Miesenberger et al. (Eds.): ICCHP 2014, Part I, LNCS 8547, pp. 226–230, 2014.
© Springer International Publishing Switzerland 2014

supporting multiple users with different communication needs with the help of grounding and reasoning capabilities. We describe how to derive the groups intention from the individual multimodal input and introduce concepts to present this information to the users. Moreover it can be used to communicate nonverbal communication elements.

2   Related Work

Most research focused on scenarios where a single user interacts with a computer (see Figure 1(a)) like in the original work from Traum and Larsson where they introduced the ISU concepts [9]. There are several conceptions for multiparty dialogs. The first obvious one was introduced in 2002 where Traum and Rickel [13] proposed a multiuser (see Figure 1(b)) and multimodal model for a game scenario, which also uses aspects of the information state theory from Traum and Larsson [9]. However Ginzburg and Fernandes [5] have relativized the work of Traum and Rickel since it does not model true multiparty dialogs (see Figure 1(c)) but rather multiuser dialogs. The multiuser model targets only parallel dialogs without any relations between the dialog flows (only one sender and one addressee). Therefore the communication between the participants and cross-related discussions about the same topic are not covered. Only with a multiparty dialog model the complex group discussion relations can be recognized.

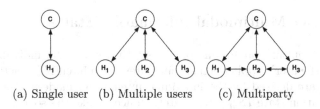

(a) Single user   (b) Multiple users   (c) Multiparty

Fig. 1. Schematic view of communication modes

Ginzburg et al. [5] also introduced in 2005 three interaction principles for realizing a system as a dialog partner. In 2008 Kronlid [8] criticizes these principles as not flexible enough and tried to extend the ISU concept by including a full-fledged multiparty turn manager. With its base in the principles of Sacks et al. [11]. In general, a turn manager tries to coordinate dialogs with the goal of a fair time distribution among the participants. Kronlid had simplified Sack's turn manager by omitting some solve strategies, which cope with complex overlapping scenarios.

In 2010 Strauß et. al. [12] extended the ISU approach for multiparty dialogs with proactive functionality by using ontologies. This is relevant to answer current research questions from a linguistic perspective. However, in our scenario there is no need for a system with communication capabilities comparable to a human. This allows us to focus on nonverbal, i.e. multimodal, aspects of the interaction with multiple users rather than forcing us to fully understand parallel ongoing discussions.

3   Scenario

We aim at a scenario in a current project to improve the participation of blind people in a brain-storming process with sighted people. Here, a mind map is used on a touch table. Here we encounter, high dynamics in the communication, like speaker changes, deictic gestures as well as frequent changes of the artifacts.

4   Dialog Management

The W3C suggests to use SCXML [2] as a dialog manager within a multimodal system. However, SCXML seems to be suited *only* to implement finite state or frame-based/form-filling dialog management approaches since they lack grounding and reasoning. Fodor and Huerta [4] demand that dialog managers should feature: (i) a formal logic foundation, (ii) an interference engine, (iii) general purpose planners and (iv) knowledge representation and expressiveness. One solution to overcome these limitations is to introduce Prolog as a replacement of an embedded scripting language [10] similar to the approach by Kronlid and Lager [7]. Embedding it as a scripting language allows to use SCXML as an ISU dialog manger compliant to the W3C MMI Architecture [3] which has the potential for more natural and flexible dialog management.

5   Multiuser Multimodal Information States

We rely on a multimodal fusion component that emits the individual events representing the user's application specific interaction intent. The actual intents of the group are derived by the individual intents and made accessible in the group information state IS_{grp}. Ultimately, concepts like the social structure of the participants ought to play a role when inferring the group intent. Figure 2 introduces the global information state.

The information state IS_{grp} comprises inferred group-related attributes as well as the actual state of the mind map, along with a history of its changes. It unifies the individual information states IS_{ind} into a coherent view. Each IS_{ind} includes, besides personal beliefs, personal attributes which includes the user's presumed mental state of the mind map. The personal attributes contain information about output related settings like *blind user*, *available* and *preferred* modalities.

The mind map's actual nodes and their relations are loaded as Prolog facts in the IS_{grp}. The IS_{ind} contains a mental model of the global map as it is perceived by the individual users. This individual mental model might differ from the actual map especially in the case of blind users. If one participant changes a node in the mind map, his mental state (in IS_{ind}) and the global mind map (in IS_{grp}) is updated. The IS_{grp} will trigger updating all other participants via

---

[2] http://www.w3.org/TR/2013/WD-scxml-20130801/

[3] http://www.w3.org/TR/mmi-arch/

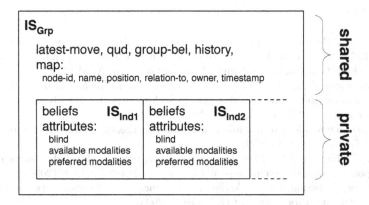

Fig. 2. Structure of adapted information state for multiuser scenarios

messages of an suitable type. Moreover, it can be used to reason when and how to deliver nonverbal communication elements.

For tracking the changes of the mind map and the discussion the IS_{grp} contains the attribute *history*. A timeout deletes expired events, because the scope or rather focus of discussion has changed.

This way we are able to provide an implementation for Strauß' and Minker's observation that not all participants share the common ground and the more participants the less common ground can be assumed [12].

6   Conclusion

This paper describes an extension of the ISU dialog management technique that integrates into the recently finalized W3C MMI recommendation. We exemplify the approach by employing it to a brainstorming session with blind and sighted participants.

The extension of SCXML via Prolog helps us to derive the groups intent and enables us to express ISU-based dialogs. In a next step, we will evaluate how this can be used to filter non-relevant events, especially for nonverbal communication, to avoid an information overload of the blind users.

Acknowledgments. This work has been partially supported by the DfG (German Research Foundation) and it has been produced out of the D-A-CH project. The D-A-CH project is a joined project between TUD, the ETH and JKU with the respective founding organizations DFG (German Research Foundation), SNF (Swiss National Science Foundation) and FWF (Austrian Science Found).

References

1. Bohus, D., Horvitz, E.: Facilitating multiparty dialog with gaze, gesture, and speech. In: International Conference on Multimodal Interfaces and the Workshop on Machine Learning for Multimodal Interaction, p. 5. ACM (2010)
2. Bos, J., Klein, E., Lemon, O., Oka, T.: Dipper: Description and formalisation of an information-state update dialogue system architecture. In: 4th SIGdial Workshop on Discourse and Dialogue, pp. 115–124 (2003)
3. Bunt, H.: Dynamic interpretation and dialogue theory. The Structure of Multi-modal Dialogue 2, 1–8 (1999)
4. Fodor, P., Huerta, J.M.: Planning and logic programming for dialog management. In: Spoken Language Technology Workshop, pp. 214–217. IEEE (2006)
5. Ginzburg, J., Fernández, R.: Action at a distance: the difference between dialogue and multilogue. Proceedings of DIALOR 5 (2005)
6. Honold, F., Schussel, F., Weber, M., Nothdurft, F., Bertrand, G., Minker, W.: Context models for adaptive dialogs and multimodal interaction. In: 2013 9th International Conference on Intelligent Environments (IE), pp. 57–64. IEEE (2013)
7. Kronlid, F., Lager, T.: Implementing the information-state update approach to dialogue management in a slightly extended scxml. In: Proceedings of the 11th International Workshop on the Semantics and Pragmatics of Dialogue (DECALOG), pp. 99–106 (2007)
8. Kronlid, F.: Steps towards Multi-Party Dialogue Management. Ph.D. thesis, Göteborgs Universitet (April 2008)
9. Larsson, S., Traum, D.: Information state and dialogue management in the TRINDI dialogue move engine toolkit. Natural Language Engineering 6(3&4), 323–340 (2000)
10. Radomski, S., Schnelle-Walka, D., Radeck-Arneth, S.: A Prolog Datamodel for State Chart XML. In: SIGdial Workshop on Discourse and Dialogue (2013) (preprint)
11. Sacks, H., Schegloff, E.A., Jefferson, G.: A simplest systematics for the organization of turn-taking for conversation. Language, 696–735 (1974)
12. Strauß, P.M., Minker, W.: Fundamentals. In: Proactive Spoken Dialogue Interaction in Multi-Party Environments, pp. 17–49. Springer (2010)
13. Traum, D., Rickel, J.: Embodied agents for multi-party dialogue in immersive virtual worlds. In: Proceedings of the First International Joint Conference on Autonomous Agents and Multiagent Systems: Part 2, pp. 766–773. ACM (2002)

Virtual Braille-Keyboard in Co-located Meetings

Emre Zaim, Markus Gruber, Gottfried Gaisbauer, Peter Heumader, Stephan Pölzer,
and Klaus Miesenberger

Johannes Kepler University, Institut Integriert Studieren, Linz, Austria
{zaimemre,ggaisbauer}@gmail.com, max.gruber@gmx.net,
{peter.heumader,stephan.poelzer,klaus.miesenberger}@jku.at

Abstract. Our daily live is no longer imaginable without touch devices. Besides standard touch devices as mobile phones and tablets also touch-tables have the chance to find their way into our daily lives. Co-located meetings can be seen as a good application area for touch-tables. They can present the artifact information layer to the whole group. On touch surfaces virtual keyboards are used by sighted people for text input and text manipulations. For blind people, such keyboards are only accessible with a decreased working speed. In co-located meetings, manipulation of artifacts (for instance bubbles of mind-maps) is very dynamic. Therefore, a decreased working speed to generate and manipulate textual inputs makes an equal participation of blind people in co-located meetings impossible. The ongoing work is concerned with the development of a virtual Braille-keyboard to allow a better integration of blind users into co-located meetings.

Keywords: Braille-keyboard, Blind user, Co-located Meetings, Touch devices.

1 Introduction

Nowadays, touch devices have found their way into many applications. Tablets and mobile phones with touch surfaces are already common in our daily live. With the ongoing hype on touch interfaces, it is very likely that also touch-tables will be used in everyday live. Possible application areas of touch tables are presented in [1] and [2]. In [3], a brainstorming scenario based on a mind-map is described, which is presented on a touch-table to the meeting's participants. In most touch-table applications, textual input is done by a virtual keyboard. Using the virtual keyboard on a touch- table decreases accessibility for blind users. Typical accessibility algorithm like scanning algorithms, as they can be used on small touch devices like smart-phones and tablets, may fail on large touch-table surfaces. Blind users may not even be able to find an appearing virtual keyboard on a large touch-table surface in a reasonable time span.

A possible solution to integrate blind persons in co-located meetings and give them the possibility to modify the content of the surface is presented in [3] by the example of a brainstorming session. In that experimental setup, the blind meeting participant uses a separate workstation equipped with a Braille-display and a standard keyboard to interact with the content on the surface, whereas the sighted persons are standing or

K. Miesenberger et al. (Eds.): ICCHP 2014, Part I, LNCS 8547, pp. 231–236, 2014.

sitting around the touch-table and make the input over a virtual keyboard. The different views for the sighted users and for the blind users represent the same information but prepared in a way so that each user can manipulate the artifact layer. Such an approach has the drawback that the blind user needs extra space for his/her workstation and input device. The blind meeting participant is excluded from taking part as an equivalent meeting participant. To overcome the problem of a separate working area for blind users in co-located meetings, virtual Braille-keyboards might offer a solution for an input device.

This paper presents an overview of today's available Braille-keyboards, discusses the possibilities of using a Braille-keyboard as an input device in co-located meetings, and presents an Android based prototype of an implemented Braille-keyboard.

2   Virtual Braille Keyboards as an Input Devices for Touch Devices in Co-located Meetings

2.1   Basic Concept of Braille-Keyboards

One of the mechanical Braille-keyboards is the Perkins Brailler (http://www.perkins.org/assets/downloads/nextgeneration/perkins_brailler_qsg _en.pdf). In general a Braille-keyboard mainly consists of six keys where each key represents a specific dot from the 6 points of a Braille-character in case of a 6 dot Braille. By using a Braille-keyboard characters are typed by pressing the according keys of the Braille-keyboard at the same time. For instance a "b" can be typed by pressing the respective keys for the upper left and middle left dots of the Braille-character. Besides the 6 keys for the characters Braille-keyboards normally have separate keys for space and backspace.

The concept of pressing the respective keys of a Braille-keyboard can be transferred to a touch device. Instead of pressing mechanical keys, specific pattern of touch points have to be analyzed and have to be mapped to a character. Different methods for analyzing and mapping exist. One approach is to use fixed defined areas of the screen. Each area represents one specific dot of the Braille character by touching the respective areas at the same time a character can be typed. Another approach is not to use fixed areas but let the user first define the areas of the dots by an initialization method. The initialization method for instance can be just to place 6 fingers at the same time to the screen. After that the areas of the dots are defined (compare 3. Implementation). Further approaches can be found in 2.2 State-of-the-Art in Touch-Based Braille-Keyboards.

2.2   State-of-the-Art in Touch-Based Braille-Keyboards

Today, several touch-based Braille keyboards and similar input strategies, which can be used by blind users, exist, as for instance SmartBraille (https://play. google.com/store/apps/details?id=jp.tmhouse.SmartBraille), Braille-Type [4], and BrailleTouch [5]. However, many of such tools are designed for small devices and not for large displays such as touch tables. For instance, BrailleTouch and BrailleType are designed in such a way, that the blind user has to place his/her fingers to specified areas as for instance edges of the touch device. Another drawback of some applications is that they are developed only for a specific operating system like iOS. A further similar input concept is presented in [6]. Input is generated by setting the pins of a Braille character line-by-line by using specific gestures (for instance a touch on the left half of the display sets the left pin of the line and a touch on the right half of the screen sets the right pin). Another interesting touch-based keyboard, which seems to overcome most of the problems, is the announced software UpSens from inpris (http://www.inprisltd.com). The tool provides a touch-based Braille-keyboard as well as an input method based on gestures. It offers a predefined set of intuitive gestures which can be extended by self-defined gestures. However, this tool is unavailable at the moment and it is announced that the first version will be for Android, and that the team is also working on an iOS version.

2.3   Possibilities of a Virtual Braille-Keyboard in Co-located Meetings

As mentioned above, touch-based Braille-keyboards allow blind users to make textual inputs on the same device as the other users in co-located meetings, which is an important step to avoid placing the blind user separately beyond his assistive technology. A further advantage of a virtual Braille-keyboard can be the working speed in comparison to virtual keyboards using special accessibility features. Scanning algorithms might be slower than typing input via Braille. Another problem for a blind user is to find the place and orientation of a virtual keyboard on large touch surfaces and searching for the virtual keyboard by the blind persons might disturb the other meeting participants. Accessibility features which use an input overlay over the whole touch surface and change the standard input behavior of the device (as it is done for instance on the iOS) only work in case that sighted users adapt their input behavior to the input modalities of blind users. A further drawback of using accessibility features for virtual keyboards is that finding a letter relies mainly on audio feedback, which can disturb the whole group in a collocated meeting. In case of a virtual Braille-keyboard, no audio feedback is necessary at least for typing letters. Only in case of checking or editing the input, audio feedback or other assistive technology has to be used.

Speech input would be another possibility to bring blind users away from a separate working area and include them better into a discussion. Compared to speech input, a virtual Braille-keyboard has the advantage that a discussion on a topic is not interrupted, but can go on while textual input is made on the touch table. Also in the case that more than one input focus is allowed a virtual Braille-keyboard gives the possibility to run in parallel to the virtual keyboards for sighted persons.

3   Implementation

The implementation of the prototype for the Braille-keyboard so far is based on an Android device. The prototype can already be included into the Android environment as a standard Android keyboard. Originally, the keyboard is designed for 6 - dot Braille, but extensions are already developed for 8 dot Braille. During the implementation, it was taken care not to restrict placing of the fingers to a special area and to give the blind user the possibility to place the fingers everywhere on the touch surface. This is an important feature as it allows the blind users to make text input everywhere on the touch interface and he/she has not to search for a special area where the virtual keyboard will popup.

The initialization of the keyboard is done by placing 6 fingers at the same time to the surface in order to calibrate the Braille-keyboard. The needed calibration at the beginning gives the possibility to set the working position everywhere on the touch surface. Figure 1 represents examples of calibration possibilities of the virtual Braille keyboard on a Tablet with 10 inches.

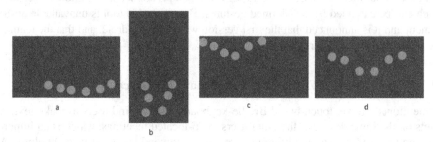

Fig. 1. Calibration Examples: a) Tablet horizontal direction and fingers are placed on the right lower corner b) Tablet in vertical direction fingers are placed on the bottom of the screen c) Tablet horizontal direction and fingers are placed on the upper left corner d) Tablet in horizontal direction and fingers are placed in the middle of the screen

Typing of letters can now be performed in the same way as typing on a hardware Braille-keyboard as for instance the Perkins Smart Brailler (http://www.perkins.org/smartbrailler/features-benefits.html). From the technical point of view the recognition of a typed character works as follows:

- Calibration points are system internally stored with a predefined radius (green points in Fig 1). The radius can be seen as a tuning parameter. By experiments, it turned out that for standard displays in the range from 7" to 10", a radius of 50 pixels works best.
- The generated touch points, when a character is typed, are system internally also represented as circles (red point in Fig 1). 40 pixels turned out to work fine for the standard devices.
- The matching of the calculated touch points to the stored calibration points is done in two ways: First, the intersection between the stored calibration points and the actual generated touch points is used. If a touch point intersects with no calibration point, but the distance between the touch point and a stored calibration point is small and the distance between the touch point and all other calibration points is high enough, the touch point is also matched to the calibration point with the small distance.
- The last step is recalculation of the calibration points after a successful recognition. Thereby, an adaptation to movements of typing positions is achieved, which leads to an increased recognition rate of the developed Braille-keyboard.

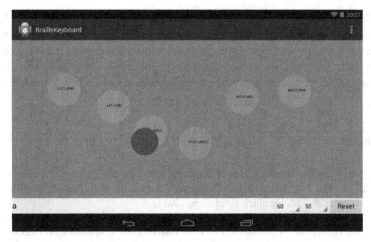

Fig. 2. Recognition of characters

Besides standard characters the following gestures are used to type special "symbols" or to call special "functions".

- swipe up: adds a space
- swipe down: adds a new paragraph
- swipe left: deletes the last typed character
- swipe right: reads the last typed word
- double swipe left: deletes the last typed word
- double swipe right: reads the whole typed text

4 Conclusion and Outlook

First user tests of the presented prototype of the Braille keyboard show the need for improvement of accuracy. Also some gestures for special characters like "space" seem to be uncomfortable for the blind user. Swips lead to the problem that the user has to take the fingers away from the calibration positions and in many cases a recalibration is needed afterwards. Therefore a redesign of the gestures for special "characters" and calls of "functions" should be considered. However touch-based Braille-keyboards have the potential to integrate blind users in co-located meetings without requiring a separate hardware device for textual input. Furthermore, virtual Braille-keyboards and more general spoken "gesture based keyboards" can be seen as an alternative to standard virtual keyboards for blind user not only in co-located meeting but also for standard devices.

Further investigation should not only focus on the possibilities of touch-based Braille-keyboards in co-located meetings, but also on the possibilities of Braille based keyboards using an unobtrusive finger based tracking system such as the Leap Motion. (https://www.leapmotion.com/).

Acknowledgements. This work has been partially supported by the FWF (Austrian Science Found) with the regional project number I867-N25 and it has been produced out of the D-A-CH project. The D-A-CH project is a joint project between TUD, the ETH and JKU with the respective funding organizations DFG (German Research Foundation), SNF (Swiss National Science Foundation) and FWF (Austrian Science Found).

References

1. Liu, J., Shi, Y.: uMeeting, an Efficient Co-located Meeting System on the Large-Scale Tabletop. In: Jacko, J.A. (ed.) Human-Computer Interaction, Part IV, HCII 2011. LNCS, vol. 6764, pp. 368–374. Springer, Heidelberg (2011)
2. Correia, N., Mota, T., Nóbrega, R., Silva, L., Almeida, A.: A multi-touch tabletop for robust multimedia interaction in museums. In: ACM International Conference on Interactive Tabletops and Surfaces (ITS 2010), pp. 117–120. ACM, New York (2010)
3. Pölzer, S., Schnelle-Wlka, D., Pöll, D., Heumader, P., Miesenberger, K.: Making Brainstorming Meetings Accessible for Blind Users. In: Encarnação, P., Azevedo, L., Gelderblom, G.J., Newell, A., Mathiassen, N.E. (eds.) Assistive Technology: From Research to Practice. Assistive Technologies Research Series, vol. 33, pp. 653–658. IOS Press, Amsterdam (2013)
4. Oliveira, J., Guerreiro, T., Nicolau, H., Jorge, J., Gonçalves, D.: BrailleType: Unleashing Braille over Touch Screen Mobile Phones. In: Campos, P., Graham, N., Jorge, J., Nunes, N., Palanque, P., Winckler, M. (eds.) INTERACT 2011, Part I. LNCS, vol. 6946, pp. 100–107. Springer, Heidelberg (2011)
5. Frey, B., Southern, C., Romero, M.: BrailleTouch: Mobile Texting for the Visually Impaired. In: Stephanidis, C. (ed.) Universal Access in HCI, Part III, HCII 2011. LNCS, vol. 6767, pp. 19–25. Springer, Heidelberg (2011)
6. Mascetti, S., Bernareggi, C., Belotti, M.: TypeInBraille: Quick Eyes-Free Typing on Smartphones. In: Miesenberger, K., Karshmer, A., Penaz, P., Zagler, W. (eds.) ICCHP 2012, Part II. LNCS, vol. 7383, pp. 615–622. Springer, Heidelberg (2012)

Accessibility of Brainstorming Sessions for Blind People

Andreas Kunz[1], Klaus Miesenberger[2], Max Mühlhäuser[3], Ali Alavi[1],
Stephan Pölzer[2], Daniel Pöll[2], Peter Heumader[2], and Dirk Schnelle-Walka[3]

[1] Swiss Federal Institute of Technology, Zurich, Switzerland
{kunz,alavi}@iwf.mavt.ethz.ch
[2] Institut Integriert Studieren, Johannes Kepler University, Linz, Austria
{Klaus.Miesenberger,Stephan.Poelzer,Daniel.Poell,
Peter.Heumader}@jku.at
[3] Technische Universität Darmstadt, Germany
{max,dirk}@informatik.tu-darmstadt.de

Abstract. Today, research focuses on the accessibility of explicit information for blind users. This gives only partly access to the information flow in brainstorming sessions, since non-verbal communication is not supported. Advances in ICT however allow capturing implicit information like hand gestures as important part of non-verbal communication. Thus, we describe a system that al-lows integrating blind people into a brainstorming session using a mind map.

Keywords: Accessibility, Mind map, Non-verbal Communication Elements.

1 Introduction

In brainstormings, coordinative, collaborative and communicative elements exist [1] in the 'level of artifacts' and the 'level of non-verbal communication' (Fig. 1).

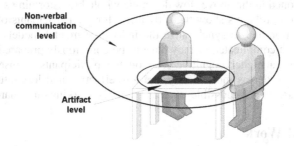

Fig. 1. Brainstorming integrates non-verbal communication and artifact level elements [2]

Within these levels, a number of challenges arise when blind and sighted persons collaborate. The challenges come from fundamentally different (and often incompatible) ways of perception and expression that cannot be easily overcome. This could bring blind people in an unwanted role, which could result in an unintended or unconscious exclusion from such a brainstorming session. In case of a brainstorming session using a mind map, the origin of the problems is twofold: they could either come from

K. Miesenberger et al. (Eds.): ICCHP 2014, Part I, LNCS 8547, pp. 237–244, 2014.

the generated elements on the artifact level, or from the non-verbal communication level. Both levels are highly interdependent, since many times non-verbal communication elements, such as deictic gestures, refer to elements on the artifact level.

1.1   Level of Artifacts

Although blind and sighted people can access the same digital information of documents by rendering it on screen/print or in Braille/audio, the way of perception leads to considerable differences in accessing or generating this information. The visual channel allows for fast and parallel perception of information, while Braille or audio could be compared to a serial perception. This difference is in particular salient for the perception of graphical elements like those of a mind map. Hence, blind people need more time for sensing the content of artifacts. This becomes even more critical when the artifacts are edited during the meeting. Moreover, jointly working on artifacts requires that each participant is aware about the state and the content of the artifacts. Due to these limitations, current tools and technologies cannot support a joint group of sighted and blind people to create and edit artifacts in a brainstorming meeting.

1.2   Level of Non-verbal Communication

A large amount of information during a meeting is transferred non-verbally by gestures, postures, facial expressions, etc., which rely on the visual channel only. Consequently, blind people are excluded from this information. Not only gestures and facial expressions are required for establishing interpersonal relationship [3], but are also important to coordinate discussions during a brainstorming, e.g. for turn-taking [4,5]. As a workaround for engaging blind people in such meetings, the implicit non-verbal communication is made explicit by verbalizing it. This evokes new problems, since non-verbal communication is parallel and thus has to be serialized in order to communicate it verbally. Moreover, non-verbal communication is done unconsciously, but it has to be consciously translated or articulated by the sighted participants. Both problems mentioned in the above slow down the whole brainstorming session.

The mentioned problems show the difficulties for the participants of a meeting to transfer information and to synchronize the individual mental models. Meetings are significantly more complicated as they have to be consciously prepared and conducted. This imposes a higher cognitive load on the participants. Consequently, such meetings tend to progress more slowly, are less effective and less intuitive. Finally, some activities are even impossible, such as intensely working on a shared document.

2   Related Work

For the chosen scenario of integrating blind people into a collocated mind map brainstorming session, we need to study the research literature on two different levels: the artifact level, and the non-verbal communication level.

2.1   Artifact Level

A vast body of research in the field of HCI (Human Computer Interaction) tackles the problem of more intuitive interaction with digital content. A major approach relies on natural user interfaces (NUIs), which enhance (or in some case, replace) a graphical user interface (GUI), buy providing technologies such as touchscreens, motions trackers, and tangible user interfaces (TUIs) [6,7,8,9] . While these interfaces are helpful for sighted persons to access and alter artifacts in an intuitive way, they support the blind users in a very limited manner.

Window Eyes [10] could output textual information to Braille displays, or audio speakers. A lot of research has been done for making graphical information accessible to the blind, both in terms of providing equivalent descriptive text alternatives [11], or using tactile and/or audio methods [12,13,14,15]. All these approaches focus on linear text and static graphics, but not on dynamically changing artifacts such as a mind map. This requires the development of systems for tracking, analyzing and displaying information and thereby tackling the problem of information overflow. Only a few approaches towards access to dynamic content exist [16,17]. Here, the user interacts with a tangible and sonic representation of a line chart. In another approach, Ferres et al. [18] translate the chart into a textual representation, which can then be accessed by conventional reading devices such as Braille displays.

However, these approaches do not investigate the dynamics of changing graphics in real-time, and they also do not include non-verbal communication elements.

2.2   Non-verbal Communication Level

While meeting support for blind people is still a largely underrepresented research area as stated by Winberg et al. [19], distributed meetings for sighted persons are well addressed in literature. Providing awareness of eye-contacts or of other gestures such as pointing or nodding supports the social presence and coordinates the teamwork [5], [4], [20]. Work presented by Ba et al. [21] provides a proximity approach to identify the visual focus of attention of a user. Morency et al. [22] show that nodding and other head movements can be successfully captured by visual tracking systems.

Deictic gestures bridge between the level of non-verbal communication and the level of artifacts. They are used by sighted people to easily refer to artifacts during a meeting. Within the very little work conducted for blind people, Oliveira et al. [23] address how to translate deictic gestures made on a whiteboard containing static content into a haptic representation. Thereby, the blind person wears a glove which guides his hand to the position on the artifact level the sighted user is pointing to. However, there is no work for deictic gestures on dynamic content.

To summarize, the integration of blind people into brainstorming sessions is still very limited. This is mainly because of the following reasons:

- Deictic gestures are not reliably captured and assigned to artifacts on the interactive surface.
- Translation of the "parallel" content of the artifact level to the serial perception of the blind user and vice versa is not well investigated.
- Lack of interfaces for blind users to interact with the artifacts

This paper thus introduces a system that allows integrating blind users in a mind map brainstorming meeting, which addresses the challenges mentioned in the above.

3   Contribution

To address the above challenges, we realized the concept of an automatic real-time translation as core of the overall system. This translation process is threefold: (1) capturing artifacts and non-verbal communication elements with dedicated sensors; (2) semantic modeling of artifacts and activities; and (3) making the information available to all participants in an appropriate and accessible representation (Fig. 2).

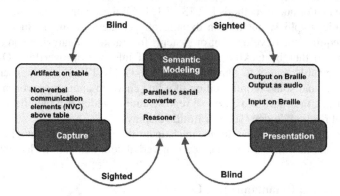

Fig. 2. General overview of the realized system

The system is realized in a multi-layer architecture, consisting of 4 layers.

3.1   Persistence Layer

The persistence layer only contains the mind map model. Although many graph-based mind map tools exist, we implemented our mind map in a tree structure. Within a tree structure, every element n the mind map represents a node in the tree model, thus having a unique path to the root. This path is made accessible to the blind users. In comparison to alternative screen exploring techniques for blind users as presented by Kane et al. [24], a tree structure can be easily navigated, interpreted and manipulated by a blind user in a way she is already familiar with.

3.2   Controller Layer

The Model Update Controller updates the persistence layer. The controller will also report changes of the model to the application layer. The model update controller also provides information to the semantic reasoner in order to properly infer the relation between deictic and other pointing gestures and artifacts.

3.3   Application Layer

The main components of the application layer are the mind map software, the reasoner, and an accessible mind map (blind user interface).

The reasoner receives the tracking information from the sensors and compares the calculated pointing direction intersection point with the positions of the artifacts on the screen in order to highlight the corresponding component. This information is given to the mind map and the accessible mind map applications, where the corresponding object is highlighted.

The mind map application is shown in Fig. 3. It currently allows adding and deleting elements, adding text to an element and freely moving it around. It is also possible to rotate an element, which is important since the sighted persons sit around the table.

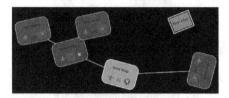

Fig. 3. Collaborative mind map Editor "CoME"

Sighted persons can move, zoom, and rotate objects by using the touch input capabilities of Microsoft PixelSense tabletop computer. All structure and content information is transferred to the blind user interface (see Fig. 4). This is in principle a serialized representation of the parallel information in the mind map. When the mind map is updated, the structure of the tree in the blind user interface is altered. The interface also offers possibilities to modify the mind map on the table, such as adding, modifying, or deleting a node in the tree. Moreover, cut and paste functionalities are available, as well as a search function or a button for further details of a node. Any modification will immediately be transferred to the mind map visualization on the PixelSense.

Fig. 4. Blind user interface and blind user testing the blind user interface

The blind user interface also contains a tree structure representing the content of the mind map. The blind user can browse this tree in a way he is already familiar with from other environments. The interface also includes a list view with the mind map's history of modifications. This allows the blind user to view modifications also in an asynchronous way. Finally, a search functionality allows searching the history as well as the tree. A message box will further notify the blind user when changes are made to the mind map or when pointing gestures highlight a certain artifact (node). All the elements can be accessed by the blind user with the Braille display (see Fig. 4).

3.4   Input/Output Layer

As described above, artifacts as well as NVCs have to be captured by the system. For our realized prototype, we choose a scenario (but are not limited to) with three sighted users and one blind user who gather around PixelSense as shown in Fig. 5.

Fig. 5. Overall physical setup

Since PixelSense is an interactive screen, any touch input for modifying the artifacts can be sensed, while text is currently still entered via the keyboard. For detecting deictic gestures as the most important representative for NVCs, three LEAP Motion sensors are used. They are placed on the PixelSense's frame to detect deictic gestures from the sighted users (see Fig. 5). The sensors are oriented in such a way that the lower boundary of the sensor's field of view is parallel to the table's surface.

4   Preliminary User Tests

The blind user interface together with the mind map editor CoME were evaluated in first trial runs. The blind users accessed the interface with a Braille display which was connected to a screen reader. Using different screen readers, the blind user interface was in general accessible, although different readers showed different performance.

In general, the blind users appreciated to present mind maps to different user groups with different adapted views. It was further seen as a good solution for the synchronization between blind and sighted users within a mind map session that there is an alert system which informs the blind user about any modification done on the mind map. Also the history of the blind user interface was very much appreciated, since it could be used if blind users missed some changes made in the mind map.

The expected irritations of sighted users by suddenly appearing nodes in the mind map – being entered via the blind user interface – were not confirmed during our first trail runs. The reason for this could be found in the fact that there was still an audio synchronization between all the team members, from which cues about the next possible interaction of the blind user could be derived.

5   Conclusion and Outlook

We introduced a system that supports a mind map brainstorming meeting between blind and sighted users. The system gives access for blind users to the generated arti-facts, and also captures and transfers non-verbal communication elements. This allows a deep integration of a blind user into a brainstorming meeting.

Our work will continue with in-depth user studies with the built system. We will then continue to integrate other NVC elements into the system, such as nodding or shrugging. For integrating these NVC elements, we will extend our current system by additional sensors. Moreover, more sophisticated filtering algorithms will be developed to avoid false interpretations and thus wrong notifications to the blind user.

Acknowledgments. This work was done in collaboration of ETH Zurich, TU Darmstadt, and JKU Linz and was funded under the DACH umbrella under the number CR2I2L_138601.

References

1. Ellis, C.A., Gibbs, S.J., Rein, G.: Groupware: Some Issues and Experiences. Communications of the ACM 34, 39–58 (1991)
2. Kunz, A., Alavi, A., Sinn, P.: Integrating Pointing Gesture Detection for Enhancing Brainstorming Meetings Using Kinect and PixelSense. In: Proc. of the 8th International Conference on Digital Enterprise Technology, ETH-Zürich, Zürich, Switzerland, pp. 1–8 (2014)
3. von Thun, F.S.: Miteinander reden 1 – Störungen und Klärungen. Allgemeine Psychologie der Kommunikation. rororo, Reinbek, Germany (1998)
4. Kendon, A.: Some functions of gaze-direction on social interaction. Acta Psychologica 26, 22–63 (1967)
5. Argyle, M., Cook, M.: Gaze & Mutual Gaze. Cambridge University Press, New York (1976)
6. Ishii, H., Ullmer, B.: Tangible Bits: Toward Seamless Interfaces between People, Bits and Atoms. In: Proc. of the SIGCHI Conference on Human Factors in Computing Systems (CHI 1997), pp. 234–241. ACM, New York (1997)
7. Fitzmaurice, G., Ishii, H., Buxton, W.: Bricks: Laying the Foundation for Graspable User Interfaces. In: Proceedings of the SIGCHI Conference on Human Factors in Computing Systems (CHI 1995), pp. 442–449. ACM, New York (1995)
8. Ganser, C., Steinemann, A., Kunz, A.: InfrActables: Supporting Collocated Groupwork by Combining Pen-based and Tangible Interaction. In: Proceedings of IEEE Tabletop 2007, pp. 1–2. IEEE, Washington (2007)
9. Hofer, R., Kunz, A.: TNT: Touch 'n' Tangibles on LC-displays. In: Natkin, S., Dupire, J. (eds.) ICEC 2009. LNCS, vol. 5709, pp. 222–227. Springer, Heidelberg (2009)
10. Window Eyes by GW Micro, http://www.gwmicro.com/Window-Eyes
11. W3C/WAI Guidelines, http://www.w3.org/WAI/intro/wcag.php
12. Yayl, L.: Huseby Zoom Maps: A Design Methodology for Tactile Graphics. Journal of Visual Impairment & Blindness 3(5), 270–276 (2009)

13. Manshad, M.S., Manshad, A.S.: Multimodal Vision Glove for Touchscreens. In: Proceedings of the 10th International ACM SIGACCESS Conference on Computers and Accessibility, pp. 251–252. ACM, New York (2008)

14. King, A., Blenkhorn, P., Crombie, D., Dijkstra, S., Evans, G., Wood, J.: Presenting UML Software Engineering Diagrams to Blind People. In: Miesenberger, K., Klaus, J., Zagler, W.L., Burger, D. (eds.) ICCHP 2004. LNCS, vol. 3118, pp. 522–529. Springer, Heidelberg (2004)

15. Petrie, H., et al.: TeDUB: A System for Presenting and Exploring Technical Drawings for Blind People. In: Miesenberger, K., Klaus, J., Zagler, W.L. (eds.) ICCHP 2002. LNCS, vol. 2398, pp. 537–539. Springer, Heidelberg (2002)

16. Petit, G., Dufresne, A., Levesque, V., Hayward, V., Trudeau, N.: Refreshable Tactile Graphics Applied to Schoolbook Illustrations for Students with Visual Impairments. In: Proceedings of the 10th International ACM SIGACCESS Conference on Computers and Accessibility (Assets 2008), pp. 89–96. ACM, New York (2008)

17. Landua, S., Welss, L.: Merging Table Sensory Input and Audio Data by Means of the Talking Tactile Tablet. In: Proceedings of Eurohaptics, pp. 414–418. IEEE Computer Society, Washington (2003)

18. Ferres, L., Verkhogliad, P., Lindgaard, G., Boucher, L., Chretien, A., Lachance, M.: Improving Accessibility to Statistical Graphs: The iGraph-Lite System. In: Proceedings of the 9th International SIGACCESS Conference on Computers and Accessibility (Assets 2007), pp. 67–74. ACM, New York (2007)

19. Winberg, F., Bowers, J.: Assembling the Senses: Towards the Design of Cooperative Interfaces for Visually Impaired Users. In: Proceedings of the 2004 ACM Conference on Computer Supported Cooperative Work (CSCW 2004), pp. 332–341. ACM, New York (2004)

20. Kunz, A., Nescher, T., Küchler, M.: CollaBoard: A Novel Interactive Electronic Whiteboard for Remote Collaboration with People on Content. In: Proceedings of the International Conference on Cyberworlds (CW 2010), pp. 430–437. IEEE, Washington (2010)

21. Ba, S.O., Odobez, J.-M.: A Study on Visual Focus of Attention Recognition from Head Pose in a Meeting Room. In: Renals, S., Bengio, S., Fiscus, J.G. (eds.) MLMI 2006. LNCS, vol. 4299, pp. 75–87. Springer, Heidelberg (2006)

22. Morency, L.-P., Quattoni, A., Darrell, T.: Latent-Dynamic Discriminative Models for Continuous Gesture Recognition. In: Proceedings of the 2007 IEEE Conference on Computer Vision and Pattern Recognition (CVPR 2007), pp. 1–8. IEEE, Washington (2007)

23. Oliveira, F., Cowan, H., Faug, B., Quek, F.: Enabling Multimodal Discourse for the Blind. In: Proceedings of the International Conference on Multimodal Interfaces and the Workshop on Machine Learning for Multimodal Interaction (ICMI-MLMI 2010), vol. (18). ACM, New York (2010)

24. Kane, S.K., Morris, M.R., Perkins, A.Z., Wigdor, D., Ladner, R.E., Wobbrock, J.O.: Access Overlays: Improving Non-visual Access to Large Touch screens for Blind Users. In: Proceedings of the 24th Annual ACM Symposium on User Interface Software and Technology (UIST 2011), pp. 273–282. ACM, New York (2011)

Emotions for Accessibility

Introduction to the Special Thematic Session

Yehya Mohamad

Fraunhofer Institute for Applied Information Technology (FIT), Sankt Augustin, Germany
mohamad@fit.fraunhofer.de

Abstract. This STS on Emotions for Accessibility is targeted towards the description of affective computing approaches e.g. emotional state detection, emotional state elicitation and their potential usage in the context of users who are disabled or older people. These user groups may gain a lot of benefits from affective computing systems e.g. in support of communication especially none verbal, management of emotional states or stress, or just improving therapy procedures etc.

Keywords: Affective computing, Accessibility, Sensors, GSR, PVB, Machine learning algorithm, Disabled person, Context, Emotion, Emotion management, User interface, e-Learning, Web-based.

1 Introduction

Affective Computing is an emerging discipline with the aim to develop computer systems that could recognize emotional states of its users and communicate with them considering the detected affective states [4]. Affective computing could support disabled persons to express their emotions to other persons e.g. users with communication disabilities like users with cerebral palsy, here a talker / communicator could change the colors and sounds of its user interface to convey none verbal aspects of user's communication to others. Similarly, an affective system based on visual sensors could help blind users to perceive none verbal emotions expressed by others.

Affective computing is based on several approaches and technologies:

- Methods used to elicit emotional data from user's feedback e.g. the semantic differential method and the Self-Assessment Manikin (SAM) method [5] and tools like the online tool TRUE (Testing Platform for Multimedia Evaluation) based on SAM technique or emotion stimulation tool compliant IADS-2 (The International Affective Digitized Sounds) [3]
- Sensor frameworks for sensing and measurement of signals for the detection of emotional states [1,2] e.g. detecting the basic emotions from the face using visual sensors, from voice using microphones or from physio-psychological signals using sensors like skin conductivity sensors (GSR), Electromyogram (EMG) that measures, muscle activity, Electrocardiogram (EKG or ECG) that measures heart activity, Electro-ouclogram (EOG) measuring eye movement and Electroencephalography (EEG, measuring brain activity).

K. Miesenberger et al. (Eds.): ICCHP 2014, Part I, LNCS 8547, pp. 245–247, 2014.

- Several machine learning techniques, they are used to recognize patterns in measured signals that indicate emotional states. E.g. Hidden Markov Model, Bayesian networks, Fuzzy Logic, Neural Network or Support Vector Machines.

2   Areas Covered by STS

The papers presented in this STS present approaches on:

- How to conduct user studies with disabled persons in the context of affective computing?
- How to involve disabled user groups in the design of such systems?
- How disabled users can benefit from affective computing systems? E.g. improving therapy procedures, emotional management systems, stress management, increase wellbeing etc.
- How does a computer recognize user's emotional state?
- What is the relation between the calculation of emotional state and face, voice, gesture and other physiological measurement such as heart rate variability (HRV), skin conductivity, and muscle movement etc.?
- How reliable or universal are these measurements?

Yehya Mohamad et al present a paper about an experimental approach to design emotional sensitive systems. We describe a system for the detection of emotional states based on physiological signals and an application use case utilizing the detected emotional state. The application is an emotion management system to be used for the support in the improvement of life conditions of users suffering from cerebral palsy (CP). The presented system combines effectively biofeedback sensors and a set of software algorithms to detect the current emotional state of the user and to react to them appropriately.

Jose Laparra et al present a paper considering emotions in the design of accessible websites. They explain the reason why the World Wide Web should be a powerful tool for enhancing the independent living of people with disabilities. On the contrary they tell about e-exclusion, because web requirements do not fit with disabled users specific needs. The first efforts were focused on Accessibility (e.g. WAI), but this does not ensure usability. Emotions are related with some of most of cognitive processes (e.g. attention or learning), key during human computer interaction (HCI), which can be measured using different physiological signals. They present a study with the aim to validate usability recommendations depending on user profiles, to check the effect of the emotional state on HCI and to identify the advantages of physiological response analysis in contrast to subjective questionnaires.

Juan-Manuel Belada-Lois et al present a paper on a system design targeted towards Diskinetic Cerebral Palsy (DCP) users, DCP is a permanent condition that causes severe motor impairments (i.e. changes in muscle tone and posture, and involuntary movements) and speech disorders (i.e. anarthria and dysarthria) which highly limit physical and social activity. The discrepancy between their intellectual potential and their actual development is primarily caused by their impaired communication and interaction abilities which hamper their learning processes and affects the way this persons are able to express emotions. This contribution shows a methodological approach for the development of a communicator for DCP users incorporating emotion capabilities in order to improve communication, emotion management and emotion awareness.

3   Future Research Areas

The presented papers are based mainly on conceptualization and application of affective computing for disabled users.

Detection of emotional states and utilization in disabled population is almost neglected area when looking to the plethora of projects going on in the area of affective computing. The challenges and unsolved problems are many e.g. the appropriate involvement of users in such projects, studies about which sensors are most suitable for which disabilities. How to elicit emotions by disabled users under specific ethical demands. Are special machine learning algorithms needed?

References

1. Calvo, R.A., D'Mello, S.: Affect Detection: An Interdisciplinary Review of Models, Methods, and Their Applications. IEEE Trans. Affect. Comput. 1(1), 18–37 (2010)
2. Calvo, R., Brown, I., Scheding, S.: Effect of experimental factors on the recognition of affective mental states through physiological measures. In: Nicholson, A., Li, X. (eds.) AI 2009. LNCS, vol. 5866, pp. 62–70. Springer, Heidelberg (2009)
3. Bradley, M.M., Lang, P.J.: The International Affective Digitized Sounds, 2nd edn. (IADS-2): Affective Ratings of Sounds and Instruction Manual, NIMH Center for the Study of Emotion and Attention (2007)
4. Picard, R.: Systems Journal 39(3&4) (2000)
5. Bradley, M.M., Lang, P.J.: Measuring emotion: The self-assessment manikin and the semantic differential. Journal of Behavior Therapy and Experimental Psychiatry, 49–59 (1994)

Detection and Utilization of Emotional
State for Disabled Users

Yehya Mohamad[1], Dirk T. Hettich[2, 3], Elaina Bolinger[3], Niels Birbaumer[3],
Wolfgang Rosenstiel[2], Martin Bogdan[2], and Tamara Matuz[3]

[1] Fraunhofer Institute for Applied Information Technology (FIT), Schloss Birlinghoven,
Sankt Augustin, Germany
[2] Department of Computer Engineering, Faculty of Science,
Eberhard-Karls-University of Tübingen, Germany
[3] Institute of Medical Psychology and Behavioral Neurobiology,
Eberhard-Karls-University of Tübingen, Germany
{yehya,moamad}@fit.fraunhofer.de,
{dirk-tassilo,hettich}@uni-tuebingen.de

Abstract. In this paper, we present an experimental approach to design systems
sensitive to emotion. We describe a system for the detection of emotional states
based on physiological signals and an application use case utilizing the detected
emotional state. The application is an emotion management system to be used
for the support in the improvement of life conditions of users suffering from
cerebral palsy (CP). The system presented here combines effectively biofeedback sensors and a set of software algorithms to detect the current emotional
state of the user and to react to them appropriately.

Keywords: Affective Computing, Machine Learning Algorithm, Disabled
Person, Context, Emotion, Emotion Management, User Interface, E-Learning,
Web-Based.

1   Introduction

Human beings are emotional, as our social interaction is based on the ability to communicate our emotions and to perceive the emotional states of others [2], [13]. A wide
range of physical disabilities involves deficits in the different stages of sensing, expressing, or interpreting of affect-relevant signals. Consequently, people with
these kinds of disabilities can be considered emotionally disabled [11]. Affective
computing, a discipline that develops systems for detecting and responding to users'
emotions [5], and affective mediation, computer-based technology that enables the
communication between two or more people displaying their emotional states [4,5],
are growing research areas that must join assistive technology research to improve the
neglected area of affective communication in disabled people [12].

Emotion detection by computers can be done using various channels such as facial
expression, voice, gestures, and postures [5]. However, this method is not reliable
in every context as individuals may be disabled and their emotions/affective state cannot be detected using these channels. In order to overcome this problem the use of

K. Miesenberger et al. (Eds.): ICCHP 2014, Part I, LNCS 8547, pp. 248–255, 2014.

psycho-physiological measurement was introduced [4,5]. Hence, it is now being actively used to acquire emotional states using different biosensors i.e. Galvanic Skin Response (GSR), Electromyography (EMG) and Electrocardiography (ECG) and [7,8].

The activation of sympathetic nerves of Autonomous Nervous System (ANS) generates authentic not alterable signals [15]. Signals from GSR, EMG and ECG are processed using different signal processing techniques and methods to convert them into meaningful data.

Machine learning techniques are used to recognize patterns in psycho-physiological signals that indicate user's affective states [16,17]. Classification of data is performed with machine learning algorithms. Different machine learning algorithms are common like support vector machine (SVN). There exist several implementations of these algorithms like the commercial Matlab or the open source data-mining tool Waikato Environment for knowledge analysis (WEKA) .

The first goal of our work is to build an affective computing detection system based on GSR and to automatically identify correlates of emotional processing in the electroencephalogram (EEG) in individuals with CP (Cerebral Palsy). The second goal is the building of an affective mediation system by implementing a web-based emotion management system to define rules that maps the actions with the corresponding emotional state, time, and location as well any other relevant context parameters.

2 Overview of the Emotional Monitoring System

To achieve the detection of the emotional state of users with CP, we have defined many parameters. All these parameters are based mainly on previous work [4] using measurements of skin conductance signals (GSR) during a time period e.g. a training session. We followed the approach of dividing the session into different periods each with its thresholds and boundaries. Similar approaches were used in pattern recognition for monitoring of failures in machines [3] or for speech recognition [6]. These parameters are used in a machine learning algorithm to detect if the user has positive or negative emotional state and the level of the emotional state.

The parameters are (a) Short-time changes - Average of signals in one minute. (b) Mid-term and average changes: Average of signals in 3 minutes. (c) Mid-term and average changes: Average of signals in 5 minutes. (d) Long-term and average changes: Baseline, an average of signals in the whole session. (e) Signal variance: which is calculated from the volatility of the signal, where high volatility of the signals is interpreted as a negative indicator and a low volatility as positive indicator of emotional state.

In addition to emotion monitoring based on GSR, the feasibility of emotion detection in the EEG is investigated in an auditory emotion induction paradigm. Electro-physio-logical correlates of emotional processing in the EEG reside in the time- and frequency domain. The late positive potential (LPP), a positive deflection in the EEG starting approximately 400 ms after stimulus onset and lasting until 1000 ms, is an event-related potential (ERP) occurring during emotional processing in the time-domain [9]. Frequency features of emotion such as inter-hemispheric, valence-dependent differences in alpha power or event-related de/synchronization effects (ERD/ERS) were also described in the literature [10]. Here, time-domain features are first identified in the EEG and then used for the classification of three distinct emotional states in terms of valence, i.e. positive, neutral, and negative, employing a support vector machine.

For emotion elicitation in users many approaches were published e.g. the International Affective Picture System (IAPS), which is a database of pictures used to elicit a range of emotions and the International Affective Digitized Sound system (IADS), which provides a set of acoustic emotional stimuli for experimental investigations of emotion and attention. [1], [17].

2.1   Emotion Detection Based on GSR

Pilot tests were conducted by users using the GSR based emotional response monitoring system. Protocols were saved out of all measurements. The measurement process of signals was conducted every 20 mills.

We tested the system in an experiment, where we have used audio stimuli to elicit the user's emotion. For the purpose of elicitation of emotions we used a standardized methodology called IADS-2 standard [1]. For that, we developed and provided a web application, where each user listened to audio recordings from the IADS-2 standard sounds. The test protocol is described as follows: The user and caregiver are briefed about the purpose of the experiment at least 15 minutes before the test. Then the sensors were attached to the left hand or any foot of the user. This signals contained artfacts due to movements.

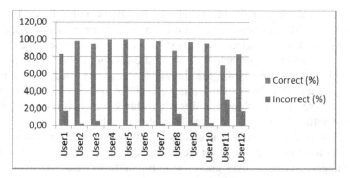

Fig. 1. Classification ratio

The users were asked to listen to a selected audio clips out of IADS-2 with a total length of 17 minutes. The system kept asking the user to enter the user's current emotional state into the system by clicking on the symbol on the screen they think matches their current emotional state. Whenever the user experiences a change in emotion, they are supposed to click on the appropriate symbol, otherwise, it will be assumed that this emotion has not changed since the previous choice. The indicated emotional states by the user and the detected ones by the algorithms were matched in our system by 5 combinations of valence and arousal: high arousal positive (HE+), high arousal negative (HE-), low arousal positive (WE+), low arousal negative (WE-) and neutral (NE). The entered data is immediately anonymized.

The resulting data contain information about user's emotion and simultaneously information about recorded sensor data. The results have shown good classification ability of the SVM machine learning algorithm (see Figure 1).

There were 13 CP users attending these experiments, among those, data from 1 user was corrupted and could not be used. We used training data from 12 users and built model based on Support Vector Machine using classes supported in Weka API. Weka is a suite of machine learning software written in Java, containings a collection of visualization tools and algorithms for data analysis and predictive modelling together with graphical user interfaces for easy access to this functionality.

2.2   Emotion Detection Based on EEG

To date, the automatic detection of emotional responses in the EEG in a healthy population employing machine learning is heatedly contested in affective research and had, until now, not yet been investigated in individuals with CP. Here we present a suitable paradigm for emotion induction in individuals with CP based on IADS-2, first results of EEG-markers of emotion in CP, as well as their automatic detection employing machine learning.

Our auditory affect induction paradigm has proven to be a suitable approach for the study of emotion in motor impaired individuals with CP who are incapable of visual fixation. All sounds from IADS-2 were divided according to their normalized rated valence, into three significantly different categories, i.e. pleasant, neutral, and unpleasant. A subset of 20 sounds per category was then selected according to valence values within categories. The final set of sounds then consists of 60 pseudo-randomized sounds, i.e. two consecutive stimuli must be from different categories. Together with each participant, we acquire a valence rating for each sound employing the self-assessment manikin (SAM) [18]. If only yes/no communication is available with the individual, we follow a binary search approach. Participants then subsequently listen to two sequences of 60 pseudo-randomized sounds. We acquired data from n=3 individuals with CP. In two cases, somewhat compromised communication was feasible, whilst in one severe case with dyskinetic CP only yes/no communication was available. To assess valence in that case, we followed a binary search paradigm limiting the number of questions. In all cases, at least one family member was present to help communicate with the participant. EEG was measured on 29 channels and 3 electrooculogram sites for later eye movement artifact correction [19].

Figure 2 depicts grand average responses to grouped stimuli categories of one participant. These first promising results show that pleasant and unpleasant sounds evoke a greater positive deflection in the EEG ~350 ms after stimulus-onset relative to neutral, as is seen in literature with healthy individuals (e.g. [9]). Participant 2 exhibits highly artefact prone data (not shown). Grand average results of participant 3 exhibit positive deflections from 400 ms to 900 ms after stimulus onset (not shown), however in all categories. Furthermore, data are also artefact prone which is attributed to involuntary muscle contractions due to the nature of CP. In the second and third case, if simple trial rejection measurements, i.e. discard every trial deviating more than 4 standard deviations from the variance of each channel, are taken into account, only an insufficient number of trials remains for analysis.

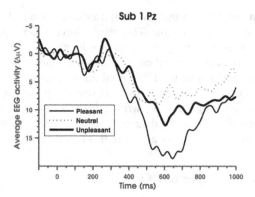

Fig. 2. Grand average responses on channel Pz in EEG time-locked to stimulus onset to pleasant (thin black), neutral (dotted), and unpleasant (thick black) stimuli. Time is depicted on x axis in ms.

As a second step of data analysis, data have been classified employing features from the time domain, as seen above. Support vector machine [20] classification with a linear kernel has been applied in a 10-fold cross validation to classify different affective categories against one another. For each participant, data of 108 trials have been used to calculate a model and then 12 trials were used for testing. Preliminary classification of these time-domain features revealed classification accuracies of approximately 51% for neutral vs. pleasant and 49% for neutral vs. unpleasant in 10-fold cross validation. Low accuracies are largely accounted for by substantially movement artifact-contaminated EEG caused by the nature of CP. Since involuntary movements are present in individuals with CP, improvements to the signal processing cascade such as optimized artifact rejection and feature extraction measures will be examined.

3   Emotion Management System (EMS)

The emotions' management system presented here has the aim to provide multimodal feedback to CP users and their caregiver based on predefined rules allowing them to improve life conditions of CP users. The EMS is able to consider not only the detected emotional state, but further parameters especially those which enable a context-aware reaction of the system, as well. The EMS is an efficient emotional management system with user interfaces targeted to two user groups, the CP users and their caregiver. This user interface provides the reactions of the system to the detected emotional state and to the predefined rules. The EMS rule authoring module targeted to the caregivers provides a user interface with a usable wizard-like editor allowing them to predefine rules for the reactions of the system.

At the core of this system is a runtime matching algorithm, which matches rules created by the caregiver (e.g. parents) with the emotional state detected by the system and all other parameters covered by the rule e.g. location. The matching algorithm acts as a scheduler and controls and influences the user interfaces of both user groups.

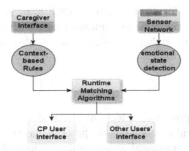

Fig. 3. Overview emotion management system

The actions are predefined set of events, which the system can implement and issue them via predefined modalities e.g. sound, vibration, text, images etc.

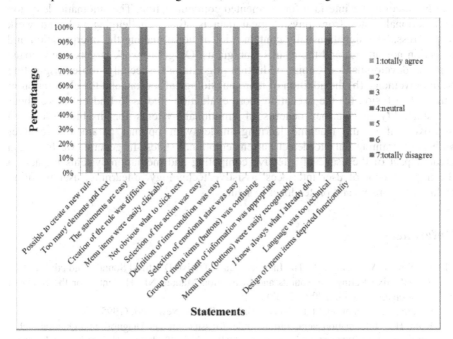

Fig. 4. Results of the usability study of the EMS

We have identified a set of actions, which will be implemented first; further actions may be implemented in later versions:

- Alerts: (a) CP user – reminders (b) caregiver/relatives – reminders - SMS – phone call
- Actions: (a) play music (b) dim light - summer – winter (c) Show favorite images, videos etc. (e) Adapt application – Games – E-learning units.

12 participants tested the EMS and answered a questionnaire. In the plot (see figure 4), x-axis represents 15 statements for the user to be evaluated, while y- axis presents

the percentage of 7 scales for each statement; each scale is represented by different color with scale 1 implies the total agreement of user with the statement and scale 7 implies the total disagreement; there are 5 additional scales in between (see Figure 4).

4 Conclusions

We have presented an approach to detect emotional states from physiological sensors in users with CP. The validation studies of the GSR based module have shown good classification rate of the emotional state compared to self or observation reports. Furthermore, first measures towards emotion detection in the EEG in individuals with CP were presented in an auditory emotion induction paradigm. Despite first low classification accuracies, this approach is a first step to expanding affective research to a clinical population of individuals with CP and therefore towards a clinical affective brain-computer interface for augmented communication. The automatic detection of emotional states from physiological data is still a challenging task and work in progress. The signals usually contain a lot of noise making the interpretation and detection not precise and the results ambiguous. On-going work targets many goals: (a) the development of noise reduction algorithms especially those originating from movements (b) the addition of more physiological sensors and the elaboration of sensor data fusion (c) the execution more evaluation studies to find out more about the suitability and further benefits of emotional systems for disabled users (d) improvement of the machine learning model with optimal parameters together with good training data to detect current emotional states. In general, we foresee a great impact of the usage of affective computing and mediation systems impact on the improvement of user interfaces, assistive technology, e-learning, user profiling techniques, sensors and biofeedback systems.

References

1. Bradley, M.M., Lang, P.J.: The International Affective Digitized Sounds, 2nd edn. (IADS-2): Affective Ratings of Sounds and Instruction Manual NIMH Center for the Study of Emotion and Attention 2007 (2007)
2. Goleman, D.: Emotional Intelligence. Bantam Books, New York (1995)
3. Kolb, H.J.: Informationsverarbeitung in der Messtechnik zur Diagnose und Qualitätssicherung. In: 43rd International Scientific Colloquium, Technical University of Ilmenau, September 21-24 (1998)
4. Mohamad, Y.: Integration of Emotional Intelligence in Interface Agents: The example of a Training Software for Learning-Disabled Children (2005) ISBN-13: 978-3832244637
5. Picard, R.: IBM Systems Journal 39(3&4) (2000)
6. Rigoll, G., Müller, S.: Statistical Pattern Recognition Techniques for Multimodal Human Computer Interaction and Multimedia Information Processing. In: Survey Paper, Int. Workshop "Speech and Computer", Moscow, Russia, October, pp. 60–69 (1999)
7. Shi, Y., et al.: Personalized Stress Detection from Physiological Measurements. In: International Symposium on Quality of Life Technology (2010)

8. Villarejo, M.V., Zapirain, B.G., Zorrilla, A.M.: A Stress Sensor Based on Galvanic Skin Response (GSR) Controlled by ZigBee (2012),
http://www.mdpi.com/journal/sensors-2012 sensors ISSN 1424-8220
9. Cuthbert, B.N., Schupp, H.T., Bradley, M.M., Birbaumer, N., Lang, P.J.: Brain potentials in affective picture processing: covariation with autonomic arousal and affective report. Biol. Psychol. 52(2), 95–111 (2000)
10. Davidson, R.J., Ekman, P., Saron, C.D., Senulis, J.A., Friesen, W.V.: Approach-withdrawal and cerebral asymmetry: emotional expression and brain physiology. I. J. Pers. Soc. Psychol. 58(2), 330–341 (1990)
11. Gershenfeld, N.A.: When Things Start to Think. Owl Books, New York (2000)
12. Sharma, N., Gedeon, T.: Objective measures, sensors and computational techniques for stress recognition and classification: a survey. Comput. Methods Programs Biomed. 108(3), 1287–1301 (2012)
13. Garay, N., Cearreta, I., López, J.M., Fajardo, I.: Assistive technology and affective mediation. An Interdiscip. J. Humans ICT Environ. 2(1), 55–83 (2006)
14. Bethel, C.L., Salomon, K., Murphy, R.R., Burke, J.L.: Survey of Psychophysiology Measurements Applied to Human-Robot Interaction. In: RO-MAN 2007 - The 16th IEEE International Symposium on Robot and Human Interactive Communication, pp. 732–737 (2007)
15. Calvo, R.A., D'Mello, S.: Affect Detection: An Interdisciplinary Review of Models, Methods, and Their Applications. IEEE Trans. Affect. Comput. 1(1), 18–37 (2010)
16. Calvo, R., Brown, I., Scheding, S.: Effect of experimental factors on the recognition of affective mental states through physiological measures. In: Nicholson, A., Li, X. (eds.) AI 2009. LNCS, vol. 5866, pp. 62–70. Springer, Heidelberg (2009)
17. Bradley, M.M., Lang, P.J.: The International Affective Picture System (IAPS) in the study of emotion and attention. In: Coan, J.A., Allen, J.J.B. (eds.) Handbook of Emotion Elicitation and Assessment, pp. 29–46. Oxford University Press (2007)
18. Bradley, M.M., Lang, P.J.: Measuring emotion: the Self-Assessment Manikin and the Semantic Differential. J. Behav. Ther. Exp. Psychiatry 25(1), 49–59 (1994)
19. Schlogl, A., et al.: A fully automated correction method of EOG artifacts in EEG recordings. Clin. Neurophysiol. 118(1), 98–104 (2007), doi:10.1016/j.clinph.2006.09.003
20. Chang, C., Lin, C.: LIBSVM: A Library for Support Vector Machines. ACM Trans. Intell. Syst. Technol. 2(3) (2011) DOI citeulike-article-id: 9306445,

Influence of Emotions on Web Usability
for Users with Motor Disorders

José Laparra-Hernández, Juan-Manuel Belda-Lois,
Álvaro Page, and Alberto Ferreras Remesal

Instituto de Biomecánica de Valencia (IBV), Valencia, Spain
jose.laparra@ibv.upv.es

Abstract. Emotions are related with many key cognitive processes during human computer interaction (HCI). The aim of this study was to validate usability recommendations depending on user profile, to check the effect of the emotional state on HCI and to compare physiological response analysis and questionnaires. 10 control users and 10 users with upper limb disorders were involved. An orthogonal design with seven usability parameters were used to generate 16 websites with different styles but with the same content. Galvanic skin response and facial electromyography on the corrugator supercilii and zygomaticus major muscles were used to assess emotional response, which are related to arousal and valence respectively; and user opinion was collected using a questionnaire. The results showed significant correlations between questionnaires and physiological signals, which are more sensitive to web parameters effect; and most of usability recommendations improve usability but only have a significant influence on users with motor disorders.

Keywords: Usability, Emotions, Physiological Response, User with Motor Disorders, Websites.

1 Introduction

The World Wide Web makes possible to access to huge amount of heterogeneous resources, from e-job to public administrations, without go out of home and independent of user allocation. Therefore, it was expected that World Wide Web would be a powerful tool for enhancing the independent living of people with disabilities and older people, helping to their inclusion on the Communication and Information Society. However, the effect has been the opposite: e-exclusion [1], because web requirements do not fit with the specific needs of these populations.

Fortunately, governments are now conscious of web access problems of these populations. The first efforts were focused on Accessibility. A clear example is the Web Accessibility Initiative (WAI), who has developed several accessibility guidelines to ensure access. However, web accessibility does not ensure web usability.

Usability involves several concepts such as effectiveness, efficiency, satisfaction, context of use, specific use, ease of use or learning [2]. Moreover, it is highly dependent on user profile and context, in contrast to accessibility.

K. Miesenberger et al. (Eds.): ICCHP 2014, Part I, LNCS 8547, pp. 256–259, 2014.
© Springer International Publishing Switzerland 2014

Emotions are related with many cognitive processes such as memory, decision making, attention or learning [3]. Therefore, emotions can play a key role for enhancing the efficiency and satisfaction during human computer interaction (HCI). User emotional response during HCI can be measuring using different physiological signals such as Galvanic Skin Response (GSR) [4] and facial Electromyography (EMG). This analysis can provide better information about user satisfaction than questionnaires. Moreover, this information can be directly gathered in real time during HCI without disturbing users.

2   Methodology

Firstly, seven of most extended web usability parameters were selected "Go Home", "Go Up", "Web site Map", "Hover and Click", "Background Image", "Breadcrumbs" and "Menu Type". Secondly, a factorial design with an orthogonal distribution was done with these parameters, generating 16 web styles applied to the same web content. Thirdly, the 16 Cascading Style Sheets (CSS) were distributed using the Federov algorithm, making a balanced test. 10 control users, without functional limitations, and 10 users with different upper limb disorders (e.g. Ataxia, cerebral palsy) were involved to check the influence of usability recommendations de-pending on user capabilities. Each user was involved in 3 sessions, performing 3 repetitions of 9 information-searching tasks using different web styles.

Fig. 1. Examples of some of the 16 web styles

EMG on corrugator supercilii (EMGc) and zygomaticus major (EMGz) muscles, and GSR were acquired using the VarioportTM system to gather user emotional response. GSR is related to emotional arousal, and EMGc and EMGz with negative and positive emotional valence respectively. Moreover, user opinion was collected using a usability questionnaire with 19 specific and 2 general items, including aesthetic issues.

On the one hand, physiological signals were filtered to reject noise and artifacts. Firstly, the phasic component of GSR (GSRp) was extracted using a 0.1Hz high pass filter. Secondly, facial EMG and GSR signals were normalized using the baseline measurement (30 seconds) of induced relax state [4]. On the other hand, Principal Component Analysis, with a Varimax rotation and Kaiser normalization, was used to transform the 20 subjective variables (items in the questionnaire) into a reduced set of independent components.

Finally, the same univariate Analysis of Variance (ANOVA) model was used for each variable, considering the principal effect of each factor (web parameters, user profile, session and repetition) and the first order interaction with the presence of motor disorders. Moreover, a correlation analysis was performed between both groups of variables.

3   Results

PCA reduced the 19 questions to 5 principal components: "Aesthetics", "Orienta-tion and Clear Layout", "Easy to find", "Simplicity and order", and "Need to learn"; explaining more than 60% of the variance.

Correlation analysis showed several significant correlations during the first session: "Aesthetics" with GSRp (0.148; $p<0.001$), "Orientation and Clear Layout" with EMGc (-0.224; $p<0.001$) and GSRp (-0.285; $p<0.001$), and "Need to learn" with EMGc (0.319; $p<0.001$) and GSRp (0.329; $p<0.001$). It should be highlighted that GSRp is related with aesthetic and usability components.

ANOVA results of physiological variables showed significant effects for most of web parameters with high levels of significance ($p<0.001$). However, ANOVA results of principal components only showed significant effects for a reduced number of web parameters and with lower levels of significance ($p<0.05$).

In relation to user profile, the presence of usability parameters have a significant influence on the emotional state during web interaction of users with motor disorders, increasing EMGz, and decreasing EMGc and GSRp. However, most of web parameters did not have any effect during the web interaction of control users. In fact, values of all physiological variables are higher for users with motor disorders, so their emotional state is more affected depending on the presence or absence of these usability parameters. Moreover, GSRp and EMGc values significant decrease along sessions for users with motor disorders, which is related with a reduction of emotional arousal and negative emotional valence respectively, being more evident the learning process.

Most of web parameters provided by usability experts had the expected effect: "Go Home", "Web site Map", "Breadcrumbs" positively affected to usability; and "Background image" negatively affected to usability. However, the effect of some parameters such as "Go Up" and "Menus" is contradictory. On the one hand, "Go up" reduced EMGc values but also reduced EMGz values. On the other hand, using two menus of one level, one on the left and other one on the upper part of the web, seems the best menu because it increases EMGz values, which is related with positive emotional valence. However, using only one menu with two levels at the upper part of the web is also a good menu because it decreases GSRp and EMGc values, which are related to reduce cognitive workload and negative emotional valence. This duality can be due o a mixed effect of usability and aesthetic issues.

4   Conclusions

Firstly, physiological response analysis detects more effects of usability parameters and with higher levels of significance than user opinion gathered with questionnaires, providing more information about the user-web interaction not only from satisfaction point of view but also from cognitive and emotional state (e.g. stress).

Secondly, web interaction influences on the emotional state of the users. Moreover, this effect is enhanced for users with motor disorders when the web design has not properly taken into account usability recommendations.

Thirdly, most of usability recommendations, provided by experts, improves usability, but the effect of other ones is not clear. The benefit of these recommendations is not clear for users without functional limitations. This highlights the need to perform more tests to adapt usability recommendations depending on user capabilities.

Fourthly, the physiological response can be affected by both aesthetic [5] and usability elements, being difficult to split both effects even in controlled experiments.

Finally, measuring of user physiological response can be useful to adapt content and complexity of interfaces depending on the specific emotional state of the users.

Future research should lean on a multimodal approach combining it with other techniques such as eye-tracking [6] and user movement analysis. Moreover, the usefulness of the methodology should be tested with real web content.

References

1. Lam, J., Lee, M.: Bridging the Digital Divide-The Roles of Internet Self-Efficacy towards Learning Computer and the Internet among Elderly in Hong Kong, China. In: Proc. of the 38th Annual Hawaii International Conference on En System Sciences, HICSS 2005, pp. 266b–266b (2005)
2. Belda-Lois, J., Helios de-Rosario, R.P., Poveda, R., Morón, A., Porcar, R., Gómez, A.: Can human movement analysis contribute to usability understanding? Human Movement Science 29(4), 529–541 (2010)
3. Nasoz, F., Lisetti, C.L., Alvarez, K., Finkelstein, N.: Emotion recognition from physiological signals for user modeling of affect. In: Proc. 3rd Workshop on Affective and Attitude User Modeling, Pittsburgh, PA, USA (2003)
4. Ward, R.D., Marsden, P.H.: Physiological responses to different WEB page designs. International Journal of Human-Computer Studies 59(1), 199–212 (2003)
5. Laparra-Hernández, J., Belda-Lois, J.M., Medina, E., Campos, N., Poveda, R.: EMG and GSR signals for evaluating user's perception of different types of ceramic flooring. International Journal of Industrial Ergonomics 39(2), 326–332 (2009)
6. Laparra-Hernández, J., Belda-Lois, J.M., Díaz Pineda, J.: Page A. A multimodal web usability assessment based on traditional metrics, physiological response and eye-tracking analysis. In: Gamito, P.S.P. (ed.) I See Me, You See Me: Inferring Cognitive and Emotional Processes from Gazing Behaviour, ch. 6, Cambridge Scholars Publishing (2014)

User Participation in the Design
of an Alternative Communication System
for Children with Diskinetic Cerebral Palsy
Including Emotion Management

Juan-Manuel Belda-Lois, Amparo López-Vicente, José Laparra-Herrero,
Rakel Poveda-Puente, and Alberto Ferreras-Remesal

Asociación Instituto de Biomecánica de Valencia. Universitat Politècnica de València
juanma.belda@ibv.upv.es

Abstract. People with Diskinetic Cerebral Palsy (DCPs) has speech
disorders limiting physical and social activity. Alternative Communication is an alternative to improve capacity. However, participation of
DCPs in the development process of DCPs is very uncommon. In this
contribution, new methodologies to improve participation of DCPs in a
new communicator using physiological signals for interaction is
described.

1 Introduction

Diskinetic Cerebral Palsy (DCP) is a permanent condition that causes severe motor impairments (i.e. changes in muscle tone and posture, and involuntary movements) and speech disorders (i.e. anarthria and dysarthria) which highly limit
physical and social activity. It is estimated that DCP affects over 125.000 people
in Europe with around 1.500 new cases each year [4],[5],[12]. It is caused by a non-
progressive impairement, imjury, or abnormality of the developing/immature
brain (before, during or shortly after birth). Over last years, prevalence of cerebral palsies has raised due to the increase in the survival rate of prematurely
born infants. The estimated lifetime cost per DCP patient is estimated at nearly
1 million [3].

Despite 78% of DCP children have a normal intelligence [8], 96% of them have
been classified as "educationally subnormal" [1]. This discrepancy between their
intellectual potential and their actual development is primarily caused by their
impaired communication and interaction abilities which hamper their learning
processes and affects the way this persons are able to express emotions.

Alternative and Augmentative Communication (AAC) systems is a wide range
of systems designd to improve communication capabilities among persons with
communication disabilities, such as in the case of DCPs. AAC systems are primarily designed by expertes based on functional aspects of the intended population, and barely on an analysis of user preferences or user needs.

K. Miesenberger et al. (Eds.): ICCHP 2014, Part I, LNCS 8547, pp. 260–263, 2014.

People use products to fulfil needs and reach objectives, the key factor on products design and development is thus to fit product requirements to user needs. There are two approaches:

1. Based on market needs [6], where attention is focused on consumers elections.
2. User Centred Design (UCD), where products should have some requirements (e.g. security, usability, aesthetic, price.) that should be perceived by users, considering user needs as the main input along design and development process [9].

The main goal of UCD is fitting product requirements to user needs [2]. However, most of standard UCD methodologies failed when are applied to users with special needs [11]. Despite the existence of some guidelines for adapting some UCD methodologies to deaf users, users with physical and speech disabilities or users with cognitive disorders [10]. This problem is reinforced on DCP users who are unable or have many problems to express their opinions in a written or verbal way.

However, several methodologies have appeared along last years to obtain user preferences without directly asking them, solving these problems. Inside this group, it should be highlighted the analysis of physiological response or behaviour patterns analysis. Many physiological signal as galvanic skin response (GSR) or heart rate variability, among others, have been used to assess from user aesthetic preferences to usability problems of one interface [7].

Therefore this contribution shows a methodological approach for the development of a communicator for DCP users incoporating Emotion capabilities in order to improve communication, emotion management and emotion awareness.

2   Material and Methods

The methodology developed in this project aims at gathering information among all the profiles related with the use of the communicators: people with DCP, relatives and carers. This approach allows to comprehensively address the assessment of their needs by considering the different points of view. Moreover, the data directly provided by DCPs can be compared with the information provided by the other profiles, extracting similarities, differences and nuances. The methodological approach has been divided into the following steps:

1. Methodology selection and adaptation: The involvement of CP people in the project required a justified choice of the most appropriate methodologies and the adaptation to CP users capabilities and skills.
2. Development of the selected techniques to involve each agent:
   (a) People with CP: Interviews, Context mapping and Card sorting.
   (b) Professionals: Focus Group, Repertory Grid Technique and Storyboard.
   (c) Family: Focus Group and Kiu Test.
3. Data analysis to identify the needs, demands and expectations of CP people to define the design requirements of the new communicator.

3 Results

The main results are briefly described:

- Data provided by the three agents is different but complementary.
- Data provided from the social environments of CP people (professional and family), without direct participation of CP people, is not enough, as this increases the risk of overlooking key aspects for communicator development.
- The adaptation of UCD techniques have allowed an effective and actively participation of people with CP.
- The involvement of CP people has required the support of professionals who were intermediaries during the communication process. People with CP have been able to provide information about their needs, demands and expectations; with the support of their caregivers as translators.
- People with CP have active and effectively participated in the creativity sessions for generating new ideas thanks to implementation of adapted methodologies.
- The necessary information to develop the new communicator has been obtained successfully with the application of the adapted techniques.

4 Conclusions

These results demonstrate that the inclusion of people with speech, written language and motor disorders, during the first phases of product design is possible, and provide different and complementary data to the information provided by other agents (professionals and relatives).

Acknowledgments. This study is part of the European Project 287774: ABC "Advanced BNCI Communication" financed Seventh Framework Programme, corresponding to the FP7-ICT-2011-7 call.

References

1. Evans, P.M., Evans, S.J., Alberman, E.: Cerebral palsy: why we must plan for survival. Archives of Disease in Childhood 65(12), 1329–1333 (1990)
2. Gould, J.D., Lewis, C.: Designing for usability: key principles and what designers think. Communications of the ACM 28(3), 300–311 (1985)
3. Honeycutt, A.A., Grosse, S.D., Dunlap, L.J., Schendel, D.E., Chen, H., Brann, E., al Homsi, G.: Economic costs of mental retardation, cerebral palsy, hearing loss, and vision impairment. Research in Social Science and Disability 3, 207–228 (2003)
4. Johnson, A.: Prevalence and characteristics of children with cerebral palsy in europe. Developmental Medicine & Child Neurology 44(9), 633–640 (2002)
5. Jones, M.W., Morgan, E., Shelton, J.E., Thorogood, C.: Cerebral palsy: introduction and diagnosis (part i). Journal of Pediatric Health Care 21(3), 146–152 (2007)
6. Kotler, P.: Marketing management. Pearson Education India (2009)

7. Laparra-Hernández, J., Belda-Lois, J.M., Medina, E., Campos, N., Poveda, R.: EMG and GSR signals for evaluating user's perception of different types of ceramic flooring. International Journal of Industrial Ergonomics 39(2), 326–332 (2009)

8. Madrigal Muñoz, A.: La parálisis cerebral (2004)

9. Porcar Seder, R.M.: Aplicación del análisis multivariante a la obtención de criterios de diseño para mobiliario de oficina. Ph.D. thesis, Universitat Politécnica de Valéncia (2000)

10. Poveda Puente, R., Barberá i Guillem, R., Sánchez-Lacuesta, J.: MUSA/IBV Método para la selección de ayudas técnicas bajo criterios de usabilidad. Instituto de Biomecánica de Valencia, Valencia (2003)

11. Poveda Puente, R., Laparra Hernández, J.: Hábitos de consumo en los mayores. mayores, p. 103 (2009)

12. Winter, S., Autry, A., Boyle, C., Yeargin-Allsopp, M.: Trends in the prevalence of cerebral palsy in a population-based study. Pediatrics 110(6), 1220–1225 (2002)

Digital Video Games for Older Adults
with Cognitive Impairment

Arlene Astell[1,2], Norman Alm[3], Richard Dye[3], Gary Gowans[4],
Philip Vaughan[4], and Maggie Ellis[5]

[1] Ontario Shores Centre for Mental Health Sciences, Whitby, Canada
astella@ontarioshores.ca
[2] Centre for Assistive Technology and Connected Healthcare, University of Sheffield, UK
a.astell@sheffield.ac.uk
[3] Applied Computing, University of Dundee, UK
nalm@computing.dundee.ac.uk, richarddye@gmail.com
[4] Duncan of Jordanstone College of Art & Design, University of Dundee, UK
g.m.gowans@dundee.ac.uk, phil_v14@hotmail.com
[5] School of Psychology & Neuroscience, University of St. Andrews, UK
mpe2@st-andrews.ac.uk

Abstract. Digital video games offer opportunities for older adults with cognitive impairment to engage in meaningful activities. However, to achieve this benefit digital video games are needed that take account of the players' cognitive impairment. This paper reports work with older adults with cognitive impairment due to dementia to find out how they can best be prompted to initiate and play games independently, what sorts of digital video activities they like to play, and if playing digital video games is engaging. The results demonstrate that older adults with cognitive impairment can learn to play new digital video activities and can be prompted to play independently through visual and auditory cues. Their behaviour indicates features of Flow similar to that reported in other gaming studies.

Keywords: Dementia, Games, Engagement, Enjoyment.

1 Introduction

Developments in Assistive Technology (AT) and Information and Communication Technology (ICT) targeting older adults have typically focused on supporting maintenance of activities of daily life such as cooking, personal hygiene and safety in the home [1]. There has been far less exploration of the potential of technologies to address more than these basic needs, for example the need for social interaction, for engagement in meaningful activities and for personal achievement and satisfaction [2]. However, these areas have been at the forefront of developments in video games and multimedia entertainment targeting other sectors of the population.

Video games have great potential as a medium for benefitting older adults with special needs, such as mobility, visual, hearing or cognitive impairment that may

K. Miesenberger et al. (Eds.): ICCHP 2014, Part I, LNCS 8547, pp. 264–271, 2014.

reduce the accessibility of other activities. The flexibility and responsiveness offered by video games make it possible to mitigate special physical and cognitive needs to enable a whole range of experiences from education to excitement to sheer enjoyment. Evidence from the applications of digital games to other groups in the population with special needs, for example children with intellectual disabilities, suggests that both "learning-purposed as well as entertainment-purposed" games can enhance their lives [3].

1.1 Games for Dementia

The Living in the Moment (LIM) project [4] started exploring the parameters for developing digital activities to provide engaging and stimulating pastimes, i.e. l'entertainment-purposed' games, for people with cognitive impairment due to dementia. Dementia is an untreatable neurological condition that affects an individual's cognitive functions and progressively worsens over time. There are several different types of dementia, each of which has its own profile of cognitive impairment alongside those aspects of cognition that are unaffected. The most common type of dementia is Alzheimer's disease (AD), which characteristically affects memory most notably forgetting recently learned information. This affects people's explicit learning ability, however implicit processes seem to be more intact [5]. This means that new activities must have very simple instructions and an intuitive interface to enable users to understand what they need to do to play the game.

Working closely with older adults with dementia the LIM project posed two questions: (i) How can they best be prompted to initiate and play games independently? (ii) What sorts of activities do they enjoy? Building on our previous findings that people with progressive cognitive impairment can interact with and concentrate on materials presented on a touchscreen [6] we created a range of digital video activities designed to present different types of challenge and stimulation. To find out how best to provide in-game prompts we presented visual and auditory cues in different ways and the results are summarized here. We looked at the ways people with dementia explored the games on the touch screen, how they used the interactive elements and how long they played for. In respect of the second question we looked at the responses from people with dementia to the different activities, with particular attention to whether they wanted to keep playing.

In trying to understand what might make an activity engaging, the concept of 'Flow' [7] has been applied to other populations [8]. Csikszentmihalyi [7] defined a Flow experience as having eight dimensions, which make it reinforcing and fulfilling and which create a desire for a person to repeat the experience. These elements are: 1. The task has clear goals, 2. There is immediate feedback, 3. There is a balance between challenges and skills, 4. Action and awareness are merged, 5. Distractions are excluded from consciousness, 6. There is no worry of failure, 7. Concern for the self disappears, 8. The sense of time becomes distorted. For an activity to be self-rewarding and maintain a person's Flow experience, the activity needs to reach a balance between the challenges of the activity, and the abilities of the participant. The presence of these features in the activity of older adults with cognitive impairment is explored in the games created during the LIM project.

2   Method

We created and tested a range of new digital video activities for touch screen over a three year period, ranging from a 3D tour round a botanic garden (Figure 1) to 'painting' a vase (Figure 2) to fairground games such as a shooting gallery. These activities fell broadly into five categories: Interactive 3D environments; Sports; Funfair and Traditional; Creative; Miscellaneous (Table 1). The Interactive 3D environments were tours around indoor and outdoor spaces and included interactive 'hotspots' for players to touch. For example, in the Botanic Garden players could 'Touch to see fish" which would launch a video of koi carp with gently rippling water sounds (Figure 1).

Fig. 1. Interactive Botanic Garden

'Sports' included activities such as tennis and skittles, while 'Funfair and Traditional' were based on activities such as knocking down slowly moving tin ducks in a 'shooting gallery' and a coconut shy. The 'Creative' activities included 'painting' and music making, along with a game based on blowing bubbles. 'Miscellaneous' activities were ones that included interacting with a pet dog, watching fish in an aquarium and making toast.

Combinations of sound - including speech and non-speech - text and movements were tested to examine their effect on supporting older adults with cognitive impairment to initiate and maintain playing.

More than 100 older adults with cognitive impairment assisted in developing and testing the new digital video activities. They were recruited from a range of services including day care, residential and nursing homes. Using an iterative design and test process each new concept was taken out to one of the partner organisations for rapid feedback from the end-users. To capture their responses all sessions were video recorded. This allows for detailed examination of how they explore and learn how to play each new activity. This approach also enables the effectiveness of different prompt types to be examined. Participants were interviewed at the end of each session.

Fig. 2. Vase painting

3   Results

Over 30 new digital video activities were developed and tested (Table 1). Of these, some were rejected straight away if the first group of participants all reacted negatively. Unsuccessful activities included many of the activities in the 'miscellaneous' category: aquarium, pet dog, planting seeds, ball course, although the picture and video viewers were positively received, as were most activities in the other four categories.

Examination of the five different activity types suggests that the participants were perfectly able to play the 'miscellaneous' activities but that these did not contain sufficient purpose or challenge to maintain participant's interest. For example, the pet dog activity offered the player the opportunity to feed the dog, stroke the dg or throw a ball. These were easily accomplished by the players but after completion did not invite repetition. This contrasts with the penalty kick game whereby players try to score a goal by touching the ball at a certain angle. On successive turns players can try to improve their accuracy or build up their score. This is true for all of the activities in the 'Sports' category.

The 'Funfair and Traditional games', such as coconut shy and shooting gallery contained similar elements of clear purpose, challenge and potential to improve. The 'Creative' digital activities appeared to offer different opportunities for achievement and accomplishment. In these activities participants were not trying to complete the task in a certain way, e.g. knock down all of the coconuts or score a goal. Rather they were able to build their skills by painting a pattern on a vase or creating a musical tune. The Interactive 3D environments offered a slightly different experience again. Participants found these interesting to explore and the enjoyed the interactive hotspots.

The post-game interviews provided useful insights into the participants' experience and views of the games. The activities people enjoyed received positive comments and expressed desire to play again, while games they not enjoy were commented on less favourably (Table 2). In addition, there was evidence from the comments that the some of the digital video activities were engaging and provided the participants opportunities for experiencing autonomy and competence (Table 2).

Table 1. New digital video activities created and tested during Living in the Moment project

Category	Digital video activity	
Interactive 3D environments	Botanic garden	Pub
	Art gallery	Sitting room
	Domestic garden	Kitchen
	House	
Sports	Golf	Skittles
	Soccer – penalty kick	Tennis
Funfair and traditional games	Shooting gallery	Pinball
	Whack-a-mole	Coconut shy
	Bingo	
Creative	Musical chimes	Vase painting
	Bubble blower	Keyboard
	Drumkit	
Miscellaneous:	Picture viewer	Video viewer
	Planting seeds	Aquarium
	Ball course	Bird House
	Flowers opening	Pet dog
	Making toast	Boiling kettle
	Frying eggs	Fish pond
	Fireworks	

4   Discussion

The main finding was that older adults with cognitive impairment due to dementia can learn to interact with and play computerised activities independently, without a caregiver being present. This is important for encouraging the development of new activities to meet the specific needs of older adults with cognitive impairment. The availability of such activities could provide opportunities for autonomy, achievement and satisfaction, which are largely missing from most other activities available to them.

In respect of the two specific questions posed by the LIM project, prompting using a mixture of built-in text, audio and visual cues can support older adults with cognitive impairment to initiate and maintain playing. For example in the painting the vase activity the player can see the paint appear on the pot as they touch it with their finger. If the player does not touch a coloured paint pot for 20 seconds one of the pots bounces up and makes a 'swooshing' noise, as of a brush stirring paint. By reminding the player they can change colour this encourages them to keep playing. Speech-based prompts were less successful, as they had the effect of making the player passively wait for the next instruction.

In respect of what activities older people with cognitive impairment enjoy, the answer is a wide range. The activities developed in the Living in the Moment project can be divided broadly into five categories: Interactive 3D environments, Sports, Funfair and Traditional, Creative, and Miscellaneous. These contrast with typical gaming typologies such as First-Person shooter, strategy, role-play, etc [9] and reflect the inspiration for the activities in the real world. Many of the new activities were created

Table 2. Comments on the digital video activities demonstrating enjoyment, engagement, autonomy and competence

Games people enjoyed	Games people didn't enjoy
"I love that"	"I don't know what it is"
"I want one of these"	"How do you stop it?"
"Can I take this home?"	"It would be much better if I knew what
"That was good, right enough"	I was supposed to be doing"
"It's something different"	"That could put you to sleep"
"I'll tell my family I want one of them"	"Not made for me is it"
Engagement	**Autonomy and competence**
"It's something to do with your brains"	"I never thought I could do that but I'm
"I could play for a good long while on	not having any problem with it"
this at home"	"I'll be able to tell my family I can do
"You could do this long enough	it"
couldn't you?"	"It's something I can do"
"That's brilliant! I'd be here all day"	"That's amazing. Everyone seems able
"I'll be playing this all weekend"	to use it"
	"It's easy when you think about it"
	"You're always learning something"

to present older adults with cognitive impairment the opportunity to carry out activities they no longer do in the real world. For instance the interactive 3D environments were developed after discussion with older adults in care homes who have very few opportunities to go out into other environments.

In respect of what makes digital video activities enjoyable for older adults with cognitive impairment the findings are very similar to other studies of gaming, in that they relate closely to several dimensions of Flow [7]. First it is very important that the games have a clear goal. For instance, one of the "Miscellaneous' activities required participants to move a ball around a course, which they could do but did not see the point of. However, when presented with a white vase and three paint pots, people happily sat and 'painted' the vase, changing colours and creating patterns as the pot slowly rotated.

Second it is important that the player receives immediate feedback. Essentially when the person touches the screen this must produce some effect, such as movement of an object or a sound or both. For instance when the person touches the bubble-blower this produces the sound of a balloon blowing up as a coloured bubble appears and grows in size before bouncing off across the screen. The players can then chase the bubble, which may change in size when touched or make a sound when 'popped'.

The activities must also contain a balance between challenges and skills. The prototype activity we developed of throwing a ball for a dog was easy to carry out but did not provide sufficient challenge to maintain interest. However, the penalty kick game, where the player can vary the angle of the shot at goal, provides the opportunity for improvement. This is reinforced by a roar from 'the crowd' when the ball goes in the net.

In respect of the other dimensions of Flow, the video recordings indicate that people become immersed in activities that are engaging and rewarding, such as painting the vase, and can be engrossed until interrupted. There was also much evidence of enjoyment as people would frequently laugh and smile when commenting on their experience. This speaks to the potential of game playing as a shared social activity for older adults with cognitive impairment. Activities such as the shooting gallery, penalty kick and coconut shy are all suitable for older adults with cognitive impairment to play together, with caregivers and with family members, including grandchildren.

Much of the lessons learnt in this project were captured using video recording. On a practical note video recording is incredibly useful as a means of collecting observational data that illuminates the process of participants exploring and learning to play. It also means that the whole team can see how the older adults react to the new activities without having to be present at the time. In addition, it is important to record the post-session interview while the activity is still on the screen, as this acts as a memory support.

In addition to the specific findings about digital activities, this research demonstrates that older adults with cognitive impairment can be active partners in the research process. They are able to express their views about what they like and dislike and make suggestions about other things they would like to do. This should encourage other researchers to engage directly with older adults with cognitive impairment to create new digital video activities.

Finally, these findings suggest that there is great potential for developing stimulating and absorbing activities for people with dementia to play alone or with others. As well as providing them with rewarding and satisfying Flow experiences, there is unexplored potential for gaming to tackle other challenges faces by older adults with cognitive impairment, such as providing cognitive maintenance, rehabilitation or education.

Acknowledgements. Parts of this work were funded by the EPSRC through grants number GR/R27013/01 to the first author and GR to the second and fourth authors. We are immensely grateful to all of the people with a dementia diagnosis who have worked with us over the past 12 years.

References

1. Astell, A.J.: Personhood and technology in dementia. Quality in Ageing 7(1), 15–25 (2006)
2. Astell, A.J.: Technology and fun for a happy old age. In: Sixsmith, A., Gutman, G. (eds.) Technology for Active Aging. Springer Science (2013)
3. Saridaki, M., Gouscos, D., Melmaris, M.G.: Digital Games-Based Learning for Students with Intellectual Disability. In: Connolly, T., Stansfield, M., Boyle, L. (eds.) Games-Based Learning Advancements for Multi-Sensory Human Computer Interfaces: Techniques and Effective Practices. IGI Global (2009)
4. Astell, A.J., Alm, N., Gowans, G., Ellis, M., Dye, R., Vaughan, P.: Involving older people with dementia and their carers in designing computer-based support systems: Some methodological considerations. Universal Access in the Information Society 8(1), 49–59 (2009)

5. Kimkowicz-Mowlec, A., Slowik, A., Krzywosxanski, L., Herzog- Krzywosxanski, R., Szczudlik, A.: Severity of explicit memory impairment due to Alzheimer's disease improves effectiveness of implicit learning. Journal of Neurology 255(4), 502–509 (2008)
6. Astell, A.J., Alm, N., Gowans, G., Ellis, M.P., Dye, R., Campbell, J.: CIRCA: A communication prosthesis for dementia. In: Mihailidas, A., Normie, L., Kautz, H., Boger, J. (eds.) Technology and Aging. IOS Press (2008)
7. Csikszentmihalyi, M.: FLOW: The psychology of optimal experience. Harper Row, New York (1990)
8. Murphy, C., Chertoff, D., Guerrero, M., Moffitt, K.: Design better games: Flow, motivation and fun. In: Design and Development of Training Games: Practical Guidelines from a Multi-Disciplinary Perspective. Cambridge University Press (2013)
9. Zelinksi, E.M., Reyes, R.: Cognitive benefits of computer games for older adults. Gerontechnology 8(4), 220–235 (2009)

"Gardener" Serious Game for Stroke Patients

Ágnes Nyéki, Veronika Szucs, Péter Csuti, Ferenc Szabó, and Cecilia Sik Lanyi

University of Pannonia, Egyetem str. 10, H-8200 Veszprem, Hungary
{nyekiagnes92,veronika.szucs01}@gmail.com,
{csutip,szabof}@vision.uni-pannon.hu, lanyi@almos.uni-pannon.hu

Abstract. This study introduces a serious game, "Gardener", which is one of the games planned within the "StrokeBack" project. The aim of this game is to support the rehabilitation process of stroke patients with upper limb impairments and damaged psychomotor abilities.

Keywords: serious game, stroke patients, rehabilitation.

1 Introduction

Within the StrokeBack project [1], founded by the EU, the goal is to increase the speed of the rehabilitation process of stroke patients. A very important criteria is that the patients are staying at home during the therapy, because their own environment has a good effect on them. With the repetition of many small exercises with the arms and shoulders, the damaged psychomotor abilities can be recovered.

The aim of this part of the project is to create games [2], [3] which make the patient to do these exercises playfully. Computer games have been demonstrated as the result of positive outcomes of the participation of people with disabilities in research and development of virtual reality [4], [5]. One of the planned games is the "Gardener" game. Playing with the "Gardener" game the user has to make repetitive movements: fingers' extension.

This game was developed by C++ programming language on Qt, because Qt provides platform independency.

2 The "Gardener" Game

The task of the player is to make the plants and flowers grow one by one. To grow a plant, the player has to water it several times with a dedicated movement. After a plant grows up, the player can continue with the next one till all of the flowers or plants in the garden are grown up. The progress bar shows how many times the actual plant needs to be sprinkled until it becomes fully grown (Fig. 1.). The count of these sprinkles is called number of Required motions.

If the player waters the plants too slowly, they will start to wither (their color will turn to grey Fig. 2.). There is a big exclamation point glowing above the withering plant to warn the player. The time interval between the last watering and the withering is called Fading time.

K. Miesenberger et al. (Eds.): ICCHP 2014, Part I, LNCS 8547, pp. 272–275, 2014.

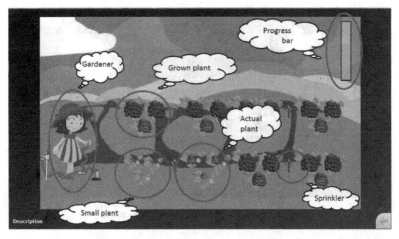

Fig. 1. The "Gardener" game: grape theme

Fig. 2. Color of grape turns grey

The player can tend many kinds of plants, for example roses, grapes or tomatoes too.

The available themes of this game are: bluebell, carrot, currant, geranium, grape, pepper, rose, strawberry, tomato, tulip.

To sprinkle a plant, the player has to make a dedicated pumping movement. If game is being played by the keyboard, press „Space" to spray. The movement of the gardener/hose is automatic; the player can only control the watering.

3   The "Gardener" Game's Level Editor

Based on the therapists' request a level editor was developed.

The level editor of The Gardener game is very simple. After setting up the main parameters of the level, the arrangement of the plants will set up automatically according to the theme.

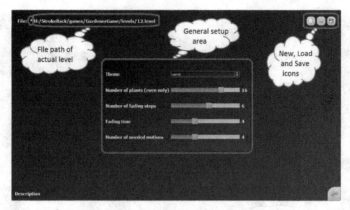

Fig. 3. Level editor of the "Gardener" game

The "new", "load", "save" icons and the Actual level's file path area are the same as in the earlier versions. To create a new level, first the "new" icon should be selected.

The parameters of a level can be set with the tools which are included in the General setup area. At the Theme label the level's theme can be selected from the drop down menu, which contains only the available valid skins. Every skin is limited by the number of plants that can be shown on the gamefield. This is because some of the plants are bigger, so less can be placed from it on the gamefield. A skin is valid, if the selected plant number on a level is under its upper limit. The limitations are the following:

- Grapes, bluebell, strawberry, and currant: 8 plants maximally
- Rose, tomato and pepper: 16 plants at maximally
- Carrot, geranium and tulip: 20 plants at maximally

The theme can be set to "Shuffle" as well, which means that the skin of the level will be chosen randomly from the valid ones.

The Number of the plants on a level can be set with a slider. It is important to notice that this should be an even number, which can be at least 4, and the maximum is specified by the chosen theme.

The next parameter is the Number of fading steps, which gives that how many steps are needed for a plant to wither when it is not watered. This can be set with a slider from 1 to 10.

The next slider is for the Fading time parameter, which means that after the adjusted amount of time the plant will start to wither. This value can be between 1 and 10.

The last parameter is the Number of needed motions, the value of which can be be-tween 1 and 10. This value shows that how many movements are required to water a plant. This is only a scale value; the real amount of required movement can be calculated with multiplying the adjusted value with 4.

4   Test by the Patients and Therapists

The first version of the game was tested by 10 stroke patients (May 2013 at the Brandenburg Klinik). The patients and therapists had several good ideas, which were installed in this new version of the game. The clinical testing of this new version of Gardener game is going to be in April in 2014. The results of this testing will be presented at the conference.

5   Conclusion

This game is a good method for training stroke patients, because while playing with them the patients will do small, funny, but important exercises, which can advance the recovery. Most of the people like to play games, so the occasionally boring practise can be made funny and pleasurable [6,7].

Acknowledgements. The StrokeBack research project is supported by the European Commission under the 7th Framework Programme through Call (part) identifier FP7-ICT-2011-7, grant agreement no: 288692.

References

1. StrokeBack project, http://www.strokeback.eu/
2. Dömők, T., Szűcs, V., László, E., Sík Lányi, C.: "Break the Bricks" Serious Game for Stroke Patients. In: Miesenberger, K., Karshmer, A., Penaz, P., Zagler, W. (eds.) ICCHP 2012, Part I. LNCS, vol. 7382, pp. 673–680. Springer, Heidelberg (2012)
3. Sik Lányi, C., Szücs, V., Dömök, T., László, E.: Developing serious game for victims of stroke. In: Sharkey, P.M., Klinger, E. (eds.) Procedings of ICDVRAT 2012, pp. 503–506. University of Reading, Reading (2012)
4. Rand, D., Kizony, R., Weiss, P.L.: Virtual reality rehabilitation for all: Vivid GX versus Sony PlayStation II EyeToy. In: Sharkey, P., McCrindle, R., Brown, D. (eds.) Proceedings of ICDVRAT 2004, pp. 87–94. The University of Reading, Reading (2004)
5. Broeren, J., Bellner, A.-L., Fogelberg, M., Göransson, O., Goude, D., Johansson, B., Larsson, P.A., Pettersson, K., Rydmark, M.: Exploration of computer games in rehabilitation for brain damage. In: Sharkey, P., Lopes-dos-Santos, P., Weiss, P.L., Brooks, T. (eds.) Proceedings of ICDVRAT 2008, pp. 75–80. The University of Reading, Reading (2008)
6. Szücs, V., Sik Lanyi, C.: Abilities and limitations of assistive technologies in post-stroke therapy based on virtual/augmented reality, Assistive Technology: From Research to practice. In: Encarnação, P., et al. (eds.) Proceeedings of AAATE 2013 Conference, pp. 1087–1091. IOS Press BV, Amsterdam (2013)
7. Szücs, V., Antal, P., Dömök, T., Laszlo, E., Sik Lanyi, C.: Developing the "Birdie" game for stroke patients' rehabilitation, Assistive Technology: From Research to practice. In: Encarnação, P., et al. (eds.) Proceeedings of AAATE 2013 Conference, pp. 1006–1012. IOS Press BV, Amsterdam (2013)

Towards an Interactive Leisure Activity for People with PIMD

Robby van Delden[1], Dennis Reidsma[1], Wietske van Oorsouw[2], Ronald Poppe[1],
Peter van der Vos[3], Andries Lohmeijer[3], Petri Embregts[2,4], Vanessa Evers[1],
and Dirk Heylen[1]

[1] Human Media Interaction, University of Twente, Enschede, The Netherlands
{r.w.vandelden,d.reidsma,r.w.poppe,v.evers,d.k.j.heylen}@utwente.nl
[2] Tranzo, Scientific Center of Care and Welfare, Tilburg University,
Tilburg, The Netherlands
{w.m.w.j.vanOorsouw,p.j.c.m.embregts}@uvt.nl
[3] Kitt Engineering Enschede, The Netherlands
{peter,andries}@kitt.nl
[4] Dichterbij Innovation and Science, Gennep, The Netherlands

Abstract. We address the possibilities of truly interactive systems for
people with Profound Intellectual and Multiple Disabilities (PIMD).
These are intended to improve alertness, movement and mood. We are
working on an interactive ball that follows body movement and an interactive floor mat for this target group. We explain the key features in
the design that are essential for the possible success.

Keywords: Snoezelen, Interactive Therapy, Profound Intellectual and
Multiple Disabilities, PIMD, Interactive Ball, Interactive Floor Mat.

1 Introduction

Interactive Entertainment is meant to be fun and might be beneficial for people
with profound mental and intellectual disabilities (PIMD) as well. Such systems
can increase alertness, mood and body movement for people with PIMD, three
goals often targeted by care staff. People with PIMD are a heterogeneous group
that generally have an intellectual developmental age of 24 months or less, have
multiple mutually reinforcing disabilities and are dependent on others for their
every-day activities [7], [9], [10]. There is a fairly limited amount of activities and
especially interactive entertainment for people with PIMD [2], [13]. Therefore,
many people with PIMD are likely to have too small an amount of non-sedentary
activities and have to do with passive activities such as watching television and
lying on a waterbed [15]. Creating interactive entertainment for people with
PIMD may help to create alternatives, but the design process is hard for several
reasons. One has to take into account a wide range of peculiarities, disabilities
and abilities. Also the process to obtain ethical approval for experiments is an
extensive procedure. The evaluation phase is complicated due to the inability
to verbally interact with the participants. Instead people with PIMD mainly

K. Miesenberger et al. (Eds.): ICCHP 2014, Part I, LNCS 8547, pp. 276–282, 2014.

communicate through body movements [14]. Affective measurements, such as indicators of happiness or agitation, are therefore often based on behavior interpreted from video recordings and on interviews with care staff [2, 3].

This user group is especially vulnerable with regard to living a meaningful life [2], [7]. At the same time it is recognized that entertainment might contribute to self-efficacy, self-esteem, autonomy and creative explorations even for people with special needs [1,2], [12]. Recent developments in technology show an array of ways to facilitate the creation of interactive systems [8]. Especially technologies such as depth cameras that can detect body posture and gross body motion (e.g. Kinect) and pressure sensors for the Arduino that are easy to implement can be useful in tapping into the limited non-verbal movement skills of people with PIMD.

Based on the interpretation of non-verbal movements more truly interactive systems can be created. This goes beyond merely turning a product on or off – it should include a developing dialog of actions and responses [2]. Such systems provide an expressive experience that is capable of captivating people in the target group [2]. We think such systems help in heightening their alertness and triggering them to move more and will result in positive effects on their mood.

In this paper we follow up with related work on electronically powered systems stimulating people with PIMD. We then describe our preliminary work, including the rationale behind two concepts we are currently developing. We finish this paper by summarizing our view and the next steps in our research.

2   Related Work

One of the few leisure activities offered to people with PIMD is *snoezelen* which takes place in a multi-sensory environment. It is intended to stimulate alertness of the people with specific needs [11], [13]. It contains, for instance, bubble tubes, aroma dispersers, projector wheels and tactile boards [4]. However, there is a lack in evidence that these environments are indeed effective. Individual differences could play a role herein, some people with PIMD might get more alert in these instrumented environments and others are more alert in their natural environments [13]. Munde et al. suggest that waves of alertness occur for this target group and that making use of these moments of alertness could help their learning abilities and overall development [9].

Several hundreds of products are available for people with special needs. Only a limited amount is suitable for people with PIMD, offering only limited interactivity (cf. [2])[1]. From these, Snoezelen® Soundbeam, an interactive music system based on movements, was one of the very few systems that we call interactive (more than a trigger button) and that seems suitable for many people

---

[1] Catalogs were selected based on Google searches with a combination of keywords including *interactive, toys and snoezelen, PIMD* or *special needs* and several catalogs suggested by therapists [4]: achievement-products.com, barryemons.nl, dragonflytoys.com, enablingdevices.com, fisher-price.com, flaghouse.com, mikeayres-design.co.uk/, snoezeleninfo.com, spacekraft.co.uk and wilkinsinternational.com.au

with PIMD as it responds to gross motor movements and produces visual and audible stimuli. Another interesting system that also targets several modalities, is the Therapeutic Motion Simulation (TMS) developed by vita-care[2]. It originates from hippotherapy but tries to provide a safer, easier, less costly way to provide a horse riding like experience, including the movement,vibration,visuals and sounds.

Between 1988 and 1995 Kitt Engineering developed the Motion Interpreted Media Interface Control (MIMIC). The MIMIC suite, provided an interactive experience with sounds, visuals and MIDI effects based on a video stream. After seeing some children with autism behaving very expressive in such an installation they were involved in a three month pilot using their system for people with special needs at the health care organization Eemeroord (currently Sherpa). The touch of an object and movements from arms and other body parts could be linked to playing sounds. For some people with special needs it stimulated movements that were not performed before.[3]

Finally, a series of interactive prototypes were developed by Lund University, including a flexible physical canvas that could be pushed for visual and auditory responses, a cuddleable toy/robot that moved and produced sounds based on the cuddling intensity, and an interactive waterbed. In evaluations, the children would take initiative for interaction and enjoy these kind of interactions [2], [5,6]. The interactive waterbed reacts to the movements of a child lying on it, see Figure 1. Based on these movements it provides an interactive *'wavescape'* consisting of sounds accompanied with subsonic vibrations. This provides a continuous non-obtrusive experience that can be tailored to the arousal of the children *[H. S. Larsen, personal communication, March 31, 2014]*. [4].

This latter research is, at least to our knowledge, the only scientific research in which *'truly interactive systems'* for people with PIMD were created. Based on the related work we conclude that people with PIMD are offered a limited amount of active leisure activities. The products that do exist have a limited interactivity. Some people do become alert in Snoezel environments, but it seems to be highly dependent on the actual person and tailored interactivity might add to the experience for more types of users. In an attempt to improve this situation by creating interactive systems, we have to address several aspects of people with PIMD in our design.

3   Our Approach and Ideas

Many people with PIMD, are showing large amounts of self-regulatory behavior, such as the stereotypical rocking, staring at fingers while moving them and making non-verbalized noises [4]. These actions can be a starting point to initiate interaction as they are likely to occur anyway. Visual impairments make

---

[2] www.vita-care.eu

[3] The original Dutch coverage of the system for Eemeroord by newspapers can be found on http://www.kitt.nl/Previous_Work_MIMIC.pdf

[4] Movies and more information can be found on http://sid.desiign.org/

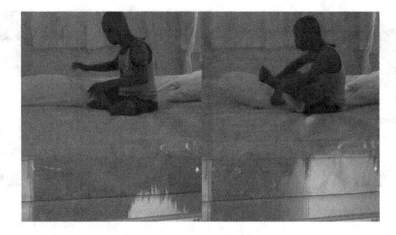

Fig. 1. The interactive waterbed, figure used with permission from the author

it hard to distinguish colors or detailed shapes, although several persons with PIMD are capable of seeing contours and objects with high contrast. Therefore, moving physical objects seem more suitable than projected images and screens.

We applied this in our first interactive concept: an interactive ball. The ball will respond to the upper body movement (e.g., the stereotypical rocking behavior) and to the head orientation of the user. The ball will be lying in front of the user. When the user is not focused on the ball, it will gently try to regain focus by playing some sounds, a wiggling movement, and LEDs changing color. When it is in focus it tries to persuade the user to move. This is done by letting the ball move according to the upper body movement of the user, and playing sounds to indicate responsiveness. The ball itself is powered from the inside, comparable to an RF car [5].

Our second concept is not yet in development. It is based on the rocking motion observed with users lying on a bed-like mat on the floor. Using pressure sensor technology in the interactive mat we can easily recognize the rocking movement. In response, the intensity and rhythm of music can be changed based on the recognized movements, rhythm of movements, and non-verbalized noises. To tailor this system for users that need more intense stimuli, this can be combined by adjusting the color and brightness in the environment.

4   Technical Implementation for an Interactive Ball

The ball we are working on moves by changing the center of gravity with three servo motors connected to weighted arms, see Figure 2. The system is powered with 10 AAA batteries. A 50 cm big pre-fabricated water-resistant expanded polystyrene ball is used for the outside. Inside there is a circular laser-cutted

---

[5] The basics of the concept are also explained in a movie that can be found on http://hmi.ewi.utwente.nl/interactive-ball-save15years-2014.mp4.

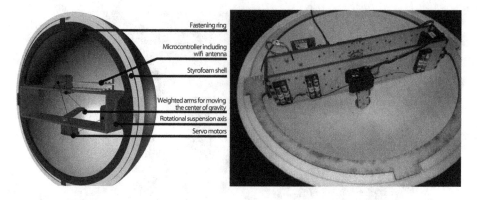

Fig. 2. A 3D-model and prototype of the interior of the ball

plywood frame holding a revolving frame containing the electronic components. In this way it should be able to move on its own in two dimensions. In our current implementation, we chose to restrict the ball to a one-dimensional left/right movement.

For tracking the head position the head joint of the upper body tracking is used of the Windows Kinect SDK 1.8. The recognition of focus towards the ball, is done with the Microsoft Face Tracking Software Development Kit for Kinect for Windows[6]. Currently we only move the ball when the face is properly detected but the upper body tracking has a higher recognition rate than the facial feature recognition and this allows for testing alternative interactions. The position of the ball is recognized with a straightforward background subtraction tracking algorithm based on a webcam feed. Based on the difference between the head position and the ball's position the ball stops, or is moved either to the left or right. In order to transmit these movements to the ball, the ball contains a local wifi hotspot and TCP/IP server. The intensity of the interaction, the intervals of grabbing attention with sounds and the type of sounds can be manually adapted to the user (during run time), in order to improve the effect of the interaction and possibly allow for a larger set of users.

5   The Next Step

Although we have been working on this topic for some time we still realize it is hard to truly understand the user group. In the coming months we are starting the first user tests, first verifying some of the technological parts on healthy people, followed by gathering feedback from therapists and responses of users in a set of pilot tests. In these pilot tests we propose to use 'within session' tests to see what settings of the ball will be optimal for the users. The alternating changes within a condition involve changing sounds and having responsive lights. They

---

[6] http://msdn.microsoft.com/en-us/library/jj130970.aspx

are convenient to overcome the mood swings of users, day-by-day variations, and large differences between users.

Subsequent exploratory long-term tests are planned to measure that an interactive system can indeed add something with respect to the dimensions of alertness, movement and mood, for people with PIMD. We will do this both with automatic measurements and more traditional measurements: interviews, observation and manual annotation. With these research activities we hope to motivate and inspire others as well to bring some extra entertainment to the lives of people with PIMD.

Acknowledgments. This publication was supported by the Dutch national program COMMIT. The authors would like to thank Henrik Svarrer Larsen and others from Lund University for their inspiring work and sharing their insights. We would also like to thank all the involved people of the health care organization of Dichterbij for their financial contributions for manufacturing of devices, their driven enthusiasm and sharing their knowledge and time for this project.

References

1. Alm, N., Astell, A., Gowans, G., Dye, R., Ellis, M., Vaughan, P., Riley, P.: Engaging multimedia leisure for people with dementia. Gerontechnology 8(4), 236–246 (2009)
2. Caltenco, H.A., Larsen, H., Hedvall, P.: Enhancing multisensory environments with design artifacts for tangible interaction. In: Proceedings of The Seventh International Workshop on Haptic and Audio Interaction Design (HAID), Lund, Sweden, pp. 45–47 (2012)
3. Dillon, C.M., Carr, J.E.: Assessing indices of happiness and unhappiness in individuals with developmental disabilities- a review. Behavioral Interventions 22, 229–244 (2007)
4. Fowler, S.: Multisensory Rooms and Environments Controlled Sensory Experiences for People with Profound and Multiple Disabilities. Jessica Kingsley Publishers (2008)
5. Hedvall, P., Larsen, H., Caltenco, H.A.: Inclusion through design - engaging children with disabilities in development of multi-sensory environments. In: Assistive Technology- From Research to Practice, Vilamoura, Portugal, pp. 628–633 (2013)
6. Larsen, H., Hedvall, P.: Ideation and ability: When actions speak louder than words. In: Proceedings of the 12th Participatory Design Conference (PDC), Roskilde, Denmark, pp. 37–40 (2012)
7. Maes, B., Lambrechts, G., Hostyn, I., Petry, K.: Quality-enhancing interventions for people with profound intellectual and multiple disabilities- a review of the empirical research literature. Journal of Intellectual and Developmental Disability 32(3), 163–178 (2007)
8. Moreno, A., van Delden, R., Poppe, R., Reidsma, D.: Socially aware interactive playgrounds. Pervasive Computing 12(3), 40–47 (2013)
9. Munde, V.S., Vlaskamp, C., Maes, B., Ruijssenaars, A.J.J.M.: Catch the wave. time-window sequential analysis of alertness stimulation in individuals with profound intellectual and multiple disabilities. Child: Care, Health and Development 40(1), 95–105 (2012)

10. Nakken, H., Joining, C.V.: forces: supporting individuals with profound multiple learning disabilities. Tizard Learning Disabil. Rev. 7(3), 10–16 (2002)
11. Shapiro, M., The, P.S.G.M.R.D.: efficacy of the snoezelen in the management of children with mental retardation who exhibit maladaptive behaviours. The british Journal of Develop, Mental Disabilities 43-2(85), 140–155 (1997)
12. van Delden, R., Reidsma, D.: Meaning in life as a source of entertainment. In: Reidsma, D., Katayose, H., Nijholt, A. (eds.) ACE 2013. LNCS, vol. 8253, pp. 403–414. Springer, Heidelberg (2013)
13. Vlaskamp, C., de Geeter, K.I., Huijsmans, L.M., Smit, I.: Passive activities: the effectiveness of multisensory environments on the level of activity of individuals with profound multiple disabilities. Journal of Applied Research in Intellectual Disabilities 16(2), 135–143 (2003)
14. Vlaskamp, C., Oxener, G.: Communicatie bij mensen met ernstige meervoudige beperkingen: Een overzicht van assessment en interventie methoden. Nederlands Tijdschrift voor Zorg aan Mensen met Verstandelijke Beperkingen 4, 226–237 (2002)
15. Zijlstra, H.P., Vlaskamp, C.: Leisure provision for persons with profound intellectual and multiple disabilities: quality time or killing time? Journal of Intellectual Disability Research 49(6), 434–448 (2005)

Blind Bowling Support System Which Detects a Number of Remaining Pins and a Ball Trajectory

Makoto Kobayashi

National University Corporation Tsukuba University of Technology, Kasuga 4-12-7,
Tsukuba City, Ibaraki, Japan
koba@cs.k.tsukuba-tech.ac.jp

Abstract. Blind bowling is known as one of the popular sports for the visually impaired people. They can enjoy the bowling with sighted assistant who tells them a number of remaining pins, a ball trajectory, and scores. Bowling is such a well-adapted sports for the visually impaired people, nevertheless they want to acquire all of the information by themselves without support by the assistant. To fill this need, a prototype system was developed as a first step. The system detects the remaining pins and ball trajectory in the area of arrow marks using simple image processing. Severe visually impaired player tested the function of remaining pins and the results proved that the system works well and it is useful and helpful for them. Addition to it, unexpected advantage was discovered. With the prototype system, bowling game became more enjoyable for the blind player since they can also acquire information of remaining pins of other players.

Keywords: Blind Bowling, Remaining Pins, Trajectory, Image Processing.

1 Introduction

Tenpin bowling is one of the popular sports for the visually impaired people including blind person. It is known as "blind bowling" and widely spread in the world, as shown in the fact that an international competition is held with over 20 national teams[1]. The visually impaired people can enjoy the blind bowling at same place, with same ball and by same regulation to the normal bowling. The only different conditions between the normal bowling and the blind bowling are as follows[2]. First, competition class is divided by the player's eye power. Second, the visually impaired players receive information of the state of remaining pins and trajectory of the thrown ball from sighted assistant(s) after throwing. Third, they use a "guide bar" that is a metal hand rail with 3.7 meters length. They use the bar to confirm the direction by touching it with the hand of opposite side to the throwing arm and they have to leave the hand off the bar when they release the ball. Under these conditions, they can enjoy playing blind bowling.

In spite of that the blind bowling is such a well-custom and a well-adapted sport for the visually impaired players, they strongly want to play it without help by sighted assistants[3]. They reported that they want to acquire at least a number of remaining

K. Miesenberger et al. (Eds.): ICCHP 2014, Part I, LNCS 8547, pp. 283–288, 2014.
© Springer International Publishing Switzerland 2014

pins and a trajectory of thrown ball. These needs were found by the questionnaire which I asked to the blind bowling players. Therefore, I decided to develop a prototype support system to fill the needs, and this paper describes the system and the results of testing it by blind bowling players.

2   System Overview

Fig. 1 shows an overview of the prototype of bowling support system. It is composed of video camera(s), HDMI-USB converter(s), a computer, a wireless bone conduction headphone, and a small wireless mouse to control a software program. Basic sequence is that the player gives a trigger to the software by clicking a button of the mouse, and he/she receives sound information via bone conduction headphone. Of course an interface device with tactile pins is available in these days instead of the sound and there are several bowling alley where is equipped with tactile pins system in Japan. However, these bowling alley is special place for the visually impaired and using special device decreases opportunities to use the system. Therefore, I decided that prototype system should start with a combination of general device like a video camera and a headphone.

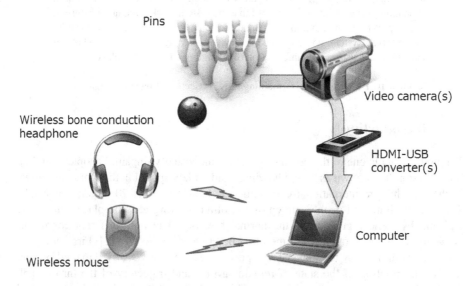

Fig. 1. An overview of the prototype system. The video camera captures image of pins and give the image information to the computer. When the player clicks the wireless mouse button, the computer answers information like a number of remaining pins via the wireless bone conduction headphone.

The position of the camera is important for this system. After several times of try and error, it was determined to set the camera around the table area on back of the lanes with a tripod. It is not just backward of the player, but backward of next lane.

The camera can capture all pins from this position, without hiding backward pins by pins in front. On the other hand, there is disadvantage that other players cannot throw ball on the next lane. Fig. 2 shows the position of the camera.

Fig. 2. Positions of video cameras. They were set at back of the next lane to the lane where the player throws a ball. The camera for counting remaining pins can captures all heads of pins without occlusions. The other camera can capture ball position in the area of arrow marks.

3   Function of Telling a Number of Remaining Pins

3.1   System in the First Phase

As a first step, a function of counting remaining pins has been implemented to the system using OpenCV and Visual Studio 2012. Before starting the main loop of the program, values of brightness at the heads of pins are memorized to the computer in advance by clicking each position manually. This operation should be done by sighted person as for now. Then, the main loop if the program starts and whenever the player clicks a button of the wireless mouse in his/her pocket, the system answers the information of remaining pins to the blind player via the bone conduction headphone. The system checks values of brightness at the positions of all pins and detects knocked down pins by the change of the value to the dark and speaks the result like "Remaining pins are, number five pin and number six pin and number nine pin." This simple algorithm allows the player to recognize the number of the remaining pins. The only things the player has to do is to click the mouse button on an appropriate timing. The timing is important because if the player clicks the button when a sweep bar or a pinsetter machine is coming down to the lane, the system may answers wrong information. The reason is that the sweep bar or the pin setter covers the position of the head of pins that is set in advance.

3.2   Testing the First System by Blind Bowling Players

Five blind players tested the prototype system described above and all of their operations and comments they made after using the system were recorded by video camera and voice recorder. As a result, it was clear that all testing players were able to operate the system correctly in spite of the difficulty of controlling the timing of clicking the mouse button mentioned above after two or three times practices. Moreover, the system was able to detected remaining pins perfectly even though original counting system equipped on the table for sighted people showed wrong information because falling pins take more time than usual case. This testing session proved that the system and its algorithm is useful and has enough reliability.

After this testing session, all players made a comment of welcoming to the system. One expert blind player said, "This system is really useful for my practice. I could practice without sighted supporter if someone set it for me." On the other hand, they gave important comments to improve the system as follows. "If we get strike or spare, the system simply says that there is no pins remains. It is not enjoyable." "Clicking a mouse operation is acceptable, but small switch is better and we'd like to put it on my finger or arm. A function of automatically detection the right timing is more helpful."

Addition to those results and comments, an unexpected effect was found in this session. One of the experienced blind player tried to test the system in a game with the other novice sighted player. During the game, information that the blind player could acquire was not only the remaining pins of himself but also of the sighted player. Using the information of the sighted player, he could even make an advice to her. It means that the system has an ability to give additional enjoyment to the blind player.

3.3   Improvement of the System

After the first testing session, several improved functions were implemented to the system by comments testing players had given. First of all, instead of the wireless mouse, small wireless switch ring which can be put on an index finger was selected as an input device. The program is changed so as to distinguish spare and strike, and to speak proper message. Automatic counting algorithm is also developed and implemented. It still needs initial setting of positions of heads though, the player does not have to click the button to hear information of remaining pins. The procedure of the automatic algorithm is as follows. At first, the system detects a sweep bar when it comes down to the floor using template matching. Then, the image after 0.8[sec] of recognized time is captured and the system speaks the number of remaining pins to the player. This time-lag is waiting time to fix the state of pins because sometimes several pins are swinging. Once the system detects the sweep bar and capture an image, the system stops detecting function for 13[sec], which is an interval time for sweeping knocked down pins and resetting remaining pins by pinsetter machine.

The spoken text sentence described the number of remaining pins is stored to the computer memory and it can be re-spoken by the player's request with pressing finger ring switch. Fig.3 shows the software appearance when the system detects sweep bar. Left side of the figure is before detecting the bar and right side of it is just after the detecting it by template matching. Large square mark on the bottom of the pins means region of interest (ROI) for template matching and small square mark means a position where is matched to the template image.

Fig. 3. A software appearance images when the system detects sweep bar. Left side is before detecting and right side is just after the detecting by template matching. Large square mark means region of interest(ROI) in which program searches matching area. Small square mark in the right image means matched position.

3.4   Testing the Improved System by an Expert Blind Bowling Player

After improvement of the system, an expert blind bowling player tested the system. He also took part in the first testing phase and already knew the principle of the system and how it works. He was explained about improved points of the system and conducted several games using the improved system.

As a result, the system worked perfectly during the games. The pattern matching program properly caught the sweep bar and told information of remaining pins to the expert blind bowling player via bone conduction headphone. When the player took strike or spare, the system told it in right way.

4   Function of Detecting Trajectory

Same as the function of telling the number of the remaining pins, the function of detecting the trajectory of the ball is realized with simple image processing. The algorithm starts with making a subtraction image between captured image and background image that is saved in advance. It makes roughly ball image that includes reflection of the ball onto the floor. Then, after noise reduction processing, the position of the ball is found by Hough Circle Transformation function of OpenCV library. Finally, the low-end point of the circle of each frame is calculated by the coordinate of the center of the circle and its diameter, and this point is defined as a trajectory points. Fig.4 shows the function of detecting trajectory. The left image of this figure is an original captured image and a circle shape which is detected by Hough Circle Transformation, and the right image of it shows subtract image and detected trajectory points in several frames before. These figures show that the system can roughly detect the trajectory of the ball. The resolution of the point is not so high because of the speed of the ball, but it is enough to distinguish between where and where arrow marks the ball go through. It might be useful though, the function should be improved in the future.

Fig. 4. Left image is original captured image and circle shape drawing over the ball which is detected by Hough Circle Transformation of right image. Right image shows subtract image after dilating and eroding process. It also shows detected trajectory points in several frames before.

5   Summary

To resolve the needs of blind bowling players, a prototype system was developed and tested. The system automatically recognizes a timing of when a seep bar comes down by template matching function and simply counts the number of remaining pins by the difference of brightness value, and tells the information to the player using wireless bone conduction headphone. The testing session indicated that it was useful and helpful for them to enjoy playing the bowling. Moreover, additional effect that they can acquire other players remaining pins and the system makes the game more enjoyable was discovered. About the other needs of the ball trajectory information, detecting algorithm utilized Hough Circle Transform is proposed.

Acknowledgement. This work was supported by JSPS KAKENHI Grant Number 25350752.

References

1. Tenpin Bowling - General information,
   http://www.ibsasport.org/sports/tenpin-bowling/
2. Rulebook for Blind Bowling, Blind Bowling Congress Japan (2002)
3. Kobayashi, M.: Application of Kinect to the sports for the blind players. 101th Research meeting of Human Interface Society Japan 15(6), 21–24 (2013)

Interacting Game and Haptic System Based on Point-Based Approach for Assisting Patients after Stroke

Mario Covarrubias, Alessandro Mansutti, Monica Bordegoni,
and Umberto Cugini

Politecnico di Milano, Dipartimento di Meccanica, Milano, Italy
{mario.covarrubias,alessandro.mansutti,monica.bordegoni,
umberto.cugini}@polimi.it

Abstract. This paper describes a system that combines haptic, virtual reality and game technologies in order to assist repetitive performances of manual tasks to patients, which are recovering from neurological motor deficits. These users are able to feel virtual objects by using a haptic device, which acts as a virtual guide taking advantages of its force feedback capabilities. A virtual environment is used forming a haptic interface between the patient and the game. The haptic device is driven under the users movements and assisted through the Magnetic Geometry Effect (MGE). Preliminary evaluation has been performed in order to validate the system in which two different tasks have been performed (throw down bricks in an hexagonal tower without and with haptic assistance) with the aim to obtain more information related to the accuracy of the device.

Keywords: Haptic interface, Virtual Reality, Post-stroke Rehabilitation, Gaming.

1   Introduction

One of the most disabling impairments resulting from stroke is the hemiparesis of the upper limb because of its impact on independence and quality of life. Stroke survivors typically receive intensive, hands-on physical and occupational post-stroke therapy to encourage motor recovery [1]. Rehabilitation after a stroke is a long process, consisting of exercises where usually the therapist guides the patient verbally as well as physically. For example, if the patient needs to perform a rehabilitation exercise consisting of a manual task, the therapist will say 'now lets start', and then the therapist begins guiding the patient's hand. Hand movement is one of the most important and complex human activities. The hand movements are controlled by the central nervous system, which regulates the activity of the hand and arm muscles to act in synergy. The central nervous system receives dynamic feedback information from visual sensors and from other body sensors located on the skin, muscles and joints while regulating the motor output. As suggested by the literature [2], [6] practice can have positive influence

K. Miesenberger et al. (Eds.): ICCHP 2014, Part I, LNCS 8547, pp. 289–296, 2014.

on the motor skill. For this reason, patients should be continuously and convincingly motivated to regularly make the exercises in order to regain the lost motor skills. The research presented in this paper aims at developing a system allowing post-stroke patients to perform rehabilitative manual tasks in a more autonomous and engaging way with respect to current practices that rely on a therapist dedicated to single rehabilitation sessions. The system is based on a previous work consisting of a Multimodal Guidance System (MGS) targeted to people affected by Down syndrome [3,4,5], which combined visual, haptic and sound technologies. The combination of these technologies was intended to be a step forward in the field of multimodal and multisensory devices for supporting unskilled people to improve their skills as well as for the assessment of manual activities. The research concerning haptic technology has increased rapidly in the last few years, and results have shown the significant role that haptic feedback plays in several fields, including rehabilitation. The interaction is enriched by the use of the sense of touch, so that also visually impaired users can identify virtual objects and perceive their shape and texture. Within the field of Virtual Reality environments and simulation tools, the sense of touch is provided by haptic interfaces [11]. They are based on devices that expose to tactile and force feedback a human user who is interacting with a simulated object via a computer [12], in order to allow him/her to feel the virtual object properties (i.e., texture, compliance or shape). The application developed for training people affected by Down syndrome implements a paradigm based on haptic guidance, which has demonstrated to have significant value in many applications, such as medical training [7], hand writing learning [8], and in applications requiring precise manipulation [9]. The haptic guidance concept has been implemented using a haptic interface, and has been extensively described in a previous publication [21]. Audio feedback has been integrated in the application, coupled with the haptic feedback. The combination of haptic and audio feedback has demonstrated to be effective, and has been used in several applications reported in literature. In [14] for example an audio-haptic interface has been used to train ophthalmic surgeon on complex optical operations. In [15] it has been implemented an audio-haptic feedback system to select target in a virtual environment; whereas in [16] it is demonstrated the efficacy of introducing an audio-haptic feedback in a virtual environment to train people in performing motor tasks. In general, acoustic feedback is used to lighten the mental workload associated with a task [17]. In the research presented in this paper it is proposed to use the haptic guidance approach for post-stroke patients rehabilitation. In case of post-stroke rehabilitation, one important factor is the patient motivation [2]. Therefore, the rehabilitation tasks proposed to the patients must be engaging and rewarding. In line with this approach, we have designed a system based on the combination of a haptic interface with Virtual Reality and gaming. The benefits of using virtual environments and gaming in rehabilitation are becoming evident as the number of such implementations and their clinical tests increase rapidly [18]. Preliminary experiments show that Virtual Reality and gaming can enhance the patients' motivation and enjoyment, which can in turn enhance their motor performances. A first prototype of the system has ben developed in order to demonstrate and prove the concept of combining several technologies, as haptics, Virtual Reality and gaming. The prototype is described in the paper and implements the haptic guidance paradigm by using the commercial Phantom Desktop device [10]. Some tests have been performed in order to evaluate the performances, benefits and potentialities of the system. Specifically, the aim of the study was to assess how the human hand can control the movements under the combination of haptic feedback integrated with virtual reality and game technology. The paper shows how the combined technology affects people performances during their rehabilitation therapy.

2   System Description and Game Concept

As mentioned in the introduction, patients after a stroke is the target group of final user for the interacting game and haptic system. The virtual reality software designed for this system has three components: the game interface, custom designed 3D haptic guidance trajectories with collision detection, and the patient interface. The haptic feedback, the sound rendering and the game interface are based on the H3D API and phyton platforms as can be seen from Figure 1. Therefore, the 3D trajectories required for the haptic guidance and all the necessary physical properties are defined through a configuration file, written in the X3D format. These software were chosen because are an open source platforms that allow to handle graphics, sound and haptic data.

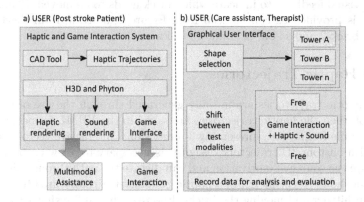

Fig. 1. System Description

3   The Graphic User Interface for Therapists

We have designed a Graphic User Interface (GUI) in order to involve therapists and care assistants during the test phase. In this way, we are also providing some training for the use of the system. Through the GUI, the therapist decides the complexity level of the game. In fact, the therapist decides for the number of bricks and the shape for the tower (quadrangular, pentagonal, hexagonal, ecc.) as can be seen from Figure 2. The phantom device provides feedback between the virtual environment and the user through the game interface, which has been developed using H3D. The purpose of the game is to haptically throw down the bricks that are used in the hexagonal tower.

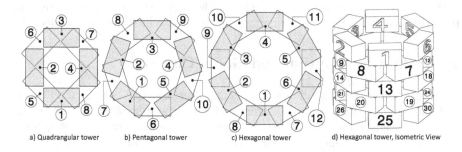

a) Quadrangular tower   b) Pentagonal tower   c) Hexagonal tower   d) Hexagonal tower, Isometric View

Fig. 2. The therapist decides for the tower shape and number of rows and bricks

The task of throw down the bricks presents visual motor integration. The shape of the tower (quadrangular, pentagonal, hexagonal, etc.) and the number of rows can be fully adjusted by the therapist to suit the needs of the user. The game provides visual feedback to indicate which brick needs to be moved. Usually, the sequence is provided as can be seen from Figure 2, starting from the brick-1, then the brick-2 and so on, in counter-clockwise.

4   3D Haptic Trajectories

The 3D haptic trajectories are initially generated through the use of a generic CAD tool, then the haptic trajectories are saved in the VRML format, which is a standard file format for representing 3-dimensional interactive vector graphics. Along with custom 3D trajectory design it is necessary to allow custom towers as they are the source of motivation and can dictate the path through the bricks. Figure 3-a shows the isometric of a haptic guidance trajectory used to assist the patient in hitting and moving the bricks. Figure2 3-b and 3-c shows the frontal and top views respectively. Figure 3-d shows the haptic trajectories inside the hexagonal tower.

5   Sound Interaction

The sound feedback of the interacting game and haptic system gives the possibility to play metaphoric sounds while the user's interact with the system. These metaphoric sounds provides information to the patients according to the type of

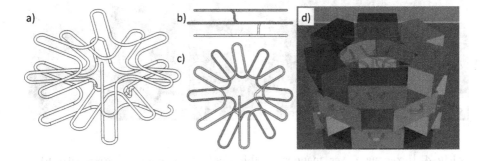

Fig. 3. Customizable haptic trajectories

task performed. In fact, once the sound feedback is enabled, the sound feedback gives the following information:

- Metaphoric sound A, if the stylus pen is not located directly on the haptic trajectories. This sound is a kind of warning alarm and means that the user's pen is located quite far from the haptic trajectories.
- Metaphoric sound B, is continuous played and is turned off when the velocity of the stylus pen is higher than an specific value. Also in this case, the sound is rendered as a warning alarm, and is deactivated when the user's pen goes too fast following the 3D haptic trajectories.

6   The Concept from the Patients Side

The stylus of the Phantom desktop is driven under the operators movement and assisted by the Magnetic Geometry Effect (MGE). When this option is activated, a spring force tries to pull the sphere of the stylus of the haptic device towards the virtual trajectory that is used as a virtual guide. In fact, this effect is used in order to assist the users hand. Figure 4-a shows the hexagonal tower with the 30 bricks in their nominal position, and then as can be seen from Figure 4-b the patient has moved the brick 1. Figure 4-c shows a patient while performing the task up to completely move the 30 bricks.

The patient hands movement has been measured using the Phantom device as input. The operations have been performed by tracking the stylus of the Phantom device through the DeviceLog command provided by the H3D API platform. The tracked sample rate is 25 Hz.

7   Results while Performing the Game

We have carried out several preliminary trials in order to test the system usability and to verify the patients improvements while performing the 3D task in which it is used the game for catching the patients attention. Table 1 shows the time results for each trial.

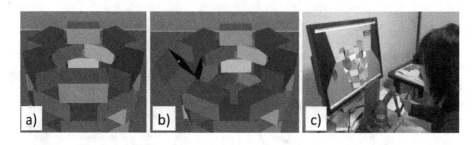

Fig. 4. Hexagonal tower, made with 30 bricks (one column and 5 rows pattern)

Table 1. Patient's time (s) while performing the task

	No assistance	First Trial	Second Trial	Third Trial
Patient 1	210	121	112	118
Patient 2	310	170	163	152
Patient 3	262	153	155	140

The results of our study showed that the haptic trajectories help patients during manual tasks by means of using the system as a rehabilitation tool. The main outcome of this pilot study is that the patients significantly reduce the time required to throw down the bricks when the haptic trajectories are enabled, which indicates that each patient learned to use the device and felt more comfortable with the exercise. In addition, we have compared the recording data obtained by using the device with and without the haptic trajectories. Performances are computed after each trial is finished, and are stored in the personal patients database. The authors are aware of the fact that the number of trials are not statistically significant, but the aim of the test was to check the effectiveness of the approach and the necessity of improvements.

8   Conclusion

The main application of the system is related to assisting patients in the assessment and training of the upper limb movements while performing gaming activities. At the current development stage, the prototype has been tested and requires to be engineered in order to become a low cost system, which can be extensively and effectively used by patients at home; this goal seems realistic. However, for the subsequent engineering process we have planned to integrate the force feedback directly into our guidance system instead of using a commercial device. This will be done on the basis of several previous works [19,20]. Therefore, the force feedback will be integrated directly into a pantograph mechanism implementing the haptic guidance paradigm. It is planned to reference the data from patients to evaluate the effect of the system in a rehabilitation program.

References

1. Sivak, M., Unluhisarcikli, O., Weinberg, B., Mirelman-Harari, A., Bonato, P., Mavroidis, C.: Haptic system for hand rehabilitation integrating an interactive game with an advanced robotic device. In: 2010 IEEE Haptics Symposium, pp. 475–481 (2010)
2. Blank, R., Heizer, W., von Voü, H.: Externally guided control of static grip forces by visual feedback age and task effects in 3-6 year old children and in adults. Neuroscience Letters 271(1), 41–44 (1999), http://www.sciencedirect.com/science/article/pii/S0304394099005170, ISSN 0304-3940
3. Covarrubias, M., Gatti, E., Mansutti, A., Bordegoni, M., Cugini, U.: Multimodal guidance system for improving manual skills in disabled people. In: Miesenberger, K., Karshmer, A., Penaz, P., Zagler, W. (eds.) ICCHP 2012, Part I. LNCS, vol. 7382, pp. 227–234. Springer, Heidelberg (2012), http://dx.doi.org/10.1007/978-3-642-31522-0_34
4. Covarrubias, M., Bordegoni, M., Cugini, U., Gatti, E., Mansutti, A.: Pantograph mechanism for increasing the working area in a haptic guidance device for sketching, hatching and cutting tasks. In: Proc. of the ASME 2012 International Design Engineering Technical Conferences and Computers and Information in Engineering Conference, IDETC/CIE 2012, August 12-15 (2012)
5. Covarrubias, M., Gatti, E., Bordegoni, M., Cugini, U., Mansutti, A.: Improving manual skills in persons with disabilities (pwd) through a multimodal assistance system. In: Disability and Rehabilitation: Assistive Technology, pp. 1–9, http://informahealthcare.com/doi/abs/10.3109/17483107.2013.799238, PMID: 23692410
6. Kurillo, G., Gregorič, M., Goljar, N., Bajd, T.: Grip force tracking system for assessment and rehabilitation of hand function. Technology and Health Care 13(3), 137–149 (2005)
7. Liu, A., Tendick, F., Cleary, K., Kaufmann, C.: A survey of surgical simulation: applications, technology, and education. Presence: Teleoperators and Virtual Environments 12(6), 599–614 (2003)
8. Teo, C.L., Burdet, E., Lim, H.P.: A robotic teacher of chinese handwriting. In: Proceedings of the 10th Symposium on Haptic Interfaces for Virtual Environment and Teleoperator Systems, HAPTICS 2002, pp. 335–341 (2002)
9. Ahlström, D.: Modeling and improving selection in cascading pull-down menus using fitts' law, the steering law and force fields. In: Proceedings of the SIGCHI Conference on Human Factors in Computing Systems, CHI 2005, pp. 61–70. ACM, New York (2005), http://doi.acm.org/10.1145/1054972.1054982, ISBN1-58113-998-5
10. PHANToM device, SenSable Technologies Inc., http://www.sensable.com (accessed October 31, 2013)
11. Burdea, G.C., Coiffet, P.: Virtual Reality Technology, 2nd edn. John Wiley and Sons Ltd, Chichester (2003)
12. Jones, L.A., Lederman, S.J.: Human Hand Function, 1st edn. Oxford University Press, USA (1951) ISBN0195173155
13. Palsbo, S.E., Marr, D., Streng, T., Bay, B.K., Norblad, A.W.: Towards a modified consumer haptic device for robotic-assisted fine-motor repetitive motion training. Disability and Rehabilitation: Assistive Technology 6(6), 546–551 (2011), http://informahealthcare.com/doi/abs/10.3109/17483107.2010.532287

14. Boulanger, P., Wu, G., Bischof, W.F., Yang, X.D.: Hapto-audio-visual environments for collaborative training of ophthalmic surgery over optical network. In: HAVE - Haptic Audio Visual Environments and their Applications, Ottawa, Canada (2006)
15. Menelas, B., Picinali, L., Brian, F., Katz, G., Bourdot, P., Ammi., M.: Haptic audio guidance for target selection in a virtual environment. In: HAID 2009 : Proceedings of 4th International Haptic and Auditory Interaction Design Workshop (2009)
16. Müller-Tomfelde, C.: Interaction sound feedback in a haptic virtual environment to improve motor skill acquisition. In: ICAD 04-Tenth Meeting of the International Conference on Auditory Display, Sydney, Australia (2004)
17. Kim, S.-C., Kwon, D.-S.: Haptic and sound grid for enhanced positioning in a 3-d virtual environment. In: Haptic and Audio Interaction Design, pp. 98–109 (2007)
18. Holden, M.K.: Virtual environments for motor rehabilitation: review. Cyberpsychol Behav 8, 187–211 (2005)
19. Campion, G., Wang, Q., Hayward, V.: The pantograph mk-ii: a haptic instrument. In: 2005 IEEE/RSJ International Conference on Intelligent Robots and Systems, pp. 193–198 (August 2005)
20. Avizzano, C.A., Portillo-Rodriguez, O., Bergamasco, M.: Assisting to sketch unskilled people with fixed and interactive virtual templates. In: IEEE International Conference on Robotics and Automation, pp. 4013–4017 (April 2007) ISSN 1050-4729
21. Covarrubias, M., Bordegoni, M., Cugini, U.: Sketching haptic system based on point-based approach for assisting people with down syndrome. Communications in Computer and Information Science 173 CCIS(PART 1), 378–382 (2011)

Exploring the Usage of 3D Virtual Worlds and Kinect Interaction in Exergames with Elderly

Hugo Paredes[1,3], Fernando Cassola[1,3], Leonel Morgado[2,3],
Fausto de Carvalho[4], Silvia Ala[1], Francisco Cardoso[1],
Benjamim Fonseca[1,3], and Paulo Martins[1,3]

[1] UTAD – Universidade de Trás-os-Montes e Alto Douro, Quinta de Prados,
Vila Real, Portugal
{hparedes,fcardoso,benjaf,pmartins}@utad.pt
[2] UAb – Universidade Aberta Av. Dr. Jacques Delors, Porto Salvo, Oeiras, Portugal
leonel.morgado@uab.pt
[3] INESC TEC – INESC Technology and Science (formerly INESC Porto),
Rua Dr. Roberto Frias 378 – Porto, Portugal
fernando.c.marques@inescporto.pt
[4] PT InS – PT Inovação e Sistemas, Rua Eng. José Ferreira Pinto Basto – Aveiro,
Portugal
cfausto@telecom.pt

Abstract. The combination of the potentialities of the interactive technologies, like exergames and the emerging motion capture devices with the ability of 3D virtual worlds for socialisation and context, can produce a platform to promote the physical activity of its users, which leverages its potential. The OnlineGym is an exploratory project based on an online 3D virtual worlds platform that allows users to interact with the system through the use of a motion capture device. This paper discusses the chosen technological approaches and the preliminary results of the experiments performed with users.

Keywords: Active Ageing, Virtual Worlds, Physical Activity, OnlineGym.

1 Introduction

Seniors commonly lack physical fitness and often suffer from severe mobility problems. Despite the lack of motivation for physical activities[3], general guidelines suggest exercising programs for elderly to strengthen muscles, balance, endurance and mobility[10].

The OnlineGym is an exploratory project based on an online 3D virtual worlds platform that allows users to interact with the system through the use of a motion capture device such as Microsoft Kinect. It aims to create an "online gymnasium": a virtual three-dimensional space where different users, physically apart, attend a shared workout session coached by a monitor, all of them connected over

K. Miesenberger et al. (Eds.): ICCHP 2014, Part I, LNCS 8547, pp. 297–300, 2014.
© Springer International Publishing Switzerland 2014

the Internet and represented by avatars directly animated by the movement captured on the Kinect devices connected to each personal computer. This scenario provides the experience of a joint participation in a group gymnastics session. The project is targeted at the elderly, who may not be able to participate in regular training sessions outside their homes, when living in lower-density areas or complex urban neighbourhoods, since that may require expensive or troublesome travel. It is hard to motivate oneself to exercise regularly alone at home[3], so exergames may help to motivate the elderly to exercise more, providing social interactions with online technologies[3,4].

This paper discusses the approaches that have been chosen to fulfil the project requirements and the preliminary results of the experiments performed with users. In the following section the background for the project is presented followed by a brief presentation of the technological platform. The preliminary experiments and results are discussed in section 4 and the paper end with some final remarks.

2   Background

In recent years, with the development of virtual reality and tracking technologies a new generation of games has risen: exergames. Such games focus on the development/leverage of the sensory and motor skills of the players, thanks to the possibility of perceptual emulation[5]. Research shows that exergames can have a positive effect on users health[10]. However, the motivation of the elderly for the games is closely related to the social factor[3]. Despite the proven potential at the interaction level, impact and visibility levels of exergames, some studies underline the need to strength the social aspects[6]. The elderly have been exposed to numerous technological changes, having telecommunications and Web brought a shift in their everyday life[1]. This change of interaction, socialisation and communication[2] facilitated connections with family and friends[1] keeping them socially connected and informed[8].

Virtual worlds environments are digital representations of real or imaginary scenarios that intend to simulate reality or compliment it and enable multiple users to be present and communicate with each other[7]. These 3D platforms, which are multi-user, collaborative, and shared virtual environments, can bring the users' experiences to a higher level and bring the being their presence[9]. Morgado et al.[7] put forward the possibility of using these online multiuser spaces becoming the place of real activities, not just simulated ones.

3   OnlineGym Platform

The OnlineGym platform is a prototype of an innovative online 3D service, which aims to contribute to the physical and mental well-being of the elderly, based on fitness group activities, where the motor skills and socialisation have essential roles. Its implementation is based on a client-server architecture through which current motion capture technologies allow the elderly to participate in group fitness sessions.

The objectives of the OnlineGym technological platform are: G1) representation of the avatars 3D movements (puppeteering); G2) remote transmission of animation control for visualisation of the entire group of gymnasts in a shared space; and G3) synchronisation of movements performed by the various participants in order to minimize the effects of communication latency. The achievement of this objectives led to the definition of an architecture with two servers: virtual worlds server and a movements' server. Three platforms that allow interaction within 3D virtual worlds using Kinect-based mocap technology were analysed: FAAST, RINIONS, NUILIB. The RINIONS platform was selected due to its capacity of reproduction of free movements, which ensures the required flexibility to the development. Achieving the objectives G2 and G3 went through adapting the RINIONS platform, jointly with its authors, to support the transmission of gestures. Management modules were also included to support the synchronisation of gestures transmission and minimise the effects of communication latency.

The OnlineGym platform was used to develop a set of experiments with users in order to technically evaluate the implemented features and impacts on the acceptance and adequacy of prototype for the users.

4   User Experiments

Experiments for technical evaluation of the OnlineGym platform were held during the development of the prototype and were made locally between the development team of the system, as well as remotely, between the various institutions involved in the project.

A pre-test with a restricted set of users was conducted to understand the degree of acceptance and suitability of the prototype. The results can not be generalised to the general population. However the given indicative data provided a more descriptive and qualitative guidance for future developments. The test was conducted with four participants and a personal trainer, all of which were accompanied by a staff member. Participants voluntarily joined the study, by invitation, and were separated geographically.

The pre-test provided important information regarding the acceptance of the OnlineGym and warned of some aspects that must be taken into account in future development, among which we highlight: the difficulty of the elderly to follow the guidelines given by personal trainer because of the speed of execution of instructions and exercises; the sound quality; the need for increased interactions and use of praise; and the accuracy of the system and the possibility of correcting the positions of the elderly in exercises. Despite the setbacks noted, participants revealed spontaneous readiness to return to use the platform which allows understanding their satisfaction with the experience carried out.

5   Final Remarks

In this paper a platform for exergames, based on virtual worlds technology, which allows natural interactions using the Microsoft Kinect motion sensor was presented. The evaluation carried out in a pre-test with users revealed the interest and importance of this project, given the positive evaluation of the participants, who were keen to re-use the system.

The preliminary study reveals the need for its continuity and suggests a longitudinal research, with a duration of at least three months, including a group of elderly, physical exercises, interviews and participatory observations, a significant sample of the population, extending the review to effects produced in the aspects of physical and psychological well-being.

Acknowledgments. This work is funded by Portugal Telecom Inovação under the Innovation Plan of the PT Group, and by FEDER funds through the Programa Operacional Fatores de Competitividade COMPETE and National Funds through FCT - Foundation for Science and Technology under the project FCOMP - 01-0124-FEDER-022701.

References

1. Ariyachandra, T., Crable, E., Brodzinski, J.: Seniors' perceptions of the web and social networking. Issues in Information Systems 10(2), 324–332 (2009)
2. Bachrach, Y., Kosinski, M., Graepel, T., Kohli, P., Stillwell, D.: Personality and patterns of facebook usage. In: Proceedings of the 3rd Annual ACM Web Science Conference, pp. 24–32. ACM (2012)
3. Brox, E., Luque, L., Evertsen, G., Hernandez, J.: Exergames for elderly: Social exergames to persuade seniors to increase physical activity. In: 2011 5th International Conference on Pervasive Computing Technologies for Healthcare (PervasiveHealth), pp. 546–549 (May 2011)
4. Gerling, K., Livingston, I., Nacke, L., Mandryk, R.: Full-body motion-based game interaction for older adults. In: Proceedings of the SIGCHI Conference on Human Factors in Computing Systems, CHI 2012, pp. 1873–1882. ACM, New York (2012)
5. von Bruhn Hinné, T., Keates, S.: Using Motion-Sensing Remote Controls with Older Adults. In: Stephanidis, C. (ed.) Universal Access in HCI, Part II, HCII 2011. LNCS, vol. 6766, pp. 166–175. Springer, Heidelberg (2011)
6. Marston, H.R., Greenlay, S., van Hoof, J.: Understanding the nintendo wii and microsoft kinect consoles in long-term care facilities. Technology and Disability 25(2), 77–85 (2013)
7. Morgado, L., Varajao, J., Coelho, D., Rodrigues, C., Sancin, C., Castello, V.: The attributes and advantages of virtual worlds for real world training. The Journal of Virtual Worlds and Education 1(1), 15–36 (2010)
8. Pettijohn, T.F., LaPiene, K.E., Horting, A.L.: Relationships between facebook intensity, friendship contingent self-esteem, and personality in US college students. Cyberpsychology 6(1) (2012)
9. Schroeder, R.: Defining virtual worlds and virtual environments. Journal For Virtual Worlds Research 1(1) (2008)
10. Waerstad, M., Omholt, K.A.: Exercise Games for Elderly People: Identifying important aspects, specifying system requirements and designing a concept. Institutt for telematikk (2013)

Games for Wireless Cubes in Cognitive Enhancement Therapy

Krzysztof Dobosz[1], Magdalena Dobosz[2], Tomasz Depta[1], Tomasz Fiołka[1],
and Marcin Wojaczek[1]

[1] Silesian University of Technology, Institute of Informatics, Gliwice, Poland
krzysztof.dobosz@polsl.pl,
{tomadep124,tomafio690,marcwoj424}@student.polsl.pl
[2] Upper Silesian Rehabilitation Center 'Repty', Tarnowskie Góry, Poland
m.dobosz@repty.pl

Abstract. Sifteo Cubes is an interactive tactile entertainment solution with own unique control interface gestures. The aim of the study was the use of games for wireless cubes in the rehabilitation of people with cognitive impairment staying in the neurology department of the hospital. Most of the exercises provided by physiotherapists can be classified into specific groups of tasks using the same way to resolve. During the analysis of sets of exercises, the following main categories of tasks are proposed: anagrams, memory games, and reflex games. As a part of a pilot program of introduction wireless cubes to the rehabilitation of people with brain injuries, three sample games, one from each category were developed.

Keywords: Wireless Cubes, Rehabilitation, Cognitive Impairment.

1 Introduction

Cognitive therapy is one of the fundamental tasks of neuropsychology [1,2]. Improvement of cognitive abilities such as memory, concentration, attention, language functions etc. is an objective of Cognitive Enhancement Therapy (CET) [3]. Impairment of cognitive functions is very often the result of brain damage which the patient suffers as a result of traffic accident or diseases such as stroke, or progressive dementia (i.e. in Alzheimer's disease). Brain injury frequently results in disorders of motor, cognitive, behavioral and social functions. Therefore, an important element of rehabilitation is appropriate diagnosis and therapy adapted to the patient's disorder. Such actions improve the quality of patient's life and extend the period in which he operates autonomously and requires less help from others.

Neuropsychological therapy uses various forms of stimulation from the most popular, using paper and pencil to such aid as boards, blocks, games, or specially prepared computer programs. Attention should be paid to the fact that patients often present motor disorder that prevents them from writing, as well as speech disorder, which does not allow for voice presentation of task solutions. These patients also often have

K. Miesenberger et al. (Eds.): ICCHP 2014, Part I, LNCS 8547, pp. 301–308, 2014.

vision problems. Therefore, it is important to seek a variety of therapeutic methods. Neuropsychological therapy is conducted by a psychologist, and is preceded by a psychological diagnosis that allows evaluating the level of cognitive functions impairment. On the basis of the diagnosis it is possible to select appropriate exercises taking into account additional information on the patient's health status. Stay in rehabilitation centers, both public and private, is limited. But there are patients for whom neuropsychological therapy should be continued after their return home. However, the independent solving of the tasks (without the help of a therapist) often is not possible.

Neuropsychological treatment of neurological patients is conducted, among others, in the Upper Silesian Rehabilitation Center "Repty" in Tarnowskie Góry (Poland). The aim of the study was the use of games for wireless cubes in the treatment of people with cognitive impairment staying in the neurology department of the hospital.

2   Related Work

Wireless cubes are not widely used in the rehabilitation of patients. A few therapists are interested in this unique technology.

An example might be Liftacube [4]. Authors realized a pervasive prototype system for training in a physical rehabilitation of person with neurological disorder or spinal cord injuries. The Liftacube prototype is composed from Sifteo cubes and the custom-made sensor board. The Sifteo cubes provide physical objects to handle in the game focusing on the key skill component. The sensor board is used to detect the height of the Sifteo cubes during the game using embedded light sensors and LEDs. The lifting height is really a determining parameter for the quality of the patient's lift movement. A separate board situated on the table with one element is used to detect if a patient lowered his arm after lifting a cube. Liftacube is able to detect the lifting of the patient's arm as well as locomotion interactions of the hands.

Another application of Sifteo cubes is used in a playful technology to engage us-ers' interrelated bodily motions to better productivity [5]. Building interactions inspired by and embodying different mindless activities, authors demonstrate the value of secondary human-computer interactions able to enhance a user's state in primary productivity tasks. There are two games prepared in that project. First game uses the idea of infinite bubble wrap – each Sifteo cube is a single bubble, and its screen shows two bubble states: inflated or popped. Pressing the screen, the user changes the cube state from inflated to popped with an audible pop. Cubes can also be formed in a sheet. Then, the user popping any one bubble starts a chain reaction of the others. Shaking the cube, the user resets the bubble with an inflation sound.

The second game shows classic physics-based toy known as Newton's Cradle. Tilting a cube, the user can simulate. Graphical objects shown on the cubes bounce off one another and screen edges. Collisions generate musical tones.

3   Sifteo Cubes

Sifteo Cubes is an interactive tactile entertainment solution [6]. It is a commercially available game technology, which engages their players through hands-on interactions.

The idea of tangible and graphical user interface platform first time was de-scribed by David Merrill and Jeevan Kalanithi of the MIT lab [7]. They described a Siftables - novel platform that applies technology and methodology from wireless sensor networks to tangible user interfaces in order to yield new possibilities for human-computer interaction. They can be physically manipulated as a group to interact with digital information and media. Then the platform was commercially distributed under the name: Sifteo cubes. The authors noted several patterns of use observed in homes and schools and identified design recommendations for display utilization on distri-buted interfaces. They also presented the process of commercializing the research prototype to create a marketable game system [8].

Sifteo Cubes platform is composed of a wireless base unit and a wireless 1.5 inch cubes (3-12 units) equipped with a tactile screen, and communicating with each other [9]. Sifteo cubes are so different from other gaming platforms that designing applica-tions for them at the first time, does not seem to be a simple task. Sifteo cubes have own unique control interface gestures. Sifteo cubes are not one device but a few, so designing an application we should think about games with multiple moving screens. It is an impediment in relation to the classical solutions dedicated to computers, and at the same time it is a chance for innovation. Sifteo cubes are characterized by the fol-lowing features [10]:

- have a relatively small size,
- each cube has its own independent screen, but they can jointly view large image fragments,
- actions can be triggered, if any two dice are neighbored,
- each of the four edges of the cube can be recognized,
- touch screen acts as one big button,
- embedded accelerometer can detect orientation and gestures.

Sifteo Cubes allow developing of games practicing cognitive skills, such as pattern recognition, strategic planning, abstract thinking, language functions, and others. Therefore, it is possible to create the games, which require recognition of colors or patterns, as well as arcade - requiring the analysis of a complex situation.

4   Implementation of Sample Games

During the rehabilitation of people with brain injuries, therapists practice the use of specially designed sets of textual and graphical tasks [11]. Each of these exercises is focused on stimulation of selected cognitive function. Some tasks presented on pages of exercise notebooks can be adapted to wireless cubes. In addition, Sifteo cubes can be used to create innovative games that do not have their counterparts in printed materials.

Most of the exercises provided by physiotherapists can be classified into specific groups of tasks using the same way to resolve. During the analysis of sets of exercis-es, the following main categories of tasks are proposed:

- anagrams - type of word play, the result of rearranging the letters of a word or phrase to produce a new word or phrase, using all the original letters exactly once; for example orchestra can be rearranged into carthorse. To this group we include also tasks, where we can build words with letters not ordered,
- memory games - card games in which all of the cards are laid face down on a surface and two cards are flipped face up over each turn. The object of the game is to turn over pairs of matching cards. To this group we also include recognition of card order, where at the beginning all the cards with numbers of different values are discovered. Then all the cards are reversed, and the player must indicate the tabs according to the numbers recorded on them.
- reflex games – The user indicates a special card as quick as possible. The card that should be indicated shows something special. A key parameter of the game is the time of displaying this card. Attention and a little bit of dexterity are important while playing the game.

As a part of a pilot program of introduction wireless cubes to the rehabilitation of people with brain injuries, three sample games, one from each category were developed. The first one is based on the idea of anagrams (Fig. 1). The user must build words using cubes lying in a line and contact with each other. Words that can be composed belong to one of selected fields: animals, clothes, flowers, occupations, body parts, food, and countries. In this game a number of cubes in the range 3-12 is used. Each area contains about 40 words. During each gameplay, the sequence of words is drawn, but every time shorter words are guessed at first. The wireless base unit automatically recognizes how many cubes are available in the closest environment. This also limits the possibility of the longest words drawn.

Fig. 1. The beginning and the end of the word building in the anagram game

The second application for Sifteo cubes is a standard memory game (Fig. 2). We need even number of cubes: 4-12. Instead of operation of turnover it is enough to touch a chosen pair of cubes. Cubes can be arranged in columns and rows, which makes them easier to remember. It is also possible to scatter the cubes at random, making the game more difficult. Game level depends on the number of cubes used in the game as well.

Fig. 2. Aligned and scattered cubes while playing in the memo game

The third game supports training of attention (Fig. 3). There is shown on the one of cube something that the user has to catch i.e. a cockroach. Then a new cockroach is shown on another, random cube. Sometimes, instead of a cockroach, a good-looking bee is presented over the several seconds. It cannot be touched. The gameplay ends when the cockroach is not caught in a certain time or when a player touches the cube showing a bee. During testing, the therapists turned their attention to the fact that the game can be enhanced by the appearance of more cockroaches than just one at a time, and the time on higher level can be shorter.

Fig. 3. Different phases of the game during attention training

5   Results

5.1   Study: Game Cubes versus Other Forms of Exercises

Introducing Sifteo cubes to the rehabilitation, we should be aware of the advantages and disadvantages brought by this technology. Over a dozen selected patients were asked about some of the most important aspects of the use of different forms of memory exercises. The study did not show a clear advantage of any of the forms of implementation of the exercise. The table demonstrates collected data. Among the most frequently mentioned disadvantages was the concern about lack of ability to use a modern technological solution as wireless cubes and the need for help of an assistant, or a therapist. Using Sifteo Cubes can be considered as a good supplement to already used tools.

5.2   Recommendations for Game Developers

Developing applications for the rehabilitation of neurological patients should be realized according to certain strict guidelines. Creators of Sifteo Cubes have published a set of recommendations for application designers [6], however, it is not addressed to specific users, which are patients in rehabilitation centers. These patients, in addition to cognitive deficits may also have motor or visual impairment. Taking into account the expectations and comments given by therapists and patients, we can define basic rules of the rehabilitation game development for Sifteo Cubes. They are:

- use a simple contrast 2D graphics, and optionally allow to select an image inversion mode,
- use of the whole available screen space of a cube to display graphics
- omit animation, effects, flicker and 3D graphics,
- use of sound to confirm the executed action (touch screen, contact ankles, shakes, etc.) and signaling a finish of a task,
- several configuration options, i.e. for memory games: find identical pairs of letters, numbers, symbols, or colors,
- several levels of difficulty to make the game interesting for patients with different levels of impairment,
- levels of difficulty can be related to the number of wireless cubes used in the game,
- measure playing time,
- create a history of previous patient's results.

5.3   Future Work

Wireless Sifteo Cubes have been introduced to rehabilitation in the "Repty" Up-per-Silesian Rehabilitation Center so far only as a pilot process. After this step, we must decide which games are correctly implemented, and in what configuration they are useful. Such information allow to use them wider. A questionnaire addressed to patients can certainly be very useful in making a decision. It should contain the following questions:

- Were the displayed graphical symbols recognizable?
- Did you hear generated game sounds?
- Were a feedback signals generated by the cubes useful in the game?
- Was the level of difficulty of the game appropriate?
- Where the configuration options appropriate?
- Would you like to use wireless cubes after leaving the hospital?

The questionnaires should be completed by the patients. Their assistants should be present and provide support when the patients write answers to questions. That is necessary, because sometimes due to paralysis of the patient, writing may not be immediately possible.

6   Conclusions

Researches so far conducted have to be regarded as insufficient, since the number of participated patients is too few. As it has already been mentioned, the exercises improving cognitive functions were used in case of neurological patients. Unfortunately most of them were elderly, who often had no previous contact with new technological solutions, and reluctantly use any electronic devices. However, cognitive therapy is sometimes a very long and hard job, and therefore another form of exercises and new kind of tasks can be more attractive, it can have a positive impact on the patient's motivation to exercise. Thus, the use of wireless cubes may be useful.

Wireless cubes are not widely used in the rehabilitation of patients. Commercial product is relatively young (since 2012), but today (April 2014) the manufacturer has already sold out all the cubes and so far said nothing about the further production. Thus their wider use in the future is questionable.

Acknowledgements. Publication supported from the Human Capital Operational Programme co financed by the European Union from the financial resources of the European Social Fund, project no. POKL.04.01.02-00-209/11; publication co-financed by the Institute of Informatics at Silesian University of Technology, statutory research no. BK/215/Rau2/2013

References

1. Sohlberg, M.M., Mateer, C.: Cognitive Rehabilitation: An Integrative Neuropsychological Approach. Taylor and Francis, Andover (2001)
2. Halligan, P.W., Wade, D.T.: Effectiveness of Rehabilitation for Cognitive Deficits. Oxford University Press, UK (2005)
3. Hogarty, G.E.: Cognitive Enhancement Therapy. Arch. Gen. Psychiatry 61, 866–876 (2004)
4. Vandermaesen, M., De Weyer, T., Coninx, K., Luyten, K., Geers, R.: Liftacube: a prototype for pervasive rehabilitation in a residential setting. In: Proceedings of the 6th International Conference on Pervasive Technologies Related to Assistive Environments, Rhodes Island, Grecee, article no. 19. ACM (2013)
5. Karlesky, M., Isbister, K.: Fidget widgets: secondary playful interactions in support of primary serious tasks. In: Proceeding of the CHI 2013 Extended Abstracts on Human Factors in Computing Systems, pp. 1149–1154. ACM (2013)
6. Sifteo Cubes, https://www.sifteo.com/cubes
7. Merrli, D., Kalanthi, J., Maes, P.: Siftables: towards sensor network user interfaces. In: Proceedings of the 1st International Conference on Tangible and Embedded Interaction, New York, USA, pp. 75–78 (2007)

8. Merrli, D., Sun, E., Kalanthi, J.: Sifteo Cubes. In: Proceeding of the CHI 2012 Extended Abstracts on Human Factors in Computing Systems, pp. 1015–1018. ACM, New York (2012)
9. Bergen, J.: Sifteo intelligent cubes use NFC to interact with each other, http://Geek.com (2011)
10. Kim, S.: 12 Tips for Making Sifteo Games, http://tech.sifteo.com/2013/01/08/12-tips-for-making-sifteo-games/
11. Buiza, C., Soldatos, J., Petsatodis, T., Geven, A., Etxaniz, A., Tscheligi, M.: HERMES: Pervasive Computing and Cognitive Training for Ageing Well. In: Omatu, S., Rocha, M.P., Bravo, J., Fernández, F., Corchado, E., Bustillo, A., Corchado, J.M. (eds.) IWANN 2009, Part II. LNCS, vol. 5518, pp. 756–763. Springer, Heidelberg (2009)

Mobile Gamebook for Visually Impaired People[*]

Krzysztof Dobosz, Jakub Ptak, Marcin Wojaczek, Tomasz Depta, and Tomasz Fiolka

Silesian University of Technology, Institute of Informatics, Gliwice, Poland
krzysztof.dobosz@polsl.pl
{jakupta656,marcwoj424,tomadep124,tomafio690}@student.polsl.pl

Abstract. The goal of the project was to create a mobile game application for Android OS platform that follows the rules of playing a gamebook. Developed application interacts with user using touch and speech interface, which is crucial in case of blind users. The paragraphs and general game data should be stored in external XML document. Game implementation introduced a form of entertainment for users with vision disabilities and established a speech and tactile interface implementation, which could be also used in implementation of other games, which target blind players.

Keywords: Gamebook, Blind People, Mobile Devices, XML.

1 Introduction

Nowadays we can find many games in leading application stores, like Google Play, App Store or Windows Phone Store, starting from simple text games and ending at graphically advanced 3D games. Even though the number of new game apps is still growing rapidly and today's mobile devices give developers an opportunity to present the content of application not only in visual form, it is hard to find a game that would target blind users or users with vision impairment. That is why the goal of this project was to discover and explore in practice the possibilities and ways of development of game application suitable for blind users, by means of creating one of them. The problem is that not all types of games can be played by a blind user. But fortunately the gamebook is an example of games that could be implemented in such way that blind user can operate it.

A gamebook is any book that presents a world of fiction that allows the reader to participate in the story by making effective choices. Those choices affect the narrative branches by means of selection of appropriate paragraph or page [1]. Reviewing the available solutions [2] we can find many implementations of gamebook, but there wasn't found any that would be adjusted for blind user.

[*] Publication supported from the Human Capital Operational Programme co-financed by the European Union from the financial resources of the European Social Fund, project no. POKL.04.01.02-00-209/11; publication co-financed by the Institute of Informatics at Silesian University of Technology, statutory research no. BK/215/Rau2/2013.

K. Miesenberger et al. (Eds.): ICCHP 2014, Part I, LNCS 8547, pp. 309–312, 2014.

2   Analysis

2.1   Functional and Non-functional Requirements

The application developed in terms of this project should fulfill following functional requirements:

- game instruction viewing – the player can check the rules of the game viewing the instruction,
- gamebook playing - the user is able to play a gamebook session,
- decision making – the player is able to make decisions during the game, which influence game's path,
- game stage saving – the player can save the state of the game,
- loading of game save – the user can load a save of a previously saved game.

Gamebook application should also meet the following non-functional requirements:

- application should be available to a wide range of Android OS – this operating system has become the most popular mobile operating system of the world [3],
- application should be optimized - taking into account that application would run on mobile devices, it should be optimized for using small amount of system resources,
- application should use external data - game content should be stored in an XML document, which structure should be valid to XML Schema,
- intuitive user interface - application provides speech and gesture interface, which is intuitive and adapted to blind users.

2.2   User Interface

Taking into account the development of an application for blind users, we have to take care of limitation that is connected with their disability. There is no possibility to interact with a user by means of graphical user interface. So in order to determine other way of interaction, developer has to consider input interface and output interface separately.

For an input interface there are two possibilities. First one is the speech recognition and second one, which is used in most of mobile applications, is touch gesture recognition. Both of those interfaces are available in most popular mobile operating systems like Android OS, iOS or Windows Phone.

Considering output interface there is a need of passing various types of information from application to user. We can treat speech and playing sounds as a medium that suits our needs. Using speech and various sounds we can provide the user with any information we want. Like in an input interface, most popular platforms provide tools for playing sounds and speech synthesis.

In order to adjust the application user interface to blind users, it was implemented in such way that makes the best use of touching the screen gestures and speech synthesis.

The user can use five basic gestures for performing actions in gamebook application:

- swipe right – horizontal move of the finger on the screen from left to right,
- swipe left – horizontal move of the finger on the screen from right to left,
- swipe up – vertical move of the finger on the screen from the bottom to the top,
- swipe down – vertical move of the finger on the screen from the top to the bottom,
- double tap – quick double touch of the screen using finger.

Gamebook application provides user information in form of a speech synthesized from a text. Using this mean of interaction the user will receive information about possible actions, decisions, character status, paragraph content etc.

3 Design

3.1 Internal Organization

Each application for Android OS is composed of parts, which are called activities. Activities in gamebook application are a bit different than in a typical Android mobile application. The difference is that activities in this application don't interact with the user by means of graphical user interface, but will use touch gesture and speech interface. Gamebook application consists of three activities:

- Main Menu – this activity is launched at a start of an application and provides the user information of all possible actions. Using this activity the user can start a new game (swipe right), load previously saved game (swipe left), open the instruction (swipe up) or simply close the application (swipe down). After performing one of the mentioned actions, the user will be informed about his decision by speach.
- Instruction – this activity provides an interface for navigating over instruction. Instruction consists of several entries. Each instruction entry provides single information about selected topic of application usage or mechanics. The user can navigate over the entries by swiping left or right. The user can close instruction activity and go back to main menu by swiping down.
- Paragraph – this activity is actually an implementation of gamebook mechanism. The whole game takes place in this activity. It can be called from Main Menu activity either by starting a new game or by loading a saved game. In the first situation new player's character is being created and his attributes are chosen randomly by dice rolling. The game starts from the first paragraph. In the second situation player's character and paragraph are retrieved from game save data.

3.2 Gamebook XML Structure

Gamebook application retrieves game description from a locally stored XML document. The whole content of game description is kept in <gamebook> tag content. This chapter describes the structure of a following document.

XML document can contain the definition of items used in gamebook. Each item has to be defined separately using <item> tag. The name of the item should be specified between opening and closing tags as text content. But there are also some attributes to be given. It is required to set a unique id of the item and to specify its type. There are four possible types of items: apparel, weapon, armor and miscellaneous. Each of them, except for the last one, requires gamebook developer to specify a character's affected attribute and numerical value of attribute change.

But the most important part of XML document is a definition of gamebook's paragraphs. Paragraph can be defined in many different ways depending on its type. But few elements are common for all types of paragraphs. One of them is a unique id attribute and other is a type of paragraph specified as attribute, but there is also a common child element <text>, which holds a paragraph's description between its opening and closing tag. Paragraphs in gamebook application come in many various types: singlepath, normal, crossroads, checkluck, food, itempick, itemloss, end, fight, dicegame. All of them have a special meaning in the game.

4   Final Remarks

The sample gamebook was tested by several users. Some of them were partially or totally blind, and some had no visual impairments. Conducted research has shown that visual impairment has no such meaning as previous experience in the use of mobile devices. Also younger users were more efficient playing the game than older ones. All of them were satisfied playing audio gamebook.

There is also a place for modifications and improvements in the application. The most important improvement of application concerns users who speak the national language, which means that application should implement speech synthesis interface with national speaker. Second modification deals with validation of XML document with gamebook description. There exists a XML schema, which defines the rules of an XML document, but current Android API doesn't provide any way to use this schema for document validation before parsing. For this modification an external solution should be implemented.

At last we need to think about different ways of realization of user interface. Good idea seems to propose alternate game configurations, where a user can play using special, big subareas on the surface of smartphone touch screen or gestures taking data of embedded accelerometer.

References

1. Demian's Gamebook Web Pages, Frequently Asked Questions,
   http://www.gamebooks.org/show_faqs.php
2. Gamebook adventures, http://gamebookadventures.com/
3. Gartner Inc.: Gartner Says Smartphone Sales Accounted for 55 Percent of Overall Mobile Phone Sales in Third Quarter of 2013 (2013),
   http://www.gartner.com/newsroom/id/

Implementation and Take-up of eAccessibility

Introduction to the Special Thematic Session

Helen Petrie

University of York, United Kingdom
helen.petrie@york.ac.uk

Abstract. This Special Thematic session presents a range of papers that address issues around the implementation and take-up of eAccessibility in the information society. Acessibility, eAccessibility, design for all and inclusive design and now all well established concepts and many resources exist for researchers and developers interested in created accessible artefacts and services. However, the overall level of eAccessibility of the information society is still low. These papers investigate why this is the case and propose a number of different ways forward.

Keywords: eAccessibility, Older Users, Disabled Users, Web Developers, Web Accessibility Guidelines, Web Design Guidelines, Web Accessibility Information Resources, eAccessibility Roadmap, Web Accessibility, Self-Service Terminals (SSTs), Automatic Teller Machines (ATMs), e-Identity.

Considerable progress has been made over the last decades in understanding the needs of people with disabilities and older people and how they can participate most fully in the emerging information society. Progress has also been made in providing assistive technologies for these user groups, allowing them to undertake tasks that they may have previously found impossible or difficult and giving them access to a wide range of mainstream technologies in ways that are more suitable for their particular capabilities and needs.

This progress addresses and challenges mainstream ICT to make products, systems and services that are truly accessible for these user groups. Many recommendations, guidelines, standards, techniques and tools have been made available to support the implementation of such eAccessibility. Nonetheless, the take up and implementation of eAccessibility is still highly fragmented and uneven. The further the information society advances, the bigger the digital divide between mainstream users and disable and older users seems to become.

This Special Thematic Session (STS) presents a range of papers addressing these issues of the uptake and transfer of eAccessibility know how into practice and the need to foster the uptake of eAccessibility by all stakeholders.

Two papers [1, 2] address the issue of providing information for a range stakeholders about eAccessibility. These papers are based on the eAccess+ Network, which has developed an online information resource, the eAccess+ Hub (http://hub.eaccessplus.eu/wiki/Main_Page) to provide information about eAccessibility

K. Miesenberger et al. (Eds.): ICCHP 2014, Part I, LNCS 8547, pp. 313–315, 2014.

and links to useful resources for different stakeholders interested in different aspects of eAccessibility.

Petrie, Darzentas and Power [2] address the issue of the lack of accessibility and eAccessibility of self-service terminals (SSTs) and why eAccessibility is so low in this sector. Based on interviews with 22 stakeholders, they propose that there is still a need to raise awareness in this sector about eAccessibility as well as a need to clear guidance on how to achieve eAccessibility of SSTs. Petz and Miesenberger [1] set out a roadmap for what is needed to achieve greater eAccessibility across three domains: web accessibility, accessible digital television, and self-service terminals, based on stakeholder interviews, desktop research, and existing regulations and guidelines.

Swallow, Power, Petrie, Bramwell-Dicks, Buykx, Velasco, Parr and O Connor [3] looked specifically at the issues faced by web developers in the creation of accessible websites and services. Based on contextual inquiry with 14 developers, they created an information resource to introduce developers to web accessibility information during development and to complement the Web Content Accessibility Guidelines [4], the Web Accessibility Information Resource (WebAIR). This resource is organized into categories oriented to the workflow of web developers; it uses their language, rather than the domain-specific language of accessibility which they they find unfamiliar and difficult; and it attempts to guide them through developing and checking for web accessibility in a lightweight manner. WebAIR was evaluated with 26 web developers and was well received.

Kamollimsakul, Petrie and Power [5] addressed the issue that many guidelines for web accessibility for older users exist, but lack evidence for their recommendations, and that these guidelines are oriented to websites in languages written in the Latin alphabet. They investigated two aspects of presentation of websites for older users in the Thai language: font type and font size. They found no differences in skim reading performance using a number of levels of these presentation aspects, but clear differences in the preferences of older Thai web users.

Finally, Schulz and Fritsch [6] investigated the very important topic of accessibility and inclusion requirements for future e-identity systems. There is no point making digital systems highly accessible if disabled and older users cannot easily and comfortably manage the security associated with systems. They consider many aspects of the requirements for accessible and inclusive e-identity systems, including content and presentation, control and operation, legal requirements, testing, help and support and highlight possible areas for future research.

References

1. Petz, A., Miesenberger, K.: Roadmap to eAccessibility. In: Miesenberger, K., Fels, D., Archambault, D., Penaz, P., Zagler, W. (eds.) ICCHP 2014, Part I. LNCS, vol. 8547, pp. 324–331. Springer, Heidelberg (2014)
2. Petrie, H., Darzentas, J.S., Power, C.: Self-service terminals for older and disabled users: attitudes of key stakeholders. In: Miesenberger, K., Fels, D., Archambault, D., Penaz, P., Zagler, W. (eds.) ICCHP 2014, Part I. LNCS, vol. 8547, pp. 340–347. Springer, Heidelberg (2014)

3. Swallow, D., Power, C., Petrie, H., Bramwell-Dicks, A., Buykx, L., Velasco, C.A., Parr, A., Connor, J.O.: Speaking the language of web developers: evaluation of a web accessibility information resource (WebAIR). In: Miesenberger, K., Fels, D., Archambault, D., Penaz, P., Zagler, W. (eds.) ICCHP 2014, Part I. LNCS, vol. 8547, pp. 348–355. Springer, Heidelberg (2014)

4. W3C/WAI, Web Content Accessibility Guidelines 2.0. (2008),
   `http://www.w3.org/TR/WCAG20/`

5. Kamollimsakul, S., Petrie, H., Power, C.: Web accessibility for older readers: effects of font type and font size on skim reading webpages in Thai. In: Miesenberger, K., Fels, D., Archambault, D., Penaz, P., Zagler, W. (eds.) ICCHP 2014, Part I. LNCS, pp. 332–339. Springer, Heidelberg (2014)

6. Schulz, T., Fritsch, L.: Accessibility and inclusion requirements for future e-identity solutions. In: Miesenberger, K., Fels, D., Archambault, D., Penaz, P., Zagler, W. (eds.) ICCHP 2014, Part I. LNCS, vol. 8547, pp. 316–323. Springer, Heidelberg (2014)

Accessibility and Inclusion Requirements for Future e-Identity Solutions

Trenton Schulz and Lothar Fritsch

Norsk Regnesentral – Norwegian Computing Center, Gaustadalléen 23a,
Kristen Nygaards hus, NO-0373 Oslo, Norway
{Trenton.Schulz,Lothar.Fritsch}@nr.no
http://www.nr.no

Abstract. Future e-identity services will need to be accessible for people with different types of abilities. We review current sets of accessibility guidelines and standards, current assistive technology, and current e-identity technology to determine accessibility and inclusion requirements for a future e-identity solution. For our project, we found that the area we could influence the most was the development of user interface for the client for e-identity and focused on these areas with the assumption that users would have access to inclusive cards and card readers. The requirements are divided into content and presentation, control and operation, legal requirements, testing, and help and support. We also provide possible areas for future research.

Keywords: Accessibility, e-Identity, Smart Cards.

1 Introduction

As society's services become digital, individuals will need to identify (or authenticate) themselves to these services to ensure the best service and experience. The classic e-identity (e-ID) of a combination of username and password has its own issues; for example, it requires the user to remember passwords, which can lead to password re-use, resulting in cascading account compromises when one password is compromised. Other ways of authentication exist. Smart cards provide a more secure method of authentication, but they are not universally accepted and not necessarily compatible with each other. Ideally, people should be able to authenticate using the type of identification they prefer as long as it satisfies the needs of service. This personalization in identification choice is also important when considering the needs of people with disabilities.

One way of dealing with the different forms of e-ID is to build infrastructure that can broker the differences between the forms of identification and then eventually authenticate the person. Much of this work can be carried on automatically, but at some point the user will likely have to be involved. At this point, an accessible, inclusive, and usable interface is necessary, especially if the ICT should meet requirements laid down by countries like Spain [15] and Norway [3].

K. Miesenberger et al. (Eds.): ICCHP 2014, Part I, LNCS 8547, pp. 316–323, 2014.

What requirements are needed for making this infrastructure accessible and usable by the most people possible? We examined the needs in the context of a software client that would work on desktops, tablets, and smartphones. The software client will serve as a frontend for people to use the method of authentication that works best for the situation. We found requirements in how information must be presented, how the interface needs to be controlled, testing the interface, and how to provide help and support.

2 State of the Art

There already exist requirements in the world of accessibility and e-inclusion and in the world of e-identity. The main requirements for e-ID are robustness of the identity token, authenticity of the identity token, user control over identity token usage, and token binding to the legitimate user. A further important aspect is identity attribute quality, which is decisive about what purposes and values an electronic identification can be trusted to protect. Finally, privacy issues (who gets to identify Internet users, why, and for how long) are tightly connected to e-ID issuance and use.

Regarding accessibility, many projects document guidelines. Yet, they can be interpreted as requirements. For example, besides standards for vending machines, the most well-known set of accessibility guidelines, the Web Content Accessibility Guidelines 2.0 (WCAG 2.0) [18], are the basis for the regulation for universal design of ICT in Norway [8]. The WCAG 2.0 is based on four principles for content: Perceivable, Operable, Understandable, and Robust. These principles are codified into 12 different guidelines. Each guideline has three different level of success (compliance) from A, AA, and AAA. The guidelines are written generically, so they can be used for content that is not necessarily targeted for the web. The guidelines are also written to be testable. This allows web pages to be run through a battery of automated tests to check their compliance.

The BBC has also used the WCAG 2.0 as a basis for its own accessibility guidelines [1], These are also extended to define guidelines for accessibility in multimedia, games, PDF's, subtitling, and screen-reader testing. There is also a draft of the accessibility requirements for mobile websites and apps for smartphones and tablets [16]. These guidelines are specific to the needs of the BBC, but they can also be used for designers and developers in similar circumstances. The Norwegian research project e-Me [12] focused on a user's whole lifetime with the user's changing abilities to use identification technology. The project concluded that service providers and identity providers should be prepared to migrate customers over to other e-ID methods when their respective abilities to handle them change.

3 Methodology

We tackled the task of finding accessibility and inclusion requirements by first taking a look at the problem space that we wanted e-identity to address. In this case,

Fig. 1. The two personas with disabilities in the project. Freidhelm (left) has poor vision and moves around with a cane and Jose (right) has dyslexia.

we wanted a solution that would work on a continental (European) scale. While drafting interdisciplinary requirements for e-inclusion and usability in the specification phase, we derived technical requirements from existing standards. In addition, we considered insight from research projects [5, 6, 12]. To accommodate discourse about user needs, we developed a set of fictitious persons (personas) with special needs using a method outlined by [14]. The personas (Fig. 1) will be used to illustrate needs to developers and technicians later in the project.

The project will evaluate the architecture that will be developed against the requirements. These evaluations will be performed using standards compliance, persona-based discourse, automated usability testing, and user observation. We determined that it was necessary to take a user-centered approach when looking at the accessibility and inclusion requirements. We investigated what parts of the e-ID service would be used directly by people. Many parts of the e-ID infrastructure (e.g., network protocols or encryption algorithms) have no impact on accessibility on their own; they exist to make authentication possible. This led us to look at things like smart cards, smart card readers, and the interface (including assistive technology) on desktops, smartphones, and tablets.

4   Work and Results

We consulted many different available accessibility guidelines for the web and the developer guidelines for different mobile and desktop systems. We examined different types of assistive technology that are available on different devices. We also looked at standards in the area of smart cards. This also required determining if any of the standards or guidelines resulted in contradictions. This did lead to some contradictions; they affected mostly presentation of textual information (e.g. line length, line spacing). In these cases, we wrote a requirement that met as many guidelines as possible. We noted that our requirements took precedence over the other guidelines.

During this process we discovered that we would have the most influence on the software that would be running on computers, smartphones, and tablets and less on smart card and smart card readers. We assumed that people using the system would have access to an accessible smart card, smart card reader, and other technology.

We divided requirements into multiple categories: *(a)* content and presentation, *(b)* control and operation, *(c)* legal requirements, *(d)* testing, and *(e)* help and support.

Overall, there were 60 different requirements with content and presentation *(a)* having the most (25). The nine legal requirements *(c)* focused on the issue of storing and using personal data for the purpose of making a system more accessible. We leave the legal requirements for a future publication, and we examine the remaining requirements here.

Content and presentation *(a)* of material is important to ensure that users will be able to understand the information. We used the WCAG 2.0 guidelines as a starting point for this, but focused on the strictest compliance level (Level AAA). We then outlined what this meant in terms of contrast for colors, how images should be used, how text should be typeset (size, spacing, line length, etc.), and how audio and video should be presented. We do not expect much video or audio to be used in the e-ID solution, but chose to highlight it since it is an important part of AAA compliance.

Control and operation *(b)* looked at the field of assistive technology that is currently available and specified what screen readers, screen magnifiers, and on-screen keyboards a client should be compatible with. We recognize that complex items like screen readers interact differently with software, but making software work with multiple screen readers can help future compatibility with other screen readers.

Beyond assistive technology, we also looked at the keyboard. We required that the client could be used with only a keyboard (with navigation following the logical layout of the client). Keyboard shortcuts were also encouraged. Some assistive technology registers itself to a system as a keyboard. Making the client work with a keyboard means that this assistive technology may work too.

Control and operation included timed events. We required that anything that could be deemed essential to using the client (i.e., if removed would fundamentally change information or functionality and could not be achieved in another way) not have a time limit. This raised issues with security as some systems may require that a session or a token can only last for so long. After some debate on this issue, we allowed an exception for this, events that happen in real-time, and things like movies. We also added a requirement that interruptions could be postponed unless it is an emergency. This should give different people enough time to carry out whatever task they need for authenticating with an e-ID.

Regarding testing *(d)*, the WCAG 2.0 guidelines are written to allow automated testing, and there are several different automated testing tools available. Yet, [17] looked at automated testing tools and found that they only covered around 50% of the success criteria. So, some sort of checking guidelines beyond automated testing was needed.

But, if a page passes all the tests in the WCAG 2.0, it does not mean that it is free of accessibility issues. [10] have shown that accessibility issues remained even when a web page had passed all WCAG tests. [9] were also surprised about the number of issues that were discovered by people with vision impairment on sites that conform to the WCAG 2.0 guidelines. The [18] state, "...even content that conforms at the highest level (AAA) will not be accessible to individuals with all types, degrees, or combinations of disability, particularly in the cognitive language and learning areas."

We included a requirement that the solution should be tested by accessibility experts who know how assistive technology will be used with the solution. This is necessary because different assistive technology result in different information presented to the user. For example, different screen readers and web browsers understand accessibility information for applications with varying levels of functionality [4].

As mentioned by [9], another way to uncover more accessibility issues is to do testing with people with disabilities. We felt that testing with users with disabilities was an important part of quality assurance and evaluating the architecture; we added specific requirements for this, preferably including different types of disabilities.

Finally, for help and support *(e)* we recognized that help material provided with the client should also be accessible and follow the requirements for content and presentation we outlined above. We also felt that additional infrastructure (e.g., calling centers or learning centers) should also ensure that content is accessible to the largest audience.

We wanted to create proper awareness for readers of the requirements. So, after the requirements were drafted, we included background information about different types of impairments; legislation about accessibility; a survey of relevant standards, guidelines, and developer guides; and information about different types of assistive technology on PCs, smartphones, and tablets. It is not an exhaustive guide, but it is a good starting point for readers that are new to accessibility and inclusion.

5   Impact

Having an accessible and inclusive e-ID solution will enable many more people to safely and securely access different public and private services on the Internet. Creating requirements helps set a baseline for work and help us know how well a solution meet, exceed, or fail the needs for a group. The requirements have been published as part of a large European project [13]. The requirements are formulated using keywords that are defined in RFC 2119 [2] for indicating requirement levels. This should make it possible to apply in other e-ID projects that wish to have a good basis for their accessibility and inclusion requirements, regardless of thematic areas. Indeed, these requirements have already been used as input to deliverables in another project related to privacy, security, and usability [7]. This is of particular importance when e-ID services adapt to changing user abilities, and when users are migrated to other e-ID base technologies.

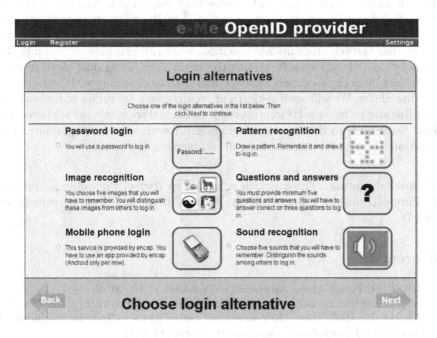

Fig. 2. Examples of accessible authentication methods [11, p. 74]

Since the basis for many of these requirements are based on electronic "living" documents, it is also necessary to keep an eye for any updates. For example, an updated draft of the BBC requirements may include items that may be useful for e-ID. We can also consider any new information found in evaluating the requirements should be pushed upstream to these documents or with developers.

A possible area to investigate is alternative forms of e-ID. The current project focuses primarily on smart cards, but other ways of authentication, such as using a mobile phone, are also candidates. [11] looked at accessible authentication beyond traditional passwords and PINs (Fig. 2), and these could also be possible to integrate into the solution. If any of these other methods are used, there will likely be some sort of user interaction with a presentation of information. It should probably be tested by people with disabilities and other help and support should be accessible. The requirements we developed should provide a basis for these possible future solutions.

6   Conclusion

In the future, all people will likely have to use some form of e-ID to access a service or verify their identity. Providing a secure and privacy-preserving solution is important, but if people find it difficult to use a e-ID, it will result in an overall less secure solution as people avoid using it or find other shortcuts. Similarly, having a solution that is accessible means that more people have the potential to use it and remain independent in society. Finally, work on accessibility can also uncover other usability issues [9].

Now that the requirements are specified, work can continue on building the e-ID solution. We will soon be testing the client software against these requirements, first by doing an expert analysis, and then later testing with actual users with disabilities. We will see if the current requirements are sufficient for building accessible and inclusive e-ID solutions or if additional requirements are necessary. Tight discourse with developers, designers and researchers on adaptability, user migration, choice, and user burden will complement the activities.

Acknowledgments. This research is funded as part of the FutureID project. The FutureID project is funded by the EU FP7 program (Grant agreement no: 318424).

References

1. BBC: BBC Future Media Accessibility Guidelines v1.10 (2014),
   http://www.bbc.co.uk/guidelines/futuremedia/accessibility/
2. Bradner, S.: RFC 2119 – Key words for use in RFCs to Indicate Requirement Levels (1997), http://www.faqs.org/rfcs/rfc2119.html
3. Diskriminerings- og tilgjengelighetsloven (DTL). Lov om forbud mot diskriminering pågrunn av nedsatt funksjonsevne (Eng: Act on prohibition of discrimination based on disability) (2008), http://www.lovdata.no/all/hl-20080620-042.html
4. Featherstone, D.: ARIA and Progressive Enhancement (2010),
   http://alistapart.com/article/aria-and-progressive-enhancement
5. Fritsch, L., Fuglerud, K.S., Solheim, I.: Towards Inclusive Identity Management. Identity in the Information Society 3(3), 515–538 (2010)
6. Graf, C., Busch, M., Schulz, T., Hochleitner, C., Fuglerud, K.S.: D.2.7 Updated Design Guidelines on the Security Feedback Provided by the "Things". Tech. rep., CURE, Vienna, Austria (2012)
7. Klein, M., Wolkerstorfer, P., Hochleitner, C., Fuglerud, K.S., Schulz, T.: D2.8 Final UI-Guidelines for the Trust Feedback Provided by the IoT. Tech. rep., CURE, Vienna, Austria (2013)
8. Kommunal- og moderniseringsdepartementet: Forskrift om universell utforming av informasjons- og kommunikasjonsteknologiske (IKT)-løsninger (2013),
   http://lovdata.no/dokument/SF/forskrift/2013-06-21-732

9. Power, C., Freire, A., Petrie, H., Swallow, D.: Guidelines are only half of the story. In: Proceedings of the 2012 ACM Annual Conference on Human Factors in Computing Systems, CHI 2012, pp. 433–442. ACM Press, New York (2012)

10. Rømen, D., Svanæs, D.: Validating WCAG versions 1.0 and 2.0 through usability testing with disabled users. Universal Access in the Information Society (September 2011)

11. Røssvoll, T.H., Fritsch, L.: Trustworthy and Inclusive Identity Management for Applications in Social Media. In: Kurosu, M. (ed.) HCII/HCI 2013, Part III. LNCS, vol. 8006, pp. 68–77. Springer, Heidelberg (2013)

12. Røssvoll, T.H., Fritsch, L.: Reducing the User Burden of Identity Management: A Prototype Based Case Study for a Social-Media Payment Application. In: The Sixth International Conference on Advances in Computer-Human Interactions, ACHI 2013, Nice, France, pp. 364–370 (2013)

13. Schulz, T., Fritsch, L., Schlehahn, E., Hansen, M., Zwingelberg, H.: FutureID Deliverable D22.7 Accessibility and Inclusion Requirements. Tech. rep., Norsk Regnesentral, Oslo, Norway (2013)

14. Schulz, T., Skeide Fuglerud, K.: Creating Personas with Disabilities. In: Miesenberger, K., Karshmer, A., Penaz, P., Zagler, W. (eds.) ICCHP 2012, Part II. LNCS, vol. 7383, pp. 145–152. Springer, Heidelberg (2012)

15. Spanish Ministry of the Presidency: Spanish Royal Decree 1494/2007 (2007)

16. Swann, H., Williams, G.F., Avilla, J.: Draft BBC Mobile Accessibility Standards and Guidelines. Tech. rep., BBC, London, UK (2013)

17. Vigo, M., Brown, J., Conway, V.: Benchmarking web accessibility evaluation tools. In: Proceedings of the 10th International Cross-Disciplinary Conference on Web Accessibility, W4A 2013, p. 1. ACM Press, New York (2013)

18. W3C Working Group: Web Content Accessibility Guidelines (WCAG) 2.0 (2008), http://www.w3.org/TR/WCAG/

Roadmap to eAccessibility

Andrea Petz and Klaus Miesenberger

Institute Integriert Studieren, Johannes Kepler University Linz, Linz, Austria
{andrea.petz,klaus.miesenberger}@jku.at

Abstract. Within three main topical areas, the eAccess+ network identified and consulted relevant stakeholder groups, analyzed and discussed the state of the art in eAccessibility, supported stakeholders in working on key issues to foster eAccessibility and disseminated experiences and knowledge all over Europe. Finally, all findings were connected and combined within a roadmap document to find appropriate future actions to support eAccessibility and its uptake.

Keywords: eAccessibility, Accessibility, Roadmap, Web Accessibility, Digital TV, iDTV, Total Conversation, Self-Service-Terminals, Accessible Documents, Accessible Tourism, Education on (e)Accessibility.

1   R&D Idea

The roadmap presented in this paper is compiled from research results and activities undertaken within the framework of the European Thematic Network eAccess+. [1]

The network put special emphasis on three topics within the wide range of eAccessibility in Europe:

- Web Accessibility
- Accessible Digital TV and Total Conversation
- Self-service terminals (SSTs) and devices for banking and financial services, public transport, tourism and cultural heritage as well as e-government

In addition to those 3 given subject areas, it became evident that there are some most important and influencing horizontal matters that need to be taken into account and researched to give both a sound researched overview and introduction to the topic within the eAccessibility universe and a map to address the right issues and persons involved to disseminate and promote eAccessibility further:

- Education on eAccessibility / Accessible Education
- Accessible Documents and Publishing
- Accessible Tourism

eAccess+ was driven by 25 core members, coming from all over Europe. It was one core task to involve stakeholders at national level and to expand the network by a group of so called "Associated Partners".

K. Miesenberger et al. (Eds.): ICCHP 2014, Part I, LNCS 8547, pp. 324–331, 2014.

By involving all stakeholder groups, like legislators, regulators, policy makers, commissioners, developers of hardware and software, user organizations, researchers, accessibility and usability experts, educators and peers, it aimed at both analyzing the state of the art and in particular the obstacles or missing links hindering a broader uptake of eAccessibility in Europe and pushing the uptake of eAccessibility further.

2   State of the Art

The eAccess+ network identified the following projects and roadmaps developed in EU-funded projects or ongoing work in that field on several areas as relevant to its work and scope:

2.1   CARDIAC

The CARDIAC project [2] aimed at generating a research agenda and priorities in accessible and assistive ICT that will favor eAccessibility. Three research lines emerged as priorities: Innovative users interfaces (including web accessibility and adaptive practical user interfaces); Holistic approach to human computer interaction (including taking into account human complexity and diversity); and advanced design and development methodologies and tools (including tools for user centered design, development of training modules, etc.). The CARDIAC project provides therefore key elements concerning the Research and development side of eAccessibility that should be considered as complementary to eAccess+ roadmap, focused on concrete implementation of eAccessibility.

2.2   GPII

The Global Public Inclusive Infrastructure project [3] is an international coalition of organizations and individuals with the aim "to simplify the development, delivery and support of access technologies and provide users with a way to instantly apply the access techniques and technologies they need, automatically, on any computers or other ICT they encounter". This coalition provides for the eAccessibility roadmap a good platform to be shared and used, providing a more EU approach. There is a great potential for the eAccess+ roadmap to become one of the reference document in the GPII, and influence their future activities.

2.3   BRAID

The "Bridging Research in Ageing and Information and Communication Technology Development" project [4] sought to 'unleash the potential of technology as a vehicle to enable people to achieve their full capacity'. The Braid roadmap gathers the results from several previous roadmaps and focuses on four main topics: independent living, health and care in life, occupation in life, and recreation in life. Focused exclusively on ageing issues, the BRAID results provide relevant insights on user needs (and especially older user needs) and recommendations on actions to be taken in that field. eAccessibility should be seen here as a transversal topic applying to all relevant areas of the roadmap. Inclusive design is a key issue in the roadmap. The eAccess+ roadmap should be read as complementary to the BRAID roadmap, providing the missing link between ageing field and eAccessibility-related issues.

2.4   AALIANCE2 Project and Roadmap

The AALIANCE2 project [5] aims to launch a network on Ambient Assisted Living and create a roadmap on upcoming challenges and technologies for future needs on this topic. The eAccess+ roadmap would here have a wide potential to influence some recommendations included in the upcoming roadmap, while benefiting from a wide range of stakeholders involved in a field where eAccessibility is a key challenge.

In addition, the eAccess+ roadmap has a great potential to be used in ongoing wide EU campaigns and actions on ICT standardization on Design for all, on freedom of movement, and on age-friendly environments.

3   Methodology

From stakeholder interviews, desktop research on legal framework(s), best practice, existing rules and guidelines as well as from own research and experience, all possible aspects of eAccessibility [6] were collected and evaluated in a relevance check with the keypersons from step 1. After identifying the relevant aspects, these items were compared, interconnected, boiled down to bigger categories and allocated within the eAccessibility universe following value chains designed for this process / purpose.

Following this important step, the project identified for every category possible tools and measures to overcome constraints and gaps as well as the key persons / institutions to be involved to make change happen. From this, milestones and success criteria were defined, leading to scenarios and possible risks in case those milestones wouldn´t be reached. This process was followed for all three major topics as well as for the most influencing horizontal matters presented above.

3.1   Web Accessibility

In terms of Web Accessibility, 20 years of research and mainstreaming led to a comprehensive set of guidelines and rules of both, mandatory (legally implemented following European or national laws) as well as informal guidelines, e.g. compiled by WAI-W3C. [7]

Nevertheless, the uptake of those quite concise and well documented rules and guidelines lack of the corresponding results:

Only 2% of websites checked for a WAI-W3C study fail concerning very basic guidelines that are crucial for web accessibility like „Alternative Texts" describing graphical content – not to speak about reaching level „AAA" that would include content and information designed following „Easy to Read"-guidelines. [8]

Approach. The approach for this part of eAccess+ was it to:

- Identify good practice and further mainstream the principles of eAccessibility (also in terms of web accessibility)
- Get in touch with stakeholders to research what they do / think / implement in terms of accessibility and where necessary find out what is lacking within this (small) aspect of eAccessibility
- Build up a comprehensive information repository collecting the most successful strategies and best practice examples as well as tailored step by step guides for different user groups with a diverse set of knowledge and competence
- Compile a roadmap identifying the most hindering issues and sign-posting who could facilitate what , why an when – especially as potentially everyone can contribute as author and information provider
- Making web accessibility, besides all rules and guidelines, a "game of chance".

3.2   iDTV and Total Conversation

In terms of iDTV, research and the set of available formal guidelines and rules is „commendably concise", leading to an overwhelming set of possible „best practice" examples and beliefs.

Following the EBU (European Broadcasting Union), the AVMS (Audiovisual Media Services) directive [9] offer a basic level of European harmonization for the European audiovisual sector as a whole but commits: „However, the way public service media is regulated essentially remains an issue for the EU Member States. The Amsterdam Protocol to the EU Treaty [10] underlines that "the system of public broadcasting in the Member States is directly related to the democratic, social and cultural needs of each society and to the need to preserve media pluralism" – what (to put it a bit exaggerated) asks for a common understanding of iDTV accessibility beyond national borders and (at least) the knowledge / the funds for implementing basic eAccessibility in this aspect in every EU member state.

Approach. The approach for this part of eAccess+ was it to:

- Identify good practice and mainstream the principles of eAccessibility
- Get in touch with stakeholders to research what they do / think / implement in terms of accessibility and where necessary find out what is lacking within this (small) aspect of eAccessibility, focusing on the „non converted" by trying both – getting in touch with decision and policy makers as well as find structures / interfaces to present them eAccessibility.
- Build up a comprehensive information repository collecting most successful strategies and best practice examples as well as tailored step by step guides for different user groups with a diverse set of knowledge and competence.
- Compile a roadmap identifying the most hindering issues and sign-posting who could facilitate what, why an when – especially as success in this aspect of eAccessibility is depending on national interest, funding and regulations.

3.3   Self Service Terminals

In terms of Accessible Self – Service- Terminals the possible eAccessibility considerations are at least two-fold:

- Architectural accessibility and reachability of the terminal and its user interface
- Accessibility of the user interface and accessibility of the information to be entered
  and/or retrieved

There are national regulations (e.g. the Austrian "ÖNorm" 16xx describing architectural considerations to include users and clients with mobility disability and gives to
some extent also basic considerations concerning users with visual constraints) dealing with the architectural dimension but no rules neither guidelines nor regulations
concerning the accessibility of the user interface or the user interaction (e.g. audible
information for blind users of an ATM).

As in most cases those kiosks also deal with "important and secure personal and
financial data", the willingness of SST providers to install accessible test systems (e.g.
with an audible, easy to use and understandable guided user instruction / user interface) is limited – first and foremost due to arguments dealing with "high security and
safety" concerning the systems in use.

Approach. The approach for this part of eAccess+ was it to:

- Identify good practice and mainstream the principles of eAccessibility
- Get in touch with stakeholders to research what they do / think / implement in
  terms of accessibility and where necessary find out what is lacking within this
  (small) aspect of eAccessibility, focusing on the „non converted" by trying both –
  getting in touch with decision and policy makers as well as find structures / interfaces to present them eAccessibility.
- Build up a comprehensive information repository collecting most successful strategies and best practice examples as well as tailored step by step guides for different
  user groups with a diverse set of knowledge and competence.
- Compile a roadmap identifying the most hindering issues and sign-posting who
  could facilitate what, why and when – especially as success in this aspect of eAccessibility is depending on satisfying security and safety considerations.

4   R&D Work and Results

The most important and influencing in depth results for the three main domains as
well as the horizontal matters can be concluded in a "Quick Start guide to eAccessibility" valid for all researched topical areas as a whole.

4.1   Educate!

- Integrate (e)Accessibility in mainstream and specialized curricula (e.g. care, service provision sector) at all levels (vocational, academic, further education)

- Implement (e)Accessibility in future calls for proposals as a compulsory evaluation criterion with the need to describe what measures are taken to comply with (e)Accessibility requirements and standards, both to carry out the project and to present the results.

4.2   Standardize and Harmonize!

- A basic framework of (legally binding and clear, genuine) accessibility standards is needed, besides W3C-WAI and ISO 9241-171:2008 [11]
- Integrate and cross-reference eAccessibility standards in other standards.

4.3   Experience!

Implement accessible solutions "subliminally" – without further advertisement in terms of "disability" or "for disabled / older adults" – just let people experience the difference.

4.4   Research!

- More research is needed to get a sound and time overview on how far we have proceeded in terms of (legal / financial / political) framework, solutions, business models / business plans, …
- More research is needed to improve the level of eAccessibility and use the potential of emerging and fast changing ICT.
- More research and development is needed in the field of Assistive Technologies as developers often spend a lot of time for working around bugs in assistive technologies rather than to conformance to standards.

4.5   Public Procurement!

- Use public procurement to drive change. Many vendors claim to deliver accessible solutions and services. Only some of them do.
- Calls for tenders and calls for research project proposals are great opportunities to communicate requirements.
- Establish skills and tools to assure that the offers and products deliver on their accessibility promises.
- Prepare textual building blocks and help-desk support for people to use in procurement both to support to the vendors, researchers and those shaping the procurement process.

4.6   Change Views on Accessibility!

In designing accessible solutions, we should move from a narrow approach that considers accessibility in a strict sense addressing specific segments of the whole spectrum of disabilities to instead adopt an inclusive approach considering the diversity of users and not only those with the most severe sensory disabilities (e.g. including young users, speakers of different languages, elderly users etc.).

Accessibility is a crucial enabler for safer, enjoyable and independent lives. To realize these benefits and to keep European businesses in a leading position, further investment in research, development and implementation as well as fundamental research in all scientific areas is still needed.

5   Impact and Contributions to the Field

Following reviewers, the "eAccess+ Thematic Network exercise and the Roadmap and HUB provide a significant integrative European resource and repository asset to take advantage of", "are top priority and challenging working domains, partly because both technologies and practices in service delivery develop quickly and there is a need to assess the development constantly in order to serve the diverse eAccessibility community with success" and the "results of the eAccess+ Thematic Network provide a sound platform for a stronger eAccessibility impact within the European scene" as well as for the long needed collaboration and co-operation with other major countries and frameworks outside Europe.

There are several key activities, like the UN Convention on the Rights of People with Disabilities [12], the EU Web Directive, the M/376 European Standardization activity, recent studies dealing with the eAccessibility cost/benefit issue including country profiles that may benefit from results of eAccess+ and its roadmap.

6   Conclusion and Planned Activities

To compile a roadmap for a complex, highly interconnected and diverse collection of topics and issues comprised within "eAccessibility" is an ongoing work in progress. Technology evolves fast and together with research, development and the gained knowledge, our lives and the way we encompass challenges and everyday situations change.

Therefore this roadmap is a snapshot showing the most important barriers and promoters of eAccessibility in Europe and strongly benefit from further development. When compiling this document, the eAccess+ Consortium was in touch with key players and major stakeholders and aimed at assuring their feedback and further involvement to keep this important work "in progress".

We found substantial support and interest from EASPD (the European Association of Service providers for Persons with Disabilities, representing over 10.000 social service provider organizations across Europe) [13] that had a lot of time for this roadmap and decided to keep track of it and co-operate with checking and further developing it within its framework on an annual basis.

Additionally, an online version of the eAccess+ roadmap will be implemented within the eAccess+ HUB that will stay up and running as one stop information repository for eAccessibility after the end of the project work. This version will have the necessary functionality to be discussed, commented and edited by registered users and will form a strong basis for strengthening the uptake of eAccessibility through sound research and up-to-date as well as on-the-point information for most diverse target groups from policy makers over developers and managers to end users.

This way, the eAccess+ roadmap has the chance to become a living part of research and development and will be an important topic and issue to be further developed and adapted to future changes and shifts.

Acknowledgements. The thematic network eAccess+ was partially funded under the ICT Policy Support Programme (ICT PSP) as part of the Competitiveness and Innovation Framework Programme by the European Community, EU SEVENTH FRAMEWORK PROGRAMME ICT PSP third call for proposals 2009: CIP-ICT-PSP-2009-3.

References

1. eAccess+ website, http://www.eaccessplus.eu
2. Cardiac website, http://www.cardiac-eu.org/
3. GPII website, http://gpii.net/
4. BRAID website, http://auseaccess.cis.utas.edu.au/
5. AALIANCE website, http://www.aaliance2.eu/
6. eAccess+ - HUB, http://hub.eaccessplus.eu/wiki/Main_Page
7. W3C-WAI guidelines, http://www.w3.org/WAI/
8. European standards for making information easy to read and to understand, http://www.inclusion-europe.org/images/stories/documents/Project_Pathways1/Information_for_all.pdf
9. EU AVMS directive, http://ec.europa.eu/avpolicy/reg/avms/index_en.htm
10. Amsterdam protocol amending the EU Treaty on public broadcasting, http://ec.europa.eu/competition/state_aid/legislation/broadcasting_communication_en.pdf
11. ISO 9241-171:2008 on the accessibility of software products, http://www.iso.org/iso/iso_catalogue/catalogue_tc/catalogue_detail.htm?csnumber=39080
12. UN Convention on the Rights of People with Disabilities, http://www.un.org/disabilities/
13. EASPD website, http://www.easpd.eu/

Web Accessibility for Older Readers: Effects of Font Type and Font Size on Skim Reading Webpages in Thai

Sorachai Kamollimsakul[1,2], Helen Petrie[1], and Christopher Power[1]

[1] Human Computer Interaction Research Group, Department of Computer Science, University of York, United Kingdom
[2] School of Information Technology, Suranaree University of Technology, Thailand
{sk750,Helen.Petrie,Christopher.Power}@york.ac.uk

Abstract. Most guidelines for making websites accessible for older people have been developed for the Latin alphabet. Currently, there are no web design guidelines for the Thai language or for Thai older people. Our research investigated the effect of font type and size in Thai on skim reading for Thai younger (21-39 years) and older (59-72 years) adults. There were two levels of font types (Conservative and Modern, which correlate to serif and sans serif types, respectively) and three levels of font sizes (12, 14, 16 point). There was a significant effect of font type on reading time per web page, but not for font size or age group. There was also a significant main effect of font type and font size on reader preferences, but no effect of age group. These findings form the basis of recommendations for evidence-based web design guidelines for the Thai language.

Keywords: Web Accessibility, Older Adults, Web Design Guidelines, Font Type, Font Size, Thai Language.

1 Introduction

There are many web design guidelines for making websites more accessible to older people [1]. However, most of these guidelines lack evidence-based research to sup-port their recommendations. Furthermore, there is some confusion when web designers want to apply these recommendations, as the guidelines often provide different and even contradictory recommendations. Two examples of such confusion are font type and font size of text on webpages.

Seven sets of guidelines make recommendations about font type: Zhao [2] recommends choosing font type based on "legibility" without explaining what that means; Agelight [3] similarly suggests choosing font type based on "familiarity and legibility"; the SPRY Foundation [4], Holt [5], SilverWeb [6], the National Institute on Aging/National Library of Medicine (NIA/NLM) [7], and the Nielsen Norman Group [8] all recommend using a sans serif font type; SilverWeb [6] warns against the use of fancy font types; and NIA/NLM [7] warns against the use of serif, novelty, and display font types.

K. Miesenberger et al. (Eds.): ICCHP 2014, Part I, LNCS 8547, pp. 332–339, 2014.

The recommendations about font size are also varied. WebCredible [9] suggests that less than 12 point is too small to read but do not recommend a specific font size; the Nielsen Norman Group [8] and Zhao [2] recommend at least 12 point; Agelight [3], the SPRY Foundation [4] and SilverWeb [6] recommend 12 to 14 point; while NIA/NLM [7] recommends 12 or 14 point.

Petrie, Kamollimsakul and Power [1] found that most web design guidelines are in English and relate to text presented in the Latin alphabet. Some research is beginning to investigate text presentation on the web in other languages such as Chinese [10], and Hebrew [11], but there are no web design guidelines which have been developed for the Thai language or for Thai disabled and older people.

This paper investigated the effect of font type and font size on skim reading tasks for Thai younger and older adults both using both objective and subjective measures with a view to developing evidence-based recommendations for websites in Thai.

2   Method

2.1   Design

A three way mixed design was used, with age group as the between participants independent variable (younger vs older adults), and font type (two levels: conservative vs modern font types) and font size (12, 14, and 16 point) as the two within participants variables. Two dependent variables are discussed here: time spent reading each webpage, and participants' ratings of their preferences, for each combination of font type and font size (measured on 5 point Likert items).

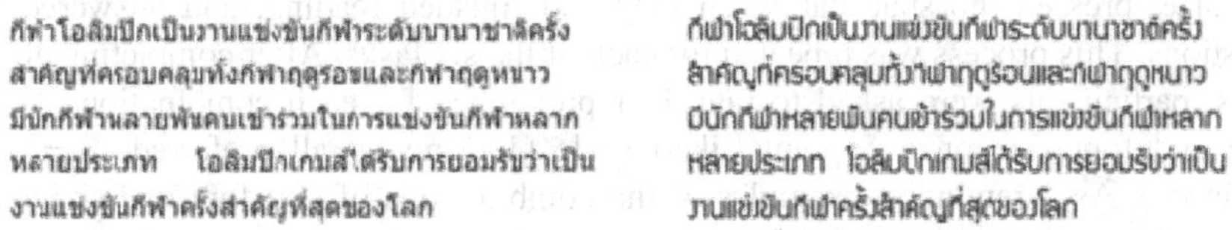

กีฬาโอลิมปิกเป็นงานแข่งขันกีฬาระดับนานาชาติครั้ง   กีฬาโอลิมปิกเป็นงานแข่งขันกีฬาระดับนานาชาติครั้ง
สำคัญที่ครอบคลุมทั้งกีฬาฤดูร้อนและกีฬาฤดูหนาว   สำคัญที่ครอบคลุมทั้งกีฬาฤดูร้อนและกีฬาฤดูหนาว
มีนักกีฬาหลายพันคนเข้าร่วมในการแข่งขันกีฬาหลาก   มีนักกีฬาหลายพันคนเข้าร่วมในการแข่งขันกีฬาหลาก
หลายประเภท   โอลิมปิกเกมส์ได้รับการยอมรับว่าเป็น   หลายประเภท   โอลิมปิกเกมส์ได้รับการยอมรับว่าเป็น
งานแข่งขันกีฬาครั้งสำคัญที่สุดของโลก   งานแข่งขันกีฬาครั้งสำคัญที่สุดของโลก

Fig. 1. An example of Thai conservative font type (left) and modern font type (right)

The Thai Conservative font type includes an extra circle at the beginning of most of consonants and vowels while the Modern font type does not, as shown in Fig 1. Thus, the Thai Conservative font type corresponds most closely to a serif font in the Latin alphabet and the Thai Modern font type correspond most closely to a sans serif font.

Each participant undertook six skim reading tasks on a specially created website about the Olympic Games, one task with each of the six combinations of font type and font size. The task was to skim read the page as quickly and accurately as possible and to then answer four multiple choices questions about the page. Skim reading was chosen as this is a very common reading task on websites. Order of presentation of the combinations was counterbalanced between participants

2.2   Participants

There were 42 participants, 21 older and 21 younger adults. All participants were native speakers of Thai.   The mean age of the older adults was 61.67 years (standard deviation 3.32, range 59 – 72 years), 11 were male and 10 were female. The mean age of the younger adults was 27.71 years (standard deviation 4.92, range 21 – 39 years), 8 were male and 13 were female.

2.3   Equipment and Materials

Participants completed the experiment on a personal computer running Windows XP and Internet Explorer 9 with 21.5 inch LED Monitor, a standard keyboard, and 2-button mouse with a scroll-wheel.

A website about the Olympic Games with six different pages of text was created for the study. Each page had 354 words of text, separated into four paragraphs. There were four multiple choice questions for each page.

2.4   Procedure

Participants were briefed about the study and completed an informed consent form and a short demographic questionnaire. Participant were asked to sit approximate 57 cm from the monitor. They were then asked to make themselves familiar with the computer, monitor, mouse, and web browser. The participants were given a practice task to familiarize themselves with the task required in the study. For each experimental trial, participants skim read the page with the appropriate combination of font type and size, pressed the spacebar when they had finished reading, and answered the questions. This process was repeated for each of the six tasks. After completing all the tasks, participants were asked to rate their preference for each combination of font type and font size on a 5 point Likert scale (1 = not at all preferred, 5 = very preferred). As a reminder, examples of the combinations of text font and size were provided.

3   Results

An Analysis of Variance (ANOVA) on the time spent per webpage found that there was a significant main effect for font type, ($F_{(1,40)} = 11.05$, $p < 0.005$), while the main effects for font size and age group were not significant. There were no significant interaction effects between any of the variables. Fig. 2 illustrates the mean for conservative and modern font types and shows that the conservative type produced significantly shorter reading times than the modern type.

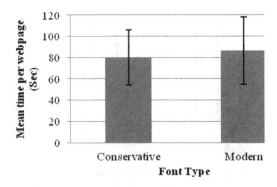

Fig. 2. Mean time spent per webpage for Conservative and Modern fonts

On the preferences ratings, an ANOVA found that there was a significant main effect for font type, (F $(1,40)$ = 168.40, p < 0.001), and font size, (F $(2,80)$ = 81.09, p < 0.001), but no main effect for age group. All participants (both young and older adults) significantly prefer the conservative font type (mean preference rating: 3.75; standard deviation: 1.08) over the modern font type (mean preference rating: 2.20; standard deviation: 1.07). In investigating the main effect for font size, an LSD post hoc analysis found that 12 point was rated significantly lower in preference (p < 0.001) than 14 point and 16 point. While 14 point was rated significantly lower in preference (p < 0.05) than 16 point (mean preference rating 12 point: 2.12 standard deviation 1.21; 14 point: 3.21 standard deviation 1.18; and 16 point: 3.58 standard deviation 1.12).

In addition, t-tests were conducted to investigate whether ratings of preference were significantly above or below the mid-point of the rating scale, to investigate whether participants were positive or negative about each font type or font size. One sample t-tests against the neutral mid-point rating of 3 showed that the ratings for the conservative font type were significant higher than neutral (t (125) = 7.75, p < .01), but the ratings for the modern type were significant lower than neutral (t (125) = 8.44, p < .001). In addition, the ratings for 12 point were significant lower than neutral (t (83) = 6.69, p < .001) while 16 point was rated significant higher than neutral (t (83) = 4.77, p < .001) but 14 point was not significant different from neutral (t (83) = 1.66, n.s.)

There was significant interaction effect between font size and age group, (F $(2,80)$ = 5.13, p < 0.01). Fig. 3 shows the means for the interaction. A Scheffé post hoc analysis showed that younger adults significantly preferred 14 or 16 point over 12 point (p < 0.005 and p < 0.05, respectively). There was no significant difference between 14 point and 16 point. While older adults show a clear significant preference for 16 point over 14 point and 12 point (p < 0.05 and p < 0.001, respectively) and they significantly preferred 14 point over 12 point (p < 0.001).

In addition, one sample t-tests against the neutral mid-point rating showed that for both younger and older adults 12 point was significant lower than neutral (younger adults: t (41) = 3.03, p < .01; older adults: t (41) = 7.49, p < .01) while 16 point was rated significant higher than neutral (younger adults: t (41) = 2.76, p < .01; older adults: t (41) = 3.94, p < .01) but 14 point was not significantly different from neutral (younger adults: t (41) = 1.86, n.s.; older adults: t (41) = 0.426, n.s.).

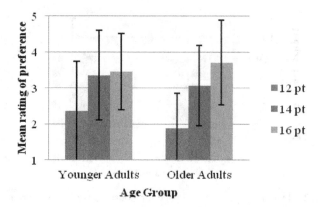

Fig. 3. Mean preference ratings for younger and older adults for 12 14, and 16 point text

There is also a significant interaction between font type, font size, and age group, (F (2,80) = 7.67, p < 0.001). Fig. 4 illustrates the mean for the interaction for younger adults for conservative and modern fonts and 12, 14 and 16 point text. A Scheffé post hoc analysis showed that, for younger adults, 12, 14, and 16 point conservative font type was not different from each other in preference rating. There was a significant difference in rating in modern font type: 12 point was rated significantly lower than 16 point (p < 0.005) but there was no significant difference between 12 point and 14 point, or between 14 point and 16 point. In addition, 12 point Modern font type was significant lower in rating than every size of Conservative font type (12 point (p < 0.005); 14 point (p < 0.001); 16 point (p < 0.001)).

One sample t-tests against the neutral mid-point of 3 showed that for younger adults, the mean rating for all point size in Conservative font type were significant higher than neutral (12 point: t = 2.22, df = 20, p < .05; 14 point: t = 6.14, df = 20, p < .001; 16 point: t = 3.44, df = 20, p < .005), but the mean rating for Modern font type

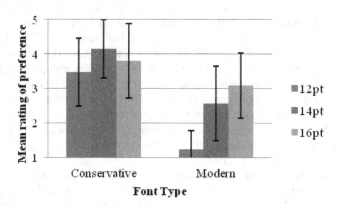

Fig. 4. Mean preference ratings for younger adults for Conservative and Modern fonts and 12, 14 and 16 point text

12 point was significant lower than neutral (t = 14.98, df = 20, p < .001) while 14 point and 16 point were not significant difference from neutral (14 point: t = 1.82, df = 20, p > .05; 16 point: t = 0.46, df = 20, p > .05).

Figure 5 illustrates the mean for the interaction for older adults for Conservative and Modern Fonts and 12, 14 and 16 point text. A Scheffé post hoc analysis showed that, for older adults, Conservative font type, 12 point was rated significantly lower in preference than 14 point and 16 point (p < 0.005 and p < 0.01, respectively). While 14 point and 16 point were not significant difference (p > 0.05). For Modern font type, 12 point was rated significantly lower than 14 point and 16 point (p < 0.05 and p < 0.001, respectively) but there was no significant difference between 14 point and 16 point (p > 0.05). In addition, 12 point Modern font type was significant lower in rating than every size of Conservative font type (12 point (p < 0.05); 14 point (p < 0.001); 16 point (p < 0.001)). 14 point Modern font type was significant lower in rating than 14 and 16 point Conservative font type (p < 0.005). 16 point Modern font type was significant lower in rating than 16 point Conservative font type (p < 0.05).

One sample t-tests against the neutral mid-point of 3 showed that for older adults, the mean rating for Conservative font type 12 point was significant lower than neutral (t = 2.26, df = 20, p < .05) while 14 point and 16 point were significant higher than neutral (14 point: t = 4.95, df = 20, p < .001; 16 point: t = 10.03, df = 20, p < .001). For Modern font type, 12 point and 14 point were significant lower than neutral (12 point: t = 20.61, df = 20, p < .001; 14 point: t = 4.18, df = 20, p < .001) while 16 point were not significantly difference from neutral (t = 1.16, df = 20, n.s.).

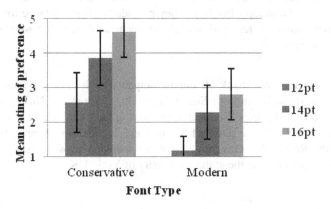

Fig. 5. Mean preference ratings for older adults for Conservative and Modern fonts and 12, 14 and 16 point text

4   Discussion and Conclusions

This study found that Thai font type had a significant effect on skim reading time, but font size did not and perhaps surprisingly, there were no differences in reading times between the two age groups. The conservative font yielded significantly quicker skim reading times across all other variables, with a 6.39 second or 7.3% increase in reading efficiency compared to the modern font.

On participants' preferences for font type, both younger and older adults preferred the conservative font type over the modern font type. For font size, the results are more complex. In general, younger adults significantly preferred 14 and 16 point over 12 point but expressed no difference in preferences between 14 and 16 point. Older adults preferred 16 point over 12 and 14 point and preferred 14 point over 12 point. In addition, there was an interaction between font type, font size, and age group. For the modern font, the pattern of preferences is similar for both younger and older adults, with 12 point rated very low by both groups. Even 16 point only reached the midpoint of the scale for older adults whereas both 14 and 16 point reached the neutral point for younger adults. However, the conservative font is generally acceptable to the younger adults, it was rated higher than the neutral midpoint for all point sizes. But for the older adults, there was a clear preference for the conservative font at 14 and 16 point over 12 point with 14 and 16 point rated higher than neutral, and 12 point rated lower than neutral.

Based on the results from the present study, proposing the conservative font type is good for both younger and older adults. While the recommendation about font size is related to font type. If web developers use the conservative type, 12 point or larger is appropriate for younger adults while 14 point or larger is appropriate for older adults. When web developers use modern font type, 14 point or larger is acceptable for younger adults and 16 point is acceptable for older adults.

These results are very unexpected if one is making predictions from web design guidelines for the Latin alphabet. Thus they provide the first evidence for web design guidelines for Thai websites, with useful evidence for developing websites for both younger and older readers.

Acknowledgements. We thank all our participants in the study for their time and effort. We also thank Institute of Social Technology, Suranaree University of Technology, Nakhon Ratchasima, Thailand for providing the room in which to conduct the study. Finally, we thank the National Science and Technology Development Agency (NSTDA), the Royal Thai Government for the scholarship, which supports the first author in his Ph.D. programme at the University of York, UK.

References

1. Petrie, H., Kamollimsakul, S., Power, C.: Web accessibility for older adults: effects of line spacing and text justification on reading web pages. In: Proceedings 15th International ACMSIGACCESS Conference on Computers and Accessibility (ASSETS). ACM (2013)
2. Zhao, H.: Universal Usability Web Design Guidelines for the Elderly (Age 65 and Older), http://www.co-bw.com/DMS_Web_the_elderly_on_the_web.htm
3. AgeLight: Interface design guidelines for users of all ages, http://www.agelight.com/webdocs/designguide.pdf

4. Holt, B.J., Komlos-Weimer, M.: Older Adults and the World Wide Web: a Guide for Web Site Creators. SPRY Foundation,
   http://www.spry.org/pdf/website_creators_guide.pdf
5. Holt, B.J.: Creating senior-friendly Web sites. Issue Brief, Centre for Medicare Education, 1(4) (2000)
6. Kurniawan, S., Zaphiris, P.: Research-Derived Web Design Guidelines for Older People. In: Proceeding 7th International ACMSIGACCESS Conference on Computers and Accessibility (ASSETS), Maryland, pp. 129–135 (2005)
7. National Institute on Aging/National Library of Medicine (NIA/NLM): Making your website senior friendly: A check list,
   http://www.nlm.nih.gov/pubs/checklist.pdf
8. Pernice, K., Estes, J., Nielsen, J.: Senior Citizens (Ages 65 and older) on the Web. Nielsen Norman Group (2013)
9. Fidgeon, T.: Usability for Older Web Users, http://www.webcredible.co.uk/user-friendly-resources/web-usability/older-users.shtml
10. Chan, A.H.S., Lee, P.S.K.: Effect of display factors on Chinese reading times, comprehension scores and preferences. Behaviour & Information Technology 24(2) (2005)
11. Parush, A., Shwarts, Y., Shtub, A., Chandra, M.J.: The impact of visual layout factors on performance in Web pages: A cross-language study. Human Factors 47(1) (2005)

Self-Service Terminals for Older and Disabled Users: Attitudes of Key Stakeholders

Helen Petrie[1], Jenny S. Darzentas[2], and Christopher Power[1]

[1] University of York, United Kingdom
{helen.petrie,christopher.power}@york.ac.uk
[2] University of the Aegean, Greece
jennyd@aegean.gr

Abstract. Self-service terminals (SSTs) are becoming an increasing important part of the service landscape for both the public and private sector. There is very little information regarding the current state of accessibility practice in this area. This paper presents the results of interviews with 22 stakeholders in the supply and deployment communities for SSTs regarding their knowledge of accessibility issues. The analysis of these interviews helps explain the current poor state of accessibility of SSTs. In addition, we analysed academic literature on self-service technology, particularly from the management and marketing disciplines, to understand their perspectives and see how these could inform the accessibility debate. Finally, building on these analyses, we make recommendations for the ways forward to improve SST accessibility and that of self-service in general and provide an initial information resource to help improve current practice.

Keywords: Self-Service Terminals (SSTs), Automatic Teller Machines (ATMs), Older People, People with Disabilities.

1 Introduction

Self-service technologies are becoming increasingly ubiquitous in everyday life. The basic concept of the self-service terminal (SST) or kiosk is not new with Automated Teller Machines (ATMs) being introduced in the 1960s [1]. However, SSTs now offer services in nearly every sphere of human activity, in both the public and private sectors, from government, education, financial, retail, travel and health services to extensive information services. Moreover, they are being deployed more and more [2]. Increasingly we find self-service solutions for checking in to hotels, airports, and even emergency departments of hospitals [3]. It is predicted that by 2020 "the customer will manage 85% of the relationship with an enterprise without interacting with a human" [4, p5].

SSTs offer many benefits for both deployers and consumers. For deployers, these benefits include: maintaining high levels of service but with reduced staffing costs with services being available 24 hours a day, 365 days a year; delivery of instructions in a range of languages as needed; provision of additional services along with the core

K. Miesenberger et al. (Eds.): ICCHP 2014, Part I, LNCS 8547, pp. 340–347, 2014.

service, for example offering travel information to train ticket buyers, or discount promotions to supermarket shoppers. Finally, the use of SSTs is perceived as a 'modern' approach, which may be good for the image of deployers.

For consumers, the most often cited benefits are: the round the clock availability of goods and services, faster service, less queuing, and more control over transactions. However there are also other, less obvious benefits. Bitner [5] found that many people preferred the impersonal interaction with SSTs, rather than dealing with "judgmental" employees for services such as train tickets. In hospitals, patients can now carry out their own administrative procedures, which may be less embarrassing but it also speeds up patient processing, and frees up nursing staff from burdensome admission procedures, so benefits both the hospital and the patients [6].

Although SSTs are now used in a very wide variety of contexts, most conform to consistent specifications and contexts of use. They are usually designed for positioning in public areas, either outside or inside buildings. Most are designed for "walk up and use", meaning a minimum of instruction and learning for consumers, and most are foreseen as being used for rapid transactions. This means that the SST style of interaction becomes familiar to consumers, and they can transfer their knowledge of use from one type of SST to another.

Despite these benefits, consumers are not always happy with SSTs. When there is a choice, many consumers will not necessarily use the self-service option. For example, in a recent study of Australian supermarket customers, only half the customers chose the self-service option in comparison to the traditional check-out, with older customers significantly less likely to choose self-service [7]. However, the traditional, human-mediated choice is often disappearing and there is an increase in the number and frequency of unattended machines and services totally unmediated by humans, and thus no other way to get some services except via an SST. More worryingly, if SSTs are not accessible to consumers with disabilities or older consumers, then the services provided by SSTs will be unavailable to them. Of further concern are the cases where there is a human-mediated service in addition to the self-service offering, but consumers have to pay extra to use the human-mediated version of the service, as is the case for some airline booking services and banking services.

Although some services such as train and airline tickets are migrating to personal devices such as smartphones and tablets, other areas of stand alone SSTs are still growing and are expected to continue to grow. For example, it is predicted that the number of ATMs could grow by 44% between 2012 and 2018, which would mean 3.7 million ATMs worldwide by 2018 [2].

2   Problems with the Accessibility of Self Service Terminals

In spite of their ubiquity in everyday life, many SSTs are not accessible to older and disabled people. Beyond the physical accessibility of the SST, there are many prob-lems of eAccessibility: problems of access to the information from the SST and inter-action with the SST controls. For example, people who are blind cannot read the screen, even if the buttons have braille on them; partially sighted people may find the print on the screen or the buttons too small or there may not have sufficient contrast between text/button and background; older people and people with cognitive disabilities, who need longer to make decisions, may find that the SSTs time out too quickly for them; people with low literacy skills (which includes not only older people and people with cognitive disabilities, but whose are not native speakers, or are not proficient in the written form of a language) may also experience problems with reading information, particularly when SSTs use terminology that is not familiar to them.

Even technologies that seem easier for people to use, such as touchscreens, can be problematic for some people with disabilities and older people. For example, older people tend to have drier hands that do not activate the touchscreen so easily and may have some tremor in the hands that makes precise positioning difficult [8].

Older people make up approximately 18% of the population in Europe [9] and people with disabilities approximately 16% of the population of working age [10]. This is a considerable number of people who are being 'designed out' of using SSTs, by which we mean that their needs were never included in the design specifications or implementations. In addition, people who are 'temporarily disabled' from accidents and injury, or from the actual context of use, such as bright sunshine or darkness on an SST screen, would also benefit from more accessible designs.

3   The View from Industry

In a recent study [11] we conducted interviews with 22 suppliers or deployers of SSTs. The interviewees included 20 suppliers of SSTs or SST components (either hardware or software), and 2 interviews with deployers of SSTs (an educational institution and a public authority). Most of the interviews took place by approaching people at trade fairs, to avoid a highly self-selecting sample of respondents already interested in ac-cessibility and eAccessibility of SSTs. These interviews showed that most suppliers and deployers of SSTs have little understanding of the need for accessibility beyond the requirements for people with physical disabilities. In particular, they had little understanding of the issues of eAccessibility of information in SSTs for visually and hearing impaired users.

The second theme to emerge from the interviews was the perceived cost of accessibility. Interviewees were very uncertain about the additional costs the might be involved in making SSTs accessible, and in what the return on investment (ROI) would be. Often interviewees believed that accessibility features would be very expensive to introduce. They also felt that the market for accessible SSTs is a small and specialist one. Finally, on the question of cost, they believed that small companies do not necessarily have the resources to deal with this issue.

The third theme to emerge in the interview was the need for clear guidelines on how to create SSTs that are accessible. Interviewees raised two complementary points of view: "tell us what to do and we will do it" and "we know we don't know what to do". These views reflect both the lack of knowledge about accessibility and eAccessibility issues but also the difficulty of taking users' needs and deployers' requirements in designing solutions.

4   The View from the Research Literature on Consumer Acceptance of SSTs

Consumers' reactions to the increase in self-service has been most extensively studied in the management, marketing and retailing disciplines. Studying mainstream consumer reactions can also help us understand the problems and solutions for older consumers and consumers with disabilities. The cost savings from "enticing customers to serve themselves" [12 p76] in a variety of ways can be extremely large. Because of this, businesses are concerned with the problem of consumer acceptance, and acquiring a deep understanding of what makes consumers adopt self-service technologies. At the same time, rejection of self-service can be very damaging, with consumers not just rejecting the particular service, but also the entire brand.

The service management literature examines consumers' intentions to adopt self-service technologies by investigating demographic and consumer trends and conducting surveys of consumers' attitudes. In the demographic studies, researchers typically study the age, gender, education and income of users and non-users of SSTs, while the traits they investigate include technology anxiety, need for interaction with a human rather than a machine, and openness to technology innovation [7, 13 - 16].

Research finds that most people can relate to frustration with SSTs, even of simple vending machines. However, many people do not voice their complaints about problems they encounter with SSTs, believing that such problems are their responsibility [17]. Some SSTs, such as supermarket self-service check-outs have been known to make even young people, who are otherwise technically literate, shy away from potential embarrassing situations that may arise in using them [7].

Other studies investigating consumer satisfaction have found that consumers will be more likely to attempt to use an SST if they are with a companion. In the case of older people, this is usually a family member. Of particular relevance here is finding that successful interactions bring a sense of achievement to both old and young users alike, but for older people it is more important than for younger people. Older consumers argue that using an SST successfully represents much more than just complet-ing a task and obtaining a service, it helps them feel independent and able to function within society, giving a feeling of self-efficacy [16].

On the whole, the rhetoric of the self-service management and marketing literature centres around understanding why people do, or do not, adopt SSTs. It makes concrete suggestions on how to encourage use. For example, it recommends that managers in enterprises deliberately close some manual service points, creating longer queues at those that are open, to encourage people try out the self-service option. In addition, it suggests mounting campaigns to attract young people by promoting the use of SSTs as 'fun' and 'cool'. Finally, in response to the finding that people who have had a bad experience will not return, it suggests staff training to try to explain to people why they have had difficulty in using the SST, and increase their self-confidence, rather than just performing the service for them [16].

However, since the literature shows that older people [18] have greater technology anxiety [19] and desire for interaction with a human rather than a machine [20], it has been recommended to deployers of SSTs that they simply avoid installing the technology where older people are the dominant user population [21]. There is no thought of designing or re-designing the machine or its interface and interaction mode, all the emphasis is on the users adopting and adapting to the machines. There is no mention of improving usability and accessibility.

5   Our Recommendations

We have presented an analysis of the reasons for the low level of accessibility in SSTs. We gathered information from suppliers and deployers, going out to trade fairs and meeting with suppliers and deployers of different types, and studying the academic literature that best represents the models under which the SST market operates.

Although awareness of accessibility and eAccessibility is low amongst both suppliers and deployers of SSTs, there is a body of research and guidelines available on this topic. However, this information is quite difficult to find. One of the aims of the European eAccess+ Network has been to create a source of information about accessibility and eAccessibility topics for all stakeholders, giving links to existing sources of information and providing brief commentaries on different sources. This has developed into the eAccess+ Hub (http://hub.eaccessplus.eu/wiki/Main_Page) which has a section devoted to SSTs (http://hub.eaccessplus.eu/wiki/Self_service_terminals). This provides information on approaches to implementing eAccessibility in the self-service technology area; case studies, examples of best practice that can provide inspiration and useful ideas; information of relevant policy and legislation, both at European and national levels; and standards and guidelines for developing and deploying accessible self-service technologies.

In addition, on the basis of our analyses, we have developed a set of recommendations for guiding efforts to increase the accessibility of the SSTs and self-service technologies in general.

Recommendation 1. Discourse on accessibility must be relevant for the SST industry.

We should tailor our discourse to industry concerns, such as the business case for accessibility (including return on investment, compliance with regulations, branding, customer loyalty, new business opportunities). Our messages must be oriented to ways of increasing revenue (by gaining more customers; by being seen to be socially responsible and ethically conscious), not losing revenue (by producing products and services that are usable by a greater number of users; and/or that comply with legislation and standards). The terminology also is different from that of researchers involved with older and disabled people, with "customer engagement" being a term more interesting to industry than "accessibility".

Recommendation 2. Make contact with well-established suppliers active in accessibility.

Those suppliers who have a long established history in SSTs are able to support the design and development costs of providing accessible solutions. However, they maintain that they are not asked by the deployers to supply accessibility features. It would be beneficial to understand more about why this is so, and to also explore the different ways suppliers can bring their influence to bear on increasing accessibility in SSTs via standards, assisting and educating deployers and so on.

Recommendation 3. Develop appropriate guidance for deployers of SSTs.
Appropriate guidance for deployers might include information about:

- the responsibility they bear to comply with legislation
- the demographics and the numbers of the population they exclude if they do not include accessibility features in the SSTs they deploy
- how to include accessibility in the tendering and procurement processes

Recommendation 4. Collect information about SST accessibility problems to be passed on to relevant stakeholders .
There is currently very little information about the accessibility of SSTs beyond the needs of people with physical disabilities. Stakeholders are often unaware of the problems that users are encountering. Individual users and user organisations need to be encouraged to give feedback to SST deployers, so they will have the necessary information to discuss their requirements with suppliers. In addition, given the nature of the industry, problems may be common across of range of deployment sectors, e.g. the soft keyboard affects airport check-in but is also found in some e-government and hotel check-in SSTs. In addition, it would be useful to collect information which looks to future uses of SSTs, e.g. the hybrid model where SSTs rely on users' own devices to complete transactions at SSTs. Such work would help to prevent inaccessibility being designed into new products, systems and services.

Recommendation 5. Make more targeted efforts within the SST industry.
We now have a clearer understanding of who should be our target groups within the SST industries, and their attitudes towards accessibility. We can better tailor our out-reach, in particular to:

- integrators: make them aware their responsibility to deployers to offer them packages inclusive of accessibility options, and for them to see this as a business opportunity.
- component suppliers: demonstrate how their products could be marketed to show that they could offer significant advantage to end users with concrete examples that are easy to implement and do not increase costs or require substantial redesign.

Recommendation 6. Raise the level of awareness from physical accessibility to eAccessibility.
Problems of physical accessibility that are easy to demonstrate and to visualise are easier to understand. However, stakeholders have little or no understanding of the accessibility of information and interaction in the digital domain (eAccessibility). There is much we have learnt from web accessibility that could be of assistance in making SSTs fully accessible. This information from web accessibility needs to be

formulated in a way that is appropriate for the SST domain and carried over to new trends in self-service, such as self service on personal mobile devices.

Recommendation 7. Work to change the perception in the SST industry that accessibility is only the responsibility of deployers.

We need to better understand the perception from the suppliers that accessibility is only the responsibility of the deployers, and work with deployers to gain insight into their needs. There needs to be cooperation between all stakeholders in the value chain of SSTs if accessibility problems are to be solved

6   Conclusions

The state of accessibility and in particular eAccessibility of the SST sector is currently relatively poor. We have found that awareness amongst the key stakeholder groups of suppliers and deployers of SSTs is quite low. We have developed a resource in the eAccess+ Hub on SST issues based on a set of interviews with stakeholders and an analysis of relevant literature to help address this lack of knowledge. Further, we have provided a set of recommendations that will help target research and practice in the area of SSTs.

Acknowledgements. This research was supported by the eAccess+ Thematic Network (www.eaccessplus.eu), an initiative of the European Commission under its ICT Policy Support Programme.

References

1. Curran, K., King, D.: Investigating the human computer interaction problems with automated teller machine (ATM) navigation menus. Computer and Information Science 1(2), 34–51 (2008)
2. RBR London, Global ATM market and forecasts 2008 as reported by ATM Marketplace (2013), http://www.atmmarketplace.com/article/220149/Growing-demand-for-cash-boosts-global-ATM-market
3. Sinha, M., Khor, K.-N., Amresh, A., Drachman, D., Frechette, A.: The use of a kiosk-model bilingual self-triage system in the pediatric emergency department. Pediatric Emergency Care 30(1), 63–68 (2014)
4. Davies, J., et al.: The Gartner CRM Vendor Guide (ID Number: G00167766) (2009), http://api.ning.com/files/BxRXMjCdcnsvaRagU5D-bDMGEFCChuyDket1Wr4kkowCLQDs6zGfuqLuukr*W2Czdl40v9mwmpyHdVzp0YZig8k1Gux5FgMm/the_gartner_crm_vendor_guide_167766.pdf
5. Bitner, M.J.: Service and technology: opportunities and paradoxes. Managing Service Quality 11(6), 37–279 (2001)
6. Slawsky, R.: Self Service Health Care (2013), http://global.networldalliance.com/downloads/white_papers/FrankMayer_Guide__Self-Service-Health-Care-for-Launch.pdf

7. Wang, C., Harris, J., Patterson, P.G.: Customer choice of self–service technology: the roles of situational influences and past experience. Journal of Service Management 23(1), 54–78 (2012)
8. Nicolau, H., Jorge, J.: Elderly text-entry performance on touchscreens. In: Proceedings of ASSETS 2012, October 22-24. ACM Press, Boulder Colorado (2012)
9. EUROSTAT. EU25 population aged 65 and over expected to double between 1995 and 2050. Eurostat News Release 129/(2006),
   http://epp.eurostat.ec.europa.eu/cache/ITY_PUBLIC/
   3-29092006-BP/EN/3-29092006-BP-EN.PDF
10. EUROSTAT. One in six of the EU working-age population report disability. Eurostat News Release 129/2006 (2003),
    http://epp.eurostat.ec.europa.eu/cache/ITY_PUBLIC/
    3-05122003-AP/EN/3-05122003-AP-EN.HTML
11. Darzentas, J., Petrie, H., Power, C.: Universal design of self-service terminals: attitudes of key stakeholders. In: Trends in Universal Design. Norwegian Directorate for Children, Youth and Family Affairs, Oslo (2013), http://www.bufetat.no/PageFiles/
    9564/Trends%20in%20Universal%20Design-%20PDF-
    %20lannsert%2016.%20januar.pdf
12. Bitner, M.J., Brown, S.W.: The evolution and discovery of services science in business schools. Communications of the ACM 49(7), 73–78 (2006)
13. Bitner, M.J., Ostrom, A.L., Meuter, M.L.: Implementing successful self-service technologies. Academy of Management Executive 16(4), 96–108 (2002)
14. Meuter, M.L., Bitner, M.J., Ostrom, A.L., Brown, S.W.: Choosing among alternative service delivery modes: an investigation of customer trial of self-service technologies. Journal of Marketing 69(2), 61–83 (2005)
15. Meuter, M.L., Ostrom, A.L., Rountree, R.I., Bitner, M.J.: Self-service technologies: Understanding customer satisfaction with technology based-service encounters. Journal of Marketing 64(3), 50–64 (2000)
16. Wang, C., Harris, J., Patterson, P.G.: The roles of habit, self-efficacy, and satisfaction in driving continued use of self-service technologies: a longitudinal study. Journal of Service Research 16(3), 400–414 (2013)
17. Robertson, N., Shaw, R.N.: Predicting the Likelihood of Voiced Complaints in the Self-Service Technology Context. Journal of Service Research 12, 100–116 (2009)
18. Dean, D.H.: Shopper age and the use of self-service technologies. Managing Service Quality 18(3), 225–238 (2008)
19. Oyedele, A., Simpson, P.M.: An empirical investigation of consumer control factors on intention to use selected self-service technologies. International Journal of Service Industry Management 18(3), 287–306 (2007)
20. Simon, F., Usurier, J.-C.: Cognitive, demographic and situational determinants of service customer preference for personal-in-contact over self-service technology. International Journal of Research in Marketing 24(2), 163–173 (2007)
21. Lee, H.-J., Cho, H.-J., Xu, W., Fairhurst, A.: The influence of consumer traits and demographics on intention to user retail self-service check-outs. Market Intelligence & Planning 28(1), 46–58 (2010)

Speaking the Language of Web Developers: Evaluation of a Web Accessibility Information Resource (WebAIR)

David Swallow[1], Christopher Power[1], Helen Petrie[1], Anna Bramwell-Dicks[1],
Lucy Buykx[1], Carlos A. Velasco[2], Aidan Parr[3], and Joshue O Connor[4]

[1] University of York, United Kingdom
{david.swallow,christopher.power,helen.petrie,
anna.bramwell-dicks,lucy.buykx}@york.ac.uk
[2] Fraunhofer Institute for Applied Information Technology (FIT), Germany
carlos.velasco@fit.fraunhofer.de
[3] Foundation for Assistive Technology, United Kingdom
aidan@fastuk.org
[4] National Council for the Blind of Ireland, Ireland
joshue.oconnor@ncbi.ie

Abstract. This paper describes the design and evaluation of a new accessibility information resource, the Web Accessibility Information Resource (WebAIR), for assisting web developers in the creation of accessible websites and applications. Evaluations were conducted with 26 web developers in which they had opportunity to use both WebAIR and an existing accessibility information resource, the Web Content Accessibility Guidelines, to perform accessibility testing on their own websites. The results indicate that a number of design decisions relating to the language, organisation and comprehensiveness of WebAIR have been successful in improving access to web accessibility information that supports web developers' practices.

Keywords: Web Accessibility, Web Developers, Web Accessibility Guidelines, Web Accessibility Information Resources.

1 Introduction

This paper presents the evaluation of a prototype information resource for helping web developers learn about web accessibility and supporting them in creating accessible websites. This resource was created as part of the i2web project[1], in which research was undertaken with web developers to understand their work practices and identify where support could be provided to them. In that work, it was highlighted that even though developers are aware of web accessibility, they struggle to develop websites that are accessible to people with disabilities [1]. A variety of contributing factors were reported and three key themes emerged as to why developers struggle with accessible web development. The first theme was that web accessibility resources do not speak the language of web developers and instead assume that

---

[1] http://i2web.eu/index.html

K. Miesenberger et al. (Eds.): ICCHP 2014, Part I, LNCS 8547, pp. 348–355, 2014.

developers are familiar with domain-specific concepts of web accessibility, such as understanding the functionality of a screen reader, or what is sufficient colour contrast between text and background. The second theme was that that web accessibility resources are often organised in ways that are different to how developers approach the creation of websites. While developers' practices are largely code-centric, web accessibility resources tend to use domain-specific groupings that are unfamiliar to web developers. The final theme was that while developers acknowledge that a substantial amount of work is necessary to make websites accessible, web accessibility resources tend to present too much information at once, which can be overwhelming when searching for specific solutions.

In order to address these issues, the i2web project created and evaluated an initial prototype of the Web Accessibility Information Resource (WebAIR), which is organised around the work practices of web developers and presents web accessibility information in developer-oriented language.

2   Related Work

Previous research has found that unclear and confusing guidelines are a major barrier to web accessibility [2, 4]. A study of 17 students taking part in a web accessibility course concluded that the Web Content Accessibility Guidelines 2.0 (WCAG 2.0) [3] are "far from testable for beginners" (p.8), attributing this to: difficulties in comprehending the language used in the guidelines; a lack of knowledge that is required to correctly evaluate the guidelines; and a reluctance to spend a lot of effort evaluating the guidelines [4]. A study of the usability of accessibility evaluation tools determined they do not make it easy for web developers to conduct web accessibility tests, due to unclear presentation of results and poor connections between identified problems and information on how to solve them [5]. Similarly, a study of the attitudes of web developers to accessibility highlighted difficulties in understanding the output of evaluation tools and stressed the need for clear descriptions of identified problems [6]. These studies demonstrate that there are problems in understanding and interpreting existing web accessibility information provided by tools and resources.

3   Design of WebAIR

Based on the requirements elicited in the i2web project [1], WebAIR was oriented towards web developers' workflows, specifically their tendency to structure their work according to the types of web content on which they are working, either during web development or testing. For WebAIR, 8 different types of web content were identified for categorising support information: forms, links, tables, images, text, multimedia, interactive content, time-limited content, within-page content and between-page content. A mapping was undertaken from existing WCAG 2.0 Success Criteria onto these categories, ensuring that coverage of existing guidelines was encapsulated in the new resource.

Each category was then populated with a list of questions for developers to use in checking their web content. For example, in the category Links, developers are asked:

Can you successfully access all links using the keyboard? The questions have been constructed to avoid the domain-specific language of web accessibility, instead the language uses web development terms or specific user actions in the interface. For each question there is a More Information page that provides developers with just-in-time training in web accessibility concepts. This allows developers to gradually learn about the domain of web accessibility and why they are undertaking specific web accessibility tests on their code while doing the tests.

Finally, in order to avoid overwhelming the developers with too much information, each More Information page contains one example solution drawn from the techniques provided in WCAG 2.0. While this is not as comprehensive in the variety of ways in which web accessibility can be achieved, it reduces the information overload problem that developers are currently encountering when trying to apply web accessibility principles and solutions to their web content.

4   Method

In order to understand whether or not the design decisions embodied in WebAIR improve access to web accessibility information for web developers, a within-participants study was undertaken. Each participant used an established web accessibility information resource, WCAG 2.0, and the new web developer-centric WebAIR. The reactions of web developers to the information resources were elicited using a combination of rating items and semi-structured interview questions.

4.1   Participants

26 web developers from the UK and Italy took part in the evaluation. The participants had between 1 and 14 years of experience of web development, with an average of 8 years (SD = 3.91). 6 participants worked for large enterprises, 15 worked for small-medium enterprises and 5 participants were self-employed freelance developers.

4.2   Materials

The evaluation was conducted using the WCAG 2.0 guidelines and WebAIR. For WCAG 2.0, participants used the official documentation provided by the W3C Web Accessibility Initiative (WAI) [3]. This multi-page website provides information on the 12 Guidelines and 61 Success Criteria (SC) of WCAG 2.0. Two pages accompany each SC: one on How to Meet that specific SC, serving as a quick reference for developers, and one on Understanding and implementing the SC.

For WebAIR, a website was created[2], comprising a main index page, listing all of the developer questions grouped by content type. Each question linked to a More Information page that contained the web accessibility support information and the

---

[2]   The prototype of WebAIR used in this evaluation is available at:
http://www.cs.york.ac.uk/hci/webair/prototype/
A revised version of WebAIR, based on the outcome of this investigation, is available at:
http://www.cs.york.ac.uk/hci/webair/

web accessibility solutions. In total there were 112-questions, with 43 having one or more follow-up questions depending on the outcome.

In order to control for the appearance of the resources, WebAIR was presented using a similar colour scheme and style to the W3C standard template.

4.3   Procedure

The study took place at a location convenient to each participant, for example their office, home or a café. Participants were encouraged to use their own computers and development tools, and they were asked to access a recent website they had developed.

Participants were introduced to each information resource in turn. For each one, they were provided with a demonstration of the structure and the locations of information before being given 10 minutes to work with the information resource in testing one of their own websites. The order of exposure to the information resources was counterbalanced to avoid fatigue or training effects.

Immediately after using each information resource, participants were asked to complete a short questionnaire comprising 9 five-point Likert items: Usefulness (1 = very low to 5 = very high), Ease of Use (1 = very difficult to 5 = very easy), Navigability (1 = very low to 5 = very high), Understandability (1 = very low to 5 = very high), Completeness (1 = very low to 5 = very high), Amount of Information Provided (1 = far too little to 5 = far too much), Number of Items to Test (1 = far too few to 5 = far too many), Organisation (1 = very unclear to 5 = very clear), and Likelihood of Using the web accessibility information resource (1 = very unlikely to 5 = very likely). Participants were also asked a number of open-ended questions to explore their opinions about the different properties of each resource. The sessions lasted approximately 60 minutes.

5   Results

Figure 1, below, shows the mean ratings for the two resources on the Likert items. A one-way MANOVA was used to investigate the effect of the type of resource on the Likert ratings. This showed a significant multivariate effect of type of resource ($F = 6.62$, df = 9,38, $p < .005$). Overall, the web developers rated the WebAIR resource significantly highly than the WCAG 2.0 resource (mean for WebAIR = 4.01, SD = 0.84; mean for WCAG 2.0 = 3.50, SD = 1.13). The univariate tests showed significant effects of type of resource on ratings of all of the Likert ratings except the number of items to test. WebAIR was rated significantly higher on usefulness ($F = 5.12$, $p < .05$, all tests df = 1,46), ease of use ($F = 47.45$, $p < .05$), navigability ($F = 13.14$, $p < .05$), understandability ($F = 36.92$, $p < .05$), organisation ($F = 18.99$, $p < .05$), and likelihood of using ($F = 8.34$, $p < .05$). WCAG 2.0 was rated significantly higher on completeness ($F = 7.59$, $p < .05$), and amount of information ($F = 15.86$, $p < .05$). These findings were elaborated in the responses to the open-ended questions.

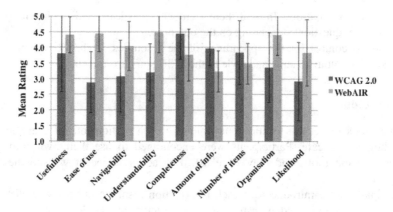

Fig. 1. Mean ratings of WCAG 2.0 and WebAIR on a range of properties

5.1   Language of the Accessibility Information Resources

The developers were asked to comment on the understandability of the language used in the information resources. One said that working with WCAG 2.0 is "fairly easy" but only if "you know what everything means." Another said: "It feels like you need a good understanding of accessibility before you can approach this, otherwise you will get lost." According to one developer, web accessibility-specific principles, such as "meaningful sequence" were not clearly defined. Another developer said: "I know that there's words that are defined in the glossary. But for actually just scanning through it, some of the language is a little bit dense." This was supported by another developer, who said: "when they started speaking about screen contrast ratios and things like that, unless you've got that concept then it doesn't make sense."

17 developers stated that they were comfortable with the language of WebAIR. One developer said: "It makes sense to us as an audience. This is the terminology that we use all the time. This is our jargon." Another said it was: "easy for someone who doesn't know a lot about accessibility to understand." The question-based phrasing of WebAIR was particularly appealing to five developers, one of whom felt the questions were "more intuitive" and "easier to understand". One developer felt WebAIR promoted "a good level of understanding", adding, "it wasn't so heavy on so much difficult language, so that was good."

Despite orienting the language towards web development terminology, six developers felt that WebAIR "still has to find its audience". One developer said: "some of the sections were more simplistic than the level I would say is about right. It is targeted at someone who knows slightly less than me, someone slightly less technical than me." Another queried why definitions are provided for basic terms, such as link and form, arguing, "even the general public would get some of that stuff." One developer believed that WebAIR underestimates the abilities of developers, stating: "It depends who you are aiming it at but people who are developing on a day-to-day basis are going to have intermediate to advanced awareness of HTML."

5.2   Organisation of the Accessibility Information Resources

Eight developers felt the organisation of WCAG 2.0 is "logical", "sensible" or "fine for that kind of specification-style document" but 15 developers found it difficult to extract relevant information. One developer said: "all the information is there but not in the same place, it's all distributed", adding, "you have to know to go through these 3 or 4 different things to find things." Three developers felt WCAG 2.0 has a "top-down" organisation that, according to one, is: "broken down in a logical fashion for describing the problems, but not for how you would fix them." One developer felt that practical information is buried too deep in the documentation, stating: "the techniques [in WCAG 2.0] tend to be really useful but the problem is they are drilled down at the bottom. You've got to mine through everything to get to them."

16 developers stated that they were satisfied with the organisation of WebAIR. One felt the grouping of information by content category made it easier to apply, saying: "it fits the structure of how I work. It's simple to follow, it's broken down into sections that can be easily skipped if they are not entirely relevant and when you're not sure why it needs to be done or how to do it, the information is there." This was echoed by another developer, who said: "I wouldn't know if it was in the 'Robust' section [of WCAG] or one of the others, whereas WebAIR makes more sense because you can think 'right, I'm working on a form, let's quickly go through the form stuff.'" 12 developers appreciated the prioritisation of practical information in WebAIR. One said: "this is a bottom-up approach, very quickly describing what problems you're likely to see, yes/no answers for just about everything."

Although the majority of developers found the organisation of WebAIR by content type useful, not all of the categories proved meaningful to them. 11 developers struggled with the "within pages" and "between pages" categories as they found these terms unusual. In addition to this, four developers struggled to understand the difference between "interactive content" and "multimedia", with one commenting that the latter was: "a dated concept, reminiscent of CD-ROMs from the late 90s."

5.3   Comprehensiveness of the Accessibility Information Resources

None of the developers questioned the completeness and thoroughness of WCAG 2.0, however, 19 developers stated that it presents an overwhelming or off-putting amount of information at once. One said: "I think there's an awful lot of information there but it's not critical information, it's just all there." Another commented that WCAG 2.0 "presents too much upfront" and suggested: "It's probably better to present a smaller amount and let people go off and study more info if they want." One developer felt the information in WCAG 2.0 "becomes redundant through being too much", while another felt it "can overwhelm you and make you feel this is a bit of an insurmountable thing to actually meet these guidelines."

16 developers were satisfied with the amount of information in WebAIR, which many of them felt was "manageable" or "a do-able amount". 18 developers felt the number of content categories (10) is appropriate and the number of questions within them (an average of 11) is reasonable. 16 developers also felt the amount of help documentation for each question is appropriate, with one commenting it is: "enough to get the gist of something" but "not too much to make you run away."

Despite being much smaller than WCAG 2.0, five developers felt the number of items to test (represented by the questions) in WebAIR is still too many. One commented: "I think to run through it for every single site, 100+ questions are perhaps too many. You're not going to want to do 100+ questions if you've not spent that long working on it."

6   Discussion

Both the quantitative and qualitative findings of this study indicate that the design decisions taken in relation to the language, organisation and comprehensiveness of WebAIR may be successful in improving the use of web accessibility information for web developers by using ways that fit into their working practices.

The developers' reactions to the change in language from domain-specific language to more development-centric language were largely positive, with many finding WebAIR more understandable and easier to use than WCAG 2.0. However, some of the language in WebAIR was found to be too basic for web developers, and more appropriate for a general audience. In avoiding domain-specific language, there is evidently a danger in over-simplifying the more familiar terminology to the extent that developers no longer feel it is relevant to developers.

The organisation of the information by web content types in WebAIR made more sense to the developers than established web accessibility categories. They found it relatively easy to navigate the information by category and quickly gain access to what they needed to do. However, the categories that did not correspond directly to specific types of content, such as those relating to within-page and between-page navigation, were considered too abstract or ambiguous to be useful. While many web accessibility problems correspond directly to specific types of content, some issues are broader in scope and relate to an entire webpage or website. Further work is needed to identify appropriate organisational structures for orienting developers within the information resource for these more global web page issues.

The results of this study are consistent with previous findings [1] that established web accessibility resources overwhelm web developers with the amount of information presented, undoubtedly in attempting to provide comprehensive information about web accessibility. Despite WebAIR being less comprehensive than the WCAG 2.0 documentation, both the ratings and the interview responses showed that developers still found it to be too large. From the interview responses, it is clear that this is partly due to the fact that web developers test their code after development of a page is nearly complete, as opposed to testing during development. Thus, further work is needed to integrate accessible design and iterative testing into development tasks and tools, something that the design of WebAIR could support.

7   Conclusions

WebAIR was designed to support web developers in creating more accessible websites. It was designed to do this by presenting just-in-time web accessibility information in the language of web developers and in an organisation that matched their workflow.

An evaluation of WebAIR indicates that these design choices have been largely successful in providing developers with a resource in which they can easily find information that is useful to them.

The evaluation has also highlighted potential areas for improvement of development processes in general. There is still a tendency among developers to see web accessibility as something to be done after completing the creation of a web page. There is a need to integrate resources like WebAIR into development tools, such as those produced in the i2web project.

In conclusion, WebAIR is a promising prototype information resource that has been designed with developers in mind. It provides a much-needed complement to existing web accessibility resources by designing and presenting information in ways that better support web developers in creating accessible websites.

References

1. Petrie, H., Power, C., Swallow, D.: i2web Deliverable 3.2: Requirements for web developers and web commissioners in ubiquitous Web 2.0 design and development (2011), http://i2web.eu/downloads/201201_I2Web_D32.pdf
2. Lazar, J., Dudley-Sponaugle, A., Greenidge, K.: Web accessibility: a study of webmaster perceptions. Computers in Human Behaviour 20(2), 269–288 (2004)
3. W3C/WAI. Web Content Accessibility Guidelines 2.0 (2008), http://www.w3.org/TR/WCAG20/
4. Alonso, F., Fuertes, J.L., Gonzalez, L.A., Martinez, L.: On the testability of WCAG 2.0 for beginners. In: Proceedings of the 2010 International Cross Disciplinary Conference on Web Accessibility (W4A) (W4A 2010). ACM, New York (2010)
5. Petrie, H., King, N., Velasco, C., Gappa, H., Nordbrock, G.: The usability of accessibility evaluation tools. In: Proceedings of the 4th International Conference on Universal Access in Human-Computer Interaction: Applications and Services, Beijing, China, July 22-27 (2007)
6. Trewin, S., Cragun, B., Swart, C., Brezin, J., Richards, J.: Accessibility challenges and tool features: An IBM web developer perspective. In: Proceedings of the 2010 International Cross Disciplinary Conference on Web Accessibility (W4A). ACM Press, Raleigh (2010)

A Multimodal Tablet–Based Application for the Visually Impaired for Detecting and Recognizing Objects in a Home Environment

Rabia Jafri[1] and Syed Abid Ali[2]

[1] Department of Information Technology, King Saud University, Riyadh, Saudi Arabia
rabia.ksu@gmail.com
[2] Araware LLC, Wilmington, Delaware, U.S.A.
syedabidali@gmail.com

Abstract. Object recognition solutions for the visually impaired based on a single modality cannot provide optimal performance under all circumstances, since each modality is best suited for particular usage scenarios. An object recognition application for the visually impaired, meant for a RFID-enabled tablet, which combines three approaches – RFID-based, visual-tag computer vision based and non-visual tag computer vision based – into a single piece of software is, therefore, presented in this paper. This solution has the benefits of being portable, accessible, low cost (the user needs only an RFID-enabled tablet, some inexpensive passive RFID tags and some visual tags (which can be printed out for free)) and more robust in a wider range of conditions than the approaches it is comprised of. The application will be adapted to other mobile platforms and devices (e.g., RFID-enabled smartphones) in the future.

Keywords: Object Recognition, Computer Vision, Blind, Visually Impaired, Mobile Application, Assistive Technologies, RFID, Visual Tags, Multi-Modal Recognition.

1 Introduction

One major challenge faced by the visually impaired is detecting and recognizing generic objects in their environment - the inability to do so causes them emotional distress, undermines their autonomy, and exposes them to injury. Though a sighted caregiver may be available to help out some of the time, however it is not possible or desirable for such a human aide to be available at all times (indeed, according to a recent report, 26% of blind adults in the United States live alone [1]). Commercial assistive technologies developed for this purpose are generally prohibitively expensive (given that 90% of the visually impaired live in developing countries earning low wages [2]) and/or require a steep learning curve (especially for the elderly, which comprise 65% of this community [2]). These facts delineate an urgent need to develop solutions which are cost-effective, intuitive and make use of commonly available technologies.

K. Miesenberger et al. (Eds.): ICCHP 2014, Part I, LNCS 8547, pp. 356–359, 2014.

RFID-based [3,4] and computer vision-based systems [5,6,7,8] have emerged as some of the most promising solutions for object recognition for the visually impaired- in particular, for indoor environments [9]. Nevertheless, both these kinds of solutions have their pros and cons as explained below.

Computer vision-based solutions are generally cost-effective, accessible, require little or no infrastructure, are typically wearable, and most of them can be installed or embedded into existing mobile computing devices. However, their performance deteriorates rapidly in uncontrolled real-world environments due to imaging factors such as motion blur, image resolution, video noise, etc., as well as changes in conditions such as illumination, orientation and scale Other limitations include vulnerability to occlusion problems and high computational cost.

A particular class of these approaches identifies objects by unique visual tags af-fixed to them (see [10] for a detailed review of these solutions for the visually impaired). Tag-based systems require relatively less computational power and storage space than their non-tag-based counterparts and are ideal for tasks that entail differentiating among a group of objects which feel the same but have different visual encoding and contents, (e.g., searching for a particular DVD in one's DVD collection). Moreover, many of these approaches do not require tags to be explicitly placed on store-bought products since these objects already have unique visual tags in the form of product barcodes. Furthermore, visual tags can be conveniently generated and printed out utilizing free online software thus, avoiding the hassle and cost involved in the purchase of non-visual tags (such as RFID or infra-red ones). However, visual tag-based systems suffer from some inherent limitations: They require careful, a-priori selection of significant objects and the correct placement of tags on those objects, their use is restricted to surroundings where objects have been tagged, the tags have to be in line-of-sight of the camera, and the tags cannot be embedded in objects (which may be aesthetically unappealing).

RFID–based solutions offer the following advantages: RFID tags are omnidirectional, do not need to be within line of sight of the RFID reader and can be embedded in the object. On the other hand, even though passive RFID tags are relatively cheap, the cost of these tags quickly becomes prohibitive if hundreds of items need to be tagged. Tagging numerous objects in a limited range may also lead to information overload with the user being unable to interpret and utilize the information about hundreds of objects presented to him simultaneously [11]. Also, such a system can operate only in a restricted environment where objects have been tagged.

It is clear - in light of the above discussion - that a system based exclusively on one of the above strategies cannot provide optimal performance under all circumstances. Rather, each of these solutions is best suited for particular kinds of tasks. For example, for locating important items in the house which the user cannot afford to misplace (such as his keys, wallet, vital medication, etc.), an RFID-based system would be preferable because of its greater robustness to occlusion and orientation changes. However, for finding generic household such as plates, glasses, cleaning products, stapler, chairs, etc., a non-tag-based computer vision approach would be the most appropriate. Moreover, for tasks that involve distinguishing among several items which are similar to each other in shape, size and texture (e.g., cans containing different soups), a visual tag-based strategy would work the best.

We are, therefore, developing an application which combines all three approaches – RFID-based, visual-tag computer vision based and non-visual tag computer vision based – into a single piece of software. This application is currently being developed for a RFID-enabled tablet - a relatively inexpensive mobile device which many users may already own. Our aim is to create an affordable, portable application that will greatly enhance the ability of the visually impaired to recognize objects in their home surroundings, boosting their self-confidence and making them more self-reliant.

The rest of the paper is organized as follows: Section 2 describes our application. Section 3 identifies some directions for future work.

2   Application Description

We are developing an application which combines an RFID-based, visual-tag computer vision based and non-visual tag computer vision based approach to aid visually impaired individuals in detecting and recognizing objects in their home environment.

The application can be used in two ways: 1) The user can choose the method for recognizing an object based on his task (as described above); the application would then proceed to identify the object using the selected approach; 2) If the user simply wants to find out what object is in front of him, he can point the tablet towards the object; the application first invokes the RFID-based method to identify the object; if that fails, it then invokes the visual-tag based technique; if that does not yield any results either, then finally it calls the non-tag based computer vision approach to recognize the object – in other words, it starts with the least computationally expensive approach and then moves towards progressively more expensive ones.

The application is being developed on an Android platform. For the visual tag-based method, the visual tags consist of semacodes [12] and the associated semacode decoding software (available for free) is being integrated into the application. For the non-visual tag computer vision based method, a SURF-based approach [13] is being employed. The RFID reader software is already present on the tablet. The front end integrates all three methods and provides various options to invoke them as described above. A speech-based interface is being used for communication between the user and the application.

The application would be available online for download and installation on a tablet PC. Upon installation, the user can immediately start using the application's non-visual tag computer vision based module. Options to purchase passive RFID tags and a link to a resource to print out visual tags would also be provided to enable the user to utilize the RFID-based and visual tag-based modules.

The strength of this application lies in its robustness to a wider range of conditions on account of its combining three different techniques as well as its low cost and accessibility: the user needs only an RFID-enabled tablet, some inexpensive passive RFID tags and some visual tags (which can be printed out for free).

3   Future Work

We plan to conduct usability testing of this application with visually impaired users and enhance it based on their feedback. We also intend to adapt it to other mobile platforms and devices (e.g., RFID-enabled smartphones).

References

1. Zuckerman, D.M.: Blind Adults in America: Their Lives and Challenges. National Center for Policy Research for Women & Families, Washington DC (2004)
2. WHO Media Center. Visual impairment and blindness: Fact sheet number 282, http://www.who.int/mediacentre/factsheets/fs282/en/
3. Murad, M., Rehman, A., Shah, A.A., Ullah, S., Fahad, M., Yahya, K.M.: RFAIDE – An RFID Based Navigation and Object Recognition Assistant for Visually Impaired People. In: Proceedings of ICET 2011, pp. 1–4. IEEE (2011)
4. Lawson, M.A., Do, E.Y.-L., Marston, J.R., Ross, D.A.: Helping Hands versus ERSP Vision: Comparing object recognition technologies for the visually impaired. In: Stephanidis, C. (ed.) Posters, Part I, HCII 2011. CCIS, vol. 173, pp. 383–388. Springer, Heidelberg (2011)
5. Sudol, J., Dialameh, O., Blanchard, C., Dorcey, T.: Looktel - Comprehensive platform for computer-aided visual assistance. In: Conference on Computer Vision and Pattern Recognition Workshops (CVPRW), vol. I, pp. 73–80. IEEE Computer Society (2010)
6. Schauerte, B., Martinez, M., Constantinescu, A., Stiefelhagen, R.: An Assistive Vision System for the Blind That Helps Find Lost Things. In: Miesenberger, K., Karshmer, A., Penaz, P., Zagler, W. (eds.) ICCHP 2012, Part II. LNCS, vol. 7383, pp. 566–572. Springer, Heidelberg (2012)
7. Winlock, T., Christiansen, E., Belongie, S.: Toward real-time grocery detection for the visually impaired. In: Conference on Computer Vision and Pattern Recognition Workshops (CVPRW), vol. I, pp. 49–56. IEEE Computer Society (2010)
8. Bigham, J., Jayant, C., Miller, A., White, B., Yeh, T.: VizWiz: LocateIt - enabling blind people to locate objects in their environment. In: Conference on Computer Vision and Pattern Recognition Workshops (CVPRW), vol. I, pp. 65–72. IEEE Computer Society (2010)
9. Jafri, R., Ali, S.A., Arabnia, H.R., Fatima, S.: Computer Vision-based object recognition for the visually impaired in an indoors environment: a survey. In: The Visual Computer. Springer, Heidelberg (2013), DOI: 10.1007/s00371-013-0886-1
10. Jafri, R., Ali, S.A., Arabnia, H.R.: Computer Vision-based object recognition for the visually impaired using visual tags. In: Arabnia, H., Deligiannidis, L., Lu, J., Tinetti, F., You, J., et al. (eds.) Proceedings of IPCV 2013, pp. 400–406. CSREA Press, USA (2013)
11. McDaniel, T.L., Kahol, K., Villanueva, D., Panchanathan, S.: Integration of RFID and computer vision for remote object perception for individuals who are blind. In: Proceedings of the 2008 Ambi-Sys workshop on Haptic User Interfaces in Ambient Media Systems (HAS 2008), pp. 1–10. ICST Brussels, Belgium (2008)
12. Semacode Corporation, http://semacode.com/about/
13. Bay, H., Ess, A., Tuytelaars, T., Gool, L.V.: Speeded-Up Robust Features (SURF). Computer Vision and Image Understanding 110(3), 346–359 (2008)

Usage Situation Changes of Touchscreen Computers in Japanese Visually Impaired People: Questionnaire Surveys in 2011-2013

Takahiro Miura[1,2], Masatsugu Sakajiri[3], Haruo Matsuzaka[3],
Murtada Eljailani[3], Kazuki Kudo[3], Naoya Kitamura[3],
Junji Onishi[3], and Tsukasa Ono[3]

[1] Graduate School of Information Science and Technology / Institute of Gerontology,
The University of Tokyo, 7-3-1 Hongo, Bunkyo-ku, Tokyo 113-8656, Japan
miu@cyber.t.u-tokyo.ac.jp
[2] National Institute of Advanced Industrial Science and Technology (AIST),
1-1-1 Higashi, Tsukuba, Ibaraki 305-8566, Japan
[3] Faculty of Health Science, Tsukuba University of Technology, 4-12-7 Kasuga,
Tsukuba, Ibaraki 305-8521, Japan
{sakajiri,ohnishi,ono}@cs.k.tsukuba-tech.ac.jp,
{mh113203,em092310,kk102304,kn122303}@cc.k.tsukuba-tech.ac.jp

Abstract. This paper demonstrates the usage of touchscreen interfaces in the Japanese visually impaired population by means questionnaire surveys conducted in 2011, 2012, and 2013. In 2011 and 2013, we carried out usage situations of touchscreens and the reasons why some of them did not use it. The surveys in 2012 and 2013 comprised the questionnaire items regarding specific manipulation situations of touchscreens. Some of the results indicate that an increasing number of visually impaired people used and required to use touchscreen computers; some of them did not want to use it because they were satisfied with conventional cell phones, and because they are waiting for the device which can feedback tactually; the users of touchscreen computers with total and partial visual impairments mainly uses double-tapping after tracing for selecting buttons and objects; The proper uses and manipulations of smartphones and tablet computers mainly depends on the application usability and the screen size, respectively.

Keywords: visually impaired people, touchscreen computers, usage conditions.

1 Introduction

Touchscreen computers such as smartphones and tablet computers are characterized by intuitive manipulation and high customizability. Currently, most predominant operating systems for touchscreen computers such as iOS (Apple) or Android (Google) ensure accessibility for people with visual impairments. These accessibility functions include screen magnification software and screen reader functions such as VoiceOver [1] and TalkBack [2]. These accessibility functions

K. Miesenberger et al. (Eds.): ICCHP 2014, Part I, LNCS 8547, pp. 360–368, 2014.

have improved with each version and the accessibility environment for visually impaired people is gradually improving. For example, iOS 5 and 6 provided input support function named AssistiveTouch for users with upper limb disorder, and the latter provided a Japanese-specific version of phonetic and exploratory reading of *Kanji* as a localized VoiceOver function [3], respectively. Some Japanese text-to-speech applications can also be installed to provide this function on Android touchscreen computers as well [4,5].

Although it has been reported that some visually impaired people are interested in and use touchscreen interfaces [6], it remains unclear how most of them use these interfaces and what properties they require from touchscreen interfaces. This is because manipulation using accessibility software is different from manipulation by sighted people. These facts lead to an insufficient amount of information about these devices being distributed among visually impaired people. As a result, specialized learning materials and lecture courses for touchscreen computers are insufficient. Ujima et al. and Miyake et al. have recently taken place the lecture courses of touchscreen computers for people with partial visual impairments in Japan [7,8], but the courses for totally blind people have hardly yet been held [9]. To ensure that accessible touchscreen computers for the visually impaired will become prevalent, it is necessary to investigate the usage situation of touchscreen computers on the visually impaired.

In this paper, our final objective is to propose effective application guidelines for touchscreen interfaces such as smartphones and tablet computers. We particularly aim to demonstrate touchscreen interface usage and interaction situations of touchscreen interface in the Japanese visually impaired population by means questionnaire surveys conducted in 2011, 2012, and 2013. In 2011 and 2013, we carried out usage situations of touchscreen computers and the reasons why some of them did not use it. The surveys in 2012 and 2013 comprised the questionnaire items regarding specific manipulation situations of touchscreen computers. Our research questions are as follows:

- How about ownership ratio change of touchscreen computers in Japanese visually impaired people?
- What kind of impressions of touchscreen computers do visual impaired non-owners find?
- What kind of gestures were preferred by visually impaired people, and are there the usage differences among visual conditions and duration of use of touchscreen computers?
- How do the some visually impaired users of both smartphones and tablet computers use for the different purpose?

2 Questionnaire Survey

In the survey, we demonstrated the usage and interaction situations of smartphones and tablet computers in the visually impaired population by three questionnaires conducted in 2011, 2012, and 2013. This paper reports some parts of the results.

2.1   Objectives

The objective of the three questionnaire was to collect the following data.

Common items in the questionnaire of 2011, 2012, and 2013

1. The individual characteristics of the participants: age, gender, disability condition, etc.
2. The usage conditions of touchscreen computers: current OS, in-use accessibility functions, location and situation of usage, etc.
3. The reasons not to use smartphones and tablet computers: the impression to these interfaces, etc.

Items investigated in different years

2011 The usage conditions of information and communication technologies (ICTs) such as personal computers, traditional cell phones, and touchscreen computers: current device models, in-use accessibility functions, desired functions, reasons for not using touchscreen computers, etc.

2012, 2013 The specific usage conditions of touchscreen computers: frequently used gestures, impressions of screen readers, etc.

2013 The different manipulation purposes of touchscreen computers in visually impaired users of both smartphones and tablet computers.

In this study, a traditional cell phone is defined as a mobile phone consisting of a display and hardware keyboard while a touchscreen computer is defined as a mobile device that does not have a hardware keyboard.

2.2   Participants

One hundred and forty (100 males and 40 females), Fifty one (36 males and 15 females), and One hundred and eighty five (132 males and 53 females) visually impaired persons, consisting of university students and personnel at NPOs for ICT penetration among visually impaired people, participated in the investigation of 2011, 2012, and 2013, respectively.

2.3   Method

The questionnaire items were determined by discussion among the authors (including totally blind persons) with reference to previous studies [11,10]. The questionnaire items numbered fifty-four (2011), thirty (2012), and forty (2013) were written in Japanese. The questionnaire was distributed in a computer-based electronic text file format, by e-mail. The participants completed the questionnaire on their own computer and returned it to the authors. Approval of the survey questionnaire was obtained from the Tsukuba University of Technology Ethics Board, and all participants had consented to participate in the survey. These surveys were conducted from 2011.12 to 2012.1, 2012.12 to 2013.1, and 2013.12 to 2014.1.

2.4 Results and Discussion

This paper mainly state the following results obtained by the questionnaire conducted in 2012 and 2013: Spread of touchscreen computers and preferable gestures in visually impaired people. The specific results of the questionnaire in 2011 were stated in [10].

Spread of Touchscreen Computers. The numbers (rates) of participants who used traditional mobiles, personal computers, and touchscreen computers (i.e., smartphones and tablet computers) in 2012 were 50 (98.0%), 50 (98.0%), and 24 (47.1%), respectively. Compared with the results obtained in 2011 [10], the rates of participants who possessed a touchscreen device increased by more than three times (from 12.9% to 47.1%) over one year.

Similar increasing tendencies can also be observed in Fig. 1. A cross-tabulation of reported visual conditions and the usage condition of touchscreen devices is presented in the upper part of Table 1 and shows that there is no significant difference between the reported visual conditions (Fisher's exact test, $p > 0.05$). However, as shown in Table 2, people with total blindness or those who can only perceive light stimuli tended to own iOS devices, while other partially visually impaired people owned a rakuraku smartphone (a Japanese-specific accessible smartphone for people with disabilities and the elderly). This is because iOS devices have a comparatively useful screen reader while the rakuraku smartphone has an eye-friendly interface but few screen reader applications, according to the participants' comments.

According to the results in 2013, seventy participants (37.8%) owned touchscreen computers; sixty-four (34.6%), twenty-five (13.5%), and nineteen (10.3%) of them owned a smartphone, a tablet computer, and the both two. This reason that the owners' rates in 2013 were less than that in 2012 were because of the number of the participants. In 2012, as a result, the survey gathered the innovators and early adopters of touchscreen users with visual impairments. The mean use periods of smartphones and tablet computers in the participants in 2013 were almost the same: 1.51 years (S.D.: 1.15) in smartphone users, and 1.46 years (S.D.: 1.16) in tablet users. These results also suggested that touchscreen users sharply increased from 2011 to 2012 and the main reason may be the release of iOS 6 that provides a Japanese specific version of explanatory expressions.

Impressions of Touchscreen Computers in Visual Impaired Non-Owners. Of the participants who did not have touchscreen computers (27 persons), twenty-three (45.1%) had never touched them and four (7.8%) had tried them but did not own them. Fig. 2 shows that 65.2% of the participants wanted to use touchscreen computers. This result, when compared to the result of questionnaire conducted in 2011 (50.0%) [10], implies that the rates of visually impaired people who do not own their own touchscreen devices but are interested in the computer is increasing. Of the participants who did not want to use a touchscreen computer, 66.7% answered that they did not because they were satisfied with traditional mobile phones and needed buttons such as a hardware keyboard. This tendency is the same as the questionnaire conducted in 2011 [10].

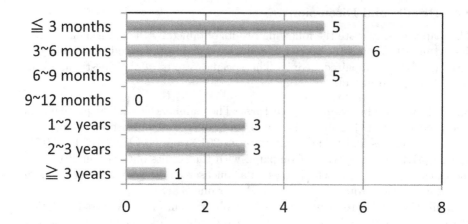

Fig. 1. Duration of use of touchscreen computer

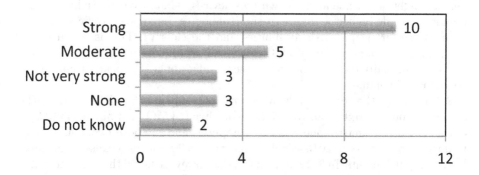

Fig. 2. Willingness to use touchscreen computer

Table 1. Reported visual condition of participants versus usage status (upper) and use experience (lower) of touchscreen computers

	Totally blind	Partially blind
In use	10	13
Not in use	13	15
In possession	10	14
Experienced but not in possession	2	2
No use experience	11	12

Preferable Gestures Gestures used by participants are shown in Fig. 3. With respect to button/icon selection (Fig. 3a), most of the participants (55.0%) traced the screen to search for the position of the button/icon, then selected

Table 2. Reported visual condition of participants versus touchscreen computers owned by participants

		Totally blind or light stimuli	Other
iOS devices	In use	12	5
($p = 0.09 < 0.10$)	Not in use	2	5
Android devices	In use	2	2
($p = 1.00$)	Not in use	10	8
Rakuraku smartphone	In use	0	3
($p = 0.06 < 0.10$)	Not in use	14	7
Other	In use	0	0
($p = 1.00$)	Not in use	14	10

Table 3. Reported visual condition of participants versus referable gestures to select a button/icon

	Totally	Partially blind
Trace the screen to find the position of a button/icon, then select it by double tap.	8	2
Search for a button/icon by Left/Right flick, then select by double tap.	1	4

it with a double tap. In addition, 15.0% and 25.0% of them used the similar gestures of split-tapping and searching objects by flick, respectively. As shown in Figs. 3b and 3c, tracing and then double tapping was most preferred by 57.9% and 30.4% of the participants when in edit mode and inputting characters, respectively. According to Figs. 3a and 3b, the participants said they preferred double-tap, flick, and split-tap in that order. Particularly, partially visually impaired users tended to select trace and double-tap more often than flick and double-tap, compared to partially visually impaired users (Table 3, p = 0.09 < 0.10). This may be because partially visually impaired users can trace and find the position of targets by residual visual sense. On the other hand, totally blind users may tend to search for objects by verbal commands. In the case of page browsing (Fig. 3d), most (76.2%) of them selected swiping vertically and horizontally with three fingers. No significant difference was observed between totally and partially visually impaired users. As shown in Fig. 3e, most of them did not use zooming in and out gestures. However, the participants with partial visual impairment used this gesture significantly more than those with total blindness ($p < 0.01$), as shown in Table 4.

Proper Use of Smartphones and Tablet Computers The 36% of the participants who used two kinds of touchscreen computers pointed to a reason of the application usability. Most of them indicated that telephone call (84.2%)

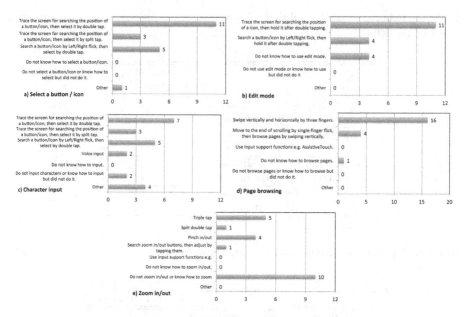

Fig. 3. Preferable gestures of participants

Table 4. Reported visual condition of participants versus usage condition of zoom gestures

	Totally blind	Partially blind
Use zoom in/out	3	8
Do not use it	9	1

and mail (73.7%) functions were mainly used in either touchscreen. Excluding the reason of the application usability, some participants properly used on predicted battery life, some stated that it is troublesome to switch many applications and is easy to use particular applications in each touchscreen, and the others used unique functions provided by careers including application of identifying bills, mobile wallet, and one-segment data broadcast receiver.

Character input methods gestures on screen keyboard did not depend on the size of touchscreen computers. Most of the smartphone and tablet computer users mainly uses split-tapping and double-tapping after tracing. Some low-vision participants used the same gesture as the sighted users employed. On the other hand, character input methods on smartphones and tablet computers were different. In both cases, most of the participants employed screen keyboard regardless of screen size (smartphone: 37% and tablet computer: 56%). However, second choices of input methods were different: 32% and 29% of the smartphone users selected voice input method and double-tapping after flicking gesture, while 36% of the tablet users employed external hardware keyboard and less of them used the voice input. We assume that input methods depend on the place to use. Many of the smartphone users manipulate their smartphone at various places with handheld conditions while Many of the tablet users use their device at stable places with their tablet on the desk or table. The future study should investigate the specific conditions to use.

3 Conclusions

Questionnaire surveys were conducted to clarify the touchscreen interface usage and interaction situations in the Japanese visually impaired population in 2011, 2012, and 2013. This paper stated the following parts of the results:

- An increasing number of visually impaired people have become used or required to use touchscreen computers. According to the mean use periods of smartphones and tablet computers in the participants in 2013, touchscreen users sharply increased from 2011 to 2012 and the main reason may be the release of iOS 6 that provided a Japanese specific explanatory expressions.
- Some of the visually impaired non-owners did not want to use it because they were satisfied with conventional cell phones, and because they are waiting for the device which can feedback tactually.
- The users of touchscreen computers with total and partial visual impairments mainly uses double-tapping after tracing for selecting buttons and objects.
- The proper uses of smartphones and tablet computers mainly depends on the application usability. However, there were various reasons of these proper uses including battery life differences and preferences of the users' likings. The preferable character input methods depended on the touchscreen size. Most of the users of smartphones and tablet computers employed software keyboard, but voice input methods and external hardware keyboard were their second choices, respectively.

This paper described the some parts of the results but could not fully stated the results of three-year questionnaire survey. Future work includes summarizing the results and then to establish a guideline for effective application design, learning materials and lecture courses of touchscreen interfaces.

References

1. Apple: Accessibility - voiceover - in depth,
   http://www.apple.com/accessibility/voiceover/
2. Talkback - google play, https://play.google.com/store/apps/
   details?id=com.google.android.marvin.talkback
3. Watanabe, T., Watanabe, B., Fujinuma, T., Osugi, N., Sawada, M., Kamata, K.:
   Major factors that affect comprehensibility of shosaiyomi (explanatory expressions)
   used in screen readers: Consideration based on classification of shosaiyomi and kanji
   writing test. J. IEICE J88-D-I(4), 891–899 (2005)
4. Document talker for android (in Japanese),
   http://www.createsystem.co.jp/dtalkerAndroidSDK.html

5. KDDI R&D Laboratories N2 TTS (in Japanese),
   http://www.kddilabs.jp/products/audio/n2tts/product.html
6. Wong, M.E., Tan, S.S.K.: Teaching the benefits of smart phone technology to blind consumers: Exploring the potential of the iPhone. J. Vis. Impair. Blind., 646–650 (October-November 2012)
7. Ujima Laboratory: Methods for taking advantage of iPad2 as educational materials and tools for visually impaired people (in Japanese), this translation is responsible for the authors, http://home.hiroshima-u.ac.jp/ujima/src/research08.html
8. Miyake, T., Noda, T., Kashiwase, M., Goto, H.: Usefulness in low-vision care of multipurpose electronic terminal, iPad2. Rinsho Ganka (Jpn. J. Clin. Ophthalmol.) 66(6), 831–836 (2012) (in Japanese)
9. Matsuzaka, H., Sakajiri, M., Miura, T., Tatsumi, H., Ono, T.: Instructions on manipulation methods of touchscreen computers to visually impaired people-through the workshops for people with total visual impairments. In: IEICE Human Communication Group Symposium 2012 HCG2012–IV–2–10, pp. 468–471 (2012) (in Japanese)
10. Miura, T., Matsuzaka, H., Sakajiri, M., Ono, T.: Usages and needs of current touchscreen interfaces in japanese visually impaired people: A questionnaire survey. In: Proc. IEEE SMC 2012, pp. 2927–2932 (2012)
11. Watanabe, T., Miyagi, M., Minatani, K., Nagaoka, H.: A survey on the use of mobile phones by visually impaired persons in Japan. In: Miesenberger, K., Klaus, J., Zagler, W.L., Karshmer, A.I. (eds.) ICCHP 2008. LNCS, vol. 5105, pp. 1081–1084. Springer, Heidelberg (2008)

Accessible Single Button Characteristics of Touchscreen Interfaces under Screen Readers in People with Visual Impairments

Takahiro Miura[1,2], Masatsugu Sakajiri[3], Murtada Eljailani[3],
Haruo Matsuzaka[3], Junji Onishi[3], and Tsukasa Ono[3]

[1] Graduate School of Information Science and Technology / Institute of Gerontology,
the University of Tokyo, 7-3-1 Hongo, Bunkyo-ku, Tokyo 113-8656, Japan
miu@cyber.t.u-tokyo.ac.jp
[2] National Institute of Advanced Industrial Science and Technology (AIST), 1-1-1
Higashi, Tsukuba, Ibaraki 305-8566, Japan
[3] Faculty of Health Science, Tsukuba University of Technology, 4-12-7 Kasuga,
Tsukuba, Ibaraki 305-8521, Japan
{sakajiri,ohnishi,ono}@cs.k.tsukuba-tech.ac.jp,
{em092310,mh113203}@cc.k.tsukuba-tech.ac.jp

Abstract. Regardless of the improvement of accessibility functions, people with visual impairments have problems using touchscreen computers. Though the size of accessible objects may differ for visually impaired users because of the manipulations under screen readers are different from those without screen readers, the characteristics of desired objects and useful gestures on the touchscreen computers for the visually impaired remain unclear. In this paper, our objective is to clarify the accessible single button characteristics and preferable gestures for visually impaired users of touchscreen computers. We studied these characteristics by evaluating the single button interaction of touchscreen interfaces for visually impaired people under a screen reader condition. As a result, the performance of task completion time on selecting task with a single button decreased as the button size became larger; they were ranked in descending order of double-tapping after flicking, double-tapping after tracing, and split-tapping after tracing.

Keywords: Visually Impaired People, Touchscreen Computers, Manipulation under Screen Reader Condition, Accessible Button.

1 Introduction

Touchscreen computers, such as smartphones and tablets, have recently become popular in the sighted population [1] because of intuitive manipulation and high customizability. Currently, most devices run iOS (Apple) or Android (Google); these systems ensure accessibility for people with visual impairments via screen magnification software and screen reader functions such as VoiceOver [2] and TalkBack [3]. These accessibility functions have improved with each version.

K. Miesenberger et al. (Eds.): ICCHP 2014, Part I, LNCS 8547, pp. 369–376, 2014.
© Springer International Publishing Switzerland 2014

In particular, iOS 6 provides a Japanese specific version of explanatory expressions (called Shosaiyomi of Kanji in Japanese [4]) as a localized VoiceOver function. Shosaiyomi of Kanji provides the speech function of phonetics reading and brief definitions to detect words with the same phonetic but different meanings in Kanji characters. (For example, the meaning of "taisho" depends on the context. This phonetic word corresponds to many Kanji characters that mean target, comparative, symmetry, or Taisho era.) Some Japanese text-to-speech applications can also be installed to provide this function on Android touchscreen computers [5,6]. Thus, the accessibility environment for visually impaired people is gradually improving.

Regardless of these improvements, people with visual impairments have problems using touchscreen computers, since the manipulations with accessibility software differs from those of manipulation by sighted people. As a result, specialized learning materials and lecture courses for touchscreen computers are insufficient. Ujima et al. and Miyake et al. have recently taken place the lecture courses of touchscreen computers for people with partial visual impairments in Japan [7,8], but the courses for totally blind people have hardly yet been held [9]. Other reasons include insufficient accessibility support of third-party applications, as with non-compliant screen reading and non-optimized button and icon designs. These situations are caused by insufficient touchscreen application design guidelines for visually impaired people and a lack of clarity regarding of the conditions of touchscreen computer usage and spatiotemporal manipulation. To ensure that accessible touchscreen computers for the visually impaired will become prevalent, it is necessary to investigate the specific interaction conditions between the visually impaired and touchscreen computers.

In this study, our objective is to embody the application guideline of touchscreen interfaces, such as smartphones and tablet computers. We particularly aim to demonstrate random single button interaction of touchscreen interface for visually impaired people by clarifying their preferable button characteristics.

2   The Method of the Single Button Interaction Experiment

2.1   Participants

Twenty visually impaired persons comprising students of a university and personnel that belonged to NPOs for ICT penetration of visually impaired people participated in this experiment. The participants included ten young (19-30 yrs.) and ten elderly (over 65 yrs.) people. Both groups consisted of five partially and five totally visually impaired people.

2.2   Outline of Evaluation Application

The experimental application shown in Fig. 1 was developed for iOS devices. The behavior of the application was derived from the application for investigating the quantitative gesture accuracy of elderly people reported by Kobayashi et al. [10].

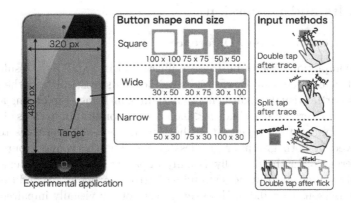

Fig. 1. Appearance of the experimental application

In the experiment, we used an iPod touch 4G (screen size: 3.5 inch with 640 × 960 pixel resolution), running iOS 6.0. The experimental application was implemented as a native application for 320 × 480 pixels. Each trial started when a rectangle button appeared at a random location on the screen. After a participant selected this target, it was dismissed from the screen. At that moment, a new target appeared at a random location. As shown in the central part of Fig. 1, the number of target shapes was three and each of them had three sizes. There were following three types of targets: square (size: 100 × 100, 75 × 75, and 50 × 50 px), wide rectangle (size: 30 × 50, 30 × 75, and 30 × 100 px), and narrow rectangle (size: 50 × 30, 75 × 30, and 100 × 30 px). These widths and heights approximately represent the optical sizes of general buttons (50 px, 8.0 mm), home screen icons (75 px, 12.0 mm), and zoomed icons (100 px, 16.0 mm).

These buttons could be selected by three gestures– double-tapping after tracing, split-tapping after tracing, and double-tapping after flicking –as described in the right part of Fig. 1. The application could log a user's manipulations, including the time to select a button, the positions touched by fingers, and the kinds of touch events.

2.3 Procedure

First, we asked the participants to be seated in front of a table and then to hold and manipulate the device with their non-dominant and dominant hands, respectively. Then, after launching the application, they were asked to select targets continuously with one of the three gestures. When they selected targets 30 times, they were allowed to have a short break and then asked to select them with other gesture. The total number of the target selection task was 270: 3 (button shapes) × 3 (button size) × 3 (gestures) × 10 (repeat count)).

3 Results and Discussion

3.1 Gestures and Group Difference

The task completion time of buttonsare illustrated in Fig. 2.As a result of employing t-test corrected by Bonferroni's method as statistical test, the participants with partial visual impairments were significantly faster in finding a button than those who were totally blind ($p < 0.05$ in each condition), in cases of double- and split-tapping, after tracing at all button shape conditions. This tendency was observed in both groups, regardless of age, but the young group showed larger differences. In the partially visually impaired group, young persons had significantly higher performances in finding buttons earlier at all conditions than did elderly persons ($p < 0.05$). However, in the totally visually impaired group, young persons had significantly higher performances at double and split-tapping after tracing than did elderly persons, but no significant superiority of the young were observed in the case of double-tapping after flicking.No significant difference between gestures were observed in the young partially blind participants, while in the others, double-tapping after flicking resulted in significantly higher performances than double- or split tapping after tracing. The difference between double- and split-tapping after tracing was the largest in the elderly totally blind participants ($p < 0.01$), as shown in Fig. 2. According to their comments, they had difficulty in split-tapping, especially adjusting their index fingers.

According to the subjective feedback obtained by interviews, the participants preferred double-tapping after flicking , double-tapping after tracing, and split-tapping after tracing, in that descending order. The results of the study indicate that the task completion times of flick then double tap was the shortest because we evaluated a single button task.

Button Size. The task completion time of various sized buttons (square, wide, and narrow rectangle, by sizes) are illustrated in Figs. 3. Among the partially blind participants, there were insignificant and slight differences between each button size in all conditions. However, the elderly participants with partial blindness were slower with almost all of button sizes and gesture conditions than their young counterparts, excluding the flick then double-tap gesture and the square and narrow buttons. According to Kobayashi et al. [10], tapping performance with 50 and 70 px buttons by elderly people were no significant and slight differences but that of 30 px button were severely decreased because of its lack of poor eye friendliness and small area. This fact indicates that the button sizes of our experimental condition was within the range of acceptable button sizes for the partially visually impaired participants.

However, for the totally blind participants, increases in the size of a button tended to decrease task completion times with using double- and split-tapping. In particular, in the condition of split-tapping to square buttons shown in the upper central part of Fig. 3, participants took 42 seconds on average to find an 8 mm button, while 4.1 seconds to find a 16 mm button. However, button size may not affect the tracing performance of flick then double-tapping in this group and

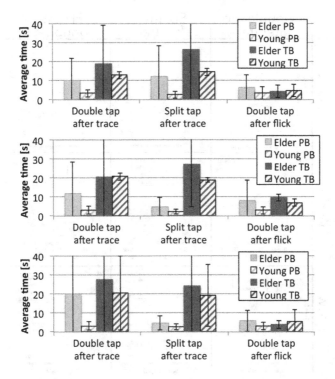

Fig. 2. Task completion time of square, wide and narrow rectangle button in three gestures. PB and TB represent partially and totally blind, respectively. Error bars represent standard deviations of corresponding task completion time.

among partially blind participants. The higher performance of tracing buttons was the results of flicking before double-tapping, double-tapping after tracing, and split-tapping after tracing, in that order. According to the comments of the participants, this order was the same as the preference of gestures.

Button Location. Figure 4 shows an example of the task completion time by the locations of a narrow rectangular button. The task completion time at the central area was significantly shorter than that of the other external sides, especially in the trials of elderly participants with total blindness. Although we assumed that it took right-handed participants longer time to trace and tap a target appearing at the side edge of their dominant hand, this effect was not be observed in this experiment. This result may be explained by the effect of the location relationship between past and present buttons, since the participants traced a next target in a zig-zag manner from the point of a previous target in the experiment. However, some of the elderly participants who were right-handed said that it was difficult to split tap at the right edge because their middle fingers sometimes tapped on the outside of the screen when they traced with their index finger and separately tapped with their middle fingers.

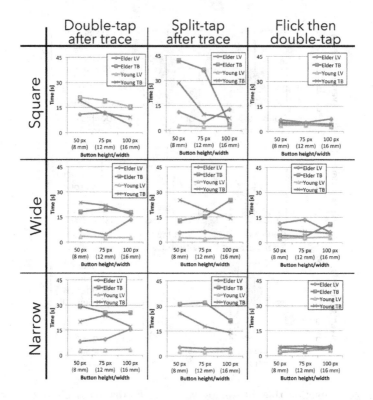

Fig. 3. Task completion time of various sizes of square buttons in three gestures. PB and TB represent partial and total blind, respectively.

Double- and split- tappings took a shorter time at the upper left and a longer time at central or upper right sides of the screen. This result may be because most of the participants were right-handed and because they started to trace from the upper left side and then continued in a zig-zag manner. In this way, they did not move their fingers straight to the right, but in an obliquely downward direction. This fact may have caused them difficulties in finding a button appearing at the upper right.

Subjective Feedback. According to the subjective feedbacks obtained by interview, they preferred double-tapping after flicking, double-tapping after tracing, and split-tapping after tracing, in that descending order. The result of the study indicates that the task completion times of flick and then double-tap was the shortest because we evaluated a single button task. The case of multiple buttons should be discussed in the future and then compared to our results.

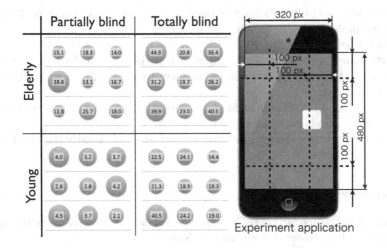

Fig. 4. An example of task completion times at various locations (Condition: narrow rectangular button, split-tapping after tracing) (left). Area segmentation on the screen (right).

Interface Design Guideline for Visually Impaired People. From the results mentioned above, a partial interface design guideline for visually impaired people can be summarized as follows:

– Developers should consider that most of the visually impaired users employed double-tapping after tracing for selecting their targets. However, partially visually impaired users tended to prefer double-tapping after tracing, while the totally visually impaired favored double-tapping after flicking.
– Buttons should be allocated at the central part of the screen. In particular, buttons at the right edge may be difficult for persons who use split tap gestures.
– Button size should be larger than 50 px for elderly partially visually impaired people. For users with total visual impairment and especially those who employ split-taps, a much larger button size is necessary for convenient.

4 Conclusions

An evaluation experiment of preferable single button was conducted to clarify the interaction situations of touchscreen interface in visually impaired people, including the young and elderly users. The results indicate the following:

– The participants with partial visual impairments were significantly faster in finding a button than those with total blindness, in cases of double- and split-tapping after tracing at all button shape conditions. This tendency was observed in both groups, regardless of age, but the young groups had larger difference.

- Double-tapping after flicking resulted in a significantly higher performance than double- and split-tapping after tracing.
- The button sizes in this study affected the target selection performances of participants with total visual impairment, while the performance of young participants with partial visual impairment were not influenced by difference in button size.
- When a target object was located at the central area, the elderly participants with total blindness most easily selected it.
- A partial interface design guideline for the usage of visually impaired people was summarized.

References

1. Smartphone ownership on the rise in Asia Pacific, whilst advertisers struggle to engage with consumers via mobile ads: Nielsen, http://jp.en.nielsen.com/site/documents/SPImr-jun12_FINAL.pdf (accessed: January 30, 2014)
2. Apple: Accessibility - VoiceOver - in depth, http://www.apple.com/accessibility/voiceover/ (accessed: January 30, 2014)
3. Talkback - Google Play, https://play.google.com/store/apps/details?id=com.google.android.marvin.talkback (accessed: January 30, 2014)
4. Watanabe, T., Watanabe, B., Fujinuma, T., Osugi, N., Sawada, M., Kamata, K.: Major factors that affect comprehensibility of shosaiyomi (explanatory expressions) used in screen readers: Consideration based on classification of shosaiyomi and kanji writing test. J. IEICE J88-D-I(4), 891–899 (2005)
5. Document Talker for Android (in Japanese), http://www.createsystem.co.jp/dtalkerAndroidSDK.html (accessed: January 30, 2014)
6. KDDI R&D Laboratories N2 TTS (in Japanese), http://www.kddilabs.jp/products/audio/n2tts/product.html (accessed: January 30, 2014)
7. Ujima Laboratory: Methods for taking advantage of iPad2 as educational materials and tools for visually impaired people (in Japanese), this translation is responsible for the authors, http://home.hiroshima-u.ac.jp/ujima/src/research08.html (accessed: January 30, 2014)
8. Miyake, T., Noda, T., Kashiwase, M., Goto, H.: Usefulness in low-vision care of multipurpose electronic terminal, iPad2. Rinsho Ganka (Jpn. J. Clin. Ophthalmol.) 66(6), 831–836 (2012) (in Japanese)
9. Matsuzaka, H., Sakajiri, M., Miura, T., Tatsumi, H., Ono, T.: Instructions on manipulation methods of touchscreen computers to visually impaired people-Through the workshops for people with total visual impairments. In: IEICE Human Communication Group Symposium 2012 HCG2012-IV-2-10, pp. 468–471 (2012) (in Japanese)
10. Kobayashi, M., Hiyama, A., Miura, T., Asakawa, C., Hirose, M., Ifukube, T.: Elderly user evaluation of mobile touchscreen interactions. In: Campos, P., Graham, N., Jorge, J., Nunes, N., Palanque, P., Winckler, M. (eds.) INTERACT 2011, Part I. LNCS, vol. 6946, pp. 83–99. Springer, Heidelberg (2011)

Tablet-Based Braille Entry via a Framework Promoting Custom Finger Spacing

Stephanie Ludi, Michael Timbrook, and Piper Chester

Department of Software Engineering, Rochester Institute of Technology Rochester, USA
{salvse,mpt2360,pwc1203}@rit.edu

Abstract. This paper outlines the development of the AccessBraille framework, an iOS framework designed to provide a Braille keyboard to an iOS application. The proof-of-concept app developed with this framework is presented as an example of how the framework can be utilized, demonstrating its use across multiple contexts where Braille entry is used. The AccessBraille keyboard framework provides a natural way for blind users to enter US Type 1 or Type 2 Braille text into an app. The keyboard allows for users to customize finger placement for comfort and hand size. User feedback was solicited through observation on the task of entering Braille using the framework at various stages of development. In addition, feedback was gathered for the deployed app itself. The feedback will provide input into the prioritization of revisions and new features.

Keywords: Braille, Framework, Tablet, Visually Impaired.

1   Introduction

On mobile devices, text entry is primarily accomplished by a virtual keyboard displayed on the screen. Over time various styles of keyboards have been developed on the Android and iOS platform, including efforts to support users with disabilities [3,4]. In this paper, we describe the design and proof-of-concept app for the AccessBraille keyboard that enables users who are blind to enter information using Braille. The AccessBraille keyboard framework is intended to address the need to have a Braille keyboard that can be reused across an app, we well as among third-party apps.

The iOS platform already has several built-in accessibility features such as the VoiceOver screen reader, color inversion, and toggle labels [1]. With VoiceOver, the user can tap on a button and VoiceOver will state what the item is (the label for the item). Braille support exists for third party refreshable Braille displays.

AccessBraille is an accessibility application for iPad that provides different modes to interactively practice Braille. The project is de-signed around educational word-based games for children in K-12 who have not mastered the (US) Grade 1 or the Grade 2 Braille system. The project goal is to be a tool for students who are visually impaired to practice the Braille. Many Braille typing machines are cumbersome and/or expensive, with limited portability and access issues for those with limited finances. By creating the iPad AccessBraille application, the ability to practice Braille or to enter text is more accessible given the ubiquitous nature of the iPad. Unlike the

K. Miesenberger et al. (Eds.): ICCHP 2014, Part I, LNCS 8547, pp. 377–382, 2014.

iPhone, the iPad's large screen facilitates typing, thus serving as an ideal device. Although Apple has a plethora of accessibility options, ironically Apple's current accessibility options do not include a Braille typing interface that does not require an external device. The developers hope to deploy the first product that successfully facilitates Braille typing while creating a more fun experience as well.

The team developed the AccessBraille application, with an underlying keyboard framework, to help pre-college students practice their US Type 1 and Type 2 Braille. This app is intended to supplement Braille instruction, and to provide practice as well as a means of entering text for use in another app such as an email app. While young users are the primary user group, anyone who is learning Braille is an appropriate user for the app.

2   Related Work

Much of the current work in enabling Braille entry has focused on seeking to enable the tactile keyboard, which involves a new screen material or an overlay for the screen. This work is a different approach than the AccessBraille keyboard framework, which can be used in existing iPad hardware. Other keyboards are intended to be adaptive in order to predict text entry [3]. While many such keyboards are useful to users, they do not serve well as a means for Braille entry or instruction where practice is important. A student project in 2011, used an approach similar to our initial circle design on the Android platform in order to show a proof-of-concept Braille entry system [2]. Such a system may be an option on the Android platform, though our user testing showed that there are user interaction issues with the approach when the keyboard is integrated into a realistic workflow (context of tasks).

In terms of the AccessBraille app itself, work is limited. Current apps tend to serve as translators to/from text (VisualBraille, BrailleWriter) and teach the alphabet for sighted users (PocketBraille, BrailleNow). The primary users for these types of apps are sighted users not individuals (much less children) who need to learn Braille in order to be fully literate. The Braille Input Editor and most other Braille editors use predefined Braille keys, which is inadequate for smaller hands. Given the project goal and approach to achieving it, the current options are lacking.

3   Design

AccessBraille can be used in standalone free typing mode, a flash card game to practice typing words, or as a text adventure. All of these modes use the keyboard framework. When users initially launch the app, they're presented with a side column of these different modes, as well as a Settings and About menu. The scope of this paper focuses on the Braille entry features.

The original keyboard design used a six-circle dot pattern (see Figure 1). The user had to press the screen with three fingers on each hand to initialize the keyboard. The circumferences of the contact points equaled the circumferences of the fingers of the user. If the user did not press at the right angle, the contact points would not appear. If the user did not press six fingers, but pressed fewer or more than six, the contact points would not appear. Audio feedback would also inform the user as to the status of the keyboard. After initial user testing, the team determined the 6-circle keyboard design was not ideal. Pressing six fingers simultaneously at the ideal angle proved to be too difficult and the design did not accommodate users who kept their fingers tightly together (as opposed to having some spacing between fingers).

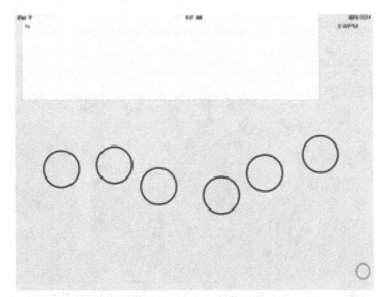

Fig. 1. Screenshot of the initial 'circle' design of the Braille keyboard

The Free Type mode provides a space for the user to freely enter letters with the Braille Keyboard. After redesign, the user must swipe 6 fingers (ideally three on each hand) upwards on the screen in order to initialize the keyboard (see Figure 2). This will present the 6 columns to type with, and will be aligned under their fingers even if the fingers are right next to each other. The columns are numbered the same as standard braille keyboards: starting from the left side of the screen the columns are numbered, 3-2-1 and 4-5-6. Throughout this paper, these columns will be known as 3-C, 2-C, 1-C, etc. The team designed the keyboard to closely resemble Braille typing devices on some tactical feedback devices. Originally based off a Perkins mechanical Brailler. The typing system corresponds to the six-dot system of Braille. The developers intended 1-C to be the location where users would place the index finger of their left hand, 2-C would be for the middle finger, and 3-C the ring finger. 4-C is where users would put their right index finger, 5-C their middle, and 6-C their ring.

By typing in the same order as the letters of Grade 1 braille the user is able to type letters. E.g., by pressing 1-C, the user will type an 'a'. The letter 'a' will be printed in a rectangular view under the typing columns.

The shift, backspace and enter functionality of the keyboard is out-side the columns. The space on the left will be referred to as 7-C and on the right 8-C, this is how 8 dot Braille's denote these extra keys. When originally implementing these functions, backspace was 8-C and 7-C toggled shift and caps lock. Enter was not a feature yet. After spending some time using a Focus Blue 40 this functionality was deemed, non-standard and the team went ahead to implement this in the same way as the Perkins Brailler.

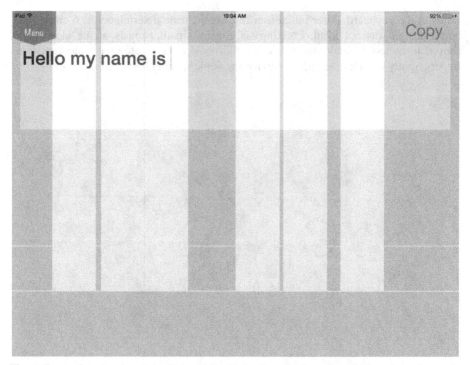

Fig. 2. Screenshot showing the redesigned Braille keyboard using columns Note that columns 2 and 1 (left hand) are very close together

The development of the AccessBraille keyboard framework trans-cends the app it-self. In particular the keyboard framework was designed for use in other apps in order to promote a consistent user experience in Braille entry on the iOS platform. Developers can easily integrate the keyboard as an option for a variety of iPad applications such as productivity or communication apps. Facilitating a build-in Braille keyboard will provide an opportunity for the blind to use Braille among their apps, which will promote literacy as well as efficiency in entering text.

4   Methodology

The keyboard, as part of the associated AccessBraille app, has been developed incrementally, with user testing at significant checkpoints during keyboard and feature development. Due to the nature of the keyboard, the tasks involved included:

1. Initiating the keyboard (to enable Braille input)
2. Typing freely, including one's name and sample sentences that exercise different letters, punctuation and complexity
3. Resetting the keyboard as needed for comfort

The team initially tested with a single Braille user in order to assess the keyboard recognition and accuracy, as well as potential recognition issues. The initial participant noted issues with recognition when the fingers are kept very close together, as opposed to having some spacing between fingers. Other than recognition issues derived from the finger spacing, no Braille accuracy issues were found.

After that initial assessment, and resulting revision to the key-board, the revised keyboard was tested with 4 visually impaired users who are Braille literate. All users ran through the 3 tasks after having the process demonstrated (since the manner of using the tablet as a Braille keyboard differs from traditional Braille entry using tactile buttons). The assessment session was conducted as a think aloud protocol, where they could ask questions as they performed the tasks as well as providing any feedback. The key aspects being assessed were satisfaction in terms of accuracy in Braille, as well as comfort. Time to complete tasks was not critical due to personal differences in Braille entry skill.

5   Results

Overall the redesigned keyboard was an improvement over the initial 'circle' version. The qualitative feedback for each of the tasks

Table 1. Qualitative feedback, broken down by task

Task	Feedback
Initiating the keyboard (to enable Braille input)	The sound feedback was needed to aid with the task, but the participants were successful within 2 attempts. They liked being able to place their fingers where they desired, and with desired finger spacing.
Typing freely, including one's name and sample sentences that exercise different letters, punctuation and complexity	Braille accuracy was high, with occasional error when any fingers were lifted off the tablet. Participants liked being able to move their fingers a bit and still have recognition of input. The voice reading the Braille was easily understood though with a bit of latency.
Resetting the keyboard as needed for comfort	3 of 4 students needed to do this as their hands traveled when typing on their lap (rather than desk). This task was done during the typing task, without interference in the Braille entry.

The issue that arose was that of the latency of the voice reading the Braille. The latency issue has since been remedied upon use of the iOS7 libraries (the initial prototype was developed in iOS6 where a third party library was used).

6   Conclusions and Future Work

While we have gathered initial results from users, we will continue to gather feedback when the AccessBraille app is deployed in the App Store in Spring 2014. As part of the ongoing feedback, user reviews and an embedded link to a satisfaction survey will be used as a mechanism to gather feedback for future releases. For exam-ple, expanding a feature to copy and paste material to other apps (e.g. email client or text message apps) will be assessed.

References

1. Apple Developer Center. Understanding Accessibility on iOS,
   https://developer.apple.com/library/ios/documentation/
   UserExperience/Conceptual/iPhoneAccessibility/
   Accessibility_on_iPhone/Accessibility_on_iPhone.html#/
   /apple_ref/doc/uid/TP40008785-CH100-SW1
2. Belezina, J.: Student-made tablet app may make dedicated Braille writers obsolete. Giz-mag, http://www.gizmag.com/touchscreen-braille-writer/20118/
3. Cheng, L., Liang, H., Wu, C., Chen, M.: iGrasp: grasp-based adaptive key-board for mobile devices. In: Proceedings of the SIGCHI Conference on Human Factors in Computing Systems (CHI 2013), pp. 3037–3046. ACM, New York (2013),
   http://doi.acm.org/10.1145/2470654.2481422,
   doi:10.1145/2470654.2481422
4. Dale, O., Schulz, T.: Easier mobile phone input using the jusfone keyboard. In: Miesenberger, K., Karshmer, A., Penaz, P., Zagler, W. (eds.) ICCHP 2012, Part II. LNCS, vol. 7383, pp. 439–446. Springer, Heidelberg (2012),
   http://dx.doi.org/10.1007/978-3-

Nonvisual Presentation, Navigation and Manipulation of Structured Documents on Mobile and Wearable Devices

Martin Lukas Dorigo[1], Bettina Harriehausen-Mühlbauer[2], Ingo Stengel[1], and Paul Dowland[1]

[1] Plymouth University, Plymouth, United Kingdom
martin.dorigo@plymouth.ac.uk
[2] University of Applied Sciences Darmstadt, Darmstadt, Germany

Abstract. There are a large number of highly structured documents, for example: newspaper articles, scientific, mathematical or technical literature. As a result of inductive research with 200 blind and visually impaired participants, a multimodal user interface for non-visual presentation, navigation and manipulation of structured documents on mobile and wearable devices like smart phones, smart watches or smart tablets has been developed. It enables the user to get a fast overview over the document structure and to efficiently skim and scan over the document content by identifying the type, level, position, length, relationship and content text of each element as well as to focus, select, activate, move, remove and insert structure elements or text. These interactions are presented in a non-visual way using earcons, tactons and speech synthesis, serving the aural and tactile human sense. Navigation and manipulation is provided by using the multi-touch, motion (linear acceleration and rotation) or speech recognition input modality. It is a complete solution for reading, creating and editing structured documents in a non-visual way. There is no special hardware required. For the development, testing and evaluation of the user interface, a flexible platform independent software architecture has been developed and implemented for iOS and Android. The evaluation of the user interface has been undertaken by a structured observation of 160 blind and visually impaired participants using an implemented software (App) over the Internet.

Keywords: Assistive Technology, User Interface, Multi-Modal, Nonvisual, Presentation, Navigation, Manipulation, Earcons, Tactons, Multitouch, Gestures, Motion, Mobile Devices, Smart Phone, Smart Watch, Smart Tablet, Wearable Devices, Document, Structure, Mathematics, Accessibility, Blind, Visual Impairment.

1 Introduction

There are a large number of highly structured documents, for example: newspaper articles, scientific, mathematical or technical literature. The document structure is very important for the user in order to efficiently handling the document content and to quickly find relevant information within the document content.

K. Miesenberger et al. (Eds.): ICCHP 2014, Part I, LNCS 8547, pp. 383–390, 2014.
© Springer International Publishing Switzerland 2014

In visual graphical user interfaces (GUIs), each logical structure element is physically presented by a specific visualization (icon). The advantage of these icons is that the user can recognize the structure much faster than if the structure is described in text only. Another advantage of a graphical user interface is that it enables direct navigation and manipulation of the document structure and content.

Blind and visually impaired persons are unable to use a graphical user interfaces and, for the emerging category of mobile and wearable devices where there are only small visual displays available or no visual display at all, a non-visual alternative for presentation, navigation and manipulation of structured documents is required too.

2   State of the Art

Screen readers like Apple VoiceOver [1], Google TalkBack [2] or Freedom Scientific JAWS [3] use text-based presentation methods like speech synthesis or braille displays only. This is an efficient method for presenting text (document content), but it is not very efficient for the presentation of non-text data like the document structure. Navigation is provided by performing key sequences on the keyboard, using the cursor routing keys of the braille display or by performing gestures on a multitouch-pad or -screen. In addition to moving the cursor forward and backward, there are many shortcuts for specific element types (for example browsing the list of headings), enabling the user to identify the element type, but it does not give any information about the level, position, length and relationship of the element. Furthermore, it is possible to explore which elements of the currently visible viewport are visually rendered at which position on the screen. But the knowledge of this physical structure does not necessary implicate the understanding of the logical structure behind it.

In addition to screen readers the following alternative approaches exist: Minatani [4] used special characters on a braille display for document structure presentation. Petit [5] developed a tool for tactile spatial exploration of web pages and James [6] tested different types of non-verbal audio for presenting HTML structures.

At the moment there is no solution which combines verbal modalities like speech with the power of non-verbal output modalities like earcons [8] and tactons [11] and the novel input modalities like multitouch and motion all provided by the emerging category of mobile and wearable devices out of the box.

3   Methodology

The following social research methods have been employed according to the guidelines of Bryman [7] using a natural science epistemological model (positivism), a quantitative research strategy and an iterative research approach:

The user interface has been developed using an inductive research approach and a cross-sectional survey research design. The concepts were measured by using single indicators with nominal and ordinal scales as well as multiple indicators using Likert scales. The participants had been selected using convenience sampling and snowball sampling as non-probability sampling methods. Data was collected by conducting structured interviews over telephone and face-to-face as well as using a self-completion questionnaire sent out over the Internet. This data had been analysed using diagrams, Linear Regression and the Chi-Square test as univariate, bivariate and statistical significance methods.

For the evaluation of the user interface, a deductive research approach employing a cross-sectional research design has been used. For data collection structured observations of participants had been conducted using a software (App) implementing the observation schedule as the research instrument. This data has been analysed using diagrams, Linear Regression and the Chi-Square test as univariate, bivariate and statistical significance methods. The results of the evaluation were fed back into a revision of the user interface.

4   User Interface

The following multi-modal user interface for non-visual presentation, navigation and manipulation of structured documents on mobile and wearable devices has been developed as a result of the inductive research:

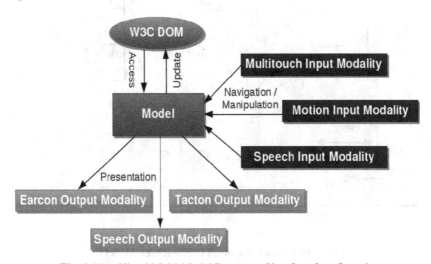

Fig. 1. Non-Visual Multi-Modal Document User Interface Overview

The document is organised and represented in a modality-neutral model. Navigation and manipulation is provided by using the multitouch, motion or speech recognition input modality. Each interaction is presented in a non-visual way using earcons [8], tactons [11] and speech synthesis, serving the aural and the tactile human sense. As a platform- and language-neutral interface, the W3C Document Object Model (DOM) [12] is used which allows the user interface to dynamically access and update the document structure and content of manifold document sources like accessibility APIs or parsers and transformers for different document formats like XML or PDF.

4.1   Model

On each hierarchy level, the element- and text-nodes of the document structure are laid-out along the structure axis in document reading order where the relative position on the axis represents the position within the document and the relative length on the axis represents the length of the text contained in it. There is a gap of one unit before and after each element. The advantages of this representation is that is enables the user to identify the type, level, position, length, relationship and text of each element. For each text node there is an additional text axis on which the contained text is laid out by word. The element types which can be inserted at a specific position are laid out along an addition insert element axis. There is a structure-, text- and insert element-cursor. Each cursor can be set to a specific position, moved forward and backward at an arbitrary speed and unset. There is a select-, active- and insertText-modifier. Each modifier can be set or unset.

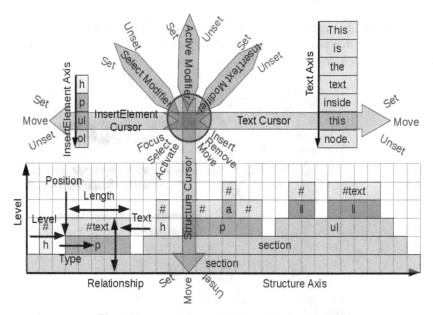

Fig. 2. Non-visual Document User Interface Model

The following interactions can be performed:

- Focus element: Set and move the structure cursor to focus all nested structure elements at the specific position.
- Focus text: Set and move the text cursor to focus text inside the focused element.
- Select selection: Set the select modifier to select the focused element or text. Move the element or text cursors to extend the selection.
- Activate selection: Set the active modifier.
- Move active selection: Move the element and / or text cursor to the target position and unset the active modifier.
- Remove active selection: Unset the cursors and afterwords unset the active modifier.

- Insert Element: Set and move the insertElement cursor to the desired elementType and set the select modifier.
- Insert Text: Set the insertText modifier, speak the text you want to insert and unset the insertText modifier afterwords.

4.2   Earcon Output Modality

Each interaction is presented by a single-pitch inherited elementary earcon [8] according to the guidelines of Brewster [9], inheriting the timbre of the element type, pitch of the element level, register of the operation, dynamics of the interaction status and duration of the interaction. These elementary earcons are rendered simultaneously as parallel compound earcons [10] to reduce the length of the audio message.

4.3   Tacton Output Modality

In the tactile modality each interaction is presented by a single-motive inherited elementary tacton [11] inheriting the rhythm (2 to 4 notes) of the element type and the tempo of the element level. These elementary tactons are rendered sequentially as serial compound tactons.

4.4   Speech Output Modality

Each interaction is presented by a inherited elementary utterance, inheriting the voice-pitch of the node level, voice-register of the operation and text of the content. If the node is a text-node, the contained text is used as the content. If the node is an element-node and contains a heading, the text of this heading is used as the content. These elementary utterances are rendered sequentially as serial compound utterances.

4.5   Multitouch Input Modality

The multitouch input modality is mainly purposed for smart phones, pablets and tablets. In this modality the pointers act relative to coordinates of the device. The actions of the model are mapped to the following gestures:

- Structure Axis: Y-Axis from the top to the bottom.
- Set Structure Cursor: Put down one pointer at the specific position.
- Move Structure Cursor: Move the one pointer up and down.
- Unset Structure Cursor: Lift up the one pointer.
- Text Axis: X-Axis from left to right.
- Set Text Cursor: Move one pointer more than 50 pixels to the left or right.
- Move Text Cursor: Move the one pointer left or right at an arbitrary speed.
- Unset Text Cursor: Move structure cursor to an other position.
- InsertElement Axis: Y-Axis from the top to the bottom.
- Set InsertElement Cursor: Slide in an addition second pointer from the top
- Move InsertElement Cursor: Move this second pointer up and down.

- Unset InsertElement Cursor: Lift up this second pointer.
- Set Select Modifier: Put down an additional second pointer at an arbitrary position.
- Unset Select Modifier: Lift up this second pointer.
- Set Active Modifier: Put down an additional third pointer at an arbitrary position.
- Unset Active Modifier: Lift up this third pointer.
- Set InsertText Modifier: Double tap and hold a second pointer at an arbitrary position.
- Unset InsertText Modifier: Lift up this second pointer.

4.6   Motion Input Modality

The motion input modality is mainly purposed for wearable devices like smart watches. In this modality the device itself is acting (linear acceleration and rotation) relative to coordinates of the word. The actions of the model are mapped to the following gestures:

- Structure Axis: Double shake the device to lay-out the structure axis along the Y-Axis in front of you from forward to backward.
- Set Structure Cursor: Put down the device 20cm at the specific position.
- Move Structure Cursor: Move the device forward and backward.
- Unset Structure Cursor: Lift up the device 20cm.
- Text Axis: X-Axis from left to right.
- Set Text Cursor: Move the device more than 20cm to the left or right.
- Move Text Cursor: Move the device left or right at an arbitrary speed.
- Unset Text Cursor: Move element cursor to an other position.
- InsertElement Axis: Z-Axis from bottom to top.
- Set InsertElement Cursor: Rotate device along the X-Axis 90° to the left.
- Move InsertElement Cursor: Move the device up and down.
- Unset InsertElement Cursor: Rotate device along the X-Axis 90° to the right.
- Set Select Modifier: Rotate device along the X-Axis 90° to the right.
- Unset Select Modifier: Rotate device along the X-Axis 90° to the left.
- Set Active Modifier: Lift up the device 20cm along the Z-Axis.
- Unset Active Modifier: Put down the device 20cm along the Z-Axis.
- Set InsertText Modifier: Rotate device along the X-Axis 180° to the left.
- Unset InsertText Modifier: Rotate device along the X-Axis 180° to the right.

5   Evaluation

To evaluate the user interface, a structured observation of 160 blind and visually impaired participants using an implemented software (App) for iOS and Android is currently on-going. The observation schedule consists of the following main steps:

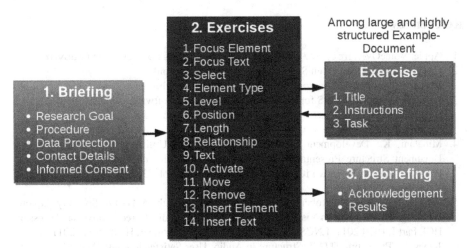

Fig. 3. Structured Observation Schedule for Evaluation of the User Interface

A briefing gives detailed information about the research goal, procedure, data protection, contact details and informed consent. After this introduction, the participant has to perform 14 exercises among a large and highly structured example document, covering all interactions provided by the user interface. Each exercise consists of a title, instructions (since the gestures for performing an interaction among the input modalities and the feedback given by the output modalities is abstract, it must be explained to the participants first) and a task the participant has to perform. Finally, the participants are debriefed. All instructions are spoken to the participants using speech synthesis.

As a measure of the concepts: the number of success or failure attempts, time taken, and the interactions performed to solve an exercise is recorded and transmitted back over the Internet.

Initial results have shown that the proposed user interface provides a potential solution.

6   Conclusions

Nonvisual presentation, navigation and manipulation of structured documents on mobile and wearable devices is very important. Therefore a multi-modal user interface has been developed as a result of inductive research with blind and visually impaired participants as a complete solution for reading, creating and editing structured documents in a non-visual way. Initial results of a structured observation of blind and visually impaired participants using software (App) for iOS and Android based on a flexible platform independent software architecture has demonstrated that the proposed user interface provides a potential solution.

References

1. Apple, VoiceOver, http://www.apple.com/accessibility/voiceover
2. Google TalkBack: An Open Source Screenreader for Android,
   http://www.google.com/accessibility/products/
3. Freedom Scientific, JAWS for Windows Screen Reading Software,
   http://www.freedomscientific.com/products/fs/
   jaws-product-page.asp
4. Minatani, K.: Development of a DAISY Player that Utilizes a Braille Display for Document Structure Presentation and Navigation. In: Miesenberger, K., Karshmer, A., Penaz, P., Zagler, W. (eds.) ICCHP 2012, Part I. LNCS, vol. 7382, pp. 515–522. Springer, Heidelberg (2012)
5. Petit, G., Dufresne, A., Robert, J.M.: Introducing TactoWeb: A Tool to Spatially Explore Web Pages for Users with Visual Impairment. In: Stephanidis, C. (ed.) Universal Access in HCI, Part I, HCII 2011. LNCS, vol. 6765, pp. 276–284. Springer, Heidelberg (2011)
6. James, F.: Presenting HTML Structure in Audio: User Satisfaction with Audio Hypertext. In: Frysinger, S., et al. (eds.) Proceedings of ICAD 1996, Palo Alto, pp. 97–103 (1996)
7. Bryman, A.: Social research methods. Oxford University Press, Oxford (2012)
8. Blattner, M., Sumikawa, D., Greenberg, R.: Earcons and icons: Their structure and common design principles. Human Computer Interaction 4(1), 11–44 (1989)
9. Brewster, S.A., Wright, P.C., Edwards, A.D.: An evaluation of earcons for use in auditory human-computer interfaces. In: Arnold, B., et al. (eds.) INTERCHI 1993: Proceedings of INTERACT 1993 and CHI 1993, pp. 222–227. ACM, New York (1993)
10. Brewster, S.A., Wright, P.C., Edwards, A.D.: Parallel earcons: Reducing the length of audio messages. International Journal of Human-Computer Studies 43(22), 153–175 (1995)
11. Brewster, S., Brown, L.M.: Tactons: Structured Tactile Messages for Non-Visual Information Display. In: Cockburn, A. (ed.) AUIC 2004 - Proceedings of AUIC 2004, vol. 28, pp. 15–23. Australian Computer Society, Darlinghurst (2004)
12. W3C - Document Object Model (DOM) Level 3 Core Specification,
    http://www.w3.org/TR/2004/REC-DOM-Level-3-Core-20040407/

Never too Old to Use a Tablet: Designing Tablet Applications for the Cognitively and Physically Impaired Elderly

Luuk Muskens, Rico van Lent, Alexander Vijfvinkel, Paul van Cann,
and Suleman Shahid

Department of Communication and Information Sciences, Tilburg University,
Tilburg, The Netherlands
{l.h.f.muskens,r.h.f.vanlent,a.a.f.vijfvinkel,p.c.d.vancann,
s.shahid}@tilburguniversity.edu

Abstract. People live longer than ever before and the population of elderly is increasing. Many elderly visit day care centres in order to avoid loneliness and continuously look for new methods of entertainment. A possible new mean of entertainment can be found in the use of tablet applications. However, due to the physical and/or cognitive impairments of these elderly, most tablet applications are not accessible. This research tries to design an elderly-friendly entertainment application. Several design guidelines were determined via a literature review and a contextual inquiry for the design of three prototypes. These prototypes successfully eliminated problems concerning button size, navigation, readability of the fonts and swiping. Furthermore, results indicated that the elderly had a strong preference for the design which had a low number of icons, a more direct way of giving information, no deep hierarchy, larger buttons with immediate feedback when pressed, a clear notification that the screens had changed and the screens which used bright colours were more effective.

Keywords: Human Computer Interaction, Design Principles, Cognitively and Physically Impaired Elderly, User Interface Design.

1 Introduction

People live longer than ever before and the population of elderly is increasing globally [1]. According to the World Health Organization [2], the number of people aged 60 has doubled since 1980. Furthermore, it is expected that on average 1 out of 10 people around the world will be older than 65 in 2025 [1]. This number will be even higher in Europe, where it is expected that 20% of its European residents will be over 65 in 2025 [3]. More often these elderly are placed in nursing homes and spending their time in day care centres. These day care centres allow elderly to maintain social contacts via social activities (e.g. reading the newspaper, watching television together and playing board games) in order to avoid loneliness. However, attempts made by day care centres are not always successful and elderly do look for new means of entertainment.

K. Miesenberger et al. (Eds.): ICCHP 2014, Part I, LNCS 8547, pp. 391–398, 2014.
© Springer International Publishing Switzerland 2014

One recent trend among many day care centres is to use gaming consoles and tablet applications for reducing boredom. Gaming consoles are mainly used for thera-py purposes and installed stationary in a particular room. Meanwhile, tablet applica-tions have a much more borderless use in terms of space, time and utility. Further-more, tablet applications can provide new means of entertainment, because of their endless features and possibilities. Unfortunately, as people age, their cognitive and/or physical abilities start to degrade and could prevent them from properly using a tablet.

The current research aimed to design an elderly-friendly entertainment-application, which takes into account the cognitive and physical impairments of the elderly. De-sign guidelines were established via a literature review and a contextual inquiry in which physical/cognitive impaired elderly reviewed existing tablet applica-tions. The design guidelines were used to create three prototypes of the entertainment applica-tion, dubbed 'De Moderne Kijkbuis (The Modern Telly)'. This research also yields new design guidelines that can be incorporated in the future applications.

2 Determining the Design Guidelines: Literature Review

2.1 General Guidelines

According to Phiriyapokanon [4] designers should consider the suitability of software characteristics for general users and extend it to cope with the limitations of specific users. His research mentions a set of guidelines that a user interface should have:

1. Reduction of Complexity: Factions that are rarely used or not necessary should be removed regarding simplicity of application.
2. Clear Structure of Task: The starting point of tasks and every step should be easily recognized and understood.
3. Consistency of Information: Avoid contradictions and inconsistencies of
4. information arrangement.
5. Rapid and Distinct Feedback: Applications should continuously provide easily re-cognizable feedback of success or failure with every action.

In addition, Phiriyapokanon [4] also mentions to minimize errors, maintain a high recoverability and provide on screen help.

2.2 Physical Impairments and Guidelines

Sensory Impairments. Elderly experience physical impairments due to different types of age related diseases (e.g. the deterioration of sensory faculties). As a conse-quence, this causes problems concerning the intake of information [5, 6]. Visual im-pairments include blurred eyesight, loss of colour vision, and a distorted perception [6]. When designing software for elderly with a blurred eyesight or distorted percep-tion, one can incorporate a screen magnifier, feedback, large button sized or enlarged spacing between buttons [7]. For elderly with a loss of colour vision, high colour contrasts can be used in the background [8, 9]. Hearing impairments causes elderly to have troubles differentiating between sounds and the direction of the sound [6].

A clear textual modality can be a solution for overcoming troubles of the deaf and hard-to-hear [7, 10].

Dexterity Impairments. Elderly experience difficulty in dexterity due to weaker muscle tissue and diseases [6]. Deterioration of the visuospatial skills causes impairments in the skills of assessing the spatial relationships between objects [5]. As a result, elderly have difficulties with making accurate movements. Using bigger button sizes and spacing can overcome the difficulties in dexterity [12, 13]. Jin, Plocher and Kiff [13] recommend a minimum button size of 11.43mm for elderly. However, Irwin and Sesto [12] state that the ideal button size is between 20x20mm and 25x25mm for elderly users. Guerreiro et al. [14] concluded that medium (12mm) and large (17mm) target sizes produced less errors compared to small target sizes (7mm). In addition, the position of a target (corner, edge or middle of the screen) did not affect performance' [14]. Spacing between the buttons is required to be between 3.17mm and 12.7mm in order to lower performance error rates for older users [13].

2.3   Cognitive Impairments and Guidelines

Praxis. Elderly have a low praxis, or the ability to perform complex tasks in response to a command or request [5]. Research suggests that one must wait until the elder complies, to proceed towards the next step [15]. In addition, a way to decrease the strain on cognitive performance is to place tasks in a step-by-step order [16]. This should be taken with care though, because to many steps can engender the feeling of 'getting lost' [17]. One has to be consistent in naming the steps, an example can be to begin a sentence with a verb (e.g. 'press this button').

Orientation. Orientation impairment causes elderly to unlearn the ability to find one's way in new surroundings [5]. Menus and usability interfaces need to be simpli-fied to minimize the amount of information which needs to be memorized, especially for elderly with limited computer expertise and confidence [11, 17]. Castilla et al. [18] mentions that an application should work independently from other applications. Furthermore, the screen should not contain any distracting elements (e.g. wallpaper, minimal amount of buttons, text etc.). Information needs to be divided into smaller, discrete chunks so elderly can absorb the information [15].

Learning. Elderly process information in a much slower pace, which causes slow reaction times in motoric and mental skills [5]. Due to deterioration of the attention skills, mental flexibility and the categorizing of information, elderly are also bad in making decisions [5]. Therefore, information needs to be consistent [15]. In addition, elderly also need more time to create an after-image. Most important is preventing the elderly to experience stress, because stress has a negative outcome on the learning ability [15].

3 Determining the Design Guidelines: Contextual Inquiry

A contextual inquiry (CI) was performed using existing tablet applications in order to gain practical insight in how the cognitive/physical impaired elderly performed on a tablet. Furthermore, findings from the contextual inquiry could further supplement the design guidelines discovered during the literature review.

3.1 Method

Participants. Fourteen participants, with a mean age of approximately 70 years and affected by different cognitive and/or physical disabilities (e.g. brain haemorrhages, rheumatoid arthritis, Parkinson's disease and amnesia). The participants had experiences with the Apple IPad 2.0 and were novice or casual users.

Materials. The literature study indicated that elderly have lesser sensory faculties, low praxis, orientation impairments, lesser visuospatial skills, slower processing of incoming information and experience lesser learning skills when pressurized. Based on this information, four existing applications (two 'simple' and two 'complex') were selected for the contextual inquiry. The two simple games were a memory game and children's game and contained big buttons and slow pacing. Afterwards, the partici-pants were interviewed based on the aspects of ISO 9126 (mainly from the accessibil-ity point of view).

Procedure. The CI and interviews took place in a separate room, were the partici-pants were not distracted. Participants were first asked about their demographical information. After this, they had to play two language-learning applications (one simple and one complex) on an Android-tablet (N=6) or an Apple-tablet (N=8).

3.2 Results

Reviews of many existing tablet applications, designed for two major platforms, show that most of the applications ignore the basic accessibility and usability guidelines and it is impossible for elderly to use these applications without external help. The contex-tual inquiry confirmed the findings from the literature review and showed that partici-pants experienced many difficulties in swiping (e.g. not enough feedback when they reached at the end of the page), pressing small buttons (e.g. too many accidental presses), navigating (e.g. unclear menu structure, labelling issues and ambiguous icons and metaphors), reading small fonts and keeping up with fast-paced changes (e.g. no control for change blindness) in the application.

4 Prototyping: 'De Moderne Kijkbuis'

In the next phase, we developed the 'De Moderne Kijkbuis (The Modern Telly)' ap-plication, according to the design guidelines determined via the literature review and contextual inquiry. This application would allow the elderly to watch television, search for television programs in the TV-guide, read the latest news and play games. The design guidelines were to provide the elderly with step by step information, no distracting elements, a clear structure of tasks, and a consistent design. This means that the information available to the user can be easily found through structure, layout, distinct feedback (e.g. a sound can be heard when a button is pressed) and a high contrast colour usage. Furthermore, the design needed to exclude swiping in order to create a press-only application with large button sizes (minimum of 12mm) and spacing (minimum of 3.17mm). We decided to design three different versions of 'De Moderne Kijkbuis', differing in complexity, button sizes/forms, mapping and aesthet-ics, in order to determine the most optimal design (see Fig. 1). Design 2 incorporated a keyboard, based on the design of No Look [19]. Three low-fidelity prototypes were created and tested with participants in the day care centre. Corrections were made if necessary, which eventually lead to the creation of the final applications.

4.1   Method

Participants. Twelve elderly (7 men), with a mean age of approximately 69 years (54-86 years) and affected with the previously mentioned cognitive and/or physical impairments, participated in the experiment. The participants had experiences with the iPad 2.0 and were novice or casual users.

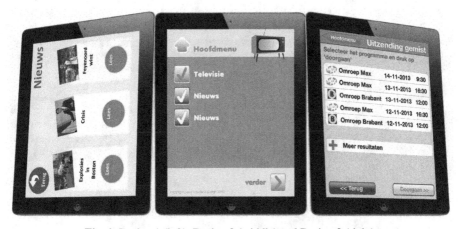

Fig. 1. Design 1 (left), Design 3 (middle) and Design 2 (right)

Materials. The materials consisted out of three applications (shown in Fig. 1) and a questionnaire based on the aspects of ISO 9126. During experiment 1, it was noticed that many of the elderly lacked the ability to speak clearly. To improve communication between the participants and the researchers, an effort was made to combine three scales from pain management to a visual five point scale (i.e. Present Pain Intensity Subscale, Rand Coop Chart and the Verbal Scale). According to research, 83% of cognitive impaired patients could indicate the severity of the pain using one of these scales [20].

Procedure. The CI and interviews took place in a separate room, were the participants were not distracted. Participants were first asked about their demographical information. After this, the participants had to interact with each design by performing pre-specified tasks (e.g. Read the news article 'Problems banking ING'). The participants had to judge each design afterwards in the interview.

4.2   Results

Observations indicated that the type of errors, noticeable during the user research, decreased in all applications. Participants navigated easily through the different interfaces, although participants did confuse the 'return to home'-button and the 'go back'-button quite often (see Fig. 2). This observation showed how a standard home or back button, used in almost all applications, is confusing for this user group. Further observations indicate that the font sizes were more readable and that participants seemed to be prone for pressing the button icons instead of the button as a whole. The button sizes/spacing was effective, since the participants stayed within the button area. However, they did not tap the tablet in the right manner (e.g. tap with nails, hold the button to long or accidently swipe during tapping), which prevented the button from becoming active. Once the participants were instructed in how to press the button properly, this error dropped. Participants were also very nervous and were trying to avoid failure by awaiting hints.

Fig. 2. Working prototype design 3

The elderly had a strong preference for design 3, which had a low number of icons, a more direct way of giving information, no deep hierarchy, larger buttons with imme-diate feedback when pressed, a clear notification that the screens had changed and which used bright colours in its design (see Fig. 2). Participants indicated that they liked this design, because they perceived the design as easy to learn.

5   General Discussion

This research tried to design an entertainment application for elderly with physical and/or cognitive impairments. 'De Moderne Kijkbuis' had multiple advantages over existing applications (e.g. no swiping, a clear mapping, and eliminating fast pacing changes). However, the elderly still required help because of their insecurity of interacting with a tablet. Furthermore, the other participants indicated that they liked the design 3, because this design was the easiest to learn. This might indicate that applications should be designed as simple as possible in order to avoid cognitive strains. Another important observation was that the elderly had major difficulties pressing two dimensional buttons. They did not receive good haptic feedback in order to determine when a button was properly pressed. One way of solving this problem is by giving haptic feedback. This technology is a layer over your standard touchscreen, which creates physical fluid filled buttons based on the visual screen below. This might help the elderly in determining if a button is properly pressed.

Our interactions with day care centres showed that these centres are consistently in search of such applications and that there is much room for improvement. This is especially the case for translating existing applications to the needs of the elderly, based on specific design guidelines. In the future, it might be possible to develop a module for teaching elderly how to use a tablet. Furthermore, instead of taking a more specific approach in designing specialized applications for elderly with a specific disease, we will be focusing on a more atypical approach. This atypical approach consists of designing general entertainment applications for the elderly with many different diseases, in order to accommodate more diverse groups. As a result, social interactions in day care centres will be richer than before.

References

1. Organization, W.H., The World Health Report 1998 - Life in the 21st Century: A Vision for All, pp. 2–8. World Health Organization, France (1998)
2. World Health Organization. Are you ready? What you need to know about ageing (2012), http://www.who.int/world-health-day/2012/toolkit/background/en/ (cited March 20, 2014)
3. Commission, E. Population Groups: Elderly (2014), http://ec.europa.eu/health/population_groups/elderly/index_en.htm (cited March 23, 2014)
4. Phiriyapokanon, T., Is a big button interface enough for elderly users?, p. 34. Mälardalen University, Sweden (2011)
5. de Jager, C.A.: Memory in the Elderly. In: Stone, J.H., Blouin, M. (eds.) International Encyclopedia of Rehabilitation (2013)
6. Medicinfo. Veel voorkomende aandoeningen bij ouderen (March 13, 2014), http://www.medicinfo.nl/%7Be826e405-d7b5-4b4b-8f3f-24cac12bc6b1%7D (cited March 15, 2014)
7. Hanson, V.L.: Web access for elderly citizens. In: Workshop on Universal Accessibility of Ubiquitous Computing 2001. ACM, Alcácer do Sal (2001)

8. Caprani, N., O'Conner, N., Gurrin, C.: Touch Screens for the Older User. In: Cheein, F.A.A. (ed.) Assistive Technologies, pp. 96–118. Intech (2012)

9. Arditi, A.: Effective Color Contrast: Designing for People with Partial Sight and Color Deficiencies (1999, 2013), http://www.lighthouse.org/accessibility/design/accessible-print-design/effective-color-contrast (cited March 6, 2013)

10. Debevc, M., Kosec, P., Holzinger, A.: Improving multimodal web accessibility for deaf people: sign language interpreter module. Multimedia Tools and Applications 54, 181–199 (2011)

11. Holzinger, A., Searle, G., Nischelwitzer, A.: On some aspects of improving mobile applications for the elderly. Universal Acces in HCI 1(2), 923–932 (2007)

12. Irwin, C.B., Sesto, M.E.: Timing and Accuracy of Individuals With and Without Motor Control Disabilities Completing a Touch Screen Task. In: Stephanidis, C. (ed.) UAHCI 2009, Part II. LNCS, vol. 5615, pp. 535–536. Springer, Heidelberg (2009)

13. Jin, Z.X., Plocher, T., Kiff, L.: Touch Screen User Interfaces for Older Adults: Button Size And Spacing. In: Stephanidis, C. (ed.) HCI 2007. LNCS, vol. 4554, pp. 933–941. Springer, Heidelberg (2007)

14. Guerreiro, T., et al.: Towards Accessible Touch Interfaces. In: ASSETS 2010, Orlando, Florida, pp. 19–26 (2010)

15. Ruholl, L.: Tips for teaching the elderly (May 1, 2003), http://www.modernmedicine.com/news/tips-teaching-elderly (cited March 4, 2013)

16. Estgate, A., Groome, D.: An introduction to applied cognitive psychology. Psychology Press, New York (2005)

17. Wilkowska, W., Ziefle, M.: Which factors form older adults' acceptance of mobile information and communication technologies. In: Holzinger, A., Miesenberger, K. (eds.) USAB 2009. LNCS, vol. 5889, pp. 81–101. Springer, Heidelberg (2009)

18. Castilla, D., et al.: Process of design and usability evaluation of a telepsychology web and virtual reality system for the elderly: Butler. Human-Computer Studies 71(3), 350–362 (2013)

19. Bonner, M.N., Brudvik, J.T., Abowd, G.D., Edwards, W.K.: No-Look Notes: Accessible Eyes-Free Multi-Touch Text Entry. In: Floréen, P., Krüger, A., Spasojevic, M. (eds.) Pervasive 2010. LNCS, vol. 6030, pp. 409–426. Springer, Heidelberg (2010)

20. Ferrell, B.A., Ferrell, B.R., Rivera, L.: Pain in cognitively impaired nursing home patients. Journal of Pain and Symptom Management 10(8), 591–598 (1995)

Tablets in the Rehabilitation of Memory Impairment[*]

Krzysztof Dobosz[1], Magdalena Dobosz[2], Tomasz Fiolka[1], Marcin Wojaczek[1],
and Tomasz Depta[1]

[1] Silesian University of Technology, Institute of Informatics, Gliwice, Poland
`krzysztof.dobosz@polsl.pl`,
`{tomafio690,marcwoj424,tomadep124}@student.polsl.pl`
[2] Upper Silesian Rehabilitation Center 'Repty', Tarnowskie Góry, Poland
`m.dobosz@repty.pl`

Abstract. The aim of this study was the analysis of existing sets of rehabilitation exercises for possible adapting them to mobile devices (tablets). We analyzed more than 300 different memory tasks presented on the pages of workbooks. Numerous tasks were classified to different categories because of the type of content and cognitive functions trained. For each type there was assigned a certain number of specific tasks. In each type the feasibility of adaptation for tablets (full, partial, impossible) and complexity of interaction (entering characters, indication, drag&drop) were evaluated. That is a big help for many older people (most of the patients in the Rehabilitation Center), because they have problems entering text with the virtual keyboard displayed on the screen.

Keywords: Mobile Devices, Memory Impairment, Rehabilitation.

1 Introduction

Upper-Silesian Rehabilitation Center "Repty" located in Tarnowskie Góry (Poland) provides rehabilitation of neurological patients. During the psychological rehabilitation of patients, a lot of exercises are used to stimulate language functions and other cognitive processes. Such exercises are usually carried out at the desk of the psychologist, using printed sheets of paper. However, there is a large part of patients whose disease has caused a paralysis of motor organs, which often makes them im-possible to move or write freehand. Therefore, exercises are often done in uncomfortable conditions at the bedside. Exercises in the form of application for tablets, probably significantly facilitate the work of psychologists. The aim of this study was the analysis of existing sets of rehabilitation exercises for possible adapting them to mo-bile devices (tablets). As a part of the work, application of sets of tasks for memory exercises has been created.

[*] Publication supported from the Human Capital Operational Programme co-financed by the European Union from the financial resources of the European Social Fund, project no. POKL.04.01.02-00-209/11; publication co-financed by the Institute of Informatics at Silesian University of Technology, statutory research no. BK/215/Rau2/2013.

K. Miesenberger et al. (Eds.): ICCHP 2014, Part I, LNCS 8547, pp. 399–402, 2014.

2   State of the Art

To improve cognitive functions, the exercises should be frequently repeated [1], which reduces the effort of the brain during collection and processing of information, and these operations are becoming faster and more automatic [2]. Repeating improves the performance of all cognitive functions, memory – as well [3]. It has been proven that each type of cognitive exercises can produce long-term memory improvement [4]. The basic cognitive exercises include [5]: language exercises (i.e. matching cards representing syllables in order to create a particular word), working memory exercises (i.e. memorizing shopping lists, phone numbers, etc.) and finding differences (i.e. comparing two illustrations).

Now there are a lot of sets of cognitive exercises prepared by experts of cognitive functions. One of them was prepared in the HERMES project [6,7]. However, due to the weakening of the memory of older people and the content of certain language tasks, developers should base on examples prepared for patients of a particular nationality, whose authors are professionals from the same country. For example, for Polish language, there are also numerous sets of memory exercises [8,9,10,11].

3   Analysis of Memory Exercises

At the first stage of the work, the analysis of the contents of memory exercises used in the Rehabilitation Center were done. We analyzed more than 300 different memory tasks presented on the pages of workbooks. Numerous tasks were classified to different categories because of the type of content and cognitive functions trained. A table containing a statement of the types of exercises was prepared. It consists of: drawing, calendar, for memorizing, language exercises, anagrams, crossword puzzles, exercises with texts of songs and proverbs, mathematical exercises, geographical exercises and associations. For each type there was assigned a certain number of specific tasks. In each type the feasibility of adaptation for tablets (full, partial, impossible) and complexity of interaction (entering characters, indication, drag&drop) were evaluated. A need to define additional resources (lists of words, images) was also specified.

Initially, we expected that each category of tasks requires a different mechanism of implementation in the prepared application. However, certain types of jobs can be applied to the same types of interactions. It appears, that from a software developer's point of view, some types of tasks are very similar to each other. It is very important for them because it allows to simplify the development and improves the efficiency of applications for tablets. In many cases, adaptation of tasks to the tablets is possible after the minor changes in the exercise mechanism i.e. writing any words should be replaced by a multiple-choice test. That is a big help for many older people (most of the patients in the Rehabilitation Center), because they have problems entering text with the virtual keyboard displayed on the screen.

4   Prototype Application

The requirements for our application are separated into functional, which are related to the implemented activities, and non-functional - which describe the expected technical expectations. Functional requirements for the application can include: creating a user associated with a particular patient, running exercises, execution time measurement, archiving workout results, summarizing of patients results. Non-functional can be as follow: proper contrast of shown images, simple and large sized graphics, sound confirmation of accepted and rejected operations performed by the user on the tablet surface, automatic voice reading the tasks content by synthesizer, adaptation of the application to the most popular tablets with 10" of diagonal.

So far, the sense of using mobile devices such as tablets in the Rehabilitation Center has not yet been confirmed. It would be unwise, to prepare an application for full functionality, allowing to practice exercises from each category. Now only a prototype application is used in the pilot studies. Screenshots (Fig.1 and Fig.2) demonstrate sample language and drawing exercises. The application language is Polish, because it was designed for the Polish-spoken patients.

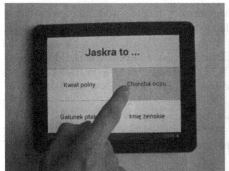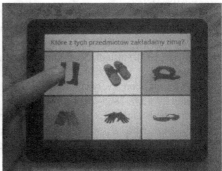

Fig. 1. Images show textual and drawing exercises that use indicating

Fig. 2. Exercise using multi-selection

5   Conclusions and Future Work

As a part of the work, there was developed the application of sets of memory exercises on the tablet with Android operating system. Pilot studies are finished, but this application must be verified during testing of a large number of patients for whom rehabilitation of cognitive impairment is carried out. Ultimately, tests will be provided in the Upper-Silesian Rehabilitation Center. It is assumed that patients will be characterized by varying degrees of cognitive impairment and manual disability. Prototype application will be improved by the introduction of larger number of difficulty levels and more varied tasks.

References

1. Kleim, J.A., Jones, T.A.: Principles of experience-dependent neural plasticity: implications for rehabilitation after brain damage. Journal of Speech, Language, and Hearing Research 51, 225–239 (2008)
2. Brown, J., Fenske, M.: The Winners Brain, pp. 219–161. De Capo Press, United States of America (2010)
3. Morrison, A.B., Chein, J.M.: Does working memory training work? the promise and challenges of enhancing cognition by training working memory. Psychonomic Bulletin & Review 18(1), 46–60 (2011)
4. Willis, S.L., Tennstedt, S.L., Marsiske, M., Ball, K., Elias, J., Koepke, K.M., Morris, J.N., Rebok, G.W., Unverzagt, F.W., Stoddard, A.M., Wright, E.: Long-term effects of cognitive training on everyday functional outcomes in older adults. National Institutes of Health 296(23), 2805–2814 (2006)
5. About the BrainHQ Exercises, http://www.positscience.com/why-brainhq/about-the-brainhq-exercises
6. HERMES – Cognitive Care and Guidance for Active Aging, FP7-ICT 216709, http://www.fp7-hermes.eu/
7. Buiza, C., Soldatos, J., Petsatodis, T., Geven, A., Etxaniz, A., Tscheligi, M.: HERMES: Pervasive Computing and Cognitive Training for Aging Well. In: Omatu, S., Rocha, M.P., Bravo, J., Fernández, F., Corchado, E., Bustillo, A., Corchado, J.M. (eds.) IWANN 2009, Part II. LNCS, vol. 5518, pp. 756–763. Springer, Heidelberg (2009)
8. Dzienniak, M., Malinowska, B.: Cwiczenia stymulujace funkcje jezykowe i inne procesy poznawcze. Czesc I i II. Lódzkie Towarzystwo Alzheimerowskie (2011)
9. Klich-Raczka, A., Piotrowicz, K., Staszczak, E., Klich, A.: Cwiczenia pamieci i innych funkcji poznawczych. Lunbeck Poland sp. z o.o (2012)
10. Ratajczak, M.: Cwiczenia usprawniajace pamiec. Merz Pharmaceuticals (2008)
11. Subela, K., Cuper, M.: Trenuj umysl. Zeszyt cwiczen do pracy z osobami z zaburzeniami pamieci. Oficyna Wydawnicza Impuls (2012)

Transit Information Access for Persons with Visual or Cognitive Impairments

German Flores, Benjamin Cizdziel, Roberto Manduchi,
Katia Obraczka, Julie Do, Tyler Esser, and Sri Kurniawan

Department of Computer Engineering, University of California, Santa Cruz, USA

Abstract. We are developing a location-based information delivery system to facilitate efficient and safe use of public transportation by people who have visual or cognitive impairments. This system comprises Wi-Fi beacons (access points) that are placed at bus stations and inside bus vehicles. Users of this system receive information on their cell phone, without the need for GPS or for Internet connectivity. The system allows one to receive information about an upcoming bus at a bus stop and to select a specific bus line. Once the desired bus arrives, the system automatically connects to the access point on the bus vehicle and remains connected while the user is riding the bus. The user can specify a desired bus stop, and the system informs the user (by a speech message) with enough advance notice when the bus is approaching the stop.

1   Introduction

Public transportation is key to independence for those who, for various reasons, cannot drive. At the same time, independent use of public transportation can be challenging for large portions of these individuals. For example, individuals with cognitive disabilities may have problems organizing and executing independent trips [5],[9]. Individual with visual impairments are also at a disadvantage when taking public transit [1],[3],[6]. A blind person cannot access printed information at a bus stop; cannot read the number of a bus arriving at a bus station; and, once on a bus, may miss the desired stop if the bus driver does not call all stops, or if the ADA-mandated audible announcement cannot be heard, for example due to loud background noise. These problems were highlighted by a survey conducted jointly by the LightHouse for the Blind and the City of San Francisco in 2007 with more than 50 blind passengers [6].

We are developing a novel approach for conveying real-time, customizable, multi-modal travel-related information to any passenger, directly on his or her own cell phone. Unlike previous research addressing a similar problem [1,2] [9], our system does not require access to the Internet, and thus does not demand subscription to a data plan. Information is pushed to one's cell phone from Wi-Fi beacons that are placed in the public transit vehicles or at bus stops. In addition, users of this system do not rely on GPS data from their cell phone (as, for example, in [8]). Note that GPS data can be inaccurate or unavailable in

K. Miesenberger et al. (Eds.): ICCHP 2014, Part I, LNCS 8547, pp. 403–410, 2014.
© Springer International Publishing Switzerland 2014

some situations (e.g. urban canyons), and continuous GPS usage quickly drains a cell phone's battery.

In our proposed system, Wi-Fi beacons are placed at bus stops as well as within bus vehicles (see Fig. 1(a)). Upon arriving at a bus station, users of this technology receive an acoustic signal from their cell phone, indicating that a connection with the local beacon was established. At that point, the user can interrogate the system to obtain information about that bus stop and about incoming bus vehicles. As soon as the desired bus arrives, a new connection is established with the in-bus beacon and maintained while the passenger is riding the bus, and more information, this time related to the specific bus ride, is made available. For example, the user is informed well in advance when the bus is approaching the desired bus stop, in time to get ready to exit the bus. Previous work [7] used Bluetooth beacons placed at bus stops to alert the user about the arrival of a desired bus. Use of Bluetooth beacons was also considered in [4] to provide information to a blind pedestrian about the status of a traffic light.

This contribution reports on current accomplishments of this project for what concerns the technical development of the system. More specifically, we discuss the implementation of the Wi-Fi beacons, the development of the client software and of the user interface, and early experiments assessing the ability of the mobile system to connect to the beacons. User studies with blind individuals are planned for the near future.

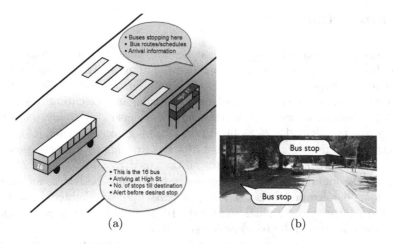

Fig. 1. (a) Conceptual system representation. Wi-Fi beacons are placed at a bus stop and inside a bus, providing different types of information to a user carrying a client software in a mobile device. (b) The location of the bus stops considered in our experiments in the UCSC campus.

2   System Description

The system consists of two main units: a client and server. The server is the access point application that communicates with the client to transmit relevant bus information. The server was designed to transmit specific information when a client is within its transmission range and the user has requested information. Users of this system interact with a client application, written in Java and implemented in an Android mobile device (a Nexus 7 tablet). Both client and server have been designed and implemented to be modular, responsive, and intuitive, allowing the user to receive relevant information when desired in a convenient modality.

2.1   Server

In our current system, Wi-Fi beacons are implemented in TP-LINK routers re-programmed with OpenWrt, a Linux-based operating system that provides a writable root file system with package management and other configurable scripts and tools. Routers are configured as Access Points (APs), and a global static primary IP address is hardcoded into each of the APs.

For our current prototype, two types of APs were reprogrammed and reconfigured: a bus stop AP and an in-bus AP. These APs look and work exactly in the same way, except for the type of information sent to the client. Bus stop APs, which are placed at bus stops, send bus routes numbers and other information such as the address or the name of the bus stop. In-bus APs, which are placed inside a bus, send the bus identifier and information about the bus stops encountered in the route. The information sent by the APs helps the client recognize the type of AP that is within range and perform adequate actions such as prompting the user to select a bus or alerting the user that their selected bus is within range and about to arrive. Note that an in-bus AP traveling on a bus may come within range of other bus stop APs (located on one or both sides of the street), or other moving in-bus APs (see Fig. 2(a)). The client must be able to differentiate between these situations and perform appropriate actions. The information exchanged must be short and compact to allow for fast lossless data transmission even when several users may be using the client application at a bus stop or inside a bus at the same time.

2.2   Client

The client is an Android application written in Java that incorporates the following hardware and software technologies: Wi-Fi, touch and gesture detection, text-to-speech (TTS) engine, socket and message communication protocols, database management system (DBMS), and Android services. Upon arrival at a bus stop, the user and the system must perform several actions that include: Start the Android application; Scan and detect nearby access points; Provide guidance to the user in order to select a bus stop and a bus to board; Provide information

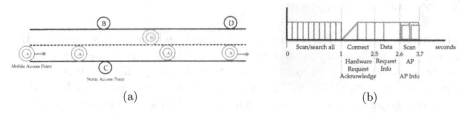

Fig. 2. (a) Possible mobile and static access point configurations. The black circles, B, C, and D, are access points that have been placed at a bus stop. The red and orange double circles, A and H, are access points that have been placed in a bus. Moving from left to right, a bus access point can be by itself, come near two bus stop access points, come near another bus access point, or arrive at a location where only one bus stop access point is present. (b) Sequence diagram of events to scan, connect, and send data between the client and the server.

about the bus routes and arrival time; Detect all of the users touch screen inputs: gestures or single and double taps; Query the local database to retrieve bus arrival information; Provide the user with auditory feedback; Listen for in-bus access points; Connect, disconnect and switch between bus stop and in-bus access points and vice versa; Stay connected to an access point; Listen for other bus stop or in-bus access points. Some of these actions must occur asynchronously and without interrupting other actions that are concurrently working or about to start. In order to fulfill this requirement, the client unit was subdivided into five main subcomponents: user activity, Wi-Fi manager service, schedule and instructions service, gesture recognition engine, and text to speech engine. The Wi-Fi manager service is the most complex component since it has to manage several threads (actions) and must be running at all times in order to listen, connect, and disconnect from access points that are within range.

These components must follow an order of execution determined by the user activity. For example, connection and initial communication with an access point must occur before transmission of data. Fig. 2(b) shows an example of a sequence of phases leading to a connection. In this scenario, it took exactly 1 second to find an access point, 1.5 seconds to fully connect to the access point, about 1/10 of a second to transmit handshake data, and 0.5 seconds to scan for selected access points. In general, the scan, connect, and data transfer phases take shorter times than in this example, depending on multiple factors including the distance to the access point and the presence of nearby obstacles.

3   User Interface

The client interface is designed to be effective at communicating proper instructions to blind users, guiding users to their desired task, and providing intuitive usage modalities. It uses multi-touch interaction techniques, text-to-speech, and tactile feedback. The user inputs data through single and double screen taps; simple instructions and information are facilitated via speech; and verbal Yes or

No words or non-speech sounds are used to provide feedback as the user single or double taps the touch screen.

Interaction with the system occurs in two main situations: when the user arrives at a bus stop and wants to be informed once a desired bus has arrived; and when the user is in the bus and wants to be informed about when to exit the bus. A typical information exchange in the first case would proceed as follows. Upon arrival at a bus stop, the client automatically detects nearby APs and iterates through each one of them, prompting the user to select one if multiple bus stop AP have been found. Once selected, the AP at the bus stop transmits relevant bus information such as the AP location and bus routes. The system then prompts the user to select one of the bus lines that he or she wishes to board. Once the bus line has been selected, the system listens and waits until the selected bus comes within range, at which point the system disconnects from the bus stop AP, connects to the bus AP, and alerts the user that the bus is arriving. In the second case, when the user is in the bus, the system is already connected to the bus AP. The system provides periodic updates such as arrival time, next stop name, and confirmation of arrival. In addition, the system allows the user to inquiry about the current route.

The set of instructions and confirmations that are used to guide the user during interaction with the system have been implemented in a hash map structure to allow for fast and easy retrieval and expansion. The client application sequentially iterates through these sets or dictionaries as a state machine, moving from a state to the next, and speaking the correct instruction, question, or confirmation given the current state of the system. For example, when the user opens the application, the system greets the user by speaking *"Welcome"* and then it asks the user *"Do you wish to connect to network X?"* Depending on the user response, the system provides a proper confirmation such as *"Bus N has been selected"* or *"The arrival time is ... "*. At any given state of the system, a phrase or word is grabbed from the dictionary, parsed to fill in any unknown information such as the bus number or the network name, and then sent to the TTS engine, which speaks it.

4   Experiments

To test the system and its various components under different conditions, we conducted a total of 41 trials comprising the following scenarios: (1) Walking from and to an access point in open and busy areas; (2) Remaining in the bus for at least 20 minutes; (3) Multiple situations at a bus stop.

Scenario 1. An AP was placed in open and in busy areas, with the user carrying the client system walking away and towards the access point. Open areas are areas with no buildings or large objects present (e.g., an open field). Busy areas are characterized by buildings and large objects surrounding the access point (e.g. a street surrounded by houses and trees). In both cases, we investigated any Wi-Fi connectivity issues that may occur due to the obstruction or disruption of the radio signal, and obtained estimate ranges for access point discovery and connectivity.

Scenario 2. We placed the AP inside a bus, with the user remaining in the same bus while connected with the AP for extended periods of time. These tests were designed to ensure that the application remained connected to the access point continuously in realistic situations.

Scenario 3. We tested the system in four different situations with a potential user arriving at a bus stop (shown in Fig. 1(b)), and with a bus subsequently arriving at the same stop. More precisely, we tested (a) connection to a bus stop AP upon user arrival to the bus stop, (b) connection to a in-bus AP when no bus stop AP was present, (c) switch from the bus stop AP to a in-bus AP upon bus arrival, and (d) connection to a in-bus AP as the user entered the bus, then remaining connected to the in-bus AP for the duration of the trip. In all of the situations mentioned above, the system was tested for discovery and connection time, connection switching performance, and transmission range were measured.

A single router, shown in Fig. 3(a), was placed at the bus stop, while another router was placed in a shuttle bus that came to the bus stop every 20 minutes. (The UCSC Dept. of Parking Transportation and the UCSC Police were notified in advance of the experiments.) The "open area" tests were performed at the UCSC West Field (a large open field without trees), while the tests in the "busy area were performed at the Science Hill bus stop (Fig. 1(b)). Transmission range measurements from and to the access point were recorded for both environments.

The application was installed in a Nexus 7 tablet and a record of the trials was kept. A trial was declared successful if the client was able to connect to an access point within a reasonable amount of time and if the client and server were able to communicate with each other without a single data packet loss. In general, results show that there were no discovery, connection time and transmission range issues for 5 out of the 6 different conditions. Only in one condition (connection switch when the bus approaches the bus stop) the system was not able to communicate properly with the in-bus access point for the initial trials; proper revision of the software led to successful connection trials in subsequent trials.

An example of connection sequence with timing information is reported in Fig. 2(b) Typical transmission ranges are shown in Fig. 3(b). It was observed that the *effective range* (i.e. the range in which the client is able to connect to the server, send information, and remain connected) was of approximately of 55 yards (165 feet). The *actual range* (i.e., the range in which the client is able to detect the server but not to connect or transmit information) was of approximately 70 yards (211 ft).

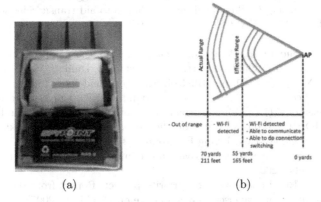

(a)   (b)

Fig. 3. (a) Access point prototype. The system consists of a pre-configured router and a 12V battery. This system was placed in a bus stop and inside a bus. (b) Transmission range of a pre-configured access point. The effective range is the range in which the client is able to connect to the server, send information and remain connected; whereas the actual range is the range in which the client is able to detect the server but neither is able to connect nor transmit information. Any access point located at a distance greater than 211 ft is considered out of range.

5 Conclusions

We have described the design and implementation of a system that will provide personalized, just-in-time public transit information to a person who, due to visual impairment or cognitive disability, may have difficulty using a bus. We are now planning for experiments with visually impaired participants who will test the system. Measurements will be taken concerning the quality of user interface on the tablet, the ability to easily navigate the menus and input data, and the ability to seamlessly switch connection to the in-bus AP once the bus arrives. Based on the results with these tests, we will adjust the system parameters and fine tune the user interface, in preparation for more thorough tests involving multiple campus shuttles and bus stops at UCSC.

Acknowledgments. The work described in this paper was supported by a contract from the National Academy of Science, issued under the Department of Transportation Award No. DC-26-7321. Dr. J. Coughlan from SKERI, Dr. A. Karshmer from USF, and Mr. P. Cantisani, provided invaluable comments to an original draft of the project report.

References

1. Azenkot, S., Fortuna, E.: Improving public transit usability for blind and deaf-blind people by connecting a Braille display to a smartphone. In: Proc. ASSETS 2010, Orlando, FL (2010)

2. Babeau, S., Labrador, J., Winters, P.L., Perez, H., Georggi, N.L.: The Travel Assistant Device: Utilizing GPS-enabled mobile phones to aid transit rides with special needs. In: Proc. 15th World Congress on Intelligent Transportation Systems, NY (2008)
3. Banâtre, M., Couderc, P., Pauty, J., Becus, M.: Ubibus: Ubiquitous computing to help blind people in public transport. In: Brewster, S., Dunlop, M.D. (eds.) Mobile HCI 2004. LNCS, vol. 3160, pp. 310–314. Springer, Heidelberg (2004)
4. Bohonos, S., Lee, A., Malik, A., Thai, C., Manduchi, R.: Universal real-time navigational assistance (URNA): An urban Bluetooth beacon for the blind. In: Proc. ACM SIGMOBILE International Workshop on Systems and Networking Support for Healthcare and Assisted Living Environments (2007)
5. Cain, A.: Design elements of effective transit information materials. FDOT Final Report (November 2004)
6. Lanzerotti, R.: Blind and low vision priority project. Report from the LightHouse for the Blind and San Francisco Mayor's Office on Disability (2007)
7. Lim, J.T.F., Leong, G.H., Kiong, T.K.: Accessible Bus System: A Bluetooth application. In: Assistive Technology for Visually Impaired and Blind People, pp. 363–384. Springer, London (2008)
8. Silva, J., Silva, C., Marcelino, L., Ferreira, R., Pereira, A.: Assistive mobile software for public transportation. In: Proc. UBICOMM 2011 (2011)
9. Winters, P.L., Barbeau, S., Georggi, N.L.: Travel Assistance Device (TAD) to help transit riders. Final report for Transit IDEA Project 52 (2010)

Indoor Navigation System for the Visually Impaired Using One Inertial Measurement Unit (IMU) and Barometer to Guide in the Subway Stations and Commercial Centers

Jesus Zegarra Flores and René Farcy

Laboratoire Aimé Cotton, Université Paris Sud, Orsay Cedex, France
`jesus.zegarra-flores@u-psud.fr`,
`rene.farcy@lac.u-psud.fr`

Abstract. The main research about indoor navigation is about the use of Wi-Fi, Bluetooth or Ultra Wide band technology for locating one person in a building. These systems give an absolute position of the person; however, it is mandatory to put the hotspots of every technology in the building for calculating this position. An Inertial Measurement Unit is usually placed on the foot because, it is easier to compute the distance. The aim of this work is to use inexpensive sensors which come in a Smart Phone, which are handheld, or belt mounted for guiding one visually impaired in two main tests: the subway station and the commercial center. We are not intending neither to put any hotspot or landmarks on the place nor to use the IMU on the foot for ergonomic reasons. The results and performances are better in the subway stations than in the commercial centers.

Keywords: Visually Impaired, Mobility, IMU, Subway Stations, Commercial Centers.

1   Introduction

The research about indoor Navigation for the visually impaired, where there is no GPS signal, includes the use of Wi-Fi [1], Bluetooth [2], or Wideband [3] hotspots, which are placed in the building for the localization of the person. All of these devices give the absolute location of the person, who carries a receiver of each technology, in the building. Other systems use a hybrid system like RFID (Radio Frequency Identification) /IMU [4].The RFID lends to locate the person using the difference of time of arrival. The IMU (Inertial Measurement Unit) is usually placed on the foot of the person [5,6]. This case has been much more investigated because it lends to compute the horizontal acceleration integration every time the foot touches the ground (when the speed is equal to 0) for obtaining the distance.

   The aim of this work is to use inexpensive sensors which come in a Smartphone (for example Galaxy S3, S4 or similar that comes with a three axis compass, a three axis gyroscope, a three axis accelerometer and a barometer that works as an altimeter)

K. Miesenberger et al. (Eds.): ICCHP 2014, Part I, LNCS 8547, pp. 411–418, 2014.

and to use computational solutions for guiding one visually impaired in two main tests: the subway station and the commercial center. We are not intending to put any hotspot or landmarks on the place. The guiding strategy used is the "recognition of each segment of the real trajectory" that will be discussed, later, in this article.

2   Materials

The Smart Phone used in these experiences is the Galaxy S3 because it comes with all the sensors required. For ergonomic reasons, we have chosen two main ways of using the device (see Fig. 1): on the hand pointing in the same direction of displacement of the person and a belt mounted on the right or left of the hip. The developed application has been adapted to be used with "Talk Back" (accessibility service in the An-droid Smart Phones) which means to use the application created swiping the finger from right to left or vice versa for passing from one function to another and to click wherever on the screen two times rapidly for accessing to the function (it was also included one vibration).

Fig. 1. Figure on the left side, user using Smart Phone in the hand. Figure on the right, user with the Smartphone on the right side of the hip.

The strategy used for the indoor navigation is to recognize each segment of the real trajectory and to eliminate the error due to the distance estimation when the user passes from one segment to another segment. In order to recognize every segment, it is necessary to know:

- The total distance the person has walked in one segment.
- If the person is in a "walking state" or "stop state".
- If the person has made ¼ of a turn right or left; or if the person has made a U turn.
- If the person walks in one straight line.
- If the person has passed from a floor to another.

The main problem about the use of the device on the hand or belt mounted is that, we cannot have accurate signals coming from the horizontal acceleration due to the damping of the joints when we walk. As a consequence, it is hard to find the initial values for starting the integration and we cannot compute the horizontal distance accurately. On the other hand, it has been proposed to count the number of steps from the vertical acceleration (pedometer basis, see Fig. 2). To set the step length, the person has to walk a premeasured distance and we divide it by the number of steps. This information is set on the application. The total distance is estimated multiplying the number of steps by this average step length. Additionally, in order to know, if the person is in a walking or stop state, it has also been used the vertical acceleration. When the person walks, the signal has big amplitudes compared to the case when he is at stop state (see Fig. 2).

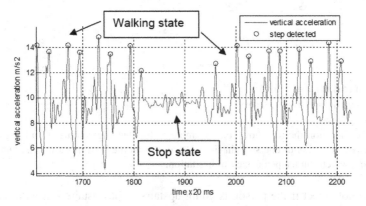

Fig. 2. Vertical acceleration of one person in a "walking state" and "stop state"

In order to know if the person has made a ¼ turn right or left, or a U turn, we use the heading of the gyroscope (relative orientation). We do not use the heading of the compass because the magnetic field is more likely to be perturbed in the subways because of the electric lines (see Fig. 3).

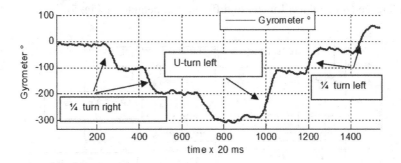

Fig. 3. Gyrometer to detect ¼ turn (+90° or -90°) or U-turn (180° or -180°)

It is also important to know if the person has walked in one "straight line" because it is considered that the person has walked in that direction with no hesitation (see Fig. 4). That is possible because we can detect one step and save the horizontal heading. Having done 6 steps, we calculate the subtraction of every heading (G6, G5, G4, G3, G2) of the gyro meter with the first G1 information. If the subtraction in all cases is less than 30°, we consider the person has done one straight line (see Figure 4).

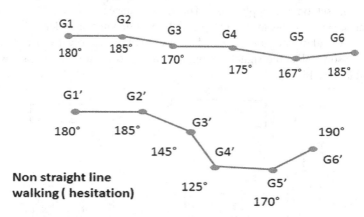

Fig. 4. The figure on the top shows one example of the heading coming from the gyroscope when one person walks in one straight line. The figure on the bottom shows one non-straight line walking which can happen in case of hesitation.

We cannot detect if the person is going upstairs or downstairs just with the information of a three axis accelerometer placed on the belt or in the hand because of the movement of the body and of the damps of the joints. In addition, the shape of the acceleration signals changes from one person walking to another person for having just one pattern of recognition. In order to know if the person has passed from one floor to another, we propose to use a barometer as an altimeter. The main limitation is that we cannot detect if the person goes down or up three or four steps because the signal is still in the noise. We need to pass at least 1or 2 meters of height for detecting the difference (Δ 0.1 hPa = 1 meter of difference of height, see Fig. 5).

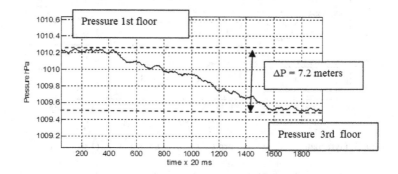

Fig. 5. Pressure signal to detect a difference of altitude

3   Methods

Two main tests have been conducted with two fully blinded people and one partially sighted person for testing the reliability and accuracy of the system. Firstly, the device is tested in three subway stations in Paris for going from one platform to other platform with paths with more than 100 meters of distance and that requires the use of stairs. Secondly, the application has also been tested in one one-floor commercial center for going to three different shops with paths with more than 100 meters of distance. None of the places was equipped with Wi-Fi or Bluetooth hotspots; therefore, we have used a previous cartography of the place for having the real path of the route that we put in the device.

The system gives the vocal information using the mobility language (one information might be "at the end of the corridor, turn right and go up the stairs"). While approaching to the end of the corridor, 7 meters before (uncertainty zone), we give the information" get ready for turning right". In order to indicate if the person has taken the right corridor, the device gives one "ok" confirmation just if the person walks in one straight line in the direction that matches with the direction of the real route. If the user has taken the wrong direction that does not match with the real route the system will say "wrong corridor taken". The system will indicate as well the place to start the navigation in order to confirm if we are in the initial position of the path.

In order to illustrate the navigation in these two places, with the corresponding vocal indications, two navigation examples will be shown (Fig. 6 and 7).

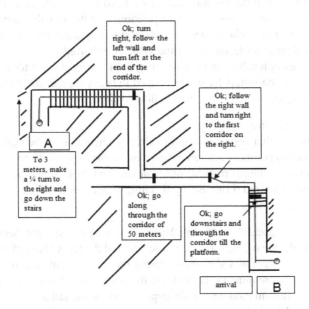

Fig. 6. Navigation in the "Place d'Italie" subway. From platform A to platform B with the vocal directions received by the user. The red line shows the trajectory done by the user. The total distance is about 100 meters.

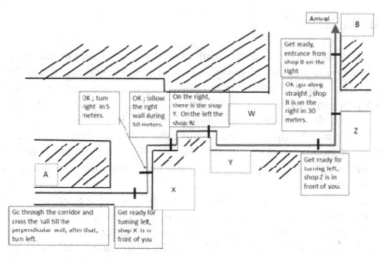

Fig. 7. Navigation in the commercial center from shop A to shop B. The vocal directions are also shown in the figure. The total distance is about 135 meters.

4   Results

The main difference found between the tests about the subway stations and the commercial centers is that in the subway station we have most of the time long corridors that can help the guidance (less degrees of freedom) for the visually impaired. On the other hand, in the commercial centers, there are wider spaces that can complicate the guidance (more degrees of freedom) for the visually impaired.

Twenty minutes of teaching the use of the system was necessary for getting familiar with the device. The testers have appreciated the easy way to use the device based on swiping the finger on the screen and the double click.

- In the subway stations:
  One problem was that two of the testers already knew one of the stations and they had their personal points of reference for going to the same platform, consequently, they did not follow the instructions of the device and they got lost and confused after some time. They redid the test by listening to the vocal indication and they arrived to the final destination.

Another problem happened in one of the stations where one right handed visually impaired put the device on the left side of the belt and the algorithm did not detect one of the turns. The problem was solved decreasing the threshold of detection of ¼ turn.

6 out of 9 paths were done in the first try, the others three were done in the second try. The guidance information was really appreciated for the testers.

The first tests about indoor navigation are very promising. The tests have also confirmed the way to guide one person by using the strategy proposed.

It is also very important that the visually impaired have a good mobility level for using the system.

- In the commercial center: In contrast to the tests in the subway stations, in the first 20 minutes, one of the testers did not arrive to the final destination. In this case, the person has to be trained to acquire one discipline of use which is neither spontaneous nor evident. For example, they have to avoid crossing places in diagonal, not to turn before the end of a segment etc. Once the person has acquired this discipline, he was able to arrive to the three destinations with no problem.

The step length of one of the subjects with hesitation was 50% the step length when he walks with a normal pace. As a consequence, the total distance calculated by using our estimation was with an error of the 50%. The case of hesitation is a critical case which is still not solved just using the IMU.

In order to anticipate one change of direction in the trajectory, the device gives one vocal indication 7 meters before arriving to the intersections. The vocal information is, for example « get ready for turning right ». This subject got confused because he thought that he had to do the turning the time he listened to the message and not at the end of the segment (intersection). We have improved the instruction, changing the message « Turning right + (name of the shop) at the end of the segment» which is clearer for the user in one commercial center where there are a lot of shops. In this way, the person has another point of reference knowing the name of the shops where he is and where he has to turn.

5   Conclusions

In this article, we have shown the possibility to guide the visually impaired people by using inexpensive sensors IMU and barometer, which come in one Smart Phone. It is possible to guide them in few hundred meters without using any special equipment placed in the indoor area. The guiding strategy proposed by the "recognition of each segment of the trajectory" seems to be accurate under the next conditions: the user has to be trained in order to understand the specific characteristics of the mobility language and the navigation and the learning of the strategies of displacement in order to avoid the failure of the IMU. Our research will continue in order to improve the algorithms to find solutions for the cases when the person hesitates a lot reducing dramatically the length of their steps.

References

1. Evennou, F., Marx, F.: Advanced integration of WiFi and inertial navigation systems for indoor mobile positioning. Eurasip Journal on Applied Signal Processing, 164–164 (2006)
2. Feldmann, S., Kyamakya, K., Zapater, A., Lue, Z.: An Indoor Bluetooth-Based Positioning System: Concept, Implementation and Experimental Evaluation. In: International Conference on Wireless Networks, pp. 109–113 (June 2003)
3. Fontanna, R.: Advances in Ultra Wideband Indoor Geolocation System, http://www.cwins.wpi.edu/wlans01/proceedings/wlan53d.pdf (retrieved from)

4. House, S., Connell, S., Milligan, I., Austin, D., Hayes, T.L., Chiang, P.: Indoor localization using pedestrian dead reckoning updated with RFID-based fiducials. In: 2011 Annual International Conference of the IEEE Engineering in Medicine and Biology Society, EMBC, pp. 7598–7601. IEEE (2011)
5. Feliz Alonso, R., Zalama Casanova, E., Gómez García-Bermejo, J.: Pedestrian tracking using inertial sensors (2009)
6. Stirling, R., Fyfe, K., Lachapelle, G.: Evaluation of a new method of heading estimation for pedestrian dead reckoning using shoe mounted sensors. Journal of Navigation 58(1), 31–45 (2005)

Communication System for Persons with Cerebral Palsy

In Situ Observation of Social Interaction Following Assisted Information Request

Yohan Guerrier[1,2], Janick Naveteur[1,2,3], Christophe Kolski[1,2], and Franck Poirier[4]

[1] Univ Lille Nord de France, Lille, France
[2] UVHC, LAMIH, CNRS, UMR 8201, Valenciennes, France
{yohan.guerrier,janick.naveteur,
christophe.kolski}@univ-valenciennes.fr
[3] Neurosciences, Université Lille 1, Villeneuve d'Ascq, France
[4] Laboratoire UMR Lab-STICC Université de Bretagne Sud, Vannes, France
Franck.Poirier@univ-ubs.fr

Abstract. People with disabilities may encounter many communication difficulties. Our main goal is to develop a communication system, called COMMOB, designed to assist people with cerebral palsy in different contexts: at home, at work and in public places. After a brief review of the different categories of assistive communication systems, our user-centered design approach is presented. It was tested in a public place in the context of a help request by a cerebral palsy person in a wheelchair. The result concerns particularly the response rate. The assistive power of COMMOB was rated from the respondents' and the user's point of view. The main lesson to be learned is that the most difficult was to attract the attention of people and to engage the interaction.

Keywords: Communication, mobility, cerebral palsy (CP), communication aid, COMMOB.

1 Introduction

People with disabilities are often marginalized, due to different processes of exclusion depending upon their physical, psychological, or cognitive functioning level. Restricted access to transportation works to isolation. Progress has been made in terms of accessibility due to architectural and technological improvements, but many individuals did not take advantage of these environments especially because of communication limitations. Fear to be unable to get information and/or help from others if they had to deal with an unforeseen situation may lead to feelings of generalized helplessness. The presence of an accompanying person (mostly usual family or professional careers) is thus often *a sine qua non* condition for travelling. However, this dependency can be seen by several disabled people as a limitation in both the development of an expected barrier-free living and their wish to have a meaningful role in the society. But requesting help from an unknown person is a challenge for many of them.

K. Miesenberger et al. (Eds.): ICCHP 2014, Part I, LNCS 8547, pp. 419–426, 2014.

The first goal of the present research program is the development of a communication system designed to assist people with communication impairments not only at home or at work with their relatives or colleagues, but also on the go with unknown individuals. This communication system also allows the communication with software applications (e.g., to write a document, to consult web sites, or to program), but the approach reported here does not exploit this potentiality. The specifications of this communication system, called COMMOB (COMmunication means for MOBility), have been published in [4,5]. The second goal is to test the efficacy of this system in real setting for both the disabled requester and the information/help providers. This paper focuses on this goal and it begins with a brief state of the art about different categories of communication systems for people with cerebral palsy. Different communication needs of such people (considered here as users) are accordingly presented. Then, our current work on the COMMOB communication system is explained. The article concludes with a discussion and research perspectives.

2   State of the Art

People with athetoid cerebral palsy (CP), i.e., multifaceted impairment syndrome secondary to lesions or anomalies of the brain arising in the early stages of development, often encounter difficulties to formulate understandable sentences due to dysarthria. They also frequently present difficulties in making gestures that prevent the production of written language with either pen or keyboard. No two patients are affected in the same way, including as for their intellectual abilities: despite mental retardation is frequent, many patients have a normal intelligence [6] allowing them to use rather sophisticated systems.

Several main categories of communication aids, more or less usable by people with cerebral palsy, can be identified in the literature: virtual keyboards (see several examples in [2], [5], [7]), physical aids (such as Guide finger [1] or EdgeWrite [12]), speech recognition system [11], brain-computer interface [13] (Please note that optical motion tracking is not considered in this study, due to the uncontrolled movements of many people with cerebral palsy). The time required for text entry using virtual keyboards is important for people with cerebral palsy; more, such devices require a significant physical effort over a long period (see an example of a study in [3]). The physical aids have the drawback that they must be used since childhood to be very effective [3]. Speech recognition is not yet effective for people suffering from dysarthria [11]. Brain-Computer Interfaces are not usable for complex tasks.

The state of the art of the different categories of communication systems for these people revealed that very few are designed for a mobile usage.

3   User-Centered Evaluation of COMMOB

A first prototype of the COMMOB communication system is available. COMMOB is part of the doctoral thesis of the first author. This system is based on pictograms that were chosen to allow quick text entry using virtual keyboards. The difficulty is not only to make the software easy to use from the user interface point of view; the users have also to be efficient in their communication tasks; too much involuntary movements would temporarily or permanently reduce their accuracy in their actions through the user interface. The communication system is used on a tablet computer, which is installed directly on the wheelchair. We chose a tablet computer to make a compromise between the size and the display surface.

The Figure 1 shows page screens of the user interface, accessible through a joystick installed on the other side of the wheelchair: from the window #1, each module is accessible; for instance, the window #2 contains a module helping a computer scientist user to program (different pictograms helping to insert Java code are available); the window #3 shows a module supporting the generation of sentences from pictograms; the window #4 shows the virtual keyboard helping to generate words and sentences which are not represented by the available pictograms (e.g., names of cities).

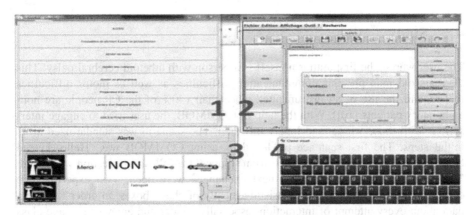

Fig. 1. Page-screens of the user interface of the COMMOB system

By definition, the system must help the user to explicit a request or exchange information without ambiguity and with a sufficiently high production rate. The performance at this level can be quantified with a series of objective parameters, such as the time needed to create a sentence and to express it to somebody, or the number of words produced per minute.

In addition to its technical performance, the system is also expected to play a role in the social interaction between the requester and the information/help provider, who is latter called "the respondent". As shown by [2], CP adults often report lower well-being that healthy controls and this seems to come from their life environment be-cause of inconvenient life in their community and few opportunities to go out. How-ever, many CP adults had self-esteem scores similar to those of the nondisabled groups [8]. The desire to be perceived as mentally competent to the greatest extent possible has also been reported [9]. Ordinary people in the street can be ignorant of the characteristics of the syndrome and its variability. The risk of failure in the information or help request is thus high, especially since uncertainty for the respondent as regards the requester can be a barrier to the social interaction. To see the technical equipment and its usage by the user will provide information about the intellectual ability of the disabled person. The respondent could thus adapt his/her behavior consequently. The present study aimed at testing this assumption in a context of mobility, in a shopping mall (Fig. 2).

Fig. 2. Cases of interaction using COMMOB in the context of mobility: information request concerning the location of the nearest station

4   Study

The user who is the first author himself is a person with athetoid cerebral palsy. This 29-years old man presents communication difficulties as well as motor difficulties that require the use of an instrumented wheelchair (40% of the CP people are non-ambulatory patients [10]). With the help of COMMOB, the user tried to engage interactions with those who attend lonely this area. The scenario was standardized at its initial steps. The first sentence produced by using COMMOB was "Hello, I need help" in French language. If the pedestrian stopped, the following question was asked: "Where is the tram station?" The next exchanges were open. Two experimenters completed an observation grid, consisting mostly of check boxes, in order to collect data about every attempt of interaction, especially gender and approximate age-class of people contacted by the user, and the outcome of the attempt of interaction. The total length of the effective interaction was measured. During the observation phase, the experimenters were situated far enough from the user and the respondent for not interfering in the social contact. At the end of his/her attempt to help the user, the respondent was interviewed by a female experimenter who came to him/her for this purpose. Questions bore on the performance of COMMOB and on the opinion of the respondent about the system. The respondent's knowledge of CP and any possible familiarity he/she might have with people suffering from CP or other disabilities were also rated. Responses were given on Likert scales or were notes between 0 and 10. Completing the questionnaire required no longer than 5 min per respondent but he/she was free to provide additional comments if he/she wished. Thereafter, the user rated the quality of the interaction from his point of view, with the possibility to add comments about his usage of COMMOB during this interaction.

Since most of the data related to the interactions presented a violation of normality conditions, non-parametric statistical analyses were performed

5   Results

Summary of the Interactions. The requester performed 281 attempts to interact with mall customers (women: 66 %); 7.6% of these people were estimated between the ages of 18-25, 55.1% between the ages 26-45, 28% between the ages 46-60, and 9.3% over 60 years old, without gender difference. Among those approached, 214 people (76%; group A) showed no signs of attention to the requester, whereas 45 did (16%; group B) but without real interaction (e.g. some just said "Hello"). Only 22 customers (8%, group C) engaged themselves in a deeper exchange with the requester. Gender differentiated these three a posteriori groups (Chi2(2)=19.2; p<.001), with a higher ratio of women in the group B (82% vs 58% in the group A, and 55% in the group C).

Ten respondents (group C) had a disabled person in their circle of acquaintances. Only one respondent knew what cerebral palsy is (just a little knowledge: 9; total ignorance: 12). The opinion the respondents had about the ability to get around alone people like the requester have ranged from a pessimistic view (0/10: "totally impossible to get around alone") to a rather optimistic view (8/10, with 10 corresponding to "they can get around without any problem"; median note: 5/10); this note was not significantly related to the other data. The requested information about the station was clearly provided by 9 respondents and was given incompletely by 7 other ones. The duration of the interaction varied between 17 s to 90 s (median duration: 41.5 s) and was not related to the other data. The shortest durations were due either to the fact that the respondent did not know where is the tram station, or to the fact that they quickly offered to accompany the requester to the station, a proposal that was not accepted.

COMMOB from the Respondent's Point of View. To the question of how the assistive system (only labeled as the 'system on the wheelchair') is helpful to disabled people such as the requester for getting around alone, the median response was 8/10 (range 3-10; Fig. 3). To the question of whether the system can incite people to help the disabled requester, the median response was 7/10 (range 2-10, Fig. 3). The notes for these two items did not significantly differ (W(22)=59, ns) and they were positively correlated between each other (ρ=0.69, p<.05).

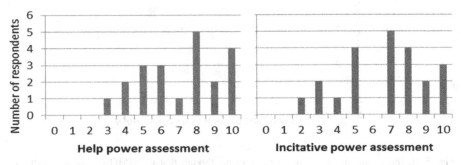

Fig. 3. Respondents' opinion (notes between 0 to 10) about the help the assistive system COMMOB can provide to disabled people, such as the requester, for getting around alone (left) and its incitative power for providing help (right)

Figure 4 showed the notes given by the respondents for the 3 items bearing on the quality of their own experience with COMMOB for reading the sentences on the tablet screen (median note: 10/10; 3 respondents were excluded since they did not look at the screen), for hearing the sentences produced by the speech synthesis (median note: 9/10), and for the communication rate allowed by COMMOB (median note: 6/10). Overall, these three notes significantly differed between themselves ($F(19,2)=6.14$, $p<.05$); the communication rate note was significantly smaller than both the reading note ($W(19)=16$, $p=.02$) and the hearing note ($W(22)=17.5$, $p<.01$), which did not significantly differed and were not significantly correlated between each other ($\rho=0.35$, ns). However, both the reading and the hearing notes were significantly related to the note provided for the communication rate (respectively, $\rho=0.49$, $p<.05$, and $\rho=0.56$, $p<.01$). The correlational approach did not significantly relate each of these three notes to the respondents' opinion about the help provided by COMMOB and about how it incites people to help the requester. However, the mean note for these three items significantly predicted the estimates of the helping power of COMMOB ($\rho= 0.43$, $p<.05$, Fig. 5; for its incitative power: $\rho=.297$, ns).

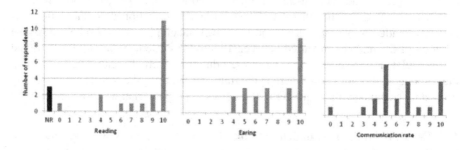

Fig. 4. Respondents' assessment of the quality of their experience with COMMOB (notes ranging between 0 and 10) for reading the sentences on the tablet screen (left side), for hearing the sentences produced by the speech synthesis (center), and for the communication rate (right)

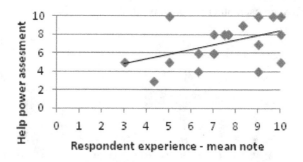

Fig. 5. Rating of amount of help the respondents though that COMMOB provides to the requester (note between 0 "not at all" and 10 "extremely") as a function of the mean evaluation of their own experience with COMMOB [(reading + hearing + communication rate)/3]

COMMOB from the Requester's Point of View. Difficulty in the access to the pictogram was reported only once by the requester ("quite a bit", due to reflection on the tablet screen). The ratings for the communication rate ("quite a bit" or "extremely" satisfactory in 81% of the cases) and for the speed of the joystick manipulation ("quite a bit" or "extremely" satisfactory in 95% of the cases) were not significantly correlated ($\rho=0.36$, ns), the lowest communication ratings given by the requester being mostly related to understanding difficulties he attributed to the respondent. Interestingly, these two ratings by the requester were far to correlate with the communication-rate note provided by the respondents (respectively, $\rho=.03$ and $\rho=.06$, ns).

As for the socio-behavioral components of the effective interactions, their initiation and the interactions themselves were rated by the requester as easy or very easy in respectively 95% and 86% of the cases, with a significant link between these two variables transformed into a 5-point scale ($\rho=.69$, $p<.01$). The correlational approach also revealed that the satisfaction of the requester with the interaction itself was significantly related to his satisfaction with the manipulation of the joystick ($\rho=.43$, $p<.05$), but not with the other factors including the communication rate ($\rho=0.34$, ns) as well as fatigue or pain (respectively, $\rho= -.17$ and $\rho=.32$, ns). Pain was experienced during 7 interactions ("a little bit" for 6 interactions and "moderately" for another one), and fatigue occurred during 15 interactions ("a little bit" for 12 interactions and "quite a bit" for 3 interactions). Overall, pain and fatigue were significantly related ($\rho=.48$, $p<.05$), and the amount of fatigue was also negatively related to the satisfaction with the joystick manipulation ($\rho=-.53$, $p<.05$).

6   Conclusions

The study confirmed the usefulness of COMMOB for helping a cerebral palsy person with strong communication limitations to request information to unknown individuals. Some technical improvements are suggested, especially to the screen location that limited the requester's gazing toward the respondent, which is an important component of the social interactions. The engaged interactions were mostly a rewarding experience for the requester towards an expected barrier-free living. However, the more crucial point was the difficulty to engage the interactions. The short-term perspectives focus on the strategies aiming at increasing the response rate with the help of COMMOB.

Other perspectives are linked to (a) the development of the COMMOB system, about new functions which can be envisaged, especially for improving the communication flow, and to (b) different types of complementary evaluations in laboratory or in mobility contexts.

Acknowledgments. This research work has been supported by CISIT, the Nord-Pas-de-Calais Region, the European Community (FEDER). The authors thank Elise Pelissier and Jordan Adelard for their contribution to the data collection. They also thank Carrefour and VPA for their hospitality.

References

1. Guide finger: http://djtechtools.com/2012/08/19/momentary-fx-in-ableton-live-advanced-midi-mappings/
2. Furukawa, A., Iwatsuki, H., Nishiyama, M., Nii, E., Uchida, A.: A study on the subjective well-being of adult patients with cerebral palsy. Journal of Physical Therapy Science, 13(1), pp. 31-35 (2001)
3. Guerrier, Y., Baas, M., Kolski, C., Poirier, F.: Comparative study between AZERTY-type and K-Hermes virtual keyboards dedicated to users with cerebral palsy. In C. Stephanidis, Universal Access in Human-Computer Interaction: Users Diversity, UAHCI 2011, LNCS 6766, pp. 310-319, Springer Heidelberg (2011)
4. Guerrier, Y., Kolski, C., Poirier, F.: Towards a communication system for people with athetoid cerebral palsy. In: Kotzé, P.; Marsden, G.; Lindgaard, G.; Wesson, J.; Winckler, M. (Eds.): Human-Computer Interaction - INTERACT 2013, 14th IFIP TC 13, LNCS, vol. 8120, Part IV, pp. 681-688, Springer Heidelberg (2013)
5. Guerrier, Y., Kolski, C., Poirier, F.: Proposition of a communication system used in mobility by users with physical disabilities, focus on cerebral palsy with athetoid problems. In: Proc. ICALT 2013, pp. 269-274, IEEE (2013)
6. Liptak, G.S., Accardo, P.J.: Health and social outcomes of children with cerebral palsy. The Journal of Pediatrics, 145(2 Suppl), pp. 36-41 (2004)
7. MacKenzie, I. S. Soukoreff, R. W.: Text entry for mobile computing: Models and methods, theory and practice. Human-Computer Interaction, 17/2002, pp. 147–198 (2002)
8. Magill-Evans, J.E., Restall, G.: Self-esteem of persons with cerebral palsy: from adolescence to adulthood. American Journal of Occupational Therapy, 45(9), 819-25 (1991)
9. McCuaig, M., Frank, G.: The able self: adaptive patterns and choices in independent living for a person with cerebral palsy. American Journal of Occupational Therapy, 45(3), 224-34 (1991)
10. Rapp, C.E., Torres, M.: The adult with cerebral Palsy. Archives of Family Medicine, 9, pp. 446-472 (2000)
11. Suanpirintr, S., Thubthong, N.: The Effect of Pauses in Dysarthric Speech Recognition Study on Thai Cerebral Palsy Children. ICreate, ACM, New York, USA (2007)
12. Wobbrock, J.O., Myers, B.A., Aung, H.H., LoPresti H.F.: Text Entry from Power Wheelchairs: EdgeWrite for Joysticks and Touchpads. ASSETS' 04, Atlanta, GA, USA, ACM Press, pp. 110-11 (2004)
13. Wolpaw, J.R., Birbaumer, N., McFarland, D.J., Pfurtscheller, G., Vaughan, T.M.: Brain–computer interfaces for communication and control. Clinical Neurophysiology, 113, pp. 767–791 (2002)

Determining a Blind Pedestrian's Location and Orientation at Traffic Intersections

Giovanni Fusco, Huiying Shen, Vidya Murali, and James M. Coughlan

The Smith-Kettlewell Eye Research Institute, San Francisco, United States of America
{giofusco,hshen,vidya,coughlan}@ski.org

Abstract. This paper describes recent progress on Crosswatch, a smartphone-based computer vision system developed by the authors for providing guidance to blind and visually impaired pedestrians at traffic intersections. One of Crosswatch's key capabilities is determining the user's location (with precision much better than what is obtainable by GPS) and orientation relative to the crosswalk markings in the intersection that he/she is currently standing at; this capability will be used to help him/her find important features in the intersection, such as walk lights, pushbuttons and crosswalks, and achieve proper alignment to these features. We report on two new contributions to Crosswatch: (a) experiments with a modified user interface, tested by blind volunteer participants, that makes it easier to acquire intersection images than with previous versions of Crosswatch; and (b) a demonstration of the system's ability to localize the user with precision better than what is obtainable by GPS, as well as an example of its ability to estimate the user's orientation.

Keywords: Visual Impairment, Blindness, Assistive Technology, Smartphone, Traffic Intersection.

1   Introduction and Related Work

Crossing an urban traffic intersection is one of the most dangerous activities of a blind or visually impaired person's travel. Several types of technologies have been developed to assist blind and visually impaired individuals in crossing traffic intersections. Most prevalent among them are Accessible Pedestrian Signals, which generate sounds signaling the duration of the walk interval to blind and visually impaired pedestrians [3]. However, the adoption of Accessible Pedestrian Signals is very sparse, and they are completely absent at the vast majority of intersections. More recently, Bluetooth beacons have been proposed [4] to provide real-time information at intersections that is accessible to any user with a standard mobile phone, but this solution requires special infrastructure to be installed at each intersection.

Computer vision is another technology that has been applied to interpret existing visual cues in intersections, including crosswalk patterns [6] and walk signal lights [2],[9]. Compared with other technologies, it has the advantage of not requiring any additional infrastructure to be installed at each intersection. While its application to the analysis of street intersections is not yet mature enough for deployment to actual

K. Miesenberger et al. (Eds.): ICCHP 2014, Part I, LNCS 8547, pp. 427–432, 2014.
© Springer International Publishing Switzerland 2014

users, experiments with blind participants have been reported in work on Crosswatch [7] and a similar computer vision-based project [1], demonstrating the feasibility of the approach.

2   Overall Approach

Crosswatch uses a combination of information obtained from images acquired by the smartphone camera and from onboard sensors and offline data to determine the user's current location and orientation relative to the traffic intersection he/she is standing at. The goal is to ascertain a range of information about the intersection, including "what" (e.g., what type of intersection?), "where" (the user's precise location and orientation relative to the intersection) and "when" information (i.e., the real-time status of walk and other signal lights).

We briefly describe how the image, sensor and offline data are combined to determine this information. The GPS sensor determines which traffic intersection the user is standing at; note that GPS resolution, which is roughly 10 meters in urban settings [5], is sufficient to determine the current intersection but not necessarily which corner the user is standing at, let alone his/her precise location relative to crosswalks in the intersection. Given knowledge from GPS of which intersection the user is standing at, a GIS (geographic information system, stored either on the smartphone or offline in the cloud) is used to look up detailed information about the intersection, including the type (e.g., four-way, three-way) and a detailed map of the intersection, including features such as crosswalks, median strips, walk lights or other signals, push buttons, etc.

The IMU (inertial measurement unit, which encompasses an accelerometer, magnetometer and gyroscope) sensor estimates the direction the smartphone is oriented in space relative to gravity and magnetic north. Finally, information from panoramic images acquired by the user of the intersection, combined with IMU and GIS data, allows Crosswatch to estimate the user's precise location and orientation relative to the intersection, and specifically relative to any features of interest (such as a crosswalk, walk light or push button); given the pose, the system can direct the user to aim the camera towards the walk light, whose status can be monitored in real time and read aloud.

In [7] we reported a procedure that allows Crosswatch to capture images in all directions from the user's current location: the user stands in place and turns slowly in a clockwise direction (i.e., panning left to right) while the Crosswatch app periodically acquires images (every 20° of bearing relative to north), making a complete circle. The system activates the smartphone vibrator any time the camera orientation is sufficiently far from horizontal, to help the user acquire images that contain as much of the visible crosswalks as possible (and prevent inadvertently pointing too far up or down). The system stitches the images thus acquired into a full 360° panorama (see Fig.1a), which was analyzed in [8] to determine the user's (x,y) location (Fig. 1b,c).

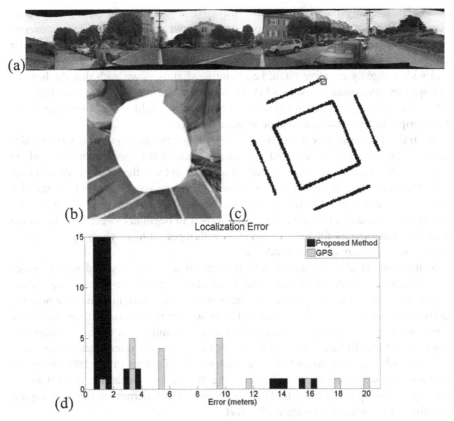

Fig. 1. Crosswatch user localization. (a) 360° panorama. (b) Aerial reconstruction of intersection based on (a) shows crosswalk stripes as they would appear from above. (c) Intersection template (i.e., map of crosswalk stripes). Matching features from (b) to (c) yields (x,y) localization estimate (shown in red, near ground truth in green). (d) Localization error of our algorithm (black) and of GPS (gray), shown as histograms with x-axis in meters and the number of counts on the y-axis, demonstrating superior performance of our algorithm.

However, capturing the full 360° panorama forces the user to turn on his/her feet in a complete circle, which is both awkward and disorienting. In this paper we describe our initial experiments with an approach that requires only a 180° (half-circle) panorama, which spans enough visual angle to encompass multiple crosswalk features in the intersection; this approach has the benefit that it can be executed by the user by moving arms, shoulders and/or hips without having to move his/her feet. The assumption underlying this approach is that the user can orient him/herself accurately enough using standard Orientation & Mobility skills, so that the 180° panorama encompasses enough of the intersection features.

We tested this new user interface in informal experiments with two blind users. The user interface was modified in two additional ways relative to the earlier (360°) version of Crosswatch: (a) in order to signal the beginning and end of the 180° sweep, the system not only issues loud audio beeps but also augments them with special vibration patterns (three short vibration bursts in rapid succession), since past experiments revealed that street noises sometimes obscured the audio tones; and (b) in order to capture more of the crosswalk stripes in the images, the camera is designed to be held with a slightly negative pitch, i.e., pointing slightly down such that the horizon line appears horizontal but somewhat above the middle of the image (see Fig. 2a); when this pitch requirement is violated, or the camera is held too far from horizontal, the smartphone vibration is turned on to warn the user.

We trained the first user to use the system indoors, before going outdoors to a single intersection, where we acquired a panorama to check that the system was working correctly. The second user was also trained indoors, and was then led outside to a total of 18 locations at a total of five distinct traffic intersections. The main challenge for this user was to orient himself sufficiently accurately so that the 180° sweep encompassed all the nearby crosswalk stripes; he tended to begin his sweeps farther to the right than was optimal for the system, even with repeated hints given by the experimenters who accompanied him outdoors.

In these informal experiments with the second user we recorded which corner he was standing at for all sweeps. The localization algorithm estimated the correct corner in 16 out of the 18 cases. While these experiments were informal, we note the following observations: (a) users were able to acquire panoramas without having to move their feet during image acquisition, by using a combination of hip, shoulder and arm movements; (b) better training is required to help users orient themselves accurately enough to encompass all important intersection features in the 180° sweep. In the future we will experiment with improving the training procedure, as well as expanding the sweep range (e.g., to 225°) in a way that still permits the user to acquire the entire sweep without moving his/her feet.

3   Evaluating Localization Estimates

In a separate experiment, we evaluated the accuracy of the Crosswatch localization estimates relative to ground truth estimates. In this experiment, one of the authors (who is sighted) photographed a total of 19 panorama sweeps (seventeen 180° sweeps and two 360° sweeps), each in a distinct location. The locations were distributed among three intersections, two of which were four-way intersections and one of which was a T-junction intersection. Another experimenter estimated the photographer's "ground truth" location for each panorama, making reference to curbs, crosswalk stripes and other features visible in satellite imagery; such ground truth is not perfect, but we estimate that it is accurate to about 1-2 meters. Using this ground truth, we evaluated the localization error of our algorithm and compared it with the localization error of GPS alone (Fig.1d). The histograms show that our algorithm is more accurate than GPS. The typical localization error of our algorithm is roughly 1 meter or less, except when gross errors occur (i.e., failure to detect one or more crosswalk stripes, or mistaking a non-crosswalk feature in the image as a crosswalk stripe). In ongoing work we are creating more accurate ground truth and decreasing the rate of crosswalk stripe detection errors.

4   Demonstration: Where is the Walk Light?

The intersection template in the GIS includes the 3D locations of features such as crosswalks and walk lights. Once the user's (x,y) location is determined, the system has enough information to help the user find a specific feature of interest, such as the walk light. We choose the walk light as a sample target of interest because a blind user will need to be given guidance to aim the camera towards it, so that its status can be monitored and reported (e.g., using synthesized speech) in real time. Fig. 2 shows an example of how Crosswatch can predict the location of the walk light even before detecting it: in Fig. 2a, a photo acquired by the second blind user in our experiment (during a panorama sweep) is marked with a red rectangle indicating the system's prediction (calculated offline in this experiment) of the approximate walk light location; the green box shows the precise location of the walk light inside (see Fig. 2b for zoomed-in portion of image), as detected by a simple walk light detection algorithm (similar to that used in [9]).

This ability to predict the location of a feature in an intersection before detecting it in an image is important for two reasons. First, using high-speed orientation feedback from the IMU, the prediction provides a way for the system to rapidly guide the user to aim the camera towards the feature, without relying on computer vision, which could greatly slow down the feedback loop. Second, the prediction may be used either to simplify the computer vision detection/recognition process (by ruling out regions of images that are far from the prediction), and is available if computer vision is unable to perform reliable detection/recognition (for instance, for features such median strips, which are extremely difficult to detect based on computer vision alone).

(a)   (b)

Fig. 2. Example of Crosswatch's prediction of the approximate walk light location (see text for explanation)

5   Conclusion

We have demonstrated new modifications to the Crosswatch user interface for acquiring panoramic imagery intended to make the procedure simpler and less disorienting for the user. A basic performance analysis of the Crosswatch localization algorithm that this user interface facilitates shows that the algorithm performs much better than GPS.

We are planning more rigorous experimental tests with more blind users, which will suggest further improvements to the system and to the user training process. Meanwhile, we are improving the localization algorithm and creating more accurate ground truth data to better evaluate its performance. Future work on Crosswatch will include integrating past work on another common crosswalk pattern (the zebra) and walk light detection into a single app, which may be accomplished by offloading some of the computations required by our algorithms to a remote server. Finally, we plan to investigate ways of creating an extensive GIS of intersections throughout San Francisco (and eventually other cities worldwide) through a combination of municipal data sources and crowdsourcing techniques, and to make the GIS data freely available (e.g., via OpenStreetMap).

Acknowledgments. The authors acknowledge support by the National Institutes of Health from grant No. 2 R01EY018345-06 and by the Department of Education, NIDRR grant number H133E110004.

References

1. Ahmetovic, D., Bernareggi, C., Mascetti, S.: Zebralocalizer: identification and localization of pedestrian crossings. In: Bylund, M., et al. (eds.) MobileHCI 2011, pp. 275–284. ACM, New York (2011)
2. Aranda, J., Mares, P.: Visual System to Help Blind People to Cross the Street. In: Miesenberger, K., Klaus, J., Zagler, W.L., Burger, D. (eds.) ICCHP 2004. LNCS, vol. 3118, pp. 454–461. Springer, Heidelberg (2004)
3. Barlow, J.M., Bentzen, B.L., Tabor, L.: Accessible pedestrian signals: Synthesis and guide to best practice. National Cooperative Highway Research Program (2003)
4. Bohonos, S., Lee, A., Malik, A., Thai, C., Manduchi, R.: Cellphone Accessible Information via Bluetooth Beaconing for the Visually Impaired. In: Miesenberger, K., Klaus, J., Zagler, W.L., Karshmer, A.I. (eds.) ICCHP 2008. LNCS, vol. 5105, pp. 1117–1121. Springer, Heidelberg (2008)
5. Brabyn, J.A., Alden, A., Haegerstrom-Portnoy, G., Schneck, M.: GPS Performance for Blind Navigation in Urban Pedestrian Settings. In: Proceedings of 7th International Conference on Low Vision, Goteborg, Sweden (2002)
6. Coughlan, J., Shen, H.: The Crosswatch Traffic Intersection Analyzer: A Roadmap for the Future. In: Miesenberger, K., Karshmer, A., Penaz, P., Zagler, W. (eds.) ICCHP 2012, Part II. LNCS, vol. 7383, pp. 25–28. Springer, Heidelberg (2012)
7. Coughlan, J., Shen, H.: Crosswatch: a System for Providing Guidance to Visually Impaired Travelers at Traffic Intersections. Journal of Assistive Technologies (JAT) 7(2), 131–142 (2013)
8. Fusco, G., Shen, H., Coughlan, J.: Self-Localization at Street Intersections. In: 11th Conference on Computer and Robot Vision (CRV 2014), Montréal, Canada (May 2014)
9. Ivanchenko, V., Coughlan, J., Shen, H.: Real-Time Walk Light Detection with a Mobile Phone. In: Miesenberger, K., Klaus, J., Zagler, W., Karshmer, A. (eds.) ICCHP 2010, Part II. LNCS, vol. 6180, pp. 229–234. Springer, Heidelberg (2010)

The Design and Evaluation of the Body Water Management System to Support the Independent Living of the Older Adult

Airi Tsuji, Naoki Yabuno, Noriaki Kuwahara, and Kazunari Morimoto

Graduate School of Science and Technology, Kyoto Institute of Technology,
Matsugasaki, Sakyou-ku, Japan
{diff.dim0505,naoking.futsal}@gmail.com,
{nkuwahar,morix}@kit.ac.jp

Abstract. Aiming for older adult's comfortable and independent outing, we are researching and developing the body water management system according to their outing schedule, their surrounding environment, and their activities like eating and drinking. In this paper, we describe our proposed system, the physiological formula for non-invasive estimation of the body water balance and the method of calculating the suggestion timing.

Keywords: Elderly People, Dehydration, Context Driven, Body Water Balance.

1 Introduction

For older adult, going out is one of the most important activities to keep their cognitive and physical abilities and gives them good stimulation and pleasure in daily-life [1]. However, many older adults have a problem managing the body water balance. Older adults tend to be the symptom of dehydration by the reduction of cell water retention capacity and dry mouth feeling [2]. Many older adults die from heat stroke in the summer. Additionally, going out is likely to become their pain for some older adults with aging, especially due to a matter of toilet. Consequently, they often tend not to drink water enough, while their outing due to the anxiety to go to a toilet. It is likely to be the cause of getting dehydrated, especially in summer. Aiming for older adult's comfortable and independent outing, we are researching and developing the body water management system according to their outing schedule, their surrounding environment, and their activities like eating and drinking. In this paper, we describe our proposed system, the physiological formula for non-invasive estimation of the body water balance and the method of calculating the suggestion timing.

2 The System Overview

We developed the body water management application that runs on the Android terminal. Fig 1 shows the system overview. The system calculates the suggestion timing of drink and toilet using the formula weight and gender, from exposure temperature of the user and notifies a voice for the user.

K. Miesenberger et al. (Eds.): ICCHP 2014, Part I, LNCS 8547, pp. 433–436, 2014.

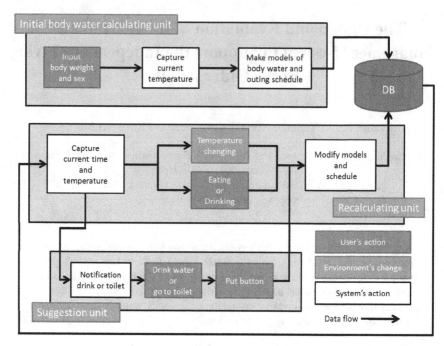

Fig. 1. The system overview

3   Estimating the Amount of Body Water

According to previous research on water balance of the human body [2,3], we've come up with the simplistic physiological formula for non-invasive estimation of the amount of body water [4]. Our system calculates the amount of body water using the formula (1), (2), (3), (4), (5), (6) and suggests user.

$$MaleU = 1500 + (W - 65.15) *1.0 - (T - 19.4)* 0.6 \tag{1}$$

$$FemaleU = 1500 + (W - 53.04)*1.0 - (T - 19.4)*0.6 \tag{2}$$

$$Toilet\ Interval = 150 / (U / 17) \tag{3}$$

$$S = W*(9.1+ (T-19.4)*2.72) \tag{4}$$

$$Drainage = (U / 17) + S + (900 / 17) \tag{5}$$

$$Drink\ Interval = (W*0.02) / Drainage \tag{6}$$

— U is the total excretion of the day [ml],
— Toilet Interval is basic toilet interval [hour],
— T is outside temperature [degrees Celsius],
— W is body weight [kg].
— S is the amount of sweat over 16.5 degrees Celsius.
— Drainage is the amount of water lost from the body per hour [ml].
— Drink Interval is the time until becoming dehydrated [hour].

4   Experimental Method

We conducted the experiment to investigate the effectiveness of the proposed system. The subjects of this experiment are five male and five female healthy (does not have any urination disease) older adults. Table 1 shows the subject's details. The one of male subject was excluded from the result because he had the severe pollakiuria which wasn't noticed. The subjects drink water and go to the toilet according to the suggestion timing that the system calculated or when they want. The number of drinking water and going to a toilet and the amount of the urine per elimination are recorded for the analysis. The amount of excretion of the subject is obtained from the changes of the body weight before and after elimination. The timing of suggestion is rearranged dynamically at every time when the subjects push buttons during the experiment. At the end of the experiment, the subjects are asked to answer the questionnaire in order to subjectively measure the effectiveness and the appropriateness of the suggestion timing. The temperature of the laboratory is kept on 22 degrees Celsius.

Table 1. Subject's details

	Number (average)	Age (average)	Body Weight (average)	Urinary Frequency Trend (5 steps)
Male	4	63-71 (66.8)	64.0-79.8 (70.23)	2-4(3.5)
Female	5	63-79 (71.8)	43.9-63.7 (55.59)	1-4(2.6)
	9	63-79 (69.5)	43.9-79.8 (62.09)	1-4(3.0)

5   Experimental Results

All subjects didn't receive drink suggestion among the experimental period. They ingested amounts of water sufficient on its own. Fig.2 shows the experimental result

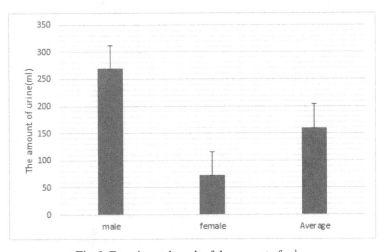

Fig. 2. Experimental result of the amount of urine

of the amount of urine. The result of female subject shows scores under 150ml. Our previous research [4] sets that the amount of water makes older adults want to urinate. However, the average of male subject result shows 275ml.

6   Conclusion

We are analyzing experimental result minutely. We will improve our system based on this result of this experiment and ought to consider about the people who are not aware of the disease.

References

1. Komatsu, Okayama, Kimura: Water intake of home-living adl-independent elderly people: its relationships with factors of their water drinking behavior. Journal of Japan Society of Physiological Anthropology 9, 25–30 (2004) (in Japanese)
2. Kimura, Negro: Simple seirigaku, 6th edn. Nankodo Co., Ltd. (2009) (in Japanese)
3. Okamato: Water balance in the elderly in summer and winter. Journal of Japanese Society of Biometeorology 35(1), 53–60 (1998) (in Japanese)
4. Tsuji, A.: Noriaki Kuwahra and Kazunari Morimoto: Study for Hydration Management in Elderly People. Journal of Human Interface Society 16(2) (2014) (in Japanese)

An Investigation into Incorporating Visual Information in Audio Processing

Ender Tekin, James M. Coughlan, and Helen J. Simon

The Smith-Kettlewell Eye Research Insitute, San Francisco, CA
{ender,coughlan,helen}@ski.org

Abstract. The number of persons with hearing and vision loss is on the rise as lifespans increase. Vision plays an important role in communication, especially in the presence of background noise or for persons with hearing loss. However, persons with vision loss cannot make use of this extra modality to overcome their hearing deficits. We propose automatically utilizing some visual information in hearing aids through the addition of a small wearable camera. Our initial results show potentially significant benefits to incorporating low level robust visual cues when the background noise is high. This technique can potentially benefit all persons with hearing loss, with substantial improvements possible for the speech perception performance of persons with dual sensory loss.

1 Introduction

In daily conversations, visual information significantly improves comprehension of speech [8], as well as providing the location and identity of the speaker. Seeing the speaker's face can account for up to 10 decibels improvement in speech perception in the presence of speech-babble noise [5]. Persons with hearing loss can use techniques such as speech-reading to significantly improve their speech perception. However, as the population in most developed countries is aging at a significant rate, the incidence of vision loss as well as hearing loss is also on the rise. Persons with such dual sensory loss cannot utilize the complementary information present in the facial cues, making communication more difficult.

The proportion of the population with vision and/or hearing loss directly correlates with age. Age related vision loss also manifests as loss in contrast/color sensitivity and temporal resolution, which cannot easily be corrected by lenses [4]. Age related hearing loss can also lead to decreased spectral and temporal resolution [4], making it harder to isolate the sound from a speaker in the presence of non-uniform noise, such as that due to other speakers in the environment, a problem known as the *cocktail party* effect. Such dual sensory loss affects more than 1 in 5 persons aged 70 years and over [6]. In this paper, we present our investigations into the benefits of utilizing the visual information in an intuitive and reliable way to enhance digital signal processing algorithms such as those used in current hearing aids. This research may lead to substantial benefits for persons with hearing loss, especially those with additional vision loss.

K. Miesenberger et al. (Eds.): ICCHP 2014, Part I, LNCS 8547, pp. 437–440, 2014.

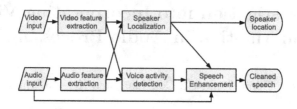

Fig. 1. Overview of the proposed system

Due to technological limitations, conventional hearing aids are unable to provide satisfactory performance in noisy and crowded environments [3]. Directional microphones can offer a 3-5dB improvement over omni-directional microphones when there is a known nearby speaker, such as at a restaurant [1]. Some microphones can even use a technique called beamforming to overcome the limitations of the static beam patterns of most hearing aids. However, there are often other sources of noise in the vicinity of the speaker that limit their effectiveness [2].

Most of these limitations may be alleviated, allowing significant performance improvements, by incorporating visual information in the audio processing stage. We propose integrating a wearable camera to obtain such visual information. This proposed system can improve the efficiency of speech processing algorithms, as well as provide information to the user regarding the identity of the speaker. There is similar, promising research into speech recognition algorithms that model head movements and lip articulations. However, these results are mostly limited to very well controlled conditions where the facial image is high resolution and well-lit. Such conditions are uncommon in the real world; as a result, we focus on using more robust cues, e.g., detection of mouth movements and the speaker in crowded environments using low-resolution videos.

2   Approach

Almost all speech enhancement techniques rely on being able to detect voice activity reliably; this allows these techniques to sample the background noise efficiently and frequently in order to enhance speech, as the statistics of noise are highly dynamic. In noisy environments, conventional algorithms can easily make mistakes since they only rely on the noisy audio cues to make their decisions. In these cases, using video of the speaker as well, voice activity may be detected more robustly; we illustrate this in Figure 1. In addition, since only certain acoustic components (e.g., signal power in different bands) will be related to a given speaker, it may be possible to learn these bands and inform the spectral speech enhancement algorithms to focus on eliminating sounds that are clearly unrelated to the speaker. We note that this proposed video information can supplement existing speech enhancement techniques, and we can build on the existing wealth of research on hearing aids and similar technologies developed for persons with hearing loss. Location and speech activity of a speaker can be obtained more reliably from the visual information which is often less noisy than audio in real-world scenarios. We have performed some initial experiments to show the feasibility of this approach. We extracted audio and video features at 30 frames per second. The audio features include Mel-frequency cepstral coefficients, long-term spectral divergence (LTSD), and energy of the audio spectrum in the frame. Video features include variance and mean intensity, as well as spatio-temporal derivatives of the mouth region of the visible speaker. These are low-level cues that may be reliably extracted from lower-resolution video as opposed to the high-definition videos used in audio-visual speechreading research.

We determined the contributions of the various features by maximizing the mutual information of the linear combination of audio and video features, i.e.,

$$\alpha^*, \beta^* = \arg\max_{\alpha, \beta} I(\alpha \cdot \mathbf{f}_a; \beta \cdot \mathbf{f}_v) \tag{1}$$

The results indicate a higher emphasis on video components such as the temporal statistics of the mouth area as captured by temporal gradients, and audio components such as LTSD and total audio signal energy in a window. We developed a simple audio-visual VAD using a linear combination of these features,

$$v = \alpha^* \cdot \mathbf{f}_a + \beta^* \cdot \mathbf{f}_v. \tag{2}$$

By comparing this value to a threshold τ, it is possible to determine whether voice activity is present. If $v > \tau$, voice activity is assumed to be present, and the speech enhancement algorithm attempts to clean the noisy speech signal. Otherwise, we assume that we are in a silence period, where the background noise estimate is updated by sampling the noise spectrum in this period.

3   Experimental Results

To establish the contribution of the visual information, a video-only VAD (where the audio components were nulled by setting $\alpha = 0$) was compared with a conventional audio-only VAD based on the long-term spectral divergence [9]. The VAD outputs were used to enhance speech using a Wiener filter, [7], on a video with one speaker, where the audio signal was corrupted by various levels of additive white Gaussian noise and speech-babble noise. Segmental signal- to-noise ratio (SSNR) values were estimated to compare the performances as SSNR has been shown to correspond better with speech intelligibility than SNR.

Figure 2 illustrates this point. In this example, increasing levels of background noise were addded a quarter and a half-way through a video. While both approaches show similar performance for lower noise conditions, the performance of the audio-only method suffers more in high-noise situations, due to the inaccuracy of the voice activity detector at such high noise levels. In this case, the output SSNR using the video-VAD was on average 8dB better, showing that video can provide complementary information when audio is very noisy.

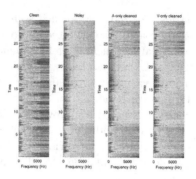

Fig. 2. Speech enhancement performance using video vs audio-based VAD's

4 Conclusion

We are exploring the potential of incorporating video in speech-enhancement technologies. Our preliminary results are promising, and we plan to validate the output using subjective evaluations by persons with dual sensory loss. A system that includes video brings some challenges in usability, but the rising popularity and acceptance of wearable technologies, as well as the potentially significant improvements in speech perception performance may make this an attractive solution for the needs of a growing population with hearing and/or vision loss.

Acknowledgements. This research was supported by the NIH-NEI Award #R21EY022200, and the DoEd-NIDRR Grant #H133E110004.

References

1. Compton-Conley, C., Neuman, A., Killion, M., Levitt, H.: Performance of directional microphones for hearing aids: real world versus simulation. J. Am. Acad.Audiol. 15, 440–455 (2004)
2. Fabry, D.A.: Adaptive directional microphone technology and hearing aids: Theoretical and clinical implications. Hearing Review (April 2005)
3. Gatehouse, S.: Electronic aids to hearing. Br. Med. Bull. 63(1), 147–156 (2002)
4. Haegerstrom-Portnoy, G., Schneck, M.E., Brabyn, J.: Seeing into old age: vision function beyond acuity. Optom. Vis. Sci. 76, 141–158 (1999)
5. Helfer, K.S., Freyman, R.L.: The role of visual speech cues in reducing energetic and informational masking. J. Acous. Soc. Am. 117(2), 842–849 (2005)
6. Horowitz, A.: Dual sensory impairment among the elderly. Tech. rep., Lighthouse International and AARP Andrus Foundation (2001)
7. Loizou, P.C.: Speech Enhancement: Theory and Practice. CRC Press (June 2007)
8. MacLeod, A., Summerfield, Q.: Quantifying the contribution of vision to speech perception in noise. Br. J. Audiol. 21(2), 131–141 (1987)
9. Ramírez, J., Segura, J.C., Benítez, C., Torre, Á.D.L., Rubio, A.: A new adaptive long-term spectral estimation voice activity detector. In: Eurospeech, Korea, pp. 961–964 (October 2004)

Indoor Positioning for Visually Impaired People Based on Smartphones

Thomas Moder, Petra Hafner, and Manfred Wieser

Institute of Navigation, Graz University of Technology, Graz, Austria
{thomas.moder,petra.hafner,manfred.wieser}@tugraz.at

Abstract. Autonomous navigation is a critical factor for visually impaired people. Outdoors, positioning based on ubiquitous signals is available, contrary indoors no ubiquitous navigation solution does exist. Because of the implementation of screen-reader software into mobile devices, visually impaired people start using smartphones. This paper focuses on the abilities of an indoor positioning purely based on sensors already present in smartphones nowadays. Therefore, algorithms specifically designed for low-cost sensors are developed. The outcome of these algorithms, which process the accelerometer, gyroscope, magnetometer and barometer data and a WiFi fingerprinting, is integrated within a mathematical filter to get a final position and heading information.

Keywords: Indoor Positioning, Visually Impaired People, Smartphones.

1 Introduction

Autonomous navigation is a critical factor for visually impaired people to master common tasks in civil life. An autonomous positioning system, that can support people with visually impairments to navigate without assistance, is a huge benefit for the society. Outdoors, positioning based on ubiquitous signals like GNSS is possible with cheap equipment and with accuracies up to some decimeters if processing techniques like precise point positioning can be used. Contrary, indoors no ubiquitous navigation solution, especially with affordable equipment, does exist nowadays.

The market introduction of smartphones with their touchscreens was a step back in the mobile phone development for the use of visually impaired people, so they may not profit from mass market developments like the huge advances within processing and sensing chips for smartphones in the last couple of years. The implementation of Apple's screen-reader software VoiceOver into the iOS operating system changed this tremendously. Visually impaired people start using smartphones like everyone else and additionally may benefit from the sensors within smartphones for positioning. If a smartphone could be used as a ubiquitous outdoor and indoor navigation device, it could support all groups of the society since the device would be already available by almost all people in some years. This paper focuses on the abilities and opportunities of implementing an indoor positioning purely based on smartphone data of sensors which are already present in smartphones nowadays.

K. Miesenberger et al. (Eds.): ICCHP 2014, Part I, LNCS 8547, pp. 441–444, 2014.

2   State-of-the-Art

Currently, companies like Ekahau [1] or Skyhook [2] are providing indoor positioning solutions. These companies developed positioning solutions based on WiFi, RFID, incorporating GNSS if the visibility is given. The achievement of room-level accuracy is claimed, however, this strongly depends on the available wireless signals present in the specific indoor environment. Additionally, just absolute positioning is provided, no robust heading information can be gathered out of these solutions.

The state-of-the-art for indoor navigation of visually impaired people are specially tailored solutions, no mass market application does exist today. These specially tailored solutions are mostly based on dead reckoning approaches with Inertial Measurement Units (IMU) which are fixed to the person's body. These techniques are called foot-mounted or waist-mounted, depending on the sensor position. Commercial foot-mounted systems for visually impaired people exist from e.g. [3], where [4] shows the possibility of a waist-mounted system for blind people. Additionally, special solutions based on infrared sensors as proposed in [5] are currently under investigation. One thing, which all systems have in common, is that they are specially tailored systems with a high monetary attribute. Therefore, such systems are not affordable as a pure navigation device for visually impaired people.

3   Methodology

An affordable navigation support for all groups of the society is the main goal of our investigations. Since the outdoor positioning is mainly solved by applying appropriate GNSS techniques, indoor-positioning just based on sensors incorporated within smartphones is presented.

The developed indoor positioning solution is based on the integrated WiFi receiver, the accelerometers and gyroscopes, the magnetometer and the barometer of the smartphone Samsung Galaxy Nexus, a roughly three year old smartphone. These sensors are available in most of today's smartphones. Unfortunately, the senor bias errors of the integrated inertial sensors are high compared to consumer grade IMU sensors, like shown in [6]. Although smartphone sensors have evolved in the last couple of years, the main purpose of these sensors never was or will be positioning, so classic sensor integration algorithms cannot be applied. Therefore, more promising Pedestrian Dead Reckoning (PDR) algorithms have been implemented within these investigations. PDR algorithms are specifically designed for low-cost inertial and magnetometer sensors and tailored to the motion of walking people. The PDR algorithm consists of three components, the step detection, the step length as well as the heading estimation. The results of a step detection and a heading estimation are shown in Fig. 1. The step detection is based on a multiple-event classification, whereas the step length estimation is calculated with previously calibrated parameters. The estimation of the step direction is conducted within a Kalman filter which filters the absolute orientation gained by the tri-axial magnetic sensors with the angular rates gained by the gyroscope.

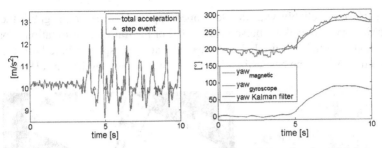

Fig. 1. Results of a step detection (left) and a heading estimation (right)

To get an appropriate absolute positioning solution out of the WiFi data, a WiFi fingerprinting is realized. This approach enables a position accuracy of a few meters by indirectly considering building structure which has a high impact on the signal attenuation. The drawback of fingerprinting is the time consuming training data generation. A data base of WiFi measurements has to be established for defined reference points in the whole building. For the real-time positioning, the actually measured signal strengths to all available WiFi access points are compared with the existing data base. The empirical fingerprinting then calculates an absolute position based on the nearest reference points with respect to the distance in signal space. For the presented solution, a prior filtering of the signal strength measurements as well as a weighted averaging of the nearest reference points is conducted.

The outcome of the PDR algorithm, which combines the accelerometer, gyroscope, magnetometer and barometer data, and the WiFi fingerprinting solution are integrated within a mathematical filter to get a final position and heading information.

The fusion of the PDR and WiFi fingerprinting data is composed of two processes, see Fig. 2. First, a Kalman filter is used to combine the WiFi based height with the barometer data to detect the floor in which the person is moving. This is necessary, since the 2D position estimation indoors is done with a Particle filter to integrate the entire information of a building layout. The geometric constraints gained by a building layout make the filtering more robust and accurate. However, this requires a pre-estimation of the floor level to integrate the right floor plan then.

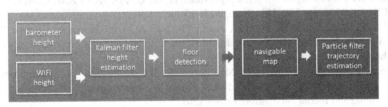

Fig. 2. Filtering concept for the indoor positioning

4   Results

The graphs in Fig. 3 show the two processes of the position filter for a test track within a four-story building. As the left graph demonstrates, the floor detection indoors can be performed reliably with the developed approach. In the right graph the horizontal trajectory of a walking person is shown. For the trajectory estimation, a particle filter with 400 particles is used. The measured state corresponds directly to the WiFi fingerprinting, where the best estimation shows the outcome of the particle filter.

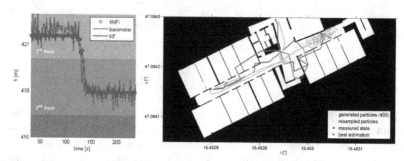

Fig. 3. Floor detection based on WiFi and barometer data (left) and trajectory (right)

5   Conclusion

Within this paper, the possibility of indoor positioning for visually impaired people with cheap, universally available signals and sensors already present in today's smartphones is presented. By applying appropriate algorithms (PDR algorithm, WiFi fingerprinting, Kalman and Particle filter) and integrating the information content of a building layout, position accuracies of a few meters can be realized.

References

1. Ekahau, Helsinki, Finland (2014), http://www.ekahau.com
2. Skyhook, Boston, USA (2014), http://www.skyhookwireless.com
3. Aionav, Bern, Switzerland (2014), http://www.aionav.com
4. Chen, D., Feng, W., Zhao, Q., Hu, M., Wang, T.: An Infrastructure-Free Indoor Navigation System for Blind People. In: Su, C.-Y., Rakheja, S., Liu, H. (eds.) ICIRA 2012, Part III. LNCS, vol. 7508, pp. 552–561. Springer, Heidelberg (2012)
5. Mehta, P., Kant, P., Shah, P., Roy, A.K.: VI-Navi: A Novel Indoor Navigation System for Visually Impaired People. In: International Conference on Computer Systems and Technologies, Vienna, Austria (2011)
6. Hafner, P., Moder, T., Wieser, M., Bernoulli, T.: Evaluation of Smartphone-based Indoor Positioning Using Different Bayes Filters. In: International Conference on Indoor Positioning and Indoor Navigation, France (2013)

Extended Scaffolding by Remote Collaborative Interaction to Support People with Dementia in Independent Living – A User Study

Henrike Gappa[1], Gabriele Nordbrock[1], Manuela Thelen[2], Jaroslav Pullmann[1], Yehya Mohamad[1], and Carlos A. Velasco[1]

[1] Fraunhofer Institute for Applied Information Technology FIT,
Sankt Augustin, Germany
{henrike.gappa,gabriele.nordbrock,jaroslav.pullmann,
yehya.mohamad,carlos.velasco}@fit.fraunhofer.de
[2] Universitätsklinikum Bonn, Bonn, Germany
manuela.thelen@ukb.uni-bonn.de

Abstract. IT-based assistive services offer the potential to support the independent living of people with dementia provided that they accommodate their specific needs. Due to their declining cognitive functions, these users face among other issues a diminishing capacity for problem solving and attention focus. As a consequence they get easily distracted and finally lost while using assistive services. To counteract such situations it is necessary to implement scaffolding features that will assist users in navigating through all relevant sub-tasks. In our user study it was evaluated whether remote collaborative interaction —obtained by offering family carers remote access to assistive services running in the homes of the relatives they care for— could serve as an extended scaffolding feature. The user study has shown promising results because the vast majority of users even in later stages of dementia understood this concept and could achieve a task in collaborative interaction with their relatives.

1 Introduction

It is a known fact that the ageing population in Europe will increase dramatically in the near future.[1] This trend has severe implications for the prevalence of the age-related decline in physical and cognitive abilities of the population, which will cause inevitably breakdowns in self-management hindering older people's chance to live independently. This, in turn, will create a high demand for independent living solutions, which seems to be one of the basic principles the vast majority of older people thrive to adhere to as long as possible (97%[2]). The wish to age in dignity, leveraged by the fact that the usage of technology to fulfil daily routines becomes more and more common, will lead to the assumption that older people

---

[1] http://bit.ly/1dFIg7n
[2] http://bit.ly/1dFIrQ8

K. Miesenberger et al. (Eds.): ICCHP 2014, Part I, LNCS 8547, pp. 445–450, 2014.

will be open to rely on IT-based assistive services. To achieve this goal it is of utmost importance that assistive services are designed according to the users' needs. In regard to assistive services for people with dementia, design issues have been the subject of several recent research projects [1, 2, 3, 4, 5]. However, the incorporation of scaffolding features guiding the user through sequences of sub-tasks to achieve their objectives and offering fall-back solutions in case a user gets lost have hardly been considered yet.

The goal of the nationally funded research project WebDA (Web-based Services for Older People and Family Carers[3]) was to create services for older people who had reduced cognitive abilities, ranging from forgetfulness influencing their proper management of everyday life up to moderate dementia. During the project, services for structuring everyday life and fostering communication skills were developed, including tools for biographical-related tasks, context-aware reminder messaging and a service to locate lost objects. To ease caring responsibilities of the family carers, all services were also accessible remotely, so they were able to support their relatives from their own homes. This feature of the WebDA services was also intended to serve as an immediately available fall-back scaffolding solution. The focus of the user study described in the following was to investigate whether such a usage scenario would allow for suitable collaborative interaction between carers and their relatives with declining cognitive skills.

The process of deteriorating cognitive abilities is highly individual. In most cases it starts with an age-associated decline in mnemonic abilities, progressing up to a mild cognitive impairment (MCI), followed by mild and several other stages of dementia. Dementia is a profound loss of cognitive abilities affecting memory functioning, problem solving skills and selective attention, inhibiting a person's ability to develop and maintain action plans to achieve personal objectives like, e.g., prepare a meal or use an IT-based assistive service for independent living.

IT-based services can compensate for such deterioration by implementing scaffolding features that support users staying on the task. For example, focusing their attention on the next step by speech messages. However, particularly when dementia is progressing, the distractibility of these users increases remarkably with the result of loss of attention and disorientation. Such situations are almost unforeseeable and human intervention is necessary, which can be provided best by carers. To avoid the escalation of such situations and its associated frustration, assistive services should intervene by suggesting to the user to contact her carer and/or inform the carer, e.g., by SMS, that her relative might have difficulties using a particular assistive service. Since carers struggle hard in most cases to balance their personal lives with work, family and carer tasks, remote access to the assistive environment of their relatives could provide an efficient means to satisfy the needs of both: the carer by facilitating supply of help from home, for instance, and the relative by achieving immediate attention. Moreover, the remote collaborative interaction could serve as an extended scaffolding feature, eventually leading to a user with dementia learning more reliably how to use an assistive service, which

---

[3] http://webda.info/ (website available only in German).

in turn fosters feelings of mastery. Research on dementia has shown that feeling in control of one's life plays a major role in slowing down the otherwise often rapidly ongoing progress of dementia [4, 5].

2 Distributed Cognition

Achievement of a task with computational assistance is a "... distribution of the cognitive act across an individual and the system" [6]. In this sense, successful achievement of a task depends on the cognitive skills of the user and on how well a system supports these skills in a given human action. Following this understanding of cooperation among personal cognitive skills and system design, the importance of a user–centred design approach thriving to leverage existing human abilities is stressed and it also depicts the potential of IT-based assistive systems to compensate for the loss of cognitive skills. Errors or mistakes in operating a system must be understood as the result of a failed interaction between a user and a system, which should be especially avoided when serving people with dementia, who are particularly vulnerable to disorientation. To allow a system to accommodate the special design requirements of people with dementia, it was found in the user studies conducted within WebDA that the animation of navigation buttons and addressing the user by speech are very efficient means for compensation [7]. Implementing such features was therefore part of the scaffolding strategy used in WebDA. Scaffolding is understood as the technique to implement distributed cognition in computational assistive systems [8].

3 The User Study

To evaluate the aforementioned setting for remote collaborative interaction with users afflicted by cognitive loss, a test scenario was developed following common standards for usability testing [9] and recommendations for testing with people with dementia [5], [10]. Beyond this, ethical standards for user testing were considered carefully, thus the test procedures, the possibility to drop out of the user test at any time, anonymous processing of test results and the like were explained to the test participants and where applicable to their appointed guardians as well.

The goal of the user study was to explore three aspects of remote collaborative interaction. First, to investigate whether users in different stages of cognitive decline (MCI to moderate dementia) are open to work collaboratively with a carer accessing their desktop remotely. This is not an immediate assumption because interpersonal relationships play a role in such interaction forms and shortcomings in operating an assistive service might convey an obvious loss of mastery to the user. The second aspect refers to the question whether users with dementia will not get confused about actions on their desktop being executed from the outside. Thirdly, we researched whether users were able to grasp the concepts of collaborative interaction, like following actions of others and taking turns for the operation of a system.

For the test a typical usage scenario was designed where the test participants with constrained cognitive skills were asked to search, in collaboration with their carers, for a specified object using the object locator service developed within WebDA (Fig. 1). To achieve this task assignment, 5 sub-tasks needed to be completed in turns, like opening the application, looking for the object by flipping pages of the object locator with searchable objects, etc. It was defined in the usage scenario whether carers or the test participants should continue with the next task, to observe whether the latter group was able to cope with the processes of remote collaborative interaction, like for instance, taking turns, and most importantly understand the action undertaken by the collaborating partner. Carers accessed the tablet PCs of their relatives running the object locator service remotely via a desktop sharing application. Communication between carers and their relatives took place via a mobile phone with loudspeakers turned on. Communication was voluntarily not offered via computer to avoid confusion when using other WebDA services for everyday management, also running on the users' tablet PCs. These services also addressed the user via speech but requested manual input.

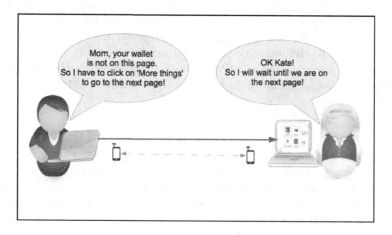

Fig. 1. Remote collaborative interaction scene

For data collection a structured questionnaire was used to gather data about the personal background and computer skills of the test participants. In addition, a structured protocol sheet was created that included comment areas for each subtask of the test scenarios to note problems arising, help provided, comments of the test participants and observations of the test conductor. Time and successful or unsuccessful completion of a sub task were also stated there. At the end of the test scenario, all test participants were asked about their opinion on the service as well as possible usability issues.

The test sample for this user study was comprised of 31 test participants (TPs) having in common a diagnosed decline in cognitive skills. The distribution of the cognitive status among the test participants was as follows: 15 TPs with a mild cognitive impairment, 9 TPs thereof were female and 6 TPs were male, ranging from 70 to 91 years (mean age 76.12). 16 TPs belonged to the group of users with dementia, ranging from mild dementia (5 TPs) to moderate (11 TPs). In this group 12 TPs were female and 4 TPs were male, ranging from 67 to 90 years (mean age 80.7). The group of test participants with dementia was dominated by TPs in later stages of dementia because it was assumed that especially this user group will need help by carers when operating an assistive service and also may have most difficulties in coping with remote collaborative interaction as an intervention strategy. In regard to computer skills, only 3 TPs of test participants with MCI had some experience with computers.

Test results showed that communication via the mobile phone worked well also to chat about the service and who is in charge of the next turn. Except for two test participants, all test participants were able to cope with the concept of remote collaborative interaction. The two test participants where this was not possible were assigned to a later stage of moderate dementia. Communication skills deteriorate remarkably in this stage, accounting partially for this test result. Their behavior appeared not to be collaborative because they were guided by the strongest stimulus perceived on the screen, which was for instance an animated navigation button, and clicked on it without communicating this to their carers. The navigation behavior was correct though, as the assistive service uses the fact that the strongest stimulus wins for people with cognitive disabilities as scaffolding technique. Two more test participants of the group of users with moderate dementia had initially difficulties with understanding the concept of remote collaborative interaction but then grasped the idea and participated in the process. All remaining 27 test participants were able to interact collaboratively by taking turns and observing actions of their carers with interest and commenting on it. As their behavior and comments showed, they understood the special circumstances of this setting and some of them were surprised that such scenarios were possible. Usability issues could not be detected and all the test participants commented this service as helpful, stressing its potential for scaffolding. Although these test results appear promising, we should mention that the usage scenario was only simulating a situation where a user needs support in operating an assistive service. To validate the applicability of the test results in real life situations, the WebDA services are now planned to be implemented in a flat shared by several people with dementia.

4   Conclusions

This user evaluation has shown that remote collaborative interaction provides a feasible approach for people with dementia and their carers to achieve together an assigned task. Furthermore, the vast majority of users with moderate dementia suffering from significant restrictions in cognitive functioning, were able to participate in the remote collaborative environment. Test results encourage to implement this approach as part of a socio-technical care environment, where IT-based assistive services support older people in managing their everyday life to prolong their stay at home. Remote collaborative interaction should ensure an appropriate use of assistive services in such care environments by providing an efficient scaffolding strategy, even for people in advanced stages of dementia. It offers the potential to ease caring activities for a relative with declining cognitive skills, because carers can access remotely the assistive care environment and communicate with their relative about its proper usage. It also invites them to participate in fulfilling caring tasks, like electronically ordering meals for the upcoming week, leveraging existing abilities of their relative not possible otherwise.

References

1. Boyd, H., Evans, N., Carey-Smith, B., Orpwood, R.: Prompting people with dementia to carry out tasks: What works and why? In: Proceedings of the First International Workshop on Pervasive Care for People with Dementia and their Carers. IEEE (April 2012)
2. Gappa, H., Nordbrock, G., Johannen, A., Schmitz, A.: Implications of dementia and age-related memory impairments on the design of it-based systems. In: Deutscher AAL-Kongress. VDE Verlag (2012)
3. Hellman, R.: Usable user interfaces for persons with memory impairments. In: Deutscher AAL-Kongress. VDE Verlag (2012)
4. Mulvenna, M., Martin, S., Sävenstedt, S., Bengtsson, J., Meiland, F., Dröes, R.M., Hettinga, M., Moelaert, F., Craig, D.: Designing & evaluating a cognitive prosthetic for people with mild dementia. In: Proceedings of the 28th Annual European Conference on Cognitive Ergonomics, ECCE 2010, pp. 11–18. ACM, New York (2010)
5. Vogt, J., Luyten, K., Van den Bergh, J., Coninx, K., Meier, A.: Putting dementia into context. In: Winckler, M., Forbrig, P., Bernhaupt, R. (eds.) HCSE 2012. LNCS, vol. 7623, pp. 181–198. Springer, Heidelberg (2012)
6. Carmien, S., Obach, M.: Back on track: Lost and found on public transportation. In: Stephanidis, C., Antona, M. (eds.) UAHCI 2013, Part II. LNCS, vol. 8010, pp. 575–584. Springer, Heidelberg (2013)
7. Gappa, H., Nordbrock, G., Pullmann, J., Mohamad, Y.: Webbasierte Dienste fürältere Menschen und Angehörige (WebDA) – Schlussbericht. Technical report, Fraunhofer FIT (2013)
8. Carmien, S.P., Koene, R.A.: Distributed intelligence and scaffolding in support of cognitive health. In: Stephanidis, C. (ed.) Universal Access in HCI, Part I, HCII 2009. LNCS, vol. 5614, pp. 334–343. Springer, Heidelberg (2009)
9. Nielsen, J.: Usability testing. In: Handbook of Human Factors and Ergonomics, 2nd edn., pp. 1543–1568. John Wiley & Sons (1997)
10. Orpwood, R., Chadd, J., Howcroft, D., Sixsmith, A., Torrington, J., Gibson, G., Chalfont, G.: Designing technology to improve quality of life for people with dementia: user-led approaches. Universal Access in the Information Society 9(3), 249–259 (2010)

Effective Application of PALRO: A Humanoid Type Robot for People with Dementia

Kaoru Inoue[1], Naomi Sakuma[2], Maiko Okada[2], Chihiro Sasaki[3], Mio Nakamura[4], and Kazuyoshi Wada[5]

[1] Tokyo Metropolitan University, Faculty of Health Sciences, Tokyo, Japan
inoue@hs.tmu.ac.jp
[2] Nursing home Shohu-en, Chiba, Japan
ugn01645@nifty.com, tf2310ji@yahoo.co.jp
[3] Tokyo College of Welfare, Tokyo, Japan
kcwgt958@icnet.ne.jp
[4] Research Institute, National Rehabilitation Center for Persons with Disabilities, Saitama, Japan
nakamura-mio@rehab.go.jp
[5] Tokyo Metropolitan University, Faculty of System Design, Tokyo, Japan
k_wada@sd.tmu.ac.jp

Abstract. PALRO is a humanoid type robot which can communicate with human through voice. This paper describes effective application for people with Dementia of PALRO. PALRO, a humanoid communication robot (Fujisoft Co Ltd.). It responds to users' speaking and even remembers faces of over 100 people. Our team wanted to see how seniors with dementia would react to PALRO and it's programs. We concluded that the effectiveness of PALRO is encourage people with dementia to interact with others, verbal and non-verbal interactions with others, et cetera.

Keywords: Communication Robot, Robot Therapy, Occupational Therapy, Dementia.

1 Introduction

1.1 Background

The number of people suffering from dementia in Japan is about 4.62 million in 2012, according to the Health, Labor and Welfare Ministry (June 6, 2013) [1]. Robots have been developed as tools to help rehabilitation and care for people with dementia. For example, PARO is a therapeutic robot modeled after a baby harp seal, developed by National Institute of Advanced Industrial Science and Technology (AIST). A substantial number of reports showed that PARO can improve Behavioral and Psychological Symptoms of Dementia; BPSD. For example, Patrizia Marti and Kazuyoshi Wada showed in their research that the use of PARO improved dementia patients' communication and sociability and also alleviated their depression [2,3]. At daycare center with nine dementia patients, team incorporated a therapeutic activity with PARO as

K. Miesenberger et al. (Eds.): ICCHP 2014, Part I, LNCS 8547, pp. 451–454, 2014.

part of the daily routine. During the test period, patients' urine samples were checked for hormone values (17-KS-S and the 17-KS-S/17-OHCS ratio). The results showed that the level of the patients' stress decreased at the end of second and fourth week. [4] In a more recent study, a research team led by Wendy Moyle conducted a small scale Randomized Controlled Trial (RCT) with PARO and proved that a group whose members interacted with PARO won highest pleasure scores [5].

PARO has been used in many institutions around the world. There are many previous studies about PARO. However, research on verbal communication robots which could understand and speak a language have not been verified sufficiently. Nowadays, there are many different kind of robots that provide different services.

The aim of the projects is to identify which activity using PALRO could be most effective to alleviate the conditions of seniors with Dementia in nursing elderly home.

1.2   PALRO

PALRO is a humanoid shaped robot produced by Fujisoft Co.Ltd.[6]. It connects to internet, to get various informations, such as news, fortune-telling, weather, forecast, etc... It can also communicate with users, walk, play music, dance, take photo, and do recreation or games, scheduling management, alarm, e-mail. In this research, we used recreation programs. Users order PALRO "PALRO, do recreation." It can carry out recreation which contains speech, physical-exercise, and games for about 20 minutes.

1.3   Dementia Care Mapping (DCM)

DCM method is designed to analyze the quality of care "through the eyes of dementia patients.

DCM mappers(observers), observed subjects for the Behavior Category Codes (BCC), such as "sleeping" and "walking," and measured the "Well-being, Ill-being Scale" (WIB Score) based on their behaviors. WIB Score is divided into six levels: +5, +3, +1, -1, -3, -5. (University of Bradford)[7].

Fig. 1. PALRO (40cm, 1.6kg, ABS/acryl/aluminum alloy, Intel RAtom"!Processor Z530(1.6GHz), memory Bus 533MHz, secondary cache 512KB, 1GB DDR SDRAM, 8GB SSD) These pictures were approved for publishing by Fujisoft Co.Ltd., volunteers

2   Method

In December, 2013, our team conducted study at a nursing home's day room when we also introduced robot "PALRO." The length of each observation was 1.5 hours long("Free session" 30 minutes; "Recreation program" 30 minutes and "Free session after recreation" 30 minutes). 25 regular members(average age: 86.6 years, 6 males, 19 females) suffering from Dementia participated in this study. The DCM version 8.0 was employed for observation tool. The three DCM mappers were two certified care workers and one Occupational Therapist.

3   Results

Group WIB Scores: 2.0 for the "Free session; 2.2; for the "Recreation program" and 1.8 "Free session after recreation." (All values are presented as average) Regarding Group Behavior Category Codes (BCC), the most remarkable results were

A   "Interacting with Others"
E   "Engaging in expressive or creative activity"
I   "Prioritizing the use of intellectual activities"
L   "Engaging in leisure, fun and recreation"
O   "Objects, verbal and non-verbal interactions with others"

People with severe dementia tended to note "O" (watching PALRO). On the other hand, seniors with mild dementia tended to note "I"," L" (enjoying games, talking) 20 out of 25 regular members showed good reactions to the PALRO program.

4   Discussions and Conclusion

These results showed that the program encouraged seniors suffering from dementia in their communication, activity expressions, intellectual activities, and fun. These results are important guideline for the future treatment.

It is effective to combine various non-drug treatments for dementia and PALRO is useful device helping patients with different activities.

PALRO is better for seniors with mild dementia, because they can enjoy PALRO program, while people with serious dementia cannot. Our group will gather many data to analyze them.

References

1. http://the-japan-news.com/news/article/0000289892 (June 6, 2013)
2. Marti, P., Bacigalupo, M., Giusti, L., Mennecozzi, C., Shibata, T.: Socially Assistive Robotics in the Treatment of Behavioural and Psychological Symptoms of Dementia. Paper Presented at the Biomedical Robotics and Biomechatronics (2006)

3. Wada, K., Shibata, T., Asada, T., Musha, T.: Robot therapy for prevention of dementia at home. Journal of Robotics and Mechatronics, 691–697 (2007); A.N. Author, Article title, Journal Title 66, 856–890 (1993)
4. Wada, K., Shibata, T.: Living with Seal Robots in a Care House - Evaluations of Social and Physiological Influences. In: Proceedings of the 2006 IEEE/RSJ International Conference on Intelligent Robots and Systems (2006)
5. Moyle, W., Cooke, M., Beattie, E., Cook, G., Gray, C.: Exploring the effect of companion robots on Emotional Expression in Older Adults With Dementia. Journal of Grrontological Nursing 39(5), 47–53 (2013)
6. PALRO (Japanese text only), http://PALRO.jp/

The Feasibility and Efficacy of Technology-Based Support Groups among Family Caregivers of Persons with Dementia

Sara J. Czaja[1], Richard Schulz[2], Dolores Perdomo[1], and Sankaran N. Nair[1]

[1] University of Miami Miller School of Medicine, Miami FL, USA
{sczaja,dperdomo,snair}@med.miami.edu
[2] University of Pittsburgh, Pittsburgh, PA, USA
schulz@pitt.edu

Abstract. With the aging of the population the numbers of people with a chronic condition such as Alzheimer's disease (AD) are expected to increase. Most people with a chronic condition, such as AD, are cared for by a family member. Although caregiving can be rewarding many caregivers experience emotional distress and physical comorbidities. In this regard, there a broad range of interventions aimed at decreasing caregiver stress. Despite the proliferation of these interventions they have only met with limited success for a variety of reasons. Information technology offers the potential of enhancing the ability of caregivers to access needed services and programs. This paper evaluated the feasibility and efficacy of technology-based psychosocial intervention for family caregivers of AD patients. Overall, the results indicated that the caregivers were enthusiastic about the program, found the technology easy to use, and indicated that the intervention enhanced their access to resources, support and caregiving skills.

Keywords: Caregiving, Technology, Dementia Patients.

1 Introduction

The population is aging at an unprecedented rate in both developed and developing countries. The growth in the number of older people, especially the old-old, has important implications for society and the healthcare system. The likelihood of developing a chronic disease or disability and the need for support and healthcare services generally increases with age. Currently about 36 million people worldwide have Alzheimer's disease (AD) or some other form of dementia and this number is expected to increase to 66 million by 2030 [1].

Most people with dementia are cared for at home by family members such as spouse (often times who is older themselves) or a daughter. Although caregiving can be rewarding and many caregivers are proud of their role and glean positive benefits, caregiving clearly creates challenges. Overall, caregiving has been shown to result in psychological distress, the adoption of poor health habits, and increased use of psychotropic medications; sleep disruption, psychiatric and physical illnesses and mortality. Caregiving also often disrupts social and family relationships and employment activities [2,3]. Given

K. Miesenberger et al. (Eds.): ICCHP 2014, Part I, LNCS 8547, pp. 455–458, 2014.
© Springer International Publishing Switzerland 2014

these consequences associated with care provision, there has been a broad range of intervention studies aimed at decreasing caregiver stress. Several studies have demonstrated significant effects in reducing caregiver burden and depression, and delaying patient placement. Despite the proliferation of these interventions, services are not always available to caregivers or caregivers are unwilling to use available services because of issues such as cost, logistic problems, or feelings of guilt about receiving help from outside of the family structure. Current information technologies offer the potential of removing these barriers and providing support and delivering services to caregivers. This study evaluated the feasibility and efficacy of using technology to deliver a psychosocial intervention to minority family caregivers of dementia patients. The intervention was modeled after the REACH II program [4].

1.1   Objectives

The focus of this paper is on the perceived feasibility and value of the support group component of the intervention. An emphasis is given to the use of technology to facilitate support group participation. In addition, ethnic differences in participation and perceptions of the support groups are discussed. We also present data on perceptions of the usability of the videophone system.

2   Methods

The VideoCare Study was a randomized trial that evaluated the effects of a technology-based intervention among an ethnically diverse sample of caregivers. Following a baseline assessment a sample of 110 caregivers (56 Hispanic Americans and 54 African Americans) were randomized into: 1) the videophone intervention condition; 2) a nutrition attention control condition; or 3) an information only control condition. Those assigned to the intervention group received a Cisco videophone that was installed in their home and connected to a DSL line and a secure server at the host site (see Figure 1, left). The Videophones were used to conduct individual skill building sessions with a certified interventionists and facilitator led support groups. Other available features included an annotated resource guide, caregiver tips: educational seminars. The features were presented in hierarchical menus in a multi-modal format (speech and text). Caregivers received training in the use of the videophone, were provided with a help card, a help feature on the menu, and access to technical support. All features were available in English and Spanish. A total of 30 participants were assigned to the intervention condition and participated in the "online" support groups. The intervention duration was 5 months, followed by a post intervention assessment. A key component of the intervention was providing caregivers with five live video support group sessions to expand their social network, provide a venue for interaction with other caregivers, and increase their knowledge and caregiving skills.

The support groups were conducted via the videophone in English and Spanish and followed a structured education/supportive format (see Figure 1, right). This included an introduction to and discussion of themes related to the caregiving experience. The group themes included: 1) Introduction to Dementia; 2) Managing Behavioral Problems; 3) Caregiver Well Being; and 4) Communication; and Planning for Life

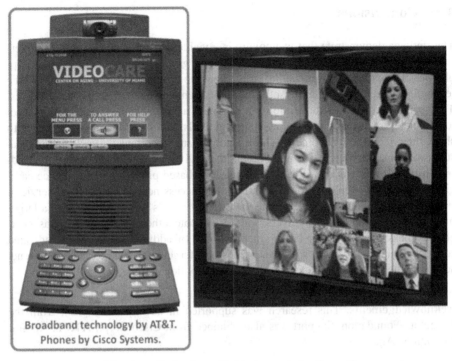

Fig. 1. Left: The Videophone Technology. Right: An example of an online support group.

Transition. The support group sessions were closed, 60 minutes in duration, and were interspersed with the individual videophone skill building sessions. The caregivers participated from their own homes via videophone.

3   Results

Overall, 73% of caregivers reported benefiting from participating in the VideoCare study with African Americans indicated a higher level of perceived benefit (86%) than the Hispanic participants (62%). The majority of the caregivers felt that study participation did not require too much work or effort 97%. Importantly 90% of the participants indicated that participation in the program made their life less stressful and 83% indicated that it helped them provide care to their loved one.

Overall, the majority of caregivers (82%) found participating in the on-line support groups was valuable, and improved their knowledge about caregiving and their caregiving skills. All of the caregivers (100%) indicated that participation in the groups helped them share their feelings about being a caregiver. In terms of the usability of the videophone technology, 96% percent of the caregivers indicated that the system was easy to use and 98% indicated that the information provided by the Videophone was easy to understand. Further, having access to the VideoCare network was ranked as the most valuable aspect of the study. This was followed by learning strategies on how to communicate with others, information about resources available in the community and participation in the support group with other caregivers.

4   Conclusions

The findings demonstrate that technology is a viable and valuable option for delivering intervention programs and conducting support groups with diverse caregiver populations. The caregivers were enthusiastic about the program and were able to use the technology. They also found it useful in terms of enhancing their access to resources. They perceived participation in the support groups as valuable, beneficial with respect to enhancing their caregiving knowledge and skills, and providing an opportunity to share their feelings with others. These findings are important as inadequate social support is linked to depression and burden in caregiver populations. Overall, the findings from this study demonstrate that technology-based programs may enhance caregivers' ability to overcome logistic barriers and access needed support and services. Further research is needed to examine the efficacy of this type of program in a larger more diverse sample of caregivers and to evaluate other outcomes such as cost-effectiveness of technology-based interventions. In addition, the project indicated some challenges associated with these types of interventions such as lack of Internet access by the majority of the caregivers that have policy implications.

Acknowledgements. This research was supported in large part by grant from the Langeloth Foundation. Support was also obtained from Cisco Corp.; AT&T; Administration on Aging.

References

1. World Alzheimer Report 2010 (2010),
   http://www.alz.co.uk/research/files/
   WorldAlzheimerReport2010.pdf
2. Pinquart, M., Sörensen, S.: Correlates of physical health of informal caregivers: a meta-analysis. Journals of Gerontology: Series B 62(2), 126–137 (2006)
3. Schulz, R., O'Brien, A.T., Bookwala, J., et al.: Psychiatric and physical morbidity effects of dementia caregiving: prevalence, correlates, and causes. Gerontologist 35, 771–791 (1995)
4. Belle, S.H., Burgio, L., Burns, R., Coon, D., Czaja, S.J., Gallagher-Thompson, D., et al.: Enhancing the quality of life of dementia caregivers from different ethnic or racial groups: A randomized, controlled trial. Annals of Internal Medicine 145, 727–738 (2006)

Making Music Meaningful with Adaptive Immediate Feedback Drill for Teaching Children with Cognitive Impairment: A Dual Coding Strategy to Aural Skills

Yu Ting Huang[1] and Chi Nung Chu[2]

[1] Department of Music, Shih Chien University, Taipei, Taiwan, R.O.C.
`yuting11@mail.usc.edu.tw`
[2] Department of Management of Information System, China University of Technology,
Taipei, Taiwan, R.O.C.
`nung@cute.edu.tw`

Abstract. Seventeen fifth graders of elementary school in Taipei were administered a web-based AIFD learning system where they practiced aural skills in response to musical intervals, pitch identifications, and rhythms then tested on their recall of these aural skills while using adaptive immediate feedback drill as cues. The pre and post-tests resulted in a significant increase in scores from the pre-test to post-test (t (16) = 2.759, p = .014). Advanced analysis showed significant differences were observed between the pre and post-tests only for the interval recognition (t (16) = 2.634, p = .018). The result of the interviews showed that the teachers and the parents hold positive views on this AIFD learning system. They were satisfied with the progress of the students' aural skills, participation during the class, and preference on music.

Keywords: Aural Skills, Intellectual Disabilities, Adaptive Immediate Feedback Drill.

1 Introduction

Aural skills which include identifying pitch, interval and rhythm are essential elements to access music [1]. Although only a few of the special children in cognitive impairment will have either the interest or ability in traditional music learning at the elementary level, those who do generally should be encouraged in their pursuits. However the inherent abstract complexity of extraction in musical variation is hard for these children with intellectual disabilities to comprehend and memorize [2, 3, 4]. In the teaching of music there would be opportunities not only for rhythms, singing, and expression, but also for listening and developing appreciation of certain musical pieces through games, dances, or even work.

The move to use technology to support learning has been an emerging development in the recent music pedagogy. Music education applications use a range of techniques to create music, to edit any aspect of it and to play it back at virtually any tempo has meant that children are now able to compose music that they cannot physically play [5, 6, 7]. However, in the learning process of identifying pitch, intervals

K. Miesenberger et al. (Eds.): ICCHP 2014, Part I, LNCS 8547, pp. 459–462, 2014.

and rhythms, children need more immediate error feedback to review, reinforce, and develop their own aural skills. The supply of learning error analyses would consolidate children's individual development of aural skills.

The Adaptive Immediate Feedback Drill (AIFD) learning system proposed in this study tries to make the musical elements accessible aurally and visually [8, 9]. To facilitate the immediate learning error feedback for children with intellectual disabilities, each classified error type of aural skills in identification with different corresponding image color cues would possess educational implications and the effects of verbal articulation from the text-to-speech engine for each specific error type of aural skills could facilitate memory recall of musical pas-sages. In such design, children with intellectual disabilities would have greater opportunities for learning independence than ever before.

2   Adaptive Immediate Feedback Drill (AIFD) Learning System

The web-based AIFD learning system is composed of assessment analysis engine and piano drill engine. The assessment analysis engine(Fig. 1)is designed to provide immediate diagnostic feedback on the melodic line assessment with pitch recognition, interval recognition and rhythm recognition(Fig. 2). Questions on the online assessment based on the pre-identified error types of aural skills were organized. All the answers of a learner made together with the corresponding information associated with each question would be analyzed and searched from the XML tree by the assessment analysis engine and saved into an XML file. A learner could receive personally adaptive feedbacks for the result of analyzed error type after taking the assessment process. With the specific error type, each learner would be transferred to the piano drill mode with more diagnosed error type of practices from the assessment analysis engine.

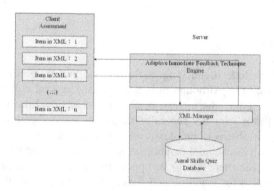

Fig. 1. The framework of assessment analysis engine

The piano drill engine(Fig. 3)is designed to provide immediate practicing feedback after the melodic line assessment with pitch recognition, interval recognition and rhythm recognition(Fig. 4).

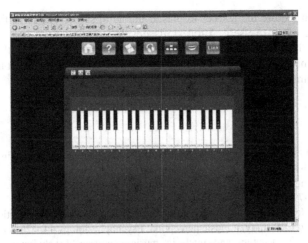

Fig. 2. The piano drill engine

3 Method and Results

Participants of this study included 17 students who attended an elementary school in Taipei. Parent permission forms were sent to all children who were receiving services in the special education classroom for children with intellectual disabilities and all were granted permission to participate in the study. They (10 males and 7 females) were fifth graders and classified as mild intellectual disabilities (IQ range 60-75, mean 71).

Participants were given pre and post-tests. The test included identifying pitch, intervals, and rhythm. After the pretests were administered, the web-based AIFD learning system was implemented for about 20 minutes per daily session over a three-month period. Children were encouraged to make self-regulating learning by manipulating the AIFD. At the completion of the learning sessions, all children were administered post-test measures. Focus interview technique was used to perform interviews on parents and teachers. The results of the interviews were used for social validity.

Result showed a significant increase in scores from the pre-test to post-test (t (16) = 2.759, p = .014). Advanced analysis showed significant differences were observed between the pre and post-tests only for the interval recognition (t (16) = 2.634, p = .018). The result of the interviews showed that the teachers and the parents hold positive views on this AIFD learning system. They were satisfied with the progress of the students' aural skills, participation during the class, and preference on music. The social validity of this manipulation was confirmed.

4 Conclusion

The adaptive immediate error feedback could move children in cognitive impairment beyond basic drill exercises to a competence that is tailored to the content of individual needs in the aural skills sequence. And the further exercises created by the AIFD learning system require the learner to master the aural skills. The remediation will be handled by the exercise itself. Aural skills development occurs when children with intellectual disabilities interact with AIFD learning system in a drill with dual coding mode. Many misconceptions could then be cleared up through the combination of practice and immediate error feedback.

References

1. McPherson, G.E.: From child to musician: skill development during the beginning stages of learning an instrument. Psychology of Music 33, 5–35 (2005)
2. Janata, P.: The neural architecture of music-evoked autobiographical memories. Cerebral Cortex 19, 2579–2594 (2009)
3. Koelsch, S., Jentschke, S., Sammler, D., Mietchen, D.: Untangling syntactic and sensory processing: An ERP study of music perception. Psychophysiology 44, 476–490 (2007)
4. Krumhansl, C.L.: Rhythm and pitch in music cognition. Psychological Bulletin 126, 159–179 (2000)
5. Solis, J., Ng, K.: Musical Robots and Interactive Multimodal Systems. In: Solis, J., Ng, K. (eds.) Musical Robots and Interactive Multimodal Systems. STAR, vol. 74, pp. 1–12. Springer, Heidelberg (2011)
6. Odam, G., Paterson, A.: Composing in the Classroom: The Creative Dream. National Association of Music Educators, High Wycombe (2000)
7. Smoliar, S.W., Waterworth, J.A., Kellock, P.R.: pianoFORTE: a System for Piano Education beyond Notation Literacy. In: Proceedings of ACM Multimedia 1995 Conference, pp. 457–465. ACM, New York (1995)
8. Clark, J.M., Paivio, A.: Dual coding theory and education. Educational Psychology Review 3(3), 149–210 (1991)
9. Henik, G.: Music and Self-Generated Images: Applying Dual Coding Theory, Generative Theory of Reading Comprehension, and Cognitive Load Theory to Web-Based Music Instruction. In: Proceedings of World Conference on Educational Multimedia, Hypermedia and Telecommunications, pp. 1129–1136 (2003)

Evaluating New Interaction Paradigms in SEN Teaching: Defining the Experiment

Paloma Cantón[1], José L. Fuertes[2], Ángel L. González[2], and Loïc Martínez[2]

[1] Consejería de Educación de la Comunidad de Madrid, Spain
pcanton@educa.madrid.org
[2] School of Computer Science and Engineering, Technical University of Madrid,
Boadilla del Monte, Madrid, Spain
{jfuertes,agonzalez,loic}@fi.upm.es

Abstract. New devices have made their way into everyday life in recent years, opening the doors to new ways of interacting with computers, providing different, and potentially better, solutions to some problems. But this raises the question of if there is any way of measuring whether or not these new devices are suitable. This paper presents a strategy for evaluating the suitability of new interaction devices in the context of teaching children with special educational needs.

Keywords: SEN, Education, Touch, Touchless, Gesture, Assessment, User Interface, Kinect, Interaction Paradigms.

1 Introduction

New devices have made their way into everyday life in recent years, opening the doors to new ways of interacting with computers. This affords the opportunity to devise new systems to exploit these new interaction paradigms and provide different, and potentially better, solutions to some problems, like the teaching of children with special educational needs (SEN).

The question raised is whether it is a good idea to use these devices in teaching systems targeting SEN users and whether there is any way of measuring the suitability of these new paradigms. Furthermore, new metaphors of interaction associated with each new device will have to be defined, and it will be necessary to validate whether or not each metaphor is suitable or needs to be tailored.

Therefore, we believe that a protocol should be established to measure and compare how usable an interaction device is and how the user would interact with the system using the respective device in a SEN context.

This paper outlines the first step towards this objective, which involves:

- selecting the user types who will participate in the tests and the device types to be compared
- developing a system that will act as a testbench for the devices

K. Miesenberger et al. (Eds.): ICCHP 2014, Part I, LNCS 8547, pp. 463–470, 2014.

- defining the information to be gathered both automatically by the system and manually by an observer
- defining the experimental procedure.

In the following we will explain the state of the art, the methodology applied to define the experiment and the conclusions and future lines of research.

2   Related Work

In recent years, many newly designed devices have changed the face of human-computer interaction. Some examples are games systems (Wii, DS), mobile devices (tablets or phones) or other devices (tactile screens and Kinect). In this section, we will look at some approaches in this field and their educational applications.

Seven years ago Apple revolutionized the field of mobile devices by providing support for user interaction via gestures and actions. Apple introduced two concepts: touches and gestures. Google built a similar touch- and gesture-based system into its Android operating system for mobile devices. Microsoft has developed a similar effort for interacting with Microsoft software using gestures (from Windows 8 to Kinect) [1].

There have been different initiatives to use these kinds of new interaction devices to improve education. Technology and education can be combined at all educational levels, but a conceptual framework should be used that identifies the required knowledge (content, teaching method , and technology) and supports teachers with technology integration [2].

In this context, children usually show clear preferences for games using relatively simpler interaction modes; they mostly prefer to play touch games (using a multi-touchable display) than computer games (using mouse and keyboard) [3].

Another interesting learning approach is based on a collaborative game played by six players with handheld motion-sensitive tangible user interfaces in front of a large shared display. The game teaches children how to cooperate with each other (social skills) and collectively reason about the cause-and-effect relationships of the different mechanisms required to move, saw and lift planks (problem-solving skills) [4].

Another type of device enables touchless gestures, that is, gestures performed in the air without touching a device. One example is Microsoft Kinect, a new device for the Xbox 360 game system launched in 2010 (which can also be used on Windows computers) [5]. Kinect set out to change the way gamers usually play videogames by converting their body into the "game controller" controlling the different elements of the game and interacting through a natural user interface using gestures and spoken commands.

Kinect was initially released as a gaming device, but it has been used as an artificial vision device in many areas of application by researchers worldwide. Research into Kinect is growing, but, so far, there is not much literature on the adaptation of this technology for children and young people with disabilities. Nevertheless, Kinect had been used effectively by people with special needs and as an auxiliary learning tool in the traditional classroom. Some successful experiences with Kinect are: improvement of the outcomes of a daily life game used by children with autism, a system of drawing via hand motion, a system to create music by arm motion [6], a system to help immigrant children learn a new language for the purposes of classroom learning and integration into local society [7], or a system for rehabbing students' motor skills, enhancing the memory of people with autism and encouraging greater sociability (helping them to cooperate with each other and gradually develop their oral expression to a point where they can give basic instructions to each other during the game) [8]. An interactive framework using Kinect for e-learning specific for presentation and assessment has also been published [9]. The goal is to create a virtual smart classroom environment rendering the classroom more interactive and exciting.

To sum up, touch and touchless gesture systems are able to enhance classroom interactions, increase participation, improve teachers' ability to present and manipulate multimodal materials, create opportunities for interaction and discussion, kindle student creativity, afford technical interactivity (including children with SEN), enhance teaching, or support learning. But as researchers are not yet clear about how the application of gesture-based computing improves learning, these devices need empirical evidence to support their legitimacy as an adequate educational technology [10] and to identify their suitability for different situations and educational environments.

3   Methodology

The process followed to develop the research was composed of the following steps:

- Identify the profile of participant users.
- Select the devices to be tested as part of this first interaction.
- Develop an educational game to test and compare devices.
- Define the information to be gathered by the system and the educator accompanying the child during the experiment (to be performed at the same time as the last step).
- Define the experiment protocol to assure reproducible and consistent results.

3.1   Identifying the Profile of Participant Users

The SEN users that most often use and find it easier to access these ICT devices have mild intellectual disability. On this ground, our study commences with this user population. This user group does not have any real trouble handling the target devices, although they do not use them as precisely, rapidly and skilfully as other users generally do. The study sets out to answer the following questions: What problems do they have? How do they show up? What influence does their intellectual disability have on the use of the selected devices?

3.2   Selecting Devices

At the start of this research project in September 2012 we found that the interaction devices that the educational field was starting to try out were mostly touch-sensitive devices and contactless gesture interaction devices. The first group includes mobile telephones, tablets and touchscreen computers. The second group includes webcams, motion sensors derived from the technology developed by PrimeSense [10] and other promising sensors like Leap Motion [11].

As the aim is to be able to develop a system to compare different types of devices, they logically had to be tested in the same environment. On this ground, we opted to develop the system on a personal computer running Windows 7 or Windows 8. The selected devices were a multi-touch screen and Microsoft Kinect.

3.3   Developing the Educational Game

We have designed an educational game that covers the most common movements used in the selected devices in order to analyse how they are performed by users and how user characteristics influence their performance.

The subject matter and operation of the game was defined in partnership with a teaching specialist, and activities in which the above movements are suitably functional and coherent were selected. The characteristics of the target users was another factor taken into account in the design of the activity, which was tailored to their educational level, the teaching goals for the user group and their gaming preferences. While the game has to be attractive, dynamic and interactive enough to motivate the users to play, it must not contain so many stimuli as to distract users and render it overly complex. Thus, the graphical interface of the games was designed to be simple and attractive.

Defining the Games. The best practice for defining the games that were to be part of the experiment was considered to be to use a subject matter that had the potential to test and compare several gestures using the selected devices. During this phase, we concluded that the actions that the user would have to perform to complete the game should include vertical, horizontal and wrist-twisting movements. We also decided that the child should be allowed to use non-educational games to learn how to operate the devices they are to use.

The first of these training activities is a bowling game, including skittles and coloured bowling balls. The player has to select and roll the respective coloured bowling ball. In the second training activity, the user has to use a set of letters to form a word. This game uses the same actions as the bowling game, plus the open action. In the same vein of gradually adding new actions to the activities, we designed a classification game organized at three difficulty levels (Fig. 1). At the easy level, the user has to select the respective element at the top of the screen (cloud), drop it on to the belt and then knock it into a round box. At the normal level, the stop box rotation and open box actions are added. At the hard level, the rotate gesture is added to the above.

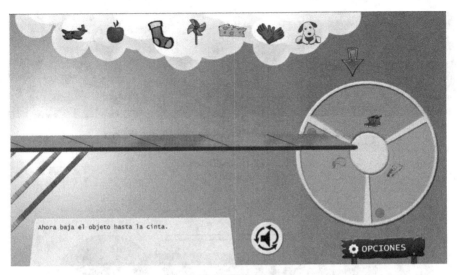

Fig. 1. Classification game

Defining the Interaction Vocabulary. The gestures denoting the actions that the user is to perform vary depending on the selected device. We focus on the gestures that are most commonly used in activities targeting younger users, which tend to be the most intuitive and look, on paper, to be the simplest to perform.

The gestures have been defined taking into account that the aim is to rate particular skills or abilities when moving certain body parts or performing hand gestures:

- Sweeping movements of arms, like up-down, sideward, in-out, rotational motions, etc.
- One-/two-handed movements: simple motions like touching part of the screen or moving right/left or up/down on the screen.
- One-finger movements: simple motions like touching or moving around the screen.
- Two-finger movements: complex motions like pinching with the index finger and thumb.

Additionally, these movements must be performed at a particular speed, which may vary. Faster movements are harder to execute properly than slower ones. These movements can be used to interact with the device applications and perform actions like select, execute, move/drag, zoom, etc.

By examining these movements and how effectively they are performed by users with an intellectual disability, we will be able to analyse what requirements the new interaction paradigms introduce and what competences users require for their performance. We believe that these gestures and body movements may be a limiting factor for users with intellectual difficulties, because, although they do not have physical handicaps, they do have problems with hand-eye coordination, precision, speed or visual-spatial processing, which can have a bearing on the effectiveness with which they perform these gestures to solve the assigned activities.

Fig. 2 shows the gesture defined for knocking an object into a box using Kinect and Fig. 3 illustrates the equivalent gesture for a tactile screen.

Fig. 2. Kinect gesture for knocking objects into the box

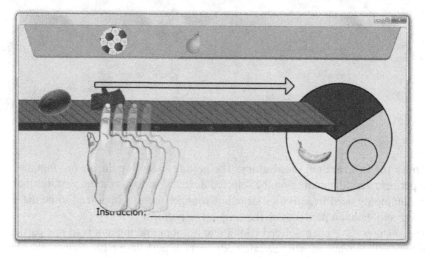

Fig. 3. Touchscreen gestures for knocking objects into the box

3.4 Defining the Information to be Gathered

There are two sources of information: information gathered automatically by the game and information gathered by the teacher after users have completed the activity.

The game is able to automatically collect a variety of generic (successes, failures...) and device-specific data. For touchscreen actions it measures gesture precision. To do this, a region is defined around the touch path trajectory. If the gesture runs through the centre of this region, precision is rated as 100%. The precision decreases as the trajectory moves away from the centre. The precision is 0% if the gesture is outside the region. This region is not visible to users. For Kinect, data are collected on how often the gesture is performed incorrectly before it is performed correctly.

In summary, the captured data will measure the number of successes, failures, precision and time taken to perform the gaming actions. From these data, we will be able to draw conclusions about the manipulative skills (precision, speed), efficiency and effectiveness of the users when performing the task and how the use of these devices influences the attainment of teaching goals.

On the other hand, the teacher completes a questionnaire designed to gather additional information regarding teaching and system user experience:

- Session data, like session time and whether or not the child had used the system before
- User personal data: any learning, visual and motor disabilities, as well as age and sex
- Data on gaming performance, recording observed gestures, postures and mobility problems
- Questions on user experience based on standard usability questionnaires.

3.5   Experimental Process

We have established a four-phase process in order to develop the experiment. Depending on the results of each phase, it may be necessary to revise the defined process and tailor the experiment in order to achieve more reliable results.

The phases are:

1. *Functionality test*: evaluate the system with 6- to 11-year-old children without SEN at our facilities. The goal is to check that the game works properly with respect to both activity performance and data collection. The questionnaire will not be used to collect data at this stage.
2. *Pilot test*: evaluate the system in a real environment (at a school) with 10 to 12 children aged from 6 to 11 years without SEN. The teacher monitoring the activity will take the survey after each child finishes using the system. This will serve to check that the system works in a real-world situation and that the questionnaire is adequate for collecting additional data.
3. *Experiment:* visit several schools that have pupils with mild intellectual disability. The pupils will perform the set activities, the system will collect data and the teacher will complete the respective questionnaires in accordance with the experimental protocol refined in phase 2.
4. *Results analysis*: the results of phase 3 will be analysed in order to determine and compare the adequacy of the multipoint touchscreens and the Kinect system for educational systems to be used by children with special educational needs.

Phase 1 was performed in February 2014 and the initial results show that the children were able to perform the tasks without too much trouble, but the gesture recognition system needed some refinement to increase its reliability. Once the system has been upgraded we will enact phases 2 and 3 from October to December 2014. If all goes according to plan, phase 4 will get under way in February 2015.

4   Conclusions and Future Lines of Research

New devices and ways of interacting with machines have emerged in recent years. But there is no standardized means of assessing which of these devices to use and how to use them in each context.

This paper reports the design of an experiment and the development of an educational application whose architecture can straightforwardly accommodate new devices and interaction paradigms. In this manner, it will be easy to compare the adequacy of each device in a particular context.

References

1. Cantón, P., González, Á.L., Mariscal, G., Ruiz, C.: Applying New Interaction Paradigms to the Education of Children with Special Educational Needs. In: Miesenberger, K., Karshmer, A., Penaz, P., Zagler, W. (eds.) ICCHP 2012, Part I. LNCS, vol. 7382, pp. 65–72. Springer, Heidelberg (2012)
2. Tse, E., Marentette, L., Ahmed, S.I., Thayer, A., Huber, J., Mühlhäuser, M., Kim, S.J., Brown, Q.: Educational Interfaces, Software, and Technology. In: Proc. CHI 2012, pp. 2691–2694. ACM (2012)
3. Yu, X., Zhang, M., Ren, J., Zhao, H., Zhu, Z.: Experimental Development of Competitive Digital Educational Games on Multi-touch Screen for Young Children. In: Zhang, X., Zhong, S., Pan, Z., Wong, K., Yun, R. (eds.) Edutainment 2010. LNCS, vol. 6249, pp. 367–375. Springer, Heidelberg (2010)
4. Goh, W.-B., Fitriani, G.C.-F., Menon, M., Tan, J., Cohen, L.G.: Action Role Design and Observations in a Gestural Interface-based Collaborative Game. In: Proc. CHI 2011, pp. 763–772. ACM (2011)
5. Zhang, Z.: Microsoft Kinect Sensor and Its Effect. IEEE Multimedia 19(2), 4–10 (2012)
6. Bossavit, B., Pina, A.: An interdisciplinary methodology for designing and implementing educational tools for children and youth with special needs. SIGAccess Newsletter 105, 4–8 (2013)
7. Mateu, J., Lasala, M.J., Alamán, X.: Tangible Interfaces and Virtual Worlds: A New Environment for Inclusive Education. In: Urzaiz, G., Ochoa, S.F., Bravo, J., Chen, L.L., Oliveira, J. (eds.) UCAmI 2013. LNCS, vol. 8276, pp. 119–126. Springer, Heidelberg (2013)
8. Boutsika, E.: Kinect in Education: A Proposal for Children with Autism. In: Proc. DSAI 2013. Elsevier (2013)
9. Sommool, W., Battulga, B., Shih, T.K., Hwang, W.-Y.: Using Kinect for Holodeck Classroom: A Framework for Presentation and Assessment. In: Wang, J.-F., Lau, R. (eds.) ICWL 2013. LNCS, vol. 8167, pp. 40–49. Springer, Heidelberg (2013)
10. Hsu, H.J.: The Potential of Kinect in Education. International Journal of Information and Education Technology 1(5), 365–370 (2011)
11. PrimeSense. 3D Sensing Technology Solutions (2014), http://www.primesense.com/
12. Leap Motion. Mac & PC Motion Controller for Games, Design and More (2014), https://www.leapmotion.com/

How to Make Online Social Networks Accessible
for Users with Intellectual Disability?

Carmit-Noa Shpigelman[1] and Carol J. Gill[2]

[1] Department of Community Mental Health, University of Haifa, Haifa, Israel
carmits@univ.haifa.ac.il
[2] Department of Disability & Human Development, University of Illinois, Chicago, U.S.A.
cg16@uic.edu

Abstract. Participation in online social networks has considerable potential to empower people with intellectual disability who might experience social isolation in the real world. However, this issue has received little research attention. In response to this challenge, we conducted an accessible online research survey to learn how adults with intellectual disability use and perceive Facebook. Results from 58 respondents indicated that they use Facebook much as non-disabled users do to connect with family members and real-world friends. At the same time, the respondents reported challenges such as privacy setting and literacy demands. We discuss these findings and how to make social networking sites accessible for this population.

Keywords: Online Social Networks, Facebook, Accessibility, Disability.

1   Introduction

Research has indicated that participation in online social networks strengthens relationships with close friends, provides social support, contributes to psychological well-being, and promotes political engagement [1,2,3]. In this sense, online social networks have considerable potential to empower people with disabilities who might experience social isolation in the real world [4]. It allows them to expand their communication channels and social circles, organize disability-rights actions, and promote disability events [5,6]. Participation in online social networks may particularly contribute to individuals with intellectual disability since they often lack peer friendships, especially after school or job hours [7,8].

The American Association of Intellectual and Developmental Disabilities [9], defines an intellectual disability (ID) as a disability that originates before the age of 18 and is characterized by significant limitations both in intellectual functioning and in adaptive behavior as expressed in conceptual, social, and practical adaptive skills. According to the U.S. President's Committee for People with Intellectual Disabilities approximately 7-8 million Americans of all ages (one in ten American families), or three percent of the general population, experience intellectual disabilities or what is often referred to in the UK as "learning disability."

K. Miesenberger et al. (Eds.): ICCHP 2014, Part I, LNCS 8547, pp. 471–477, 2014.
© Springer International Publishing Switzerland 2014

McClimens and Gordon [10] explored the potential of the Internet and particularly blogs to increase the range of contacts available to people with ID outside their immediate family or professional support networks. The participants who were all adults with ID composed and posted blogs, supported by volunteer students. The findings indicated that blogging promoted the self-expression of people with ID. Mazurek et al. [11] also found that youth with cognitive impairments were more likely to engage in online social interactions (email and chat rooms) than those with autism. The above studies highlight the opportunity that social media offer people with ID in terms of sharing personal stories, exchanging information, and expanding their social circles.

However, participation in social media requires managing the challenges of accessibility and usability that people with ID might encounter. An online service where the user has to sign up for an account, sign in using a username and password, and then understanding the concept of the specific online social network and its terminology might be difficult for people with cognitive impairments. This process requires relatively high literacy skills which are not common among people with ID [12,13]

This issue of how people with ID use online social networks, including potential benefits and risks and how to make this service accessible for them has received little research attention. We addressed this issue by conducting an accessible online research survey to reach a pool of adults (18 years and older) with ID who use Facebook and document their online experiences, accessibility challenges and desires. Our primary research aim was to learn how adults with ID use and perceive Facebook. The secondary research aim was to produce practical recommendations from the users themselves about future accessibility of Facebook.

2   Method

We applied a method – a self-report online survey – to maximize participation of people with ID in responding to our questions toward better understanding of the experiences, capabilities and desires of Facebook users with ID. Currently, there are no data about how many people with disabilities, and ID, in particular, use Facebook. The online survey allowed us to include the voices of people with ID in the developing knowledge base about use and accessibility of online social networks. As our survey platform, we used SurveyGizmo, an online software program for designing and conducting Internet surveys.

The target population was adults (18 years old or over) with ID such as Down syndrome or other disabilities that make learning hard or slower, who use Facebook. To enhance accessibility to people with ID, the questions were framed in plain language. The volunteer participants could complete the online survey by themselves or ask for assistance, as stated in the online consent: "You should decide the answers to the survey questions by yourself (no help). However, if you need help putting your answers into the survey, ask someone you trust for help. This person can be someone like a family member, staff person, or friend."

The online survey consisted of 52 questions. The first part included 20 multiple-choice questions focused on how the participants with ID use Facebook; most of these questions were rated on a 4-point scale. Then, there were 18 questions focused on how the participants perceive Facebook. These questions were rated on a 2-point scale (agree vs. disagree), as indicated in Table 1.

Table 1. The second part of the online survey: Facebook perceptions (selected items)

Here are some sentences - Please tell us if you agree or disagree with them:
1.   Facebook is not accessible
2.   I wish others (such as my guardian, family, etc.) would allow me to use Facebook more
3.   I feel good when I am on Facebook
4.   When I have a problem in life, I can always ask for advice from people on Facebook
5.   When I am on Facebook, I feel like everyone else
6.   I wish Facebook included   pictures to communicate with friends (instead of text)
7.   Facebook is too boring
8.   Facebook makes it is easy to make new friends
9.   It is dangerous to use Facebook
10. I feel more comfortable talking with people on Facebook than in person (face-to-face)

In addition, there were 11 demographic questions such as gender, age, education, occupation, ethnicity, etc. The final part of the survey included an open-ended question about recommendations for future change of Facebook in order to make it accessible for users with ID: "What changes would you recommend on Facebook?"

By the end of the survey period, 71 people with disabilities had logged in to the survey. We excluded partial participation (13 respondents), resulting in a total sample of 58 respondents who completed the survey. We used primarily descriptive statistics to convey the characteristics, experiences and perceptions of people with ID who use Facebook. In addition, we compared Facebook experiences and perceptions across demographic variables (such as gender, living style, etc.) using nonparametric tests (Chi-Square and Kruskal–Wallis). We also used a qualitative approach to analyze the responses to the open-ended question [14].

3   Results

The majority of the respondents with ID were female (57.9%), 30 years and older (57.9%), and residents of the U.S. (84.5%) who had learning disability and/or ADD/ADHD as a secondary disability (51.2%). We found that the respondents visit Facebook at least once a week (67.2%) from their own device which is connected to the Internet, such as personal computer, mobile phone or tablet (67.8%). Most of them (82.8%) reported that they use Facebook with no assistance from a caregiver or friend and use it primarily for connecting with people they meet in face-to-face settings (e.g., friends, family members, caregivers). Only a few (10.5%) use Facebook for connecting with people they meet only online.

3.1   Quantitative Results

A nonparametric test (Kruskal–Wallis test: P(2)=1.00, p > 0.05) revealed a non-significant difference between the living style of the respondent with ID (guardian, alone, friends/roommates/ supported living) and the frequency of using Facebook (once two (or more) months, at least once a month, at least once a week, at least once a day). We also used this test to compare Facebook experiences/activities (e.g., send, accepting or deleting a friend request, looking for people that the respondent contacts face-to-face, looking for old or new friends, hit "Like" on posts or photos of friends, sending private messages, asking for help, chatting, updating the status, uploading photos, etc.) between male and female respondents. Of the 17 experiences, only one -- "hit "Like" on posts or photos your friends put on Facebook"-- was significantly different between male and female respondents ,i.e., women hit "Like" more than men (P(1)=4.27, p < 0.05).

When we compared Facebook experiences of respondents who use Facebook by themselves with respondents who get help, we found significant differences only on three experiences: (1) Respondents with ID who use Facebook by themselves significantly tend to look for people that they know (contact every day, week or month) (P(1)=4.07, p < 0.05); (2) Respondents with ID who use Facebook by themselves significantly tend to ask for help from someone else on how to use Facebook (P(1)=10.42, p < 0.001); (3) Respondents with ID who use Facebook by themselves significantly tend to chat with a friend on Facebook (P(1)=12.81, p < 0.001).

The respondents also asked to rate their perceptions of Facebook on a binary scale (1- Agree, 2 – Disagree). The results indicated that they, on average, perceive Facebook positively (M= 1.33, SD= 0.17). Female and male respondents with ID seemed to perceive Facebook similarly (non-significant differences), except in regard to the information presented on Facebook. Male respondents said there is too much information to read on Facebook compared to female respondents ($\chi2$=4.14, p < 0.05).

3.2   Qualitative Results

Thirty-one respondents took time to answer the open-ended question. The respondents suggested how to make Facebook accessible for users with ID. Many of them viewed Facebook timeline (a recent profile page design) as a negative change since they had to relearn how to use Facebook: "Stop changing so much. Every time there is a change it takes me a long time to figure it out. The timeline scares me. I hope I do not have to get it"; "Not slowly changing everyone's page to the timeline. And going back to the way it used to be before it started making all those changes." They recommended developing a simple version of Facebook that will allow users with ID to adjust the level of complexity.

In addition, the majority of the respondents said that Facebook should become easier for users with ID through speech-to-text software (voice-control programs) and should include more graphics and less text: "I can read but not everyone can read"; "More graphic and explanations like how to." Other respondents referred to the privacy settings that should protect the safety of Facebook users with ID. They asked to make the privacy settings more set to the user's control: "I think that Facebook should change the way they prevent personal information of a Facebook user from getting out to the world." One respondent suggested adding a function of online help guided by a trusted adviser or mentor.

4   Discussion and Conclusions

The results indicated that, as is true for all Internet users (62% male users compared to 72% female users), Facebook is more popular with women with ID [15]. Accordingly, more female than male users with ID reported that they significantly hit "Like" on posts or photos of their Facebook friends [16]. In general, the respondents with ID positively perceive and use Facebook. They use it primarily for connecting with family members and real-world friends i.e., people they meet in face-to-face settings, similar to Facebook users in general [17]. Some of them reported that by participating in Facebook they feel "like everyone else" which means it contributes to their sense of belonging to the general community [18].

Previous studies have shown that people with ID have problems using typical computer interfaces including web browsers [19,20]. Nonetheless, the majority of respondents in our study reported they use Facebook with no assistance which might imply that individuals with ID who have basic cognitive abilities can surf the Internet and participate in social networking sites. However, they did report challenges they face while using Facebook.

Supporting findings in the literature [21,22], the respondents in the present study found the privacy settings and the frequent changes in the user interface (e.g., the timeline) hard to understand and navigate. In an online service where most of the communication is text-based, literacy support is essential, especially for users with ID. A simplified version of Facebook (http://m.facebook.com) that was originally intended for users with vision impairments or people who use the service over a slow network connection [23] might be valuable also for users with ID. However, it seems that the respondents in our study were not familiar with this version, except for one respondent who raised the idea of "Simple Facebook" or "Easy Facebook" which allows users to keep clicking until they are comfortable with the level of complexity. The other respondents also suggested solutions for making Facebook more accessible. These included voice-control programs (such as speech-to-text application) and graphics to overcome difficulties with writing, reading and reading comprehension. Future development of the Internet and its social services should follow the concept of universal design, meaning that the web has to be maximally accessible for all users whether they have disabilities or not.

References

1. Hampton, K.N., Goulet, L.S., Rainie, L., Purcell, K.: Social networking sites and our lives: How people's trust, personal relationships, and civic and political involvement are connected to their use of social networking sites and other technologies. The Pew Research Center's Internet & American Life Project (2011),
   http://www.pewinternet.org/Reports/2011/Technology-and-social-networks.aspx

2. Mauri, M., Cipresso, P., Balgera, A., Villamira, M., Riva, G.: Why is Facebook so successful? Psychophysiological measures describe a core flow state while using Facebook. Cyberpsychology, Behavior, and Social Networking 14, 723–731 (2011), doi:10.1089/cyber.2010.0377

3. Steinfield, C., Ellison, N.B., Lampe, C.: Social capital, self-esteem, and use of online social network sites: A longitudinal analysis. Journal of Applied Developmental Psychology 29, 434–445 (2008), doi:10.1016/j.appdev.2008.07.002

4. Albert, B. (ed.): In or out of the mainstream? Lesson from research on disability and development cooperation. The Disability Press, Leeds (2006)

5. Haller, B.A.: Representing disability in an ableist world: Essays on mass media. The Advocado Press, Louisville (2010)

6. Thackeray, R., Hunter, M.A.: Empowering youth: Use of technology in advocacy to affect social change. Journal of Computer-Mediated Communication 15, 575–591 (2010), doi:10.1111/j.1083-6101.2009.01503.x

7. Buckley, S., Bird, G., Sacks, B., Archer, T.: A comparison of mainstream and special education for teenagers with Down syndrome: Implications for parents and teachers. Down Syndrome News and Update 2, 46–54 (2005)

8. D'Haem, H.: Special at school but lonely at home: An alternative friendship group for adolescents with Down Syndrome. Down Syndrome Research and Practice 12, 107–111 (2008)

9. American Association of Intellectual and Developmental Disabilities (AAIDD): Intellectual disability: Definition, classification, and systems of supports, 11th edn. AAIDD, Washington (2010), http://www.aaidd.org/media/PDFs/CoreSlide.pdf

10. McClimens, A., Gordon, F.: People with intellectual disabilities as bloggers: What's social capital got to do with it anyway? Journal of Intellectual Disabilities 13, 19–30 (2009), doi:10.1177/1744629509104486

11. Mazurek, M.O., Shattuck, P.T., Wagner, M., Cooper, B.P.: Prevalence and correlates of screen-based media use among youth with autism spectrum disorders. Journal of Autism and Developmental Disorders 42, 1757–1767 (2011), doi:10.1007/s10803-011-1413-8

12. Sevilla, J., Herrera, G., Martínez, B., Alcantud, F.: Web accessibility for individuals with cognitive deficits: A comparative study between an existing commercial web and its cognitively accessible equivalent. ACM Transactions on Computer-Human Interaction 14(3), 1–25 (2007)

13. Hoffman, M., Blake, J.: Computer literacy: Today and tomorrow. Journal of Computing Sciences in Colleges 18, 221–233 (2003)

14. Patton, M.Q.: Qualitative research and evaluation methods, 3rd edn. Sage Publication, Thousand Oaks (2002)

15. Duggan, M., Brenner, J.: The Demographics of Social Media Users – 2012. The Pew Research Center's Internet & American Life Project (2013),
    http://www.pewinternet.org/Reports/2013/Social-media-users.aspx (retrieved from)

16. Rainie, L., Smith, A., Duggan, M.: Coming and Going on Facebook. The Pew Research Center's Internet & American Life Project (2013),
    http://www.pewinternet.org/Reports/2013/
    Coming-and-going-on-facebook.aspx (retrieved from)
17. Lenhart, A., Madden, M.: Teens, privacy, & online social networks. The Pew Research Center's Internet & American Life Project (2007),
    http://www.pewinternet.org/Reports/2007/
    Teens-Privacy-and-Online-Social-Networks.aspx (retrieved from)
18. Kampert, L.A., Goreczny, J.A.: Community involvement and socialization among individuals with mental retardation. Research in Developmental Disabilities 28, 278–286 (2007), doi:10.1016/j.ridd.2005.09.004
19. Davies, D.K., Stock, S.E., Wehmeyer, M.L.: Enhancing independent internet access for individuals with mental retardation through use of a specialized web browser: A pilot study. Education and Training in Mental Retardation and Developmental Disabilities 36, 107–113 (2001)
20. Li-Tsang, C., Yeung, S., Chan, C., Hui-Chan, C.: Factors affecting people with intellectual disabilities in learning to use computer technology. International Journal of Rehabilitation Research 28, 127–133 (2005)
21. Haller, B.A.: Representing disability in an ableist world: Essays on mass media. The Advocado Press, Louisville (2010)
22. Sevilla, J., Herrera, G., Martínez, B., Alcantud, F.: Web accessibility for individuals with cognitive deficits: A comparative study between an existing commercial web and its cognitively accessible equivalent. ACM Transactions on Computer-Human Interaction 14(3), 1–25 (2007)
23. Sillanpää, N., Älli, S., Övermark, T.: Easy-to-use social network service. In: Miesenberger, K., Klaus, J., Zagler, W., Karshmer, A. (eds.) ICCHP 2010, Part 1. LNCS, vol. 6179, pp. 544–549. Springer, Heidelberg (2010)

Improving Social and Communication Skills of Adult Arabs with ASD through the Use of Social Media Technologies

Alaa Mashat, Mike Wald, and Sarah Parsons

University of Southampton, UK
{aam1f11,mw}@ecs.soton.ac.uk,
s.j.parsons@soton.ac.uk

Abstract. People with Autism Spectrum Disorder (ASD) find it hard to communicate and interact with other people. Although technology has been involved in sup-porting people with ASD in developed countries, research on such technologies has been mainly related to Western culture. Arab adults with ASD require sup-port for improving their social skills. However, cultural differences could limit the usability of existing technologies. The proposed study aims to investigate the use of social networks for supporting Arab adults with High-Functioning Autism or Asperger syndrome in order to improve their abilities in social situations such as family relations and friendships, considering the influence of culture and tradition views on the usability and sociability of social media technologies.

Keywords: Accessibility, Usability, Autism Spectrum Disorder, Arabs, Adults, Social Media, Technology, Social Skills, Communication.

1 Introduction

Autism Spectrum Disorder (ASD) is a lifelong developmental disability, varying from High-Functioning Autism (HFA), or Asperger syndrome, to Low-Functioning Autism (LFA) [1]. HFA and Asperger syndrome are the less severe levels of autism. People with ASD find it hard to communicate and interact with other people [2]. The National Autistic Society (UK), following DSM-5 "The Diagnostic and Statistical Manual of Mental Disorders" [3] identifies the main difficulties people with ASD face as social communication and interaction, and restricted, repetitive patterns of behaviour, interests, or activities.

In Arab countries, the situation of social communication is more difficult, as communicating with the opposite gender is already an issue with many people in certain Arab countries [4]. In addition, awareness of ASD in these countries is limited [5], and families are more likely to hide their diagnosed child to prevent themselves from feeling ashamed and from the harsh judgment of society, which could increase the isolation of people with ASD from social interaction. Many studies have been implemented with the aim of improving social skills for people with ASD; however, most research in the ASD field has been concerned with children, with only a few research

K. Miesenberger et al. (Eds.): ICCHP 2014, Part I, LNCS 8547, pp. 478–485, 2014.

projects on the use of technology by adults, some of which will be mentioned in Section 3. A high number of adults with ASD face problems in face-to-face communication and try to avoid social interaction situations and group activities [6,7]. About 60%-75% of adults with ASD have been found to have poor outcomes in their adult experiences, such as friendships, education, employment and independent living [8].

In addition, almost all of the studies and innovations have appeared in developed countries, and are mainly relevant to Western culture [9,10,11]. People with ASD receive less attention in the Arab world, and the use of technology is not widely considered. Services and support for improving their communication and interaction skills are also limited. This research is focused on investigating the use of social technologies for supporting Arab adults with High-Functioning Autism or Asperger syndrome in order to improve their abilities in social situations, considering the influence of culture and tradition on the usability of social media technologies.

2   ASD in Arab Countries

A number of studies have shown that the average number of diagnosed individuals in Arab countries is lower than in developed countries [9], [12,13]; however, there is also a significant difference between the numbers of ASD diagnoses in different Arab countries. This might be due to the differences in beliefs, customs and relationships or to economic problems [14]. It has been claimed by different studies [9,10], [12], that the assumption of this low percentage in countries such as Saudi Arabia, Oman and the UAE is due to the lack of information identifying children with ASD, underdiagnosis and under-reporting of cases. These point to a number of possible factors such as cultural differences, level of education, lack of services, and low levels of experience and professional training. Although, people with ASD used to receive less attention in the Arab world and fewer health care services [9], this has changed and more consideration is now given to support this group. More support centres for people with ASD have been established in different Arab countries and events and work-shops are organised to raise awareness [15,16]. However, in some Arab countries, qualified experts, and specialists are still needed in this field, in addition to support services [17]. As one of the supportive tools used in Western countries for people with ASD, technology could be used to bring its interest and usefulness to the life of people with ASD in Arab countries [18].

3   Social Technologies and ASD

Several studies on the use of technology have shown a potential impact on the quality of lives for people with ASD in developed countries, and the improvement of social skills [18]. Moore & Calvert found that children with ASD enjoyed working with computer technologies, and experienced greater learning results [19]. In addition, it has been reported that users with ASD prefer to interact with technology such as computers and robots, rather than real humans because they find it safer and more interesting [20]. When it comes to socialising, observably, social networking sites have been popular in the past few. Social networks offer a type of human-human interaction rather than just a computer-human interaction [21], that allows users to connect and socialise without the pressures of time and immediacy that they face in real-life social situations, which could be helpful for people with ASD.

A number of studies have investigated the usability of online social networks for persons with autism spectrum conditions. These studies showed that adults with ASD could benefit from using social networks to support them in social communication, interaction, building and maintaining friendships and receiving advice. For example, a project developed by Autism Connections Europe (ACE) was presented to help adult individuals with ASD to make friends: ACEbook aims to enable friends to meet via Facebook, according to a specific interest, and then arrange personal meetings around Europe to strengthen their friendship [22]. This project has shown some improvements in social and communication skills, independence, mood, and in overcoming fear among the participants [22]. Thinking about encouraging Arab users with ASD to use a social network such as the ACEbook might raise different opinions and views due to cultural differences.

In addition, managing timing, schedules, daily life activities and self-care is also important. By working on improving these skills, people with ASD can have a better chance to be employed, be in a relationship, have friends, increase independence, have a better life and be part of the community [2]. One example of this effect comes from the Graphics, Visualization & Usability Centre in Georgia, and is a social supportive technology for adults with ASD, implemented by Hong et al. [23]. The aim was to help adults with ASD to be more independent and to learn daily life skills, by providing them with on-demand support, with an idea similar to prompting systems. The design is called the SocialMirror; the name was driven from the idea of the device which is an interactive display integrated into a mirror and connected to an online trusted social network.

For adolescents and adults with ASD it is important to practice their social skills and learn social rules in order to improve their communication and interaction with people. In addition, a more recent study considered the use of a supportive social network aiming to provide young adults and adolescents with ASD the opportunity to gain support from a group of family and friends, instead of over-relying on one caregiver. The idea was to use circles (a feature in social networks that combines a group of people interested in a particular topic, or people with a common social connection) in order to seek information and advice, and build independence [24]. These studies showed that including social networks in assistive technologies could bring their benefits to the life of an individual with ASD.

4   Preliminary Study

The studies mentioned above established the usefulness of social networks for adults with ASD in Western countries. However, this may have a different perspective when considering Arab users. Based on the literature and the cultural perspective of the researcher, we have identified some cultural and traditional factors that might have an influence on Arab users with ASD when using technologies, creating a Framework for Autistic Arabs' Social Communication and Interaction Technology (FAASCIT).

Some of these factors are grouped under technical issues such as: Internet access and cost, availability of technology services, language and accents, usernames and passwords, variety of devices and software, cultural differences in technologies, abbreviations and Internet language and the use of Arabic language using Latin letters, which is known as "Arabizi" [25]. The other factors were grouped under personal issues, such as spoken language, accents, gender differences in the use of technology, playing music in the technology, and some related to social rules such as the restrictions towards communicating to the opposite gender, building relationships and the validity of publishing personal information and photos online. Additional factors included the level of knowledge of people with ASD and/or their parents, autonomy and independence, lack of public services and offering technologies and support.

Preliminary interviews were implemented by the researcher in the current study, aiming to gather information regarding services provided for people with ASD in Saudi Arabia, and, in addition, to find out to what extent the factors mentioned above affect the usability and accessibility of technologies by adult Arabs with ASD.

Two types of flexible, semi-structured interviews were designed, each specified for a particular group of participants: (1) a group of experts or members of staff specialized in the field of Autism, and (2) a group of adults (16 years or older) with ASD. Twelve members of staff and experts participated in this contextual review from eleven centres in different Saudi Arabian cities. Three participants were interviewed who had been diagnosed with ASD. All three were male adults aged 20, 21 and 24. However, at this stage not all the factors could be considered in the interview questions. The data collected from the interviews were in the form of text, driving the research strategy to be qualitative research.

5   Preliminary Findings

It was concluded that there is a lack of support for adults with ASD in Saudi Arabia and the services provided are mainly for children. Only three centres actually accept adults with ASD. One centre stops providing services at the age of 14, and one stops at the age of 16. All other centres are only for children and they do not have any facilities to support adults. One of the centres was for males only, and all other centres were for both male and female children. However, there is a segregation age at each centre at which the males and females are separated, at least in classes. The age of segregation differs between centres, ranging from 5-13 years. In addition, five of the centres do not provide Internet access to the children. Four had both Arabic and English sections, the other centres only used Arabic and did not have any English sessions. Five of the specialists reported a lack of technologies for people with ASD in the Arabic language. It was also pointed out by three of the specialists that they had faced some problems with children speaking with different accents and dialects. It was also observed that there may be some people who are not happy listening to music, but this does not really form a significant concern.

In regard to the use of social media, the three participants with ASD were not very familiar with the use of Facebook or Twitter. Two of the participants were using Whatsapp[1], which "is a cross-platform mobile messaging app that allows you to exchange messages without having to pay for SMS". Even though they seemed

---

[1] http://www.whatsapp.com/

interested in computers, they only use it for basic things such as Google search, YouTube or viewing photos of people on Twitter. For presenting their personal information and pictures online, two of the participants did not have a problem; the third participant said he would not want to add his picture online. This was interesting because it was noticed that he does display his photo as a profile picture on "Whatsapp", and he had been interviewed on a T.V program before, which is now available on Youtube. In the Arabic culture, males usually do not have a problem with publishing their personal data online; this might differ with female participants.

In regard to the small number of participants, finding the right participants is challenging, as it is difficult to reach adults with HFA or Asperger syndrome in Arab countries. This could be because they may be hidden, not diagnosed or do not admit to having the disability. Widening the study to include participants from a number of other Arab countries, such as the UAE, Qatar, Kuwait and Jordan, will be considered in the further implementation of the present study.

6   Research Strategy

According to the Social Media Update 2013, the percentage of adults on social networking sites is 73% of online adult users, with Facebook having the highest number of users; 71% of online adults [26]. The 5th edition of the Arab Social Media Report indicates that the use of social networks has been increasing in the Arab world [27]. This significant increase in the usage of social networks could be connected to the Arab Spring, as reported in the Arab Social Media Report, [28]. In 2012 the number of Facebook users in Saudi Arabia was over six million, 90% of whom use it in the Arabic language [29].

It has been reported in different studies that people with ASD are more interested in visuals and pictures than in text [30,31]. Putnam and Chong in [32] report that people with ASD desire to include social skills in the technologies in order to overcome their difficulties, as well as developing organisational skills and academic skills. According to Cooper [33], photos, with a percentage of about 93%, represent the most engaging posts on Facebook, compared to links, videos or text-based posts.

For the implementation of the proposed research, the role of photos across social networks (in particular Facebook) will be investigated. The idea is to examine conversations and comments posted by Arab adults with ASD over the photos on Facebook, and how their interest in photos and their interaction can influence their social relationships with family and friends online. Participants' profiles and their activities around photos will first be evaluated. They will be given specific tasks related to photos, as part of the study, such as using tags. The activities will be evaluated after a period of time using data collected from Facebook API and face-to-face interviews.

In addition, the impact of the cultural and traditional factors during the study will be measured by creating a profile throughout the process of testing the tasks in the study, to identify the cultural factors that are important for the Arabs with ASD when using social networks, in order to develop the final framework regarding culture, and usability and sociability issues (Fig.1).

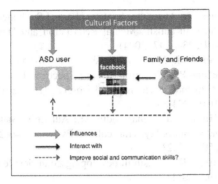

Fig. 1. Research strategy: main components and relationships

7   Conclusion

From the literature and the interviews, it is clear that adults with ASD in Arab countries still require more attention and support in order to improve their social and interaction skills to help them build and strengthen their relationships, and to be integrated into the society. However, Arab culture and traditions raise issues when using social networks. Our future research will investigate the effect of cultural factors on the usability and accessibility of social networks by adult Arabs with ASD, with the goal of enabling them to use the technology more easily in a way that accommodates their own cultural context and helps them to use social networks effectively for improved communication and socializing.

References

1. Newschaffer, C.J., Croen, L.A., Daniels, J., Giarelli, E., Grether, J.K., Levy, S.E., Mandell, D., Miller, L., Pinto-Martin, J., Reaven, J., Reynolds, A., Rice, C., Schendel, D., Windham, G.: The epidemiology of autism spectrum disorders*. Annu. Rev. Public Health 28, 235–258 (2007)
2. Grandin, T., Attwood, T.: Different...Not Less: Inspiring Stories of Achievement and Successful Employment from Adults With Autism, Asperger's, and ADHD: Future Horizons Incorporated (2012)
3. American Psychiatric Association, Diagnostic and Statistical Manual of Mental Disorders DSM-IV (1994)
4. Alsheikh, T., Lindley, S., Rode, J.: Understanding Online Communication through Arab Eyes. In: CHI 2010, Atlanta, Georgia, USA, April 10-15, pp. 1–4 (2010)
5. Essa, M.M., Guillemin, G.J., Waly, M.I., Al-Sharbati, M.M., Al-Farsi, Y.M., Hakkim, F.L., Ali, A., Al-Shafaee, M.S.: Increased Markers of Oxidative Stress in Autistic Children of the Sultanate of Oman. Biological Trace Element Research 147(1-3) (2012)
6. Bishop, J.: The Internet for educating individuals with social impairments. Journal of Computer Assisted Learning 19(4), 546–556 (2003)
7. Burke, M., Kraut, R., Williams, D.: Social Use of Computer-Mediated Communication by Adults on the Autism Spectrum. In: Proc. of the 2010 ACM Conference on Computer supported cooperative work (CSCW 2010), pp. 425–434. ACM, New York (2010)

8. Seltzer, M.M., Shattuck, P., Abbeduto, L., Greenberg, J.S.: Trajectory of development in adolescents and adults with autism. Mental Retardation and Developmental Disabilities Research Reviews 10(4), 234–247 (2004)

9. Al-Farsi, Y.M., Al-Sharbati, M.M., Al-Farsi, O.A., Al-Shafaee, M.S., Brooks, D.R., Waly, M.I.: Brief Report: Prevalence of Autistic Spectrum Disorders in the Sultanate of Oman. Journal of Autism and Developmental Disorders 41(6) (2011), doi:10.1007/s10803-010-1094-8

10. Al-Salehi, S.M., Al-Hifthy, E.H., Ghaziuddin, M.: Autism in Saudi Arabia: Presentation, Clinical Correlates and Comorbidity. Transcultural Psychiatry 46(2) (2009), doi:10.1177/1363461509105823

11. Samadi, S.A., McConkey, R.: Autism in developing countries: lessons from Iran. Autism Research and Treatment (2011)

12. Eapen, V., Mabrouk, A.A., Zoubeidi, T., Yunis, F.: Prevalence of pervasive developmental disorders in preschool children in the UAE. Journal of Tropical Pediatrics 53(3) (2007), doi:10.1093/tropej/fml091

13. Yazbak, F.E.: Autism seems to be increasing worldwide, if not in London. British Medical Journal 328(7433), 226–227 (2004)

14. Hussein, H., Taha, G.R., Almanasef, A.: Characteristics of autism spectrum disorders in a sample of Egyptian and Saudi patients: transcultural cross sectional study. Child and Adolescent Psychiatry and Mental Health 5 (2011), doi:10.1186/1753-2000-5-34

15. Ashoka Arab World Internet Report: Raising autism awareness in the Arab region (2008), http://ashokaarabworld.wordpress.com/2008/05/07/raising-autism-awareness-in-the-arab-region/

16. Qabbani, B.: Dubai urged to step up for autism awareness' The National (2011), http://www.thenational.ae/news/uae-news/dubai-urged-to-step-up-for-autism-awareness

17. Muhammad, F.: Saudi Gazette, Internet Report: Autism turning into regional epi-demic, experts warn (2013), http://www.saudigazette.com.sa/index.cfm?method=home.regcon&contentid=20130128150896

18. Bolte, S., Golan, O., Goodwin, M.S., Zwaigenbaum, L.: What can innovative technologies do for Autism Spectrum Disorders? Autism 14(3), 155–159 (2010)

19. Moore, M., Calvert, S.: Brief report: Vocabulary acquisition for children with autism: Teacher or computer instruction. Journal of Autism and Developmental Disorders 30(4) (2000), doi:10.1023/a:1005535602064

20. Benford, P.: The use of internet-based communication by people with autism. University of Nottingham, Nottingham (2008)

21. Spolsky, J.: It's Not Just Usability, Joel on Software (2004), http://www.joelonsoftware.com/articles/NotJustUsability.html

22. Autism Europe. Improving quality of life for people with autism (2011), http://www.autismeurope.org/publications/press-releases/document-497.html

23. Hong, H., Kim, J.G., Abowd, G.D., Arriaga, R.I.: Designing a social network to support the independence of young adults with autism. In: Proceedings of the ACM 2012 (2012)

24. Hong, H., Yarosh, S., Kim, J.G., Abowd, G.D., Arriaga, R.I.: Investigating the use of circles in social networks to support independence of individuals with autism. In: Paper Presented at the Proceedings of the SIGCHI Conference on Human Factors in Computing Systems. ACM (2013)

25. Ghanem, R.: Arabizi is destroying the Arabic language. Arab News (2011), http://www.arabnews.com/node/374897

26. Duggan, M., Smith, A.: Social Media Update 2013. Pew Research Center (2013),
    http://pewinternet.org/Reports/2013/Social-Media-Update.aspx
27. Arab Social Media Report: Transforming Education in the Arab World: Breaking Barriers
    in the Age of Social Learning, 5th edn. Dubai School of Government (2013)
28. Arab Social Media Report: Social Media in the Arab World: Influencing Societal and Cultural Change? Dubai School of Government 2(1), 29 (2013)
29. The Social Clinic. The State of Social Media in Saudi Arabia 2012 (2013),
    http://www.thesocialclinic.com/
    the-state-of-social-media-in-saudi-arabia-2012-2/
30. Habash, M.A.: Assistive Technology Utilization for Autism An Outline of Technology
    Awareness in Special Needs Therapy. Paper presented at the Second International Conference on Innovations in Information Technology (2005)
31. Kana, R.K., Keller, T.A., Cherkassky, V.L., Minshew, N.J., Just, M.A.: Sentence comprehension in autism: thinking in pictures with decreased functional connectivity. Brain
    129(2006), 2484–2493 (2006)
32. Putnam, C., Chong, L.: Software and Technologies Designed for People with Autism:
    What do users want? Paper presented at the Proceedings of the 10th International ACM
    SIGACCESS Conference on Computers and accessibility, Canada (2008)
33. Cooper, B.B.: 7 Powerful Facebook statistics you should know for a more engaging
    Facebook page. buffer (2013), http://blog.bufferapp.com/
    7-facebook-stats-you-should-know-for-a-more-engaging-page

The Role of User Emotional Attachment in Driving the Engagement of Children with Autism Spectrum Disorders (ASD) in Using a Smartphone App Designed to Develop Social and Life Skill Functioning

Joseph Mintz

Institute of Education, University of London, London, UK
j.mintz@ioe.ac.uk

Abstract. There has been, in the last ten years, a fast developing interest in the potential use of mobile technology in the classroom and in particular, in the use of such technology to support children with ASD (Autistic Spectrum Disorders). The HANDS project developed a software application for mobile Smartphones based on the principles of persuasive technology design, which supports children with ASD with social and life skills functioning – areas of ability which tend to be impaired in this population. Issues with the application of a behaviorist approach to the complex social field of special educational needs are considered. An argument is made for the need for 'thick' persuasive applications which take account of such complexity including the role of mediating factors. Particular focus is given to qualitative results indicating that user emotional attachment is one such key factor.

Keywords: User Emotional Attachment, Autism, Special Educational Needs, Instructional Design, Persuasive Technology.

1 Introduction

Impairments in social and communicative reciprocity and in adaptive, flexible regulation of self and behaviors in individuals with ASD lead to significant difficulties in social participation both in simple situations, such as shopping and catching a bus to school as well as more intensely in complex social transactions, such as building relationships, or fitting in with classroom rules in educational contexts [1]. Perhaps un-surprisingly, there has been some hope invested in the potential of assistive technology, and particularly since the launch of the iPhone in 2007, in the use of mobile technology to support individuals with ASD in overcoming these barriers to social inter-action. In an exploratory study, Mechling et al. [2] evaluated the use of a mobile device with multiple prompt levels, indicating its potential to increase efficacy in completion of novel tasks and transitioning within and between tasks. Gentry et. al. [3] used standardized measurement tools to evaluate the efficacy of mobile devices as cognitive aids in a sample of high school students with ASD, indicating positive initial outcomes. Reports have also being published on the use of mobile technology

K. Miesenberger et al. (Eds.): ICCHP 2014, Part I, LNCS 8547, pp. 486–493, 2014.

specifically to support social skills development. For example, Tentori and Hayes [4] report on the initial implementation of a smartphone app designed to give children social cues in specific social situations. Such research findings form the basis of support for the development and systematic evaluation of a fully integrated and flexible cognitive support tool on a mobile smartphone which can offer a wide range of interventions personalized to the individual needs of a student with ASD. More recently, a number of small scale studies, such as Neely et al. [5] and Mechling, Foster and Ayres [6], have been published on the use of tablet technology for similar purposes.

One such system was developed in the HANDS (Helping Autism Diagnosed Navigate and Develop Socially) research project, which created a cognitive support smartphone app which allows teachers to flexibly develop interventions on such de-vices to support children with ASD in developing social and life skills. The software design for this system was based on the principles of Persuasive Technology [7]. This paper reports on aspects of the use and evaluation of the HANDS system.

2 Persuasive Technology

The initial development of persuasive design principles by Fogg [7] was rooted in social psychology, but also influenced by behaviorism, cognitive psychology and communication theory. Fogg also drew on the Computers as Social Actors Approach developed by Nass et. al. [8] in which a social rule or dynamic for human-human interaction is adapted so that instead of two humans interacting, we have a computer and a human interacting in a social context. There has been considerable use and development of persuasive systems in healthcare and commerce/marketing (see [9] for recent examples).

Fogg [7] highlights several specific design principles for bringing about behavior change that are particularly well suited to incorporation in to technology systems:

1. Reinforcement – reinforce target behaviors positively when they happen or negatively when they don't
2. Reduction – make a complicated task simpler by removing stages in the process
3. Self monitoring – allow the user to monitor their behavior
4. Suggestion – perform an intervention at the most opportune moment when the user has both motivation and the ability to act.
5. Surveillance – the person's behavior is monitored and observed by other people
6. Tailoring – use of personally relevant information as part of the intervention.
7. Tunneling – sequencing tasks, to reduce cognitive load on the user, and thus support completion of the overall goal.

2.1   Credibility and Kairos

Fogg also makes extensive use of the two other concepts - source credibility and Kairos. The former is typically categorized in the literature as having two dimensions – trustworthiness and expertise [10]. Trustworthiness indicates the perceived goodness or morality of the source and expertise indicates the perceived knowledge and skill of the source. Tseng and Fogg [11] consider specific features which can influence perceived computer credibility, including interface design features such as color tones and balanced layout. Fogg regards credibility as a central issue for the design of persuasive systems because the inherent inflexibility of computer systems means that design errors in this area can very easily lead to irretrievable losses of perceived source credibility.

Fogg also highlights the concept of Kairos, namely that messages are more likely to be persuasive if they are delivered at the right time and place. Fogg [7, 12] considers Kairos as being particularly relevant for mobile persuasive systems. He argues that as mobile phones, integrated with social networking technology, become more and more a central part of the lives of students, mobile offers opportunities for interventions to be delivered at a time and place when they are receptive to receiving them.

2.2   The HANDS System

Modeling the HANDS software on persuasive technology design resulted in development of the following key functionalities: 1) an interactive calendar function with prompts, 2) a "Personal Trainer" training and support function that allowed teachers to flexibly develop specific interventions including step by step guidance sequences incorporating video and audio content. These interventions were designed on a server based application and then uploaded to the client application on the child's smartphone. The Personal Trainer is the key arena for the expression of persuasive design principles in the software, further exploiting persuasive principles including tailoring to the specific needs of the individual, personalization (such as choosing the audio and visual skin of the app), reduction (step by step instructions that reduce cognitive load), credibility, and rewards. The first prototype of this software was implemented during the 2010 school year. Following a training programme, teachers worked with individual children to develop tailored interventions using the smartphone app, with ongoing support from the academic and technical team. Evaluation of this prototype was fed in to the development of the second prototype which was similarly implemented in the 2011 school year. Implementation took place at four special schools across Europe and involved 20 teachers and 40 children.

3   Special Educational Needs and Persuasive Technology

From one perspective, special educational needs, such as Autism, Attention Deficit Hyperactivity Disorder, Oppositional Defiant Disorder, Down's Syndrome etc. are synonymous with medical categories. Autism is a psychiatric (i.e. medical) definition, conceived primarily as a developmental disorder of the human nervous system. Psychiatric definitions of autism are clearly located firmly within a medical model (see Barton 1988's seminal discussion [13]), and as such, when introduced in to the social field of education have been subjected to sociological critiques which note that 'normal' modes of social and emotional communication can be thought of as socially constructed, and that greater recognition might be given, in educational setting in particular, to seeing this is difference rather than deficit, and that as such the diagnostic labels themselves could even be considered as negatively pathologizing groups of children [14,15]. These two accounts (psychiatric and sociological) are in fact often both extant, frequently with considerable tension, in the minds of teachers and in the national and local discourses and debates on policy on special educational needs.

This discussion is of particular relevance to the use of persuasive technology for special educational needs because of persuasive technology's provenance. As discussed, Fogg brought together these strands from the existing disciplines of rhetoric, social psychology and persuasion research in his 'new' discipline of persuasive technology. However, the behaviorist slant of Fogg's work is clear. It is reasonable to postulate that there is a tension which arises when an approach derived from behaviorism (although certainly not in Fogg's case a naïve variety) is applied to special educational needs, a field where the debates between medical versus social conceptualizations of the object of activity put in to question the linear relationship between action and object that a behaviorist approach implies.

This analysis points towards the complexity of the social field in to which persuasive applications are applied. In 'traditional' persuasive technology, applications are designed to apply to a tightly defined area of behavior, i.e. to persuade a person to undertake one clearly specified behavior in one clearly specified context. For example, Kim, Hong, and Magerko [16] discuss a comparative study of the effectiveness of two PC-based widget applications, each designed to give a visual metaphor for the energy consumption when the PC is on but not in use, thus persuading users to switch their PC off when not being used. Thus we have a clearly specified behavior – switch your PC off when you are not using it, in a clearly specified context; that is, the use of your PC. In addition, 'traditional' applications are relatively context free; that is, there is very limited information available about individual target users, and thus applications focus on interventions and persuasive messages that can be easily replicated for use across large populations with a low level of individualization. Although tailoring has been identified as a persuasive strategy, the implementation of this strategy in typical persuasive applications generally uses a very limited data set about individual users. In educational contexts the area of behavior targeted as well as the context are typically diffuse. Persuasive technology design to date has resided outside of a defining social context and empirical research has paid attention to persuasive effects rather than studying and using the social context. Yet when you are discussing persuasive effects in relation to special educational needs, where even the terms are contested and complex, persuasion needs to be considered differently. However, I argue that it is perfectly possible to develop what can be termed "thick" persuasive applications which explicitly take account of the social context and can be applied to a more complex range of behaviors such as those related to special educational needs in the classroom. Where then does the potential benefit of persuasive design for special educational needs lie? In many diagnostic conditions, including autism, ADHD, Oppositional Defiant Disorder, Developmental Coordination Disorder, we see impairments in social communication, emotional regulation and social interaction, linked to difficulties with adaptive, flexible regulation of self and behaviors. Consequently, a major objective of the education of young people with these conditions is the modification of behaviors associated with impairments in social and life skill functioning [17]. Thus persuasive technology has the potential to help children with special educational needs who want to change their behavior (and one of Fogg's key principles [7] is that persuasion via technology is only effective when the 'target recipient' wants to change their behavior on some level). However, 'thick' applications need to take account of the complex social field, one aspect of which is that whether a persuasive message delivered by technology is effective depends on how it is mediated in that social field. One of those factors is user emotional attachment.

4   User Emotional Attachment

Writing from a general HCI perspective, Meschtscherjakov [18] and Wehmeyer [19] have noted that mobile device users develop a relationship with their mobile devices and that their level of engagement with the device generally and with particular functions is dependent on the quality of that relationship. They use the terms "user attachment" or "user emotional attachment" to signify that mobile devices can act as an expression of an individual's personality or a symbol for group membership, and as such act as an extension of or form part of an individual's sense of identity. Wehmeyer [19] and later Geven et. al. [20] note that personalization (i.e. the tailoring of mobile phone functions such as wallpaper, screensavers etc.) can be one aspect of the process whereby users become "attached" to their mobile devices on an emotional level. Fogg and Eckles [12] use the analogous term "mobile marriage", which is the development of an intensive positive relationship between the user and the device, based on repeated interactions over a period of time. Fogg and Eckles also employ the term "mobile loyalty", which is the perception by users that a device exists to serve their needs and wishes first. The existence of such a perception is postulated as increasing the level of credibility of the persuasive messages provided by on the device, credibility being a key principle of persuasive design. Clearly both concepts are interdependent, as a user who has developed a positive emotional attachment to their device via repeated interaction (user device attachment) is potentially more likely to view persuasive messages on the device as being more credible.

5   Research Methodology

The objectives of the interpretivist qualitative analysis reported on here were to gain an understanding of the factors mediating engagement with the app. A linked quantitative analysis measuring the extent to which the software had an impact on developing social and life skills is reported elsewhere [21]. Classroom observations and linked semi-structured interviews were carried out with 15 teachers working with children using the app using the across the four test school sites, and a linked questionnaire was completed by an additional 15 teachers. Interviews were also undertaken with 18 children across the four schools, and with 16 parents.

6   Data Analysis

A thematic analysis of the full data set was undertaken. This followed Fereday & Muir-Cochrane [22] in using a combined deductive / inductive procedure for the coding of the data facilitated by the Nvivo software package. Identification of themes and patterns in the data was based on a descriptive cross case comparison [23, 24]. Each instance of a teacher working with a child (teacher-child dyad) was considered as a case. Firstly a case study summary was constructed for each case, with emerging themes and patterns being highlighted. Then each case was iteratively compared to the others, and the identified themes and patterns modified during this process to ensure a best fit to the overall data set.

7   Results and Discussion

The key factors mediating engagement (the 'thick' aspects of persuasive technology use with this group of children with special needs) are indicated in Table 1.

Table 1. Factors Mediating Engagement

Factor	Number of Cases +ve	Number of Cases -ve
Technical factors	14	15
Graphical User Interface Design	6	11
Source Credibility	13	0
User Device Attachment	18	
Kairos	23	0
Home-School Collaboration	20	0

Cases are +ve where the influence on engagement was positive and –ve where the influence on engagement was negative

As indicated in Table 1, user emotional attachment was identified as a mediating factor in 18 cases (see Mintz et. al. [21]) for a discussion of other factors identified). Teacher, child and parent interviews and teacher questionnaires demonstrated high levels of individual usage of the mobile functions and the width and breadth of functions that the children used, and that in the perception of teachers and parents, broader engagement with these wider phone functions influenced the children's level of engagement with the intervention app and responsiveness to persuasive messages designed to develop social and life skill functioning.

The qualitative analysis gives some support to the proposition that user device attachment is a relevant factor influencing how children using persuasive mobile systems engage with their device and with specific persuasive functions. Certainly it seems clear that overall attachment is influenced, as suggested in the persuasive design literature, by repeated positive interactions with a range of cognitive and social functions on the device.

This paper also lends support to the contention that thick persuasive applications, which take account the complex social field which children with special educational needs, their parents and their teachers inhabit, could have a positive effect on behavior change. However, for this to happen, consideration of relevant mediating factors, in other words, how these interventions are assimilated in to the world of the child and made meaningful for the user is crucial. User emotional attachment could be conceived of as a conceptualization of the point that children with autism (and likely with ADHD, ODD etc.) do enter in to a type of emotional connection with their device, and it is this emotional connection to the whole device, rather than to just a persuasive app, which is meaningful for them. Persuasive technology may have behaviorist roots, but when it takes proper account of what technology means for individual children, and the complexities that are involved for teachers in working with such children, it can have a role to play with children with special educational needs. Such a conclusion also implies that qualitative research methods as applied here are crucial in letting us uncover those meanings.

References

1. Howlin, P.: Outcome in Autism Spectrum Disorders. In: Handbook of Autism and Pervasive Developmental Disorders, pp. 201–220. Wiley, Hoboken (2005)
2. Mechling, L.C., Gast, D.L., Seid, N.H.: Using a personal digital assistant to increase independent task completion by students with autism spectrum disorder. J. Autism Dev. Disord. 39, 1420–1434 (2009)
3. Gentry, T., Wallace, J., Kvarfordt, C., Lynch, K.B.: Personal digital assistants as cognitive aids for high school students with autism? Results of a community-based trial. J. Vocat. Rehabil. 32, 101–107 (2010)
4. Tentori, M., Hayes, G.: Designing for interaction immediacy to enhance social skills of children with autism. In: Bardram, J., Langhenreich, M., Truong, K., Nixon, P. (eds.) Proceedings of the 12th ACM International Conference on Ubiquitous Computing, pp. 51–60. ACM Press, New York (2005)
5. Neely, L., Rispoli, M., Camargo, S., Davis, H., Boles, M.: The effect of instructional use of an iPad on challenging behavior and academic engagement for two students with autism. Research in Autism Spectrum Disorders 7, 509–516 (2013)
6. Mechling, L.C., Foster, A.M., Ayres, K.M.: Navigation Between Menu Screens and Multiple Touch Points on a Touch Screen Tablet to Access and Complete Multi-Step Tasks Using Video Prompting. Inclusion 1, 121–132 (2013)
7. Fogg, B.J.: Persuasive Techonology. Using Computers to Change what We Think and Do. Morgan Kaufman Publishers, San Francisco (2003)
8. Nass, C., Steuer, J., Tauber, E.R.: Computers are social actors. In: Conference Companion on Human factors in computing systems - Computer Human Interaction 1994, pp. 72–78. ACM Press, New York (1994)
9. Berkovsky, S., Freyne, J. (eds.): PERSUASIVE 2013. LNCS, vol. 7822. Springer, Heidelberg (2013)
10. McGinnes, E., Ward, C.: Better liked than right: trustworthiness and expertise in credibility. Personal. Soc. Psychol. Bull. 6, 467–472 (1980)
11. Tseng, S., Fogg, B.J.: Credibility and computing technology. Communications of the ACM 42, 39–44 (1999)
12. Fogg, B.J., Eckles, D.: Mobile Persuasion: 20 Perspectives on the Future of Behavior Change. Stanford Captology Media, Stanford (2007)
13. Barton, L.: The Politics of special educational needs. Routledge, London (1988)
14. Molloy, H., Vasil, L.: The Social Construction of Asperger Syndrome: The pathologising of difference? Disabilty and Society 17, 659–669 (2002)
15. Bogdashina, O.: Theory of mind and the triad of perspectives on autism and Asperger syndrome: a view from the bridge. Jessica Kingsley Publishers, London (2006)
16. Kim, T., Hong, H., Magerko, B.: Designing for persuasion: toward ambient eco-visualization for awareness. In: Ploug, T., Hasle, P., Olmas-Kukkoonen, H. (eds.) PERSUASIVE 2010. LNCS, vol. 6137, pp. 106–116. Springer, Heidelberg (2010)

17. Jordan, R.: Managing autism and Asperger's syndrome in current educational provision. Pediatric Rehabilitation 8, 104–112 (2005)
18. Meschtscherjakov, A.: Mobile attachment – Emotional attachment towards mobile devices and services. In: Oppermann, R., et al. (eds.) Proceedings of the 11th Mobile HCI 2009, Article 102, ACM, New York (2009)
19. Wehmeyer, K.: Assessing users' attachment to their mobile devices. In: The Proceedings of the 6th International Conference on Mobile Business, ICMB 2007. IEEE Computer Society, Toronto (2007)
20. Geven, A., Schrammel, J., Tscheligi, M., Mayer, M.: Cell phone design for teenage use. In: Cunliffe, D. (ed.) HCI 2008 Proceedings of the Third IASTED International Conference on Human Computer Interaction, pp. 236–241. ACTA Press, Anaheim (2008)
21. Mintz, J., Gyori, M., Aagaard, M.: Touching the Future Technology for Autism? In: Lessons from the HANDS Project, IOS Press, Amsterdam (2013)
22. Fereday, J., Muir-Cochrane, E.: Demonstrating Rigor Using Thematic Analysis? A Hybrid Approach of Inductive and Deductive Coding and Theme Development. International Journal of Qualitative Methods 5, 1–11 (2006)
23. Yin, K.: The Case Study Crisis: Some Answers. Adminstrative Science Quarterly 26, 58–65 (1981)
24. Sada, A.N., Maldonado, A.: Research Methods in Education. Sixth Edition by Cohen, L., Manion, L., Morrison, K. Taylor & Francis, Routledge (2007)

Gamification for Low-Literates: Findings on Motivation, User Experience, and Study Design

Dylan Schouten[1], Isabel Pfab[2], Anita Cremers[3], Betsy van Dijk[2], and Mark Neerincx[1]

[1] Faculty of Electrical Engineering, Mathematics and Computer Science,
Delft University of Technology, Delft, The Netherlands
{D.G.M.Schouten,M.A.Neerincx}@tudelft.nl
[2] University of Twente, Enschede, The Netherlands
Isabelpfab@gmail.com,
E.M.A.G.vanDijk@utwente.nl
[3] TNO, Soesterberg, The Netherlands
Anita.Cremers@tno.nl

Abstract. This study investigated the effects of the gamification elements of scaffolding, score and hints on the user enjoyment and motivation of people of low literacy. In a four-condition within-subjects experiment, participants performed mental spatial ability tests with the aforementioned elements. Quantitative results were inconclusive, but post-test interviews provided insights on the limited effectiveness of the gamification elements. Complex questionnaire wording, high task difficulty, and an improperly situated task environment all contributed to ceiling effects in the influence of scaffolding. Score was found to be ineffective without proper contextualization connecting the numerical score to clearer performance measures. Finally, the underused hints functionality has indicated the need for adequate 'mixed initiative' support.

Keywords: Literacy, Gamification, Motivation, User Enjoyment.

1 Introduction

In modern Dutch society, people of low literacy engage in low levels of societal participation, due to an insufficient grasp of information and communication skills. Computer tools to support societal participation learning for this demographic already exist, but the design of these tools is not optimal. First, people of low literacy suffer from low self-efficacy with regard to learning and the use of information and communication technology (ICT), which translates into reduced motivation to act. And second, the current tools are experienced as complicated and unengaging. This study aims to experimentally investigate whether or not gamification elements can improve the user enjoyment and raise the motivation of people of low literacy using software.

The paper is set up as follows. This chapter provides background information on low literacy and low societal participation in the Netherlands, the issues with current computer support tools related to societal participation learning, and the concept of gamification. Chapter 2 presents the experimental methodology, including information

K. Miesenberger et al. (Eds.): ICCHP 2014, Part I, LNCS 8547, pp. 494–501, 2014.
© Springer International Publishing Switzerland 2014

on experimental design, measurement operationalization, participant demo-graphic information, and materials used. Chapter 3 gives an overview of the results. Chapter 4 offers discussion on study outcomes and recommendations for future work.

1.1 Low Literacy, Societal Participation, Information and Communication Skills

At around 1.1 million people, close to 10% of the Dutch work force is currently classified as being 'low-literate' [6]. The concept of low literacy encompasses not only a deficient grasp of basic reading and writing ability, but also indicates a lack of the information and communication skills needed to effectively participate in modern information societies [14]. Murray et al [10] report on a standard of functional literacy that is associated with higher societal participation, independence and learning, which is seen as the minimum level required for effective participation in society [14].

Societal participation is the common term for goal-directed behaviors enacted in the context of a social structure. Schouten [13] provides a model of societal participation consisting of two axes: a formal-to-informal social context axis and an information-to-communication skill axis. Examples of problematic societal participation for low-literates in this model are engaging with formal institutions through writing and through interactive voice response systems, reading and understanding traffic signs while driving, and using email and Skype to stay in touch with far-away friends.

1.2 Support Tools, User Enjoyment, Motivation

One common method for assisting low-literate people in language learning and societal participation is the use of software support tools. However, Schouten [13] asserts that currently available tools in these areas are not optimal. Particularly in the areas of user enjoyment and motivation, low-literate users often run into issues. Schouten [13] posits that people of low literacy often suffer from low levels of self-efficacy with regard to both learning and ICT use, which negatively impacts motivation. Negative affect towards learning and towards ICT play a role as well. While many low-literate people express a desire to learn, the (perceived) complexity of support tools acts as an additional impediment.

User enjoyment, a subset of user experience, indicates users' general pleasure or displeasure with a system. Based on Gajadhar et al [3], user enjoyment encompasses several concepts. Positive and negative affect refer to the user's general affective state towards the software. Annoyance measures judgment about the software's usability. Finally, competence and challenge indicate respectively the user's sense of being good at using the software, and the difficulties encountered during use. All of these concepts are self-reported. Preliminary reports from low-literate user workshops [13] show issues with regard to support software and user enjoyment. High levels of complexity exacerbate negative attitudes towards ICT, causing frustration and annoyance.

Motivation is a powerful predictor for software use and learning outcome. This study specifies four kinds of motivation, based on Guay et al [4]. Intrinsic motivation refers to engaging in an activity 'for its own sake'. Extrinsic motivation, engaging in an activity to obtain a certain goal, is divided into identified regulation (where the activity itself is seen as valuable and self-chosen) and external regulation (where the activity is strictly seen as a means to an end). Finally, amotivation refers to a lack of desire to engage in an activity.

1.3   Gamification

Gamification is becoming increasingly ubiquitous. Deterding et al [2] define it as "the use of game design elements in non-game contexts" (p.1). Within the context of this study, gamification could prove useful in increasing user enjoyment and motivation with regard to societal participation support. Gamification has already been applied in astronaut training software to improve individual motivation [1] and to improve user engagement in e-learning [9].

Three specific gamification elements are seen as being particularly interesting in this context. Scaffolding refers to gradually increasing difficulty level and reducing guided support in track with user progress [2]. This matching of user skill and task difficulty could make the user feel more competent at tasks, and implementations of similar ideas have been shown to influence intrinsic motivation [12].

Hints, implemented as helpful guides and comments designed to facilitate progress and avoid frustration [16], can be seen as a form of learning support, aimed at reducing experienced challenge. Good use of hints supports players in solving problems on their own, rather than just 'giving' them the solution [12]: hints used in this learning-support way could increase intrinsic motivation.

Finally, Zichermann and Cunningham [17] consider the numerical performance measure of score to be "an absolute requirement for all gamified systems" (p.36). Score and reward systems have been linked to increased extrinsic motivation in users [16]. Furthermore, score's provision of feedback and social-competitive context to the user [17] links it to possible higher positive affect with regards to a task.

1.4   Research Question

To our knowledge, studies into gamification specifically with low-literate users are nonexistent. There are reasons to suspect that general findings about gamification do not directly apply to a low-literate demographic, however. Information and communication skill deficiencies cause problems with software use at large, likely impeding the effectiveness of gamification [14]. The addition of extra elements to software can create perceptions of high complexity and necessitate learning new functionality and new information structures, which would exacerbate problems derived from this. Finally, van Linden and Cremers [8] report that low-literates, among other things, often show reduced abstract thinking skills: this could reduce the effectiveness of certain gamification elements, such as score.

This study aims to investigate the effectiveness of the gamification elements of scaffolding, score and hints in improving the user enjoyment and motivation of people of low literacy. The principal research question is: Can the use of gamification in ICT software applications enhance motivation and user enjoyment for people of low literacy using these applications? The following hypotheses are tested:

1. Scaffolding
   (a) Scaffolding increases intrinsic motivation in low-literates.
   (b) Scaffolding increases self-reported competence in low-literates.
2. Score
   (a) Score increases external regulation in low-literates.
   (b) Score increases positive affect in low-literates.
3. Hints
   (a) Hints increase intrinsic motivation in low-literates.
   (b) Hints decrease experienced challenge in low-literates.

2   Method

2.1   Experimental Design

This study employed a counterbalanced mixed-method within-subjects design. To measure the effect of gamification on user enjoyment and motivation, four experimental conditions were used: three conditions corresponding to the scaffolding, score and hints gamification elements, and one control condition.

Each condition consisted of the participants completing a mental spatial ability test (SPAT). Developed by Neerincx et al [11], the SPAT involves matching a provided three-dimensional figure with a correctly rotated version of that same figure, chosen from a set of alternatives. While this test is non-verbal, it has a high base level of difficulty and complexity that supposedly provides room for support initiatives like gamification to have clear effects. Research shows that low-literate participants perform relatively poorly at this test, exacerbating this effect [8]. Figure 1 shows a screenshot of the SPAT-application used during the experiment.

Fig. 1. Screenshot of Spatial Ability Test (SPAT) software used in the study. The participant should indicate which of the three right-most figures is identical to the left-most figure.

In the control condition, participants were asked to solve a set of 15 SPAT puzzles. Puzzles ranged in difficulty from 2 to 5 answer possibilities, and a predetermined random difficulty order was used. Each puzzle had a time limit of 15 seconds. Other conditions were differentiated as follows: in the scaffolding condition, the predetermined random difficulty order was changed to a sequential difficulty order, gradually increasing the puzzles in difficulty level: 2 answer categories, then 3, then 4, then 5. In the hints condition, a 'hint' button was added to the user interface: participants could click this button once per puzzle to remove one incorrect answer, a maximum of ten times total. In the score condition, participant performance was displayed at the end of the condition, in a '[number correct]/15' format.

2.2   Participants

With the help of the Dutch Stichting Lezen & Schrijven, 17 low-literate participants were recruited for this study. 12 female and 5 male subjects participated, ranging in age from 33 to 71 years (mean=51.94 years, SD=11.255).

2.3   Measures

In order to measure user enjoyment and motivation in low-literate participants, a short questionnaire was created. This questionnaire was adapted from the Game Experience Questionnaire (GEQ) [7] and the Situational Motivation Scale (SIMS) [4], containing five questions to measure self-reported competence, annoyance, challenge, and positive and negative affect, and four questions to measure intrinsic motivation, identified regulation, external regulation, and amotivation. All questions were rated on a 5-point Likert scale. Question wording was simplified to better fit the low-literate participants. Participant performance on the test, defined as the number of puzzles solved correctly, was also measured in all conditions.

2.4   Procedure

Two participants were present in each experimental session, participating in parallel. A brief introduction of the task was given before starting. The test was demonstrated, paying special attention to operation, and any questions were answered.

Each participant completed all four experimental conditions in sequence: condition sequences were counterbalanced. Participants filled out the enjoyment/motivation questionnaire after each condition; experimenter help in reading questionnaires was offered, but not enforced. After completing the experiment, participants also filled out a questionnaire measuring demographic information, computer experience and gaming preferences. Finally, short interviews were held. The intent of these interviews was to gain more in-depth insights into participant motivation and enjoyment. Interviews were semi-structured: questions like 'what did you think of this game?' and 'did you notice any differences between different play sessions?' were used as predetermined starting points, with follow-up questions based on insight.

3   Results

Questionnaire results were analyzed using linear and quadratic regression analysis. Scores for positive affect, intrinsic motivation and identified regulation were high across participants, while other scores (including SPAT scores) were more varied, with no immediate trends. None of the six hypotheses were confirmed (see Table 1).

Table 1. Overview of regression analysis results as related to the six hypotheses

1a: Scaffolding, Intrinsic Motivation	$F_{(3.64)} = .082$	$p = .969$	Unconfirmed.
1b: Scaffolding, Competence	$F_{(3.64)} = .777$	$p = .511$	Unconfirmed.
2a: Score, External Regulation	$F_{(3.64)} = .104$	$p = .957$	Unconfirmed.
2b: Score, Positive Affect	$F_{(3.64)} = .022$	$p = .995$	Unconfirmed.
3a: Hints, Intrinsic Motivation	$F_{(3.64)} = .118$	$p = .960$	Unconfirmed.
3b: Hints, (Experienced) Challenge	$F_{(3.64)} = .476$	$p = .700$	Unconfirmed.

The follow-up analysis found two interesting significant results. First, a linear relation between competence ($R^2=.066$, $F_{(2,64)}=4.57$, $p=.36$) and performance indicates that self-reported competence was a good predictor of actual competence. And second, a quadratic relation between positive affect ($R^2=.209$, $F_{(2,64)}=4.671$, $p=.000$), intrinsic motivation ($R^2=.109$, $F_{(2,64)}=3.931$, $p=.023$), identified regulation ($R^2=.216$, $F_{(2,64)} = 8.800$, $p=.000$) and performance seems to indicate a relation between skill and enjoyment. Analysis of computer self-efficacy and gaming preferences showed no significant outcomes: values for both constructs measured across the range, with no trends to speak of.

4   Discussion and Conclusions

Based on quantitative analysis, none of the hypotheses could be confirmed. As this represents a deviation from expectations, possible explanations are offered next.

Generally speaking, this study seems to have underestimated the issues low-literates experience with regard to information and attention complexity. Simply dealing with the 'base' SPAT proved complex enough for participants to require their full attention. Furthermore, questionnaire wording was found to be overly complex, even after editing. The motivation questions were particularly misunderstood, with participants often verbalizing one answer and noting another. The concept of 'motivation' may be too abstract for this demographic to be measured in questionnaires.

This study reaffirms the vital importance of strongly taking the constraints associated with low literacy into account (c.f. [8]). While attempts were made to adapt measuring instruments to the target demographic, issues of complexity, abstraction, and information overload were still encountered.

The lack of results for scaffolding can be attributed to two ceiling effects. First, almost all participants reported high motivation and enjoyment, both in questionnaires and in post-test interviews, simply from participating in the study. The experimental task was too 'fun', and seen as a game, which led to a high baseline for enjoyment and motivation even in the control condition. These findings confirm the importance of properly situated test design [14]. An experimental design that was less enjoyable, framing the situation as a problem or a test, could have avoided this issue.

Task difficulty presented a second ceiling effect. Perceived difficulty did not change as a function of the number of answer possibilities, but instead seemed dependent on participant skill levels: participants were either consistently good at the task, or consistently bad, with little change between conditions. Particularly for the latter group, and counter to expectations, the difficulty of the experimental task influenced outcomes in an undesired way: the base task difficulty was so high that the effect of the experimental manipulations was too small to make any real difference.

It could also be argued that since the SPAT measures the stable trait of mental rotation skill, little room would be left for difficulty manipulation through scaffolding to begin with. While this notion does not invalidate this study's scaffolding manipulation, given that measurements focused on more affective factors, it does provide a compelling alternate reason for why this manipulation had so little effect.

The lack of results for score can be attributed to insufficient context: displaying score in only one condition lacked any progress and skill information. Participants also did not always report 'seeing' the post-test score screen; as no equivalent screen existed in other conditions, this could be due to information overload or attentional division. Finally, the numerical nature of score was difficult to some participants.

Earlier assumptions about the application of this gamification element should be rethought. The combination of information and attention overload and interpreting numeric information could mean that a visual representation of score as a motivator is simply not suited for low-literates. Future studies should attempt to clarify this.

The lack of results for hints can be attributed to two factors. First, about 50% of participants reported not 'seeing' the hints button in the condition it was present: as with score, this could represent information or attention issues. Second, the participants that did see the hints button reported a desire to not use it: they saw the test as a game, and wanted to test their skills. A similar attitude was visible with the questionnaires: participants would never ask for help with reading the questions, but any offer of help was always gladly accepted. These findings seem to indicate the need for better design of support options: mixed initiative design principles could be used to achieve a better balance in offering and enforcing help [5].

Finally, the quadratic relation between positive affect measures and performance seems similar to flow theory and the Zone of Proximal Development [12], which present the optimal user experience as a between frustration and boredom. The notion that societal participation learning for low-literates is subject to flow considerations could be used as a starting point for designing better software to this effect.

References

1. Cornelissen, F., Neerincx, M.A., Smets, N.J.J.M., Breebaart, L., Dujardin, P., Wolff, M.: Gamification for Astronaut Training. In: The 12th International Conference on Space Operations, Stockholm, Sweden (2012)
2. Deterding, S., O'Hara, K., Sicart, M., Dixon, D., Nacke, L.: Gamification: Using Game Design Elements in Non-Gaming Contexts. In: Proceedings of CHI 2011, pp. 1–4. ACM (2011)
3. Gajadhar, B.J., de Kort, Y.A.W., IJsselsteijn, W.A.: Influence of social setting on player experience of digital games. In: CHI 2008. ACM, Florence (2008)

4. Guay, F., Vallerand, R.J., Blanchard, C.: On the Assessment of Situational Intrinsic and Extrinsic Motivation: The Situational Motivation Scale (SIMS). Motivation and Emotion 24(3), 175–213 (2000)
5. Horvitz, E.: Principles of mixed-initiative user interfaces. In: Proceedings of the SIGCHI Conference on Human Factors in Computing Systems: The CHI Is the Limit (CHI 1999), pp. 159–166. ACM (1999)
6. Houtkoop, W., Allen, J., Buisman, M., Fouarge, D., van der Velden, R.: Kernvaardigheden in Nederland: Resultaten van de Adult Literacy and Life Skills Survey (ALL). Uitgave Expertisecentrum Beroepsonderwijs (2012)
7. IJsselsteijn, W.A., de Kort, Y.A.W., Poels, K.: Game Experience Questionnaire (2007), http://www.gamexplab.nl
8. van Linden, S., Cremers, A.H.M.: Cognitive Abilities of Functionally Illiterate Persons Relevant to ICT Use. In: Miesenberger, K., Klaus, J., Zagler, W., Karshmer, A. (eds.) ICCHP 2008. LNCS, vol. 5105, pp. 705–712. Springer, Heidelberg (2008)
9. Muntean, C.I.: Raising engagement in e-learning through gamification. In: Proc. 6th International Conference on Virtual Learning ICVL, pp. 323–329 (2011)
10. Murray, T.S., Kirsch, I.S., Jenkins, L.B.: Adult Literacy in OECD Countries: Technical Report on the First International Adult Literacy Survey, National Center for Education Statistics, USA (1997)
11. Neerincx, M.A., Pemberton, S., Lindenberg, J.: U-WISH Web usability: methods, guidelines and support interfaces (Report TM-99-D005). TNO Human Factors Research Institute, Soesterberg, The Netherlands (1999)
12. Obikwelu, C., Read, J., Sim, G.: The Scaffolding Mechanism in Serious Games. In: Fun and Game 2012, Toulouse, France (2012)
13. Schouten, D.G.M.: Improving Societal Participation for Low-Literates and Non-Natives Through Computer Support Tool Design (2013) (Unpublished)
14. Schouten, D., Smets, N., Driessen, M., Hanekamp, M., Cremers, A.H.M., Neerincx, M.A.: User Requirement Analysis of Social Conventions Learning Applications for Non-Natives and Low-Literates. In: Harris, D. (ed.) EPCE 2013, Part I. LNCS, vol. 8019, pp. 354–363. Springer, Heidelberg (2013)
15. van Staalduinen, J.P., de Freitas, S.: A Game-Based Learning Framework: Linking Game Design and Learning. In: Kyhine, M.S. (ed.) Learning to play: exploring the future of education with video games, pp. 29–54. Peter Lang, New York (2011)
16. Warren, S.J., Dondlinger, M.J., Barab, S.A.: A MUVE Towards PBL Writing: Effects of a Digital Learning Environment Designed To Improve Elementary Student Writing. Journal of Research on Technology in Education 41(1), 113–140 (2008)
17. Zichermann, G., Cunningham, C.: Gamification by Design. O'Reilly, Sebastopol (2011)

Designing Tangible and Multitouch Games
for Autistic Children

Weiqin Chen[1,2]

[1] Oslo and Akershus University College of Applied Sciences, Oslo, Norway
Weiqin.chen@hioa.no
[2] University of Bergen, Bergen, Norway
Weiqin.chen@infomedia.uib.no

Abstract. Tangible multitouch tabletops allow multiple users to interact with physical and virtual objects simultaneously and afford natural and intuitive social interactions. Although some applications have shown that multitouch tabletop technology is an applicable technology with potentials for children with ASD, more research is need to understand how to take advantage of the affordance of this technology. This research presents an effort in exploring the potentials of tangible and multitouch games for children with ASD.

Keywords: Autism Spectrum Disorder, Tangible User Interfaces, Multitouch, Tabletop Games, Children.

1   Introduction

Autism Spectrum Disorder (ASD) is a set of neurodevelopmental disorder characterized by impairment in social interaction, communication skills and in behavior, which is restricted and repetitive. Recent statistics have shown that autism is the second most prevalent neurodevelopmental disorder among children and is estimated to be 1–2 per 1000 children. Meanwhile ASD is estimated to affect about 6 per 1000 children. The spectrum of ASD is continuous and includes many variations. However, all types of ASD present three common well-defined difficulties known as the Triad of Impairments: impairments of social interaction, of social language and communication, and of flexibility of thought and imagination [1].

Computer-based applications are considered to be useful tools for therapeutic and educational purposes for children with ASD because they are predictable, consistent, free from social demands and specific in focus of attention [2]. In recent years there has been a large body of research on tangible and multitouch tabletop interfaces. Tangible user interfaces (TUIs) augment the real physical world by coupling digital information to everyday physical objects and environments [3]. Tangible multitouch tabletops allow multiple users to interact with physical and virtual objects simultaneously and afford natural and intuitive social interactions.

Although some applications have shown that multitouch tabletop technology is an applicable technology with potentials for children with ASD, we still need to understand how to take advantage of the affordance of this technology in order to provide

K. Miesenberger et al. (Eds.): ICCHP 2014, Part I, LNCS 8547, pp. 502–505, 2014.

the best possible support for children with autism, their families and professional who support them. This research is one of the efforts in exploring the potentials of tangible and multitouch games.

2   Related Work

Multitouch technologies, which allow multiple users' simultaneous input, provide more opportunities for flexible collaboration compared with traditional interfaces. They allow direct and simultaneous manipulation of digital objects on the interface and provide possibility of non-verbal and gestural communication. The past few years have seen a great increase in research on multitouch technologies for autistic children. These researches range from enhancing social interactions and communication skills to improving imaginations [4,5]. Most recently Hourcade et al. [6] developed applications and activities on multitouch tablets for promoting social skills among children with ASD. They observed increased pro-social behaviours such as collaboration and coordination and augmented appreciation for social activities. They also found that these applications provided children with novel forms of expression. Tangible technologies, which have shown to be able to help children with social skills [7], have also been investigated by researchers on their affordance in supporting autistic children to collaborate and communicate. For example, Farr, et al. [8] compared the activities of autistic children in two conditions, one where the children played with Topobo, a constructive assembly system with kinetic memory, and one where they played with LEGO building blocks. The research found that more cooperative play occurred when children used Topobo. In our research we aim to investigate the joint benefits of tangible and multitouch technologies on children with ASD.

3   The Design of a Game Suite

Inspired by previous research in tangible and multitouch technologies and their applications, based on game design principles, and through communication with ASD experts, family and caregivers of ASD children, we have identified the requirements for the application and implemented a suite of games. The game suite is developed on the Samsung SUR40 multitouch table using Microsoft PixelSense. Byte Tags are used to mark physical objects such as dog food and Frisbee so that the table recognizes these objects. Depending on where and which objects are placed on the table by the children, the system will take different actions and give different feed-back.

3.1   Requirements

The games in the suite should be designed for different purposes and different levels of difficulties so that teachers, parents, and caregivers can choose which game to give to the children based on the conditions of the children [9]. Children themselves should also have the opportunities to choose which game they would like to play.

The game suite should include both single-player games and multi-player games. Preferably the games should have single-player mode and multi-player mode. In multi-player games and multi-player mode, tasks should enforce collaboration and communication, rather than dividing the tasks to individual children. Turn-taking should be built into each game as collaborating sometimes means to compromise one's interest for the interest of the whole group [6]. The children should have the possibility to decide for their own turn-taking system, as this can make the game more challenging than simply following the machine's instructions [4].The games should allow children to make mistakes, rather than using constraints to prevent children from making mistakes. Children should learn to handle their own mistakes as well as others' and to control and manage the frustration resulting from the mistakes.

3.2   Game Examples

Circles is a two-player game (Fig. 1a). The two circles (light blue and red ones) are to be moved to the end of the maze without touching each other or the walls. Each circle is controlled by one player. If a collision happens, the players have to start again from the beginning. The game mainly trains four skills: collaboration, communication, physical coordination and handling mistakes. The players have to collaborate and communicate to give their partners possibility to anticipate the next moves. The mistakes involve both players and the objective is to have the children overcome these obstacles by recognizing their mistakes or by forgiving the other player's mistakes. Faces is designed to help autistic children recognizing facial expressions and relating the expressions with feelings (Fig. 1b). When an image appears, the player touches a word label representing the feeling. In Pets the players have to offer different objects in order to reply to different needs of the pets (Fig. 1c). The mood of the pet changes according to the player activities and the object it received. The players should recognize this association to make the right choice. This game is based on the research that shows the positive effect of animal-assisted therapy on autistic children [10].

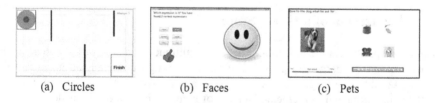

(a)   Circles   (b)   Faces   (c)   Pets

Fig. 1. Interfaces

4   Discussion and Future Work

The combination of tangible and multitouch technologies has the potential to provide support for autistic children beyond each of the individual technology. In this research we aim to increase the understanding of the affordance and potentials of this combination. In addition, the development of the game suite provides the teachers, parents, and caregivers the opportunity to choose games based on the children's conditions. The children themselves can also choose which game to play based on their own or joint interests. This flexibility could enhance the engagement of the children [5]. We are currently planning a formative evaluation, which will be carried out soon.

Acknowledgement. The author would like to thank the two groups of EPS (European Project Semester) students in autumn 2012 and spring 2013 for their contribution to the project.

References

1. Wing, L., Gould, J.: Severe impairments of social interaction and associated abnormalities in children: epidemiology and classification. Journal of Autism and Developmental Disorders 9, 11–29 (1979)
2. Murray, D.: Autism and information technology: therapy with computers. In: Powell, S., Jordan, R. (eds.) Autism and learning: A guide to good practice. David Fulton Publishers, London (1997)
3. Ishii, H., Ullmer, B.: Tangible bits: towards seamless interfaces between people, bits and atoms. In: Proceedings of the ACM SIGCHI Conference on Human factors in computing systems (CHI 1997), pp. 234–241. ACM Press (1997)
4. Piper, A.M., O'Brien, E., Morris, M.R., Winograd, T.: SIDES: a cooperative tabletop computer game for social skills development. In: Hinds, P.J., Martin, D. (eds.) Proc. of the 20th Anniversary Conference on Computer Supported Cooperative Work, pp. 1–10. ACM, Banff (2006)
5. Giusti, L., Zancanaro, M., Gal, E., Weiss, P.L.: Dimensions of collaboration on a tabletop interface for children with Autism Spectrum Disorder. In: Conference on Human Factors in Computing Systems (CHI 2011), pp. 3259–3304. ACM Press, Vancouver (2011)
6. Hourcade, J.P., Bullock-Rest, N.E., Hansen, T.E.: Multitouch tablet applications and activities to enhance the social skills of children with autism spectrum disorders. Personal and Ubiquitous Computing 16, 157–168 (2012)
7. Hendrix, K., van Herk, R., Verhaegh, J., Markopoulos, P.: Increasing children's social competence through games, an exploratory study. In: Proceedings of IDC 2009, pp. 182–185 (2009)
8. Farr, W., Yuill, N., Raffle, H.: Social Interactional Benefits of a Tangible User Interface for Children with Autistic Spectrum Conditions. Autism 14, 237–252 (2010)
9. Zarin, R., Fallman, D.: Through the Troll Forest: Exploring Tabletop Interaction Design for Children with Special Cognitive Needs. In: Conference on Human Factors in Computing Systems (CHI 2011), pp. 3319–3322. ACM Press, Vancouver (2011)
10. Martin, F., Farnum, J.: Animal-Assisted Therapy for Children with Pervasive Developmental Disorders. West Journal of Nursing Research 24, 657–670 (2002)

You Talk! – YOU vs AUTISM

Alessandro Signore[1], Panagiota Balasi[2], and Tangming Yuan[3]

[1] Westhouse Italia Srl, Centro Direzionale Milanofiori, Assago, Italy
lex25288@gmail.com
[2] Codix SA Systems Integration, Athens, Greece
balgiota@hotmail.com
[3] Department of Computer Science, University of York, York, United Kingdom
tommy.yuan@york.ac.uk

Abstract. This paper reports our work in developing a mobile application, which helps autistic children communicate with those around them, by using PECS symbols to formulate a sentence and later on speak it out loud. The application in question has gone through a rigorous development process: both the requirements gathering and evaluation for this project have been conducted with experts in the world of autism in order to further establish the soundness of the work. All the issues that were found throughout the evaluation, which was carried out as a cognitive walkthrough, were fixed and suggested additional functionalities were taken into consideration in order to enhance the application with more features. A user-based evaluation, which was conducted in order to further establish the validity of the work, proved that the application was well accepted by the autistic community in the virtual world.

Keywords: Autism, Autistic, Verbal Impairment, PECS, Makaton.

1 Introduction

Autism is a disorder, affecting more than 400.000 individuals in the UK alone [1], which is characterized by a marked impairment in non-verbal communication, peer relationship development, delay or absence of verbal communication from a very young age. This last impairment, which is this project's main focus, is usually overcome in the real world by the employment of communication methods, such as the Picture Exchange Communication System (PECS) and the Makaton. Concepts from both communication methods will be used in this application in order to provide a technological solution that autistic people can use to interact with the world around them.

Researchers have been testing out other methods to make communication possible, namely one of these being computer-aided interaction. As [2] shows, multimedia programs provided with visual and auditory stimuli can be successfully used to teach important skills to individuals affected by autism, as they can in fact introduce them to fundamental social communication concepts such as language, emotion recognition and social skills. All attention will be narrowed down to the first of these three in this

K. Miesenberger et al. (Eds.): ICCHP 2014, Part I, LNCS 8547, pp. 506–512, 2014.

paper. According to [3], computer-aided communication seems to prove as quite an efficient and effective choice when it comes to individuals affected by autism. Most of these individuals have in fact, not only been shown to prefer the visual channel to the auditory one, but have also been known to have quite an eidetic memory.

The chief concern of this paper is the development of a PECS-based software application that is to be used by autistic children with verbal communication difficulties. It is expected that the application will not only be beneficial to children affected by high-functioning autism but also adults affected by a low-functioning one, since they also show a substantial lack in both verbal and non-verbal communicative skills. The remainder of this paper is organized as follows. It starts with a critical review of the existing applications followed by the design principles that are followed at the development stage. It then discusses the requirement and the design process of the intended application. Finally, the evaluation of the application is documented and results are discussed.

2 Design Principles

Four key user interaction related aspects have emerged in the primary steps of this project, which will be of vital importance throughout the course of it all, and these are [4,5]:

- It is of the utmost importance to catch the child's interest;
- Interaction modalities must be kept simple, ergo an application should not include different kinds of them all popping up on the screen at the same time (e.g. allowing the user to either type in text or speak it via voice recognition should not be an option);
- Children should be able to learn from their own actions, this will be achieved by providing them with repetitive and recursive steps;
- User interfaces should not be over-cluttered with symbols as this may impede users from successfully establishing a connection.
- There seem to be two different communication systems that represent viable and already well-tested ways of interacting with children with special needs: the Makaton and the PECS. The PECS is out of the two the one that caught much attention because of the engagingness and colorfulness its symbols have, since, as it was established earlier, one of main goals of the items in the user interface would have to be to attract the user's attention.
- One of the Makaton's traits will also be taken and integrated into this project. The sentences in this project will in fact be formulated using key-word symbols, as:
- Symbol reading would prove far too advanced for the children the application is intended for and they would not be benefitting much from it;
- Functional reading would not be useful because the information the receiver of the conversation would be given would not be sufficient for them to understand the needs of the sender.

3   Requirements Elicitation

The list of requirements for this project was elicited with the help of several experts in the field, one of whom was especially vital to its fruition. All requirements have been gathered keeping in mind the stakeholders of the application:

- Individuals affected by autism;
- Parents/guardians;
- The specialist teachers with whose help the requirements for this project have been gathered;
- Experts in the field who might benefit from the development of such a project.

An extensive background reading alongside discussions with a lecturer from the Department of Psychology at the University of York, specializing in language development in autism and specialist teachers working for a school for children with special needs in York, have served as a mean to further define the requirements.

The requirements that have emerged are as follows:

1. The symbols that shall be used within the application are PECS symbols. Though they are highly customizable and, as such, do not themselves retain a standard; they represent one of the most used communication systems for people with learning difficulties and can allow us to successfully achieve the objectives posed by this project.
2. The application shall guide children and allow them to learn from their mistakes. Since many teachers suggest that most of them tend to be error-prone.
3. Autistic children lack the ability to abstract and should therefore not be distracted from achieving their goal by having to look for the symbol they are after in different folders. Therefore items shall not be over-categorized, though one categorization level would not be too deterrent.
4. The children's first goal is expressing their needs and not someone else's. As such, the formulation of sentences like "the girl eats an apple" would be of no interest to them. The formulation of sentences that are not strictly correlated to the user shall not be possible.
5. As it's been gathered, the average autistic user's disabilities demand that steps be recursive and repetitive (as mentioned earlier).
6. All the sentences shall be spoken out in British English. As many teachers have in fact pointed out, most applications tend to be aimed at an American audience and children here in the UK find it hard to relate to them because of the different accent.
7. It is not yet clear at this stage the level of language that shall be required in the application. That is if the application should enforce the use of proper sentence formulation, despite the fact that some sentences might result harder for the average autistic child to grasp.

4   User Centred Design

User centered design was used as the development process. Going from the previously gathered requirements, new prototypes have been drawn until an agreement between the stakeholders could be reached.

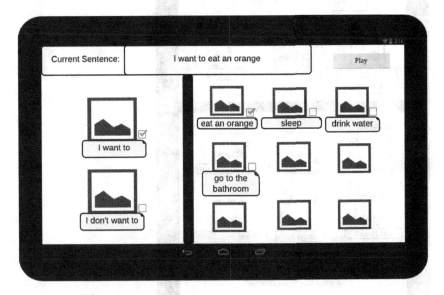

Fig. 1. First prototype

The first prototype in figure 1 was drawn without the input of either users or experts; it was merely sketched up going from the pieces of information gathered during the requirements elicitation. It was in fact drawn on the basis that:

- An autistic child may only wish to express their own wants (hence the I want to and I don't want to) and no one else's;
- There should be no excessive need for navigation, because, as already stated earlier, this might drive the children to not accomplishing their goal.

The feedback the was received from a specialist teacher was fairly positive but a need for sequentiality was expressed along with the need of asking for help, wanting to sleep and going to the bathroom, which led us to drawing the second and final prototype for the application shown in figure 2.

As can be seen from this prototype, the clear portrait layout, opted for instead of the landscape one, along with the division between the steps that need to be undertaken in order to get to the formulation of a sentence, gives a clear sense of sequentiality and navigation which was, what had been said, was missing in the first prototype. The validity of the second prototype was verified with a colleague of the specialist teacher the first one had been looked over by.

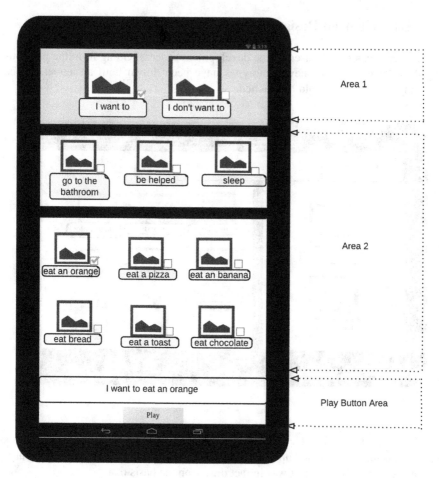

Fig. 2. Second and last prototype

5   Evaluation

Out of all the different ways this application could have been evaluated, a setting not involving users [6] was chosen, the reason for that being that it would have been extremely difficult to get them to cooperate in an evaluation with an expert, given their indisposition as both children and autistic users.

The expert evaluation was conducted in two different iterations: the first was conducted with a former specialist teacher and whilst second with the mother of an autistic child.

The former specialist teacher was working at York City Council as a reviewer for applications and programs alike, to judge if they be fit to be used by people with mental disabilities in an educational environment.

Her deep knowledge of autism combined with an experience in evaluating software convinced the author that her expertise should be used to evaluate the application.

Not only did she guide me through some of the usability issues an autistic child could experience whilst attempting to use the application, but also gave me an insight into how the application could be better improved in terms of choice of symbols, language syntax and coloring.

The approach the author used was quite straightforward and simple: a cognitive walkthrough [7]. Since another kind of walkthrough had been used throughout the design stage with the prototyping and had proven fruitful it was thought the same would be done again.

The mother of the autistic child also proved immensely helpful in terms of choice of symbols and even allowed the author to indirectly further test the application at home with her son. The test lasted one month and proved quite positive as it served as a way to further define the symbols for the application.

A user-evaluation was also conducted by putting the application online on the Play Store at the following link:

`https://play.google.com/store/apps/details?id=com.SeGle Nx.youtalk`

As of the writing of this paper, the application has awarded 3.5 out of 5 stars and out of the 421 downloads it has had, it is still being used by 211 people.

6   Project Overview

This project has started out with an overview into autism, which delved into its different categorizations, the non-computer-aided communication tools already in place for dealing with this disorder and finally a thorough critique of already existing applications that address this or similar problems.

It then progressed onto the requirements elicitation process that was achieved by combining what was uncovered in the literature review with discussions with several experts in the field.

A user-centered approach was used throughout the entire project and extreme care was taken whilst designing the application to make sure it complied with the usability needs of autistic children. The design went in fact through two prototyping iterations, which have been discussed and evaluated by experts in the field. The prototype, which was agreed upon, was then enhanced with the functionalities required in order to meet the requirements for this project.

Based on this design, an Android application was then developed. The implementation also went through two iterations. After the first one, a cumulative evaluation by an expert and the mother of an autistic child was carried out and a reviewed implementation was provided in order to address all the problems that had been found in the previous evaluation.

Rigorous testing was conducted in order to make sure it complied with the requirements that had been set out and that it worked according to design.

A user-based evaluation was then conducted by publishing the application on the Google Play. It was awarded 3.5 out of 5 stars and the Google Play statistics showed that 50% of the people that downloaded the application decided to keep it, meaning that they must have found it useful.

7   Conclusion

This project's aim was to address the verbal impairment autistic people suffer from. This was achieved by developing an Android application that allowed users to formulate sentences using symbols in the PECS (a well establish communication method in the autistic community).

The application that has been developed addressed several usability issues, that had been found in other applications currently available, by breaking the sentence formulation in different area of the screen: as such the conversation starters can only be found in the top part of the screen, after which the other symbols can be found (with their own ramifications). This clear division allows the user to better focus their attention and the background of the area containing all the items that can be interacted with at a certain point of the sentence formulation process, is given a yellow coloring indicating that the user should only concern themselves with those specific items for the time being.

By using this application, the user will hence be able to formulate sentences via PECS symbols and speak them out loud, and the people in their near proximity will be able to understand their needs without being in a strict contact with them.

The immediate further work is to continue the user-based evaluation and fix any issues thence found.

References

1. Autism.org.uk,
   http://www.autism.org.uk/about-autism/myths-facts-and-statistics/statistics-how-many-people-have-autism-spectrum-disorders.aspx
2. Wainer, A.L., Ingersoll, B.R.: The use of innovative computer technology for teaching social communication to individuals with autism spectrum disorders. Research in Autism Spectrum Disorders 5(1), 96–107 (2011)
3. Pozzar, R.: Autismo, comunicazione facilitata e tecnologie. Tecnologie didattice 22(1), 59–60 (2001)
4. Designingforchildren.net,
   http://www.designingforchildren.net/papers/w.keay-bright%20designing%20for%20children.pdf
5. Makaton.org,
   https://www.makaton.org/Assets/Store/Downloads/FreeResources/EventPosters.pdf
6. Bass, L., et al.: Software Architecture in Practice, 3rd edn. SEI series in software engineering. Addison Wesley / Pearson Education, New Jersey (2012)
7. Rogers, Y., et al.: Interaction Design: Beyond Human-Computer Interaction, 3rd ed. John Wiley & Sons, Chichester, United Kingdom (2011)

A Game-Based Intervention
for Improving the Communication Skills
of Autistic Children in Pakistan

Muneeb Imtiaz Ahmad[1], Suleman Shahid[2], and Johannes S. Maganheim[1]

[1] Didactics of Computer Science, Computer Science Education Group,
Department of Computer Science, University of Paderborn, Paderborn, Germany
muneeb06@gmail.com, jsm@uni-paderborn.de
[2] Tilburg Centre for Cognition and Communication,
Department of Information and Communication Sciences,
University of Tilburg, Tilburg, The Netherlands
S.Shahid@uvt.nl

Abstract. In this paper, we discuss the design and evaluation of a computer game "Guess Who" which was used as a tool to encourage social interaction in autistic children. We performed an evaluation of the game for a span of six weeks at an autistic school in Pakistan. We present the qualitative results collected from the weekly feedback taken from teachers against every child's behavior. We also present the video analysis results that give us information about the amount of social interaction among children while playing the game.

Keywords: Autistic Children, Games, Social Communication.

1   Introduction and Motivation

Autism Spectrum Disorders (ASDs) are intricate, enduring neurodevelopment and behavioral disorders found in beginning or early childhood. Children diagnosed with ASD shows signs of communication, emotional and social impairment, and the severity of which varies from mild to severe. Researchers have designed and evaluated several assistive technologies comprising of computer [1], multi-touch table [2], mobile based applications [3] and games [4] to address these problems. However, one of the major problems with these solutions and evaluations is that they are mainly performed in the developing countries and a little attention has been paid on the children of developing countries. Recent research has shown that Autism is a severe problem in many developing countries particularly in South Asia.

In this paper, we discuss the design and evaluation of a collaborative computer game "Guess Who" which was used as a tool to encourage social interaction in children with ASD. Games are interactive, engaging, and entertaining but they are no longer just used as a tool for entertainment. Researchers have used them for several serious purposes for instance; education, learning, and helping people with special needs. SIDES [2] is a good example of a tabletop computer game which is designed for developing social skills in individuals with Asperger Syndrome. Another good and

K. Miesenberger et al. (Eds.): ICCHP 2014, Part I, LNCS 8547, pp. 513–516, 2014.

recent example is open autism software based games on tablet devices, which have been used to encourage social interaction in autistic children [3]. In addition, there are several other mobile apps [5] and games [4] which have been used to encourage face to face interaction among these children.

2   Guess Who? Game and Its Objectives

Guess Who? is a simple board game in which each player hides one card from the deck of 24 cards. Each player takes turn to ask questions about card properties to guess the card selected by their opponent. The player, who guesses the first, wins the game. We developed a computer version of the Guess Who? board game. The whole functionality of the game was replicated using two windows tablets used by two players and connected via the Internet. It has also been described as a useful tool for helping autistic children in recognizing and describing different faces [6]. In this study, we used both manual and computer version of the 'Guess Who?' game with high functioning autistic children as a tool or a platform to evaluate our hypothesis 1) Can we encourage these children to work collaboratively in an interactive environment, 2) Can we improve their social and communication skills by assuring social interaction among them during the game play.

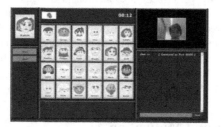

Fig. 1. "Guess who?" Game

3   Evaluation of Guess Who? Game

We designed a longitudinal evaluation study of six weeks to evaluate our hypothesis. The game was evaluated with a group of 8 children aged between 8 to 12 years at a school in Lahore, Pakistan. In the first round of evaluations, we performed 'Super Skills Profile for Social Discovery' questionnaire with all children to know their current state. The reason behind evaluating paper and computer versions was to compare the effectiveness of both platforms and to see if the computer platform had any added value. Children played both manual and computer version of the game for six weeks. We performed a within-subject study with the game. Each team consisted of two children and his/her teacher. The children and their teacher sat in front of each other. Teachers facilitated and continued to help these children in playing the game when required. Each session lasted between 25 to 30 minutes. We recorded the weekly feedback of teachers about their observation on child's behavior. We analyzed their feedback to measure the usability and impact of our game. In addition, all of the evaluation sessions were video tapped. We also performed video analysis for all sessions to measure the amount of social communication among these children.

4   Evaluation Results

We discuss qualitative results based on the weekly feedback of parents and results generated from the video analysis. Initially children were able to hide the cards with the help of their teachers. They used to repeat questions asked by their teachers or opponents during the game play. On average, 4 to 8 sentences were uttered per minute during the game play. Children were able to show verbal interaction by saying sentences during their opponents' turn. They were also pointing their fingers to different cards. Overall, children asked and repeated questions and answers with prompts like "Is he male?", "Yes, he is male", "He has brown eyes". Previous research has shown that this kind of a repeating, prompting and recognizing behavior is very important for the development of communication skills of autistic children [3], [5]. Children also showed progress with every passing week. They were able to distinguish between male and female card characters more easily. Their understanding of different cards' properties (e.g. person with a hat, smiling character, etc.) was also improved. From the third week, most of the time children were able to ask questions without prompt for both app and no app of the game. Teachers also noticed this positive changed in their behavior and reported, "He been able to recognize the properties of the cards."

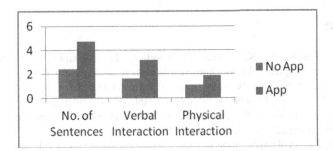

Fig. 2. X-axis represents the mean value of all children; y-axis represents the minimum and maximum value parameters for no of sentences, verbal interaction, and Physical Interaction per minute for app and no app

The videos were coded for the following parameters: no of sentences, verbal interaction, supportive comments, discouraging comments, and physical interaction. All of these parameters were coded as numbers. The coding was performed by two researchers. One of them did not participate in the evaluation process. We transcribed all the sessions. All of the video were of different length, so we normalized the occurrence of above mentioned parameters per minute. We tested whether the data was normally distributed using Kolmogorov-Smirnov's (K-S) test. If normal distribution was found, we compared sessions with manual and computer versions using paired t-test. The results showed statistically significant difference between manual and computer version of the game for no of sentences ($p < .001$), verbal interactions ($p < 0.01$) and physical interactions ($p < 0.01$). The results are showed in figure 2. Children were more engaged, used more sentences to communicate and showed much stronger physical interaction while playing using the computer version as compared to the manual version. The results also showed that the number of sentences spoken, verbal interactions and physical interactions also significantly increased over every week. However, there were no differences found for supportive and discouraging comments.

5   Conclusion and Future Work

In general, we conclude that "Guess who?" game proved to be a useful tool for initiating collaboration among children. It was also able to encourage them to socialize and communicate with their peers. Over the weeks, their communication skills improved slowly but steadily. Overall, the evaluation results were promising; the school also requested a copy of the game and they are also using it at the school on a regular basis. To the best of our knowledge, this is the first study of such kind in Pakistan that has attempted to improve the communication skills of autistic children in Pakistan using novel games and in future, we intend to design more card decks for teaching children about different emotional expressions and social behaviors in detail. We also plan to use the one player version of the game where children can play against the computer.

References

1. Davis, M., Dautenhahn, K., Nehaniv, C., Powell, S.: Towards an interactive system eliciting narrative comprehension in children with autism: A longitudinal study. In: Designing accessible technology, pp. 101–114. Springer, London (2006)
2. Piper, A.M., et al.: SIDES: a cooperative tabletop computer game for social skills development. In: Proceedings of the 2006 20th Anniversary Conference on Computer Supported Cooperative Work. ACM (2006)
3. Hourcade, J.P., et al.: Evaluation of tablet apps to encourage social interaction in children with autism spectrum disorders. In: Proceedings of the 2013 ACM Annual Conference on Human Factors in Computing Systems. ACM (2013)
4. Sampath, H., Indurkhya, B., Sivaswamy, J.: A communication system on smart phones and tablets for non-verbal children with autism. In: Miesenberger, K., Karshmer, A., Penaz, P., Zagler, W. (eds.) ICCHP 2012, Part II. LNCS, vol. 7383, pp. 323–330. Springer, Heidelberg (2012)
5. Venkatesh, S., et al.: TOBY: early intervention in autism through technology. In: Proceedings of the SIGCHI Conference on Human Factors in Computing Systems. ACM (2013)
6. 20 Best Social Games for Children With Autism, Aspergers, ADHD, http://autismsd.com/20-best-social-games-for-children-with-autism-aspergers-adhd/ (accessed December 25, 2013)

Access to Mathematics, Science and Music
Introduction to the Special Thematic Session

Arthur I. Karshmer

University of San Francisco, San Francisco, USA
akarshmer@usfca.edu

Abstract. Mathematics and related subjects are the most difficult disabilities to design and develop helping tools in the domain of assistive technologies. In the current session we will present 17 short and long papers that deal directly the problems associated with math, science and music for the blind and visually impaired. While these three areas seem a bit disparate, they really are in close proximity to each other and the attention of our special session.

Keywords: Mathematics, Music, Blindness.

1 Introduction

Math, science and music are three areas of life that require special languages that are not easily understandable to those with vision impairments. The basic problem in these domains is the fact that their languages are two dimensional while Braille and other notations for the blind are strictly linear. Being linear implies that Braille cannot express these notations in a manner that is directly manipulated by the user. The solutions to these issues normally require a complex representation delivered in what is called a content sensitive language. Content sensitive languages, present yet another set of problems to the blind.

2 What's in Our Session

This year, ICCHP has received an interesting collection of new ideas for our special thematic session, as well as further reporting of improvements to ideas presented in the past. Additionally we have seen a set of authors and institutions new to participation in ICCHP. This is a very positive sign for the future of ICCHP and the world of improving the lives of the disabled. Some of the papers presented will be in the following domains

1. Using gestures in math education
2. Intelligent tutoring in math
3. Nemeth code in 8 dot Braille
4. Auditory functions in math functions and tables
5. The Markdown system

K. Miesenberger et al. (Eds.): ICCHP 2014, Part I, LNCS 8547, pp. 517–518, 2014.
© Springer International Publishing Switzerland 2014

6. Graph theory algorithms and the blind
7. Braille and accessible e-textbooks
8. MathMelodies
9. Effectiveness of computer assisted instruction
10. Learning linear algebra by the blind
11. The LEAN system for math learning
12. SVGPlott audio tactile math
13. A Music presentation system
14. Free tools to help the blind
15. Multi modal interface for learning algebra
16. Performance metrics and their ability to render mathematics

These papers, the hallway chats and QandA sessions look very interesting this year. Please come to join us in a lively and interesting session. You will surely walk away with new ideas as well as adding new and interesting concepts to the rest of the group.

Intelligent Tutoring Math Platform Accessible for Visually Impaired People

Piotr Brzoza and Michał Maćkowski

Silesian University of Technology, Gliwice, Poland
{piotr.brzoza,michal.mackowski}@polsl.pl

Abstract. Nowadays there are many problems with the access to scientific and educational materials for visually impaired people. It especially refers to learning mathematic. Only a small number of such materials is published in a form accessible for blind and low vision people. Particularly, it limits significantly disabled persons to participate in education research and engineering works in many science and technology disciplines. Fortunately new technological solutions, such as e-learning become more and more popular, and many universities use it to improve educational offer and create new possibilities for disabled people. However, in many cases it may cause the problems with accessibility. The article presents developed, intelligent, interactive tutoring platform for math teaching. Currently, the platform is used in the process of education of students from Faculty of Mathematics at Silesian University of Technology, and disabled students from others faculties of the University. The research results clearly indicate the improvement of learning quality by visually impaired people, and also confirm the efficacy of designed rules for adapting mathematical formulas to visually impaired people needs.

Keywords: e-Learning, Mathematics, Accessibility, Visual Impaired.

1   Introduction

Visually impaired people have limited access to scientific and educational materials. Only a few of them are published in alternative form accessible for blind and low vision people. Particularly, it limits significantly disabled persons to participate in education research and engineering works in many science and technology disciplines. Nowadays, more and more Universities use e-learning platforms to improve educational offers. It creates new possibilities for people with disabilities but, at the same time may cause accessibility problems.

The enormous obstacle in learning mathematic by visually impaired people is the shortage of mathematic course books published in Braille form. It is mainly due to the high cost of adaptation and complexity of this process. What is more, mathematical Braille notations are differentiated depending on the country, which makes it difficult to use foreign mathematical books in Braille form.

Authors of works [1,2] present the developed Lambda system, which offers the alternative presentation of mathematical formulas on Braille displays, edition by visually

K. Miesenberger et al. (Eds.): ICCHP 2014, Part I, LNCS 8547, pp. 519–524, 2014.
© Springer International Publishing Switzerland 2014

impaired people and graphic presentation on computers display. The only disadvantages of the presented solution are the proposed 8- points Braille mathematical notation which vary from the nationals Braille mathematical notations, and the high cost of Braille monitor. The other solution presented in papers [3,4,5] is the mathematical extension of Daisy standard allowing Daisy browsers the alternative presentation of mathematical formulas.

Presented solutions of accessibility to mathematical formulas are not applied in interactive alternative presentation of mathematical formulas during exercise solving. The further part of the paper presents the developed and implemented platform for interactive math learning suited to the needs of visually impaired people.

2   Problem-Oriented Interactive Learning of Mathematics

The project ForMath – intelligent tutoring system in mathematics aims to create an interactive platform for supporting education in mathematics. It can be used by technical students to self-study of selected fields of mathematics and expanding knowledge in these fields. The platform is primarily a collection of exercises, in which there is possibility to appeal to theory (e-books), or get hints on how to solve a specific problem (at any stage of solving the exercise). It contains exercises of varying difficulty within different branches of mathematics. Errors and mistakes made by students are registered, analyzed and then are the basis for preparing individual lists of exercises tailored to the student's level of knowledge. In case of repeated difficulties the student is directed to the remedial exercises sessions.

During the project pedagogical and cognitive research are conducted, which help to choose the best learning solutions. This platform exploits elements of the constructivist theory of learning that focuses on activation and motivation the student and application of the principle 'the more we know, the more we can learn' by adjusting the difficulty level to the level of knowledge of the learner, and gradation the difficulty of subsequent exercises.

3   Platform Implementation

To implement the developed platform LaTeX and PHP languages were used. Student has to login to the platform and can choose a problem to learn. After some sessions, system would be able to propose some problems. To make it possible, the platform must register the student activity. A solution of a problem (exercise) is divided into screens. Each screen presented to a student contains an exercise and some possible actions to make. The user can make some decisions: choose some expression from a list or write some number or text to an input field. After that, the student can choose an action by clicking on a button. Each button is connected to one or more screens and moving to the next screen depends on the user decision. Figure 1 presents the example of the exercise from 4Math platform. In this case student has to choose the correct solution (integral function) from the proposed list of solutions. After selected it, the student press the Next button. If the selection is correct, the exercise is finished, and in other situation the platform helps student to resolve the problem by providing guidance, theorems and math definitions.

So the solution can be described as a graph, and the student is moving through that graph, choosing a path. Of course, there are some terminal screens, and after reaching these screens student can move to another exercise or log out.

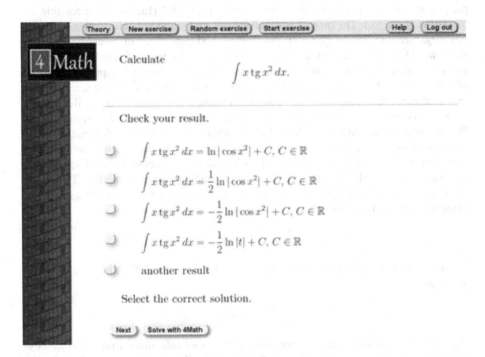

Fig. 1. The example of exercise screen which allows user to select the right integral function (the exercise solution)

Teachers give the access code to the platform for theirs students. So after logging into the platform student's activity is saved into data base. Student can choose a group of problems or system can propose new problem to solve automatically. After the decision is made, the PHP file with the start page is presented to a student. Then the user has to solve the problem or can go to page with tips leading to solution of the problem. After clicking a button, the platform analyse the user decision and presents the new screen with the next part of the exercise.

On each screen there are some standard buttons. Log out button, which end the session, theory button to present contents of a problem to student on each screen. Also a new exercise button to break solution of current problem and jump to another one.

All mathematical exercises available on the platform were prepared by experienced math teachers who have been teaching students from different technical university faculties. Teachers defined classes of typical errors made by students during resolving math exercises. Based on this grouped of errors, the scenarios of exercise resolving were prepared. Such interactive exercises give the opportunity to exam of student's math knowledge. The platform implement the intelligent algorithms for automatic assessment of mathematics understanding by students and selecting of new exercises which allow to improve student's math knowledge.

4   Platform Accessibility

The concept of alternative presentation of mathematical formulas based on results of previously conducted European research project EUAIN (European Accessible Information Network). The project was carried out by Institute of Informatics, universities, organizations for people with disabilities, and publishers of printed and digital materials. One of the main project objectives was development of standards for accessibility adaptation materials to the needs of impaired people. In this project, Institute of Informatics carried out a research referring to an alternative access to scientific and technical materials, which contain structural information (tables, schemas, diagrams).

At the beginning of the research the common used mathematical terminology for Polish language was analyzed. Next, the examples of basic and complex mathematical expressions from various areas of mathematics were prepared. All mathematical formulas were consulted with mathematicians and math teachers in terms of appropriate reading, in order to design the principles for their alternative presentation. The results of preliminary research indicate diverse (ambiguous) way of vocal reading of mathematical formulas by various people. For examples the equation:

$$\frac{1+x}{1-2x} + 3 = 10 \tag{1}$$

Is read: *"fraction nominator 1 + x denominator 1 − 2x + 3 = 10"* and can be misinterpreted as:

$$\frac{1+x}{1-2x+3} = 10 \tag{2}$$

The above verbal notation does not convey the exact information on the content of denominator, hence it is insufficient for understanding the expression by visually impaired person. Thus, it is necessary to enclose an additional information about the end of a fraction, e.g.: *"fraction nominator 1 + x denominator 1 − 2x end of fraction + 3 = 10"*. The presented way of reading aloud the expression ensures its correct analysis and understanding by visually impaired person.

In many languages there are no precisely specified rules for reading mathematical formulas. Understanding mathematical formulas being read aloud, requires the access to their visual presentation. For clearly understanding the formulas by visually impaired people, it is necessary to design a set of rules used for describing the structure of formulas. It can be done by defining additional vocabulary, e.g. fraction, end of fraction, end of power, etc.

In the following phase of the research the exemplary mathematical expressions, described according to defined rules were read to the visually impaired persons with a different level of knowledge of mathematics. The results confirmed the high level of understanding the mathematical formulas and their structures.

The alternative descriptions of entirely formulas included in exercises on Intelligent Tutoring Math Platform were prepared according to designed principles. For example the alternative accessible presentation of equations (possible solutions) in Figure 1 is as follow:

- Proposal 1

$$\int x \, tgx^2 \, dx = \ln|cosx^2| + C \qquad C \in R \tag{3}$$

"Integral of x tangents of x power 2 end of power dx = natural logarithm of absolute value of cosines of x power 2 end of power end of absolute value end of natural logarithm + C, C is an element of the set R"

- Proposal 2

$$\int x \, tgx^2 \, dx = \frac{1}{2}\ln|cosx^2| + C \qquad C \in R \tag{4}$$

"Integral of x tangents of x power 2 end of power dx = fraction nominator 1 denominator 2 end of fraction natural logarithm of absolute value of cosines of x power 2 end of power end of absolute value end of natural logarithm + C, C is an element of the set R"

- Proposal 3

$$\int x \, tgx^2 \, dx = -\frac{1}{2}\ln|cosx^2| + C \qquad C \in R \tag{5}$$

"Integral of x tangents of x power 2 end of power dx = - fraction nominator 1 denominator 2 end of fraction natural logarithm of absolute value of cosines of x power 2 end of power end of absolute value end of natural logarithm + C, C is an element of the set R"

- Proposal 4

$$\int x \, tgx^2 \, dx = -\frac{1}{2}\ln|t| + C \qquad C \in R \tag{6}$$

"Integral of x tangents of x power 2 end of power dx = - fraction nominator 1 denominator 2 end of fraction natural logarithm of absolute value of t end of absolute value end of natural logarithm + C, C is an element of the set R"

The prepared descriptions of formulas can be read by visually impaired people, who use screen readers, such as Jaws or Window-Eyes. For better understanding the mathematical formulas, their descriptions can be read interactively by visually impaired users. The alternative description of mathematical formulas and interactive elements of user interface for each exercises is stored in XML files that describe the logical structure of all screens representing mathematical exercises.

Additional, alternative description of mathematical formulas does not influence the appearance of exercise screens, but it is accessible to screen reader programs by hiding the descriptions behind the screen thanks to the use of CSS (Cascading Style Sheets).

5 Summary

The research was conducted with cooperation of visually impaired university students and pupils from schools for visually impaired people. The exercises were also consulted with teachers of such students. Thanks to the platform application, visually impaired students are provided with single-handed, interactive exercises solving. It increases their level of mathematical knowledge, and can be reflected on the improvement of learning opportunities in the fields of engineering.

Currently, the platform is used in the process of education of students from Faculty of Mathematics at Silesian University of Technology, and disabled students from others faculties of the University. The platform includes hundreds of exercises from various branches of mathematics with varying degrees of difficulty, of which about 30% has been adapted for visually impaired people. In the future it is intended to automate the process of adapting new exercises and design new rules for exercises with graphical elements such as charts and diagrams.

The research results clearly indicate the improvement of learning quality by visually impaired people, and also confirm the efficacy of designed rules for adapting mathematical formulas. Therefore, it is planned to automate the process of translating the mathematical formulas written in LaTeX, into their alternative presentation adapted for visually impaired people, as well as developing additional rules for alternatives description of mathematical formulas dedicated to visually impaired students with a good knowledge of mathematics. What is more, for exercises including complex graphic elements a special files will be prepare in order to enable preparation of tactile pictures that can be printed on braille printer.

Acknowledgments. This work was supported by the European Union from the European Social Fund (grant agreement number: UDA-POKL.04.01.01-00-106/09).

References

1. Nicotra, G., Bertoni, G., Bortolazzi, E., Formenti, L.: Innovative Methods for Accessing Mathematics by Visually Impaired Users. In: Miesenberger, K., Klaus, J., Zagler, W., Karshmer, A. (eds.) ICCHP 2010, Part II. LNCS, vol. 6180, pp. 423–430. Springer, Heidelberg (2010)
2. Bernareggi, C.: Non-sequential Mathematical Notations in the LAMBDA System. In: Miesenberger, K., Klaus, J., Zagler, W., Karshmer, A. (eds.) ICCHP 2010, Part II. LNCS, vol. 6180, pp. 389–395. Springer, Heidelberg (2010)
3. Brzoza, P., Gardner, J.A., Soiffer, N.: Life Cycle of a DAISY Book with Math: From Authoring to Players. In: Conference Technology and Persons with Disabilities (CSUN 2008), Los Angeles, USA (2008)
4. Brzoza, P.: Multimedia MathReader for Daisy Books. In: Miesenberger, K., Klaus, J., Zagler, W.L., Karshmer, A.I. (eds.) ICCHP 2008. LNCS, vol. 5105, pp. 875–878. Springer, Heidelberg (2008)
5. Fitzpatrick, D.: Mathematics: How and What to Speak. In: Miesenberger, K., Klaus, J., Zagler, W.L., Karshmer, A.I. (eds.) ICCHP 2006. LNCS, vol. 4061, pp. 1199–1206. Springer, Heidelberg (2006)

Gesture-Based Browsing of Mathematics

Shereen El Bedewy, Klaus Miesenberger, and Bernhard Stöger

Institute of Integrated Study, Johannes Kepler University Linz, Linz, Austria
shereen_elbedewy@hotmail.com,
{k.miesenberger,bernhard.stoeger}@jku.at

Abstract. This paper is introducing a new concept which is combining gestures and speech in applications to help people navigate through Mathematica notebooks. The application can be used by all people, but it is targeting visually impaired people specifically. On the basis of the $1 gesture recognition algorithm our definition of gestures started and advanced to include the enhancements that took place in the $1 gesture recognition itself. The prototype system allows users to navigate through the Mathematica notebooks on the basis of the tree structure receiving speech as an output. Finally the evaluation and the conclusion that sums the basic concept and the user feedback is also provided in this content.

Keywords: Mathematics, Mathematica Notebooks, Touch Gestures, Visually Impaired People, Speech Output, Gesture Recognizers.

1 Introduction

Mathematics plays an important role not only in our educational life but also in our daily life. Therefore people try to make mathematical content accessible in an easy way. On one hand mathematical representation is always assisted by visual aids as drawings and notes which illustrate the main content as geometrical figures (lines, curves), graphical notes (strokes, underlines, highlighting some parts of the material or links between different terms). Moreover, mathematical functions or equations are usually displayed in two dimensions, which help the reader to convey the general structure of the formula. [1] On the other hand, in order to ease the mathematical accessibility people also considered the Software tools, as Matlab, Mathematica and R. Which help people perform the mathematical tasks and their representation in an advanced clear way. In both cases either considering paper-pen or software in accessing math, one can notice the fact that the sight plays an important factor in providing an understanding of the mathematical expressions. The reader can perceive the structure of an expression, localize its elements, and access each of these elements by a deep look into any mathematical expression. After considering the importance of sight in accessing the mathematical content, let us have a look on the case of its absence. Visually impaired people face great challenge in dealing with complex mathematical content. Therefore they have to rely on other communication channels that are available to convey the mathematical contents as audio and tactile.[2] One

K. Miesenberger et al. (Eds.): ICCHP 2014, Part I, LNCS 8547, pp. 525–532, 2014.
© Springer International Publishing Switzerland 2014

example for the audio channel is speech and for the tactile channel is Braille. But both speech and Braille are basically linear, which means that formulas need to be linearized and in most cases this linearization generates a much longer representation, expressions cannot be presented in two dimensions and the immediate access to the structure of the mathematical expression is lost. [3] Sometimes an initial scan of the equation is recommended, as this allows the readers to imagine the representation of the equation structure, followed by a detailed imagination when moving from an element to another. This would overcome the difficulty blind people face when they hear scientific content with equations represented in a strictly linear form.

2   State of the Art

Many projects and applications tried to combine tactile and audio to help the visually impaired people. Their main aim is to support the work of blind users, facilitating their understanding and helping them to carry out calculations. The first example, Audio System for Technical Reading (ASTER) system aims to produce accurate renderings of documents. ASTER system provides mechanisms to control the multiple ways of the audio presentation. [1] The second example, the Maths Genie is a formula browser that facilitates understanding formulas using voice.[4] The third example, Lambda is a mathematical reading and writing system that supports the Braille and is designed for blind students. [3][5] The fourth example, Infty is an editor which allows people with and without visual disabilities to share the same technical content through three main modules, which are InftyReader, InftyEditor and ChattyInfty.[2]

3   Specification of the System

The approach introduced in this paper relies on tactile "gestures" as an input mode from the user and audio as an output mode to the user. The main aim of the application is to build an interface to accept gestures from the users and according to these gestures, the user will be able to navigate through the Mathematica notebooks. The Mathematica notebooks could hold any type of cells (text, proofs, mathematical expressions and equations). A combined set of cells is simply the structure of the Mathematica notebook. The application supports navigating through existing notebooks and exploring their content. The definition of gestures in this content is a special motion by one finger on a touch slate to indicate a shape, based on each shape an action will be performed. One of our main concerns was to minimize the number of gestures used to make the memorization processes easier for the users. The hypothesis question we are asking is: Can blind people use gestures for browsing mathematical content?

3.1   Mathematica as a Choice

As Mathematica is our main program we are using and we are interested in exploring its notebooks. Knowing that it is a high-level programming language, this was the main reason behind implementing our application and its programming phase using Mathematica and make great use of all its capabilities. Moreover writing the main code and implementation in a Mathematica notebook will require no external link to the kernel. The style Mathematica notebooks is using to display mathematical content is the tree based technique. This way of illustration works better for blind people than the linear Braille display technique, because it preserves the structure of the mathematical contents, decreases the representation space and prevents the effort of reading math in a linear fashion. This is reflected in our implementation, how blind users were able to traverse mathematical content in a tree form than a linear form.

3.2   The GBM System

The GBM (Gesture Based Browsing of Mathematics) system is well developed as a prototype system. The state of the art of this paper is not only in providing a new access to blind people, which is gestures and speech but also in the gesture detection algorithm itself. Allowing $1 algorithm to detect horizontal, vertical and diagonal lines is a fresh new feature which is discussed in the coming sections in details.

The system starts as the user initiates the interaction by performing any gesture from the defined ones on the touch slate which is in the current state the touch pad embedded in any laptop. Then this gesture is read into a notebook defined as the "Main Program" it holds all the programming of the system and it translates this gesture into an action, sends this action to the Mathematica kernel through the link between the notebooks and the kernel known as "MathLink". The kernel performs this action on the Notebook the user chose to interact with, then the output of the performed action is spoken out loud to the user. As we can notice everything is implemented and runs in Mathematica, the advantages of this approach is obvious in its speed and the quick speech response to any gesture the user enters. The system has two modes, the first mode is the "Practice Mode", it is activated as the user presses on the button "P", it is designed specially to help starting users to get to know the GBM system and practice the gestures and know their responses. The second mode is the "Interaction Mode", it is activated as the user presses on the button "I", it is the real mode where all the gestures perform actions and the user starts the real navigation and an exciting trip into the notebook. The gestures are defined in the points below given the "Gesture Name, Symbol, Abbreviation and Action" respectively in each point.

- Left Square Bracket → [→LSqB →Go to the next neighboring left child on the same level of the tree.
- Right Square Bracket →] →RSqB →Go to the next neighboring right child on the same level of the tree.
- Diagonal Right Line → \ → DRL →Go to the outermost right child of the current node.
- Diagonal Left Line →/ →DLL →Go to the outermost left child of the current node.

- Vertical Line → |→VL →Go to a level upward in the tree.
- Horizontal Line → — →HL →Explore the current node of the tree.

4 Implementation

The approach used in this paper is based on "$1 Algorithm for Gesture Recognition". The simplicity of $1 algorithm is obvious in the shapes selection as geometrical basic shapes, for example as circles, triangles, square shapes and brackets.[6] One can notice the advantages of $1 algorithm, as it is invariant to rotation, scaling and translation. Invariance means that the gesture doesn't get affected by the transformations applied on it. Therefore $1 doesn't require any prior feature selection it is very flexible to transformations and can accept any change. Above all it results in a very high percentage recognition rate. $1 algorithm restricts the focus of the user to uni-stroke movement which means the user moves one hand with gentle pressure over a surface typically once; these are defined as gestures that unfold over time. Some of the gestures supported by $1 algorithm and used in this project are "Caret == ∧" , "Left Square Bracket == [" and "Right Square Bracket ==]" shapes. The candidate points are then sampled at a rate determined by the sensing hardware which is laptop touch-pads in our case. By defining a list of templates $\{T_1, \ldots, T_n\}$, one should try to find a perfect match to the gesture entered by the user from this list. This is considered a challenge in the recognition process because due to the fact that human nature is different, some people draw gestures quickly and others draw them slowly which results in different number of points. People have different sizes of fingers which result in different sizes of gestures.

4.1 The $1 Algorithm

The recognition proccess follows the steps of the $1 algorithm:

1. *Resampling:* First, all the gestures should be resampled to overcome the movement speed variance from one user to another; this challenge will affect the number of input points in the gesture. Therefore to make gestures comparable with each other all gestures are resampled to contain 60 points.
2. *Rotation:* Second, all the gestures should be rotated to allow the two lists of points being compared, to best align on each other.
3. *Scaling and Translation:* Third, all the gestures should be scaled in a non-uniform fashion to acquire same boundaries, followed by a translation to a reference point.
4. *Optimal Angle and Best Score:* Fourth, is to find the optimal angle and the best score between the entered gesture and the list of stored templates. At this point the real recognition takes place where an entered gesture is compared to each stored template T_i in order to find the average distance between the set of points. The least average distance to the entered gesture is considered the best match of the recognition process.

Although $1 algorithm results in high precision recognition though it has some limitations, one of these limitations which we are trying to enhance is that $1 algorithm includes 2D space only no 1D or 3D space are recognizable. And that $1 algorithm cannot differentiate between shapes that differ in orientations, aspect ratios, or locations. For instance, to differentiate between squares and rectangles, circles and ovals, or directions as arrows directed upward or downward is not possible. For example when the users requested to draw gestures as horizontal and vertical lines, these gestures had to be scaled in a non-uniform fashion and due to the fact that lines run in the 1D spaces categorization, this affected the recognition process. And the system couldn't distinguish between the direction of the line or its orientation. This brings us to the approach suggested in this paper to overcome the line recognition challenge. We start by defining a new term which is dynamic templates, they are templates that are computed by each entered gesture by the user, not pre-stored in the program as fixed templates like the ones we introduced before [Square Brackets and Caret].[7] The dynamic way helps us to compute the best fitting line between lists of Candidate points. As the user enters a new gesture in the form of a list of points, the function which fits the best line between these points is being invoked and it returns the equation of the best fitted line. We determine from this equation the starting and the ending points of the line by projection. Taking into account the starting and ending points of the line we construct a line between these two points, where it has 60 equidistant points. This is to guarantee that the line template we just formed has the same number of points of the entered gesture after running in the resampling process. Afterwords, this template is being stored in the list of templates $\{T_1, \ldots, T_n\}$ and the gesture entered by the user is compared to it and to all the previously stored templates. The least distance between these templates and the gesture is being selected as the best match of the recognition process. If it happened to be that the best match was our template line we just constructed, then we get the angle of this line and decide where it occurs on the Cartesian plane and which line direction it indicates. The only disadvantage of the dynamic template approach is its time consumption and speed limitations, when computing a dynamic template to each entered gesture.

Figure 1, illustrates the range of angles on which one can decide what type of line it is. If the user entered the red dashed line with angle α, therefore the system can recognize the line according to the α location on the Cartesian plane. If α lies in the red region $110° \leq \alpha \leq 160°$ or $290° \leq \alpha \leq 340°$ then it is a diagonal left line. If the α lies in the blue region $20° \leq \alpha \leq 340°$ or $160° \leq \alpha \leq 200°$ then it is a horizontal line. If the α lies in the green region $70° \leq \alpha \leq 110°$ or $250° \leq \alpha \leq 290°$ then it is a vertical line. Finally, if the α lies in the yellow region $20° \leq \alpha \leq 70°$ or $200° \leq \alpha \leq 250°$ then it is a diagonal right line. The case of the red dashed line with angel α, it appears to lie in the last case the yellow region which is a diagonal right line.

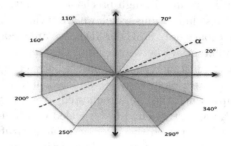

Fig. 1. Range of Angles

At this point the gesture recognition is completed by returning a number indicating which template was chosen, from the template list including the dynamic template we just constructed, and finally according to the returned number a certain action is performed to navigate through the notebook.

4.2   Navigation

Now, how does the navigation take place and what is its structure?

When people open any book, notebook, section or paper usually they like to browse it first, know the sections and the subsections it consists of, know the titles and subtitles and finally they can read it and go through it in details. This way of reading and exploration of the hierarchy before going in details is very beneficial, as it structures the piece of reading in the brain in the same way it is structured in reality. Therefore we divide the program into two main levels, "Higher Level of Interaction" which is the Notebook and "Lower Level of Interaction" which is the Cell.

Higher Level " Notebook Level". The notebook the user chooses and wants to browse can be treated in the form of a tree structure, where the root of the tree is the notebook list with all the cells and the cells are the children of this root. By having a pointer which points to the current position in the notebook tree, this pointer gets updated whenever the position in the notebook changes. Taking into consideration the two levels we are interacting with. The tree structure of the notebook is quite different from that of any other tree, as the notebook tree relies on the pattern matching concept in Mathematica.

Pattern Matching. Each time the user performs an action the current position in the notebook will lie in any of the pattern matching cases. The switch command applies the pattern matching concept, it will compare the current position in the tree and will select one of the cases. In each case the user can perform further actions according to the category the position lies in. Category one is the case of having a list with any number of cells. This case takes place when the notebook pointer points to the root of the notebook. Category two is the case of having a Cell containing another group of any number of cells. Category three is the case of having a single cell with a String type. This string could be an Input/Output or a title, section or subsection form. If the type of the cell is an Input/Output then the user has the option to switch to a cell interaction technique. Otherwise the cell is a title, section or subsection then it is spoken out loud to the user. And finally category four is the base case and an error handling method, it holds the possibility that the notebook pointer ran out of boundaries or if the user wishes to access a child's node where this node happens to be a leaf.

Lower Level "Cell Level". As we want to move from the higher level and go further to lower level to the cell level, as the global variable is assigned a new cell expression, a pointer is initiated to point at the position in the cell and is treated as a tree which traverses its nodes. The gestures that the user can perform in a cell level are the ones defined in the points we mentioned before in the "The GBM System" part, each of these gestures when applied results in its corresponding action in the cell level.

These are the cases the user can perform in both the higher and the lower level of the notebook. Each gesture has a specific meaning and a specific number, the number is sent back to the GBM system when this gesture is performed. Regardless of which level the user is standing at and at which position the pointer is pointing to, these gestures are defined for certain actions.

5 Evaluation and Future Work

The overall GBM system feedback was pleasant, the state of the art was applicable and joining touch gestures to sound feedback turned out to be successful. The gestures that were used were easy to learn and to memorize by the users, adding the lines to the gestures were of a great help as they are easy to draw and to memorize and finally the speech output was satisfying the need. Some of the coming challenges were solved in the first phase of the GBM system and the others will be handled in the future phases:

1) The visually impaired people requested a practice mode to train themselves on the gestures and to memorize the output and action of each before they start the real interaction. Therefore we made this affordable by running the whole system in the practice mode.2)One of the issues that appeared while the users were drawing the gestures is that they accessed the menu bar of Mathematica by mistake. Therefore a solution to this was to let the gesture drawing notebook in a "FullScreen" mode. 3) The initial mouse position is a challenging issue, as after the user draws the gesture he/she becomes lost where the mouse position ended up. A solution to overcome this problem was to provide the user the button "M" which provides the user with the current position of the mouse and guides him/her where to move the mouse in order to initiate a new gesture. As a future work for this issue is to set the mouse position automatically at the outer most left side of the screen once the user ends a gesture, so as to possess the space to draw another gesture.4) To integrate the GBM system with Braille is

a marvelous step that could be applied in the future, then the user will have all the options and possibilities to interact with the GBM system and other systems simultaneously. The users will be able to write/edit to the notebooks, not just reading and navigating through them. 5) A future step could be supporting bigger touch slates to draw the gestures for example as the size of the tablets.

6   Conclusion

In this paper, we undertook a first investigation of the idea of combining touch gestures and speech, which was introduced as a novel concept in the field of mathematics for visually impaired people. We saw its impact in the evaluation phase, how it offered a nice environment for the blind people to navigate through mathematical notebooks and access mathematics in a new fashion. The pros and cons were discussed together with the challenges that appeared during the implementation and testing phases. These challenges opened many doors to the future, such that we are planninbg to extend the system according to the aspects listed in the preceding section.

References

1. Archambault, D.: Non visual access to mathematical contents: State of the art and prospective. In: Proceedings of the WEIMS Conference, pp. 43–52 (2009)
2. Archambault, D., Stoeger, B., Fitzpatrick, D., Miesenberger, K., et al.: Access to scientific content by visually impaired people. Digital Journal of CEPIS (Spanish version was published in Novatica 8(2), 29–42 (2007)
3. Archambault, D., Stoeger, B., Batusic, M., Fahrengruber, C., Miesenberger, K.: Mathematical working environments for the blind: what is needed now? Interaction et usages des modalities non visuelles accessibilities des continues complexes, 36 (2007)
4. Karshmer, A.I., Bledsoe, C., Stanley, P.B.: The architecture of a comprehensive equation browser for the print impaired. In: Miesenberger, K., Klaus, J., Zagler, W.L., Burger, D. (eds.) ICCHP 2004. LNCS, vol. 3118, pp. 614–619. Springer, Heidelberg (2004)
5. Stoeger, B., Miesenberger, K., Batusic, M., Archambault, D.: Multimodal interaction with mathematical formulae: Access, communication and support for blind people in doing mathematics. Interaction et usages des modalités non visuelles, accessibilité des contenus complexes, 48 (2005)
6. Wobbrock, J.O., Wilson, A.D., Li, Y.: Gestures without libraries, toolkits or training: a \$ 1 recognizer for user interface prototypes. In: Proceedings of the 20th Annual ACM Symposium on User Interface Software and Technology, pp. 159–168. ACM (2007)
7. Windsteiger, W.: Personal communication (2013)

Towards the 8-Dot Nemeth Braille Code

Aineias Martos[1,2], Georgios Kouroupetroglou[1],
Vassilis Argyropoulos[2], and Despina Deligiorgi[1]

[1] Speech and Accessibility Lab., National and Kapodistrian University of Athens, Greece
{martos,koupe}@di.uoa.gr, despo@phys.uoa.gr
[2] University of Thessaly, Department of Special Education, Volos, Greece
vassargi@uth.gr

Abstract. In this work, a language-independent design methodology for the systematic development of an 8-dot braille code, has been applied to the Nemeth code. First, we set the design principles: compression, intra-similarity, inter-similarity, unambiguity, consistency and foresight. Then, we follow the Nemeth principles: non enclosure, just in time information, be true to the print, good mnemonics and continuous notation. Finally, we introduce 24 transition rules from 6- to 8-dot Nemeth code. Indicative results of the methodology are also presented.

Keywords: Braille, 8-Dot Braille, Nemeth Code, Assistive Technologies.

1 Introduction

8-dot braille [1,2] has been introduced as an extension to the 6-dot braille for specific tasks where the 63 braille 6-dot cells seem insufficient. The extended 8-dot braille character set, with 255 combinations, adds dots 7 and 8 in the last row. These characters are typically presented through a refreshable braille display. An 8-dot braille code is not meant to substitute the 6-dot braille. A language-independent design methodology for the systematic development of an 8-dot braille code, to be adopted by 6-dot braille readers, have been recently designed and developed by Kacorri and Kouroupetroglou [3]. Nemeth code [4] is a well-known braille system for mathematics and science used not only in North America but also in other countries. In the current study, we present our effort towards the development of an 8-dot Nemeth braille code by adopting the methodology of [3].

2 Methodology and Results

In the first phase, we have applied the following design principles [3]: compression, intra-similarity, inter-similarity, unambiguity, consistency and foresight. Moreover, in this phase, we retained the following set of principles suggested by Nemeth [5]:

- Non enclosure principle: don't put any phantom parentheses or other enclosures into the braille that are not in the print.

K. Miesenberger et al. (Eds.): ICCHP 2014, Part I, LNCS 8547, pp. 533–536, 2014.

- Just in time information principle: give the reader the needed information exactly when it is needed. Don't make him/her have to go looking for it.
- Be true to the print principle: don't make any braille notation that does not correspond to the print notation.
- Good mnemonics principle: give to the reader symbols that are grouped together logically when the print symbols are grouped together logically. Preserve symmetry of notation.
- Continuous notation principle: don't interrupt the reader's reading with letter signs and number signs unless some specific indication is needed.

During the implementation phase, the results from the first phase were taken into account to specify the required transition rules from the 6-dot to the 8-dot Nemeth braille code. Thus, we have introduced the following 24 rules:

1. Retain compatibility with the original 6-dot Nemeth as much as possible.
2. Retain compatibility with ASCII braille where it is possible and it does not abuse rule 1.
3. Use unique symbols borrowed from ASCII braille when it is possible, even changing original Nemeth symbols where it is possible to replace double cell symbols.
4. Use dots 7, 8 or both to get unique symbols or to eliminate double cell symbols.
5. Do not create a specific braille symbol for each representation of the same symbol in ink or screen.
6. Define an open and close symbols to show bold, italics etc. Similar symbols are used in original Nemeth code to denote superscript and subscript.
7. Always use subscript indicators (as in the original Nemeth code) to separate the base of the logarithm.
8. Avoid numeric sign usage. Only lower part numbers are allowed.
9. Allow double cell braille symbols as an exception only when it is impossible to avoid ambiguity with unique 8-dot symbols.
10. Avoid 3 cell braille symbols (allowed in some cases in original Nemeth) by creating at least 2 cell symbols if it is not possible to generate unique 8-dot symbols.
11. Retain language indicators as they are used in original Nemeth code.
12. Retain original Nemeth symbols that contain letters such symbols for section mark paragraph mark etc.
13. Where only dot 4 is used as a prefix in 6-dot Nemeth replace it with dot 8 if it leads to a unique character. If dot 8 leads to an ambiguous character or a clash then try dot 7 or both dots 7 & 8 to avoid ambiguity.
14. If applying rule 13 leads to ambiguous character then retain 6-dot representations or try to apply another rule in order to remove ambiguity.
15. If a decimal dot (.) is used as a prefix in 6-dot Nemeth try first to borrow from ASCII braille to replace the 2 cell symbol.
16. If applying rule 15 leads to ambiguous results or to a clash then try to replace symbol by using dot 7 or 8 or both to get a unique symbol or to avoid ambiguity.
17. Apply rule 15 and 16 in the case dots (4, 5, 6) or ASCII braille (_) is used as a prefix.

18. Use the underline symbol (_) to open bold face. Close bold face with dot 5, like returning to the baseline in the original Nemeth code.
19. Open italic with decimal point. Close with dot 5 similar to returning to the baseline in the original Nemeth.
20. Try the above rules as follows: First, try rules to borrow from ASCII braille. Second, try rules related to dots 7, 8 or both. Third, retain the original Nemeth representation.
21. Treat the comma and the decimal point as numeral symbols in the case a comma or a decimal point is followed by one or more digits.
22. Treat comma and decimal point as punctuation symbols in the case a comma or a decimal point is followed by a letter or space.
23. The dash symbol is retained from the original 6-dot Nemeth and is used as hyphen too. The distinction between its usage as a minus or a hyphen is done by using the appropriate spacing.
24. Use the symbol (4, 5, 6, and 7), borrowed from the 8-dot ASCII braille, as a large dash when it is preceded and followed by a space.

Then, we propose the following subtasks to be followed: (i) apply the transition rules to the existing 6-dot Nemeth braille code; (ii) debug each one rule, e.g., eliminating any errors; (iii) check for consistency between transition rules' results, e.g., ensuring that the application of two or more rules produces no conflicts; and (iv) provide a list of unbounded 8-dot characters available.

Tables 1 and 2 present indicative results of the above methodology in the cases of (6) and (4,5,6) array of the Nemeth symbols respectively.

3   Conclusions

Further work includes: a) application of the above methodology to the whole set of the Nemeth code and b) user evaluation of the resulted 8-dot Nemeth code.

Table 1. Example of 8-dot Nemeth code for the (6) array

Unicode	Symbol	6-dot Nemeth	braille dots	8-dot Nemeth	braille dots	Description
0x0028	(		1,2,3,5,6		1,2,3,5,6	left parenthesis
0x0028	(		6 1,2,3,5,6		1,2,3,5,6,7	enlarged left parenthesis
0x0029	)		2,3,4,5,6		2,3,4,5,6	right parenthesis
0x0029	)		6 2,3,4,5,6		2,3,4,5,6,7	enlarged right parenthesis
0x005B	[		4 1,2,3,5,6		1,2,3,5,6,8	left square bracket
0x005D	]		4 2,3,4,5,6		2,3,4,5,6,8	right square bracket

Table 2. Example of 8-dot Nemeth code for the (4,5,6) array

Unicode	Printed Symbol	6-dot Nemeth	braille dots	8-dot Nemeth	braille dots	Description
0x002E	.		4,5,6 2,5,6		2,5,6,8	full stop
0x002C	,		6		6,8	comma
0x003B	;		2,3		2,3,7	semicolon
0x00AB	«		4,5,6 2,3,6		2,3,6,8	left pointing double angle quotation mark
0x00BB	»		4,5,6 3,5,6		3,5,6,8	right pointing double angle quotation mark
0x0027	'		3		3	apostrophe
0x0021	!		4,5,6 2,3,5		2,3,5,8	exclamation-mark
0x005F	_		4,5,6		4,5,6	under bar
0x003A	:		2,5		2,5,8	colon
0x20AC	€		5 1,5		5 1,5	euro sign
0x0023	#		3,4,5,6		3,4,5,6	number sign
0x00AF	‾		1,5,6		1,5,6	macron

Acknowledgements. This research has been co-financed by the European Union (European Social Fund – ESF) and Greek national funds through the Operational Program "Education and Lifelong Learning" of the National Strategic Reference Framework (NSRF) under the Research Funding Project: "THALIS-University of Macedonia- KAIKOS: Audio and Tactile Access to Knowledge for Individuals with Visual Impairments", MIS 380442.

References

1. ISO/TR 11548-2:2001, 1st ed., Part 2: Communication aids for blind persons–Identifiers, names and assignation to coded character sets for 8-dot Braille characters - Latin alphabet based character sets. International Standards Organization. Zurich, Switzerland (2001)
2. APH: 8-dot Computer Braille Table (2013), http://tech.aph.org
3. Kacorri, H., Kouroupetroglou, G.: Design and Developing Methodology for 8-dot Braille Code Systems. In: Stephanidis, C., Antona, M. (eds.) UAHCI 2013, Part III. LNCS, vol. 8011, pp. 331–340. Springer, Heidelberg (2013)
4. Nemeth, A.: The Nemeth Braille Code for Mathematics and Science Notation, 1972 Revision. American Printing House for the Blind (APH), Louisvillem Kentucky (1972)
5. Nemeth, A.: The Nemeth Code. In: Dixon, J.M. (ed.) Braille: Into the Next Millennium, pp. 120–127. National Library Service for the Blind and Physically Handicapped, Washington, D.C (2001)

AudioFunctions: Eyes-Free Exploration of Mathematical Functions on Tablets

Marzia Taibbi[1], Cristian Bernareggi[1,2], Andrea Gerino[1,2], Dragan Ahmetovic[1], and Sergio Mascetti[1,2]

[1] Dept. of Computer Science, Università degli Studi di Milano, Milano, Italy
[2] EveryWare Technologies, Milano, Italy

Abstract. It is well known that mathematics presents a number of hindrances to visually impaired students. In case of function graphs, for example, several assistive solutions have been proposed to enhance their accessibility. Unfortunately, both hardware tools (e.g., tactile paper) and existing software applications cannot guarantee, at the same time, a clear understanding of the graph and a full autonomous study. In this paper we present *AudioFunctions*, an iPad app that adopts three sonification techniques to convey information about the function graph. Our experimental evaluation, conducted with 7 blind people, clearly highlights that, by using *AudioFunctions*, students have a better understanding of the graph than with tactile paper and existing software solutions.

1 Introduction

Visually impaired students face many difficulties while studying scientific subjects. This is due to the fact that many concepts are harder to understand without their graphical representations (e.g., a graph). In some cases, typical exercises actually require to deal with graphical information (e.g., drawing geometrical symmetries). Mathematics is probably the clearest example and indeed the hindrances of accessing this subject have been extensively studied in the literature [1]. In particular, in this paper we address the problem of rendering functions graphs accessible.

Traditional solutions to this problem include tactile drawings printed by a tactile embosser as well as on swell paper or produced with pen and sheets (e.g., by a Sewell kit). These solutions have some drawbacks. First, these drawings cannot be changed once printed, therefore the whole drawing has to be printed again to correct a mistake. Moreover, direct interaction with tactile drawings (both embossed or on swell paper) is not possible. For example a student who is given the tactile graph of a function cannot draw the symmetric function on the same drawing. Direct interaction is possible with a Sewell kit, but very good manual skills are required. One more drawback of tactile drawings concerns tactile labels (e.g. Braille labels) that are often too large to be embedded in a drawing without overlapping with lines or other labels. For example, a Braille label on the orthocentre of a triangle may easily overlap with the heights.

K. Miesenberger et al. (Eds.): ICCHP 2014, Part I, LNCS 8547, pp. 537–544, 2014.

Software solutions have also been proposed. Among the others we mention mainstream calculus programs that can be used to generate value tables of functions (e.g. Octave, MatLab, Mathematica, etc.) and programs for graph function sonification (e.g. Audio Graphing Calculator [1] and Sonification Sandbox [2]). Value tables are very useful to get quantitative information about the functions. Nonetheless this solution presents many drawbacks. First of all, it takes a long time for a blind student to understand the curve trend. Moreover, since the exploration is basicly sequential (from left to right or from right to left along the abscissa-axis), global features such as symmetries as well as absolute maximum and minimum points can hardly be recognized by a blind student [3]. Some local features, like concavity, are very difficult to understand too.

Sonification programs enable blind students to understand the trend of a curve and the existence of local maximum and minimum points as well as intersections with the abscissa-axis [4]. Nonetheless, no quantitative information is straightforwardly provided by these programs while a blind student is exploring the curve. Hence, it turns out to be very difficult to find out global features depending on quantitative information (e.g. absolute maximum and minimum points) and features depending on exact numeric values (e.g. the coordinates of a given point such as the axes intersection points, the beginning and the end of a given interval, and so on). Moreover, the sound feedback is not enough to convey information about the asymptotic behaviour of a function (e.g. to find out an horizontal asymptote) and concavity in a given interval. One more drawback concerns the difficulty for a blind student to understand mutual relations between two distant points or between distinct portions of a curve (e.g. it is very hard to find out whether three points are on the same line or to find out symmetries).

In this paper we present *AudioFunctions*, an iPad prototype that makes it possible to overcome the problems highlighted above and that highly increases the independence of the student as well as the comprehension of the functions graphs. *AudioFunctions* presents two major improvements with respect to existing software solutions. First, being a tablet application, it benefits from the non-mediated interaction, which is typical of touchscreen devices. This in turns makes it possible to design an interaction paradigm that is based on the use of proprioception. Indeed, the second improvement consists in a set of three techniques to explore a function graph. Two of these techniques highly rely on proprioception.

We show experimentally that *AudioFunctions* tremendously improves, with respect to the other software solutions, the effectiveness of the application in terms of how clearly the user understands a function graph. Actually, *AudioFunctions* is so accurate that the testing users better recognized the function's properties with it (after five minutes of training only) rather than with tactile drawings (that every tester was well trained to use). Clearly *AudioFunctions* also has the great advantage, with respect to tactile drawings, to allow the user to study function graphs in total autonomy.

The remainder of this paper is organized as follows: in Section 2 we describe in more details the existing solutions (both hardware and software). In Section 3 we describe *AudioFunctions* and, in particular, the three techniques to explore a function graph. Our experimental evaluation is presented in Section 4 while Section 5 concludes the paper.

2 Related Work

The problem of function graphs accessibility for blind and sight impaired people has been tackled with a number of ICT solutions in the field of assistive technology for education. These solutions can be grouped in four categories: embossing tactile drawings, understanding graphs through query languages, sonification of function graphs and haptic tools for exploring diagrams.

Techniques for embossing graphs on paper have been improved over the years [1]. Indeed, at present, there are many tools to create and emboss high quality graphs on paper [5]. Nonetheless, some drawbacks still exist. First, tactile graphs cannot be edited once embossed, so the mistakes cannot be corrected and students cannot draw on the same graphs (e.g. to draw symmetric curves). In addition, Braille labels can easily overlap with lines or other labels, so they must be very short and in many situations even one letter Braille labels render difficult graph understanding [6].

The second category of techniques concerns understanding graphs through query languages. The student can understand the properties of a graph by querying information to a software application through a formal language (e.g. a calculus program such as Mathematica or Matlab) or through natural language [7]. These techniques do not provide a global understanding of the graph trend and require the student to know concepts of mathematical calculus even while exploring function graphs for the first time (e.g. what is a maximum, a minimum, concavity, etc.).

The use of sonification to enable sight impaired people to access function graphs has been studied through Audio Graphing Calculator [1] and Sonification Sandbox [2] applications. These sonification programs provide a sound description of a function graph by using simple sound [1] and midi sound [2]. Sonification enables blind students to understand the trend of the graph and relevant points such as maxima, minima and intersections [4]. Unfortunately, no quantitative information is straightforwardly provided by these programs while a blind student is exploring the curve. Moreover, the sound feedback is not enough to convey information about the asymptotic behaviour of a function (e.g. to find out an horizontal asymptote) and concavity in a given interval. One more drawback concerns the difficulty for a blind student to understand mutual relations between two distant points or between distinct portions of a curve (e.g. it is very hard to find out whether three points are on the same line or to find out symmetries).

Finally, haptic and audio-haptic systems have also been proposed to make possible non-visual graph exploration and manipulation [8]. The main advantage of these systems consists in the ability of touching and manipulating the graph. Moreover, guided exploration is also possible. The hand of the student is guided by the arm of an haptic device (e.g. the Phantom) along the curve. Unfortunately, haptic devices are still very expensive. Moreover, the workspace is limited (about 15 by 15 cm), so graphs with many details can be hardly understandable.

3   The *AudioFunctions* Prototype

The use of *AudioFunctions* can be divided in two main activities: the specification of the function expression as well as of its drawing properties and the function graph exploration.

3.1   Specification of Function Expression and Drawing Properties

To specify a function expression, a user can choose a template and then edit it (see Figure 1(a)). The template can be chosen from the list of "default" expressions (i.e., a pre-defined set of common functions, like $y = x$, $y = x^2$ or $y = sin(x)$) or from the list of recently used expressions, as they were edited by the user (in Figure 1(a) the list of recently used expressions is hidden by the keyboard). To edit the function expression, *AudioFunctions* presents an ad-hoc keyboard, that is similar to a calculator keyboard and that contains keys for the digits and for the most common arithmetic and trigonometric operators.

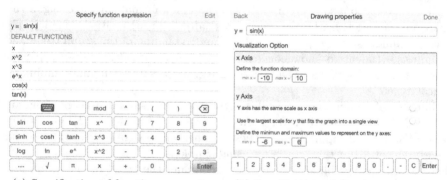

(a) Specification of function expression   (b) Specification of drawing properties

Fig. 1. Specification of the function expression and its drawing properties

The function drawing properties (see Figure 1(b)) include options to define the domain and the scale on the two axes. With the first option, the user can set the function domain in terms of the minimum and maximum values of x to be represented. The second property is a boolean value indicating if the y axis should have the same scale as the x axis. If this property is set to "true" (the default value) then the next two options are disabled. In case this property is set to "false", with the third option the user can choose to automatically scale the

y axis, which means that *AudioFunctions* chooses the largest scale for the y axis such that the function graph fits in the screen. If "automatic scale" is disabled, then the user can manually choose the scale for the y axis, by indicating the minimum and maximum values to represent on the y axis.

3.2   Function Graph Exploration

The exploration of the function graph supports three "exploration modes" (see Figure 2). The first one, that we call "non interactive", is analogous to the solution proposed in Audio Graph Calculator and Sonification Sandbox: by using a "double two finger tap" gesture[1] *AudioFunctions* starts playing the function sonification, which is obtained as follows. As shown in Figure 2(a), *AudioFunctions* divides the function domain into a set of intuitively small intervals (e.g. the rectangle r). For each interval, given the sonification direction starting from the lowest and up to the highest x coordinate, the app computes the value of $y = f(x)$ where x is the minimum value of the interval and reproduces the "value-sonification" for y, i.e., a sound whose pitch is proportional to the value of y with respect to the range of y values.

Example 1. With the function $y = sin(x)$, for $x \in [-10, 10]$, when $x = \pi/2$ we have $y = 1$ which is also the maximum value for y and hence the value-sonification for $x = \pi/2$ has the highest pitch. Vice versa, if we draw $y = x$, for $x \in [1, 10]$, the sonification for $x = 1$ has the lowest pitch, because 1 is the smallest value represented for y.

We call the second exploration mode "mono-dimensional interactive" (Figure 2(b)). The user can slide the finger along an horizontal bar positioned at the bottom of the view that represents the x axis.

While sliding the finger, *AudioFunctions* uses the value-sonification technique to represent the value $y = f(x)$ where x corresponds to the current finger position. The clear advantage of this exploration mode is that, thanks to proprioception, the user can perceive the current x position. Also, the user can move forward and backward along the x axis, at the desired speed, hence, for example, focusing more on some parts of the functions that are more relevant for the user (e.g., a minimum point).

The third exploration mode is called "bi-dimensional interactive". The overall idea is to make it possible for the user to follow with one finger the graphical representation of the graph. The shape of the graph is then perceived thanks to proprioception. This mode adopts a different sonification, that we call "position-sonification", since the aim is not to encode the y value, rather to guide the user while following the plotted line. When the user touches on the function line, the position-sonification reproduces a sound with the highest pitch. When the user touches outside the line, the pitch diminishes as the minimum distance between the touched position and the line increases. For example, in Figure 2(c), point

---

[1] This is the gesture that on iOS devices is associated, for example, to start and pause music reproduction.

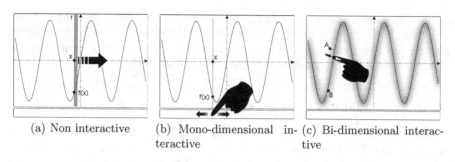

(a) Non interactive   (b) Mono-dimensional in- (c) Bi-dimensional interac-
                            teractive   tive

Fig. 2. Function exploration screen and Exploration modes

A is more distant from $f(x)$ than point B. Therefore, when the user touches A a low pitch sound will be played while touching B will yield a high pitch sound.

The two interactive modes have some additional features. First, while exploring, *AudioFunctions* reproduces some additional sounds in case the function intersects some "interesting points", like intersection with the axis, local minimum and maximum and changes in the concavity. Second, interaction with two fingers is supported. This is very useful, for example, when it is necessary to maintain a reference point in the exploration. To achieve this, when a second finger touches the screen, *AudioFunctions* starts reproducing the sound associated to that finger, ignoring the first one. Third, by double tapping, *AudioFunctions* reads details on the current position, including: the values of x and $f(x)$ and the function concavity in that point. This is useful because function concavity is easily understandable by sight, but hard to figure out with these sonification techniques.

4   Experimental Evaluation

The main objective of *AudioFunctions* is to let the user perceive the shape of a function graph. Therefore we focused our experiments to determine how precisely a user can recognize the function properties from the exploration. To measure the level of understanding of the function, we asked each user to explore the graph and to answer 8 questions (e.g., "which is the concavity of the function for $x = 0$?"). We scored each answer with a mark of 0 (totally wrong answer or no answer), 1 (partially correct answer) or 2 (correct answer). We run the experiment with 7 blind users, all with some education in Mathematics (at least high school) and acquainted with tactile drawings. During each test session we first described *AudioFunctions* in about 2 minutes and then we left 3 minutes to let the user get familiar with the app. After these 5 minutes training we started the test that was divided into three steps, each one involving a different tool: *AudioFunctions*, tactile drawings and "Audio Graphing Calculator" (AGC). The order of the three steps was random. During each step we chose a random function expression from a set of pre-defined functions presenting the corresponding graphs to the user and posing him/her the 8 questions. While answering each question the user was free to interact with the exploration tool. We recorded the answers and the time needed to provide them.

Figure 3(a) shows, for each user and technique, the sum of the scores obtained in all the questions (we recall that the maximum is 16). Intuitively this metric represents the overall understanding of the function obtained by each user with each technique. We can observe that every user obtained much better results by using *AudioFunctions* with respect to AGC. *AudioFunctions* also proved to be more effective also compared with the tactile drawings that, we recall, all the users were acquainted with. Indeed, every user, except user 7, obtained better results with *AudioFunctions* than with tactile drawing and for most of the users the results with *AudioFunctions* are much better than with tactile drawings (e.g., users 2, 4, 5 and 6).

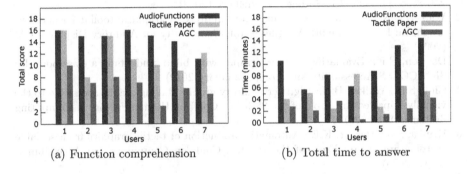

(a) Function comprehension   (b) Total time to answer

Fig. 3. Results of the experimental testing

Figure 3(b) compares the total time required by each user to answer the 8 questions by using each technique. Results show that, by using AGC, users provided answers more quickly (about 2 minutes on average) than with tactile drawings (about 5 minutes on average) and *AudioFunctions* (about 9 minutes on average).

5   Conclusions and Future Work

In this paper we presented *AudioFunctions* a tablet prototype that allows visually impaired students to explore function graphs. *AudioFunctions* presents three exploration modes, two of which use propriception by taking benefit from the direct interaction with the tablet touchscreen. The experimental evaluation that we conducted with 7 users shows that *AudioFunctions* allows the users to have a much better understanding of the function graph than existing software solutions. *AudioFunctions* allows the users to have a better understanding also when compared to tactile paper. This was not expected, as the users only trained with *AudioFunctions* for a few minutes, while they were all acquainted with mathematical exercises on tactile paper.

While the aim of *AudioFunctions* was to explore different interaction paradigms, as a future work we intend to focus on the sonification technique, to compare different solutions and identify the one that best suites each exploration mode. We also plan to engineer *AudioFunctions* and distribute it on the Apple-Store. This would allow a large distribution of the app, which in turn can have positive effects on future research. Indeed, by remotely collecting usage data, it could be possible to evaluate the solution with a much larger number of users, possibly in the order of hundreds or thousands.

References

1. Gardner, J.A.: Access by blind students and professionals to mainstream math and science. In: Miesenberger, K., Klaus, J., Zagler, W.L. (eds.) ICCHP 2002. LNCS, vol. 2398, pp. 502–507. Springer, Heidelberg (2002)
2. Walker, B.N., Cothran, J.T.: Sonification sandbox: A graphical toolkit for auditory graph. In: Proc. of the 9th Meeting of Int. Community for Auditory Display. ACM (2003)
3. Davison, B.K.: Evaluating auditory graphs with blind students in a classroom. In: SIGACCESS Accessibility and Comp. (January 2012)
4. Choi, S.H., Walker, B.N.: Digitizer auditory graph: Making graphs accessible to the visually impaired. In: Proc. of the 28th Int. Conf. on Human Factors in Computing Systems. ACM (2010)
5. Krufka, S.E., Barner, K.E.: Automatic production of tactile graphics from scalable vector graphics. In: Proc. of the 7th Int. Conf. on Computers and Accessibility. ACM (2005)
6. Gardner, J.A., Bulatov, V.: Scientific diagrams made easy with iveotm. In: Proc. of the 10th Int. Conf. on Computers Helping People with Special Needs. Springer, Heidelberg (2006)
7. Ferres, L., Lindgaard, G., Sumegi, L., Tsuji, B.: Evaluating a tool for improving accessibility to charts and graphs. ACM Trans. Comput.-Hum. Interact. (November 2013)
8. Ramloll, R., Yu, W., Brewster, S., Riedel, B., Burton, M., Dimigen, G.: Constructing sonified haptic line graphs for the blind student: First steps. In: Proc. of the 4th Int. Conf. on Assistive Technologies. ACM (2000)

Markdown – A Simple Syntax for Transcription of Accessible Study Materials

Jens Voegler, Jens Bornschein, and Gerhard Weber

Technical University Dresden, Institute of Applied Computer Science, Dresden, Germany
{jens.voegler,jens.bornschein,gerhard.weber}@tu-dresden.de

Abstract. Transcription of study materials into accessible formats is a challenging but necessary task. The sources of study materials vary from images to multimedia files, which often have to be transcribed manually. A fully accessible target format such as HTML is the goal of every transcription process, supported by guidelines and helpful tools. Therefore the transcribers have to deal not only with the content but also with the right usage of the used tools. We show that the usage of the easy to use Markdown language can improve the technical quality and accessibility of the resulting documents. For further improvements of the transcription process several helping tools are presented to simplify and speed up the process as well.

Keywords: Transcription, Image Description, LaTeX, HTML, Markdown, SVG, Accessibility, Transcription Process Optimization, Pandoc, Gladtex.

1 Introduction

During their studies students require a large amount of study materials such as slides of lectures, books and tutorials. The content varies from plain text, plain and animated slides up to video and audio files, e.g. in language trainings. All these different media can be inaccessible to students with disabilities. Depending on the specific impairment of a student assistive technologies are used, e.g. StickyKeys, screen reader or magnifier. Our team has experience in transcription of study material for visually impaired and blind students. The transcription process focuses on HTML, but we improve the quality of the transcribed material and accelerate the transcription.

2 Transcription Process

The TU Dresden Support Center for blind and visually impaired students transcribes lecture material and books into HTML (see 2.1). The process is divided into three steps: preparation, transcription and quality check. In step one an inquiry for the copyright and original sources of the material is sent to the publisher or lecturer. Although copyright has been always granted in the past, it is time-consuming to identify the proper person for the request. Publishers and lecturers send files in different file formats such as PDF, plain text, LaTeX, Powerpoint or MS Word files.

K. Miesenberger et al. (Eds.): ICCHP 2014, Part I, LNCS 8547, pp. 545–548, 2014.

The transcription self is done by students from various faculties of our university. Therefore they are using various editing tools, depending on their knowhow and preferences because some of those tools offer helpful features such as syntax-highlighting, XML-Validation and many more. Supplementary the source files can be transcribed automatically into HTML.

LATEX2HTML (`http://www.latex2html.com/`) is such a tool, but it is often necessary to check and edit the generated files afterwards manually. Therefore most of the work is done by copy and paste of short text passages and adding the HTML tags manually. After the transcription the result is checked for quality by a senior member of our Center and is due for revision if necessary.

2.1   HTML as Book Format

Our students read all transcribed books either in Braille on a Braille display or visually impaired using appropriate magnification tools. While Windows is predominately used some students rely also on Linux. HTML is independent of any operating system and it is accessible for screen readers. Visually impaired people can zoom in and use their own styles to adapt the visual presentation.

In cooperation with blind and visual impaired students an authoring guideline for text transcription was developed in the 1990s. The guidelines describe all textual and visual elements of a book and how to transcribe them. A consistent naming convention for the used file and directory structures is defined and ensures further flexibility of the transcription process.

2.2   Quality and Quantity of the Transcribed Material

Student workers of various faculties transcribe the material. Therefore the knowledge/background of the transcribers is different and also the quality of the transcribed material is diverse. For example a student of psychology explains a psychological picture but he normally does not know so many details on HTML, validation and tools. Common problems are linking errors, invalid HTML-code, incorrect data structure, insufficient description of complex pictures.

These problems can be alleviated by proper editing software. Some editing applications offer helpful features including syntax-highlighting, XML-Validation and many more. In our experience some expert transcribers develop their own shell script for automatic removal of elements or adding markup content. In the following we describe a new approach for transcription using a different markup language to generate accessible HTML.

3   Markdown

"Markdown is intended to be as easy-to-read and easy-to-write as is feasible."[3]. It is a simple Markup language and highly accessible to print-disabled people.

The syntax of Markdown covers only a small subset of HTML tag. Furthermore LaTeX code can be embedded for example for mathematical expressions by enclosing the formula with $$. If additional HTML elements are needed, HTML tags can be inserted. An advantage of Markdown over HTML is its brevity. "...the single biggest source of inspiration for Markdown's syntax is the format of plain text email." [3].

After the transcription into Markdown it can be converted in several different formats, e.g. Docx, HTML, PDF, OpenDocument, DocBook or MediaWiki markup by using Pandoc[4]. Pandoc is a universal document converter offering also different methods for rendering the embedded LaTeX math code in HTML:

- translation to MathML
- rendering by MathJax as image (http://www.mathjax.org/)
- using gladtex (http://sourceforge.net/projects/gladtex/)

Gladtex is a preprocessor for LaTeX math. Rendering of LaTeX math by gladtex consists of two steps. In step one the LaTeX math is enclosed in the tag <eq>. Gladtex processes the resulting file and creates an image of the formula and link to it in the second step.

4   A Plug-in for the Transcription with Markdown

We developed a plug-in for the editor Sublime Text [4]. The plug-in supports the transcription process and helps to comply with our authoring guidelines. The following functions are supported:

- creation of the file and folder structure
- insertion of Markdown syntax for a heading, lists, block quote and code blocks
- adding navigation structure
- adding metadata of the creator and additional information
- creation of the index file and generating the table of content
- generating HTML by using pandoc.

Some of these functions just add Markdown syntax. Other ones have a GUI for user input, e.g. for adding URLs or the file names of images.

5   Pilot Study

We conducted a pilot study with two different groups of transcribers. A plug-in was developed and used by 5 inexperienced volunteers (Group A). The volunteers got a tutorial in Markdown to become familiar with the plug-in and all shortcut keys.

Their tasks were to transcribe some lectures and some chapters of a text book over the course of 4 months. In parallel 3 other participants (Group B) used the authoring guidelines in combination with an editor of their own choice and personal modification like shell scripts (Group B). The participants in Group B have more experience in transcription of books, because they are working in our working group at least 6 month. All 8 students are studying computer science and are familiar with HTML.

The resulting HTML files were checked by using LinkChecker. and were validated by a XML tool. The LinkChecker results show that errors of Group A were less than in Group B. The identified errors made by Group B were wrong named files, missing anchors incorrect file paths. The validation results show that the files of Group A are valid and well-formed. On the contrary some files of the Group B were invalid and not well-formed. Feedbacks of blind students on the quality of the HTML were sent by mails. One very import hint is that the quality of the description of the image should be done by persons who have the necessary scientific background.

The answers show participants of Group B are using a variety of tools and also test their results in different ways. Some are using validation tools and shell scripts, e.g. for the generation of table of content.

6   Further Works

We are developing our plug-in for the editor Kate and adapt our author guidelines to reflect also Markdown. The plug-in should also support the named functions (see 4) and will have additional functions like a link checker, which presents the results in the Kate-GUI. A more simple way for the creation of complex tables has to be realized. For the description of complex images it is planned to test whether it is possible to split the transcription process of describing the image done by experts and transcription of the material to Markdown by students. Furthermore it has to be evaluated whether it is possible to convert a source file like PDF, DOCX, PPTX to Markdown while relying on project Leibniz for preprocessing of source documents. Then the mistakes of the conversion can be corrected manually and additional information can be added and finally the HTML files can be generated. Additionally gladtex is adapted that the conversion fulfills our author guideline.

Acknowledgements. We thank Sebastian Humenda for his work on the gladtex, the pandoc converter and the kate plugin.

References

1. Studienzentrum für Sehgeschädigte (SZS), Karlsruhe Institute of Technology: "ASCII-Mathematikschrift (AMS)", Karlsruhe, Germany (2001)
2. Markdown, http://daringfireball.net/projects/markdown/
3. Pandoc document converter, http://johnmacfarlane.net/pandoc/
4. Sublime Text, http://www.sublimetext.com/

Making Graph Theory Algorithms Accessible to Blind Students

Lukáš Másilko and Jiří Pecl

Masaryk University, Brno, Czech Republic

Abstract. The authors of the proposal are teachers of mathematics for students with visual impairment at Masaryk University (Brno, Czech Republic). When giving instruction, they face the following problem: how can blind people use a given mathematical algorithm in view of the fact that they follow all the information in linear way. Often the instructors have to decide whether to adapt such an algorithm or let blind students work with it in the same manner as their sighted peers do. Their goal is to find an optimal set of methods which would respect blind people's linear manner of working with information and at the same time be sufficiently effective. In their paper, the authors will present several adaptations of two algorithms of Graph Theory. They will assess the pros and cons of all the proposed modifications.

1 Introduction

There are many projects aimed to develop an application for mathematical documents' conversion into the format accessible to blind readers. However, active work with mathematical expressions (editing, simplifying, computing a value) is not discussed very often. What is more, the issue of adapting mathematical algorithms based on visual manipulation with objects is usually ignored completely. Nevertheless, one can find algorithms in many areas of mathematics, such as graph theory, linear algebra or mathematical analysis, which are part of the curriculum for students of technical universities and natural sciences.

We are trying to change this situation. We want to help teachers who ask their blind students to perform an algorithm that requires arranging the input data spatially and modifying them. With respect to the linear manner of working with information the teacher should consider in advance

1. how to present the input data to a blind user,
2. how the blind user can work with these data,
3. if the proposed method of the algorithm procedure is sufficiently effective,
4. and if the written procedure is understandable to other people (fellow students, other teachers, etc.)

Our goal is to provide teachers with general hints explaining how to solve the situation and what to focus on. We use our own knowledge and experience to prepare proposals of adaptations of algorithms, and share them with other people interested in this issue.

K. Miesenberger et al. (Eds.): ICCHP 2014, Part I, LNCS 8547, pp. 549–556, 2014.

2   The Methodology Used

To evaluate the effectivity and usability of proposals of adaptations, we enter a dialogue with the target group. First we introduce the selected algorithm and explain its standard practical application. Then we discuss its pros and cons with respect to blind users and try to motivate the participants of the discussion to suggest possible modifications of the algorithm. Once everybody understands the principles of the algorithm procedure, we elucidate our own adaptations and ask the participants to assess them. We consider primarily the effectivity of the blind person's work, memory and time requirements, and comprehensibility to other people.

All the adaptations should respect the blind person's manner of processing information. Therefore we include proposals of input data arrangement and notation or the tool for manipulation with them. The traditional arrangement of objects being used during the standard algorithm procedure can be an obstacle for blind persons. When looking for a specific piece of information they spend a lot of time by following other objects and their details which are not important at that moment. They do not have the opportunity to work with objects generally without concentrating on their specific values or properties. With respect to the blind person's manner of processing the information we have to ensure easy and quick access to the objects we actually work with during the computation. Therefore, in many cases, it is not useful to respect their traditional arrangement, although it can help the blind to understand single steps of the computation more deeply when getting to know the algorithm. [1]

The dialogue with the target group is mostly realized on two occasions: individual instruction for blind students or consultation with their teachers, and a meeting with a larger group of interested people blind students and their teachers, specialists preparing learning materials, or developers of ICT designed to facilitate access to mathematical documents.

Participants of individual instruction or consultations know the algorithm or at least understand the context of its application. Therefore they can immediately decide whether blind users can use the algorithm in a standard way. On the other hand, they examine the given proposals of adaptations based on their personal perspective and take into consideration their individual abilities (blind student) or possibilities (teacher). They are therefore likely to choose a solution which is ideal with regard to their own preferences and fail to consider other criteria, such as those mentioned above. The main advantage of meetings with a larger group of people is a great variability of their assessments. We spend a lot of time and energy explaining the principles of algorithm procedure but receive a richer and often unexpected feedback.

3   The Research Work

We presented the results of our previous work at international conferences Universal Learning Design 2013 and Ahead Conference 2013. We used three well-known algorithms of linear algebra and mathematical analysis (polynomial division, matrix multiplication, function graph analysis), described their adaptation proposals and compared these modifications with results of published works focusing on didactics of mathematics for the blind (see [2], [3] and [4]).

4   The Current Research Introduction and Related Work

Graph Theory is a field of mathematics with a lot of interesting algorithms used to solve many practical problems. These algorithms are based on active manipulation with graphs' elements such as nodes and edges which users highlight or whose labels they edit. When all the steps of the procedure are completed, the modified graph serves as the final solution of the task. Blind people often prefer reading graphs in a tactile form respecting the spatial arrangement of nodes and edges. If they wish to modify such a tactile graph, they are confronted with limits of current technologies. The developers of tools for tactile graphics production expect blind users to use these tools mainly for reading.

The IVEO Hands-on-Learning System by the American company ViewPlus (see [5]) is one of the examples. A teacher using the system can import or recognize a picture, modify it and divide into areas which are provided with two-level descriptions. A blind student then puts a tactile version of the picture on a touchpad. Tapping on a certain area he can listen to the description using a screen reader. However, the system in its current state does not enable editing of area descriptions while the user is exploring the picture on the touchpad.

Members of research centers have been exploring other possibilities of enabling access to graphics for the blind by non-visual means, for example:

1. Multimodal Interactive System (MIS) based on human-computer interaction. An object is represented by a virtual model. We can observe its shape, surface and other properties using a special device that provides force feedback (Phantom, Novint Falcon etc.) See [6].
2. Vibrotactile feedback together with sonification available on any device with a touchscreen. One can distinguish shape, surface and other properties of objects by regulating the intensity of vibrations accompanied by acoustic signals. Diagram Center and its researching team led by Markko Hakkinen are currently working on a project called Integrating Haptic Feedback for Image-based STEM Assessments within eTextBooks. The preliminary results were presented at the CSUN 2014 conference.

Our goal is to provide blind students with algorithm adaptations which are easily available with regard to technologies and procedures. They need only a computer equipped with a screen reader, refreshable braille display and standard editors for text, spreadsheet or mathematical expression processing.

5   The Research Results

The authors of the proposal have chosen two essential algorithms of Graph theory:

1. Dijkstra's algorithm is used to search for the shortest path from an initial node to all the other nodes of an undirected graph with non-negative edge path costs and
2. Kruskal's algorithm is designed to find a minimum spanning tree of an undirected graph.

5.1 Dijkstra's Algorithm

Original Procedure of the Algorithm. We work with a weighted undirected graph $G = (V, E, w)$, where V is a set of nodes, E is a set of undirected edges and w is a weight of any edge. At the beginning of the algorithm we add the value $A/0$ to the label of the initial node A and X/∞ to labels of all the other nodes X with unknown distance from A. We repeat performing the following three steps until we cannot process any other node:

1. Select the unvisited node X/n with the smallest tentative distance n from the initial node A.
2. Perform the following two steps for every edge e coming out from the node X/n to any unvisited node Y/m:
   (a) if $m > n + w(e)$, modify the current tentative distance of the node Y to $m = n + w(e)$.
   (b) otherwise keep the label of the node Y as it is.
3. Mark the node X as visited.

When performing Dijkstra's algorithm we change labels of nodes only. We update their current tentative distance from the initial node or we mark them as visited.

Proposals of Adaptation

1. *Work with a graph on a sheet of a spreadsheet:* We add labels of all the nodes to the first column starting with the initial node. All the other cells on the row for a node X are reserved for edges coming out from X and are written as n-Y where n is a weight of the edge and Y is the end node of the edge, see Table 1. We modify labels of the nodes in the first column, values of the other columns are to be read only. We mark visited nodes by asterisk to avoid proceeding them in the following steps of the algorithm. We finish the algorithm when all the nodes are marked by asterisk (they are all visited).
2. *Work with a graph on two sheets of a spreadsheet:* There is only one change in comparison with the first method of adaptation. We use the first sheet to explore edges whereas the second sheet includes only one column with the nodes' labels to be consecutively modified.
3. *Work with a tactile version of a graph, use of any editor to modify tentative distances of nodes:* the method is similar to the previous one and differs only in representation of the graph which is offered as a tactile image. a student combines tactile reading of the graph with editing labels of nodes written in any text editor or spreadsheet.

Table 1. Example of a graph represented by a table

$A/0$	1-B	3-E	6-D		
B/∞	1-A	1-E	3-C		
C/∞	1-E	2-F	3-B		
D/∞	4-E	6-A			
E/∞	1-B	1-C	3-A	4-D	4-F
F/∞	2-C	4-E			

Discussion of Pros and Cons. It is clear the first method is advantageous to teachers. The graph is well arranged and understandable, all the nodes and edges are in one place. Nevertheless, blind students do not find the method good. Performing the algorithm is not effective because of the frequent movement between rows and columns of one sheet of the table.

The second method eliminates the disadvantage. When switching from one sheet to another the cursor remains in the same position as it was previously and therefore a user gets all the processed data immediately without searching for them for a long time. Furthermore, the second method is more economical concerning memory requirements. When switching between the two sheets the student needs to hold only the tentative distance of the current node from the initial one in his/her memory. All the other data s/he needs are easily and quickly accessible. One of the blind students came with an interesting proposal of improvement: "I could change the name of the sheet and put there the information about currently processed node. I have it on my refreshable braille display all the time I work with the sheet, therefore I need not keep it in my memory."

The third method respects the spatial arrangement of the graph preferred by sighted users of the algorithm and blind ones assessed it as the best one too. "I prefer working with a tactile version of the graph. One gets a better idea of the relationships between nodes. When working with the graph in a table, nodes are arranged alphabetically even though they need not be neighbours," said one of the visually impaired students of our university. All the experienced blind users came up independently with a proposal to write nodes on one line of a plain text editor instead of separating them, each node on one line, which was recommended first. As they have a refreshable braille display they can immediately observe all the (un)visited nodes.

5.2 Kruskal's Algorithm

Original Procedure of the Algorithm. We work with a weighted undirected graph $G = (V, E, w)$, where V is a set of nodes, E is a set of undirected edges and w is a positive weight of any edge.

1. At the beginning of the algorithm initialize a subgraph $T = (V, \emptyset)$ containing all the nodes of the graph G and an empty set of edges.[1]
2. Sort the edges of the graph G according to their weight and process them consecutively from the shortest one.
3. Check if addition of the current edge to the subgraph T establishes a cycle. If not, add the edge to the subgraph T.
4. After processing the last edge the subgraph T becomes the minimum spanning tree of the graph G.

When processing the algorithm in the standard way we work with a visual representation of a graph. When adding an edge to the subgraph T we highlight it directly in the graph (using a different color or any other means of highlighting). There is a graph H with seven nodes in Fig. 1 demonstrating the situation before processing the fourth edge between the nodes D and G. After the first three steps of the algorithm the edges CF, DE, CD were added to the subgraph T. The next one (DG) does not establish a cycle and therefore we can add it to the subgraph T as well.

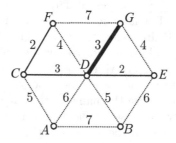

Fig. 1. Weighted undirected graph H, highlighting edges of the subgraph T and a currently processed edge

Proposals of Adaptation

1. *Edges of a graph are organized in a table according to nodes, and a subgraph is created in another document (sheet):* the graph is converted to a table. We add labels of the nodes to the first column. All the other cells on the row for a node X are reserved for the edges coming out from X and are written as X-n-Y where n is a weight of the edge and Y is the end node of the edge. We use another sheet or a separate text file to add the edges of the subgraph T consecutively and to organize sets of nodes connected together by existing edges of the subgraph T. Let's take the same graph H with seven nodes illustrated in Fig. 1. The following two tables demonstrate the situation after addition of the first two edges to the subgraph T. The second part of the Table 2 demonstrates the following fact. The first two edges

---

[1] At the termination of the algorithm the subgraph T becomes a minimum spanning tree of the graph G.

of the subgraph T connect two sets of nodes $\{C, F\}$ and $\{D, E\}$. Before adding the next edge C-3-D we have to check if it does not imply a new cycle at the subgraph T. a sighted student checks that visually while a blind one does so by organizing sets of nodes connected together by edges of the subgraph T. If both nodes of a processed edge belong to the same set of nodes, s/he immediately knows a cycle is going to be created. Otherwise s/he can update the Table 2 (second part), add the processed edge to the subgraph T and modify the sets of nodes connected together. S/he should not forget the currently processed edge was kept in the Table 2 twice therefore it is necessary to delete it at both places.

Table 2. Edges organized in a table according to nodes and a subgraph T

A	A-5-C	A-6-D	A-7-B			
B	B-5-D	B-6-E	B-7-A			
C		C-3-D	C-5-A			
D		D-3-C	D-3-G	D-4-F	D-5-B	D-6-A
E		E-4-G	E-6-B			
F		F-4-D	F-7-G			
G	G-3-D	G-4-E	G-7-F			

MST - Edges:	C-2-F	D-2-E		
MST - Sets of vertices:	C, F	D, E		

2. *Edges are organized in two rows of a table, a subgraph is created in another document (sheet):* the graph is again converted to a table but edges are organized differently. They are completely described in the first column as strings X-n-Y where symbols X, Y indicate nodes connected by an edge with a weight n. The second column serves to repeat the weight of the edge. Most of the spreadsheet applications enable users to arrange data according to values of a certain column. Therefore a blind student can sort edges in ascending order with regard to weights kept in the second column. To consecutively prepare the subgraph T and sets of nodes connected by the subgraph's edges we use the second sheet or a separate document. We process the algorithm in the same manner as previously.

Discussion of Pros and Cons. Let us state in advance that blind students find the second method of adaptation better. There are three main reasons for that:

1. they can immediately find the edge which should processed;
2. they spend less time moving the cursor between rows and columns of the table;
3. they do not need to delete the processed edge twice.

When using the first method they have difficulties finding the edge with the lowest weight. They can solve the problem if they search for them by finding strings as -1-, -2-, etc. One of the students came up with a proposal to leave the concept of the graph representation by means of a table and use the same arrangement of edges in any plain text editor. Edges of a certain node would be positioned on a line separated by commas or spaces. In that case blind students can use keyboard shortcuts or a refreshable braille display and its functions to work with a text effectively.

6   Conclusion and Planned Activities

Students of mathematics and informatics encounter many algorithms. Some of them can be performed by blind people in a standard manner, but there are still many algorithms that should be adapted due to the reasons mentioned above. The authors of the proposal plan to continue working on this. They would like to share proposals of selected algorithms adaptations with all the interested people (teachers, students and assistive technologies experts); they would also appreciate other peoples ideas, comments and solutions. To meet this objective, they created web pages that allow users to discuss didactical issues concerning the instruction of mathematics for the blind. The URL of these sites is http://www.teiresias.muni.cz/amalg.

References

1. Másilko, L., Pecl, J.: Mathematical Algorithms and their Modication for Blind Students. In: Proceedings of the Conference Universal Learning Design, Brno 2013, pp. 99–108. Masaryk University, Brno (2013)
2. Project Math Access (online). Research and Development Institute, Inc., c1997-2006, http://s22318.tsbvi.edu/mathproject
3. del Campo, J., Nicotra, G., Formetti, L.: Lambda: Matematica e Braille - Didactics, http://learninglambda.veia.it/it/didattica
4. Bernareggi, C.: Non-sequential Mathematical Notations in the LAMBDA System. In: Miesenberger, K., Klaus, J., Zagler, W., Karshmer, A. (eds.) ICCHP 2010, Part II. LNCS, vol. 6180, pp. 389–395. Springer, Heidelberg (2010)
5. ViewPlus Technologies, Inc. IVEO Tactile Hands-on Learning System ©2014, http://www.viewplus.com/products/software/hands-on-learning
6. Bernareggi, C., Comaschi, C., Dalto, G., Mussio, P., Parasiliti Provenza, L.: Multimodal Exploration and Manipulation of Graph Structures. In: Miesenberger, K., Klaus, J., Zagler, W.L., Karshmer, A.I. (eds.) ICCHP 2008. LNCS, vol. 5105, pp. 934–937. Springer, Heidelberg (2008)

Braille Capability in Accessible e-Textbooks for Math and Science

Katsuhito Yamaguchi[1], Masakazu Suzuki[2], and Toshihiro Kanahori[3]

[1] Junior College Funabashi Campus, Nihon University 7-24-1 Narashinodai,
Funabashi, Chiba 274-8501, Japan
eugene@gaea.jcn.nihon-u.ac.jp
[2] Institute of Mathematics for Industry, Kyushu University 744, Motooka, Nishi-Ku,
Fukuoka 819-0395, Japan
suzuki@isit.or.jp
[3] Research and Support Center, Tsukuba University of Technology 4-12-7, Kasuga,
Tsukuba, Ibaraki 305-8521, Japan
kanahori@k.tsukuba-tech.ac.jp

Abstract. DAISY or accessible EPUB3 could be a good solution to make e-textbooks more accessible. However, unfortunately, a good method to include Braille in them is not established, yet. Due to complicated Situations in Braille notations, automatically converting print contents, especially, ones for math/science into Braille has its own problem. Furthermore, Braille translation in Japanese is usually context-dependent. After reviewing those situations and how Braille is currently treated in DAISY, what are required for Braille capability in DAISY/ accessible EPUB3 are discussed. Based on our DAISY/EPUB3 authoring tools, "ChattyInfty3," and Braille editor, "BrailleInfty," a practical solution to realize the Braille capability is given.

Keywords: Braille, e-textbook, mathematics, DAISY, Accessible EPUB3.

1 Introduction

In Japan, so-called "digital textbooks" (the official name of an e-textbook in Japan) are supposed to be fully adopted in elementary and junior-high school in April, 2020. However, now, a large number of those digital textbooks, especially ones for math and science are not necessarily accessible. Establishing a good method to make them accessible is our important task.

As is well known, "The Digital Accessible Information System (DAISY)" [1] now becomes a standard format of accessible e-books. Actually, "the International Digital Publishing Forum (IDPF)" [2] decided to adopt DAISY4 XML as a part of EPUB3 standards in 2011. Since EPUB3 will be certainly one of standard formats in e-textbooks, DAISY (accessible EPUB3) is an excellent solution for provide accessible digital textbooks to people with various print disabilities.

However, there remain unsolved problems in DAISY technical content to deserve greater attention. One of the most important ones is that the current

K. Miesenberger et al. (Eds.): ICCHP 2014, Part I, LNCS 8547, pp. 557–563, 2014.
© Springer International Publishing Switzerland 2014

DAISY has no Braille capability. In DAISY, a reader can access a math formula in MathML character by character, symbol by symbol with speech synthesis, magnifying or highlighting, etc. However, the blind cannot access technical DAISY contents in Braille. In order to use DAISY/accessible EPUB3 textbooks for the blind in school, Braille-output capability should be required.

In this paper, after reviewing difficulties in translation of Japanese technical contents into Braille, complicated situations in Braille conversion of technical notations and Braille capability in DAISY briefly, we discuss what is required for DAISY/accessible EPUB3 and give a practical solution to realize that, based on our assistive tools.

2   Problems in Translating Technical Contents into Braille

2.1   Problems in Translating Japanese Contents into Braille

There is seriously complicated situation in Braille translation in Japanese. Four different character sets are used simultaneously in print: Chinese characters (Kanji), Hiragana, Katakana and alphanumeric letters. While Hiragana and Katakana are essentially kinds of phonetic symbols, a single Kanji character or their compound usually has several ways of pronouncing, according to its context. Math/science technical terms or the proper nouns such as the name of a person/a place, particularly, historical ones are often read in a different manner from the usual.

For instance, as was reported in the ICCHP 2010 [3], we made a brief survey on the ambiguity in Japanese aloud-reading of mathematical or mathematics-related technical terms consisting of Kanji. While 416 words can appear in both mathematical and nonmathematical contexts, 110 words (26.4% of them) have more than one pronunciation according to context; that is, they should be read out in a different manner from the usual in a technical context.

To avoid this ambiguity, a Japanese printed document often includes so-called "Ruby" characters to specify how to pronounce each Kanji or their compound. It is a kind of phonetic description typically written in hiragana or katakana to the side of the original Kanji in a small (Ruby-type) font. However, Ruby characters are not necessarily placed alongside all Kanji. In addition to that, a Japanese-text sentence in print has no explicit breaks except for punctuation marks. All the words are always written continuously.

On the other hand, there is only one character set in Japanese literal Braille code, which is essentially corresponding to Katakana. A word in Braille should be separated from each other with a space like European languages. When translating a printed Japanese document into Braille, at first, we have to convert all Kanji characters into Katakana, based on their pronunciation and put a space between words before the translation.

Thus, the translation of a Japanese textbook ranging from math to history is heavily context-dependent. Consequently, popular Braille-translating software for Japanese seems to make mistakes quite frequently in converting not only technical contents but also other many non-technical ones. Furthermore, it cannot treat math formulas at all.

2.2   Problems in Translating Technical Notations into Braille

In terms of technical notations, there is another complicated problem in Braille translation, which occurs commonly also in many countries other than Japan. As is well known, since the ordinary Braille consists of 6 dots, only 63 different characters (besides a space) can be represented in a single Braille cell. Thus, all those single-cell Braille characters are assigned to basic literal print characters in each local language such as the (lower-case) alphabet. The other print characters/symbols including capital letters should be represented in so-called "a Braille code," which is a sequence of multiple Braille cells. A particular Braille-code system such as a Braille math code is usually defined in a different manner from the literal Braille code system of each language.

Since such code systems have been developed independently from each other in local community/country, many different systems have been developed for a same field. For instance, the math notation in print is definitely the most universal language in the world. However, a Braille math notation in a country is usually different from ones used in the other countries, even if a national language is the same. In addition, another confusing problem is that a print symbol is often assigned to several different Braille symbols in different fields even in one country. For instance, the Braille symbol for the plus sign, $+$, in math is different from one in computer science in Japan.

"The International Council of English Braille (ICEB)" has been working on a project: "Unified English Braille (UEB) Code" to aim at unifying all of technical and non-technical Braille notations (except for music) in the ICEB-member countries. Since In 2012, finally "the Braille Authority of North America (BANA)" decided to adopt UEB officially [4], the complicated situation will be remarkably improved, at least, in those countries in near future.

However, for quite a while (or from now on), two different types of technical Braille codes: the Nemeth and the UEB codes are used simultaneously in USA. They are significantly different from each other. Here, some samples in each code are shown below.

- Digits: 1 2 3 4 5
  Nemeth:

  UEB:

- Equation: $2x + 3y = -5$
  Nemeth:

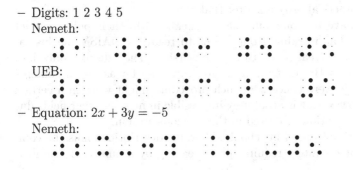

UEB:

⠨⠴ ⠿ ⠒⠶ ⠀⠶⠶ ⠨⠿ ⠒⠶⠶ ⠿ ⠀⠶⠶ ⠀ ⠶⠶ ⠨⠶ ⠶⠶

Remark:

In the UEB code, many Braille symbols used in algebra are usually of two

cells such as $1 = $ ⠨⠴ ⠿ . On the other hand, in the Nemeth code, they are usually represented as a single-cell symbol. However, when writing a number

next to a space, so called "Number sign," ⠼ should be put prior to it. That

is, ⠼ ⠂ is the Number sign and a number, 1.

Thus, even in USA, a print math expression can be described in two different manners in Braille. Since the BANA does not give a definite rule to switch them, we cannot assume beforehand which code should be used for a certain document.

There are hundreds of technical Braille codes in the world. Consequently, computerized conversion of a technical print document into Braille is usually a very complicated job. Nevertheless, in terms of math-to-Braille conversion, several remarkable results have been achieved until now. Archambault, et al. has been worked on an open-source project, "Universal Math Conversion Library (UMCL)." They provide tools to convert LaTeX/MathML formulas into several Braille math codes [5, 6, 7]. The Duxbury Braille Translator, which is the most popular Braille translator in the world, also can converts a LaTeX document including math expressions into several Braille codes. "The LEAN (Linear Editing and Authoring Notation) Editor" [8] allows a user to convert a MathType [9] formula embedded in a Microsoft Word document into Nemeth Braille code used in USA, and vice versa. There also have been some other challenging activities such as conversion from MathML into Nemeth by Stanley and Karshmer [10], the Lambda Project [11], etc. However, completely automatic Braille translation of technical contents seems to be still an impossible mission.

3   Braille Capability in DAISY

Unfortunately, it is currently impossible to prepare a DAISY XML file that can automatically output Braille. In 2008, the Braille-in-DAISY Working Group in the DAISY Consortium worked out a final report on their survey [12]. They discussed what should be required for DAISY-to-Braille translation; however, there has been no practical progress after that time.

In addition, we have to point out that, to begin with, their policy cannot suit our necessity. That working group seems to regard a DAISY file just as a source for automatic (real-time) Braille conversion. They discuss only how to do it efficiently with Braille translator (software). As far as literal contents in European language were concerned, such procedure might work in a certain level. We believe, however, it is absolutely impossible in most of other fields due to the complicated situation discussed in the previous section.

In terms of e-textbooks used in school, all Braille descriptions must be completely correct. That definitely requires proof reading by a human transcriber.

The approach by the Braille-in-DAISY Working Group cannot meet this demand. We have to give another practical approach, at least, for e-textbooks; particularly, ones for math or other technical subjects.

We believe that only possible and practical solution for that is to embed correct Braille descriptions into DAISY/EPUB3. Two different ways can be considered to realize that. The simplest one is to embed Braille directly into a DAISY/EPUB3 XML (source) file, itself like an alternative text for an image. However, it seems to be inefficient since this approach requires to produce multiple kinds of Braille-embedded XML files for the same print contents, to correspond to changing a Braille-code system, for instance.

The other approach is to prepare a separate file set of Braille descriptions and call them at each part of DAISY/EPUB3 XML. In a multimedia DAISY, audio files are treated in this manner. We believe it is a better solution.

4 How to Produce Braille-Embedded DAISY

We have developing several assistive tools for print-disabled people to access STEM (science, technology, engineering and math) [13, 14]. "ChattyInfty3" is authoring tools for accessible multimedia contents of STEM in DAISY/EPUB3 [15, 16].

As was reported in ICCHP 2012 [15], in DAISY, we need a way to control how to read out each technical term in Kanji characters, symbol or mathematical formula locally according to their context. We refer to this new concept of assigning a pronunciation as "Yomi" (a Japanese word that means "a manner of aloud reading"). To realize the Yomi function in DAISY, we tentatively gave a method based on DAISY4 (EPUB3) Ruby tag. Although we already referred to Ruby in the previous section, it should be noted that Ruby and Yomi are conceptually different from each other. Although Ruby is included in an original print document, Yomi is not. The reading given with Yomi, therefore, should not appear explicitly in the DAISY version, unlike the case for Ruby. However, Yomi has to control speech output as well as Ruby.

As was discussed previously, to convert technical contents into Braille in Japanese, at first we have to give a correct aloud-reading to each of Kanji characters or their compounds included in technical contents before the conversion. The development of the Yomi function helped us with constructing a dictionary for this conversion.

Although it has not been reported so far, we also develop a Braille editor, "BrailleInfty" and a Braille-translation engine for math formulas. A sighted user can author STEM contents in an intuitive manner with BrailleInfty. The translating engine allows us to convert math formulas in MathML into one in the Japanese math/Science Braille code. By combining our Braille-translating engine with a popular Japanese Braille translator, a ChattyInfty3 file can be easily converted into BrailleInfty.

Based on these tools, we established a new method to embed Braille into DAISY (accessible EPUB3) XML. As is well known, a source text including a

MathML formula in DAISY XML is divided into multiple small elements enclosed with span tags: `<span>` and `</span>`. Each span element is a unit for highlighting, aloud-reading, etc. If the audio attribute were set at the span tag, a DAISY player would call an audio file such as recorded human voice stored in an audio folder and play back it at that position.

We defined a new attribute for the span tag: "a Braille attribute." Embedding Braille descriptions into DAISY/EPUB3 with the Braille attribute is performed through the following steps.

1. At first each span element in ChattyInfty3 is listed in a table.
2. Then, they are translated into their Braille description with our engine. A human transcriber can correct all errors in the table with BrailleInfty.
3. Finally, the result (a correct Braille description), which is connected with the original span element automatically, is stored in a Braille folder. Each span element corresponds to one Braille file.

A DAISY/EPUB3 player could call a Braille file like an audio file and output to a refreshable Braille display.

For the present, our Braille translator can convert MathML into Japanese math/science Braille code only. However, combining our system with another engine such as UMCL, we would become able to create Braille-embedded technical e-textbooks in another language.

5   Conclusion

As is discussed, to output completely correct Braille descriptions in e-textbooks, we have to embed them into DAISY/EPUB3 XML. Here, we give a practical manner to realize that.

Unfortunately, however, there is no available device that can treat them for the present. Although "Braille Sense series" [17] is probably only one portable Braille device that can play back DAISY audio/text contents as well, it cannot output Braille embedded in our DAISY e-textbooks. KGS Corporation is now developing a new portable all-in-one device with a refreshable Braille display, "Braille Memo Smart" [18]. Braille-output capability for our DAISY e-textbooks is supposed to be implemented on it in near future.

One problem in our method is that too many Braille files corresponding to each span element must be prepared in the Braille folder. In the next revision of EPUB3, EPUB3.01, so called "Rendition Mapping" is supposed to be realized [19]. Using this function, we will become able to give information of mapping between elements in EPUB3 and Braille contents. Then, we may simply prepare a single Braille file that has the same content as the original EPUB3 book. In this approach, the Braille contents, itself, could be printed out easily if necessary. We are now working on upgrading ChattyInfty3 so that it can support the EPUB3 Rendition-Mapping function.

References

1. The DAISY Consortium, http://www.daisy.org/
2. The International Digital Publishing Forum, http://www.idpf.org
3. Yamaguchi, K., Suzuki, M.: On Necessity of a New Method to Read Out Math Contents Properly in DAISY. In: Miesenberger, K., Klaus, J., Zagler, W., Karshmer, A. (eds.) ICCHP 2010, Part II. LNCS, vol. 6180, pp. 415–422. Springer, Heidelberg (2010)
4. The Braille Authority of North America, http://www.brailleauthority.org
5. Archambault, D., Fitzpatrick, D., Gupta, G., Karshmer, A.I., Miesenberger, K., Pontelli, E.: Towards a Universal Maths Conversion Library. In: Miesenberger, K., Klaus, J., Zagler, W.L., Burger, D. (eds.) ICCHP 2004. LNCS, vol. 3118, pp. 664–669. Springer, Heidelberg (2004)
6. Moço, V., Archambault, D.: Automatic Conversions of Mathematical Braille: A Survey of Main Difficulties in Different Languages. In: Miesenberger, K., Klaus, J., Zagler, W.L., Burger, D. (eds.) ICCHP 2004. LNCS, vol. 3118, pp. 638–643. Springer, Heidelberg (2004)
7. Universal Maths Conversion Library, http://sourceforge.net/projects/umcl/
8. LEAN Editor, http://www.access2science.com/mathml/LEANMath_Manual.html
9. Design Science, http://www.dessci.com/en/
10. Stanley, P.B., Karshmer, A.I.: Translating MathML into Nemeth Braille Code. In: Miesenberger, K., Klaus, J., Zagler, W.L., Karshmer, A.I. (eds.) ICCHP 2006. LNCS, vol. 4061, pp. 1175–1182. Springer, Heidelberg (2006)
11. The Lambda Project, http://www.lambdaproject.org/home/
12. Braille-in-DAISY Working Group, http://www.daisy.org/project/braille
13. InftyProject, http://www.inftyproject.org/en/
14. Science Accessibility Net, http://www.sciaccess.net/en/
15. Yamaguchi, K., Suzuki, M.: Accessible Authoring Tool for DAISY Ranging from Mathematics to Others. In: Miesenberger, K., Karshmer, A., Penaz, P., Zagler, W. (eds.) ICCHP 2012, Part I. LNCS, vol. 7382, pp. 130–137. Springer, Heidelberg (2012)
16. Yamaguchi, K., Kanahori, T., Suzuki, M.: Authoring Tools for EPUB3 Math Contents. In: Proc. the 29th CSUN Annual International Conference on Technology and People with Disabilities, BLV-051, San Diego (2014)
17. HIMS International, http://www.himsintl.com/
18. KGS Corporation (Japanese only), http://www.kgs-jpn.co.jp/
19. EPUB Multiple-Rendition Publications, http://www.idpf.org/epub/renditions/multiple/epub-multiple-renditions-20131209.html

MathMelodies: Inclusive Design of a Didactic Game to Practice Mathematics

Andrea Gerino[1,2], Nicolò Alabastro[1], Cristian Bernareggi[1,2],
Dragan Ahmetovic[1], and Sergio Mascetti[1,2]

[1] Dept. of Computer Science, Università degli Studi di Milano, Milano, Italy
[2] EveryWare Technologies, Milano, Italy

Abstract. Tablet computers are becoming a common tool to support learning since primary school. Indeed, many didactic applications are already available on online stores. Most of these applications engage the child by immersing the educational purpose of the software within an entertaining environment, often in the form of a game with sophisticated graphic and interaction. Unfortunately, this makes most of these applications inaccessible to visually impaired children. In this contribution we present *MathMelodies*, an iPad application that supports math learning in primary school and that is designed to be accessible also to visually impaired children. We describe the main challenges we faced during the development of this didactic application that is both engaging and accessible. The application, currently publicly available, is collecting enthusiastic reviews from teachers, who often contribute with precious insight for improving the solution.

1 Introduction

A large number of commercial applications exist to support learning of primary school children. While some of these solutions are in the form of websites or applications for traditional devices (desktop and laptop), recently these applications have been developed for mobile devices, in particularly for tablets. For example, more than 65,000 educational applications are available for iOS devices[1].

Most of these applications engage the child by immersing the educational purpose of the software within an entertaining environment, often in the form of a game, generally with sophisticated graphic and interaction. Unfortunately, this results in most of the existing applications being inaccessible to visually impaired children which are already discriminated in the access to the print-based exercises and would actually benefit significantly from the autonomous use of educational applications. Also, the lack of accessible mobile applications can limit the social inclusion of visually impaired children.

In scientific literature many different interaction paradigms have been investigated to make entertaining educational games accessible to visually impaired children. These interaction paradigms include, in particular: auditory user interfaces and audio-haptic interaction. Educational auditory games have been

---

[1] Source: http://www.apple.com/education/ipad/apps-books-and-more/

K. Miesenberger et al. (Eds.): ICCHP 2014, Part I, LNCS 8547, pp. 564–571, 2014.

proposed both as desktop applications and recently as mobile applications [1]. While auditory user interfaces solve many interaction challenges [2], they also require attention and good memory skills [3]. Hence, especially in education (e.g. in presenting mathematical puzzles), auditory feedback alone is not the best solution. Auditory user interfaces have been extended with haptic or tactile feedback in order to help blind people to construct a mental representation of the scene. Audio-haptic educational games have been proposed both with general purpose haptic devices [4] and with new hardware devices employing vibro-tactile feedback [5,6], specifically designed to generate tactile stimuli which reinforce audio cues. These solutions proved to be more usable by blind people, but they are far more expensive and, as far as specific devices are concerned, they are currently only available as prototypes.

To address these problems, in this paper we present *MathMelodies*, an iPad application that supports primary school children in learning Mathematics. *MathMelodies* has been designed and implemented to be enjoyable by both visually impaired and sighted children. The software has been first developed as a university prototype and then, thanks to a crowdfunding campaign, engineered and distributed as a commercial application[2].

In this contribution we describe the main design challenges of *MathMelodies*. We adopted a user-centered design methodology, driven by a number of tests and on-the-field evaluations. In particular, we report the results of three evaluation sessions: an expert-based evaluation, a test conducted with the first prototype of the app and a more qualitative evaluation conducted on the commercial version of the application. Finally, we describe the feedback we have received so far and how they impact the application design.

2   Related Work

Non-visual interaction paradigms to make interactive games accessible to visually impaired people have been extensively studied in scientific literature. These paradigms are based on sensory substitution: the visual elements dynamically displayed on the screen are substituted with multimodal non-visual stimuli that guide the sight impaired player in the game [7]. The most frequently adopted non-visual interaction modes include auditory feedback as well as tactile and haptic stimuli.

Auditory feedback has been successfully employed to replace the sense of sight in many interactive games. In [8], Roden et al. illustrate a framework to generate audio game in a 3D audio environment. In [9], Vallejo et al. investigate sonification techniques in point and click games. Miller et al. [10] propose audio cues in games inherently based on audio feedback (e.g. where the player is required to reproduce a rhythmic pattern), but that are inaccessible to sight impaired people because of visual instructions. Ramos [11] and Ng [12] have recently evidenced the advantages of informative sounds in interactive games. Furthermore, in recent years, many auditory interfaces have been specifically

---

[2] https://itunes.apple.com/us/app/math-melodies/id713705958?mt=8

designed for games on mobile devices [1,13]. Nonetheless, all auditory interaction paradigms for games require much attention, memory skills and the ability to recognize even slightly different sounds. Furthermore, while auditory interfaces that employ spatial sound (e.g. 3D sound) can be successfully used with headphones that isolate the player from the surrounding environment, this may prevent the user from interacting with other players.

Auditory games have been extended with haptic or tactile feedback in order to reduce the cognitive load required to sight impaired people to construct a mental representation of the scene. Audio-haptic educational games have been proposed both with general purpose haptic devices [4] and with new hardware devices employing vibro-tactile feedback [5,6], or haptic gloves [14] specifically designed to generate tactile stimuli which reinforce audio cues. These solutions proved to be more usable by sight impaired people than auditory interaction paradigms only. Nonetheless, haptic devices are currently still very expensive, most of these devices are available as prototypes only and they are not designed to be used with mobile devices.

3   Design Challenges

During the design and development of *MathMelodies* we faced three main challenges. First, the application has to present exercises that are accessible to visually impaired children. In the preliminary prototype we experimented two main interaction paradigms that we called "sonification-based" and "object-based". With sonification-based interaction the application presents a generic image that can be explored through audio-feedback with a solution similar to the one adopted in [15]. For example, the application can guide the student to identify a triangle by reproducing a sound when the boundary is touched. Vice versa, with the object-based interaction paradigm, the application shows some objects on the screen, each one associated with an audio feedback that represents the object itself. In this case, the audio feedback is independent on the position of the touch within the object. For example, touching the figure of a dog, the application plays a sound of a dog barking. Similarly a digit is read when it is touched. The experimental evaluation has shown that the object-based interaction paradigm is less cognitively demanding for the students, hence resulting more enjoyable for the users and more suitable to represent complex exercises. According to these results, we designed a set of 13 different types of exercises relying on the object-based interaction paradigm. To further simplify the interaction model, we decided to organize the objects into a grid layout that, as we observed in our evaluation, helps reducing the time and mental workload required to explore the entire screen. Another choice driven by the need of simplifying the interaction consisted in the definition of two input techniques: a simplified on-screen keyboard to insert the digits only (e.g., for the addition exercises, see Figure 1(a)) and a multiple choice dialog (e.g., to answer an exercise like the one shown in Figure 1(b)). Finally, we observed that the interaction with the exercises without any preliminary explanation is not intuitive for some children.

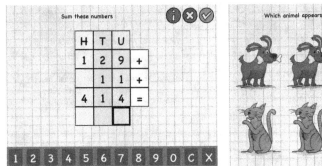

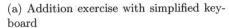

(a) Addition exercise with simplified keyboard

(b) Counting exercise

Fig. 1. Two exercises of *MathMelodies*

Also, for some exercises, the eyes-free exploration of the screen can be time consuming. To address these two problems, we decided to add a short explanation that is read when a new type of exercise is presented.

The second design challenge is to stimulate children to play the exercises several times hence taking benefit from reinforcement learning. To address this challenge, we designed the exercises to have up to 6 difficulty levels. For example, in the "easy" addition exercise the child is asked to add two single-digit numbers, while at an harder level (designed for 3rd grade students) the aim is to add three numbers, each one with up to three digits as in Figure 1(a). For the same reason, the exercises are defined in terms of their type and difficulty level and not according to their actual content that is randomly generated each time the exercise is presented to the student.

Another important aspect to stimulate children to play the same exercise several times is to entertain them. We pursued this objective by presenting, in most of the exercises, what we call "audio-icons": amusing drawings, each one associated with an easy-to-recognize and funny sound. Also, the application gives a reward to the child in the form of a short piece of music when a correct answer is provided. As a future work we also intend to create a more sophisticated reward mechanism that takes into account the number of wrong answers the child provided before giving the right one. For example, zero mistakes can be rewarded with 3 "golden stars".

The last design challenge is to immerse the educational activities in an accessible entertaining environment that also links the exercises together and motivates children to keep on playing. We addressed this challenge with a tale, divided into 6 chapters, organized in increasing difficulty levels (two chapters for each grade). Each chapter is further divided into "pages", each one comprising a background image, some text (read by a speech synthesizer) and some "audio-icons" (see Figure 2). Pages are intertwined with the exercises and there are about 30 exercises in each chapter.

(a) A page with a piano audio-icon   (b) A page with a frog audio-icon

Fig. 2. Two pages of *MathMelodies* story

Overall, the tale and the audio-icons have also the objective of triggering children's interest. This is similar to the approach adopted in most textbooks that heavily rely on colorful images. The difference is clearly that in *MathMelodies* this solution works for visually impaired children too.

4   Implementation of *MathMelodies*

During the app implementation we had to face a number of technical issues and here we describe two of them. The first issue deals with the large amount of app content, i.e., the story text, images (backgrounds and icons), and audio (sounds and music). Indeed, it is clearly impractical to define the app by hard-coding the content into the program. Instead, we defined a format for the "content file" that describes, for example, the structure of each chapter, each page, etc. A "content engine" in *MathMelodies* reads this file and presents the content to the user, in the form of exercises, pages, etc... Thanks to this approach, it is possible to define the app content independently from the app implementation.

The second issue is related to the implementation of the object-based interaction paradigm that is built on top of the system accessibility tools. On iOS devices, there are two sets of tools that render the system accessible to visually impaired users. One set is designed for low-visioned users and includes the "zoom" screen magnifier, font size adjustment and color inversion. While some ad-hoc gestures are defined to use the zoom functions, the overall interaction paradigm is analogous to the one for sighted users. The second set of tools is globally called "VoiceOver" and defines a totally different interaction paradigm. The overall idea is that, when the user taps on a graphical object (e.g., a button), VoiceOver gives it the focus and describes it both with a speech synthesizer and an external Braille display (if connected). To activate a focused object (e.g., to press a button), the user double taps anywhere on the screen. In addition to this basic behavior, VoiceOver has several additional gestures to make the interaction more efficient.

In order to enhance the app usability for visually impaired users that rely on residual sight, we used large fonts and high contrast between the front objects (i.e., text or pictures) and the background image. Although we did not evaluate this solution with a sufficiently large number of low-visioned users, we expect the app to be accessible to most low-visioned students by using the default accessibility tools. For what concerns blind users or low-visioned users that cannot totally rely on residual sight, some issues arose in the implementation of the object-based interaction paradigm. Indeed, the simplest solution to implement this paradigm would be to fully rely on VoiceOver (i.e., not implementing any custom behavior for app accessibility). This approach would make it possible to develop an app that is totally consistent with the system-wide interaction paradigm. However, this solution suffers from a major drawback, as it is not suitable to address all design challenges. For example, without defining any custom behavior it is not possible to develop the audio icons that reproduce the associated sound upon getting the focus. Other features that call for a custom behavior are multi-tap exploration and automatic reading of pages. Clearly, to achieve a deeper customization of the interaction paradigm a larger coding effort is required and it is quite involved to mimic VoiceOver standard behavior as well as to guarantee the consistency with the system-wide interaction paradigm. For example, the current version of *MathMelodies* (1.0) uses some custom objects in the story view: to enable the automatic reading of a page, story text is "hidden" to VoiceOver and "played" automatically with iOS 7's integrated text-to-speech synthesiser. We chose this approach because we wanted the app to be of immediate use also to users that are still not acquainted to standard VoiceOver gestures. Our preliminary tests, presented in Section 5, validated this approach. However, after app publication we received feedback that led us to reconsider our choice. Indeed, with this solution the text is not shown on external Braille displays. To address this issues we are now working on a new version of *MathMelodies* that minimizes the use of objects with custom behavior.

5   Experimental Evaluation

During the whole design and development process we took benefit from the feedback obtained from one of the designers who is blind and experienced in education for blind persons. In addition, we organized three evaluation sessions.

The first session was organized with four teachers expert in education for blind students[3]. The evaluation was divided in two steps. In the former, we presented a list of the exercises derived from Italian educational directives and integrated with workbooks and online resources. For each exercise we asked the experts to evaluate the importance of the exercise in the education of a blind person and to rate how difficult it is to practice it with existing solutions. In the second step of the evaluation we presented the preliminary prototype implementing sonification-based and object-based interaction paradigms. All four experts

---

[3] From the center for the blind people in Brescia, Italy.

independently agreed on the fact that object-based paradigm would be quicker to learn and also more adaptable to a larger variety of exercises.

The second session was conducted as a test with three blind children. After a short training with the prototype, we asked each child to solve three exercises with object-based interaction and one exercise with sonification-based interaction. All students have been able to complete and correctly answer exercise 1 (counting) and 2 (position in a table). Vice versa, one student has not been able to complete (and hence to provide an answer to) exercise 3, a spelling exercise, and exercise 4 consisting in recognizing a triangle by a sonification-based interaction. Overall, all students reported that the object-based interaction is easier to understand and two of them also highlighted that it is funnier.

The third evaluation session was conducted with three blind children in primary school and with two sighted children in primary school. All children were required to complete all the exercises in the first chapter consisting in counting exercises, sums, etc. All blind children were enthusiast while using the application. Two out of three reported that they were entertained and engaged especially by the sounds used (e.g. the call of animals and the rewarding melodies). All of them experienced some difficulties in the early exploration of the tables, and needed some help by a sighted supervisor. However, after at most 2 minutes of supervised training, all children got familiar with the application and were able to solve the exercises autonomously and, most of the times, providing a correct answer at the first attempt. The two sighted children enjoyed the application as well. One of the two children experienced some difficulties, at the beginning, in understanding how to answer. This was partially due to the fact that the child didn't pay much attention to the exercise explanation. After explaining how to answer, no more help was needed. To solve this problem we intend to create introductory exercises in which the focus is not on the exercise itself rather on how to use the application.

6 Conclusions and Future Work

To the best of our knowledge, *MathMelodies* is the first app for math learning on mobile devices that is specifically designed to be accessible to visually impaired children. In this paper we describe the main challenges that we had to face in the app design and implementation as well as the results of the experimental evaluations that shows how *MathMelodies* is actually accessible and entertaining.

Currently, the app is freely available on the AppStore and it has been downloaded 700 times in the first two months after the English version has been released. Since the app publication we received feedback from about 10 people, in most of the cases teachers for blind students. This feedback has a high value for us and is driving the design of the next version of *MathMelodies*.

As a future work we intend to take an even larger advantage from the app distribution to the public and we intend to automatically collect usage data and to use them to evaluate the app itself. In this perspective, 700 users are about 100 times as much as we could expect to involve in the evaluation conducted with the physical presence of the users.

Another future improvement consists in developing a collaborative system that allows the teachers to directly participate in the development of the app content. This crowdsourcing system can drastically reduce the development costs of the next versions of *MathMelodies* and ease the scalability of this solution.

References

1. Mendels, P., Frens, J.: The audio adventurer: Design of a portable audio adventure game. In: Markopoulos, P., de Ruyter, B., IJsselsteijn, W.A., Rowland, D. (eds.) Fun and Games 2008. Mendels, P., Frens, J, vol. 5294, pp. 46–58. Springer, Heidelberg (2008)
2. Stefik, A., Hundhausen, C., Patterson, R.: An empirical investigation into the design of auditory cues to enhance computer program comprehension. Int. J. Hum.-Comput. Stud. 69(12), 820–838 (2011)
3. Stanley, P.: Assessing the mathematics related communication requirements of the blind in education and career. In: Miesenberger, K., Klaus, J., Zagler, W.L., Karshmer, A.I. (eds.) ICCHP 2008. LNCS, vol. 5105, pp. 888–891. Springer, Heidelberg (2008)
4. Gutschmidt, R., Schiewe, M., Zinke, F., Jürgensen, H.: Haptic emulation of games: Haptic sudoku for the blind. In: Proc. of the 3rd Int. Conf. on Pervasive Technologies Related to Assistive Environments. ACM (2010)
5. Raisamo, R., Patomäki, S., Hasu, M., Pasto, V.: Design and evaluation of a tactile memory game for visually impaired children. Interact. Comput. 19(2) (2007)
6. Kuber, R., Tretter, M., Murphy, E.: Developing and evaluating a non-visual memory game. In: Campos, P., Graham, N., Jorge, J., Nunes, N., Palanque, P., Winckler, M. (eds.) INTERACT 2011, Part II. LNCS, vol. 6947, pp. 541–553. Springer, Heidelberg (2011)
7. Westin, T., Bierre, K., Gramenos, D., Hinn, M.: Advances in game accessibility from 2005 to 2010. In: Stephanidis, C. (ed.) Universal Access in HCI, Part II, HCII 2011. LNCS, vol. 6766, pp. 400–409. Springer, Heidelberg (2011)
8. Roden, T., Parberry, I.: Designing a narrative-based audio only 3d game engine. In: Proc. of the Int. Conf. on Advances in Computer Entertainment Technology. ACM (2005)
9. Vallejo-Pinto, J.A., Torrente, J., Fernández-Manjón, B., Ortega-Moral, M.: Applying sonification to improve accessibility of point-and-click computer games for people with limited vision. In: Proc. of the 25th BCS Conf. on Human-Computer Interaction. British Computer Society (2011)
10. Miller, D., Parecki, A., Douglas, S.A.: Finger dance: A sound game for blind people. In: Proc. of the 9th Int. Conf. on Computers and Accessibility. ACM (2007)
11. Ramos, D., Folmer, E.: Supplemental sonification of a bingo game. In: Proc. of the 6th Int. Conf. on Foundations of Digital Games. ACM (2011)
12. Ng, P., Nesbitt, K.: Informative sound design in video games. In: Proc. of the 9th Australasian Conf. on Interactive Entertainment: Matters of Life and Death. ACM (2013)
13. Kim, J., Ricaurte, J.: Tapbeats: Accessible and mobile casual gaming. In: Proc. of the 13th Int. Conf. on Computers and Accessibility. ACM (2011)
14. Yuan, B., Folmer, E.: Blind hero: Enabling guitar hero for the visually impaired. In: Proc. of the 10th Int. Conf. on Computers and Accessibility. ACM (2008)
15. Yoshida, T., Kitani, K.M., Koike, H., Belongie, S., Schlei, K.: Edgesonic: Image feature sonification for the visually impaired. In: Proc. of the 2nd Int. Conf. on Augmented Human. ACM (2011)

An Interactive Workspace
for Helping the Visually Impaired Learn Linear Algebra

Bassam Almasri, Islam Elkabani, and Rached Zantout

Department of Mathematics and Computer Science,
Faculty of Science, Beirut Arab University, Lebanon
{bza148,islam.kabani,r.zantout}@bau.edu.lb

Abstract. In this paper an interactive workspace designed to help visually impaired students practice the fundamentals of linear algebra is introduced. Unlike most of the approaches, this interactive workspace aims at enhancing math manipulation abilities for students who are visually impaired, mainly dealing with linear algebra expression that requires more complicated techniques in accessing. Read-expression, Hide-Row/Column, and Text-Tools are examples of techniques that the workspace implements. Such techniques are invoked by hot access keys which in turn with audio feedback allow the user to navigate and edit the linear algebra expression, access its elements especially matrices, find the solution and save it for further review and edit. The methodology followed is to list all the operations required in Linear Algebra. Then the tasks which require visual abilities were isolated and implemented in the framework.

Keywords: Accessibility, Linear Algebra, Visually impaired.

1 Introduction

Linear algebra is one of the most important branches of mathematics, and is part of many areas of science in general. Thus, it is required for students majoring not only in mathematics, but also in engineering, physics, and economics [1]. Around the world, many high schools provide linear algebra courses as essential parts of the mathematics curriculum [2,3,4]. The number of high school students with visual impairment is significant. For example in the USA, according to the National Federation of the Blind (NFB) 1,061,600 visually impaired students were enrolled in high school diploma or a GED in 2011 [5].

Visually impaired students avoid learning linear algebra in high school. This is usually due to them facing a lot of challenges while dealing with linear algebra. For example, matrices which are an essential part in linear algebra expressions are by nature two dimensional (2D). Thus, solving a simple operation like adding two matrices will pass through two steps: (1) check if the two matrices have the same size, (2) add the numbers in the matching positions and write the results in a new matrix. These two steps require repeated scans and jumps between the entries of the two matrices. Similarly, finding the number of rows or columns, determining the type of

K. Miesenberger et al. (Eds.): ICCHP 2014, Part I, LNCS 8547, pp. 572–579, 2014.
© Springer International Publishing Switzerland 2014

matrix, or accessing elements of a diagonal sequentially can be easily done by sighted students while it takes much longer by students who are visually impaired. Unlike other approaches that help visually impaired students solve only the one dimensional (1D) algebraic expressions; this approach facilitates the manipulation process of two dimensional (2D) linear expressions. For example scans and jumps between sub-expressions to solve an algebraic equation differ than scans and jumps between two matrices to solve multiplying operation which requires jumps in two dimensions.

In this paper, we propose an interactive workspace, aiming at enabling high school students who are visually impaired to learn linear algebra. The workspace described in this paper provides several techniques and system operations in order to support the manipulation of linear algebra expressions.

In section 2, prior research is summarized. Section 3 details the methodology of deriving the tasks that require help for the visually impaired. In section 4 the overall framework and its components is described. Section 5 describes the implementation of the tasks. In section 6 a plan of system evaluation is presented. Section 7 concludes the paper with a summary of achievements and future research ideas.

2   Prior Research

Many research projects are designed to overcome barriers and problems associated with visually impaired accessibility in mathematics. Two main categories of approaches exist: static and dynamic. In static approaches such as MAVIS [6] and BraMaNet [7],the mathematical content is statically converted into a format that is reproducible using assistive devices or that can be printed on Braille paper. The document is mostly viewed as a passive entity (akin to a printed document presented to a sighted user), while the active component is represented by the user, who uses an assistive device (e.g., a refreshable Braille display) to move around the document, reading parts, skipping other parts, or backtracking. On the other hand, dynamic approaches require a conversion process to allow navigation in accordance with the mathematical structure. In this case, the document itself becomes an active component, its semantic structure is exposed and information overload on the user reduced.

AsTeR [8] is a system that helps produce rendering audio of electronic documents. It allows navigation of the formulas, exploring the expression as a tree-based structure and tagging certain nodes for easy recall. MathGenie [14] is specially designed for visually impaired students in the sciences. It allows the user to navigate MathML formulas through a simple key combination, focusing only on representation of formulas rather than semantics. Mathplayer [9] is a plug-in for Microsoft Internet Explorer that reads MathML input.

Despite the number of approaches aimed at promoting accessibility of mathematical formulae (i.e., reading or writing), there have been relatively limited efforts to enhance mathematics manipulation technologies (i.e., doing mathematics). In [10] visually impaired students are given the ability to manipulate algebraic equations through an interactive non-visual workspace. This workspace enables manipulating mathematics in a convenient, accessible, and usable way. By using the selection technique of this workspace, students are able to select sub-expressions of interest as well as manipulate functions. However, this workspace only supports doing and manipulating algebraic expressions and does not support linear algebra.

3   Methodology

In this paper, manipulation of linear algebra expressions by visually impaired students is simplified through providing them with an interactive workspace. The aim of such a workspace is to enable the visually impaired student to interact with linear algebraic content as effectively as possible as a sighted student. The first step towards building such a workspace was to identify which tasks required the student to use his/her sight. Syllabi of linear algebra courses in high schools were reviewed [2,3,4], as well as books and papers written for the purpose of teaching linear algebra [11,12,13]. The following topics were identified [13]: Matrix Addition and Multiplication, Systems of Linear Equations, Determinants, Properties of R^n, Eigenvalues and Eigenvectors, and Orthogonality. Each topic was then broken into several subtopics. "Gaussian elimination" and "elementary matrices" are examples of subtopics of the topic "Systems of Linear Equations". Each sub topic was further broken into basic operations. The basic operations were then grouped into several categories according to their type. Table1 lists the basic linear algebra operations that were obtained from all the identified subtopics and their categories. Each basic operation was then broken down into tasks. For example the operation "Scalar multiplication" was broken down into the following tasks:

Task 1: Create a new matrix for the result.
Task 2: Access the scalar value.
Task 3: Access the current entry in the matrix.
Task 4: Multiply the entry by the scalar value.
Task 5: Write the result in the new matrix in the same position.
Task 6: Repeat the tasks 2, 3, and 4 for each entry in the matrix.

Tasks were then filtered based on whether or not they needed visual abilities. For example, among the tasks of "Scalar multiplication" only tasks 1, 2, 3 and 5 required visual abilities. The list of all tasks requiring visual abilities was then analyzed to determine the following visual abilities needed in linear algebra:

V1: Find the number of rows/columns in a matrix.
V2: Access the entries of a single row/column sequentially.
V3: Access the entries of the diagonal of a matrix sequentially.
V4: Return to a bookmark.
V5: Access a specific entry in a matrix.
V6: Create a new matrix of certain size.
V7: Hide row/column of a matrix.
V8: Unhide row/column of a matrix.
V9: Check whether entries of a matrix in strategic places were equal.

Table 1. Basic Operations and their categories

Category	Basic Operation
Matrices Arithmetic	Adding/Subtracting
	Multiplying by a constant (Scalar Multiplication)
	Multiplying by another matrix
Determinant Matrix	Determinant of a 2x2 matrix
	Determinant of a 3x3 matrix
Transpose Matrix	Transpose
Inverse Matrix	Inverse of a diagonal matrix
	Inverse of a 2x2 matrix
	Inverse of a 3x3 matrix
Elementary Row/Column operations	Interchange two rows/columns
	Multiply each element in a row/column by a non-zero number
	Multiply a row/column by a non-zero number and add the result to another row/column.

Table 2. Techniques and their description

Techniques	Description	Visual abilities
Read-Expression	Read the selected expression, identify a matrix by its position and size (number of rows, number of columns).	V1
Read-Matrix	Read the selected matrix entry by entry after initialize the pointer and direction of reading (row, column, or diagonal). Stop after read each entry.	V2, V3, and V5
Next-Row/Column	Continue the reading to the next row/column	V2
Feedback	Inform the end user about the ending of row, column, or matrix.	V2, and V3
Text-Window	End user can any time open an auxiliary text window then close it.	V4
Write-Matrix	The end user can any time write an empty matrix with specific size.	V6
Text-Tools	Select, Copy, Paste, Delete, Write.	V6
Hide-Row/Column	Hide a row/column from the selected matrix.	V7
Unhide-Row/Column	Unhide a row/column from the selected matrix.	V8
Identify-Properties	Inform the end user about the location of zeroes and ones in a matrix.	V9

In order to help the visually impaired students do these visual tasks, the proposed workspace provides one or more techniques for each task. The implementation of these tasks will evaluate by several usability metrics and the result will collected and reported. In Table2, the techniques are presented along with their descriptions. In addition, each technique is mapped to the visual abilities that it supports.

4   Design and Structure

The system consists of three main modules: Interface, System Technique, and System Object, as shown in Figure1.

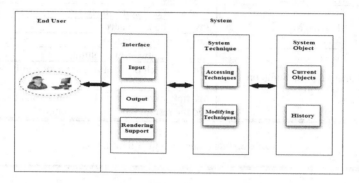

Fig. 1. The general architecture of the proposed system

The Interface module is the space where interaction between the user and the system occurs. One of the goals here is effective operation and control of the system on the user's end. Another goal is feedback from the system, which aids the operator in making operational decisions. Interface contains three sub-modules: Input module which allows the users to manipulate the system by using several techniques such as Write-Matrix technique, and Output module which allows the system to indicate the effects of the users' manipulation by using audio feedback. The audio feedback is used to keep the visually impaired students oriented to the manipulation process. For example, the system provides audio information about each single entry. Rendering Support module, which supports the module of interface by one or more render techniques such as TTS technique. The System Techniques module implements the system operations that help the end user in performing the basic linear algebra operations mentioned previously. These techniques are classified into two sub-modules: Accessing Techniques which allow the user to access the expression, its elements, and the history of the manipulation, and Modifying Techniques which allow the end user to write or modify his/her solution. The System Object module is devoted to store the objects of the system and its data. It consists of two sub-modules: Current Objects module which contains the current objects, and History module which contains all the manipulation steps.

After accessing a file that contains a MathML content the system automatically detects and converts the linear algebra expressions into objects which make them much easier to be navigated, edited, and updated. Dealing with objects allows the user to stop at each element in the matrix and call one of the available techniques such as Next-Row/Column.

5   System Description

The ultimate goal of this workspace is to facilitate the manipulation process of a linear algebra expression for visually impaired students. This workspace allows the student to navigate expressions, select a certain matrix, and navigate its entries by using hot access keys and audio feedback. Using audio, the workspace starts with a brief description of the available options. The user has the ability to either choose to read from a specific file stored locally or online from a web page. The system will then detect the MathML content and convert the linear algebra expressions to objects. All objects identified are then grouped in a list which the user can navigate using the arrow keys. The system will then inform the user about the number of expressions available. The user can then choose an expression and the system will read the expression for the user.

Matrices in an expression are read to the user as the letter m followed by an index along with the size of the matrix. The number of rows and columns, and the location of zero's and one's; are examples of the information about the selected matrix that the system provides to the user. Moreover, the system allows the user to select a matrix in order to navigate its entries. By using the available techniques in the system like Next-Row/Column and Feedback techniques, the user can access the entries and know the nature of the matrix by using Identify-Properties technique.

Editing an expression in order to solve it is available to the user during the navigation in the main window. By using suitable hot access keys, the user is able to update, delete, and add a component to the expression. The system provides several techniques in order to help the user handle the linear algebra expression such as: Hide-Row/Column, Text-Tools, Write-Matrix and more. The user has also the ability to save the results of his/her manipulations. Saving the results will update the MathML file to include a MathML representation of the new results so that when the user reopens the file later on he/she will be able to navigate the results as well as edit them.

Using arrow keys in navigating instead of several hot access keys for each system's component will reduce the amount of memorizing by the user. For an example, the h button in the keyboard is devoted to invoke the help function that is used for finding out the current status or reviewing the list of available hot access keys. The tab button in turn allows the end user to access different available windows. In addition the arrow keys employed by the system to help the user in navigating the names of existing files, the available expressions, the elements of an expression, and the entries of a matrix.

Figure 2 illustrates the interface of the workspace. The user is able to navigate and select a linear algebra expression by using the available techniques such as Read-Matrix technique. In addition, the user can edit any selected expression, perform the operation, and save the solution. Also the user has the ability to move freely between the available forms using hot access keys as shown in the figure below.

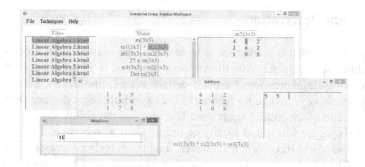

Fig. 2. The workspace of the system

6   System Evaluation

The system is currently under evaluation with visually impaired students enrolled in Lebanese High schools and Universities. Several experiments using a system proto-type will be conducted for evaluating the system. The prototype involved most func-tional features of the designed workspace: Adding two matrices, Multiplying two matrices, Transpose a matrix, and more. A number of participants who have vision impairment will be involved in the experiments. In each of the experiments, partici-pants will be asked to do specific tasks by two approaches: first through the conven-tional way they use (CCTV or Braille writer), then through the system after it will be fully introduced to them by a demo. Time needed by each student to accomplish the tasks, answers reached, mistakes made, will be recorded in order to measure the effectiveness and efficiency of the system.

7   Conclusion and Future Work

Students with visual impairments have unique learning needs that must be addressed if they are going to access the general education curriculum. In this paper we pre-sented an interactive workspace that is designed for helping visually impaired students in practicing the fundamentals of linear algebra. After listing all the basic operations required in linear algebra and identifying the tasks that require visual abili-ties, a set of techniques was constructed in order to help the visually impaired students perform these tasks. The implementation of these techniques was then described and followed by the plan for the usability test. In the near future, we will work on the enhancement of the system based on the results of the ongoing usability test and eva-luating its benefits on other categories of visually impaired students. Also it would be of interest to extend the current workspace to serve visually impaired students in other areas of mathematics.

References

1. Bogomolny, M.: The Role of Example-Generation Tasks In Students' Understanding of Algebra, Simon Fraser University, Canada (2006)
2. Stanford High School, Linear Algebra,
   `http://ohs.stanford.edu/syllabi/syllabus_UM51A.pdf`
3. Stuyvesant High School, Math Courses,
   `http://stuy.enschool.org/apps/pages/index.jsp?uREC_ID=127571`
   `&type=d&termREC_ID=&pREC_ID=253244`
4. Pukekohe High School, Linear Algebra,
   `http://www.pukekohehigh.school.nz/WebSpace/1473`
5. National Federation of the Blind: Statistical Facts about Blindness in the US in 2011 (2011), `https://nfb.org/factsaboutblindnessintheus`
6. Karshmer, A., Gupta, G., Geiiger, S., Weaver, C.: Reading and writing mathematics: the project. In: Proceedings of the Third International ACM Conference on Assistive Technologies, pp. 136–143. ACM Press, Marina del Rey (1998)
7. Schwebel, F.: BraMaNet: logiciel de traduction des mathématiques en Braille,
   `http://handy.univ-lyon1.fr/projects/bramanet`
8. Raman, T.V.: Audio Systems for Technical Reading, Ph.D. thesis, Department of Computer Science, Cornell University, NY, USA (1994)
9. Soiffer, N.: Mathplayer: web-based math accessibility. In: The 7th International ACM SIGACCESS Conference on Computers and Accessibility, Assets 2005 (2005)
10. Alajarmeh, N., Pontelli, E., Son, T.: "From "Reading" Math to "Doing" Math: A New Direction in Non-visual Math Accessibility". In: Stephanidis, C. (ed.) Universal Access in HCI, Part IV, HCII 2011. LNCS, vol. 6768, pp. 501–510. Springer, Heidelberg (2011)
11. Day, J.M., Kalman, D.: Teaching Linear Algebra: What are the Questions?, American University, USA, Washington (1999)
12. Idris, I.M.: Toward a Right Way to Teach Linear Algebra, Mathematics Department, Faculty of Science, Ain-Shams University, Cairo, Egypt (2003)
13. Carlson, D., Johnson, C., Lay, D., Duane Porter, A.: The Linear Algebra Curriculum Study Group recommendations for the first course in linear algebra. College Mathematics Journal 24, 41–46 (1993)
14. Karshmer, A.I., Bledsoe, C., Stanley, P.B.: The architecture of a comprehensive equation browser for the print impaired. In: Miesenberger, K., Klaus, J., Zagler, W.L., Burger, D. (eds.) ICCHP 2004. LNCS, vol. 3118, pp. 614–619. Springer, Heidelberg (2004)

The LEAN Math Accessible MathML Editor

John A. Gardner

ViewPlus Technologies, Inc., Corvallis, OR, USA
john.gardner@viewplus.com

Abstract. This article describes the new LEAN Math application. LEAN Math will input MathML and convert it to an internal representation from which any number of accessible formats can be generated. It is useful for reading math, but its real importance is that it fills a void for blind people who need an efficient, usable tool to create, edit, and manipulate math equations in braille and/or audio. The first application of LEAN Math is as an editor for MathType equations in MS Word, the most popular scientific authoring system today. The editor can open and edit existing equations or create new ones. It also puts a word description or braille translation of the equation into the MathType alt text property. This alt text is read by any screen reader, making MathType equations in MS Word fully accessible. This paper gives a brief overview of its features.

Keywords: Accessible Math, Reading Math, Writing Math, Manipulating Math, MS Word, MathType.

1 Introduction

1.1 Accessible Methods for Reading Math

Math in scientific web and e-book documents can be directly accessible to people with print disabilities provided the math is expressed in the MathML[1] markup language. Some web browsers, including older versions of Internet Explorer with the MathPlayer[2] plugin and Chrome with the ChromeVox[3] speech display provide audio-access to MathML. Safari on iOS systems with VoiceOver[4] provides both audio and braille access to MathML. Specialized applications such as the EASYReader[5] and GH ReadHear[6] provide access to electronic books in formats adhering to accessibility standards set by the International Digital Publishing Forum[7]. There is hope that future electronic books and web documents will adhere to such standards, making math in all web and e-books accessible.

---

[1] http://w3.org/math
[2] http://www.dessci.com/en/products/mathplayer/
[3] http://www.chromevox.com/
[4] http://www.apple.com/accessibility/osx/voiceover/
[5] http://www.yourdolphin.com/productdetail.asp?id=9
[6] http://www.gh-accessibility.com/software/readhear-pc/
[7] http://idpf.org/

K. Miesenberger et al. (Eds.): ICCHP 2014, Part I, LNCS 8547, pp. 580–587, 2014.
© Springer International Publishing Switzerland 2014

Math in PDF documents is not directly accessible, but such documents can be indirectly accessible if the author's manuscript is available. Most modern authors use MS Word with the MathType math editor to write scientific documents, though a substantial number still use LaTeX and similar variations of the TeX family of markup languages. LaTeX source files are directly readable by any screen reader, and generations of blind people have had good access to scientific documents by becoming experts in reading LaTeX[1].

MS Word+MathType documents can also be accessible to blind readers, be-cause MathType permits one to display equations in LaTeX. The user must develop sufficient knowledge of LaTeX to read the equations, but it is only the math that is expressed in LaTeX. It is much easier to read MS Word with LaTeX equations than to read a corresponding LaTeX document, because the latter generally has pages of text markup that must be read past. This slows the reading process and interferes with comprehension. Blind people who know math braille have a better option for reading MS Word documents. Several translators are available to convert MS Word+MathType documents into braille.

1.2   Accessible Methods for Writing and Manipulating Math

Blind people who know math braille can write math equations compactly in braille. Braille is not as flexible as a pencil – one cannot easily cross off terms, trans-pose them to the other side of the equation, etc. One can only write equation after equation with appropriate changes. Braille is also not easily converted to a main-stream form. Computer translation from any conventional math code to a mainstream representation is notoriously unreliable. So if the math is intended for mainstream use (eg for a sighted teacher), the translation must be done by a human math braille expert, and there are not many of these.

For several decades, LaTeX was the only accessible route by which a blind person could create a mainstream document with math. LaTeX is a complex lan-guage, and compiling it to the final document is a non-trivial task. It is unreasonable to expect that any student needing to write math equations must become a LaTeX expert, particularly if the student has no intention of becoming a professional scien-tist. Learning enough LaTeX to write equations in MS Word+MathType is a less onerous task. Unfortunately, there is no feedback when those equations are converted to standard form. It is very easy to make mistakes, so the user is never sure that the equation is actually what is intended.

The ChattyInfty[8] editor was developed originally to provide access to documents recognized by the Infty Reader[9], the only Optical Character Recognition (OCR) application that recognizes math expressions. Chatty Infty can export in several mainstream formats, including MS Word, LaTeX, and XHTML, but it does not import these formats. It is somewhat expensive but does offer several nice features, including an image of the equation in standard visual form during the creation/editing process.

---

[8] http://www.sciaccess.net/en/ChattyInfty/
[9] http://www.inftyreader.org/

1.3   LEAN Math

LEAN Math was developed so that blind people would have an easy and affordable way to write and manipulate math. When LEAN Math for MS Word is installed, two applications are installed, LEAN-In and LEAN-Edit. LEAN-In inserts alt text in selected MathType equations. LEAN-Edit is the main application that allows the user to create MathType equations or edit existing ones. LEAN-Edit's preference menu includes choices of format for saving alt text. LEAN-In saves in the currently-selected preference. LEAN Math is a commercial product whose beta test phase is expected to end in mid-2014. It will be a commercial product but will be licensed free to blind individuals.

2   The LEAN User Interface

The LEAN Editor User interface is a dialog with four lines. The top line shows the equation in LEAN notation. LEAN uses a special Unicode set with special characters for open-root, close-root, open-fraction, fraction-line, close-fraction, etc. These particular

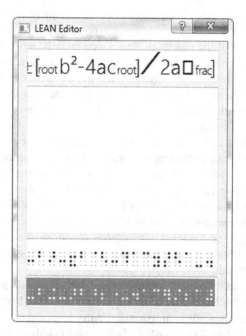

Fig. 1. The LEAN Math Editor User Interface. The top line is the LEAN notation, the second is for messages spoken during editing, the third is the equation in LEAN Braille notation, and the bottom line in the user's choice of conventional math braille. Focus is on the bottom line, which is Nemeth.

LEAN symbols are shown in Figure 1, which shows the LEAN interface when the editor contains the equation

$$x = \frac{-b \pm \sqrt{b^2 - 4ac}}{2a} \tag{1}$$

3   Basic Features of the LEAN Editor

The first-time user needs to know how to install the LEAN Editor and needs to know the following items to get started:

- LEAN_Edit is started by clicking on the icon in the desktop.
- MS Word must be open when starting LEAN Editor or else an error occurs.
- MathType must be installed or LEAN will not work.
- Keyboard characters are entered normally into LEAN equations. Only a few (@ ^_) are special hot keys. Other characters must be entered by opening an appropriate list with a function key.
- The function keys play the role of pull-down menus in LEAN Editor. ALT keys are hot keys. They do not pull down menus as in most Windows applications.
- Once LEAN Editor is open, press CTRL+h to access a thorough list of help topics. These are an internal manual for LEAN. LEAN can be learned by reading these help topics.

3.1   Help Files

Pressing CTRL+h in the LEAN Editor brings up a list of help topics. These topics cover basically every feature of LEAN_Edit and LEAN_In. Users should arrow up and down to find a topic, then press ENTER to open it. Navigation is standard. Up/down arrows move line to line, right/left arrows move letter by letter, CTRL+right/left move word by word. The * key navigates by sub topic and reads it. The line length is user-selectable to match the length of a braille display if desired. The length is set in the preference menu as discussed below.

3.2   Preference Menu

CTRL+p opens the preference menu. Preferences are used to control display parameters but do not affect the actual equation. One navigates the menus with up/down arrow and makes selections with right/left arrows. Pressing ENTER accepts a new preference, and pressing ENTER twice makes it the default. Defaults are non-volatile.

3.3   Function Key Selections

Function key F1 plays its normal Windows role. It is the context-dependent help key. When focus is on an object in the equation or on an item in some list, F1 brings up a dialog with a description of the item. One may browse the dialog and close it with the ESC key. All other function keys open menus.

- F2 opens a menu of common non-keyboard math characters, including dot and cross product, plus minus, minus plus, infinity, and degree.
- F3 opens a menu of structures including fraction, square root, subscript, super-script, and squared. All these can be inserted with a single hot key. The hot key is given in the list so that beginners can use the menu and learn the hot keys as they become power users. There are of course many structures in this list that are less common and do not have a dedicated hot key.
- F4 opens a menu of lists including the lists opened by F2 and F3. Many of these lists, eg integrals, tables, can be opened with hot keys, and the hot keys are given.
- F5-F10 bring up lists of advanced characters and are arranged in alphabetic order of the type of symbol.
- F5 opens a list of arrow characters as well as lists of several sets of specialized arrow symbols.
- F6 opens a set of binary operators. Binary operators are symbols that "operate" between two characters. The "+", "=" symbols are common binary operators. These two are available from the keyboard so are not given in the F6 list.
- F7 opens a set of symbols common in calculus including differential, partial diffe-rential, integral sign, etc.
- F8 opens a list of geometry symbols.
- F9 opens a list of modifier symbols. Modifiers are symbols that combine with another symbol. Examples are the dagger and prime symbols.
- F10 opens a set of symbols used in set theory. Examples are the union and inter-section symbols.
- F11 is presently unused.
- F12 lists all navigation commands and is intended as a reference for finding the right key to use for less common navigation procedures such as table navigation, compacting equations, and clipboard commands.

3.4   Clipboards

The Lean Editor has three types of clipboard. All are non-volatile, so any-thing saved in a clipboard will not be changed when the editor is closed or even if the computer is re-booted. One can copy or cut to a clipboard and paste from it. Partial expression cannot be copied. An attempt to do so results in an error dialog.

- The normal clipboard is modeled on the standard Windows clipboard. One selects a character or string of characters by holding the shift key and moving forward or backward through the equation. The copy command is CTRL+c, cut is CTRL+x, and paste is CTRL+p. Apart from the restriction of copying only complete ex-pres-sions, this is normal Windows behavior.
- The Selectable Clipboard. The selectable clipboard is actually a set of ten clip-boards. One selects a string just as one does for the normal clipboard and copies to the selectable clipboard with SHIFT+CTRL+c. Then one either types a number

from 0 to 9 or arrows down to the clipboard with that number, and then presses ENTER to complete the copy command.   SHIFT+CTRL+x is identical to copy except that it cuts the selected region.   SHIFT+CTRL+v pastes from the selectable clipboard in a similar manner.

- The Fraction Clipboard. The fraction clipboard is dedicated to copying, cutting, and pasting fractions. To copy a fraction it is necessary only to put the cursor on the open or close fraction symbols or anywhere inside the fraction.   When one presses ALT+c or ALT+x, the smallest fraction enclosing the cursor is copied or cut respectively. ALT+v pasts from the fraction clipboard.   The fraction clipboard is also manipulated with other commands. ALT+I pastes in the inverse of the fraction in the clipboard. ALT+u converts the numerator of a fraction to a non-fraction string and cuts the denominator to the fraction clipboard.   These are all very useful commands for manipulating algebraic equations while "doing math" as opposed to simply writing math.

4   Advanced Features of the LEAN Editor

4.1   Structures

LEAN does not permit the user to insert the open or close symbol for frac-tions, roots, or any other structure.   One may insert structures only by inserting the full structure and then inserting the various parts of the structure.   For example, a fraction is entered by finding it in the F3 menu or by pressing ALT+f. The cursor is automatically placed on a numerator place-holder symbol.   One then creates the fraction numerator, presses the right arrow to move to the denominator and then creates it. Consequently it is relatively difficult to create a LEAN equation that is not valid MathML.

4.2   Special Features for Manipulating Equations

The fraction clipboard was described above. It is largely intended for the kinds of manipulation frequently needed while solving algebraic equations. One can cut a fraction from one side of an equation with one keystroke (CTRL+x) and insert its inverse on the other side with one more keystroke (CTRL+i.   One can cut the denominator from a fraction and convert the numerator to a string in the same place with CTRL+u. One can convert a selected string to the numerator of a fraction and place the cursor in an empty denominator with ALT+t. These are all extremely useful commands for manipulating algebraic equations.

4.3   Compound Elements

The LEAN Editor has internal structure that permits multiple-character quantities such as multiple-digit numbers and multiple-character scripts to be part of a compound character.   These permit numbers to be spoken more intuitively and for cognitively simpler browsing of complex equations.   The user can hear x sub ijk super abc instead of something like x sub {ijk} super {abc}.

4.4   Compacting Equations

LEAN Math permits users to create a compact view of a long equation and then view the various terms by gradually decomposing the parts. The parts are the structures that make up the equation or portion of equation that the user compacts.

4.5   LEAN Braille

LEAN Braille is an invention of the author. It was developed as a braille equivalent of the LEAN notation and has many advantages over conventional math braille codes. It is unique and not context-dependent and therefore can be back-translated more robustly than can conventional math braille. It also permits nice features such as the compact view, which conventional braille codes cannot.

LEAN Braille is inspired by the GS Braille Code research done by Gardner and Salinas (http://dots.physics.orst.edu/gs.html). GS is a dual 6/8dot braille code originally begun because of the displeasure of the researchers with Unified English Braille committee's insistence on adopting literary braille numbers. The GS Braille research was terminated with the untimely death of Prof. Salinas.

GS and LEAN Braille use the Antoine numbers that are used in DIN (Central European) computer braille. These are derived from literary numbers by dropping the number sign and adding a dot-6 to each of the letters a-I that represent the digits 1-9. The zero is represented by dots346, because adding a dot-6 to "j" is a "w", and unfortunate consequence of "w" not being included in French when M. Louis Braille developed the braille character set. The great advantage of Antoine numbers is that they do not conflict with any non-accented letter. In fact non-contracted English braille does not have these ten characters at all.

LEAN adopted the basic features and most of the symbols of GS. The author created LEAN Braille symbols for the LEAN special symbols. Math equations expressed in LEAN Braille are quite compact when the 8-dot form is used.

5   Beta Testing and Commercialization

Commercial product testing proceeds quite differently than research beta testing. The author has been both a research scientist and a commercial developer and understands the difference. Research testing must begin by determining whether the research direction is sensible. For commercial products, a company must make a prior judgment that the product is sensible in order to justify the usually considerable development expense. So the purpose of commercial product testing is to help the developers correct bugs, tune features, and make the product as user-friendly as feasible. Normally product beta testers are given prototypes and asked to use them in their daily work or recreation. Feedback is normally in the form of unstructured commentary. LEAN Math is being beta tested as a commercial product, not a research project. Although approximately fifty people are on the beta test list, the number of dedicated beta testers is only approximately five. They have helped with finding bugs, and some have suggested feature improvements, including the compacting feature. At least two beta testers are also using LEAN Braille to some extent and appreciate its compactness and lack of context sensitivity.

LEAN Math will be a part of several ViewPlus information accessibility "solutions". It was never intended to be a money-making product in its own right, so licenses will be given free to blind individuals. Companies and educational institutions may purchase LEAN Math as part of a ViewPlus solution and receive training and support.

Acknowledgements. The author is grateful to Michael Whapples, Courtney Christensen, and Yuemei Sun for software assistance in developing this product.

Reference

1. Maneki, A.P., Jeans, A.: LaTeX: What Is it and Why Do We Need it? Braille Monitor Publisher National Federation of the Blind (2012),
   https://nfb.org/images/nfb/publications/bm/bm12/bm1207/bm120704.htm

SVGPlott – Generating Adaptive and Accessible Audio-Tactile Function Graphs

Jens Bornschein, Denise Prescher, and Gerhard Weber

Technische Universität Dresden, Institut für Angewandte Informatik, Dresden, Germany
{jens.bornschein,denise.prescher,gerhard.weber}@tu-dresden.de

Abstract. Curve sketching is a hard task for blind and visually impaired pupils and students, but it is an essential part in education. To help those students as well as their colleges, teachers and other people to prepare good tactile function plots the platform independent console program *SVGPlott* was developed. It enables users without any special knowledge about creating graphics for blind or visually impaired people to prepare highly adaptable mathematical function plots in the SVG format, which can also be used for audio-tactile exploration. *SVGPlott* was developed in a user-centered design process, including teachers and users. We show that blind and sighted users can prepare function plots including key as well as an automatically generated textual description not only for tactile, audio-tactile and print output, but also for usage on a dynamic tactile pin device and as a high contrast visualization for low vision people.

Keywords: Accessible SVG, Science and Mathematics, Function Graph Plots, Tactile Graphics, Audio-Tactile Graphics, Adaptability of Graphics, Style Sheets, User Groups, Blind and Visually Impaired Users, Tactile Pin Device, Accessibility.

1 Introduction

Mathematics is a basic course every student has to take. The graphical aspect of the curve sketching task is a big challenge for blind and visually impaired students – not only creating function graphs by their own, but also reading previously prepared graph plots of classmates, colleges or teachers with less experience in creating such kind of graphics for special reader groups.

There are several systems for making mathematical function graphs accessible. Existing hardware calculators, such as *Orion TI-84 Plus Talking Graphing Calculator* [1], or software calculators, such as *MathTrax* [2], sonify the graph and give audio feedback about the trend of the graph via pan and pitch of sound signals corresponding to x- and y-values of the function. With the *Accessible Graphing Calculator* [3] the user can plot more than one function to find intersections. The *TermEvaluator* [4], for example, offers a highly adaptable user interface. Some of these tools have the opportunity to print out the resulting graphics. Providing an additional description of the function graph can help to better understand the graphic. Some programs automatically create descriptions of the graph and its distinctive characteristics [2].

K. Miesenberger et al. (Eds.): ICCHP 2014, Part I, LNCS 8547, pp. 588–595, 2014.
© Springer International Publishing Switzerland 2014

In the following we describe a simple java- and gnuplot-based [5] console program that can create graph plots for mathematical functions as adaptive Scalable Vector Graphics (SVG) for audio-tactile output. The program allows the user to easily create graphical representations of mathematical functions that can be printed, displayed on screen or used for audio-tactile (including Braille) or visual exploration. Existing functions can also be adapted for user groups with special needs.

2   The SVG Graph Plotter Program

Using a tool to calculate function values of a graph often results in a list or a table of numerical values. To convey a qualitative meaning of this data to the reader, the relationship between the points can be displayed, for example, by sonification, which is also very abstract, or in a graphical manner. In mathematics education a graphical representation can help students to perform curve sketching tasks. Commonly, there are tasks such as "find the main features of the curves", "find the turning point", "find the x-intercepts" etc. In addition, a tool which allows such a graphical output should also permit the combination of more than one function in one coordinate system. In this way, further mathematical exercises, for example comparing two functions or finding their intersections, will be possible.

For this reason, we aim at designing *SVGPlott* as a tool that allows visually impaired students as well as their teachers to create tactile graph plots of mathematical functions for curve sketching including support for Braille. For a better understanding of the tactile output it should be enriched with additional textual information that can be accessed, for example, with an audio-tactile system, such as *IVEO* [3].

The program can plot an unlimited number of planar functions in one coordinate system, but it is optimized for up to three different functions for a tactile output. As the heterogeneous usage of special mathematical notations for writing function terms is a problem producing inconsistencies, every function can get a freely-assignable title. This title can be an intuitive name or the function term written in another mathematical language, such as LaTeX or Nemeth-code, in cases the function call differs.

A key (legend) is generated as an independent SVG file containing the line styles used in relation to the plotted functions, the optional individual function title as well as a description of the axes' scales and their ranges. Supplementary, a textual description is generated as structured HTML. It explains the chosen view port, plotted functions and feature points of the plots in structured lists for an easy exploration with a screen reader. This description can be used as an alternative text placed, for example, in a DAISY book.

3   Adaptability of Graphics

As the main feature, the output should be easy to adapt in style to several different output media or user groups. A subsequent adaptation of graphical output is not straightforward. If the image is pixel based, special programs with graphic tools and filters are necessary for editing. Even if the picture is available as a vector graphic, which can theoretically be edited without any quality and information loss, special tools, knowledge and programs are required. Vector based image formats, such as SVG, have the advantage that image elements are declared in a programmatic, mathematical way by describing how an object has to be painted. For this a vector image can be increased without quality loss and, theoretically, can be read in text by a user.

The features supported by the XML based SVG format allow the adaptation in a simple, fast and powerful manner. Changing the style information for several parts of the image is possible and gives the opportunity to adapt a wide range of visual as well as tactile properties of an image. This can be achieved by using Cascading Style Sheets (CSS), which allow the declaration of simple rules for color, size and other visual properties of elements. It is also possible to define separate representations for different output media in one file. One can distinguish between a view on a screen and a printer or embosser. This makes it possible to define a view for a Braille reader on paper and a view for a sighted college or teacher on a screen in the same file. A big advantage of SVG is that the files can be viewed with every current web browser.

To support this flexibility, the SVG has to be well prepared. Nearly every object of the SVG has to get a unique identifier as well as a meaningful class name that groups associated elements in their visual representation. These names and identifiers can be used by the different implemented style sheets.

3.1   Tactile Optimization

One of our main goals for the development of *SVGPlott* was to find an easy way of creating tactile graphs for blind students. This means basic characteristics for tactile imaging should be followed, for example keeping the image as simple as possible and not presenting image elements too small allowing a good tactile recognition. Adaptation with style sheets cannot add further information to an image or change the whole composition. For that reason the basic image structure has to be well designed.

A basic implementation for tactile output, especially for *Tiger* embossable tactile images, is created. Three highly different line styles for the plotted curves were designed, so that they can be immediately distinguished by the reader from their tactile shape. More than three different lines in one plot seem not to be reasonable, but are possible. The lines of the plotted functions have to be the most noticeable ones in the graphic, followed by the coordinate axes. Thereby, variations between two different function lines can be only presented through diverse patterns in a tactile output. We chose to use a continuous line for the first curve, a dotted line for the second and dashed lines for any further curves (see Fig 1). The different line styles vary in their ease of tracking. Therefore, the user has to select the used line style by sorting the functions by complexity. The most complex function has to get the continuous line and should be inserted as first and so on.

Other elements of the graphic are adjusted for tactile print as well. For example, all texts inside the key or the titles of the plot and the axes, will be set to Braille. Lines of the underlying grid as well as the coordinate axes are styled in gray values which will appear as different embossing depths on the tactile paper.

Induced by user feedback the feature to mark special points in graphs or to paint only some points into an empty coordinate system was integrated. Thereby, the user can set up several lists of points, name them and place them into the graph (see Fig. 1, left). The points will be described in the key and in the textual description as well, but they will not be labeled in the plot itself. Therefore they have to be intuitively identifiable and distinguishable in visual and tactile shape. For a better recognition some free space around the points is realized by a border defined in the style sheet. This prevents points from falling together with axes, function lines or other points. Infinite amount of point lists are possible, but more than two different point lists and styles should be avoided in the context of a usable tactile graphic.

SVGPlott also addresses user who want to plot integral functions. It is possible to define integrals between the x-axes and a function or between two functions, delimited by the image section or by manually adjustable limits. The integral area is filled with a tactile pattern, overlapping the underlying grid. The axes and the function lines overlap the integral area and are separated to the filling pattern by some free space for a better recognition, too. The area can be filled with two different diagonal line style patterns (left oriented and right oriented, see Fig. 2) or with a freely selectable color.

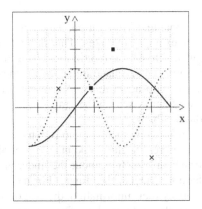 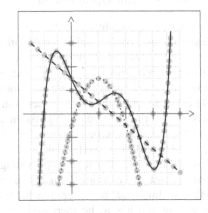

Fig. 1. Plot of sine/cosine functions and two point lists optimized for tactile output (left) and plot of three functions with visible overlay regions (light gray) for audio-tactile output (right)

We also tested the possibility to adapt the output of *SVGPlott* to the two-dimensional refreshable Braille display *BrailleDis7200* (see Fig. 2), which has a resolution of 10 dots per inch and therefore is comparable to a normal Braille text embosser with equidistant setting [6]. As a consequence of the low resolution different line styles for the function graphs are not feasible, therefore only one function – except the combination with another easy function, such as a line – should be displayed in one plot. Different styles for marked points are a problem, too, as well as Braille text. It cannot be ensured that Braille is rendered correctly on the device, because of interpolation problems when rescaling the rendered SVG image to the low resolution of the pin device. In contrast to a static embossed printout on paper users of the pin device have the opportunity to pan and zoom in the displayed image, comparable to the using of magnifier software. This allows the reader to have a more detailed look at difficult regions in the plot. But this also makes it difficult to display Braille because the rendered Braille text will be zoomed as well and will be unreadable again. To overcome this problem we define all texts not in Braille, but in uppercase sans-serif font type. The reader can have a look at the tactile ink-print by zooming in (letters can be identified from a size of nine pins on the pin device [6]) or can use a standard screen reader to get access to the textual value of the labels. To reduce the information in the plot the underlying grid will be hidden on the pin device.

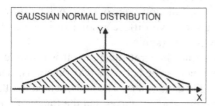 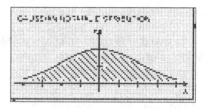

Fig. 2. Plot of the Gaussian function optimized for pin device (left) and its representation on the pin device where black pixels will be set as raised pins (right)

3.2   Audio-Tactile Optimization

Some parts of the graphic are enhanced by additional text information, which provide feedback on their name, value, or intention, for example the axes. This is done by using the SVG feature of giving those elements a title and a description. Using title and description can also support the understandability of an image for sighted readers, for example by showing the title as a mouse-over pop-up in the web browser. In a tactile exploration on the *IVEO* system blind users can touch on the graph with their fingers and get the title and description via audio feedback.

For that purpose, important points have to be marked as special regions, which can be realized by defining overlays in the SVG. Therefore, the chosen points are overlaid with invisible, selectable regions providing further information about the underlying centering point. An individual small point is hard to select with a finger. For making sure that the important points are reachable to convey their information, the size of the selectable region has to be increased for getting that information. The regions are distributed over the function curves and the coordinate system (see Fig. 1, right). Care is taken that no of these additional information regions overlap, so every region can be selected. Therefore a hierarchy for distributing such regions is implemented: 1) intersections between the functions, 2) turning points, 3) x intercepts (null), 4) function points crossing the underlying x-grid values, 5) further spread function values between the main feature points, 6) points on the given axis scale.

How can the readability of the function plot be supported when no audio output is available? As previously mentioned, an underlying grid is plotted. With this grid, which resolution is twice as high as the axes scales, the user can easier count and estimate the function values across the plot. Furthermore, an unlimited number of reference lines in x and y direction can be added to the picture, helping the reader to identify special values.

3.3   High Contrast Optimization

Plots can be created not only for tactile output, but also as high contrast version for low vision users by simply loading another style sheet. For example, the functions will be drawn in different highly contrasting light colors, such as yellow, magenta and lime green, on a black background with white coordinate axes and grid (see Fig. 3). Marked points also will be painted in white with different shapes. For people with a defective color vision the functions should be additionally plotted with different line styles as in the tactile version. Integral areas will be filled with a less opaque version of the tactile filling patterns resulting in a structured light gray plane that is easily recognizable (see Fig. 3, right). As in the tactile version important elements, such as axes, functions and marked points, have some free space surrounding and separating them. For printouts the style sheet contains a media switch for a black on white print version of the image while the user is looking at a high contrast version on the screen. The group of low vision and visually impaired users is very heterogeneous in their preferences and needs, so no general recommendation for styling of such plots can be given.

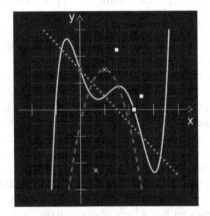 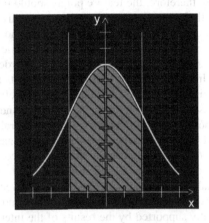

Fig. 3. High contrast versions for plot of three functions and two point lists (left) as well as a Gaussian function with a marked integral area (right)

4 Evaluation

In the context of user-centered design we did a first pilot study with two blind subjects, in which the program's usability and its results for tactile and audio-tactile output were tested. Both subjects are late blinded students of information technology, which are experienced users of command line tools and gnuplot, have a good knowledge about curve sketching, but are less experienced with the *IVEO* system. After a short briefing on the usage of the program the subjects should create a plot containing two given functions. Because the program is fully portable and platform independent, the subjects could run the test setup on their own, well known Linux and Windows computers. The tactile outputs (graphic and key) were embossed by a *TigerPro* on DIN A4 paper.

As their first task the subjects had to find the value 1 on the x-axis by interpreting the grid and the key. The second task was to estimate the feature points on the tactile graphs. In the third task the subjects had to redo the second task with the audio-tactile support of the *IVEO* system, using the same tactile graphic as in the first task (compare Fig. 1, right). Thereby, the feature points, estimated by the subjects in a view range from -8 to +8 in both axe-directions, deviated from the real numeric solution in average about 0.04. Without *IVEO* support the mean error was about 0.29. Finally, several previously prepared plots of different shapes and numbers of functions were presented and the users were asked to give some more feedback about the intelligibility and distinguishability.

In a second step, interviews with three sighted teachers of science and mathematics for blind and visually impaired pupils were conducted. Thereby, we asked them about didactic requirements for such a tool aiming at pupils/students and teachers, after the available features of *SVGPlott* and the resulting graphics were presented. It became clear that the given structured description can help the user to better understand the tactile graphic or can be used as an alternative of the printout. To get an overview about the characteristics of a function the textual description should follow its trend and, therefore, the feature points should be sorted by their x-value instead of grouping by their type (interceptions, turning, null). To this it is also important to declare from which quadrant the graph is entering and leaving the coordinate system. In this way, the reader can walk along the graph while reading it from a low x-value to the higher ones visiting all feature points in their order of appearance.

In further tests with two blind subjects the point symbols and the suitability for the tactile pin device were analyzed. Therefore, specially prepared plots for *Tiger* embosser and the pin device were shown and the subjects had to identify and follow the function lines and axes as well several marked points placed on the function line and freely somewhere inside the coordinate system. After finding all points they had to sort the different point symbols by recognizability and distinguishability. As mentioned before, only two different point symbols should be used in one graphic. A small filled square was rated best followed by a plus symbol as they are highly distinguishable to each other and also fast and easy to recognize. This rating is independently supported by the results of the interviews with teachers who also have the best experience with small solid points surrounded by some free space and sharp line symbols, such as a cross or plus symbol.

In a fourth test the high contrast version was tested with a low vision student normally using magnifier software. High contrast versions of several function plots were presented (three function plot, plot with different marked points, integral function) and the user should follow the function lines and identify and distinguish the marked point without using magnifier software. It became clear that solid lines are better to recognize and to follow as structured lines. The subject was not able to follow all the function lines without using the zoom feature of the standard web browser. Similar to the subjects in earlier tests, the low vision subject mentioned that all solid objects seem to appear as the same, but were easy to distinguish against a cross or a plus symbol. The subject also used the key and the additional textual information by hovering over them with the mouse and reading the appearing small pop-up.

5   Conclusions and Outlook

We showed that the developed console program can be easily used by blind students to successfully create tactile function plots. The tactile results can be used for solving classical curve sketching tasks. This can be done by the normal tactile version of the graph as well as by the audio-tactile version on the *IVEO* system which can increase the accuracy of the results. The SVG plot can be customized via style sheets to other user groups.

In the future a fully accessible graphical user interface should be developed so that a wide range of users have a better joy of use while using *SVGPlott*. The extensibility of the program has to be increased that users can freely define and use their own filling pattern or point symbols. Features for measurable or equidistant coordinate systems are desirable as well as functionalities for doing scatter plots. To overcome problems of low resolution on the pin device the novel opportunities of this medium should be used by implementing animations and interactions, such as blinking or active hiding of objects inside the SVG, which is possible with standard SVG-features or embedded JavaScript. *SVGPlott* will be freely available as an open source project.

Acknowledgements. We thank Gregor Harlan for his fundamental work on SVGPlott. The Tangram project is sponsored by the Federal Ministry of Labour and Social Affairs (BMAS) under the grant number R/FO125423.

References

1. Meddaugh, J.: What's New from The 28th Annual International Technology and Persons with Disabilities Conference, CSUN 2013 Wrap-up, vol. 14(3) (March 2013)
2. Moskovitch, Y., Walker, B.N.: Evaluating Text Descriptions of Mathematical Graphs. In: Proceedings of the 12th International ACM SIGACCESS Conference on Computers and Accessibility, Orlando, Florida, USA (2010)
3. Gardner, J.A.: Access by Blind Students and Professionals to Mainstream Math and Science. In: Computers Helping People with Special Needs, Linz, AU (2002)
4. Liese, W.: Formeln und Gleichungen am PC: LiTeX stellt umfassende Moeglichkeiten fuer den mathematisch-naturwissenschaftlichen Unterricht mit Blinden und Sehbehinderten bereit. In: Zeitschrift fuer das Sehgeschaedigten-Bildungswesen, pp. 13–29 (2007)
5. Racine, J.: Gnuplot 4.0: A portable interactive plotting utility. Journal of Applied Econometrics 21(1), 133–141 (2006)
6. Prescher, D., Nadig, O., Weber, G.: Reading braille and tactile ink-print on a planar tactile display. In: Miesenberger, K., Klaus, J., Zagler, W., Karshmer, A. (eds.) ICCHP 2010, Part II. LNCS, vol. 6180, pp. 482–489. Springer, Heidelberg (2010)

Free Tools to Help Blind People with Musical Learning

Nadine Jessel

IRIT, Université Paul Sabatier, Toulouse, France
baptiste@irit.fr

Abstract. This paper describes solutions to improve the access to music for blind people. These solutions are proposed during the European project Music4VIP. The objective of the project is to help teacher to teach music to blind pupils and to create tools which will enable blind people to learn music independently. A method base on SUS questionnaire is described and used to have a quick feedback for users. These first results indicate that users perceive our solution as good but these results have to be consolidated with further surveys with a large number of respondents.

1 Introduction

As Antonio Quatraro said in 2009, during the conference for the Commemoration of the Bicentenary of Louis Braille's Birth, access to music for blind people is on the decrease. We can see this clearly in a moving film, Braille – My Musical Language, [2] in which three Blind musicians, through their own stories emphasize the importance of Braille Music. Music is the only totally accessible art for blind people but it is difficult for them to learn it. In the past, music was learnt in specialized schools and a lot of blind people became very good musicians or at least gained a good musical culture. Due to the decrease of specialized schools and the integration of blind people into mainstream schools their musical education is poor. Braille music is not widely taught because music teachers are reluctant to learn it themselves. At the same time, the number of people who are able to transcribe musical scores in Braille is also on the decrease so it is difficult to find musical scores in Braille. This alarming situation requires the help of computer tools to transcribe, edit and read musical scores.

This paper describes the solutions proposed by the European project Music4VIP. In the first part of this project we researched the requirement and the current state of the art for accessible music. In the second part we describe the Music4VIP solutions that will enable teachers to teach music to blind pupils and tools which will enable blind people to learn music independently. Finally, we propose a methodology for the evaluation of these tools and didactic solutions.

2 Requirement and State of the Art

Based on the analysis of the results of the questionnaire carried out during the first step of the project music4VIP we can structure the requirement in six following areas:

K. Miesenberger et al. (Eds.): ICCHP 2014, Part I, LNCS 8547, pp. 596–601, 2014.

- *Students, Teachers and Music Schools:* For children at a young age it is important to encourage them to study music and introduce soon and step by step the use of Braille music. With the help of IT technology children can use easily Braille but the problem is the teacher who is not up-to-date with IT technologies in this specific area. Teacher need training courses to adapt their teaching methods, to communicate with Blind children and to give equal importance to studying by ear than to learning by reading Braille music.
- *Availability of Braille Texts:* It is necessary to obtain Braille score easily which correspond as precisely as possible to the print editions but also which can be manage and reduce following the user needs.
- *Braille Music and Informatics [IT]:* Numerous software exist for editing music for sighted people, most of them use MusicXML and Midi to code a musical score. To exchange musical score and to produce them quickly in Braille, it is necessary to use software making the conversion of scores from Braille music into staff notation and vice versa. A computer program to manage and edit Braille score helps blind teacher or blind student to exchange their production with sighted musicians. Hear and read the music on the same system is important to facilitate the memorization. Most people prefer embossed copies when they read musical score but some of them prefer to use a computer when they read Braille music. The program should support some presentation customizations such as presentation section by section or bar over bar. The software should be easy to use with a simple documentation, using shortcuts and should be accessible using screen reader technology.
- *Web Service:* As it exists for Braille text, the creation of an international Braille music catalogue should permit to find quickly Braille musical scores produce in several countries and to improve the communication between production centers.
  Braille music syntax: The Braille music syntax is well defined in the new international manual of Braille music notation [3] but some dialects exist, it is a complex syntax because it depends of the context and Braille music is a linear code which not permits to Blind people to have a complete vision of a music score. The Braille music in electronic form contains Braille and Midi information so it is easy to hear and read the musical information, the electronic form permits to read the Braille music using a screen reader.
- *Support for Braille Music Pedagogy:* It is important to adapt the pedagogy to get an overall picture of the score, to re-duce the reading speed, to not refer to the musical information with the visual aspect.

Responding to this different requirement, we propose the solutions defined and realized during the Music4VIP project. A proposal of evaluation of the usability of these solutions will be explain and the results will be analyzed.

3   Music4VIP Solutions

The Music4VIP project aims to develop the best possible use of new technologies to help with the teaching and learning of Braille music. We propose some free technical tools as well as some guidelines and videos which can help teachers to teach music to blind students.

3.1   Technical Tools

Thanks to the previous work done during the Contrapunctus project [4] to create a code able to code musical information in Braille (BMML Braille Music Markup Language) [5] we propose a number of free tools to manage musical information in Braille. BMML has been designed to code the structure and content of music Braille notation according to the New International manual of Braille Music Notation. BMML facilitates the conversion to and from other music notation codes and permits the flexibility to code Braille music variants.

We have developed a free online conversion module which is able to convert a MusicXML file score into BMML and vice versa. This module is accessible for blind people using a screen reader and very easy to use also for teachers who want to produce Braille music files.

We also offer free software called BMR (Braille Music Reader) which can read BMML files and facilitates the reading of musical information in Braille, by sound and in spoken form. With BMR the musician can explore the score, hide some parts or elements and access all the musical information. BMR has the same functionality to read a score as BME (a commercial product) [6] which can also edit a score in Braille.These different tools are necessary but not sufficient to help blind people in their musical learning. We propose some guidelines, video and pedagogical scenarios to help teachers and students in their use.

3.2   Pedagogical Aids and Scenarios

We propose several video lessons and choose to present four of them which aim to help a sighted teacher to teach music for blind student.

The first video gives a history of Braille notation and several principles for normal text.

The second video addresses the theme of the musical education of young blind people, with particular reference to aural teaching within musical studies. In this video we talk about perception and classification of various sounds, focusing on the main similarities and differences between auditory perception and perception based on data coming from other sensory canals (sight, smell, touch).

The third video proposes guidelines for efficient and effective communication with blind students.

The fourth video describes Braille music principles and computer tools that facilitate the management of musical scores.

Having viewed these lessons a teacher will be able to teach blind pupils more efficiently.

Teachers have to adapt their teaching and the following scenarios can help. We propose for example a scenario to teach a song and one to construct a didactical unit for a piano student. In each case the teacher has to prepare the score in MusicXML or in BMML using the transcription module and send them to their blind pupils. The first scenario is a suggested lesson plan designed to teach the two-voice "Ode to Joy" to a class. The second scenario describes practice strategies for developing agility at the piano, based on Hanon's exercises.

We also propose a music theory book and some acoustics lessons with examples in BMML which can be studied directly and independently by blind pupils or with the help of a teacher.

To evaluate the usability of our different tools and guidelines we propose to use the SUS (system usability scale) [7] questionnaire which is very simple (10 questions) but efficient to provide subjective feedback for the users. We focus our attention on two groups of users, one composed of teachers and one of blind music students.

3.3   Methods and Results of This Questionnaire

We use the SUS (System Usability Scale) which is a very simple questionnaire based on 10 items with a scale from 1 to 5 based on Likert scale. The Likert scale is based on forced-choice questions which indicate the degree of agreement or disagreement with the statement. Table 1 shows the adapted SUS.

Table 1. Adapted SUS

		Strongly disagree				Strongly agree
1	I think that I would like to use this system frequently	1	2	3	4	5
2	I found the system unnecessarily complex	1	2	3	4	5
3	I thought the system was easy to use	1	2	3	4	5
4	I think that I would need the support of a technical person to be able to use this system	1	2	3	4	5
5	I found the various functions in this system were well integrated	1	2	3	4	5
6	I thought there was too much inconsistency in this system	1	2	3	4	5
7	I would imagine that most people would learn to use this system very quickly	1	2	3	4	5
8	I found the system very cumbersome to use	1	2	3	4	5
9	I felt very confident using the system	1	2	3	4	5
10	I needed to learn a lot of things before I could get going with this system	1	2	3	4	5

- For the teachers we propose two questionnaires: In the first questionnaire we change "the system" to "the video lessons" and delete the question 5 because in this case it will make no sense. For this questionnaire concerning video lesson the score of question 5 is calculated with 3.
- For the second questionnaire we change "the system" to "the conversion module".

- In the questionnaire for the students we change "the system" to "BMR" (Braille Music Reader).

Perhaps we have also to add a questionnaire for the students with the conversion module because in some cases the teacher gives them a MusicXML file and the student has to make the conversion.

At the present time, we are not asking for feedback concerning the conversion module because there remain some problems with the version of MusicXML files and with some MusicXML files found on the web. The conversion module frequently responds it is not an XML file.

So, we focus our attention on the teachers' answers concerning the video lessons and the students' answers concerning the BMR module.

To calculate the SUS score, as indicated in [7], we sum the score contributions from each item and multiply the sum of the scores by 2.5 to obtain the overall value of SUS. SUS scores have a range of 0 to 100.

For items 1,3,5,7 and 9 the score contribution is the scale position minus 1.

For items 2,4,6,8 and 10, the score contribution is 5 minus the scale position.

We analyze the results with the help of the result done in the figure 1 in the article [7] which qualifies the SUS score with adjective rating.

Table 2. SUS Score and adjective rating

SUS Score	Adjective Rating
SUS score <25	Worst imaginable
25 < SUS score < 38	Poor
48 < SUS score < 52	OK
52 < SUS score <72	Good
72 < SUS score < 85	Excellent
85 < SUS score	Best imaginable

We have very few answers (less than ten for each questionnaire) but all of them qualify as Good or Excellent.

- For the teachers' questionnaire the average is 75 and the answers are in the range 70-80 which puts the responses between Good and Excellent. The open question at the end of the questionnaire contains no answers.
- For the student questionnaire the average is 77 with range of [75-80].

Several suggestions appear in the open question such as:

- BMR is better for beginners
- BMR runs well with Jaws and NVDA
- I need help with my Braille table to manage my Braille display.

These first results indicate that users perceive our solution as good but these results have to be consolidated with further surveys with a large number of respondents.

4   Conclusion

We propose several tools and guidelines to facilitate Blind pupils in their musical studies. All the tools are free and teaching material is in CC BY-NC creative commons licenses. As the copyright laws concerning musical scores are not the same in different European countries each teacher must choose which scores to convert into Braille. The work done has to be tested on a large scale but the preliminary tests, explained in this article, are good. It will be useful to create an open archive in which each teacher or student can exchange their lessons and can comment on the lessons proposed by others. In this case, it is necessary to add metadata information in LOM (learning object metadata) [8] format to use a research engine efficiently to find spe-cific resources for class teaching or individual teaching. This prospect is not so easy due to the multilingual and different musical curricula in the different European countries.

Acknowledgements. Part of this work have been undertaken in the European project Music4VIP, I have to thanks all the partners of the project.

References

1. Music4VIP, http://www.music4vip.org
2. Braille – My Musical Language, http://www.nota.nu/braillefilm
3. Braille Music Notation,
   https://archive.org/details/newinternational00bett
4. Contrapunctus project, http://www.punctus.org
5. Encelle, B., Jessel, N., Mothe, J., Ralalason, B., Asensio, J.: BMML: Braille Music Markup Language. The Open Information Systems Journal 2009(3), 123–135 (2009)
6. BME, http://www.veia.it/en/bme2_product
7. SUS – System Usability Scale,
   http://www.usabilityprofessionals.org/upa_publications/jus/2013february/JUS_Brooke_February_2013.pdf
8. LOM – Learning Object Metadata,
   http://hmdb.cs.kuleuven.be/publications/files/Lorsurvey.pdf

The Development of a Music Presentation System by Two Vibrators

Nobuyuki Sasaki[1], Satoshi Ohtsuka[2], Kazuyoshi Ishii[3], and Tetsumi Harakawa[4]

[1] Tsukuba University of Technology, 4-12-7, Kasuga, 305-0821 Tsukuba, Japan
nsasaki@cs.k.tsukuba-tech.ac.jp
[2] Gunma National College of Technology, 580 Toribamachi,
371-8530 Maebashi, Japan
ohtsuka@ice.gunma-ct.ac.jp
[3] Ishii Lab., Ohtaniminami, Ebina-shi, Japan
k-ishii@sun.ocn.ne.jp
[4] Maebashi Institute of Technology, 460-1, Kamisadoricho,
371-0816 Maebashi, Japan
harakawa@maebashi-it.ac.jp

Abstract. We have been developing the Body-Braille system, which transmits Braille characters to disabled people through vibrations on any part of the body. Five years ago, we began working on music applications of this. Using 9 micro vibrators, any melody with a sound range less than 2 octaves can be expressed by vibration. Last year, we developed the music presentation system using only two vibrators. Using special equipment (Pocket-Body braille, Pocket-Bbrll), we performed two experiments and obtained successful results for applying a small number of vibrations to music expression. The details of the system to present music tone by vibration and the results of the experiment are described.

Keywords: Body-Braille, Vibration, Deaf-blind People, Music.

1 Introduction

Since 2002, we have been developing the Body-Braille system, which transmits Braille characters to disabled people through vibrations by six vibrators on any part of the body [1]. We have performed several experiments for the support of disabled people's daily life. Although we could obtain several successful results, affixing six vibrators on the surface of the body was still not a simple matter. So, we developed a "two-points system" to transmit Braille characters [1]. In this system, the two vibrators are driven three times for each Braille cell. With this simpler Braille code, we can use fewer vibration motors, which is convenient for body parts having a small area and makes it possible to use much smaller equipment (Pocket- Bbrll).

Five years ago, we began to develop musical applications of this technology; that is, presentation of a melody by vibration. First, using nine micro vibrators, we developed the system in which any melody with a sound range less than

K. Miesenberger et al. (Eds.): ICCHP 2014, Part I, LNCS 8547, pp. 602–605, 2014.
© Springer International Publishing Switzerland 2014

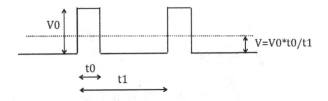

Fig. 1. Illustration of a PWM duty cycle

two octaves can be expressed by vibration [2]. Second, from two years ago, taking advantage of the "two-points system", we have also been developing music presentation by two vibrators. This paper describes the details of this system.

2   Music Presentation System

In the previous system, we developed a music presentation system by using nine vibrators, which means two Braille cells are used. Seven out of nine vibrators correspond to the notes (Do Re Mi Fa So La Ti) and two vibrators correspond to the half tone and octave. Nine fingers of both hands were used to detect the vibration. Using this system, almost all the songs used in the experiment were recognized by experimental participants. If this music presentation system is realized by using only two vibrators, a very small and portable musical equipment could be used. Disabled people can enjoy music by vibration anywhere, and it would help the study and practice of singing or playing a melody. Two years ago, we began to develop a music presentation system which uses only two vibrators to express any melody with a sound range less than two octaves. In this system, PWM (Pulse Width Modulation) technology is used to control the intensity of vibration, and the seven levels of intensity correspond to the seven notes. We propose two modes of presentation, "fixed system" and "moving system".

3   Expression of a Melody by Two Vibrators

In this system, since we have only two vibrators, we decided to use the intensity of vibration to express the note. The length of each note is expressed in the same manner as in the previous system; that is, by the vibration continuation time. To control the vibrator intensity, we adopted the PWM technology. By switching the voltage to drive a vibrator very rapidly, the vibration intensity would be proportional to the average power. In other words, if the pulse duty cycle becomes larger, the intensity of the vibration would be stronger (see Fig. 1). We set seven levels of PWM duty cycle corresponding to the intensity of each note (Do Re Mi Fa So La Ti). Two vibrators take charge of two octaves, which realize the presentation of a melody. We call this the "fixed system" (see Fig. 2). We also tested another system, which uses Phantom Sensation. A phantom sensation occurs when a user feels as if the vibration is occurring somewhere between the two vibrators although there is no actual vibration at that location. If the

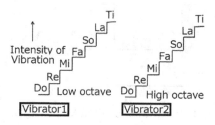

Fig. 2. Fixed System

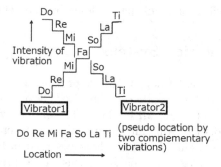

Fig. 3. Moving System

intensity of two vibrators (m1, m2) is set in complementary fashion like k & (1-k) respectively, the pseudo-location would be L*(1-k) from the m1 location. Here, L is the distance between m1 and m2. Thus, if the intensity of the vibration has seven levels, distance L is divided into seven locations and the imaginary vibration would be moving around within the seven pseudo-locations. As such, a melody whose sound range is less than one octave can be expressed by the movement of the phantom sensation. We call this the "moving system" (see Fig. 3). Several melodies are written into the ROM of Pocket-Bbrll and played back by vibration with these two systems (fixed and moving).

4   Experiment and Results

Fig. 4 shows a picture of the experimental set-up. In this experiment, the left arm was used and the two vibrators were settled near the wrist and near the elbow. We had two participants, a partially sighted man and a blind woman. Both of them were very familiar with music. Seven easy and well-known Japanese nursery songs were used. At first, the title of each song were told to the subjects beforehand and melody by vibration were recognized by them. Following are some opinions and comments from the participants:

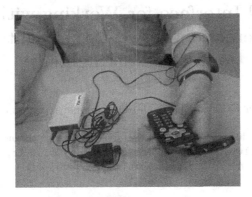

Fig. 4. Experimental Set-up

- Almost all the notes of test melodies could be recognized in the "fixed system". The "fixed system" would be very useful in music education for disabled people.
- The transition from the low octave note to the high octave feels unnatural.
- One subject felt the "moving system" was interesting and useful.

5   Conclusion

We tried to apply the Body-Braille technology to the entertainment field, particularly in the presentation of a music melody by vibration. Using only two micro vibrators, any melody whose sound range is less than two octaves can be expressed. We tested two kinds of presentation system, the "fixed system" and the "moving system". Through the two experiments, we obtained successful results for applying a small number of vibrations to music expression. In the near future, a very small and portable apparatus by which hearing, studying, and appreciating music anywhere can be implemented.

Acknowledgments. A part of this work was supported by JSPS KAKENHI 23500667.

References

1. Ohtsuka, S., Sasaki, N., Hasegawa, S., Harakawa, T.: Body-Braille System for Disabled People. In: Miesenberger, K., Klaus, J., Zagler, W.L., Karshmer, A.I. (eds.) ICCHP 2008. LNCS, vol. 5105, pp. 682–685. Springer, Heidelberg (2008)
2. Ohtsuka, S., Sasaki, N., Hasegawa, S., Harakawa, T.: Development of a Musical Score System Using Body-Braille. In: Miesenberger, K., Klaus, J., Zagler, W., Karshmer, A. (eds.) ICCHP 2010, Part II. LNCS, vol. 6180, pp. 443–446. Springer, Heidelberg (2010)

Multimodal Interface for Working with Algebra: Interaction between the Sighted and the Non Sighted

Silvia Fajardo-Flores and Dominique Archambault

EA 4004 – CHArt-THIM Université Paris 8, France
silvia.fajardo-flores@etud.univ-paris8.fr,
dominique.archambault@univ-paris8.fr

Abstract. In an integrated school environment for Mathematics learning, effective communication and collaboration between sighted and non sighted students and teachers is a crucial aspect. Common activities in the classroom as doing dictations, exercises and exams, become cumbersome without an adequate support. We have developed a prototype interface to support these activities using visual, speech and braille output modalities. User testing with students showed that the interface facilitated writing, manipulation and communication.

Keywords: Visual Disability, Accessibility, Mathematics, HCI.

1 Introduction

At present, non sighted students still struggle to follow Mathematics courses, and very few of them pursuit higher level Mathematics related studies. Students need to understand concepts, take notes, make questions and submit homework amongst other activities. While they can manage to use braille to perform most of these activities, they need the help of an intermediary to communicate with their sighted peers and teachers. At times, they also face the problem of following verbal descriptions based in spatial aspects of the concepts being explained. Taking into account the needs of sighted and non sighted students and teachers, we developed a prototype interface where sighted and non sighted students can produce and manipulate mathematical contents, and visualize them in a synchronised way. A set of features that aim to facilitate the resolution of basic algebra equations is included in this interface. The possibility to use such an interface could bring some advances working in an integrated environment.

2 State of the Art

Regarding the access and work with mathematics with a sighted-non sighted collaborative orientation, there exist software to visually represent mathematical contents including speech output, such as the Math Genie [9], InftyReader [13],

K. Miesenberger et al. (Eds.): ICCHP 2014, Part I, LNCS 8547, pp. 606–613, 2014.
© Springer International Publishing Switzerland 2014

braille output such as the MAWEN prototypes [1], or both, such as LAMBDA [5]. LAMBDA uses a linear visualisation of expressions and allows copying and pasting terms as an aid for solving. The MAWEN prototypes includes assistants to support manipulation and simplification [12], though the results showed that they needed improvement. Other research projects concern the analysis of the audio output using prosody, earcons, spearcons and lexical cues [4], and presentation modalities based in complexity [3],[6], amongst others. Aiming to support more advanced studies in mathematics, other projects use LATEX as input, and either braille or audio as output. LABRADOOR [10], converts LATEX into the Marburg braille code; the LATEX-access project [8] produces mathematical braille according to the Nemeth code, and the project PSLM (Programme Spécialisé de Lecture Mathématique à l'Usage des Non-Voyants) takes a LATEX input to produce an audio output in French. These projects have facilitated to some extent the access to mathematics for the blind, though most of them, with the exception of LAMBDA and InftyReader, are research projects which are not available to end users as AT products. There exist as well another type of software with advanced capabilities as symbolic calculators aimed for the general user, such as Sage, Axiom and Mathematica. However, the use of this type of software is not recommended for educational purposes since it performs automatic transformations which can affect the development of the student's algebraic symbolism [2,11]. On the other hand, most of them are based in graphical interfaces which are, most of the time, not accessible to screen readers.

3   The Interface

We have developed an interface with the aim to facilitate the edition, comprehension and resolution of algebraic equations using visual, speech and braille output modalities. The development of the interface followed a User Centered Design approach, after which design is based upon an understanding of users and the tasks to be undertaken, and potential users are involved in the development.

Firstly we analysed the actions of sighted and non sighted students while solving linear equations, as well as those of mathematics teachers while explaining the resolution. Teachers were also interviewed regarding the didactical aspects to be considered. The results of the analysis are reported in [7].

The development followed an iterative process which began with the implementation of edition and navigation according to the needs detected in our first analysis. A first prototype was reviewed by users and modified according to their suggestions. A second round of functions were implemented in the latest version, whose evaluation we present in this article.

The latest version of the interface has the following features:

- Edition of basic algebra equations, involving exponents, fractions and square roots, using the computer keyboard and the braille keyboard. We use delimiters to indicate the beginning and the end of fractions and square roots. Writing delimiters with the computer keyboard implies the use of shortcut keys, or menus.

- Possibility to visually display expressions in a bidimensional and linear way.
- Synchronised visual, audio and braille display.
- Folding and unfolding of sub expressions.
- Display and navigation by semantic blocks according the levels of the expression tree.
- Search of parts of the expression, search of common terms.
- Marking of terms and shortcuts to "jump" between them.
- Possibility to keep the cursor in the last visited position of each line.
- Possibility to read and copy marked terms independently of the position of the cursor.
- Possibility to save contents on file in MathML format.

The interface was developed in the Mozilla Platform, using XUL for the graphical interface, Python for the back-end and MathML for the visual representation. The MathML expression tree is transformed dynamically as elements are typed. Marking and folding of terms are indicated internally by the use of additional boolean attributes. The synchronisation to braille is achieved through a conversion table; a string representing the audio output is built and then passed on to the screen reader. NVDA is used to control the audio and braille output on Windows.

We used a Model-ViewController (MVC) architecture to facilitate implementation and modification of the interface components (see Figure 1).

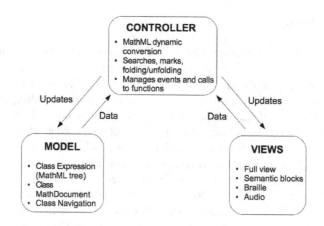

Fig. 1. Model-View-Controller Architecture

The interface and its views is shown in Figure 2. An example of expression is written in the bidimensional and linear modalities in line 1 and 2 respectively. The braille output is the same for both. The block view and the audio string reflect the active term.

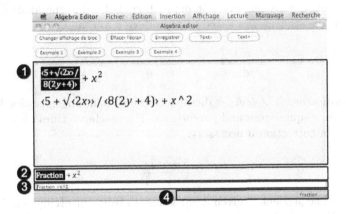

Fig. 2. Bidimensional and linear writing of an expression. Views : 1) Full expression, 2) Semantic blocks, 3) ASCII Braille, 4) Audio string.

4   User Testing

The purpose of the evaluation was to observe the possible difficulties while typing with the computer keyboard or the braille display, the ease of verification of the written terms by audio or/and braille, the recognition and recovery from typing errors, the memorisation of shortcuts, the difficulties in understanding expressions, the efficacy of communication teacher-student and the possibility to execute the desired strategy for solving.

The participants were :

- 4 mathematics teachers : 3 with normal vision, 1 partially sighted.
- 6 students: 2 non sighted students from high school, and 4 from junior high school, of which 3 are non sighted and 1 is partially sighted.

The test consisted of four parts:

1. *Writing/Reading Expressions:* Participants (teachers and students) wrote expressions using either the keyboard or the braille display, following a practical demonstration on how to write exponents, fractions and square roots.

$$3x^2 - 6 = 3(x^2 - 2) \qquad \frac{2x}{x+2} = \frac{4}{x-10} \qquad \sqrt{x+4} \quad (1)$$

2. *Comprehension:* The student is given three nested fractions of increasing complexity, in order to analyse each of them using the audio output. We wanted to observe the efficacy of the audio output, as well as the participant's use of the navigation by blocks. The features were demonstrated to each

participant, but its use was not mandatory. Following the analysis of each fraction, the student was asked to reproduce it verbally.

$$\frac{a + \frac{b}{c}}{d + e} \qquad \frac{\frac{a+b}{c+d}}{x - y} \qquad \frac{\frac{x+1}{8+y}}{\frac{x-1}{9+z}} \tag{2}$$

3. *Communication:* The teacher dictates to the student an expression involving a fraction, a square root and parenthesis. The teacher verifies the output and proposes a correction if necessary.

$$\frac{5 + \sqrt{2x}}{8(2y + 4)} \tag{3}$$

4. *Solving:* The student is given 3 equations to solve, involving simplification, distribution, clearing of fractions and parentheses. This part was done exclusively with audio output.

$$7 - \frac{x + 3}{x} = 5 \tag{4}$$

$$x + 2(x + 2(x + 2)) = x + 2 \tag{5}$$

$$(3a^2 + 2a + 7)(a + 5a - 4) \tag{6}$$

The tests were executed on Windows XP and 7, with a Papenmeier Braillex Trio. The partially sighted teacher used a computer with Mac OS X Mountain Lion and the system zoom. The tests were performed in three different high schools in France.

5   Results and Discussion

Writing. Students have different levels of knowledge on the use of the computer, the braille display and the mathematical braille code; therefore they had different abilities and preferences for the input/output modalities. Typing exponents, fractions and square roots did not present important difficulties, though the users require to get used to using shortcuts in order to write bidimensional structures using the keyboard. They agreed that the audio output is comprehensive, but it can be very tiresome if used alone. Participants got used to identify and correct errors in a short time. The braille input, whose interactions were more limited in implementation than those of the computer keyboard, allowed participants writing fractions, roots and exponents.

Comprehension. Teachers expressed that understanding a mathematical expression involves recognising the symbols, understanding the organization of the expression, and knowing how to start the solving process. In the activity of listening and reproducing the structure of the nested fractions, students were able to reproduce correctly the structure of all three. In general students preferred to listen to the full fraction, even if it meant to listen to it 2 or more times. We observed that they were more susceptible to use the navigation by blocks as fractions became more complicated. On the other hand, students expressed that in cases like this is when one can really appreciate the braille representation.

Communication. The direct communication between student and teacher was very effective in all cases. The teacher dictated the expression in the way he is used to; some teachers consider that dictation must be particular for blind students, for example : "now I'm going to tell you the terms in the numerator", while others would dictate the same way they would to sighted students. The student wrote the expression and the teacher validated the writing or made corrections. Since the students had already written fractions and roots, they did not make significant errors. The immediate visualization of the student input during dictation was greatly appreciated by teachers.

Solving. Not all participants were able to do this part of the evaluation since they did not have the required knowledge of algebra. Only the 2 students from high school were able to do the solving exercises. Junior high school students participated in the edition, reading and dictation exercises, but their teachers mentioned that the students had not learned operations with fractions, and that the exercises were too complex for them. Only one of the junior high school solved a linear expression proposed by her teacher; this student was not familiar with the computer keyboard, so she used the braille device.

The two students who were able to perform this part expressed some kind of frustration when presented with a simplification of multiple terms and the distribution of 2 factors of 3 terms each, but they did not express discouragement when realising the complexity of a double nested expression, or the expression involving the clearing of a fraction. Both students solved correctly the expression with nested parentheses. Figure 3 shows the solution of one of the students, who identified an initial simplification and then carried on with distribution.

Students used the functions to fold and unfold sub expressions while exploring exercise 6 (see Figure 4). We observed that the possibility to go back to the last visited position of each line was very useful, especially during distributions, since it allowed students to follow up the order of multiplications. One of the students used the search for common terms after the simplification of quadratic terms, in order to make sure he had considered them all.

For most of the activities, students tried to replicate on the interface their usual work in text editors or in the braille display. They did not use the navigation by blocks very often, and they did not use the function for marking terms. This could be due to the recent introduction of this functions in their usual work environment and the mental load of having presented all the features and shortcuts at the same time. Further exposure to such features during real exercises could allow us to observe whether they support resolution or not. While the interface provides basic braille input and output, the braille implementation

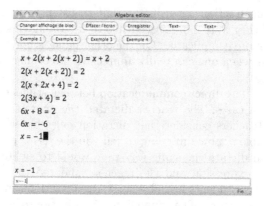

Fig. 3. Student's solution to equation 5

$$\boxed{PRODUCT}$$
$$\leadsto \boxed{FACTOR}\, FACTOR$$
$$\leadsto (3a^2 + 2a + 7)\,\boxed{FACTOR}$$
$$\leadsto (3a^2 + 2a + 7)(a + 5a - 4)$$

Fig. 4. Unfolding sequence on exercise 6

for interaction must be improved so that it also allows reverse pointing with its correspondent visual highlight. On the other hand, it was observed the need to personalize shortcut keys and levels of verbosity of speech.

6 Conclusion

Communication is probably the most critical aspect for the integration of a non sighted student in a mainstream environment. This communication does not only involves visualizing what the other is doing, but also being able to do it while using their preferred method for writing and reading contents. Users have different backgrounds and preferences; offering multiple modalities on an interface it is also part of the consideration for user diversity. We performed a second type of tests in a cognitive walkthrough modality with Mathematics teachers with experience working with non sighted students, in order to verify the pertinence of the features regarding didactical aspects. While the results of the tests are encouraging for this level of education, we need to open up the possibilities for students in more advanced levels. Higher studies of Mathematics currently demand the knowledge of LATEX for working with complex documents; however, the verbosity of LATEX makes it hard to use with a screen reader and a braille display. It would be interesting to analyse the implementation of the dynamic visualisation, synchronisation and access features proposed in our work, in order to create and maintain LATEX documents in a more straightforward way.

References

1. Archambault, D.: Non visual access to mathematical contents: State of the art and prospective. In: Proceedings of the WEIMS Conference 2009, pp. 43–52 (2009)
2. Artigue, M.: Learning mathematics in a cas environment: The genesis of a reflection about instrumentation and the dialectics between technical and conceptual work. International Journal of Computers for Mathematical Learning 7, 245–274 (2002)
3. Awde, A., Bellik, Y., Tadj, C.: Complexity of mathematical expressions in adaptive multimodal multimedia system ensuring access to mathematics for visually impaired users. International Journal of Computer and Information Engineering 2(6), 393–405 (2008)
4. Bates, E., Fitzpatrick, D.: Spoken mathematics using prosody, earcons and spearcons. In: Miesenberger, K., Klaus, J., Zagler, W., Karshmer, A. (eds.) ICCHP 2010, Part II. LNCS, vol. 6180, pp. 407–414. Springer, Heidelberg (2010)
5. Bernareggi, C.: Non-sequential mathematical notations in the lambda system. In: Miesenberger, K., Klaus, J., Zagler, W., Karshmer, A. (eds.) ICCHP 2010, Part II. LNCS, vol. 6180, pp. 389–395. Springer, Heidelberg (2010)
6. Abu Doush, I., Pontelli, E.: Building a programmable architecture for non-visual navigation of mathematics: Using rules for guiding presentation and switching between modalities. In: Stephanidis, C. (ed.) UAHCI 2009, Part III. LNCS, vol. 5616, pp. 3–13. Springer, Heidelberg (2009)
7. Fajardo Flores, S., Archambault, D.: Understanding algebraic manipulation: Analysis of the actions of sighted and non-sighted students. In: Yamaguchi, K., Suzuki, M. (eds.) The International Workshop on Digitization and E-Inclusion in Mathematics and Science (DEIMS 2012) (2012)
8. Irving, A.: The latex-access project (2007), http://latex-access.sourceforge.net/
9. Karshmer, A., Bledsoe, C., Stanley, P.: The architecture of a comprehensive equation browser for the print impaired. In: Miesenberger, K., Klaus, J., Zagler, W.L., Burger, D. (eds.) ICCHP 2004. LNCS, vol. 3118, pp. 614–619. Springer, Heidelberg (2004)
10. Miesenberger, K., Batusic, M., Stöger, B.: Labradoor: Latex-to-braille-door (1998), http://www.snv.jussieu.fr/inova/publi/ntevh/labradoor.htm
11. Monaghan, J.: Computer algebra, instrumentation and the anthropological approach. International Journal for Technology in Mathematics Education 14(2), 63–72 (2007)
12. Stöger, B., Miesenberger, K., Batušić, M.: Mathematical working environment for the blind: Motivation and basic ideas. In: Miesenberger, K., Klaus, J., Zagler, W.L., Burger, D. (eds.) ICCHP 2004. LNCS, vol. 3118, pp. 656–663. Springer, Heidelberg (2004)
13. Suzuki, M., Kanahori, T., Ohtake, N., Yamaguchi, K.: An integrated ocr software for mathematical documents and its output with accessibility. In: Miesenberger, K., Klaus, J., Zagler, W.L., Burger, D. (eds.) ICCHP 2004. LNCS, vol. 3118, pp. 648–655. Springer, Heidelberg (2004)

Performance Metrics and Their Extraction Methods for Audio Rendered Mathematics

Hernisa Kacorri[1,2], Paraskevi Riga[1], and Georgios Kouroupetroglou[1]

[1] University of Athens, Department of Informatics and Telecommunications, Athens, Greece
{c.katsori,p.riga,koupe}@di.uoa.gr
[2] The City University of New York, Computer Science Program, New York, USA
hkacorri@gc.cuny.edu

Abstract. We introduce and compare three approaches to calculate structure- and content-based performance metrics for user-based evaluation of math audio rendering systems: Syntax Tree alignment, Baseline Structure Tree alignment, and MathML Tree Edit Distance. While the first two require "manual" tree transformation and alignment of the mathematical expressions, the third obtains the metrics without human intervention using the minimum edit distance algorithm on the corresponding MathML representations. Our metrics are demonstrated in a pilot user study evaluating the Greek audio rendering rules of MathPlayer with 7 participants and 39 stimuli. We observed that the obtained results for the metrics are significantly correlated between all three approaches.

Keywords: Math Audio Rendering, Metrics, Accessibility, MathML, Usability.

1 Introduction

Acoustic modality is one approach often favored by researchers to create an accessible platform for mathematics [1-6]. It is essential to evaluate and compare the accuracy of mathematical expressions provided by a rule-based system with speech output. Recently, we introduced the EAR-Math methodology [7], along with a number of associated novel metrics, to automatically calculate their performance through quantitative methods in audio rendered mathematics. However, one limitation is the requirement for "manual" steps required in computing these metrics. The focus of this paper is to explore and compare alternative ways to calculate the proposed metrics with and without human intervention. This would allow for more robust results with fewer human errors during the data processing steps. Furthermore, we present results of a pilot study in evaluating the Greek audio rendering rules with MathPlayer [8].

2 Related Work

Relatively few researchers have evaluated the quantitative performance of their math audio-access approaches. We reviewed the methods adopted for assessing the accuracy of these approaches as perceived by the users. In the user evaluation of MathTalk

K. Miesenberger et al. (Eds.): ICCHP 2014, Part I, LNCS 8547, pp. 614–621, 2014.
© Springer International Publishing Switzerland 2014

[9], participants' response was considered correct if the perceived formula retained over 75% of the rendered formula's content and its major structural features. However, no further details on the calculation of these accuracy metrics were available. The transcriptions of participants during the evaluation of I-Math [10] were compared linearly to the original textual expressions. The number of correct words and positions were evaluated using precision, recall, and F-score. Last, TechRead's evaluation [11] and the user study in [12] asked participants to choose among multiple un-weighted answers the one that best matched the audio stimuli. The differences in these evaluation approaches and metrics pose challenges for future researchers to compare their findings to previous work.

3   Performance Extraction for Audio Rendered Mathematics

Evaluation of Audio Rendered Math (EAR-Math), proposed in [7], is as an experimental methodology for user-based performance evaluation of mathematical expressions rendered by a rule-based system with audio output. Mathematical expressions, non-linear in nature, make it challenging to define a fine-grained error rate metric that describes a rendering system's performance. To measure the distance between the intended math expression and the one perceived by the users, EAR-Math proposes three error rate metrics. They are tailored to account for both content and structure and are derived by first aligning the two mathematical expressions and then computing the number of insertions, deletions, and substitutions in the perceived expression compared to the reference over the total number of elements in the reference expression for each of the three categories of elements:

$$SER = \frac{\#Ins + \#Del + \#Sub}{\#StructuralElem} \tag{1}$$

$$OER = \frac{\#Ins + \#Del + \#Sub}{\#Operators} \tag{2}$$

$$INER = \frac{\#Ins + \#Del + \#Sub}{\#Identifiers + \#NumericalValues} \tag{3}$$

- Structure Error Rate (SER) involves structural components of a math formula such as fractions, roots, and arrays.
- Operator Error Rate (OER) is focused on mathematical operators e.g. plus, minus, and times.
- Identifier and Number Error Rate (INER) represent the number of errors for identifiers and numerical values within the expression.

The key step in the calculation of the error rates for the performance metrics SER, OER, and INER is the comparison of the intended mathematical expression and the one perceived by the users. It requires a representation and alignment method that allows for fine-grained labeling of the elements in the expressions as structural, operators, numerical, and identifiers. We compare three approaches that use tree transformations and discuss their pros and cons with respect to the adopted alignment process. For each approach we illustrate an example of alignment for two math expressions: the intended expression rendered by the system (Reference) and the one perceived by a user (Perceived). The box in the Perceived expression indicates the part which the user was unable to include in the response.

$$\text{Reference: } x = \frac{a^2 + \sqrt{b-1}}{c} \tag{4}$$

$$\text{Perceived: } x_2 = \frac{a_3 + \sqrt{b}}{} \tag{5}$$

3.1 Syntax Tree Alignment

As in [7], the first approach is to draw the Syntax Trees for both reference and perceived expressions. Next, we 'manually' perform the alignment of the perceived tree to the reference tree and count their differences such as insertion, deletion, and substitution, to calculate the error rate metrics. In this approach, the leaves of the tree are considered identifiers or numbers and the inner nodes operators (e.g. +, -, *) or as structural elements (e.g. frac, sub, (,), cos, log, sum). Fig. 1 illustrates the application of this error rate extraction method on the example expressions. While identifying the operator, identifier, and number errors is a straightforward process, structural errors may be more challenging, especially when the correct structural element is improperly positioned in the tree. The approach counts this disposition as a double error, deletion and re-insertion. A drawback of this approach could be the required cognitive load and ambiguity in the alignment process, especially when the perceived expression is sparse compared to the reference.

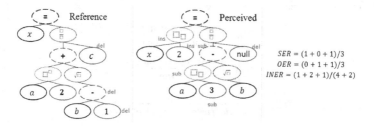

$$SER = (1 + 0 + 1)/3$$
$$OER = (0 + 1 + 1)/3$$
$$INER = (1 + 2 + 1)/(4 + 2)$$

Fig. 1. Syntax Tree Alignment of the two math expressions

3.2 Baseline Structure Tree Alignment

The Baseline Structure Tree [13], introduced for the recognition of handwritten mathematics, captures the layout of a formula without committing to any particular syntactic or semantic representation. Horizontally adjacent symbols in the expression, considered to be in the same region, are represented as ordered siblings in the tree. Thus, we can draw the tree unambiguously by exploiting its reading order even for a sparsely perceived math expression. Next, we 'manually' perform the alignment of the perceived tree to the reference tree and count their differences such as insertion, deletion, and substitution to calculate the error rate metrics. In this approach, the structural elements are defined by regions (e.g. center, over, under) and are placed at even tree depths, while the operators (e.g. frac, sub, +, -), numericals, and identifiers, i.e. all the printable elements, are positioned in odd depths. Fig. 2 illustrates the application of this error rate extraction method for the example expressions. The approach inherently counts the disposition of structural elements in the perceived tree. A drawback of this approach is that the resulting trees are more verbose than the Syntax Trees and is more tedious especially if the alignment and error rates are "manually" calculated.

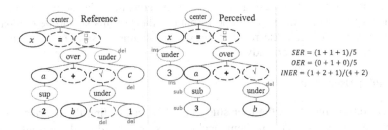

$$SER = (1 + 1 + 1)/5$$
$$OER = (0 + 1 + 0)/5$$
$$INER = (1 + 2 + 1)/(4 + 2)$$

Fig. 2. Baseline Structure Tree Alignment of the two math expressions

3.3   MathML Tree Edit Distance

Tree alignment is an optimization problem well defined in computational biology. It searches for the minimum operation number of node insertions, deletions and substitutions that are required to transform one tree into another, a measure called edit distance. To automate the calculation of the performance metrics, we apply the edit distance algorithm proposed in [14] to Presentation MathML encodings of the reference and perceived formulae. In particular, we parse the Presentation MathML trees into regular expressions and use the edit distance implementation in [15] (RTED) to obtain the optimal alignment of the trees. We further modified the RTED implementation to print the labels of the nodes in the tree and to assign them to the error rates categories: structural (<mrow>, <mfrac>, <msup>, etc.), operators (<mo>), and identifiers or numbers (<mi> and <mn>). Fig. 3 illustrates the application of this error rate extraction method for the example expressions.

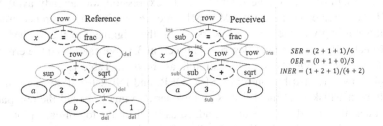

$$SER = (2 + 1 + 1)/6$$
$$OER = (0 + 1 + 0)/3$$
$$INER = (1 + 2 + 1)/(4 + 2)$$

Fig. 3. MathML Tree Edit Distance Alignment of the two math expressions

A requirement of this approach is that similar MathML notations should be used for both formulae, e.g. the same tool generates them. If the MathML code is already available for the reference formula, then it is suggested to copy and modify it accordingly for the perceived formula. One of the major advantages of this approach is that it provides more robust results while minimizing the required human intervention in the calculations of the proposed metrics.

4   Comparison of Extraction Methods in a Pilot User Study

While future researchers focusing on the pros and cons may choose one of the above approaches to evaluate their system performance, their results should be comparable. Therefore, we investigate the relationship of the obtained results from all three approaches within a pilot user study.

4.1   Pilot User Study

We revisited the results of the user study in [7] by calculating the metrics based on each of the approaches. The mathematical expressions, based on the formulae set for the ASTeR demonstration [16], were rendered through the Dimitris voice of Acapela Greek Text-to-Speech [17] driven by MathPlayer with lexical and prosodic cues.

Of the 7 participants recruited for the study: 2 were congenitally blind and 5 were sighted. All participants had been exposed to more complex mathematical expressions than the stimuli. There were 5 men and 2 women of ages 20-34 (average age 25.9). During the study, participants would listen to mathematical expressions and write down the perceived formulae. They were allowed to make changes to their initial guess two more times. We collected all three perceived versions for each of the expressions. After the experimental session, blind participants would read their notes and describe their answers to a sighted member of the team who would then visualize the expression in two-dimensions.

4.2   Results

As in [7], we 'manually' drew and aligned the trees for the perceived and reference formulas for the first and second approach and recorded the errors. For the third approach the MathML tree of the reference math expression was already available in MathML. To create the perceived MathML tree we copied the reference tree and edited it accordingly to the users' answers. Then, the alignment of the MathML trees was automatically performed as described in section 3.3. We calculated the error rates for the aggregated elements among all stimuli, as shown in Table 1.

Fig. 4 shows the distribution of the SER, OER, and INER for all three methods as boxplots with whiskers at the 1.5 IQR (inter-quartile range). To aid the comparison, mean values, illustrated with a star, are added as labels at the top of each plot. For all attempts, we observe that the MathML Tree Edit Distance results share similarities with the Syntax Tree results though the former shows higher variance and mean. We speculate this is due to the inherent verbosity of the MathML representation compared to the abstract representation of the Syntax Trees.

Table 1. Overall error rates in the stimuli set for the three approaches

	Syntax Tree (1)			Visual Tree (2)			MathML Tree (3)		
	SER	OER	INER	SER	OER	INER	SER	OER	INER
1st Attempt	0.18	0.12	0.11	0.16	0.17	0.14	0.24	0.14	0.13
2nd Attempt	0.1	0.06	0.04	0.08	0.09	0.06	0.14	0.07	0.07
3rd Attempt	0.07	0.04	0.02	0.04	0.06	0.03	0.09	0.05	0.04

The Visual Trees approach seems to have shifted the weight of the structural errors to the operators. This makes sense given that the structure in the mathematical expression is now represented by the layout and not by the semantics. We also observe that participants tend to improve their performance the second and the third time they listen to the mathematical expression and this is captured by all three approaches. This suggests that the audio rendering might have been accurate, but other factors (such as audio memory and familiarity with the system) may have an effect on the results and should be taken into account when designing the experiment.

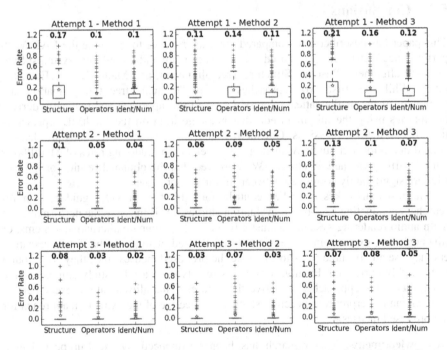

Fig. 4. Error rate distributions for user attempted responses by methods (Method 1: Syntax Tree, Mehod 2: Baseline Structure Tree, Method 3: MathML Edit Distance)

We performed a correlation analysis to the obtained results to further investigate the relationship of the error rates across the approaches. Table 2 displays the Spearman's rho correlation values for SER, OER and INER. The rho value is shown for each pair of approaches by error rate category. We note that all correlations were found to be significant. This indicates that future researchers may choose either of the approaches to calculate their metrics. We also observe that the aforementioned speculations about the similarities of the first and third approaches are supported. There is a significantly strong correlation between SER1 and SER3. While the second approach shifts the structure errors to operators, the identifiers and numbers are almost identical to the first approach. This is also supported by the significantly strong correlation between their INER metrics.

Table 2. Correlations (Spearman's rho) between the three approaches. All values were found to be highly significant (p < 0.001).

	Method 1 & 2	Method 1 & 3	Method 2 & 3
SER	0.79	0.831	0.662
OER	0.73	0.529	0.789
INER	0.975	0.668	0.674

5   Conclusions

This paper has described and compared three approaches to calculate the EAR-Math performance metrics for user-based evaluation of math audio rendering systems: Syntax Tree alignment, Baseline Structure Tree alignment, and MathML Tree Edit Distance. While the first two approaches require "manual" tree transformation and alignment of the mathematical expressions, the third approach automatically derives the metrics using the minimum edit distance algorithm on the MathML representations of the math expressions. Our metrics and their extraction methods are demonstrated in a pilot user study evaluating the Greek audio rendering rules of MathPlayer with 7 participants and 39 stimuli. We observed that the obtained results for the metrics are significantly correlated between all three approaches.

This research makes three key contributions. First, it provides guidance for researchers conducting user-based evaluation studies to: (i) measure the performance of math audio rendering systems against a baseline, (ii) compare alternative systems, or (iii) iteratively evaluate improvements/styles. Second, it suggests that future researchers may use any of three ways to calculate the proposed metrics since they were found to be highly correlated. Finally, it provides results from a pilot study comparing the three alternative approaches to derive the metrics. This allows future researchers to compare and interpret results across studies irrespective of the extraction approach for the proposed metrics.

Acknowledgments. This research has been co-financed by the European Union (European Social Fund – ESF) and Greek national funds through the Operational Program "Education and Lifelong Learning" of the National Strategic Reference Framework (NSRF) under the Research Funding Project: "THALIS-University of Macedonia-KAIKOS: Audio and Tactile Access to Knowledge for Individuals with Visual Impairments", MIS 380442.

References

1. Freitas, D., Kouroupetroglou, G.: Speech Technologies for Blind and Low Vision Persons. Technology and Disability 20, 135–156 (2008)
2. Archambault, D., Stoger, B., Fitzpatrick, D., Miesenberger, K.: Access to scientific content by visually impaired people. UPGRADE VIII(2), 1–14 (2007)
3. Bates, E., Fitzpatrick, D.: Spoken mathematics using prosody, earcons and spearcons. In: Miesenberger, K., Klaus, J., Zagler, W., Karshmer, A. (eds.) ICCHP 2010, Part II. LNCS, vol. 6180, pp. 407–414. Springer, Heidelberg (2010)
4. Kouroupetroglou, G., Kacorri, H.: Deriving Accessible Science Books for the Blind Students of Physics. Proceedings of the American Institute of Physics 1203, 1308–1313 (2010)
5. Karshmer, A., Gupta, G., Pontelli, E., Miesenberger, K., Ammalai, N., Gopal, D., Batusic, M., Stöger, B., Palmer, B., Guo, H.: UMA: A System for Universal Mathematics Accessibility. In: Proceedings ASSETS 2004, the 6th Intern. ACM SIGACCESS Conference on Computers and Accessibility, Atlanta, Georgia, USA, October 18-20, vol. 196, p. 55. ACM (2004)
6. Tsonos, D., Kacorri, H., Kouroupetroglou, G.: A design-for-all approach towards multimodal accessibility of mathematics. Assistive Technology Research Series 25, 393–397 (2009)
7. Kacorri, H., Riga, P., Kouroupetroglou, G.: EAR-Math: Evaluation of Audio Rendered Mathematics. In: Stephanidis, C., Antona, M. (eds.) UAHCI 2014, Part II. LNCS, vol. 8514, pp. 111–120. Springer, Heidelberg (2014)
8. Soiffer, N.: A flexible design for accessible spoken math. In: Stephanidis, C. (ed.) UAHCI 2009, Part III. LNCS, vol. 5616, pp. 130–139. Springer, Heidelberg (2009)
9. Stevens, R.D.: Principles for the design of auditory interfaces to present complex information to blind people. Doctoral dissertation, University of York (1996)
10. Wongkia, W., Naruedomkul, K., Cercone, N.: I-Math: an Intelligent Accessible Mathematics system for People with Visual Impairment. Computational Approaches to Assistive Technologies for People with Disabilities 253, 83–108 (2013)
11. Fitzpatrick, D.: Towards Accessible Technical Documents: Production of Speech and Braille Output from Formatted Documents. Doctoral dissertation, Dublin City University (1999)
12. Murphy, E., Bates, E., Fitzpatrick, D.: Designing auditory cues to enhance spoken mathematics for visually impaired users. In: Proceedings of the 12th International ACM SIGACCESS Conference on Computers and Accessibility, pp. 75–82 (2010)
13. Zanibbi, R., Blostein, D., Cordy, J.R.: Baseline structure analysis of handwritten mathematics notation. In: Proc. of the 6th Int. Conf. Document Analysis and Recognition, pp. 768–773. IEEE (2001)
14. Zhang, K., Shasha, D.: Simple fast algorithms for the editing distance between trees and related problems. SIAM Journal on Computing 18(6), 1245–1262 (1989)
15. Pawlik, M., Augsten, N.: RTED: A Robust Algorithm for the Tree Edit Distance. PVLDB 5(4), 334–345 (2011)
16. Raman, T.V.: Mathematics for computer generated spoken documents–ASTeR Demonstration, http://www.cs.cornell.edu/home/raman/aster/demo.html
17. Acapela text-to-speech, http://www.acapela-group.com/

Developing Tactile Graphic Output Functions Necessitated in the Performance of Research Using Statistical Methods by Blind Persons

Kazunori Minatani

National Center for University Entrance Examinations,
Komaba 2-19-23, Meguro-ku, Tokyo, 153-8501 Japan
minatani@rd.dnc.ac.jp

Abstract. It is difficult for blind persons to conduct research using statistical methods in an effective and independent manner. Jonathan Godfrey emphasized the usability of R for blind persons. His BrailleR package can be said to use is the "method of transcribing values represented in graphics into characters." The author has shown that the advantages of the "method of converting graphics into a tactile graphic." This research realized access by blind persons to graphics output by R using that method with no human intervention. The software developed through this research was employed the approach of interpreting SVG output produced by RSVGTipsDevice. It was configured that dot size and inter-dot pitch could be defined. An experiment showed that the question of which method is more effectively applied differed according to the experiment participant.

Keywords: Blind Persons, Tactile Graphics, Statistics, R, SVG.

1 State of the Art

The access blind persons have to presentations of graphical representations is severely constrained. As such, it is difficult for them to conduct research using statistical methods in an effective and independent manner. In such research areas, presentations of graphical representations are used to perform research and communicate the results of that research to other companies. This is particularly true for exploratory study, whose basis is the task of analyzing data from various viewpoints and identifying its characteristics. In order to efficiently perform that task, visualization using graphical representations, particularly graphs, is typically applied.

Actual examples of three methods for presenting graphical representations to blind persons and their respective advantages and disadvantages [1] have been outlined in Table 1. When considering the use of the three presentation methods by blind persons for the purpose of effectively and independently performing such research, the "method of translating graphics to explanatory sentences," which absolutely requires human intervention, is inappropriate. With respect to the

K. Miesenberger et al. (Eds.): ICCHP 2014, Part I, LNCS 8547, pp. 622–629, 2014.

Table 1. Three methods for presenting graphical representations to blind persons

Methods	Translating graphics to explanatory sentences	Transcribing values represented in graphics into characters	Converting graphics into a tactile graphic
Examples and Remarkable R&Ds	Descriptions to a graphics using the ALT attribute; TapTapSee[2]	Charts that show the source data in numerical form; To provide a spreadsheet file as substitution of graphs; BrailleR[7]	Embossed graphics; Way(1997)[3]; Tiger Software Suite[4]; TMACS[5]
Critical Advantages	Unified media	Presents values exactly	Shared graphical images with sighted people
Critical Disadvantages	Human intervention is required	Lack of an intuitive understandability	Limited to things understandable as tactile graphics
Mental Workload	Low	Heavy	Varies according to object
On-the-Fly Support	Not feasible	Feasible	Feasible
Presentation of visualized objects effectively	Not feasible	Not feasible	Feasible

task of developing an environment conducive to the efficient and independent performance of research using statistical methods by blind persons, Jonathan Godfrey and his series of ongoing efforts have yielded significant results. Godfrey investigated the accessibility of leading statistical analysis software by blind persons, and emphasized the usability of R in this respect. [6] The BrailleR package [7] has been implemented based on those findings. R's plot(), boxplot() and other high-level plotting functions, when used in tandem with its print() function, enable the essential portion of values that make up drawn data to be displayed in numerical form. One of the principal functions of BrailleR Package promotes substitute display functions for graphics using values similar to the print() function, and achieves output in the form of numerical values and characters (text) that makes it easier for blind persons to grasp the nature of graphic displays.

Among the methods indicated in Table 1, the one that the BrailleR can be said to use is the "method of transcribing values represented in graphics into characters." Consequently, the advantages and disadvantages under that method also apply to BrailleR. In other words, as stated above, BrailleR allows on-the-fly support of graphical output, and does not require human intervention. Moreover, values displayed are also accurate. At the same time, that method causes intuitive understanding of graphical presentation to suffer, and also requires a heavy mental workload for understanding the content of the graphics. With that method, it is difficult to present objects that are most effectively served by graphical representations, such as details of trends represented by line graphs and complex topography represented by maps. By virtue of its advanced graphics output functions, in addition to the output of graphs, R is utilized in the output of maps using GIS data. When this is considered, the constraints of that method are regrettable.

Methods employed by the BrailleR package require individual support tasks for drawing functions. With this problem in mind, in order to effectively support a wide range of high-level plotting functions, the BrailleR package uses utilizes the methods and class mechanisms possessed by R. And yet, it is impossible to eliminate the necessity of individual support tasks for drawing functions. For example, BrailleR is compatible with `hist()`, R's standard histogram drawing function. Although this function utilizes the method established by Sturges, [8] when data deviates from normal distribution, the applicability of that method deteriorates. The `truehist()` function contained in the MATH package using the method established by Scott, [9] which is believed to be superior in this fashion, is currently not supported by BrailleR.

The author has shown that the advantages of the "method of converting graphics into a tactile graphic" can yield sufficient benefits in cases where the graphics output of software meets certain conditions. [1] For the purpose of this paper, the "certain conditions that the graphics output of software should meet" are defined as the intermediate format that handles graphic data within that software consisting of primitive drawing commands in vector format (as opposed to bitmap format) and character output commands that handle characters in the form of code (as opposed to glyphs). To demonstrate this, the author simultaneously implemented prototype software that converts graphic output by R into tactile graphics.

2   Approaches of This Research

2.1   Significance and Possibility of Applying the "Method of Converting Graphics into a Tactile Graphic" to R

This research realized access by blind persons to graphics output by R using the "method of converting graphics into a tactile graphic." In accordance with the analysis presented by Godfrey, this research shares the perception that among statistical analysis software currently in distribution, from the standpoint of access by blind persons, R is by far the most superior. At the same time, the "method of converting graphics into a tactile graphic," while not used by BrailleR, holds promise in the utilization of R by blind persons. This method, which can present objects effectively represented to the user graphically (such as graphs and maps), is defined by the crucial advantage it demonstrates with respect to graphics output by R. Godfrey emphasized that blind persons should also possess understanding with respect to graphs viewed by other people. [7] Through the advantage the above method offers by providing advanced support of graphical representations viewed by other people (with normal sight), it is safe to say that Godfrey's position would be realized with a higher level of completeness. Meanwhile, the disadvantage of the above method in that it carries the constraint of limiting objects to things that are easy to understand using tactile graphics does not pose a major problem when the purpose of using R is considered.

To a certain extent, the approach taken in this research mitigates the impracticability of tactile graphics output in statistical learning and research environments as indicated by Godfrey. [7] Writing with refreshable tactile displays in mind, Godfrey did not consider tactile graphics output in such environments as a practical choice due mainly to the following reasons: (1) blind persons cannot widely access tactile graphics output (due to its high cost); (2) there are constraints on the quality of graphics that can be presented. This impracticability cited by Godfrey can be mitigated to a certain extent when a braille embosser equipped with graphics output functions is used instead of a refreshable tactile display. Braille embossers, which can also be used to print general character text in addition to graphic representations, have general versatility, and as such rank higher on lists of equipment for establishing learning and research environments for blind persons. Moreover, braille embossers also top refreshable tactile displays in terms of the graphics quality they can present. For example, on a Dot View DV-2 [10] refreshable tactile display sold by KGS, a single dot type can only be displayed with a pitch of 2.4mm. On the other hand, the ESA721 Braille Embosser [11] can emboss three sizes of dots: large (1.7mm in diameter), medium (1.5mm) and small (0.7mm). Plotting accuracy is 0.32mm horizontally and 0.35mm vertically.

Additionally, when pondering the actual performance of tasks for statistical analysis, an inherent level of effectiveness can be expected of the approach proposed by this research. Plotting multiple data sets on a single graph plane and eliciting an intuitive understanding of their correlation makes statistical analysis work significantly more efficient. Comparisons of chronological trends of such multiple data sets are difficult with numerical chart-like formats such as those outputted by the BrailleR package.

2.2   Limits of Prototype Software and Image Formats Supported by This Research

As touched upon above, the author implemented prototype software that converts graphic output by R into tactile graphics. Using said prototype software, the author loaded graphics data saved by R in PiCTeX format and converted it into tactile graphic data. Due to the use of PiCTeX format files as the data source, this approach has critical two limitations.

- **Limited Means of Presentation:** As PiCTeX was developed with only monochrome output in mind, it cannot output in color. When reverting output to tactile graphics, there is more room to utilize the color data belonging to the source graphics (discussed below).

- **Uncertainty Surrounding Maintenance:** The `help()` function of R's GRdevice mechanism contains a disclaimer that the PiCTeX driver is "of historical interest only."

Given the above limitations, among image formats for graphics output supported by the R version 2.15.1 contained in Debian GNU Linux 7.0, the author searched for formats that fell under the condition of consisting of primitive drawing commands in vector format and character output commands that handle characters in the form of code. At last, it is revealed that all vector formats–pdf, postscript, cairo_pdf and svg–do not fulfill the above condition perfectly.

As a graphics output driver that fulfills the above condition, the author used RSVGTipsDevice. [12] This SVG [13] output driver was released as an add-on package for R. The main purpose behind its development was to add graphics output functions to R that use JavaScript to enable dialogic commands. SVG files outputted by RSVGTipsDevice differ from those outputted by the R-standard SVG graphics output driver in that when RSVGTipsDevice outputs character strings, the files use commands—in other words, SVG `text` tags—that handle characters as code. Moreover, RSVGTipsDevice supports color outputting and continues to undergo active development.

3 Software Developed

The software developed through this research was given the provisional name of "RSVG2TVG" (short for "RSVGTips to Tactile Vector Graphics"). A processing flow for parsing XML using the pull-parser method was introduced for the loading of line units and the detection of PiCTeX commands through pattern matching conducted by the prototype software. By employing the approach of interpreting SVG according to XML-based planning, in addition to SVG output produced by RSVGTipsDevice, RSVG2TVG successfully attained the possibility of rendering output by various forms of graphic software that support SVG-format output in tactile graphic form. For implementing RSVG2TVG, the programming language Ruby, which is highly competent in processing character strings and is equipped with an advanced XML parser module as a standard, was used. Using Ruby enables RSVG2TVG to run on a multi-platform basis similar to R.

For incorporating character strings in graphics into tactile graphics, methods that utilize the prototype software [1] — replacing as one character label and generating a chart sheet matching these labels and original strings — were applied. Tactile graphics data outputted using RSVG2TVG can be printed as embossed graphics using an ESA721 braille embosser. [11] RSVG2TVG was configured so that dot size and inter-dot pitch could be defined for each color used in SVG files. In statistical graphs, the presentation method of using different colors for each data set to plot multiple data sets on a single graph plane and realize intuitive comparisons between those data sets is used with great frequency. In outputting graphical representations using a braille embosser, the corresponding method is adjusting dot size and inter-dot pitch. With the use of RSVG2TVG, when preparing graphs using R, users can adjust the dot size and inter-dot pitch for embossed graphs by making appropriate adjustments to colors in accordance with the data set at hand. This corresponding relationship between colors and dot presentation can be freely changed by using YAML to state that relationship. SVG supports presentation using 65,536 RGB gradations, meaning that there are essentially no constraints on corresponding dot presentation.

As an output sample, Figure 1 indicates a line graph used to plot Nikkei closing share price averages and dollar-yen exchange rates for 2013. In embossed this graph in the same figure, the black lines have been outputted with a small dot size and an inter-dot pitch of 2mm, and the red lines a large dot size and an inter-dot pitch of 4mm. In consideration of paper printing, for the SVG data for the source graphics, the line type for the red line was changed. This graph can be safely assumed to help facilitate analysis that assumes a correlation between share prices and the currency rate.

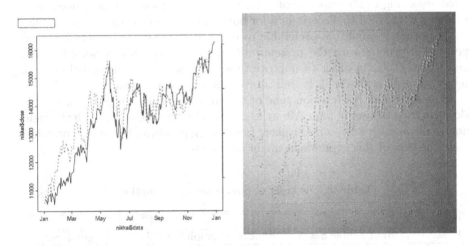

Fig. 1. A line graph used to plot Nikkei closing share price averages and dollar-yen exchange rates for 2013 (left) and .the embossed output of that (right).

4   Results—Evaluation Experiments

An experiment was performed to verify which of the following two methods is effective in allowing blind persons to ascertain the nature of graphics output using R when said methods are used: the presentation method employed by BrailleR; and the presentation method employed by RSVG2TVG. The tasks under this experiment were established in conformity with the practical usage of R. Average monthly temperature data for 2012 was acquired for four cities in the Northern Hemisphere and four cities in the Southern Hemisphere from http://www.climate-charts.com/. These eight total data items were outputted line graphs for each data set using RSVG2TVG and braille tables for each data set (modeled after output applied to `hist()` functions in BrailleR Package) were used. "Set A" and "Set B" were formed consisting of four graphs or tables that combined the two cities from the Northern Hemisphere and the two cities from the Southern Hemisphere. Experiment participants discerned the data on the Northern Hemisphere cities contained within each set. The order of presenting each condition is shown in Table 2. Participants were three blind undergraduate or graduate university students who use braille every day.

Correct Rates: One out of three participants made perfectly correct answers in all conditions. Two out of three participants, one judging from the braille table set and the other from the embossed graphs set, were unable to discern that Bangkok was a Northern Hemisphere city.

Reaction Times(Table 3): There was a participant who discerned the braille table set quickly, one who discerned the embossed graph set quickly, and one whose discernment time did not change based on the presentation method.

Observations: The question of which method is more effectively applied differed according to the experiment participant. The presence of experiment participants who failed to discern data for both embossed graphs and braille tables suggests that it would be preferable to outfit R usage environments for blind persons in general with the presentation methods employed in both BrailleR and RSVG2TVG in order to improve those environments. The distribution of response speed is also a likely indicator of the same conclusion.

The participant b's reaction time of the embossed graph set was remarkably slow. He tried this set at first. After the experiment, he explained that he thought how to distinguish a city's Hemisphere from its temperature. Pursuing a practical task, the task of this experiment might be too complicated.

Table 2. The order of presenting each condition

Participants	A	B	C
First	Braille table Set A	Embossed graph Set B	Embossed graph Set A
Second	Embossed graph Set B	Braille table Set A	Braille table Set B

Table 3. Reaction times (seconds)

Participants	Braille table	Embossed graph
a	37	29
b	42	155
c	39	39

5 Discussion

It is possible that the "method of converting graphics into a tactile graphic" may result in advantages that potentially cannot be enjoyed using the "method transcribing values represented in graphics into characters;" moreover, RSVG2TVG realizes that possibility. One may conclude that there is a need to establish environments in which BrailleR and RSVG2TVG can both be used in a complementary manner based on which software is appropriate for the situation at hand.

Through supporting output by drawing applications by RSVG2TVG, such software can be utilized as tactile graphics creation software. Moreover, graphs outputted with R can also be outputted as post-processed tactile graphics.

References

1. Minatani, K.: A Proposal for an Automated Method to produce embossed graphics for Blind Persons. In: Stephanidis, C., Antona, M. (eds.) UAHCI 2014, Part II. LNCS, vol. 8514, pp. 144–153. Springer, Heidelberg (2014)
2. TapTapSee - Blind and Visually Impaired Camera, http://www.taptapseeapp.com/
3. Way, T.P., Barner, K.E.: Automatic Visual to Tactile Translation—Part II: Evaluation of The Tactile Image Creation System. IEEE Transactions on Rehabilitation Engineering 5(1), 95–105 (1997)
4. Tiger Software Suite, http://www.viewplus.com/products/software/braille-translator/
5. Minatani, K., Watanabe, T., Yamaguchi, T., Watanabe, K., Akiyama, J., Miyagi, M., Oouchi, S.: Tactile Map Automated Creation System to Enhance the Mobility of Blind Persons—Its Design Concept and Evaluation through Experiment. In: Miesenberger, K., Klaus, J., Zagler, W., Karshmer, A. (eds.) ICCHP 2010, Part II. LNCS, vol. 6180, pp. 534–540. Springer, Heidelberg (2010)
6. Godfrey, A.J.R.: Statistical Software from a Blind Person's Perspective: R is the Best, but we can make it better. The R Journal 5(1), 73–80 (2013)
7. Godfrey, A.J.R.: The BrailleR Project. In: Proceedings of Digitization and E-Inclusion in Mathematics and Science, Tokyo, pp. 1–7 (2012)
8. Sturges, H.A.: The choice of a class interval. Journal of the American Statistical Association 21(153), 65–66 (1926)
9. Scott, D.W.: Multivariate Density Estimation: Theory, Practice, and Visualization. John Wiley, New York (1992)
10. DV-2, http://www.kgs-jpn.co.jp/ index.php?%E8%A3%BD%E5%93%81%E8%A9%B3%E7%B4%B0#s46a1117 (in Japanese)
11. ESA721 Ver 1995, http://www.jtr-tenji.co.jp/products/ESA721_Ver95/ (in Japanese)
12. Plate, T.: An R SVG graphics device with dynamic tips and hyperlinks, http://cran.r-project.org/web/packages/RSVGTipsDevice/ RSVGTipsDevice.pdf
13. Scalable Vector Graphics (SVG) 1.1, 2nd edn., http://www.w3.org/TR/SVG/

The Study of a New Actuator
for a Two-Point Body-Braille System

Nobuyuki Sasaki[1], Kazuya Nakajima[1], Satoshi Ohtsuka[2],
Kazuyoshi Ishii[3], and Tetsumi Harakawa[4]

[1] Tsukuba University of Technology, 4-12-7, Kasuga, 305-0821 Tsukuba, Japan
`nsasaki@cs.k.tsukuba-tech.ac.jp`
[2] Gunma National College of Technology, 580 Toribamachi,
371-8530 Maebashi, Japan
`ohtsuka@ice.gunma-ct.ac.jp`
[3] Ishii Lab., Ohtaniminami, Ebina-shi, Japan
`k-ishii@sun.ocn.ne.jp`
[4] Maebashi Institute of Technology, 460-1, Kamisadoricho,
371-0816 Maebashi, Japan
`harakawa@maebashi-it.ac.jp`

Abstract. We have been studying the Body-Braille system that transmits Braille characters to disabled people through vibrations on any part
of the body. Two years ago, we began to use a SMA (Shape Memory Alloy) device instead of a micro-vibrator. As a result, several advantages
were obtained such as smaller equipment size, high resolution transmission, and low power consumption. This year, we developed test equipment for the SMA device which can supply flexible PWM (Pulse Width
Modulation) parameters and performed several tests for Braille reading.
The test results reveal several possibilities for using a SMA device as a
communication channel.

Keywords: Body-Braille, Vibration, Deaf-blind, SMA.

1 Introduction

Since 2002, we have been developing the Body-Braille system, which transmits
Braille characters to disabled people through vibrations by six vibrators on any
part of the body [1]. We have experimented with Body-Braille in several systems
such as the "Tele-support system", which is a remote support system for deaf-
blind people, "an independent support system" for deaf-blind people's urban
mobility using RFID, and "Helen Keller phone system" for deaf-blind people's
communication. Through these experiments, we realized that we could reduce
the number of vibrators. We call this new system the "two-point Body-Braille
system". In this system, the two vibrators are driven three times for each Braille
cell. With this simpler Braille code, we can use fewer vibration motors which are
convenient for body parts having a small area and it makes it possible to use
much smaller size equipment.

K. Miesenberger et al. (Eds.): ICCHP 2014, Part I, LNCS 8547, pp. 630–633, 2014.

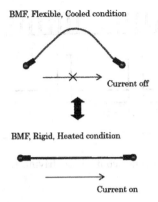

BMF, Flexible, Cooled condition

Current off

BMF, Rigid, Heated condition

Current on

Fig. 1. The BMF self-elasticity [3]

For the vibration device, we used an inexpensive and easily obtained device, which was a micro vibration motor that is often used in mobile phones. But its size, resolution, response, lifespan, consumption power and waterproofness are problematic. In order to overcome these several problems, we began to apply a new vibration device technology to our application (mainly to the "two-point Body-Braille system") from three years ago. The details are described in this paper.

2   What's SMA?

SMA is a functional device which changes thermal energy to kinetic energy. In particular, since SMA made from Ti-Ni is stable and has high electric resistance, a new device as an actuator using the heat by sending the current directly is being developed recently [2]. Bio Metal Fiber (BMF), one of the SMA devices, has self-elasticity like a muscle — normally softly pliant. But once it has an electric current, it shrinks strongly. When the electric current is removed, it becomes pliant again and expands, returning to its original length. This movement makes the vibration [3].

3   Research of SMA and Application

We researched various types of SMA and found that Bio Metal Fiber from Toki Corp. is the easiest to obtain and has excellent features as a vibration device by the repetition of extension and contraction [3]. Several applications have been developed and tested previously [4]. By using SMA as a tactile display equipment, a Braille display system and entertainment uses were realized [4]. We experienced those devices and we felt the need for some practice, especially for six-point Braille reading. So, we decided to apply the SMA device to our "two-point Body-Braille system".

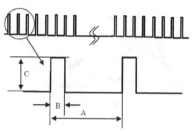

A:Pulse interval, B:Pulse width, C:Pulse voltage

Fig. 2. PWM pulse control for driving the SMA

Fig. 3. Picture of the mounting state of BMF devices

4   Driving SMA

As described above, it is necessary to turn on and off the current repeatedly in order to get vibration in a SMA device. For that purpose, we used PWM technology (see Fig. 2) in which it is possible to give heat to SMA by average current. Cooling is done by dissipation. Three parameters of SMA — pulse voltage, pulse width and pulse interval — must be decided correctly to get the best vibration. Following the previous study [4], we developed a flexible experimental equipment to decide the best parameters. As a result, we decided that for the BMF100 device, the optimal parameters were as follows: pulse voltage is 2.6V, pulse width is 1ms and pulse interval is 30ms. To get the stronger vibration, we placed two devices adjacently as parallel drive. Fig.3 shows the picture of the mounting state of the BMF devices.

5   Experiment

We performed three experiments with two subjects: a partially sighted man and a blind man. First, we performed an experiment to compare the present system with a previous system using two micro vibration motors and we obtained a result that is equivalent to using SMA device in terms of the reading accuracy in the two-point Body-Braille system. After that, we tested many parts of the body for reading Braille code. The results and observations are below.

1. Qualitative observations
   - Vibration is very clear and comfortable.
   - Older people tend to feel a little uncomfortable.
   - After feeling continuous vibration for a long time (not in Braille code case), heat is felt, but Braille code was fine.
   - The accuracy depends on the angle and pressure applied to the SMA device. How to settle the device on the body surface is problematic.
2. Comparison of body surfaces for device placement
   We tested the sensitivity of many body surfaces for reading Braille characters such as the tip of the index finger on both hands, finger root, palm, wrist, arm, elbow, neck, ear, back, abdomen and leg. Results show that the fingertip is the best, back and abdomen are difficult, and other parts are usable (the preferable part depends on the subject).
3. Braille code reading
   A Braille code reading test was done by using original software which generates and presents one random character (Japanese Kana) for subjects to identify. Fingertip, finger root, arm, wrist, neck, ear and leg were tested and on all the surfaces except the arm, we got more than 80 percent of correct answers.

6 Conclusion

We applied a new vibration device to the two-point Body-Braille system. We developed the experimental equipment by which we could determine suitable PWM parameters. Using these parameters, we tested many surfaces on the body and selected several suitable surfaces. Furthermore, we performed a Braille character reading test and obtained a high percentage of correct answers on many surfaces of the body. Consequently, we could observe the possibility of using a new vibration device instead of a micro vibration motor. In the near future, we would have more experiments and develop the new equipment using SMA.

Acknowledgment. A part of this work was supported by JSPS KAKENHI 23500667.

References

1. Ohtsuka, S., Sasaki, N., Hasegawa, S., Harakawa, T.: Body-Braille System for Disabled People. In: Miesenberger, K., Klaus, J., Zagler, W.L., Karshmer, A.I. (eds.) ICCHP 2008. LNCS, vol. 5105, pp. 682–685. Springer, Heidelberg (2008)
2. Homma, D., Nakazawa, F.: Development of Functional Anisotropic Shape Memory Alloy Fiber and Application. Denki-Seiko (Electric Furnace Steel) 77(4), 277–283 (2006) (in Japanese)
3. http://www.toki.co.jp/biometal/products/WhtsBM.php
4. Mizukami, Y., Uchida, K., Sawada, H.: Tactile Transmission by Higher-level Perception Using Vibration of Shape Memory Alloy Thread. Information Processing Society of Japan 48(12), 3739–3749 (2007) in Japanese

Design Guidelines of Tools for Facilitating Blind People to Independently Format Their Documents

Lourdes M. Morales[1], Sonia M. Arteaga[2], Peter Cottrell[1], and Sri Kurniawan[1]

[1] University of California, Santa Cruz, 1156 High Street, Santa Cruz, CA 95064
{lommoral,pcotterl,skurnia}@ucsc.edu
[2] Hartnell College, 411 Central Avenue Salinas, CA, 93901
sarteaga@hartnell.edu

Abstract. In professional and educational settings, a document's presentation can be as important as its content. Thus, blind people often rely on sighted help for fear of having their documents treated dismissively or misinterpreted as lack of professionalism or education, by sighted readers when the documents do not meet presentation 'standards'. Still, most work on helping blind people with word-processed documents focuses on the content rather than the formatting. Our work aims to enable the development of efficient tools to help blind people independently format their documents. We first sought to understand blind peoples' experiences and issues with document formatting and sighted readers' strategies and expectations regarding well-formatted documents. As a result, we compiled a set of guidelines for such tools and present them here.

Keywords: Assistive Technology, User Interface, Blind Users, Word Processors, Screen Readers.

1 Introduction

In professional and educational environments, some documents' presentation can be as important as their content (e.g. resumes, thesis, project proposals, research papers). Hence, a person's career can vastly depend on being able to communicate through written word in a way that is professional, visually appealing and similar to one's peers. Even for sighted people this is not always easy, but the formatting tools and references are easily available (and accessible) to them. Unfortunately, the same cannot be said for blind people.

Blind people feel less comfortable when presentation is key and the readers are 'important' (e.g. employers, recruiters, peers), because they are aware their written works are treated dismissively when they do not meet sighted reader's formatting 'standards' [1], [3], [6] and, as we found, they feel their badly-formatted works are misinterpreted as lack of professionalism or education. Further, the study reported in [3] found that documents produced by blind people, while well written grammatically, often contain formatting and layout errors (a formatting error is the incorrect or inconsistent formatting of text and a layout error is

K. Miesenberger et al. (Eds.): ICCHP 2014, Part I, LNCS 8547, pp. 634–641, 2014.
© Springer International Publishing Switzerland 2014

the incorrect or unusual positioning of text on a page). In theory, blind people can check their documents to locate formatting errors by using a word processor like Microsoft (MS) Word along with a screen reader software. But, as we found through interviews with 15 blind people and [3] reported, the task can be painstaking, tedious, slow, frustrating, overwhelming, and sometimes impossible. It is not surprising then that blind people often rely on sighted help for a secondary check or even the creation of documents, because otherwise their work is unlikely to be treated fairly or accepted [1], [3], [6]. Moreover, sighted help is not always cheap or available, which further hampers blind peoples' productivity. In sum, blind persons cannot be as productive as their sighted peers.

Still, there is not much work on supporting blind people create well-formatted documents. Document preparation that separates content and style as in LATEX can mediate the issues, but it usually requires quite advanced technical knowledge and this would unavoidably exclude a percentage of blind persons. In the 1980s there were works on producing word processors specifically for blind people, but these mainly concentrated on supporting blind persons in the more general tasks associated with writing documents rather than formatting [5]. Moreover, word processors specifically targeted at blind users appear to have been superseded by the widespread use of standard word processors with screen readers. In [3] they studied documents produced by blind persons to determine and classify the most common formatting and layout errors produced by blind persons, and based on this they developed two prototype tools: one for creating letters and another that checked for the common errors, notified the user of possible errors and suggested how to correct them (it did not give the user the option to directly edit the text). Hence, there is still a need for work that focuses on facilitating blind people to independently format their documents.

The work presented here focuses on the design characteristics of tools that will help blind people independently format their documents. For this, we surveyed and interviewed blind persons to learn about their experiences and issues with document formatting. In addition, we interviewed and observed sighted people to investigate their expectations and strategies regarding well-formatted documents. As a result, we extracted a set of preliminary design guidelines for tools that will help blind people format documents and present them here.

2   Survey among Blind Persons

We ran a survey on the concept of document formatting and the tools used to format documents among 21 people who: 1) are blind (with at most some light perception), and 2) use word processors and screen readers. For the qualitative data, we analyzed open-ended responses by doing open-coding and theme extraction. Participants were between the ages of 18 and 56, 81% reported being blind since birth or infancy, 76.2% said MS Word is the word processor they use most often, 76.2% said JAWS is the screen reader they use most often, they were all aware of the concept of document formatting before the survey, 70% learned about the concept when they were less than 18 years old and 55% while in high school, and 90% knew or had formatted documents without sighted help. Participants that did not know about the concept or had not formatted documents on their own wanted to learn how to format documents to make them visually appealing and be certain they do it correctly.

Participants that knew how to format documents on their own learned with tools such as: screen readers, Braille NoteTaker, and word processors' built-in formatting functions. Among these, 33.3% prefer getting sighted help when formatting documents for reasons such as: accessibility issues with word processors and screen readers, sighted people can do it better, it is hard or impossible, and it is for the sake of the sighted reader. Still, these participants said they would be motivated to do it themselves if they: understood document formatting better, could take a class on it, or had a good tool for it (i.e. one that is reliable, informative, and accessible). The other 66.7% prefer to format their documents themselves (although some said sometimes they use sighted help) for reasons such as: the satisfaction and advantage of doing things independently, aversion to requesting assistance, and to save time.

Most of the participants that prefer to format their documents themselves said that the word processor they use most often when formatting documents has the necessary features and is easy to use, but some still said they have issues with: accessibility, efficiency, getting the necessary information, or understanding how to use formatting functions. Also, some said they use additional tools, such as embossers and braillers, to format their documents but it is hard and time consuming. When these participants were asked whether they thought a better tool for formatting documents was needed, the ratio of those that answered "yes" to those that answered "no" was 5 to 7. Those that answered "no" felt that: 1) screen readers and word processors are sufficient even though the accessibility can be improved, or 2) that other resources, such as tutorials or guides on how to format properly and check a document's formatting with existing tools, should be created instead. In contrast, those that answered "yes" felt that tools for formatting need to be: easier to use, more accessible (especially the formatting features), straightforward, informative (e.g. provide better feedback on whether the formatting is appropriate), helpful (e.g. make visual information, such as graphs or figures, straightforward), reliable, and efficient (i.e. it should enable them to format their documents independently as well as and in the same amount of time as a sighted person).

Finally, most participants (95.2%) thought that it is important for blind people to know how to format documents for reasons such as: independence, one less barrier towards equality, it makes them more competitive in professional and educational environments (they thought badly or unformatted documents might lead people to erroneously believe they are careless, unprofessional or uneducated) and hence, it can improve one's quality of life.

3 Interviews with Blind Persons

We interviewed another 15 blind people to learn more about their document formatting experiences (i.e. strategies, issues, tools) and the functionalities they wish for in a tool to help them format documents. We found that adventitiously blind participants' mental models and techniques were different from those of congenitally blind participants, due to their prior experience seeing formatted documents. Hence, we analyzed the interviews from the 10 adventitiously blind participants and the 5 congenitally blind participants separately:

3.1 Results from Congenitally Blind Participants

Interviewees occupations included: attorney, specialist in technology and computer support for blind people, vocational rehabilitation counselor, and student. They primarily use screen readers, some also use Braille technologies (e.g. Braille NoteTaker, Braille display), and most use MS Word. Three main topics emerged:

Formatting Strategies and Problems. Most participants write content first (sometimes they change everything to plain text to avoid unwanted formatting), then check the document line by line for content errors, and finally format in a linear fashion going line by line. Some stated that they use an established style guide for their documents, such as the Modern Language Association style. Still, some said that accessing and implementing style guides is a bit difficult and they cannot be sure they are using them correctly without sighted help. The formatting problems that participants mentioned included: difficulty with indentation (it can be hard to do correctly or catch, so when delineating paragraphs they use a line space instead), font styles, footers, and headers; and errors that were due to them forgetting they had made changes or not realizing that MS Word had automatically changed the formatting. Some said they get around the problems with screen readers by using Braille technologies, because Braille contains many formatting symbols that can help them get a sense of the location of the formatted element and thus, make the formatting process easier.

Existing Tools Are Not Helpful for Some Formatting Tasks. Some participants stated having problems with word processors (e.g. when MS Word automatically changes formatting), Braille technologies, and screen readers. The problems with Braille technologies included: having to guess the number of spaces needed for indentation (when using the Braille NoteTaker) and margins being limited by the physical size of the display area on the device, which makes formatting larger documents difficult. Similarly, the problems with screen readers included: the output (listening to every space and formatted item is tedious, slow, a huge memory load, distracting, frustrating, and just overwhelming), not getting all the necessary information (e.g. the number of spaces between words), and the difficulty with jumping back and forth within a document to find the appropriate formatting style, which slows down the formatting process. Still, some participants stated that some screen readers have improved their capabilities for skimming documents and checking for extra spaces and describe font style and font color. In general, participants believe that screen readers need improvements to effectively help users: 1) better understand the content of the documents they are reading, 2) better edit and format their documents, and 3) navigate documents. On that note, participants said screen readers should give users more control over the output and how they navigate documents.

Characteristics of a Formatting Tool for Blind Persons. Participants' ideas on the characteristics of a tool that will help them with formatting included: automatically checks the document's formatting, makes suggestions in a linear fashion (similar to MS Word's grammar and spelling checkers) instead of performing automatic corrections, gives the user the choice to either accept or reject suggestions, allows users to correct similar instances throughout the document, runs with shortcut keys, callable at anytime, provides the functionality and usability necessary for them to use the application on their own to confidently format documents, gives tips on how to format based on the document's type (e.g. essay, resume), and provides templates (that apply the proper formatting to whatever is typed in) of various document types.

3.2   Results from Adventitiously Blind Participants

Interviewees occupations included: counselor, program manager, college student, clinical psychologist, computer system analyst, blogger, writer, magazine editor, retired VP of a bank's marketing team, and retired medical secretary. The technologies they use included: screen magnifiers, document scanners, Braille Notetakers, Eudora for email, and screen readers. As before, 3 main topics emerged:

Formatting Strategies and Problems. To format their documents, they usually stick to formatting styles they are familiar with and know will look good (many of these participants lost their sight after high school and thus, remembered formatting styles). They also use: formatting approaches that are easier to implement with current tools (e.g. line space to delineate paragraphs), templates that are document type specific (to get a better idea of how to format) or that they created, and documents that they are able to use as a guide by scanning through the formatting with a screen reader. To check their documents for formatting errors they either go line by line and character by character across the whole document, or use sighted help to also check for visual appeal and graphical content, especially when writing books in Braille, emails, letters, proposals, papers, etc. Still, participants stated that they feel that they do not have enough time and sighted help (since it is not always available when needed) for the number of documents they create. In addition, these participants use Braille writers and readers to format, because these provide a better idea of the locations of various formatting features and they feel this makes the formatting process easier. The problems participants mentioned having included: finding accessible versions of documents and forms they needed to work with, working with pictures and graphs or any document element that has location or direction associated with its presentation, dragging and dropping items, creating works cited pages, using certain websites, adding page numbers to documents, and in general, formatting. Another problem they mentioned was that most of their errors are introduced when MS Word automatically formats text that is typed or pasted into the document, and that these are hard to catch because they are unexpected and unannounced.

Existing Tools Are Not helpful for Some Formatting Tasks. Similar to the congenitally blind interviewees, these participants also encountered difficulties with their screen readers not being able to read all the formatting information (e.g. borders, paragraph indentation, highlighting, and hanging indents). They believe that screen readers need to have better formatting feedback that does not load their memory, and is fast and clear in conveying information.

Characteristics of a Formatting Tool for Blind Persons. Participants stated that a tool to help them format their documents must provide: recommendations on how to format different types of documents, information on why a specific formatting was applied and why it is needed, and accessible style guides and templates that include a description of the formatting for different types of documents. Also, the tool must help them put pictures, tables, and graphics in their documents; and it must be affordable or free. Some even suggested that it have an alternate interface, such as speech or tactile (they felt it would be helpful to be able to touch the area on the screen where they want the formatting done), to improve feedback and interaction.

4   Study with Sighted People

We ran a study with 14 sighted people (all MS Word users, which have been using it for at least a year to create or edit documents at least once a week) where we: 1) observed them and recorded their on-screen actions while they formatted a document to learn about their formatting techniques (especially those that may be difficult to do without sight with current tools) and 2) inquired about what they expect in a well-formatted document. For the first part, participants were asked to use MS Word 2007 or higher to format a given two-paged document that contained formatting errors commonly found in documents produced by blind people [3] and to use the Thinking Aloud protocol [2] so that we could learn about their thought process with regards to their formatting decisions. For the second part, we transcribed the interviews and analyzed them by doing open-coding and theme extraction.

Formatting Techniques. We observed the following commonalities in the formatting techniques of participants: they learn about the desired formatting style (e.g. font size and type of headings) before proceeding with formatting, look at formatting at paragraph level (not word-by-word like blind people), and approach the formatting task in a top-down manner (i.e. starting at the top of the document, they format linearly until they reach the end of the document) but occasionally jump back to review a previous formatting style (this is something blind people have difficulty doing with current tools). Also, they focus on headings more than the body of text, use style sheets they created or an existing one that requires the least amount of changes in the document (some blind people have difficulty accessing and implementing styles), correct inconsistent formatting (observing visual consistency for blind people can be difficult for they need to hear the formatting attributes of similar items and they cannot do this with existing tools as easily as sighted readers), and they use the mouse to navigate the document (something blind people cannot do) and shortcut keys or the formatting functions on the MS Word ribbons to quickly format the document.

Expectations Regarding Well-Formatted Documents. We gathered that sighted readers expect well-formatted documents to have visual consistency in terms of positioning of text (spacing, justification and layout) and font (size, type, and color), look good and professional, and be easy on the eyes (a difficult concept to convey to a blind person, especially a congenitally blind one).

5   Summary of Results – Preliminary Design Guidelines

Consolidating the previous studies with blind and sighted people through an affinity diagramming exercise, we came up with the following preliminary design guidelines with regards to the functional requirements of a formatting tool for blind people (we only took the first level of the affinity diagram that we created):

1. Check document in a linear top-down approach
2. Accessible at anytime and from anywhere inside a word processor
3. Functions must be callable using intuitive shortcut keys
4. Minimize memory load–give info on formatting incidences and functions only
5. Provide the option to ignore, change or correct the formatted occurrences.
6. Correct in real-time.
7. Work well with various screen readers.
8. Explain formatting error and suggest how to fix it, do not just correct it.
9. Notify when the word processor changes the formatting automatically
10. Provide and explain templates and/or styles for various document types.

6   Conclusion

The main goal of our work is to facilitate blind people to independently produce documents that meet sighted readers' presentation standards. For this, we surveyed and interviewed blind people to understand their experiences with document formatting. Also, we interviewed and observed sighted persons to understand their strategies and expectations regarding well-formatted documents.

In sum, the contributions of this work are: 1) a better understanding of blind people's formatting problems with current tools and their strategies regarding document formatting, and 2) a set of 10 preliminary design guidelines for creators of tools to help blind people independently format documents.

7   Future Work

To verify some of the guidelines and see if new ones emerged, we developed a prototype tool and tested it with 8 blind participants. Due to space limitations, details on the prototype and its evaluation will be presented in a future paper. The next steps would be to improve the prototype based on the feedback, test it and iterate until we determine the optimal design characteristics. Also, like [3] did in 2003, we plan to study documents created by blind people to validate and find their most common formatting and layout errors, and develop a prototype tool that helps check for and correct those types of errors. We will keep collaborating with blind people and sighted people through user studies, surveys, and interviews to determine and validate what such tools need to do in order for them to work correctly and efficiently.

Acknowledgments. This material is based upon work supported by the National Science Foundation through the Graduate Research Fellowship grant No. DGE-1339067 and the HCC grant No. 1054984. We thank all of the participants and Jennifer Lui who helped with the study with sighted persons.

References

1. Diggle, T., Kurniawan, S.H., Evans, D.G., Blenkhorn, P.: An Analysis of Layout Errors in Word Processed Documents Produced by Blind People. In: Miesenberger, K., Klaus, J., Zagler, W.L. (eds.) ICCHP 2002. LNCS, vol. 2398, pp. 587–588. Springer, Heidelberg (2002)
2. Ericsson, K.A., Simon, H.A.: How to study thinking in everyday life: Contrasting think-aloud protocols with descriptions and explanations of thinking. Mind, Culture, and Activity 5(3), 178–186 (1998)
3. Evans, D.G., Diggle, T., Kurniawan, S.H., Blenkhorn, P.: An investigation into formatting and layout errors produced by blind word-processor users and an evaluation of prototype error prevention and correction techniques. IEEE Transactions on Neural Systems and Rehabilitation Engineering 11(3), 257–268 (2003)
4. Morales, L., Arteaga, S.M., Kurniawan, S.: Design guidelines of a tool to help blind authors independently format their word documents. In: CHI 2013 Extended Abstracts on Human Factors in Computing Systems, pp. 31–36. ACM (2013)
5. Vincent, A.T., Turnbull, S.D.: Word processing for blind people. Microprocessors and Microsystems 8(10), 535–538 (1984)
6. Wang, K., Barron, L.G., Hebl, M.R.: Making Those Who Cannot See Look Best: Effects of Visual Resume Formatting on Ratings of Job Applications with Blindness. Rehabilitation Psychology 55(1), 68–73 (2010)

Contribution to the Automation of the Tactile Images Transcription Process

Yong Chen, Zehira Haddad, and Jaime Lopez Krahe

THIM CHART, Université Paris8, St Denis, France
ychen09@etud.univ-paris8.fr,
{zhaddad-bousseksou,jlk}@univ-paris8.fr

Abstract. This paper presents an image conversion process on tactile maps intended for the use by people with blindness. This process is based on the image processing which includes image segmentation, shape recognition and text recognition. The proposed approach can be applied to different types of images.

Keywords: Accessibility for Blind People, Image Segmentation, Shape Recognition, Text Detection, Fuzzy Methods.

1 Introduction

This work aims to develop tools to facilitate the accessibility of images for visually impaired people. Indeed, for these people, the multimedia progress which is based on the exchange of visual information constitutes a real obstacle. It is evident that visual information is a very rich source of information: unfortunately, visually impaired people cannot benefit from it. This work is precisely dedicated to the development of specific solutions for this problem.

Despite the proposed solutions of tactile access for written information, for example Braille transcription, the automation of this process is not easy in the case of images. Currently, the transcription of images is made manually. This requires a lot of time and resources. In fact, this transcription process is very delicate because there are certain limitations in the sense of touch that do not exist for the visual sense. Of course, in contrast to the sighted person who can easily distinguish a rich number of colors and other visual information, the blind person can only distinguish a relatively small number of textures by using touch. Also, when we pass from one textural area to another, this is not as obvious for a blind person as it is for a visually impaired person. By consequently, the contours of the different textural areas required to be enhanced for a better exploration and understanding by non sighted people. In addition, given the fixed font size written in Braille, it is more appropriate in most cases to establish an independent image caption and introduce the labels in this image to refer to the legend. All these specific constraints of tactile transcription images are generally taken into account for manual transcription of tactile image maps [1]. The main objective of the presented work is to contribute to the automation of the transcription process, taking into account all the parameters related to visual deficiency.

K. Miesenberger et al. (Eds.): ICCHP 2014, Part I, LNCS 8547, pp. 642–649, 2014.
© Springer International Publishing Switzerland 2014

2   Methodology

In order to automate the image transcription, the proposed approach begins by detecting and classifying the various regions contained in an image. The detection of the different areas is done by a segmentation algorithm. Then, the separation of the various elements provided by the previous step is achieved via a post treatment. After this, we affect textures on the different extracted regions. Otherwise, the recognition of forms takes place, in which a feature vector is calculated for each form. This vector is then used to identify the form by applying a fuzzy clustering algorithm. For the text region, we extract and recognize the different text areas so that they can be transcribed into Braille language. Thus, the proposed approach contains the following steps: segmentation, post treatment applied for each segmented region, shape recognition and text transcription into Braille.

2.1   Segmentation and Post Treatment

The main objective of this step is to identify and extract the different regions of the image. The applied algorithm is the FCM (Fuzzy C-Means) segmentation [2,3]. It is based on color.

First, we estimate automatically the number of colors by using the RGB histogram. This number is done by the number of predominant colors in the image histogram. Afterwards, we determine the number of classes (colors), we apply the segmentation method. This method is based on a fuzzy clustering algorithm which optimizes a quadratic criterion of classification where each class is represented by its center of gravity. A fuzzy partition of the image is then obtained by assigning to each pixel a degree of membership in a given region.

After this, we use a post treatment for each region detected by the FCM segmentation step. This treatment is essential for the validation of the previous step. The used algorithm is based on the analysis of connected components [4]. It permits to improve the segmentation results by distinguishing between the different regions dedicated to be transformed on textural regions. Indeed, each detected region will be assigned a well differentiable texture in the corresponding tactile image. However, knowing that a blind person cannot effectively distinguish more than five different textures, we impose a maximum limit on the number of textures used by tactile map: five distinctive textures for each transcribed card. In this work, we propose also to smooth and improve the contour of each textured area. Thus, in order to provide a better understanding and exploration of the tactile card, the contours of different regions (textured areas) are smoothed and heavily accented.

In figure1, we represent the results of this step.

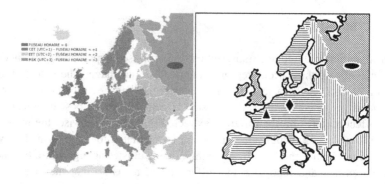

Fig. 1. Results of segmentation and post treatment

2.2   Intelligent Shape Recognition

Generally, we can find in images, specific known forms which correspond to particular information. We treat here the case of geometric forms. These different forms have special properties that characterize them. We propose in this phase an intelligent algorithm which can detect and recognize these shapes. This algorithm is based on the characteristic features of a form. Thus, to characterize a shape, we propose to use the mathematical parameters done by Table1:

- The number N of peaks, given by Harris detector [5](Figure2),
- The ratio between the concave surface and the convex surface A/Ach,
- The mathematical eccentricity E,
- The ratio between the concave surface and the bounding surface of the casing A/Ab,
- The ratio between the squared perimeter of the convex hull and the surface Pch2/Ach,
- The ratio between the perimeter of the shape and scope of its convex hull P/Pch.

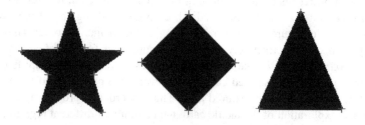

Fig. 2. The vertices of a shape

In figure3, we represent the difference between the convex hull (blue line) and the bounding box (red line).

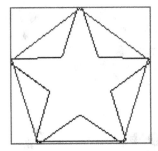

Fig. 3. Representation of the convex hull and the bounding box

Table 1. Mathematical features corresponding to different forms

	Number of Vertices	Eccentricity	A/A_{ch}	A/A_b	P_{ch}^2/A_{ch}	P/P_{ch}
Triangle	3	X	1	0.5	X	1
Square	4	0	1	1	X	1
Rectangle	4	X	1	1	X	1
Rhombus	4	X	1	0.5	X	1
Circle	0	0	1	$\pi/4$	4π	1
Ellipse	0	X	1	$\pi/4$	X	1
Star	10 (5 on the convex hull)	X	0.6	0.4	X	X

Then, based on the calculation of these parameters, a feature vector representative of the shape is extracted. Thus, we apply for each detected region in the segmentation step, the fuzzy classification algorithm [6] in order to automatically recognize the form [7,8]. So, each geometric form can be automatically identified in the image and transmitted with a specific tactile code described in the legend.

2.3 Text Transcription

In this step, we detect the text in image by applying SWT (Stroke Width Transform) [9,10]. This transform captures the only text effective features and use the geometric signature of text to filter out non-text areas. So, this system can be used to recover the regions that may contain text regardless of its size, direction, font, color and language of these regions. Therefore, it provides reliable text region detection (Figure 4).

The text transcription steps are:

- Location of the text region using SWT.
- Extraction of the text region via the approach of Boris Epshtein [11].
- Automatic recognition of character using the Tesseract OCR.
- Transformation of each letter in Braille [12].

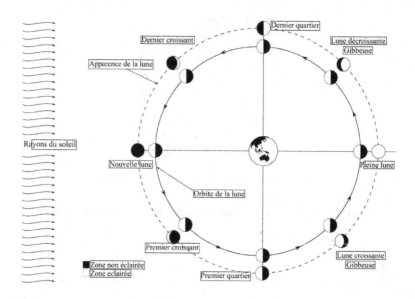

Fig. 4. Text region detection with SWT

For the text recognition step, we use Tesseract OCR. Then, we apply a Braille transformation in order to propose a tactile access of the written information. Note that given the constraints of tactile exploration that fixes a certain size for Braille text, we propose to put it in a "legend card" other than the tactile map representing the image.

3   Experiment Results

In this work, we used different types of images including geographic maps and pedagogic images where we can find various contents: geographic areas, geometric forms and text. The results of the different phases corresponding to the tactile transformation of these images are illustrated in the following figures:

The obtained results show the interest of this approach. However, the limits observed in our experiments are mainly those of the OCR step. Indeed, despite the advance of OCR systems, their performance is not complete. In our application, this limit is mainly due to the frequent overlap enough text with different outlines of the images. Nevertheless, according to the context of the image, it is possible to introduce specialized dictionaries according to the domain of interest of this image. This will have as results to limit errors generated by OCR.

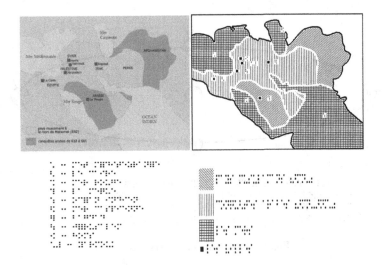

Fig. 5. Geographic image: The Arab World in the year 631 and 661

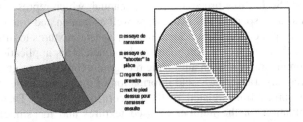

Fig. 6. Pedagogic image: Reaction of people deal with a coin on the ground

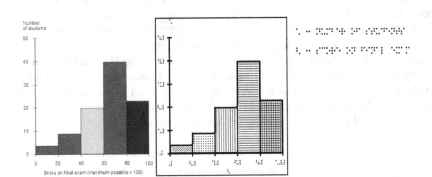

Fig. 7. Pedagogic image: Score of final exam

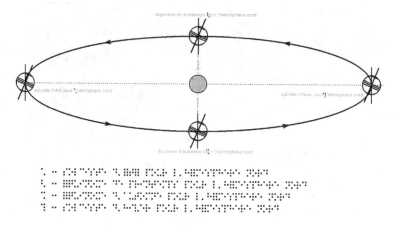

Fig. 8. Astronomy image: The 4 seasons

4   Conclusion

The goal of this work is to propose a tool for the automation of the tactile image transcription process. So far, this process is purely manual, which represents several constraints related to time spent in this process, as well as human and financial resources.
We developed an application that permits to apply special textures to different regions
of the image so they are well distinguishable by touch. This application also allows
text transcription in Braille and an automatic recognition of different geometric forms.
In order to effectively transcribe visual information of image on tactile maps, we have
proposed a few precautions related to the concerned disability. These precautions
include the limitation on the number of used textures and the smoothing and enhancement of the different contours. In addition, in order to meet the constraints on
the size of Braille font, we proposed to place the legend on another card than the transcribed picture. It is true that in the work we present, the complete automation of the
process does not give a success rate of 100% for all the tested images. However, to
overcome this limitation, we propose to introduce a user verification for each step.
The user would validate the different steps of the process. He corrects the errors. Otherwise, for simple images, we notice any intervention of user.

As future work, we collaborate with the blind students of the National Institute for
the Young Blind in order to enrich our basic tests and improve the proposed application. Indeed, this work may have different applications, such as the accessibility in
learning or the documentation access in general. In addition, we can use it to treat
images from map libraries by generating toponymic databases in order to address and
localize.

References

1. Bris, M.: Recommandations pour la transcription de documents, documentation du service des documents adaptés pour les déficients visuels. INSHEA, Suresnes, 2004.
2. Bezdek, J.C., Ehrlich, R., Full, W.: FCM: The Fuzzy C-Means Clustering Algorithm. Computer & Geosciences 10(2-3), 191–203 (1984)
3. Chen, C.W., Luo, J., Parker, K.J.: Image Segmentation via Adaptive K–Mean Clustering and Knowledge-Based Morphological Operations with Biomedical Applications. IEEE Transactions on Image Processing 7(12) (December 1998)
4. Bouman, C.A.: Connected Component Analysis. Digital Image Processing (January9, 2012)
5. Harris, C., Stephens, M.: A Combined Corner and Edge Detector. In: Proceedings of The Fourth Alvey Vision Conference, Manchester, UK, pp. 147–151 (1988)
6. Fonseca, M.J., Jorge, J.A.: Using Fuzzy Logic to Recognize Geometric Shapes Interactively. In: The 9IEEE International Conference on Fuzzy Systems, FUZZ IEEE 2000 (2000)
7. Lopez-Krahe, Alamo-Cantarero, T., Davila-Gonzalez, E.: Discrete line and circles: application to pattern recognition. ENST. D ISSN 0751-1345
8. Llados, J., Marti, E., Lopez-Krahe, J.: A Hough-based method for hatched pattern detection in maps and diagrams. In: 1999 Proceedings of the Fifth International Conference on Document Analysis and Recognition, p. 479 (1999)
9. Jung, C., Liu, Q., Kim, J.: A stroke filter and its application for text localization. PRL 30(2) (2009)
10. Epshtein, B., Ofek, E., Wexler, Y.: Detecting Text in Natural Scenes with Stroke Width Transform. In: IEEE Conference on Computer Vision and Pattern Recognition (2010)
11. Epshtein, B., Ofek, E., Wexler, Y.: Detecting Text in Natural Scenes with Stroke Width Transform. In: 2010 IEEE Conference on Computer Vision and Pattern Recognition (CVPR), June 13-18 (2010)
12. Code braille français uniformisé pour la transcription des textes imprimés. Deuxième édition (Septembre) (2008)

Dots and Letters: Accessible Braille-Based Text Input for Visually Impaired People on Mobile Touchscreen Devices

Elke Mattheiss[1], Georg Regal[1], Johann Schrammel[1], Markus Garschall[1,3], and Manfred Tscheligi[2,3]

[1] CURE – Center for Usability Research & Engineering, Vienna, Austria
{mattheiss,regal,schrammel,garschall}@cure.at
[2] ICT&S, University of Salzburg, Salzburg, Austria
manfred.tscheligi@sbg.ac.at
[3] AIT Austrian Institute of Technology GmbH, Vienna, Austria
{markus.garschall,manfred.tscheligi}@ait.ac.at

Abstract. Tailored text input methods for visually impaired and blind users are needed on touchscreen devices to support their accessibility. Therefore, we developed a new Braille-based text input method named EdgeBraille, which allows entering Braille characters by swiping one finger along the edges of the touchscreen. The approach was compared with the current standard method of a talking keyboard, first in a short-term lab study (14 participants) and then during two weeks of daily training (7 participants). Overall EdgeBraille was perceived well by the users. In terms of user performance we found no significant differences between the two methods. Based on the evaluation results and the feedback of our participants, we discuss advantages and disadvantages of Braille-based methods in general and EdgeBraille in particular, as well as possibilities for improvements.

Keywords: Text Input Method, Touchscreen, Mobile Devices, Braille, Visually Impaired and Blind Users.

1 Introduction

Many visually impaired and blind (VIB) people are intense technology users and use mobile devices regularly. With the emerging era of smartphones, touchscreen devices without keypads are becoming increasingly common, thus the improvement of touchscreen accessibility is an important issue to address.

An important aspect of interaction with smartphones is the ability to enter text, for example in order to write short messages or emails. The common way of making soft keyboards accessible for VIB users is based on the "talking fingertip technique" [1]. VoiceOver for iOS and TalkBack for Android are commercial products using this technique, which allows the device to read onscreen elements (such as letters of the keyboard) to the users, when they touch them with their fingers. A disadvantage of using a soft keyboard for entering text on touch devices is that the entire alphabet has

K. Miesenberger et al. (Eds.): ICCHP 2014, Part I, LNCS 8547, pp. 650–657, 2014.

to fit on the screen, which hampers the selection process. This is why a number of alternative solutions for non-visual text input have been presented in the scientific literature (e.g. pie-menu-based [2], gesture-based [3] and Braille-based text input [4]), aiming to reduce the number of elements on the screen.

In this paper, we present the design of a new Braille-based text input method for touchscreens named EdgeBraille and reflect on Braille-based methods in general as well as possibilities for improvement.

2   Related Work

Braille-based text input for blind people, which in the basic version uses six dots for one letter, was presented as a promising possibility in accessibility research. Previous Braille-based input methods can be differentiated into those who allow entering a Braille letter in one single step, and those who split the entry into several steps.

With TypeInBraille [4] three steps are needed to enter one Braille letter. For each row, users can select no, one or both dots. Perkinput [5] supports entering a Braille letter in one or two steps. For small screens such as smartphones, characters can be entered in two steps with three fingers. When using two small screens or one larger screen such as a tablet, two hands can be used simultaneously in order to input both columns of a Braille character in a single step.

Input of Braille letters in one step is used in BrailleType [6] and BrailleTouch [7]. Both approaches use six targets on the screen that represent the six dots of a Braille character. In the BrailleType system, target dots can be selected successively by touching them. BrailleTouch uses a multi-touch paradigm. Therefore the mobile phone is used with the screen facing away from the user, with three fingers of each hand resting over one of the six targets (three on each side).

Table 1. Summary of evaluation results reported by previous work on Braille-based methods (N = the number of participants, # = the number of sessions, wpm = the measured words per minute). BrailleTouch [7] reported the performance values captured in the last of 5 sessions. For the remaining methods the reported value is the average over all sessions conducted. TypeInBraille [8] calculated the error rate by dividing all errors through the length of the text. The rest of the methods used metrics proposed by [9]. BrailleType [6] reported the old MSD error-rate, Perkinput [5] the uncorrected error-rate and BrailleTouch [7] the total error-rate.

Method	N	#	wpm	error rate
TypeInBraille [8]	7	1	6.30	3.00 %
VoiceOver			5.20	4.00 %
BrailleType [6]	13	1	1.49	7.00 %
VoiceOver			2.10	14.12 %
Perkinput [5]	8	7	6.05	3.52 %
VoiceOver			3.99	6.43 %
BrailleTouch [7] Expert performance	6	5	23.20	14.50 %
BrailleTouch [7] Moderate performance	3	5	21.00	33.10 %
BrailleTouch [7] Poor performance	2	5	9.40	39.30 %

Considering previous work related to Braille-based text input, our goal was to create a new Braille-based method, which allows entering a Braille letter fast and in one single step. For comparison Table 1 provides an overview of evaluation results of the different Braille-based input methods and the values reported for VoiceOver. Furthermore the method should be convenient and usable with one finger, following findings by Paisios [10], who reports that one-finger interaction was rated best by blind users.

Inspired by previous research concerning text input with edge-supported Graffiti strokes [3], we developed EdgeBraille. We use a screen layout similar to BrailleType [6] and BrailleTouch [7], but the input paradigm differs significantly. BrailleType uses a multi-touch approach, which is indeed fast but requires the users to hold the phone with both hands. With EdgeBraille users can hold the phone with one hand and they only need one finger to enter the Braille letter. BrailleTouch uses tap-based input of each dot at a time, which is not very fast and requires accurate tapping. We expect a swipe-based approach along the display's edges to be faster and easier. Our design approach is described in detail in the following section.

3   Prototype Design of EdgeBraille

The structure of the screen relates to the structure of a Braille letter. The top two and bottom two dots (diameter: 12mm) of the Braille letter are placed in the corners of the display. Two points halfway along the side edges of the screen are used for the two middle dots.

A letter is entered by sketching an arbitrary sequence of Braille dots. Each dot can be activated by moving the finger on the dot, and revisiting a dot deactivates it. Examples of different strategies to write a letter can be found in Fig. 1.

Fig. 1. Possibilities to enter the letter "N" with EdgeBraille. (a) Selecting the dots using the shortest path (b) Selecting the dots column wise circling around dot no. 2 (c) Selecting the dots by first activating dot no. 2 and then deactivating it on the way back from dot no. 3.

A space is entered by tapping anywhere on the screen but not on a dot. To prevent accidentally deactivating a dot, the zone for deactivation is approximately 1.7 mm smaller than the zone for activation. When activating and deactivating, vibro-tactile feedback is provided and different sound files are played for activation and deactivation.

For users with residual vision also visual feedback is provided, as the dots are highlighted green when activated and grey when deactivated. When the finger is lifted, the activated dots are registered and the letter is spoken to the user and displayed on the screen. To prevent accidentally writing a letter, a threshold of 75 milliseconds for lifting the finger was defined.

The edges of the touchscreen are used as guardrails by marking them with a mechanical frame. Thus, we assume that this will ease orientation for the VIB people and speed up the process. This assumption is supported by Kane et al. [11], who reported that blind people preferred gestures that used screen edges and corners. For the short-term evaluation we built a cardboard frame to provide physical guidance. For the longer-term evaluation we used a commercial cover (Griffin GB01902 Survivor Cover) as shown in Fig. 1.

4   Short-Term Evaluation

In a short-term evaluation we compared the participants' performance and opinion towards EdgeBraille along with Android's talking keyboard method TalkBack. We did this for two reasons: first talking keyboards still are the standard accessible method for text input on touchscreens provided by mobile operating systems and secondly, the Braille-based approaches presented in the related work were not available for comparison at the time we conducted our research. For the short-term evaluation we used a HTC Desire S with Android 2.2.3.

For the evaluation 14 VIB participants (9 male, 5 female) with a mean age of 33.00 years (standard deviation = 12.22) were invited to participate. All participants were able to read and write Braille letters and five of them already had a lot of experience with touch-based mobile phones and the talking fingertip method. They were provided with a short description and five minutes of training with each method. To assess the training effect throughout usage, participants had to enter 16 two-word texts successively with each input method. Participants were told to enter the text as quickly and accurately as possible and they could not correct incorrectly entered characters. We measured the words per minute (wpm = number of correct characters per minute divided by five) and MSD error rate [9] for the methods and compared the beginning (i.e. first four tasks) with the end (i.e. last four tasks) of the test, to analyze the training effect.

The results show that EdgeBraille achieves the same performance as TalkBack at the end of the test (wpm: EdgeBraille=3.97 ± 1.00, TalkBack=3.64 ± 1.35, $F_{1,13}=0.793$, p=.389; error rate (in percent): EdgeBraille=8.43 ± 5.21, TalkBack=10.58 ± 9.99, $F_{1,13}=0.46$, p=.512). Regarding the training progress, it is not surprising that the wpm rates are significantly higher (p<.000) in the last four tasks (mean=2.94 ± 1.03) than in the first four tasks (mean=3.81 ± 1.18). The further data analysis showed a significant increase for EdgeBraille ($t_{13}=-6.14$, p<.000), as well as for TalkBack ($t_{13}=-2.76$, p=.016). The results are also shown in Fig. 2 (left figure). Regarding the participants' preference, we found that EdgeBraille was preferred by eight users, while TalkBack was only preferred by four (and two were indecisive).

5   Longer-Term Evaluation

To understand how the users' performance and opinions evolve over time, a two-week evaluation with a subset of seven users of the first evaluation was conducted. Five men and two women with a mean age of 38.86 years (standard deviation = 14.29) participated; two of them were users of the talking fingertip method.

For the longer-term evaluation we used the iPhone 4 (with iOS 5.1.1), which was configured to work exactly in the same way as TalkBack in the short-term evaluation. Participants had to enter given texts (92 to 99 characters per method) in a specific sequence every day with EdgeBraille and VoiceOver. The input was logged to ensure participants conducted all training sessions. At the beginning, the 8th and the 15th day of the study, a lab session was organized to assess the participants' performance and opinion.

At the end of the two-week training, participants were able to enter text at an average with 7.17 (±2.14) wpm with EdgeBraille and 6.29 wpm (±2.60) with VoiceOver ($F_{1,6}=1.92$, p=.215). The data analysis shows a significant trainings effect ($F_{2,5}=12.76$, p=.011), and a significant difference in wpm between the first and the third test for EdgeBraille ($t_6=-3.72$, p=.010) as well as VoiceOver ($t_6=-4.86$, p=.003). Regarding the preferences, we allowed the participants to state multiple preferences. We found a clear preference for VoiceOver in the first session (five participants preferred Voice-Over, one EdgeBraille, and two were indecisive). This changed in the second session, where EdgeBraille was the most preferred input method (five preferred EdgeBraille, two VoiceOver and one was indecisive). In the last session the preference for Edge-Braille and VoiceOver was balanced (four preferred EdgeBraille, four VoiceOver, and one was indecisive).

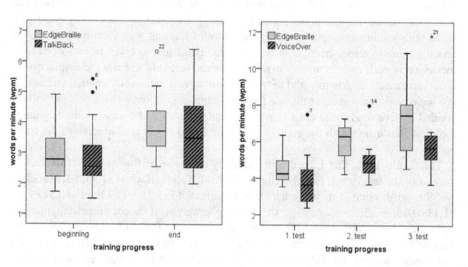

Fig. 2. Text input rate (wpm) in short-term (left) and longer-term (right) evaluation

6   Discussion

With regard to performance measures, our results show that there is no difference between EdgeBraille and the talking keyboard approaches. Also, looking at reported results from related work, EdgeBraille has a comparable input speed as TypeInBraille and Perkinput, but seems to be faster than BrailleType and slower than BrailleTouch.

In our research, participants stated that Braille-based methods are especially suitable for people who do not know the QWERTY keyboard layout very well. On the other hand for people familiar with the keyboard it is easy to find specific letters. Two disadvantages of Braille-based methods compared to keyboard-based methods are the need to know all Braille characters by heart and that it is not clear, which characters exist, as they cannot be directly accessed with the talking fingertip technique. Regarding the prototypical implementation of EdgeBraille, participants were missing some control characters such as delete, enter, cursor back and cursor forward. These could be implemented by assigning unused Braille combinations, although those are not standardized and therefore could decrease learnability.

However, our participants appreciated that with EdgeBraille there are fewer elements on the screen compared to talking keyboard and that the elements are larger. Due to the lower number of target elements in Braille-based approaches (typically six elements) compared to keyboard implementations (typically more than 26 elements) the Braille-based interfaces can be designed much smaller. This concurs with the feedback obtained from participants, that they would prefer a smaller version of EdgeBraille and expected it to be faster than the full-screen version.

Another aspect worth noticing is that the currently used 6-point Braille version could be extended to improve text input performance. By the implementation of Grade-2 Braille, contractions and abbreviations could be entered instead of whole words.

Based on these insights, EdgeBraille offers specific possibilities of further improvement of Braille-based methods. EdgeBraille could be used in scaled down versions, which do not occupy the whole screen's real estate. Therefore it could better be integrated with applications, because text input is no goal in its own but typically used in combination with other interface elements. This applies also to TypeInBraille and BrailleType but not to Perkinput and BrailleTouch as the size of the interface is directly related to the user's hand size and could not be scaled down to very small configurations.

Finally, all Braille-based methods discussed in this paper – including EdgeBraille – use 6-point Braille. Though it seems that for text written with a mobile phone 6-point Braille is sufficient, participants of our research activities call for the 8-point version to have a greater repertoire of characters. EdgeBraille (as well as Perkinput, TypeInBraille and BrailleType) could be easily extended to an 8-point version. In the case of BrailleTouch an extension to 8-point would be problematic, as users will en-counter difficulties in handling the device in a stable manner.

7   Improvements and Future Work

To analyze the identified improvement potential – smaller size and 8-point Braille – we developed a version of EdgeBraille allowing input of 8-point Braille, which was scalable to different sizes. We created two versions of 8-point EdgeBraille, one scaled by the factor 0.5 (occupying a quarter of the screen, see Fig. 3) and one scaled by factor 0.3 (occupying a ninth of the screen). These smaller versions could seamlessly be used as alternative text input method instead of the talking keyboard, by integrating it with typical smart phone use cases (e.g. writing emails).

To provide tactile feedback, we used regular screen protection foil where the area occupied by 8-point EdgeBraille was cut out, to create a perceptible edge for guidance of the input finger. This approach for providing tactile feedback is similar to the one presented by [12]. The authors found that that haptic structures can serve as additional feedback in non-visual situations (demonstrated for an in-vehicle application).

In the 8-point version of EdgeBraille we also extended the range of functions. We added the possibility to delete characters and to search for unknown characters, by assigning unused Braille combinations. For example, to delete a character the unassigned dot 7 (down, left corner) was used. Moreover the text written so far could be spoken to the user by the text to speech engine. A double tap anywhere on the screen triggers the text to speech engine. By these means the text input method could be used in a more realistic manner than before.

Fig. 3. 8-point Braille version of EdgeBraille (scale 0.5), guidance with display protection foil

A first proof-of-concept user study with 7 participants revealed that users are able to enter text including special characters using the 8-point version of EdgeBraille in both sizes (0.5 and 0.3). Input speed and error rate differed widely depending on the experience with Braille-based input in general and knowledge of 8-point Braille in particular. However, from the initial results we see that the 8-point version of Edge-Braille is a promising approach for entering special characters, which is cumbersome to do with the talking keyboard approaches.

Moreover we could show, that it is possible to use a scaled down version of Edge-Braille with a perceptible edge provided by cut out screen protection foil. All participants stated that the guidance by screen protection foil was helpful, although two participants stated that in real life they would only use it if possible without foil, as the edges provided by the foil may be distracting when performing other tasks than text input. Regarding size the 0.5 version was perceived well, the 0.3 version was perceived as too small by five participants. Providing the user the possibility to tailor the size of the input element to their preferences might be a suitable option.

In future work we plan to examine the optimal size that balances speed and error, and analyse text input performance of the 8-point EdgeBraille approach in detail.

8 Conclusions

In this paper we presented a new Braille-based text entry method and discussed different approaches of text entry for VIB people on touchscreen devices. Braille-based text entry mechanisms are an important possibility to complement current text input paradigms based on talking keyboard.

Overall EdgeBraille was perceived well by the users, possesses favourable handling characteristics, and performed comparable to talking keyboard. Especially when considering the improvements, EdgeBraille has potential to become a convenient form of text input for Braille literate users.

References

1. Vanderheiden, G.C.: Use of audio-haptic interface techniques to allow nonvisual access to touchscreen appliances. In: 40th Annual Meeting of the Human Factors and Ergonomics Society (1996)
2. Yfantidis, G., Evreinov, G.: Adaptive blind interaction technique for touchscreens. Universal Access in the Information Society 4(4), 328–337 (2006)
3. Wobbrock, J.O., Myers, B.A., Kembel, J.A.: EdgeWrite: A stylus-based text entry method designed for high accuracy and stability of motion. In: Proc. UIST 2003, pp. 61–70 (2003)
4. Mascetti, S., Bernareggi, C., Belotti, M.: TypeInBraille: A Braille-based typing application for touchscreen devices. In: Proc. ASSETS 2011, pp. 295–296 (2011)
5. Azenkot, S., Wobbrock, O., Prasain, S., Ladner, R.: Input finger detection for nonvisual touch screen text entry in Perkinput. In: Proc. GI 2012, pp. 121–129 (2012)
6. Oliveira, J., Guerreiro, T., Nicolau, H., Jorge, J., Gonçalves, D.: Blind people and mobile touch-based text-entry: Acknowledging the need for different flavors. In: Proc. ASSETS 2011, pp. 179–186 (2011)
7. Southern, C., Clawson, J., Frey, B., Abowd, G., Romero, M.: An evaluation of Braille-Touch: Mobile touchscreen text entry for the visually impaired. In: Proc. MobileHCI 2012, 317–326 (2012)
8. Mascetti, S., Bernareggi, C., Gerino, A.: TypeInBraille: Quick typing on smartphones by blind users. Rapporto interno N. 39 11 RT, Uni. of Milano
9. Soukoreff, R.W., MacKenzie, I.S.: Metrics for text entry research: An evaluation of MSD and KSPC, and a new unified error metric. In: Proc. CHI 2003, pp. 113–120 (2003)
10. Paisios, N.: Mobile accessibility tools for the visually impaired. PHD Thesis (2012), http://cs.nyu.edu/web/Research/Theses/nektariosp.pdf (retrieved online September 19, 2012)
11. Kane, S., Wobrock, J., Ladner, R.: Usable gestures for blind people: Understanding Preference and Performance. In: Proc. CHI 2011, pp. 413–422 (2011)
12. Zimmermann, S., Rümelin, S., Butz, A.: I Feel it in my Fingers: Haptic Guidance on Touch Surfaces. In: Proc. TEI 2014, pp. 9–12 (2014)

Real-Time Text Tracking for Text-to-Speech Translation Camera for the Blind

Hideaki Goto[1] and Takuma Hoda[2]

[1] Cyberscience Center, Tohoku University, Sendai, Japan
hgot@isc.tohoku.ac.jp
[2] School of Engineering, Tohoku University, Sendai, Japan

Abstract. Some mobile devices have been developed for helping the visually-impaired people to obtain useful information from text on documents, goods, and signboards. However, it is still difficult for the blind to find or even notice the text in the environment and to capture the images suitable for character recognition and speech synthesis. We developed a prototype of reading assistant device with a scene text locator that shows the text location by sound signals. To improve the device further, this paper proposes a real-time text tracking method that enables character recognition on-the-fly and also helps the users to obtain the text information easily and efficiently with less searching efforts. The presented method is based on our former one, and provides a new feature that it is tolerant of temporary occlusion or out-of-view of text regions.

Keywords: Reading Assistant, Scene Text Detection, Text Tracking, OCR (Optical Character Recognition), Text-To-Speech.

1 Introduction

Some text information acquisition devices have been proposed in order to help the visually-impaired to obtain useful information from text on documents, goods, and signboards [1]. It is difficult for the blind to find or even notice the text in the environment and to capture the text images suitable for character recognition. Particularly, some objects such as signboards are difficult to find since they cannot be touched by the users' hands. To help the blind, we developed a framework of reading assistant device with a scene text locator that shows the text location by sound signals, and built a prototype device by combining the scene text locator, Optical Character Recognition (OCR) engine, and text-to-speech engine [2]. Figure 1 shows the block diagram of the device. A lot of visually-impaired people have tried our device at the Sight World 2012 exhibition in Tokyo, an annual event for the visually-impaired people, volunteers, supporting companies, etc., and we have confirmed its usefulness, found the limitations and some problems to solve.

We assumed user's active reading actions, i.e. the user was supposed to press the capture button when he/she wanted the device to read out the located text. When we think about the case where the user is walking down the street or

K. Miesenberger et al. (Eds.): ICCHP 2014, Part I, LNCS 8547, pp. 658–661, 2014.

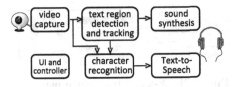

Fig. 1. Block diagram of the reading assistant device [2]

corridor, for example, and just wants to "hear" the prominent text in the scene, the above manual mode is not so helpful. Active reading mode, in which the device actively finds all text regions in the scene and notifies the user, must be very useful in such a situation.

This paper proposes a real-time text tracking method designed for text-to-speech translation cameras for the blind. Text tracking is a technique for keeping track of each text region in the video sequence. The new method is based on our former one [3], and provides a new feature that it is tolerant of temporary occlusion or out-of-view of text regions.

2   Real-Time Text Tracking for Wearable Camera

Our revised wearable camera device for the blind captures the scene images continuously, detects text regions on-the-fly, and translates the text into speech using the OCR engine and the text-to-speech engine. The device needs to know which text region in the current video frame corresponds to which one in the previous frame since the text regions are found independently between different video frames. The user does not want to hear the same text over and over. Therefore, text tracking is required to keep track of each text region, to pick up clear images for OCR, and to avoid repeating voice synthesis for the same text.

Scene text tracking for wearable camera is different from the typical object tracking or caption tracking in the following aspects.

- Since scene text is sticking to the background, we cannot use a popular object/ background separation method such as background subtraction.
- Text region movements are jerky in the video captured by a wearable camera compared with a steady camera.

In our former method [3], we employed the pyramidal Lucas-Kanade tracker combined with the Harris corner detector, and developed a nearest-neighbor cross-checking region matching. Although the method works much better than its predecessor, it cannot keep track of text regions once they get out of the camera's view. To deal with the problem, we have introduced the object tracking using SURF (Speeded Up Robust Features) descriptor [4]. The other parts are basically the same as the ones in our previous method. The overall algorithm is as follows.

MSER-based text detection [5] is applied to the video sequence once every $T_{int} = 30$ frames. This interval is for achieving a real-time processing as the

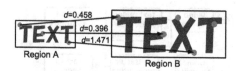

Fig. 2. SURF-based text region matching

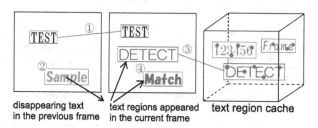

Fig. 3. Text tracking using SURF

precise text detection and localization are computationally expensive in general. For each text-detecting frame (TD frame hereinafter), text regions are found by grouping text-like blocks. Harris corners are extracted from every video frame, and the Lucas-Kanade object tracking method is applied to the non-TD frames. In this way, the text regions are tracked until the next TD frame comes.

Figure 2 shows the SURF-based region matching. A SURF is represented by a 64-dimensional vector. SURFs are calculated for each text region. Let τ_1 and τ_2 be pre-defined parameters. The correspondence is considered "good" if $d < \tau_1$, where d is the Euclidean distance between two SURFs. We examine every SURF combination between the two regions, and count the number of the good correspondences, N. The contents of the two regions are considered same, i.e. the same text, if $N > \tau_2$.

Some text regions may appear or disappear during the tracking process. As shown in Fig.3, the following four cases can occur at the TD frame.

1. The same text appears and the tracking continues.
2. The text has disapeared. The SURFs are put into the cache (temporary memory).
3. The text has appeared again. (Corresponding data is found in the cache.)
4. A new text has appeared. (No corresponding data exists.)

3   Experiments

We have tested the proposed method in an indoor scene with a plain wall as the current text detection cannot deal with complex backgrounds. The test video was captured using JVC GZ-HM670 video camera at 640×480 pixels, 30fps. The parameters were empirically set to $\tau_1 = 0.9, \tau_2 = 8$. Figure 4 shows an example of the text tracking. The proposed method can deal with jerky movements and keep track of text regions going out of the camera view. Text0 and Text1 are tracked correctly after they disappear temporarily.

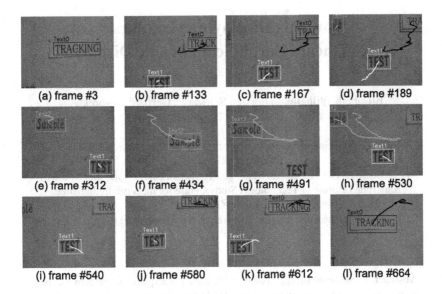

(a) frame #3	(b) frame #133	(c) frame #167	(d) frame #189
(e) frame #312	(f) frame #434	(g) frame #491	(h) frame #530
(i) frame #540	(j) frame #580	(k) frame #612	(l) frame #664

Fig. 4. Experimental result of the text tracking

4   Conclusions

This paper has proposed a real-time text tracking method to be used in a wearable text-to-speech translation camera device for the blind. The new method is tolerant of temporary occlusion or out-of-view of text regions thanks to the SURF-based matching technique.

Developing a prototype of wearable text-to-speech translation camera equipped with the proposed text tracking method is under way. Some more improvements in the text detection/localization/tracking are included in our future work to deal with complex scenes.

References

1. Mancas-Thilou, C., Ferreira, S., Demeyer, J., Minetti, C., Gosselin, B.: A multifunctional reading assistant for the visually impaired. EURASIP Journal on Image and Video Processing, 1–11 (2007)
2. Goto, H.: Text-to-Speech Reading Assistant Device with Scene Text Locator for the Blind. In: Proc. of AAATE 2013, pp. 702–707 (2013)
3. Pégeot, F., Goto, H.: Scene Text Detection and Tracking for a Camera-equipped Wearable Reading Assistant for the Blind. In: Park, J.-I., Kim, J. (eds.) ACCV Workshops 2012, Part II. LNCS, vol. 7729, pp. 454–463. Springer, Heidelberg (2013)
4. Bay, H., Ess, A., Tuytelaars, T., van Gool, L.: SURF: Speeded Up Robust Features. Computer Vision and Image Understanding 110(3), 346–359 (2008)
5. Koo, H.I., Kim, D.H.: Scene Text Detection via Connected Component Clustering and Nontext Filtering. IEEE Trans. on Image Processing 22(6), 2296–2305 (2013)

Towards Displaying Graphics
on a Cheap, Large-Scale Braille Display

Elisabeth Wilhelm[1], Thorsten Schwarz[2], Gerhard Jaworek[2],
Achim Voigt[1], and Bastian E. Rapp[1]

[1] Karlsruhe Institute of Technology, Institute of Microstructure Technology,
Karlsruhe, Germany
`{elisabeth.wilhelm,achim.voigt,bastian.rapp}@kit.edu`
[2] Karlsruhe Institute of Technology, Study Centre for the Visually Impaired,
Karlsruhe, Germany
`{thorsten.schwarz,gerhard.jaworek}@kit.edu`

Abstract. Large-scale Braille displays will make participation in modern media society easier for visually impaired people. At the moment extensive research is done on developing new technologies for affordable refreshable Braille displays. However, the developed displays often do not match the user requirements. This is because most of the engineers entrusted with the development know little to nothing about the potential users of their systems. To bridge that gap we carried out an online survey. Within this survey 69 people who either are visually impaired themselves or take care of someone who has lost his/her sight stated their opinion on how a large-scale refreshable Braille display should be designed. The results of this survey were used to build a first prototype of a large-scale refreshable braille display for displaying text and tactile graphics. This prototype relies on cheap, energy efficient microfluidic phase change actuators.

Keywords: Refreshable Braille Display, Braille, Tactile Graphics, Computer Display for the Visually Impaired.

1   Introduction

People who have lost their sight rely substantially on touch and hearing for obtaining information about their environment. Accordingly, displays that plot digital data such as text and graphics for visually impaired users must address at least one of these senses. While today speech output is integrated in nearly every technical device the development of tactile displays falls short of expectations. Because of the high priced actuators that are used in tactile output devices, such as refreshable Braille displays, many of these devices are limited to one line of text only. Using such a display makes it impossible to view graphics. Besides this the limited window makes it difficult to navigate through programs and web sites which have been written for sighted people using normal screens. One of the first attempts to provide a large-scale refreshable Braille display was done by combining several Braille lines to an array using traditional

K. Miesenberger et al. (Eds.): ICCHP 2014, Part I, LNCS 8547, pp. 662–669, 2014.
© Springer International Publishing Switzerland 2014

actuators [1]. However as the price scales almost linear with the amount of actuators these displays are unaffordable for most members of the blind community [2].

In general the approaches of tactile displays can be divided into three groups depending on the stimuli they provide for the receptors located in the skin [3]. Basically these receptors can be addressed mechanically e.g., by pressure or by vibration, electrically or thermally [4]. Until today electrical systems where not commercialized because of their invasive nature which discourages potential users [3]. It has been proven that heat flow is able to influence the sense of touch and may be used for providing additional information for the reader. As to our knowledge all attempts to transfer data like text or pictures via heat flow failed [2]. The most successful approaches are those that use mechanical actuators. Apart from the approaches based on surface acoustic waves nearly all mechanical displays rely on pins that can be lifted or lowered individually. The pins resemble the so-called tactile pixels (taxels). This group can be further divided into the so-called dynamic displays and the static displays. Dynamic displays are small pin arrays that are situated on a moveable device e.g., a computer mouse. During reading the fingertips of the reader are resting on the pin array. In order to explore larger graphics the device is moved around. Depending on the position of the device the pin array changes its content. The advantage of such devices lies in the reduced amount of actuators required. Unfortunately the actuators of such devices can only apply pressure to the fingertips. The signal that is obtained from that kind of stimulus is not as big as the one that people feel when reading paper braille. This is due to the lack of shear forces which address other neurons than pressure. In addition the neurons which are excited by pressure grow accustomed to the sensation if the same taxel is raised for a longer period of time [2]. The static displays, which are also called large-scale refreshable Braille display, comprise a huge amount of taxels. Like normal screens these displays display the whole picture or text at a time. The reader can then explore the surface with both hands. Since this takes some time the actuators can react a bit slower than the once that are used in dynamic displays. If the actuators are bistable the display does not consume any energy during reading [2]. Electromagnetic displays which contained suitable latching mechanism were the first displays to be invented [5]. However like the piezoelectrically driven devices these actuators are expensive. The approach to replace the actuators with microfluidic actuators in which a membrane is bulged by pressurized air [6] failed because these actuators are not bistable. The same applies to thermopneumatic actuators in which a material is heated. When heated the material expands thereby deforming the membrane [7]. However, both pneumatic and thermopneumatic actuators are very cheap. Recently several attempts of using so-called smart materials for these applications have been made. These include shape memory alloys, electro active polymers, magnetorheological fluids as well as light activated polymers [3], [8]. As these materials are still in the stage of development one cannot say which of them will meet the requirements of a large-scale Braille display best. At the moment the actuators that can achieve a sufficient displacement for displaying Braille letters are either very big or require high voltages.

In this paper we present a cheap method for building large-scale microfluidic Braille displays by using a bistable microfluidic actuator that relies on a phase change mechanism. By this we can reduce the power consumption of the display to a minimum. This is especially useful if the display is fabricated as portable device. The portability of such devices is one of the most important features that a large-scale Braille display must meet. We derive this information from an online survey which we conducted recently and whose results we present in this paper. In this survey 69 people who either suffer from blindness themselves or care for someone who is blind were asked for their opinion on the ideal microfluidic Braille display.

2   Identifying the Needs of Blind Users by Means of an Online Survey

Although several attempts have been made to identify technologies that can replace the expensive piezo-actuators none of these inventions reached market maturity. This may be due to the fact that many people who were entrusted with the research on alternative Braille displays do not suffer from blindness themselves. Therefore their knowledge of the context in which such a display may be used is limited. To overcome this problem we carried out an online survey which gave visually impaired people, their supervisors and teachers the opportunity to influence the development of the refreshable Braille display which we present in this paper at a very early stage. For this purpose we developed a barrier-free accessible questionnaire by using the forms provided by Google Drive. This tool was chosen for carrying out the interviews because an online survey makes it easier to contact a small, distributed group of people. However, by using online surveys we are only able to reach people who are using computers with web access [9]. In our case this limitation is applicable as potential users working with computers are, at the moment, those that will most likely buy a large-scale refreshable Braille display in the future.

Within three months 69 people aged 17 to 70 years returned the questionnaire. 42.03 % of these people were born blind. Another 28.99 % of the participants were late blind making a total of 49 blind participants. 2.9 % of all participants work as teacher or professor for blind people while 5.8 % said that they are supervising a visually impaired person. 23.19 % of the participants were not able to assign themselves to either of these groups. Most of those are people that are visually impaired but do not suffer from complete loss of sight. Two people assigned themselves to two groups which was possible because one can e.g. be blind and at the same time be a teacher of a blind person. Nearly all of the participants (75.36 % of all participants) said that they are working with a computer for six to seven days a week. The time that each person spends in front of his or her PC per day varies widely ranging from less than two hours (7.25 %) to more than eight hours (20.29 %). For the questions on the economic potential as well as the design of the display multiple answers were allowed. 62.32 % of the participants said that they would buy a large-scale display either for themselves, for their students or for the person they supervise. 31.88 % of all participants stated they would not buy such a device. Those were asked to give reasons for their decision. Most of these people are afraid that such a display would be too expensive. Only a few people are either not able to read Braille or are only working with text for which they can use the small refreshable Braille displays. When asked how much they would pay for such a large scale microfluidic Braille display, 29.19 % of all participants said that they would spend less than 1.000 €. 21.74 % of the participants would spend between 1.000 € and 3.000 €. Only 4.35 % of all participants would spend more than 10.000 €. 47.83 % of the participants would only buy a display, if health insurance or their employer would pay for the system. On the one hand the large group of people willing to buy a display shows that there is a significant market for large-scale refreshable Braille displays. On the other hand the amount of money which these people would spend for such a display confirms the need of cheaper actuators.

After checking the economic boundary conditions we tried to find out what visually impaired people expect from a large-scale refreshable Braille display. Most of them (68.12 %) stated that the refreshable Braille display should be a portable device which one can use in combination with a laptop. 36.23 % of the participants said that they want a special tablet PC for blind people and only 23.19 % of the participants voted for a stationary system. This tendency was also found by asking how big and heavy such a display should be. Here the majority (42.03 %) voted for the size of a tablet PC while 31.88 % of the participants wanted the display to be as big as a DIN A4 page. 14.49 % of the participants wished a display with the size of a postcard and 17.39 % of the participants thought that the size of a smartphone would be the adequate size for such a display. 40.58 % of the participants said that the display may be as heavy as a laptop (2-3 kg) while 50.72 % of the participants said that they wanted a display which is as heavy as a tablet PC (500 g). These answers indicate that the new Braille actuators need to be lighter than the ones used in refreshable Braille cells today. We then asked in which environment the participants would use their large-scale refreshable Braille displays. 68.12 % of the participants said that they would use it at home, 55.07 % of the participants wanted to use it in an office, 31.88 % of the participants would use it in a classroom or auditorium. All these places have in common that they are indoors and normally have some kind of temperature control. However 26.09 % of the participants stated, that they want to use their refreshable Braille displays outdoors e.g., in the garden. This sets higher requirements to the temperature and moisture stability of the actuators to be used in such a display. More constraints are added when one wants to fulfill the wish of 27.54 % of the participants who want to use their displays in environments where the usage of radio waves is regulated, e.g., hospitals or air planes. Another 7.25 % of the participants want to use their refreshable Braille displays in environments that are subject to regulations of explosion protection e.g., gas stations.

Further requirements regarding the actuators are that they need to be fast. 66.67 % of the participants said that the taxels should change their state within 10 s, 23.19 % of the participants would wait 10 to 30 s for the actuators to switch, 4.35 % of the participants said that 30 to 60 s would be an appropriate time and only 1.45 % of the participants voted for more than 60 s. 42.03 % of the participants said that all taxel should refresh at the same time whereas 53.62 % of the participants quoted that the taxels can refresh in a serial manner e.g., line by line. According to 63.77 % of the participants the resolution of the display which sets limits to the size of the actuators should be somewhere in between the resolution of Braille scripture and the resolution of 20 DPI which is used to print tactile graphics. Besides this the actuator should be able to latch in several heights in order to encode additional information e.g., colors as 71.01 % of the participants stated. This would also be helpful for 46.38 % of the participants who wanted to adjust the height of the taxels according to their needs. 53.62 %

of the participants said that displaying colored pictures that contain taxels with different heights should take the same time as displaying a page of text.

According to 81.16 % of the participants the display should come with integrated control items such as buttons for both placing the cursor and scrolling. Additional buttons for zooming and changing the heights of the taxels were wished by 53.62 % and 44.93 % of the participants, respectively. Another special feature which could be integrated in such a display is touch feedback. 44.93 % of the participants stated that it would be good if the display could detect where the hands of the reader are. Thus the next page could be loaded in advance. A real touch feedback which uses gesture control is wished by 44.93 % of the participants. Even though some kind of touch feedback is integrated in most modern refreshable Braille displays 30.43 % of the participants of the online survey stated that this is not useful. Another special feature would be the possibility to display the content not only in a tactile manner but also such that it is visible as well. 40.58 % of the participants said that such a feature would be unnecessary, 40.58 % of the participants said that it should be clearly visible which taxels are activated. 44.93 % of the participants would like to have a display that can display blackprint as well as tactile content.

3   The Concept of the Microfluidic Braille Display

The results of the online survey underline the need for cheap actuators which are able to display braille letters. As described above membrane actuators which are commonly used in Lab-On-Chip devices represent a cost-effective alternative as they either rely on air or paraffin as actuation material. Unfortunately both actuator types consume energy in form of electricity or pressure constantly while displaying taxels. If such a device is built using these actuators portable gas- and/or electrical energy storage of significant capacities must be implemented. In order to reduce the amount of energy that the display needs we designed an actuator which only consumes energy while it changes its state. Thus the whole display only consumes energy while the content that is displayed changes. During the time the user needs to read this content no energy is consumed. Basically our display consists of a microfluidic channel network, which links the individual actuators. The channel network has one inlet. This channel splits in multiple channels each of which ends at a dead end. The dead ends are blocked by a deformable membrane which forms the tactile surface of the refreshable braille display. Beneath the membrane small microfluidic actuators such as phase change valves are located (see Fig. 1). While turned off these actuators completely block the channel. So even if pressure is applied to the channel systems the membranes will not deform. By addressing the actuators via an electronic platform the valves can be opened individually.

Whenever a valve is open, the pressure that is applied to the channel system e.g., using a syringe pump, will bulge the membrane of the channel ending directly above this specific valve. For stabilizing the bulged membrane, which effectively acts as a taxel, the valve is turned off while the channel system is pressurized. After the valve is completely closed the pressure is turned off. The taxel will stay as it is until the valve is opened again. If the valve beneath a bulged membrane is opened while no pressure is applied to the system, the restoring force of the membrane will cause the taxel to decline.

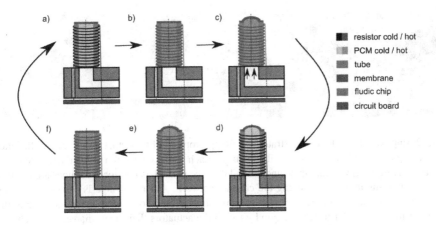

Fig. 1. Working principle of the microfluidic actuators. Each actuator of the display consists of a tube which is filled with a phase change material (PCM) (a). The tube which is placed on a microfluidic chip is covered with an elastic membrane. A heating wire is wound around this tube. This wire is connected with a circuit board using the through holes that are integrated in the microfluidic chip. If the individual taxel is turned on, the wire will start heating the tube (b). During this time the PCM inside the tube starts melting. Then pressure is applied to the microfluidic channel system (c) deflecting the membranes of those actuators which are located above the tubes with molten paraffin. When the taxel has reached its full size the heating wire is turned off. The PCM solidifies thereby stabilizing the taxel. After the PCM has solidified completely the pump/syringe which provides the pressure is disconnected (d). The taxel is now stable and will maintain its height until the heating wire is turned on again (e). Once heated the restoring forces of the membrane, will push the liquid back into the channel within a few seconds.

4   Setup and Test Results with the First Actuator Prototypes

In our setup the microfluidic actuators are small tubes which are filled with a phase change material (PCM) e.g., paraffin. The actuators are covered with a membrane that forms the tactile surface of the display. In order to provide optimum heat transfer into the phase change material the heating resistors are fabricated by winding a heating wire around the filled tubes (see Fig. 1). Using actuators with an inner diameter of 1.4 mm taxel actuation times of 11 s (+/-1 s) were measured. Fig. 2 depicts the prototypes of these tubular phase change actuators. In order to provide a better view on the details the actuators were manufacture with an inner diameter of 2 mm. The time that is required for stabilizing the taxel is highly dependent on the temperature of the surrounding environment. In order to speed up the solidification process a fan may be added to the setup. The height of the individual taxel is dependent on the pressure that is applied to the membrane. By controlling this pressure the taxel can be set to different heights. This additional option may be used for encoding additional information such as color.

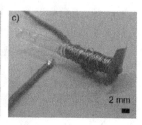

Fig. 2. Implemantion of a demonstrator and first prototypes of the actuator. a) One Braille letter consisting of six individually controllable taxels. Each taxel consist of a silicon tube filled with paraffin. A heating wire that is wound around the tube is used as resistor. The tubes are inserted into a microfluidic chip containing the channel network. A 5 ml syringe is used for applying pressure. A membrane fabricated from polydimethylsiloxane covers the actuators forming the tactile surface. In order to allow a good view on the actuators their inner diameter was chosen to be 2 mm and the spacing between the actuators was increased. The bistability of the actuator principle is proven with a single prototype (b). When pressure is applied to this actuator using a syringe the membrane is bulged. As soon as the PCM has solidified completely the taxel will remain in its state even when the syringe is disconected (c).

5   Future Work

In the near future we will build up an array containing more than 100 actuators. These actuators will have the size of standard Braille taxels. They will be arranged with a pitch of 2.5 mm according to the rules of equidistant Braille [10]. Using this array we will conduct readability tests. Furthermore we will optimize the production of the tube actuators. At the moment the costs of the actuators are dominated by the amount of manual work required for assembly. By increasing the degree of automation in the production process we will reduce the prize of the display even further. Another important factor which we identified during our online survey is the time each actuator needs to perform an actuation cycle. For diminishing this time PCMs with lower melting temperatures will be evaluated. In addition the length of the actuator tubes will be optimized further. Doing so we will be able to decrease the amount of PCM used in the actuator which will also shorten up the actuation cycles.

Acknowledgements. This work has been funded by the German Federal Ministry of Education and Research (BMBF) research grant 16SV5775.

References

1. Völkel, T., Weber, G., Baumann, U.: Tactile Graphics Revised: The Novel BrailleDis 9000 Pin-Matrix Device with Multitouch Input. In: Miesenberger, K., Klaus, J., Zagler, W.L., Karshmer, A.I. (eds.) ICCHP 2008. LNCS, vol. 5105, pp. 835–842. Springer, Heidelberg (2008)
2. Vidal-Verdu, F., Hafez, M.: Graphical tactile displays for visually-impaired people. IEEE Transactions on Neural Systems and Rehabilitation Engineering 15(1), 119–130 (2007)

3. Chouvardas, V.G., Miliou, A.N., Hatalis, M.K.: Tactile displays: Overview and recent advances. Displays 29(3), 185–194 (2008)
4. Chouvardas, V.G., Miliou, A.N., Hatalis, M.K.: Tactile displays: a short overview and recent developments. In: ICTA 2005: Proceedings of Fifth International Conference on Technology and Automation, pp. 246–251 (2005)
5. Lindenmueller, H.-P., Schoenherr, K.-P.: Tactile indicating device. Google Patents (1976)
6. Wu, X., et al.: A Refreshable Braille Cell Based on Pneumatic Microbubble Actuators. Journal of Microelectromechanical Systems 21(4), 908–916 (2012)
7. Kwon, H.-J., Lee, S.W., Lee, S.S.: Braille dot display module with a PDMS membrane driven by a thermopneumatic actuator. Sensors and Actuators A: Physical 154(2), 238–246 (2009)
8. Camargo, C.J., et al.: Light-actuated CNT-doped elastomer blisters towards braille dots. In: 2011 16th International Solid-State Sensors, Actuators and Microsystems Conference (TRANSDUCERS) (2011)
9. Evans, J.R., Mathur, A.: The value of online surveys. Internet Research 15(2), 195–219 (2005)
10. Prescher, D., Nadig, O., Weber, G.: Reading braille and tactile ink-print on a planar tactile display. In: Miesenberger, K., Klaus, J., Zagler, W., Karshmer, A. (eds.) ICCHP 2010, Part II. LNCS, vol. 6180, pp. 482–489. Springer, Heidelberg (2010)

Author Index